STRANGE POWER

Strange Power
Shaping the parameters of international relations
and international political economy

Edited by
THOMAS C. LAWTON
Royal Holloway University of London, UK
JAMES N. ROSENAU
The George Washington University, USA
AMY C. VERDUN
University of Victoria, Canada

Ashgate

Aldershot • Burlington USA • Singapore • Sydney

Published by
Ashgate Publishing Ltd
Gower House
Croft Road
Aldershot
Hants GU11 3HR
England

Ashgate Publishing Company
131 Main Street
Burlington
Vermont 05401
USA

Ashgate website: http://www.ashgate.com

British Library Cataloguing in Publication Data
Strange power : shaping the parameters of international
  relations and international political economy
  1.International relations   2.International economic
  relations
  I.Lawton, Thomas C.   II.Rosenau, James N. (James Nathan),
  1924– III.Verdun, Amy C.
  327

Library of Congress Cataloging-in-Publication Data
Strange power : shaping the parameters of international relations and international
political economy/edited by Thomas C. Lawton, James N. Rosenau, Amy C.
Verdun.
     p. cm.
  ISBN 0-7546-1324-0 (HB)
     1. International economic relations—Political aspects.   2. International
  relations.   3. Globalization.   4. World politics—1989–   5. Power (Social
  sciences)   6. Strange, Susan, 1923– Retreat of the state.   I. Lawton, Thomas C.
  II. Rosenau, James N.   III. Verdun, Amy, 1968–

  HF1359.S767   2000
  337–dc21   00-036348

ISBN 0 7546 1324 0 (Hbk)
ISBN 0 7546 1329 1 (Pbk)

Typeset by Manton Typesetters, Louth, Lincolnshire, UK.
Printed and bound in Great Britain by MPG Books Ltd, Bodmin, Cornwall

Contents

PART VII   CONCLUSIONS

List of Figures and Tables

Figures

Tables

Foreword

ROBERT O. KEOHANE

My earliest memory of Susan Strange is not of her in person, but of her 1971 book, *Sterling and British Policy*. I have a vivid memory of being in the Stanford University Library thinking about her discussion of how the British government responded to financial markets in the first quarter-century after World War II. Of course, I also remember Susan Strange in person: the pierced brow when one said something she doubted, the quick retort, her wonderful sense of humor and joy in life. Her winning irreverence was never better exhibited than at her Presidential Address to the International Studies Association (ISA) in 1995, when she advised her audience: 'Don't take too much notice of the barons and the top brass. Have the courage to do your own thing, and say what your really think, not what other people have told you to think' (Strange 1995: 295). She always did, and we are wiser for it.

As Strange said in the preface to *States and Markets* (1988), she and I were part of the same 'extensive invisible college', even though, as she wrote, 'there are many things on which we do not always agree' (Strange 1988/1994: acknowledgement). I am proud to have been part of her invisible college, even if 'we do not agree' loomed rather large in her discussions of my own contributions. At any rate, my plan in this foreword is to seek to identify the themes that I perceive in Strange's work, as well as the themes on which she showed great ambivalence. I only wish that she could be here to point out to me, once again, how I have missed the point!

Five themes seem to me to dominate Strange's approach to the analysis of international political economy. I refer to themes rather than to moods – such as her mood of pessimism about the world economy and its financial system. I focus on her analysis of the underlying relationships between politics and economics, rather than on her arguments with respect to particular sectors of the world economy. These five themes might not be the ones that Strange herself would have chosen but they are the themes in her work that have made the most impression on me and, I believe, constitute the essence of her intellectual legacy to international studies.

The first theme that I want to emphasize is that structural power is crucial to the study of international political economy. Strange was interested in structures rather than processes, which she regarded as derivative and often misleading to academics because of the dissimulation engaged in by practitioners.[1] For her, structural power is 'the power to choose and to shape the structures of the global political economy within which other states, their political institutions, their economic enterprises, and (not least) their professional people have to operate' (Strange 1987: 565). She identified four domains of structural power: security, production, finance and knowledge. For her, structural power was more fundamental than either bargaining or agenda setting through international regimes.

To say that Strange privileged structure is not to argue that she ignored agency. In my analysis, a focus on agency is her second theme. Throughout her writings, she emphasized the role of self-interested agents, seeking control over valued outcomes such as security, wealth, the freedom to choose, justice, protection from risk (1994: 18). For her, the core of international political economy lies in the relations between 'markets and authorities'. She declared in 1994 that this is how she should have entitled her seminal work, *States and Markets* (ibid.: x). I find the authorities–markets formulation illuminating – and complementary to Robert Gilpin's emphasis on the intersecting pursuit by agents of power and wealth. Strange's method followed from her focus on agents: 'you should look for the key bargains in any situation', then assess which bargains might change (Strange 1988/94: 39). In my view, this is excellent advice. Don't look for paradigms, look for bargains!

The world Strange portrayed was a tough one, whose agents were fundamentally out for themselves. She often complained that they could not see their self-interest, that they were caught up in competitive activity that was self-defeating, or even that they were irrational (*Casino Capitalism*, 1986; *Mad Money*, 1998). She urged them often to pursue their interests in more sensible and sustainable ways; but she never urged them 'to be good', or to put the 'global interest' (a phrase she never would have used without irony) over their own. That, she thought, would have been foolish.

I now turn to criticism of Strange's linked themes of structural power and agency. Surely she was right to insist on structural power in the political economy, at a deeper level than the political arrangements that some of us call regimes. This argument goes back at least to Marx and is certainly implied by such thinkers as Schumpeter, Hirschman and Gilpin. Bargaining takes place with such structures of power in mind. She was also right that power should not be viewed as purely material in character, and that it cannot be analyzed *simply* in terms of explicit bargaining. Yet in my view she conflated the key distinction between power as a set of capabilities – not necessarily exclusively material – and power as the ability to affect outcomes (1996: 21–7).[2]

If structure is the ability to affect outcomes, then it will *necessarily* determine power relationships, as a matter of definition. To conflate resources and outcomes is not helpful in generating testable explanations of the role of different potential sources of influence. If, on the other hand, we think of structure as the resources themselves – in the domains of security, production, credit and knowledge – then the analyst needs to specify causal mechanisms that link specific resources with outcomes. Strange's disdain for theory, it seems to me, made her impatient with the distinctions that are necessary if we are to test different structural conceptions of power.

For Strange, international political economy concerned: 'the social, political and economic arrangements affecting the global systems of production, exchange, and distribution, and the mix of values reflected therein' (1988: 18). Yet her third theme, in my interpretation, was a pervasive skepticism about international organizations and international regimes. She continually insisted that 'international organizations are not free agents. ... Governments have always been extremely careful not to take even the smallest step which would let an international organization usurp any of the fundamental prerogatives of the state' (1986: 171). She did not even like the use of the term 'regime' to describe international governance arrangements, describing it as 'a rather strange use of the word' (1994: 21). In her famous article in the regime's special issue of *International Organization*, she warned against the concept and its emerging use, declaring that 'there be dragons' (Strange 1983). She regarded 'interdependence' as a 'euphemism for asymmetric dependence'; about the notion of 'global governance' she was even more scathing (1996: xiii).

Here I detect a contradiction. When one speaks as she did of 'arrangements affecting global systems', one refers to institutions – rules, practices, organizations – created through historic time as a result of processes of interaction and bargaining. Strange privileged structures, often with enlightening results. In my view, however, she did not pay sufficient systematic attention to the way human-constructed arrangements (institutions) affect agents' views of their interests and the strategies they pursue. She was too 'put off' by the euphemistic semantics of the rhetoricians of interdependence, to see how an incentive-oriented view of institutions actually fits well within her worldview. 'Process', after all, is another word for bargaining within the context both of particular distributions of power resources and of institutional characteristics.

Strange's allergy to the bureaucratic obfuscations of international organizations (IOs) and their leaders, may have contributed to her skepticism about them. Indeed, sometimes her antagonism seemed almost visceral, a reaction to a pomposity that she detested. But no serious student of international organizations sees them as free agents. The issue is how their capabilities, and the restraints of international regimes – created by states – influence the strategies of states, firms, NGOs and the IO bureaucracies themselves.

These three themes – an emphasis on structural power, a focus on self-interested agents and skepticism about international institutions – may make Strange look like a 'realist' as the term is often used in international political economy. Her critique of the regimes volume (Strange 1983) can indeed be viewed as a realist argument, and in 1984 she defended the study of international relations as the best starting point for the study of international political economy, partly with the argument that security is the prime value (Strange 1984: 184). However, her views on power were always more sympathetic to Gramscian views, such as those of Robert Cox, than to strict realism. Furthermore, between 1984, when she published her chapter on the study of international relations, and 1994, she decisively broke with the state-centric assumption of realism. Indeed, she swung with characteristic force to the other pole, entitling her 1996 book *The Retreat of the State*.

She prepared the way for this shift with her concept, in *States and Markets*, of structural power in four areas: security, production, credit and knowledge. Once the subject-matter had been defined in terms of structural power, the role of state became not *the* subject of inquiry, a constant as in realism, but a variable. Making this move opened many intellectual doors, although Strange may have run too far from realism's cozy little house when she declared 'the retreat of the state'. Indeed, her own emphasis on agency should have made her more cautious, since she recognized that agents adapt their behavior to new situations. In a remarkable passage in *The Retreat of the State*, she says:

> Censorship, police power and state control over information flows all belong to the past. That is clear. But what the social innovations will be that will follow the technology, just as surely as banks, conscript armies, post offices and civil services followed the industrial innovations of the nineteenth century, still lie hidden in the future. (1994: 53)

In other words, states take on new functions in response to change. Changing functions is not the same as 'retreat'. Broadly speaking, the fourth theme that I attribute to Strange's work – abstracting from the issue of 'retreat' – is the emphasis on competition among authorities, within different sectors of the world market economy, as they struggle for mastery. At her best, she neither dismissed the state nor privileged it, but inquired about its role and the extent of actual state ability to influence outcomes.

The last of Strange's themes that I want to emphasize is her consistent claim, throughout the 1980s, that America remained hegemonic. Her emphasis on structural power and her study of British seapower in the 19th century, sensitized her to the many ways in which the United States continued to dominate world politics in the 1980s, despite its relatively low proportion of world exports and imports and the decline in its share of world gross domestic product (GDP). She emphasized that the United States was the orchestrator rather than the victim of the collapse of the Bretton Woods system in 1971 (1986: 67–8); she declared in 1988 that she suspected that American power had actually increased, not declined; and in 1987 she published a sustained critique of the 'persistent myth of lost hegemony' (Strange 1987). She emphasized throughout her work how US dominance in the security realm enabled it to justify 'finding other ways than taxes to have its defence policies paid for' (1998: 5). She certainly thought that a book properly entitled *After Hegemony* would have to be about the distant future, and she was right. On this point, I simply concede; I should have listened to her earlier.

Her pursuit of these five themes, in prose that was pungent and memorable, meant that, to me, Strange was a valuable colleague whose ideas helped to shape my own; a persistent if sometimes irritating critic; and a worthy adversary. As she said, and as I have indicated, we did not always agree. But in a field in which tedious repetition often passes as scholarship, she was always interesting – and sometimes right!

Although Strange wrote vigorous prose and enjoyed taking positions, she was ambivalent on the biggest normative issue in our field: how the world economy should be governed, and by whom. She was clear that there is a need for governance. Throughout her writings, she disparaged the hyper-liberal notion that markets would operate smoothly by themselves. For Strange, markets are firmly embedded in politics; they are influenced by politics and their stability depends on political support and occasional intervention. No hyper-liberal would have written books on the world financial system entitled *Casino Capitalism* and *Mad Money*!

Her view of markets could have led Strange to an argument close to my own: that increasing interdependence creates potential gains from cooperation that leaders of states can anticipate, and that they therefore devise institutions, in limited and partial ways, to perform the functions that are essential for such cooperation to occur. Indeed, in *The Retreat of the State*, Strange said that her own view 'might be called functionalist, if the word had not been so widely used in the study of international organizations' (1996: 42). She could not use this particular f-word since it would imply that her view was similar to mine! She certainly would not have wished to be associated with any view that overlooks fundamental issues of power and distributional bargaining – as my arguments have sometimes been misinterpreted as doing. Much less would she have wanted to be associated with an 'American' view that is sometimes interpreted as emphasizing management of the world economy, in US interests, rather than analysis of how authority and markets interact.

Strange rejected functionalism as used by institutionalists such as myself, and she rejected our remedy: more multilateral cooperation. But she did not have faith in private, decentralized authority – bankers, CEOs of corporations, leaders of insurance companies – either to have the vision or the capability to regulate global capitalism. In *Casino Capitalism*, she appealed to the United States (often the object of her criticism) to exercise 'a wise hegemony over the world market economy' (1986: 171). Later she characterized that admonition as reflecting 'a naive hope', and asked for 'a transnational coalition of forces concerned for the long-term welfare and indeed survival of global civil society and of the managed market economy that sustains it' (Strange 1995: 294).

As these quotations suggest, Strange was profoundly ambivalent about the United States. She loved the openness and irreverence of American society. As she admiringly said, 'This is the only country I know where you can buy T-shirts that say, "Question Authority"' (Strange 1995: 204). In a sense, she was by instinct and temperament a woman of the American West. Yet she was also offended by the arrogance of American power and of American academics. Perhaps her strident attacks on the United States were the result in part of an unrequited romanticism about what only the United States could achieve, not by altruism, but by putting 'its own house in order' (1986: 175).[3]

Following Kindleberger, Strange believed that world financial order had rested on the lender of last resort role of hegemonic central banks: the Bank of England under the gold standard and the US Fed after World War II. These periods of order were not functionally determined but were political 'accidents', which 'may never be repeated'. The unanswered question, she believed, was 'how to recreate that authority for the integrated world financial system and thus for the good of the world economy' (1996: 194–5). In thinking about this question during the 1980s, Strange had appealed to the American state, perhaps because she had discarded both the hyper-liberal and institutionalist alternatives, and could think of nothing else. During the 1990s, she offered the uncharacteristically utopian notion of a 'transnational coalition of forces' or simply left the question for the next generation. As she said in *Mad Money*:

Our problem in the next century is that the traditional authority of the nation state is not up to the job of managing mad international money, yet its leaders are instinctively reluctant to entrust that job to unelected, unaccountable (and often arrogant and myopic) bureaucrats. We have to invent a new kind of polity but we cannot yet imagine how it would work. (1998: 190)

With this statement, made at the end of her last major work, I entirely agree. I believe that the new kind of polity that we need will involve international institutions, but they will have to be accountable to publics in quite a new way. To understand how such a polity would work, we are deeply indebted to the work of Susan Strange. We will have to grasp her major arguments to understand what is happening in the world political economy: in particular, to examine how self-interested authorities interact with markets, in the context of structural power; and to problematize the role of the state in that process. We honor her memory not only by thinking of her as a person – a vibrant woman, loving life – but by remembering, reinvigorating and critiquing the themes of her work.

Notes

1 See her discussion in *Mad Money* (1998: 6), of the pretense that international monetary reform remained under serious discussion after 1973, contrasting with the reality of 'anarchy'.
2 For an example of claims about structural power, followed by empirical examples that seem to involve similar analysis to that of others relying on the distinction between resources and abilities to influence outcomes, see *States and Markets*, pp.25–34.
3 In *Mad Money*, the sequel to *Casino Capitalism*, I could find no praise for American hegemony, indeed, no reference to her earlier call for a wise hegemony.

References

Strange, Susan (1983), *Cave! Hic Dragones:* a critique of regime analysis', in Stephen D. Krasner (ed.), *International Regimes*, Ithaca: Cornell University Press, pp.355–68.

Strange, Susan (1984), 'What about international relations?', in Susan Strange (ed.), *Paths to International Political Economy*, London: George Allen & Unwin.

Strange, Susan (1986), *Casino Capitalism*, Oxford: Basil Blackwell.

Strange, Susan (1987), 'The persistent myth of lost hegemony', *International Organization*, 41(4) Autumn, 551–74.

Strange, Susan (1988), *States and Markets*, 2nd edn 1994, London: Pinter Publishers.

Strange, Susan (1995), 'ISA as a microcosm', *International Studies Quarterly*, 39(3) September, 289–96.

Strange, Susan (1996), *The Retreat of the State: The Diffusion of Power in the World Economy*, Cambridge: Cambridge University Press.

Strange, Susan (1998), *Mad Money: When Markets Outgrow Governments*, Ann Arbor: University of Michigan Press.

Preface

Susan Strange was a leading figure in international studies during the latter half of the 20th Century and a pioneer of international political economy as an academic discipline. This book is a tribute to her life and thought. It seeks to embed Susan's work in the discourse that shapes the parameters of modern international studies. However, in the spirit of Strange as a critical thinker, we also critique the precision and the limitations of her ideas. In so doing we attempt to develop a balanced approach to a study of the world political economy.

Susan was very aware that a central role of the academic was that of educator. Consequently, the contributors were asked to reflect on Susan's work in relation to the wider literature of the field so that the book would be of value to future generations of students.

We invited contributions from both senior and junior scholars, students of Susan as well as colleagues, and aimed at a fair representation from various countries and regions of the world. The volume therefore brings together an eclectic group of contributors from diverse academic backgrounds. The group is representative of scholars from the US, Canada, Africa, Israel and numerous European countries. Moreover, the combination of approaches and experiences provides an indepth and multifaceted view of contemporary International Relations/International Political Economy theory and practice. We wish to thank all of our contributors for subscribing to the spirit of the endeavor, particularly under what often proved to be rather challenging time constraints.

A book of this nature could not be completed without the generous help and support of many people and organizations. First of all, we would like to thank all of our contributing authors for delivering their papers on time. Several of the papers were presented at the International Studies Association (ISA) annual convention in Los Angeles in March 2000. Our thanks are also extended to the participants at that conference for useful comments and suggestions. Secondly, support was provided by the home universities and through grants held by the editors. Thomas Lawton would like to thank the

School of Management at Royal Holloway University of London; Amy Verdun extends her gratitude to the Department of Political Science at the University of Victoria and the Robert Schuman Centre at the European University Institute, Florence; and James Rosenau continues to be grateful for the support of The George Washington University. We would furthermore like to acknowledge the excellent research and editorial assistance of Robin Kells. Her assistantship was funded by a Grant of the Social Sciences and Humanities Council of Canada (SSHRC Grant: 410-99-0081) held by Amy Verdun.

Finally, we would like to thank the staff and management of Ashgate Publishing for their support of and enthusiasm for this project. Our editorial manager, Ann Newell, was extremely helpful and accommodating in her dealings and highly professional in her approach. Tony Waterman proved a meticulous proof-reader of the book's final draft. Our commissioning editor, Kirstin Howgate, deserves a special word of thanks. Her initial suggestion helped kindle the project and her commitment and hard work have been unwavering.

Susan was a colleague or mentor but above all, a friend, to all involved in the writing of this book. Each of us has his or her own personal tribute and anecdote that combined, could fill another volume. She frequently mused that 'the youth has the future' and believed that open-minded students who challenged accepted wisdoms were fundamental to the advancement of international studies. We dedicate this book to Susan's enduring legacy and living memory.

Thomas C. Lawton, James N. Rosenau, Amy C. Verdun
London; Washington D.C.; Victoria, B.C./San Domenico di Fiesole
May 2000

Contributors

Benjamin J. Cohen is Louis G. Lancaster Professor of International Political Economy at the University of California, Santa Barbara. He has previously taught at Princeton University and the Fletcher School of Law and Diplomacy, Tufts University.

A. Claire Cutler is Associate Professor of Political Science at the University of Victoria, British Columbia, Canada, where she teaches International Law and Organization and International Relations Theory. Her publications include the co-edited book, *Private Authority and International Affairs* (New York: SUNY Press, 1999).

David C. Earnest is a Ph.D. candidate in political science at the George Washington University, Washington, DC. A specialist in international relations theory and political methodology, his research focuses on the impact of global migration on the stability of political coalitions.

Robert Gilpin is Eisenhower Professor of Public and International Affairs, Emeritus, Princeton University. He is the author of several books on international affairs. His most recent book is *The Challenge of Global Capitalism: The World Economy in the 21st Century* (Princeton University Press 2000).

Judith L. Goldstein is Professor of Political Science, Chair of the International Relations Program and Chair of the International Policy Studies Program at Stanford University. Her work includes *Ideas, Interests and American Trade Policy* (1993) and (with Robert Keohane) *Ideas and Foreign Policy* (1994). She is currently writing a book on the GATT/WTO.

Stefano Guzzini is Associate Professor of Political Science, International Relations and European Studies at the Central European University, Budapest College. He is the author of *Realism in International Relations and International Political Economy: The Continuing Story of a Death Foretold* (Routledge 1998).

Eric Helleiner is an Associate Professor in the Department of Political Studies at Trent University in Canada. He is author of *States and the Reemergence of Global Finance: From Bretton Woods to the 1990s* (Cornell University Press 1994) and co-editor of *Nation-States and Money: The Past, Present and Future of National Currencies* (Routledge 1999).

Robert O. Keohane is James B. Duke Professor of Political Science at Duke University, Durham, North Carolina. He is co-author (with Joseph S. Nye, Jr.) of *Power and Interdependence* (1977; 2000) and author of *After Hegemony* (1984) and *International Institutions and State Power* (1989).

Thomas C. Lawton is Lecturer in European Business and Corporate Strategy at the School of Management, Royal Holloway University of London. He is the author of *Technology and the New Diplomacy* (Avebury/Ashgate 1997) and editor of *European Industrial Policy and Competitiveness* (Macmillan Business/St Martin's Press 1999).

Anna Leander is Assistant Professor of Political Science at the Central European University and research fellow at the Copenhagen Peace Research Institute. She has recently published 'A Nebbish Presence: Undervalued contributions of sociological institutionalism to IPE', (*Acta Oeconomica*, 50(1–2), 1999, pp.37–57).

Jean-Pierre Lehmann is Professor of International Political Economy at IMD in Lausanne, Switzerland. He has held academic positions in universities and institutions in most East Asian and Western European countries and has been advisor to both governments and multinational corporations. He has written extensively about Japan and the modern world economy.

Sandra J. MacLean is an Assistant Professor of Political Science and a Fellow of the Centre for Foreign Policy Studies at Dalhousie University, Halifax, Canada.

Christopher May is Senior Lecturer in International Political Economy at the University of the West of England, Bristol, UK. His book, *A Global Political Economy of Intellectual Property Rights: The New Enclosures*, is published by Routledge. His current research includes a critical account of the global information society and an international history of intellectual property rights.

Kevin P. Michaels is a Ph.D. Candidate at the University of London. He has fifteen years private sector experience in a variety of assignments including strategic planning, management consulting, and engineering. He holds an MSc in International Relations from The London School of Economics and MBA and engineering degrees from the University of Michigan.

Lynn K. Mytelka is Director of the United Nations University Institute for New Technology (UNU/INTECH) in Maastricht, the Netherlands. Her publications include *Competition, Innovation and Competitiveness in Developed Countries* (OECD Development Centre 1999) and *Technological Capabilities and Export Success in Asia* (Routledge 1998).

Maria Nzomo is an Associate Professor at the Institute of Diplomacy and International Studies of the University of Nairobi. She is widely published on issues of governance, gender studies, and Civil Society. She is currently the Director of the Civil Society Programme at CODESRIA, Dakar, Senegal.

Louis W. Pauly is Professor of Political Science and Director of the Centre for International Studies at the University of Toronto. His publications include *Who Elected the Bankers? Surveillance and Control in the World Economy* (Cornell University Press 1997).

Julie Pellegrin is a Research Fellow at the Institute for German Studies, University of Birmingham, UK, where she works on the microeconomic foundations of regional integration dynamics in Europe.

James N. Rosenau is University Professor of International Affairs at The George Washington University, Washington D.C. His publications include *Thinking Theory Thoroughly* (2nd edn 2000, with Mary Durfee), *Along The Domestic-Foreign Frontier* (1997) and *Turbulence in World Politics* (1990).

Timothy M. Shaw is Professor of Political Science and International Development Studies at Dalhousie University in Nova Scotia. He is also Visiting Professor at Stellenbosch and Western Cape Universities in South Africa and at Mbarara University of Science and Technology in Uganda. He is general editor of the Macmillan/SMP Series on IPE and editor of the Ashgate series on new regionalisms.

Jonathan Story is the Shell Fellow in Economic Transformation and Professor of International Political Economy at INSEAD in Fontainebleau, France. His publications include (with Ingo Walter) *The Political Economy of Financial Integration in Europe: The Battle of the Systems* (MIT Press 1998) and *The Frontiers of Fortune* (Pitman 1999).

Roger Tooze has taught at the Nottingham Trent University, the University of Wales, Aberystwyth, the London School of Economics, the University of Southern California and Ruskin College, Oxford. He has published widely on the theory of IR/IPE and is completing a book called *Reflections on IPE Theory*. He is Susan Strange's literary executor.

Alfred Tovias is Associate Professor of International Relations at the Hebrew University in Jerusalem and Visiting Fellow at the Centre for International Studies at the London School of Economics. His publications include *Tariff Preferences in Mediterranean Diplomacy* and *Foreign Economic Relations of the European Community*.

Geoffrey R.D. Underhill is Professor of International Governance at the Universiteit van Amsterdam. His books include *Industrial Crisis and the Open Economy: Politics, Global Trade, and Textiles in the Advanced Economies* (Macmillan 1998), *The New World Order in International Finance* (ed. Macmillan 1997) and *Non-State Actors and Authority in the Global System* (edited with R. Higgott and A. Bieler, Routledge, 2000).

Bertjan Verbeek is Associate Professor of International Political Economy at the School of Public Affairs of the University of Nijmegen, the Netherlands. He is co-editor of a forum on bureaucratic politics and foreign policy analysis in the *Mershon International Studies Review* (1998/2) and co-editor of *Autonomous Policymaking by International Organizations* (Routledge 1998).

Amy C. Verdun is Associate Professor of Political Science and Director of the European Studies Program at the University of Victoria, British Columbia, Canada. She is the author of *European Responses to Globalization and Financial Market Integration: Perceptions of Economic and Monetary Union in Britain, France and Germany* (Macmillan/St. Martin's Press 2000).

G.P.E. Walzenbach is Lecturer in European Politics at the University of the West of England, Bristol and a Research Fellow at the Centre for Economic and Social Science Research. He is the author of *Coordination in Context: Institutional Choices to Promote Exports* (Ashgate, 1998) and has published articles in the field of West European Politics and Comparative Political Economy.

PART I
THE POWER PILLARS OF THE WORLD POLITICAL ECONOMY

PART I.
THE POWER PILLARS OF
THE WORLD POLITICAL
ECONOMY.

1 Introduction: Looking Beyond the Confines

THOMAS C. LAWTON, JAMES N. ROSENAU AND AMY C. VERDUN

International relations stands as the one social science with barriers to entry so low that anyone can jump them. It has been and will remain the richer for keeping those barriers low. (Strange 1988)

Introduction

International Political Economy (IPE) has traditionally been viewed as a subset of international relations (IR). Its domain of research was generally perceived as international economic affairs, such as trade negotiations and economic sanctions. Ultimately, the paradigm was state centric: IPE was the study of the international economic activities of nation states. This perception dominated international relations literature from the discipline's emergence in the post-World War I era. It was only in the latter part of the 20th century that orientations began to change. Fuelled by the research of a handful of lateral-thinking intellectuals, IPE came to embody much more than state–state economic relations, challenging the realist assumption that states were all that mattered in the international system. First markets and then firms emerged as important international actors, as did other non-state players. International power resided not with or in states *per se* but rather in a set of global power structures. Certain states could shape the nature and direction of international relations through controlling access to these power structures. For example, the United States emerged as a global hegemon in the post-World War II era in part because US companies were at the forefront of new technological developments such as the invention of the microchip. Through its preferential access to this new meta-technology, the US government exercised structural power and therefore possessed relational power relative to other governments. This new way of perceiving international relations revolutionized the discipline.

A major scholar of this paradigm shift, one could say its 'intellectual midwife', was a British academic named Susan Strange. During the course of her long and illustrious career, Strange sought to legitimize her unique perspective and, in so doing, reshape the parameters of IPE. Even more than this, Strange undertook to reconceptualise IR more broadly. She evoked significant criticism even as she stimulated considerable debate with her claim that IR is a subset of IPE and not the other way around. She thus contributed to resetting the parameters for much of the discourse in contemporary IPE and IR. Strange contributed to the literature on IR and IPE in a variety of ways. She criticized the dominant IR theories for being too state-centric. She stressed the importance of also considering markets, firms and other non-state actors and the need to focus on the key power structures (finance, technology, security and production) in the international system. US scholars of IR and IPE were often criticized for having too narrow, too American a view of global politics.[1] Similarly, she criticized them for giving in to 'fashions' in methodology and theory (see, for example, Strange 1982). She was concerned about the fact that the *problématique* dealt with by international politics was too narrow, and advocated instead looking at the realm of politics as including much more than its traditional terrain. In her view crime, poverty the effects of politics on households and people's safety across the globe should be included in the study of international politics. The focus should be on the entire system. In addition, she prophesied the need to broaden the concept of power: it should include structural and relational power, the power to influence the ideas of others, their access to credit, security and prosperity (Strange 1988: 172). Strange's analyses and theories served to help shape the conceptual frameworks of many students and scholars of the global political economy.

The ensuing contributions are not intended as an uncritical account of one person's work. Rather, they are designed to bring together a set of ideas and findings that collectively shape the parameters of IPE. Whilst the book focuses on the contribution of Strange to IR/IPE, the remit is sufficiently wide to encompass a whole range of seemingly disparate themes and topics. In effect, the chapters amount to a critical and reflective work, relevant for scholars and students alike. The various themes covered fit together to form a unique perspective on the contemporary global economy and thus provide readers with analytic tools that better enable them to understand and interpret international relations in the era of the contemporary global economy. Furthermore, in line with Strange's overarching structural power theory, three spheres of contemporary structural transformation[2] are woven throughout the various chapters: first, the overarching power relationship in the global political economy, that is, whether or not a hegemonic form of power exists or will be maintained; second, the nature of political authority or authorities (the dominance of states in the world system); third, globalization – the inexorable movement towards a world market, functioning according to principles of economic liberalism.

Explaining International Political Economy

Gilpin (1987) argues that the tensions and interactions between politics and the economy constitute the stuff of political economy. He contends that central concerns of international political economy are the impact of the world market economy on the relations of states and the ways in which states seek to influence market forces for their own advantage (Goddard *et al.* 1996: 22). Other commentators argue that IPE was initially defined by the topics that it investigated such as trade, finance and multinational corporations (Katzenstein *et al.* 1998: 645). These perspectives were rejected by Strange as being too narrow, as failing to account for non-state actors in the international system. In particular, Strange was concerned with the role of large firms and the power that they often wielded in the world. In her later work, she also considered the role of other non-territorial sources of authority such as organized crime networks and non-governmental organizations like Greenpeace (Strange 1996: x).

Most importantly, Strange always advocated multidisciplinarity as essential to understanding change and outcomes in the international political economy (1996: xv). She advocated that IR and IPE scholars should listen to what other social scientists from a variety of disciplines have to say: scholars in business schools, economic historians, geographers, psychologists, sociologists and so forth. She believed that the discipline of international relations has lost ground, that separatist specialization is often rendered analytically inadequate in the complex and rapidly changing modern world political economy. However imperfect the findings may be, international studies scholars must attempt to synthesize and blend approaches and perspectives in their research.

IPE scholars have traditionally been seen as coming from one of three main ideological camps: Liberalism, Marxism and Realism. Each of the three schools of thought adopts its own set of principles and ideals to help make sense of a complex reality. A key differentiating factor is their respective units of analysis. Within international political economy, Liberals emphasize the individual, Marxists focus on class and Realists concentrate on the state. As Frieden and Lake

(1995: 32) point out, divergence also emerges on the inevitability of conflict within the political economy, and the relationship between economics and politics. Liberals believe that economics and politics are largely autonomous spheres, Marxists maintain that economics determines politics, and Realists argue that politics determines economics. As the IPE (sub)discipline emerged, it developed two main research domains: the international system and the interaction between domestic politics and the world political economy. The work of Strange was firmly located in the first of these fields. It may in fact be argued that she considered this to be the true focus of IPE as a distinct discipline, given its emphasis on the system rather than its subsets or players. Put differently, a central concern of IPE has to do with how the world is structured and who has systemic power.

The Dominant Debate: Neorealism versus Neoliberalism

Within international relations theory, there are continuing differences between neorealism and neoliberalism over which paradigm best explains the contemporary international system. According to Baldwin, the two camps agree that anarchy exists within the international system (1993: 4). However, they differ fundamentally over the extent of anarchy and thus the degree of independence which powers experience in decision making within this anarchical international system. Neorealists[3] argue that states still determine their own policies, based on self interest. This includes decisions concerning whether or not to participate in international alliances. Neoliberals argue that state autonomy is a myth, due to global interdependence (Milner 1988: 70; 81–2). The neoliberal position may be interpreted as contending that states cannot – as neorealists argue – make decisions based solely on national interest; but that systemic factors impinge on these decisions and restrict a country's ability to negotiate and legislate independently.

Neorealism[4] focuses much more than classical realism on the distribution of power as a determinant of outcomes (Keohane 1993: 271). It is particularly concerned with the constraints imposed on and incentives provided to states by the international system. Emerging from Waltz's seminal work, *Theory of International Politics* (1979), Keohane refers to Waltz's deductive theorization of political realism as 'structural realism' or 'neorealism'. Neorealism denotes both the 'intellectual affinity' of Waltz's approach 'with the classical realism of Morgenthau and Herz' and its own 'elements of originality and distinctiveness' (Keohane 1986: 15–16). Keohane acknowledges the emphasis placed by neorealists such as Waltz on system level theory, as it allows us 'to understand the context of states' actions before accounting for the actions themselves' (ibid.: 18). However, following on from the work of Keohane and Nye (1977), Keohane argues that Waltz's notion of structure is not sufficient to understand the international system in all its complexity. He contends that a more inclusive theory should account for economic processes and international political institutions (1986: 18). Furthermore, Keohane asserts that a more systematic bridging of the gap between external and internal environments is needed, through the development of improved theories of domestic politics and decision making (ibid.: 191). In partial response to Keohane's criticisms, Waltz acknowledges the need to complement any theory of international politics with a theory of domestic politics. He argues, however, that to do so is in fact fully in accordance with – and not contrary to – realist assumptions (Waltz 1986: 331).

Liberalism went through a different development process to realism. The updating of liberalism to neoliberalism occurred via institutionalist theory (often referred to as 'neoliberal institutionalism'). Keohane argues that the basis of institutionalist theory is moulded as much by realism as by liberalism (1993: 272). Neoliberal institutionalists accept that states are the primary actors in world politics and that realism/neorealism therefore 'provides a good starting point for the analysis of cooperation and discord [in the international system]' (Keohane 1984 : 245). However, as Keohane argues, realism 'does need to be reformulated to reflect the impact of information-providing institutions on state behavior' (ibid.: 246).

According to neoliberal institutionalists, institutions – defined by Keohane (1984) as 'sets of practices and expectations' rather than formal organizations *per se* – are central to our understanding of successful inter-state cooperation. Institutions (or 'regimes') are not perceived as instruments or organs of 'world government', approving the actions of nation states. Rather, they are viewed as facilitators of 'interstate agreements and decentralized enforcement', enabling governments to 'pursue ther own interests through cooperation' (ibid.: 246).

Ultimately, it would appear that the intellectual divide between neorealism and neoliberalism is not as great as some commentators would have us believe. Fundamentally, both schools of thought accept the primacy of states in world politics. However, through the incorporation of institutionalist ideas, neoliberalism goes further in providing a comprehensive theoretical lens on world politics.

The Structural Power Paradigm

Both neoliberal institutionalism and neorealism underrate the role played by non-state actors within international bargaining, and both fail to account for the impact which the system *per se*, and changes therein, can have on governmental trade and competitive positions. To trace these links we are led to examine the utility of structural power models. The structuralist approach to international relations was developed during the late 1960s and early 1970s from Marxist interpretations of world order (Frank 1967; Wallerstein 1974). The basic premise of this approach is that the proliferation of transnational cultural and economic interactions has led to the development of a global system. The structuralist school refers to this as the world economy (Palan 1992: 22). Their objective was, in the view of Wallerstein, 'to describe the world-system at a certain level of abstraction, that of the evolution of structures of the world system' (1974: 8).

The classical Marxist structuralist approach, however, was weakened by its underestimation of the role that states play within the world system. As Palan (1992) points out, a more balanced approach has since emerged which places the state centrally within any analysis of the international system. These scholars come from a disparate mix of disciplines, and adopt the view that the international system should not be approached as a one-dimensional, monolithic entity, but rather, should be viewed as a system containing numerous interlinked power structures (Braudel 1979; Strange 1988).

Strange handled these interlinkages by defining power as the capacity to make decisions on four basic societal needs in the modern world economy – security, knowledge, the production of goods and services and the provision of credit and money (1989: 165) – and by proposing (1988) that two types of power are exercised in the international political economy. One is power in the traditional realist sense of the authority (or power) of an international actor (always a state, according to the traditional realist approach) to force other actors in the system to do that which they would not do voluntarily. The other type is structural power, which exists at a different level and involves

> the power to shape and determine the structures of the global political economy within which other states, their political institutions, their economic enterprises and (not least) their scientists and other professional people, have to operate; structural power, in short, confers the power to decide how things shall be done, the power to shape frameworks within which states relate to each other, relate to people, or relate to corporate enterprises. (Strange 1988: 24–5).

Strange (1988) proceeds to argue that the structural power approach is of much greater utility when dealing with the international political economy, given its non-distinction between economic power and political power. It is, in fact, a more actor-neutral theory (compared with the traditional power framework) and thus allows for the consideration of non-state actors in determining the nature and course of international relations.

Strange develops her argument further by contending that a number of separate but interdependent power structures exist within the international system. These may be seen as the four pillars of the international political economy. Strange argues that structural power is the unevenly distributed systemic ability to define the basic structures of these four pillars: security, credit, production and knowledge (ibid.: 15). All other elements of the international political economy (for example, global issues such as trade or more specific sectoral items such as integrated circuits) are secondary structures, being moulded by the four fundamental power structures. In Chapter 2, Story will consider the nature of these four pillars and comment on their implications for IR/IPE.

A final point worth noting is the claim that technology (stemming from the knowledge structure) is of central importance, both in gaining traditional power and in strengthening the other three pillars of systemic power. This primacy of technology and the knowledge structure within the contemporary international political economy corresponds to the rise of what Drucker described as the symbol economy (1986: 781). Drucker describes this as the emergence of a global economy that is driven by flows of invisible assets such as capital and credit (and we might add technology). Such an information-driven economy has become intertwined with the real or tangible economy, that is, the flow of goods and services (ibid.: 782). Thus invisible assets drive the economy and technology is the most crucial of invisible assets. The knowledge structure has therefore come to dominate other structures such as finance and production.

Strange argued subsequently (1996: x) that the notion of structural power in world politics, society and economy liberated the study of international political economy from the realist tradition in the study of international relations. Put differently, the structuralist approach also seeks to identify how international relationships are shaped by both state actions and systemic developments, thereby merging the realist state-centric and the system interlinkage approaches.

This merger is also consistent with Drucker's (1986) argument that the society of states is now overlaid by a complex, interdependent, world economy.[5] Moreover, the notion of structural change enables us to understand why and how the power of firms has increased relative to governments, and consequently changed the nature of international relations. Strange argued that structural changes in finance, information and communications systems, defense equipment and production methods have together played the most important role in redefining the relationship between authority (government) and market (firms). The fundamental catalyst encompassing all of these changes is technology. The changing nature of technology has altered the allocation and exercise of structural power, through its transformative effect on the central pillars of structural power (Strange 1991: 38).

To clarify the determinants of change at a systemic level, it is accepted that the state, the market and technology together comprise the three broad vehicles of transformation (Strange 1991). Each of these three systemic players shapes the nature of the four pillars of structural power. However, the degree of influence is the key factor: government and market influence have been, and continue to be, considerable, but the rate of change introduced by technology is, and continues to be, far greater in terms of its scope and depth. In addition, it is important to realize that, although technology is the central player in structural change, it is not a tangible, structured entity. Therefore one must attempt to determine who or what controls both its form and results. Such direct control rests, for the most part (that is, excluding government/military research and development laboratories), with corporate enterprises. It follows that considerable power and authority within the international system has been lost to the market, thus significantly enhancing the role and strength of firms within the state–firm bargaining process.

Overview of the Book

This volume is divided into seven parts and 21 chapters, plus an annotated bibliography. Part I sets out the broad parameters of Strange's approach to international political economy and critically examines her power structures. In this chapter we have sought to suggest how Strange's work has shaped the nature and discourse of contemporary international political economy and how it links into the relationship between international political economy and international relations, with an emphasis on the importance of the four structural power pillars to an understanding of this relationship.

In Chapter 2, Jonathan Story points out that a key feature of Strange's writings was her argument that states were not the sole authorities in the world political economy. This statement was directed back to the realists, such as Morgenthau, who dominated debates in the 1960s over the cold war. The statement was then directed against US interdependence/regime theorists who came to dominate IR discourse from the mid-1970s on. Strange's major positive statement developed the idea of the attributes of power, providing a canvas of authorities much broader than traditional writers on international relations. Yet there were significant ambiguities regarding the role of states in her work, particularly when she attacked the exponents of world financial markets from a traditional Keynesian perspective.

Chapter 3, by Lynn Mytelka, looks closely at the relationship between states and firms in the creation of a structure of power in which knowledge figures centrally. It does so by focusing upon the changing nature of knowledge as a structural basis for power in the international political economy. The chapter examines the role of the state in the relationship between power and production in historical perspective and then proceeds to introduce three critical changes that have enhanced the role of knowledge as a vector for power in the international economy. These are the privatization of knowledge and the role now played by knowledge-intensive production and innovation-based competition in global competitiveness. The final section of the chapter examines the way in which power derived from the knowledge structure has increasingly shaped international rule making at the turn of the millennium.

In Chapter 4, Thomas Lawton and Kevin Michaels are concerned with production, another pillar of Strange's structural power concept. Contrary to recent critical thought, something has changed between the globalization process of the late 19th century and that of the late 20th century. There has been a fundamental change in what Strange defined as the production structure. Specifically, inter-firm trade in intermediate products has become far more important than foreign direct investment in terms of international economic growth. Lawton and Michaels begin by examining Strange's notion of the production structure and its place in structural power. They proceed to discuss the changing process of globalization and the growth in intermediate products, deconstructing Michael Porter's value chain concept in the process. They argue that, in addition to developments in communications, the 'new globalism' is characterized in large part by changes in the production structure. For governments to adapt to this new environment, they need to think in terms of how to gain or maintain comparative advantage in a particular part of the value chain.

The link between money and power in world politics was one of the most enduring themes in Strange's work. The second part of the volume is therefore devoted to a fourth pillar of structural power – finance. Considerable attention is given to this component, in part because of the emphasis which Strange placed upon the role of money and finance in the international political economy and in part because finance and money is a primary field of IPE.

In Chapter 5, Amy Verdun focuses on Strange's analysis of how the structure of the financial system implies a set of embedded power relations underpinning the international system of states. These power relations affect the relative roles of state and non-state actors in the constitution of the international political economy and Strange's arguments furthermore imply the need to challenge state-centric conceptions of international political economy. The chapter also discusses Strange's criticism on the study of international politics, as well as the other scholars' criticisms of Strange's approach.

In Chapter 6, Benjamin Cohen concentrates on the link between understanding power in international relations and the global monetary system. He looks at the impact of money and finance on the international *political* system, with particular emphasis on the role of money as a power variable in inter-state relations. The chapter also explores the exact nature of state power in monetary affairs and how it changes over time. It also examines the consequences of alternative distributions of monetary power for the management of global finance. The focus is strictly on inter-state relations.

In Chapter 7, Geoffrey Underhill carries forward the insights of Verdun and Cohen and investigates how Strange's analysis of monetary and financial order, including the prominent role of non-state actors in the emergence of global financial markets, informed her understanding of the role of the state in an era of global economic integration. The chapter also challenges Strange's 'retreat of the state' thesis and develops resultant theoretical implications for an understanding of the global political economy and the state.

Part III is concerned with critical perspectives on international relations. Beginning with Chapter 8, Bertjan Verbeek considers whether the current debate regarding the nature of international relations, and international political economy in particular, is related to different views of various academic communities, roughly along an American/non-American cleavage. He argues that any claim about American intellectual hegemony obscures the main issue at stake: are international politics and international economics related, but clearly distinct, spheres, or do they constitute one integrated research subject? The answer to this ontological question sets limits on the theoretical and methodological approaches available. This chapter argues in favor of the second perspective.

In Chapter 9, Claire Cutler examines various approaches to critical theory of IR. The chapter aims at reflecting on the work of Susan Strange and drawing comparisons with other critical thinkers in the field of IR theory. Some scholars have claimed that Strange in fact was a Marxist or at least part of the historical–materialist tradition. This chapter traces that debate and analyses the extent to which Strange's work indeed can be categorized as such. It also emphasizes the specificity of her approach and the extent to which it has influenced the discipline of international relations.

Roger Tooze's Chapter 10 attempts to develop a critical analysis of ideas, ideology and knowledge in the global political economy (GPE). It seeks to review the way we think about the nature of ideology and knowledge by situating them within a critical political economy of knowledge, and from this revised conception it illustrates the necessary role of 'neoliberal ideology' in constructing and maintaining the current configuration of power in the GPE.

Part IV examines state power and global hegemony. In Chapter 11, Robert Gilpin rebukes 'the retreat of the state' thesis, arguing in favor of the continued relevance of realism to an understanding of international relations and international political economy. In so doing, he discusses the role and power of the state in the modern international system and reflects on the globalization debate. He contends that the state has not lost its economic autonomy and that it does continue to have considerable latitude in the formulation and implementation of economic policies.

Chapter 12, by Stefano Guzzini, argues that Strange's realism displays a central duality. Traditionally, the discipline of international relations conceives of realism in opposition to idealism, to utopian thinking. This chapter shows that Strange fits rather well some of the central tenets of realism so understood. She did not spare her criticism of those fellow realists who did not seem to appreciate what she considered to be major shifts in the nature of global affairs. Strange, the anti-idealist realist, was the champion of a power-materialist discipline of International Political Economy which subsumes, if not swallows, classical International Relations and its more narrow-minded scholars, as she would see them. But then, in political theory, realism has also seen IPE as a development of realism.

In Chapter 13, Eric Helleiner provides a commentary on one of the central debates that Strange generated in IPE during the last phase of her career, the debate about the trajectory of US power in the world economy. Helleiner highlights how Strange's views were not in fact all that different from the US school's hegemonic stability theory. Whereas in Chapter 8, Verbeek stresses how Strange critiqued US IR/IPE thought, Helleiner emphasizes how in fact she shared some similar assumptions with US advocates of the hegemonic stability theory. Her disagreement concerned how the theory was applied historically and in the current day. Strange, for instance, argued throughout the 1980s and early 1990s that US scholars were overstating the decline of US hegemony, especially in finance, and that they were thus misinterpreting the roots of global economic instability. Helleiner contends that this position has essentially been proven right in the 1990s, when US dominance in global finance has once again been apparent.

In Chapter 14, Judith Goldstein examines the recent history of US trade policy and the role of the US in shaping the development of the

World Trade Organisation (WTO). She considers the extent to which the WTO has been shaped in America's image, compounding the argument, advanced by Strange and by Helleiner in the previous chapter, that US global hegemony is ongoing and enduring. The chapter also considers the extent and nature of US influence and control over other international trade and investment regimes such as the North American Free Trade Agreement (NAFTA) and the extent to which this regional grouping represents differing perspectives on international trade and investment, or acts merely as a vehicle for US economic power.

The book's fifth part shifts the emphasis away from more general system theory and towards applied regional political economies. The emergence of a global economic order has been accompanied by the consolidation of regional economic groupings such as NAFTA, the Association of South East Asian Nations (ASEAN), and the European Union (EU), which embodies a new form of governance of the economy as well as a combined regional economic power in the global system.

In Chapter 15, Julie Pellegrin states there is no doubt that the question as to whether and how the EU will be able to consolidate and improve its competitiveness will have wide repercussions for the global economy at large. But whose competitiveness are we talking about? Her chapter echoes Strange's point on the ambiguity of the notion of competitiveness and applies it to the case of the enlargement process of the EU. Enlargement is indeed one decisive factor in the definition of Europe's relative competitiveness. By uniting two areas at different levels of development characterized by large gaps between living standards and cost levels, enlargement unleashes unprecedented potentials for trade, investment and rapid economic growth. The chapter asks whether and by whom these potentials are seized: states, firms and/or EU *societies*?

The dramatic rise and fall of Japan has been an important subject of discourse in modern IPE. In Chapter 16, Jean-Pierre Lehmann examines Japan's failure in the 1990s to rise to globalism due to its inability to engage in the creative destruction of its obsolescent statist, nationalist model. He argues that only by bringing about a domestic sea change in genuinely opening up the country and all its institutions to the forces of globalization will Japan be reinvigorated. The chapter also includes an assessment of the impact of globalization on East Asia, with particular stress on the crisis of 1997 and how the East Asian political economy may evolve in light of the collapse of the Japanese model. The effects that developments in Japan and East Asia will have on the international political economy are considered. The chapter concludes by asking whether Strange's perspectives on the evolution of the emerging actors within the nation state and the relations between states that are thereby derived fit into the Japanese/East Asian paradigms.

The completion of the Uruguay Round in 1993 and the creation of the WTO have not halted the formation of trading blocks, although the process is slower than before 1993. There are clear signs of the world trading system shifting towards regionalism if not regional trading blocks. In Chapter 17, Alfred Tovias discusses the way in which trading blocks can be seen as a potent way of conducting struggles in the international political arena. The chapter reflects on both IR theories and IPE theories, and argues that the latter offer much more potent frameworks of analysis for understanding contemporary international politics.

In Chapter 18, Anna Leander argues that an interesting two-way critique of economic development emerges from Strange's ideas on the place of the developing world in IPE. This critique first accuses classical economics of not accounting for the systematic and structural impediments that retard Third World economic development. However, it also accuses the developmental/dependency school of not recognizing the potential benefits of foreign direct investment and the harmful effects of protectionism. This dual-pronged critique is evident in several of Strange's later works and culminated in a genuine concern about the fragmenting of the world economy and the increasing prosperity gap between the rich north and the poor south.

Part VI of the volume focuses on emerging research agendas in IPE. In Chapter 19, Walzenbach argues that, while Strange's work in the IPE field has been generally acknowledged, her thoughts as a comparativist are either neglected or oversimplified as a sweeping anti-institutionalist critique. In this chapter, he traces this second perspective throughout her most influential works, to assess its shortcomings and to discuss how, nevertheless, it could be utilized for innovative and refreshing research. It is argued that new insights could be gained by confronting the Strange-type realism with more recent attempts to combine the various strands of political economy in a common analytical framework.

Chapter 20, by Timothy Shaw, Sandra Maclean and Maria Nzomo, argues that we should go beyond the outdated and misleading orthodoxies of both realism and international political economy by bringing in civil societies. In this they are picking up on one of Strange's final areas of interest. This involves focusing on the way non-governmental organizations (NGOs) and other elements in civil society seek to maximize their global activity and visibility.

The final section of the book draws together some of the overarching ideas and issues raised throughout the volume. An annotated bibliography is also provided in an addendum to the text. In Chapter 21,

David Earnest, Louis Pauly and the editors advance a final commentary on analyses pursued in several previous chapters, discussing the extent to which Strange succeeded in blurring a number of established 'academic boundaries' in IR/IPE. These are primarily the boundaries between economics and political science and the cultural boundary between American and European international studies scholarship. We also reflect on the significant epistemological boundary between non-normative political science and normative political theory. In addition, the authors discuss the global governance agenda and Strange's views on this important theme in modern IPE. Finally, we attempt to illustrate how the collection of chapters in this book, inspired by the work of Susan Strange, have enabled a more integrated and realistic view of the world political economy.

The book concludes with an annotated bibliography of Susan Strange's academic lifework. This represents an impressive array of critical insights into various aspects of international studies, spanning half a century. Christopher May lists the works in chronological order and briefly relates the content of each item to the development of Strange's thought.

Final Comments

We conclude this introduction with a note about a strand of Strange's work that is not an explicit focus of any of the chapters. None explicitly focuses on the concept of security, which, it will be recalled, Strange regarded as one of the pillars of structural power. The omission of a security chapter is due partly to the limits of available space, but mainly it stems from the absence of IPE specialists for whom security questions are a major concern. Many of them focus so fully on the political aspects of economic phenomena that they tend to take security questions for granted. Not so with Strange. She devoted considerable attention to exploring the premise that, in the future as in the past, 'the world's economic order will depend ... on developments in the global security structure' (1988: 59). Stated in more general terms, Strange's conception of IPE was not a narrow one. Rather, it roamed widely across the terrain of IPE and, in so doing, achieved a rare and edifying coherence. Although we lack an explicit focus on security, many of the chapters do include security considerations in their analyses and arguments. Moreover, national and international security considerations are seldom far from the minds of the editors and from the overall theme of this book.

Notes

1 When Strange referred to 'Americans', she was referring to US Americans.
2 First identified by Robert Cox, in Morgan *et al.* (1993).
3 Keohane and Nye argue that the key difference between realism and neorealism is that the latter concept 'aspires to the status of science' (1989: 247).
4 The term 'neorealism' is generally attributed to Robert Cox.
5 Peter Drucker (1986), cited in Susan Strange (1994: 212).

References

Baldwin, D.A. (1993), 'Neoliberalism, Neorealism, and World Politics', in David A. Baldwin (ed.), *Neorealism and Neoliberalism: The Contemporary Debate*, New York: Columbia University Press.

Braudel, F. (1979), *Civilisation Matérielle, Economie et Capitalisme: XVe–XVIIIe Siècle*, Paris: Colin.

Drucker, P. (1986), 'The Changed World Economy', *Foreign Affairs*, Spring.

Frank, A.G. (1967), *Capitalism and Under-Development in Latin America: Historical Studies of Chile and Brazil*, New York: Monthly Review Press.

Frieden, J.A. and D.A. Lake (1995) *International Political Economy: perspectives on global power and wealth*, Routledge: London.

Gilpin, R. (1987), *The Political Economy of International Relations*, Princeton, NJ: Princeton University Press.

Goddard, C.R., J.T. Passé-Smith and J.G. Conklin (1996) *International Political Economy: state–market relations in the changing global order*, Boulder, CO: Lynne Rienner.

Katzenstein, P.J., R.O. Keohane and S.D. Krasner (1998), 'International Organization and the Study of World Politics', *International Organization*, 52(4), 645–85.

Keohane, R.O. (1984), *After Hegemony: Cooperation and Discord in the World Political Economy*, Princeton, NJ: Princeton University Press.

Keohane, R.O. (ed.) (1986), *Neorealism and Its Critics*, New York: Columbia University Press.

Keohane, R.O. (1993), 'Institutional Theory and the Realist Challenge After the Cold War', in David A. Baldwin (ed.), *Neorealism and Neoliberalism: The Contemporary Debate*, New York: Columbia University Press.

Keohane, R.O. and J.S. Nye (1977), *Power and Interdependence: World Politics in Transition*, Boston: Little & Brown Publishers.

Milner, H.V. (1988), *Resisting Protectionism: Global Industries and the Politics of International Trade*, Princeton, NJ: Princeton University Press.

Morgan. R., J. Lorentzen, A. Leander and S. Guzzini (eds) (1993), *New Diplomacy in the Post-Cold War Era: Essays for Susan Strange*, London: St. Martin's Press.

Palan, R. (1992), 'The Second Structuralist Theories of International Relations: A Research Note', *International Studies Notes*, International Studies Association, 17(3), Fall, 22–29.

Strange, S. (1982), 'Cave! Hic Dragones: A Critique of Regime Analysis', *International Organisation*, 36(2), Spring, 479–97.

Strange, S. (1988), *States and Markets: An Introduction to International Political Economy*, London: Pinter.

Strange, S. (1989), 'Towards a Theory of Transnational Empire', in E-O. Czempiel and J.N. Rosenau (eds), *Global Changes and Theoretical Challenges: Approaches to World Politics for the 1990s*, Lexington: Lexington Books.

Strange, S. (1991), 'An Eclectic Approach', in Craig N. Murphy and Roger Tooze (eds), *The New International Political Economy*, Boulder, Co.: Lynne Rienner.

Strange, S. (1994), 'Wake up, Krasner! The world *has* changed', *Review of International Political Economy*, 1(2), Summer, 209–19.

Strange, S. (1996), *The Retreat of the State: The Diffusion of Power in the World Economy*, Cambridge: Cambridge University Press.

Wallerstein, I. (1974), *The Capitalist World Economy*, Cambridge: Cambridge University Press.

Waltz, K.N. (1986) 'Reflections on *Theory of International Politics*: A response to my critics', in R.O. Keohane (ed.), *Neorealism and Its Critics*, New York: Columbia University Press.

2 Setting the Parameters: A Strange World System

JONATHAN STORY

Introduction

During the decades when Strange was most active as an international relations scholar (from the 1960s through to the 1990s), the world political economy prompted four related transformations. The first of these was the transformation of the state system as the United States grew into its eminence as the world's sole great power, the number of states multiplied as former European colonies claimed political independence, and the major powers sought to minimize the risks of war between themselves. The second component was the relentless retreat of any alternative forms of government to 'market democracy', as oligarchies, military juntas or various forms of fascism and communism failed the test of time, as illustrated by the long line of failures, defeats and disasters that accompanied their often turbulent demise. The third of these transformations was the recreation of the world market by the Western powers, and by the United States in particular, to reach a level of integration unknown since the first decade of the 20th century. But unlike the situation in the earlier period, trade and investments after 1945 were overwhelmingly by large industrial corporations, financed by the explosive growth of global financial markets. These financial markets would never have reached the size they did without the expansion in government debt which accompanied the move by all industrial countries to fund expenditures through the issue of bonds, and by the related development of speculative foreign exchange markets. The fourth of these transformations was the growth of the industrial or service corporation, initially based in a home country, and with subsidiaries or market outlets in host countries, towards becoming a transnational group with subsidiaries and markets located around the globe, and with a widely dispersed shareholder community, and a non-national

19

recruitment policy. All available indicators, such as the estimated global sales of foreign subsidiaries, pointed to the continued expansion of international production and the deepening of interdependence in the world economy, beyond that achieved by international trade alone.

These four, interrelated strands of a global transformation were simultaneous in that they interacted in a myriad of ways over the years, but they were not synchronized. Unravelling cause and effect thus became an arduous task and generated much theoretical exploration in the field of international relations. A key feature of Strange's writings was her argument that states were not the sole authorities in the world political economy. This statement was directed back to some, but not all of the realists, such as Morgenthau (1967) and Bull (1997), who dominated debates in the decades following World War II, and focused their writing on states as the key units in the international system or society of states; but it was directed much less at other writers, usually associated with the realist school, such as Aron (1962) and E.H. Carr (1939). Aron and Carr, unlike Morgenthau and Bull, took into consideration the ideological, social and industrial dimensions of power in world politics. Waltz (1979) discussed the limits to market interdependence as rooted in the state system, but underplayed market dynamics on his state structure. Strange's statement was then directed against US interdependence/regime theorists who came to dominate IR discourse from the mid-1970s on, and who incorporated market transactions into the heart of their thinking. Strange approved of their cross-disciplinary approach, but attacked them for developing theories which exonerated the United States from acting responsibly in world affairs, and that failed to address the crucial links between the international political system, economic disorders and diverse values.

To Strange, the defining characteristic of the late 20th century was that humanity was undergoing major structural change, and that conventional frameworks of analysis failed to take these dynamics into account. Strange's writings are haunted by memories of the 1930s, the breakdown of the world economy, the slide to war, and the disasters that ensued (Strange 1986: 192; 1998b: 90–95). Hers was an appeal to recognize the urgency of developing a theory to bring politics and economics together to guide policy in a dynamic world system. Her world system was not composed of two political and economic systems gliding by like ships at night; they are one and the same system (Strange 1976: 20) and their core is the modern corporation, markets and technology (Strange 1991b). Her 'new realist' approach is based on an empirical study linking state policies to corporate strategies, the new diplomacy transforming world politics and markets. The following sections discuss Strange's theoretical objectives, her analysis of the dynamics of change, her warnings about the traps to avoid in the prolonged US debate on hegemons, and finally her model of structural power and its applicability to international political economy.

Strange Objectives

Reforming the agenda of international relations was Strange's prime objective. In *Sterling and British Policy* (1971), she concludes that British policy makers connived with successive US administrations and economists in misdirecting attention to sterling and the alleged weaknesses of the British economy and the British balance of payments, when in effect the root of the British problem lay in its vulnerability to the policies of the United States, the world's top currency country. In part, this was the result of a failure in Whitehall to appreciate that traditional reflexes were no substitutes for carefully crafted policies in a post-war world. But the failure was also due to the atrophy in the study of international relations. Instead of developing a modern study of international political economy, its protagonists had allowed a yawning gulf to widen yearly between international politics and international economics. International economic relations were left to the economists whose writings were both partial and naïve (Strange 1970: 304). They were partial because their focus on the mechanics of market transactions derived from the methods taught in US universities, the headquarters of the economics profession, and served to direct attention away from more fundamental questions. They were naïve because they wrote as if political factors did not exist, as if economic policies were made after careful analysis of economic costs and benefits, and not out of ambition, fear or 'totally irrelevant considerations and irrational emotions' (ibid.: 314).

Political science was no better. The focus in international relations was resolutely on the diplomatic–strategic arena of the cold war, despite the paramount significance of economic development to the poorer countries, and of international economic relations to the members of the West's 'affluent alliance'. European integration studies, too, were dominated by neofunctionalists, whose assumptions about international organizations filching the sovereignties of states by stealth had recently received rude treatment at the hands of President de Gaulle. Abstract theories, such as systems analysis and game theory, could only be applied by political sophisticates; in the hands of the uninitiated, they were nitroglycerine. 'Vague and woolly words' (Strange 1997: xii) were no substitute for placing political factors once again at the heart of economic analysis.

The basic tenet of international relations theories challenged by Strange is the assumption of the state as the sole unit to be taken into account in world affairs (Strange and Tooze 1981: 4–5). The tenet is predicated on the presumption of the separability of the domestic domain of the territorial state, and the system of states where no authority is endowed with a monopoly of violence. Within its frontiers, the politics of a state is a complex affair, arranged differently according to the country's political culture, the degree of loyalty paid by citizens to the state, the nature of the political system and the control exercised by the state over citizens and territory alike. Externally, states coexist in rivalry with other states, fed by the insecurity that is endemic to the condition of membership in this 'anarchical society' of states. The major political issue is how to preserve some minimal order and to prevent or to minimize the risk of war between states. The behavior of states among each other is thus different in nature to domestic politics. Confronting a hostile world, states demand loyalty of their citizens and act as a unitary front in relations with others. They seek to supplement their weaknesses by making alliances in order to draw on the strengths of others. But as all states seek to maximize power and wealth, their calculations on the expected benefits and costs rarely coincide. To the extent that alliances can be harnessed to the service of a temporary order, they have to be the instruments of the great powers, differentiated from lesser states by their capabilities. Great powers rise and fall, but world politics only shifts from one structure to another. According to this view, all that has happened over the course of the last century is that, with the collapse of the Soviet empire, the world is back to an unstable multipolar order. In place of the bipolar balance between the two superpowers and their respective alliances, there are five great powers – the United States, the EU, Japan, China, possibly Russia – much as there were five or six great powers in Europe, prior to the outbreak of war in 1914 (Strange 1994a: 5). It is against this position that little fundamental has changed in the nature of world politics that Strange rebels, and the 'fiction' she attacks is the separability of national and international politics, which makes it possible to argue that the study of national politics and the study of international politics are different in kind.

Why then did Strange differ from the theorists of transnational relations and of economic interdependence who successfully recorded the permeability of state authority in an increasingly integrated world economy? Their conclusions, after all, were compatible with Strange's position that the state-centred paradigm was not an adequate foundation for the study of a world in transformation. Nor was there much to distinguish between their respective positions regarding 'the end of sovereignty' thesis. 'And what, anyway, do we understand by this "economic sovereignty"?', she asks rhetorically. 'Is it not, after all a concept which never could be defined in any absolute terms, and which in contemporary terms is increasingly drained of meaning?' (Strange 1976: 21). The answer to the question of where she differed lies in the very different emphases of the two studies conducted in parallel on international economic relations in Chatham House and in Boston. The Chatham House study on the international economic relations of the Western world in the 1960s insisted on challenging the assumptions of both international (liberal) economics and international politics, whereas the Boston study on cooperation and conflict in a system of 'complex interdependence' borrowed from neoliberal institutional theory, and placed states once again center stage (Keohane and Nye 1977). Neoliberal institutionalists maintained that organizations or regimes arose in response to the unequal distribution of information between agents in conditions of imperfect competition. Keohane and Nye (1977) went on to theorize that regimes changed as a function of the overall power structure, the economic process, the relative powers of states in particular 'issue areas', and bargaining within international organizations. Strange's position in the Chatham House volume was to warn against illusions that people and governments would develop a sense of collective responsibility, and drew attention to 'the nature of the limiting factors, the reservations and qualifications which were attached on various occasions to international co-operative actions' (Strange 1976: 24). This skepticism then developed into two central arguments. The first held that regime theory helped to explain how states sought to control outcomes abroad and at home, but failed to explain nondecisions to allow non-regimes to survive (Strange 1986: 25–59). The second argument drew attention to the fact that states and societies do not subscribe just to liberal economic values of efficiency, based on the individual pursuit of private interest, but to other values also such as security, equality and justice (Strange 1988a: 9–22).

Strange's ambition was either to develop herself, or to cajole colleagues in international relations departments to develop, a theoretical approach that could be used by people with different value preferences. The essential condition for such an approach was that it took into account the dynamics of change in the international system, and therefore of the state. What she proposed was a Cartesian synthesis of opposed paradigms in international studies: the realist, the idealist and the structuralist (Strange 1995: 55). Since the 1930s, she argued, there had been a triangular dialogue of the deaf between realists, idealists and Gramscian structuralists. From the 1930s to the 1960s, and then in revived form in the subsequent two decades, the debate had been dominated by the realists, who despaired of changing an international political system based on states. So the most they could recommend was awareness of the institutions that sustained and moderated state behavior in 'the anarchic society', or to develop ideas, such as regime theory, to enable states to cope better. Idealists sought for ways to reduce conflict and to foster cooperation between states through the creation of international institutions, agreement on general principles of conduct, and the elaboration of rules, regulations and procedures. Their aim was, and is, gradually to transform the international system, so as to bring the 'anarchic society' of states more under a common law, similar to domestic law in individual states. The structuralists, named after the Italian Communist Party leader, Gramsci, favored radical structural change of social and economic relations in the world, and regarded the state system as one facet, and one facet only, of an unjust structure of power. That structure was based on what Robert Cox (1987) has called the 'production structure' of how the world does its work. For Cox, reform of that structure also entails going beyond the existing state system to a 'post-Westphalian' design where state sovereignties no longer serve as an excuse for predatory conduct internationally (Cox 1997). Strange's contribution lies in bringing this Marxian and postmodern vision of world politics to the center of her analysis.

Dynamics of Change

The dynamics of change in the second half of the 20th century, and especially from the 1960s on, were not located in states and international organization – the focus of realist and idealist approaches to the study of international relations – but in markets and corporate organizations. That is Strange's central thesis. Most of the 'string of vague and woolly words' conceived to describe the diffusion of power in the world economy are state-centric or plain euphemisms for the export of American culture and preferences. 'Globalization', for instance, means anything from the sale of hamburgers to the internet, but in effect is associated with Americanization, just as the word 'multinational' corporation was coined by IBM, a quintessentially US corporation, to present a non-national image to the world. 'Global governance', by contrast, is state-centric in that it refers to cooperation and harmonization or standardization of practice between governments of territorial states, just as 'interdependence' stands for asymmetric dependence of smaller states on the world's hegemon. They are therefore partial descriptives, and cannot serve as an objective vocabulary to develop a viable theory for international political economy. Yet Strange acknowledges that the United States, with its federal law, huge state sector, large corporations and financial institutions, universities and publicly as well as privately funded research laboratories and vast internal market, is the epicentre of a world market, reconstituted under US patronage after 1945. It is the impersonal forces of world markets, integrated over the postwar period more by private enterprise in finance, industry and trade than by the cooperative decisions of governments, [that] are now more powerful than the states to whom ultimate political authority over society and economy is supposed to belong. (Strange 1997: 4)

From this flow a number of propositions central to her conception of international political economy. The first is that war and peace between states is no longer a prime concern, compared to the economic and political dimensions of world markets. Governments of all major states have to deal with materialist societies. Their demands can only be pursued by the pursuit of wealth within their own territory, and definitely not by engaging in war for power over more territory. Populations want trade, not because it brings cooperation between peoples, but because without trade wealth could not be achieved. Indeed, governments can only fund the development costs of weapons by sales on world markets, thereby greatly altering the prospects of achieving a reasonable degree of world order. But at the same time, citizens of the affluent alliance are increasingly rejecting war with other major states as too dangerous an option. All these developments have shifted the agenda of governments from the political concerns of foreign offices to conduct relations of power and prestige between states, to business concerns for market access, product promotion or foreign exchange regimes. If states compete, it is not over territory, but for market shares, as success in the pursuit of wealth may contribute to cementing the domestic consensus. States are concerned primarily to ensure that business conditions within their own jurisdiction are sufficiently attractive to foster wealth-creating activities and to attract inward investment by multinational corporations. This requires changing the economic policy framework away from offering privileged conditions to 'national champions', and towards forging alliances with multinational corporations.

The second proposition is that the power of states is in decline. States, Strange argues, are not obsolete, and the boundaries of states have not disappeared yet to allow us to talk of a global society (Strange 1997: 33). But all states have found their power and authority hollowed out, as they have had to share functions with an ever wider range of interested parties. Their powers to ensure the security and wealth of their citizens are shared with other governments, and with firms; they share powers with the financial markets to set the value of their currencies; their powers to raise revenues are shared in many countries with political parties and mafias, while the development of the internet threatens to provide citizens with the means to place their incomes outside the state's territorial jurisdiction. States, in other words, are one among many actors on the world stage, but it nonetheless remains the case that the authority of states has been differently affected by the spread of market exchanges (Strange 1995). Consider the case of the United States, which, she argues, has lost authority to the world markets which US diplomacy so assiduously encouraged. But the United States has not lost power to other states, or to other international organizations. It is other states which have become more vulnerable to the forces of world markets, the global reach of US authority, and the determination of US economic diplomacy to create more open access around the world for the products, patents and services of US enterprises. In the EU, by contrast, states have lost powers to international organizations, seen powers seep downwards to local authorities and bargained with firms to meet the materialist aspirations of citizens. In the wider world, many traditional functions of the state to provide for their citizens are no longer discharged at all, given the combination of circumstances created by the dispersion of authority between states and other actors and the integration of the world economy.

The third proposition is that 'the pace of development in the international economic system has accelerated, is still accelerating and will probably continue to accelerate; and that in consequence, it is outdistancing and outgrowing the rather more static international political system' (1970: 305). This pace of development, and the resulting shift in the balance of power between states and markets, is generated by two key factors: one is the accelerating pace of technological change and the second is the development of financial markets capable of funding the capital cost of most technological innovations (Strange 1997: 7). The key agent of change is the multinational corporation and the globalization of production that has been the result of the corporation's need to recuperate the cost of investment in new technologies. Corporations need access to world markets and have to negotiate the terms with governments. States may deny access, but once the go-ahead has been granted, the corporation decides where, how and when to invest (Strange 1991b: 246). The wider the spread of its facilities around the globe, the more the corporation becomes a diplomatic partner with many states, and has to engage in a complex juggling act with many ministries, many labor unions and many suppliers or distributors. Indeed, it is the corporation that is transforming the world political system by establishing transnational networks of alliances and arrangements with other corporations, and by entering bargains on a bilateral basis with states. This 'new diplomacy' (Strange 1991b: 1–31) is quite distinct from traditional economic diplomacy between states. The new diplomacy is characterized by bargains between states and corporations, where control over outcomes can be negotiated; by contrast, traditional economic diplomacy is unable to control the outcomes decided by the global financial markets. The United States used these traditional channels and its powers to make crucial non-decisions to create what Strange calls the Frankenstein of the world market, with the result that the markets have escaped US control, and the pretensions of the Group of Seven industrialized countries to manage them are hollow (Strange 1988b: 16).

The fourth proposition thus holds that the world polity is pluralist. After three centuries in which state authority over society was centralized, the trend is in the opposite direction with the world moving forward to a 'new medievalism' (Strange 1988a: 229–32; Strange 1997: 30–43). Strange means by this that competing authorities coexist in world politics and markets, as power has become more dispersed: the problem is that this 'new medieval' world has no pope and no emperor. The world is materialist, driven by greed and self-interest, while the emperor – the United States – is unwilling or unable to behave responsibly. Consequently, the principles of pluralist (domestic) politics developed in the 1950s and 1960s to challenge the old view of the state as in charge of its domestic affairs, she suggests, should be applied to world politics. These principles are best suited, she contends, to a world more than halfway to a world economy and a world society. A pluralist perspective reduces the significance of the traditional distinction between domestic and international, and populates the world system with more authorities than states. Politics, the pluralist school argues, is not just what politicians do. Politics occurs whenever individuals seek support from others to achieve objectives. This definition presents politics as ubiquitous, and populates its arena with a broad fauna of organizations and individuals. Following Easton's famous definition of politics as 'the authoritative allocation of values in the system' (1965), Strange defines politics as those processes and structures through which the mix of values in the system – freedom, equality, security, justice – are distributed among groups and individuals. She also deploys Lasswell's (1950) formulation, of politics as who gets what, when and how, and refers to Dahl and Lindblom's (1953; also Lindblom 1977) concept of 'polyarchy': the power structures of public officials and societal elites and their ability to define 'issue areas' in promotion of particular interests. If these are the definitions to work with, then any study of politics must examine the sources of authority, the process and the values by which these 'issue areas' are defined. Who defines the 'what' (the contested issues) and how the process is decided is the task of the political economist (Strange 1994a: 7).

Obfuscations and Hegemons

Like the pluralists, Strange asks the question, what is power in human relations and who has it? Her answer, like theirs, is that we should look at objectives and outcomes if we are to identify where power lies. If government wants X, and people want Y, but the outcome is X, then it is government that has power. Converting this definition from the domestic arena to the world system, and ending up in a 'new medieval' interpretation of world affairs, requires her to venture out onto the field of ideas and do battle. And the reason is simple: converted to inter-state affairs, the objectives–outcome definition of power is as absolutist a definition of asymmetry between sovereign states as can be imagined. State A wants X, state B wants Y, and the outcome is X, so state X has power. State A is the greater and state B is the lesser power. For Strange, this is not adequate to define the complexity of world affairs. 'Better,' she writes, 'catholic complexity than protestant parsimony' (Strange 1994b: 218). 'The whole point of studying international political economy rather than international relations is to extend more widely the conventional limits of the study of politics, and the conventional concepts of who engages in politics, and of how and by whom power is exercised to influence outcomes' (ibid.). International relations studies, by definition, emphasize the relational power of one state directly to another. If B cedes to A, it can only be for one of two reasons: A's capabilities exceed those of B, which does not wish to risk confrontation, so cedes; or A's will prevails over B. As capabilities alone are not automatically translated into outcomes, we are left with 'will'. But 'will' is not quantifiable, as resources are. Its invocation amounts purely to a statement that state A has will if its outcomes triumph, and that state B lacks will. Or its absence can be deployed as a prayer: 'if only', the sigh goes up, member states had shown more 'will', the League of Nations would have been fine (Strange 1970: 309).

This is the root of Strange's attack on hegemonic stability theory. It is prayer disguised as analysis. This 'loose and ambiguous' theory (Strange 1987: 554) means different things, points to different conclusions, and diverts attention from its assumptions. The theory has two variants: the strong version has the hegemon produce stability in world order when it uses power to enforce order on others (Wallerstein 1974); a weak version states that the hegemon is a necessary, but not sufficient, condition for world order. In other words, the presence of a hegemon is a partial explanation as to why order prevails some times, but not others. The weaker version became popular in the early 1970s, when US diplomacy was seeking to extricate the troops from Vietnam and President Nixon announced the end of the dollar's convertibility into gold at $35 an ounce. US scholars elaborated on Kindleberger's study, *The World in Depression, 1929–1939*, which came out in 1973, to advance the case of disorder in world affairs as due to the hegemon's relative decline. Great Britain had been unable, and the United States had been unwilling, in the inter-war years, to play the role of the hegemon, and provide open markets, countercyclical spending and a stable currency to the world economy. Disorder on a world scale was the result. The pattern, the theoreticians argued, was being repeated in the 1970s, as the United States lost power, measured in terms of capabilities (Keohane and Nye 1977; Gilpin 1987), relative to the economies of rivals, or as economic and social sclerosis set in as vested interests came to enjoy special benefits (Olson 1982). The basic assumption of all this literature was that power was associated with the resources of a territorial state: as the hegemon's relative capabilities declined, the capabilities of others rose and challenged the hegemon. Its conclusions were contradictory: one set of conclusions predicted a free-for-all; others, like Keohane (1984), proposed cooperation between the advanced industrial states. Its two basic propositions went unchallenged: that the United States had lost power in and over the system; and that this decline accounted for disorder in the system.

Hegemonic stability theory begets international regime theory. This holds that the hegemon's preferences in international relations are injected through international organization into the world financial or trade regimes, or into bilateral regimes, defined as 'sets of implicit or explicit principles, norms, rules and decision-making procedures around which actors' expectations converge in a given area of international relations' (Krasner 1983). Strange castigates the theory for being too value-biased, too static, too state-centric and too US-centric (Strange 1981; 1982). It is value-biased in that regime means rule, implying a value preference for order, whereas the 'anarchic society' of states is characterized by the precariousness of the international order, the dispersion of authority, the weakness of international law and a large number of unresolved problems and conflicts. All international arrangements that go by the name of regime are easily upset, for instance because some parties may consider that the regime does not provide security, justice or wealth for them. In other words, the theory assumes that order is a value that has priority over others. It understates the dynamics in world affairs, and pays too much attention to the end result, and too little to determining factors originating in markets and technology which are apt to bring it about. The theory is too state-centric, and pays too much attention to what governments can do or agree, rather than to what they cannot do and do not agree. It therefore leaves in shadow all areas where regimes do not exist, tends to present regimes as areas of agreement rather than as agreements to disagree, and reflects the touching belief that international institutions can somehow change state behavior.

Finally, it is too US-centric in that the theory understates the asymmetries of states' dependence on regimes. Given the inter-state and market hierarchy, with the United States at the pinnacle, the less regime or governance there is, the more vulnerable will groups be in lesser states to the power structures of the market. It cannot serve, in short, as an adequate guide for international political economy.

Hegemonic decline and regime theories both suggest that there is little that can be done in a world where political authority is fragmented. Strange has no truck with such obfuscations. There never has been, nor ever is likely to be, an abundant store of international collective responsibility on which leading states can draw in their efforts to sustain world order. Management of common concerns in the 'anarchic society' has always been improvised, and crisis-ridden, especially when 'the most powerful and most ruthless member of the affluent alliance' (the United States) neither proposes regimes which are binding on itself, nor is prepared to impose 'a measure of tyranny' (Strange 1976: 359) on the Europeans or the Japanese. Rather, successive US governments have been swayed by short-term considerations, rather than by awareness of the long-term national interest in building a healthy, well-ordered and stable financial system, 'capable of sustaining a healthy, stable and prosperous world economy' (Strange 1986: 23). This proclivity to the short-term has shown up in a series of non-decisions by US authorities, not so much in relations with other states, as in their own relations to markets. The failure to bring order into the US regulatory jungle, the financing of both warfare and welfare through the double budget and current account deficits, the support for offshore tax havens, or the non-regulation of foreign exchange markets have prompted the emergence of 'casino capitalism' and the merry-go-round of 'mad money'. On closer inspection, the school of US decline has grossly overdone the Cassandra act (Strange 1988b: 3). What has happened, Strange maintains, is that there has been no decline at all, 'only a change in the basis of American power, as when a person shifts weight from one foot to another' (ibid.: 1). Simply, the US 'corporation' empire spills out over its frontiers, and is consolidating an entirely new kind of non-territorial empire. It is this non-territorial empire (of corporate investment, financial institutions, the media, the dollar markets, the military bases, the oil pipelines) that is truly the 'flourishing economic base' of US power, not the goods and services produced in the United States.

The US Empire

US power has no historic parallels, and has created a non-territorial empire 'the likes of which have never been seen before' (Strange

1988b: 13). As this empire is the definitive feature of the world political economy for most of the past century and as far as the eye can see into the next, it is not adequate to analyze the world system equipped with outdated tools from the past. That is not to say that the history of world politics or economics is to be discarded, that the comparative analysis of states is not to be encouraged, that the foreign policy process of states is not to be studied, or that the 'anarchic society' of states is not to be analyzed. Quite the contrary: Strange considers them all relevant to the study of the world system. But they have to be subsumed, she suggests, in a new construct more appropriate to the world as it is, and as it is becoming. Taking aim at the US school of hegemonic stability and regime theorists, she proposes to replace regimes with structures, issues with values, and capabilities with outcomes (Strange and Tooze 1981; 1988b).

Let us start with the last. The objectives–outcome definition of power dispenses with capabilities as a sufficient condition for answering the question of who gets what: it is not enough to know that X is well endowed with resources relative to Y to anticipate the outcome. The way resources are distributed does not tell us what X or Y's policy choices will be: Strange is no determinist, Marxist or 'econocrat'. For her, outcomes are shaped in part by bargaining, where bargaining skills are not uniformly distributed between participants and during which value preferences may be modified. Bargaining furthermore is inter-group, including state–state relations. In other words, the arena of bargaining is pluralist and dynamic. That is where values trump issues. In a pluralist world of many authorities, issue areas are not likely to be decided in a consensual mode. There will be some broad symbolic, 'motherhood and apple pie' areas of agreement, and a consensus on a few issue areas among some participants. But in a wide community of authorities, there will be very different value preferences, and consequently major tensions among them. The same point is made by Bull or Aron when they argue that the world system of states no longer shares the same values as its European predecessors in previous centuries. Under such conditions, many authorities are more likely to reach non-decisions, or, if they have reached decisions, they are likely to be incomplete or temporary or both. Different value preferences, Strange suggests, is a key source of change in regimes, which, by contrast to structures, are as solid as the last treaty or as substantial as an international organization. Structures are defined as basic political functions, which authorities may exercise in relation to the system of production, exchange and distribution of goods and services. Power is thus exercised in terms of the relationship of authority to market. Those who hold power decide the mix of values, and the source of their power. Those who hold structural power (as defined in the previous chapter) decide on the mix of values and the sort of outcomes.

Strange's definition of structural power, already discussed in Chapter 1, leads her to argue that whoever possesses or controls all sources of the power structure is able to shape the choices of others, without directly putting pressure on any of them. As already stated, these four sources are control over security, production, credit and knowledge and beliefs or ideas.

The security structure is state-centered, but greatly affected by the dynamics of technologies and markets, and provides or withdraws security from individuals, social groups and corporate enterprises. The main threat to security arises from disagreements among the many authorities in the international political economy about the limits of their respective authority. It is advisable, Strange suggests, to reject use of the concept of legitimacy, implying the existence of countersocieties, and to consider the security structure as jeopardized when one authority challenges the domain rights of another. In the state system, conflicts arise when the decline of great powers, such as the Ottoman empire, open up opportunities for misperceptions about the tolerated limits of competing authorities, or when status quo powers are challenged by revisionist powers. What counts is the belligerency of a state, not the nature of its domestic arrangements. World economic order depends greatly on what happens in the security structure.

The production structure is how people at work are organized, with the key change being the accelerated internationalization of production (see Chapter 4), the combined result of state policies, technological innovations, management strategies and market trends. In terms of values, the dominant production structure scores well on efficiency, having allowed a sharp average rise in living standards alongside an unprecedented rise in world population. Clearly, it has wrought fundamental changes in the security structure, and affects class relations and corporatist arrangements. Strange is on sure ground in suggesting that the production structure's record on justice is highly controversial, as its effects on distribution of benefits and costs have been highly uneven, complex and subjective. But she is unsure whether the difficulties that corporations pose for states should be taken as an indication that they are filching power from states. This ambiguity about whether or not state powers are or are not in decline is a permanent feature of her thought, despite her forceful assertions to the contrary.

The financial structure is defined as the way credit is created, and the monetary system through which relative values of the different monies in which credit is denominated are set (see the chapters by Verdun, Cohen and Underhill, this volume). It is composed of a global market linking financial centers and a series of national credit and money systems. Its key feature is its instability, which Strange equates with the trend to market liberalization, while castigating the United States for its series of non-decisions in promoting it. Not surprisingly, her financial structure scores high in US values of efficiency and freedom, but very poorly on security and distributional justice. The workings of the financial structure prompt citizens to clamor for more welfare handouts, engendering a state hyperactivism. This is a trend that Strange warns against confusing with effective state execution of its traditional functions as a sovereign. In similar vein, Strange considers the debates between Keynesians and monetarists in the 1970s and 1980s as being too state-centric, particularly in the case of the United States, to account for the workings of what is a global financial structure.

Strange's knowledge structure (discussed further in Chapters 3 and 5) is defined in terms of what knowledge is discovered, how it is stored, who communicates it, by what means and to whom on what terms. This is an area where she prefers to lay down a marker for future investigation, rather than to make any original statements. In many ways, her concept of a knowledge structure is similar to Nye's concept of 'soft' as compared to 'hard' power, which enables states through cultural attraction, ideologies or international organizations to get others to do what they would want. The workings of the knowledge structure within the state system create, she suggests, competition between states for the acquisition of knowledge, and a growing asymmetry between them. But she also notes the growth in the flow of information, which stimulates the growth of service jobs, facilitates global production and marketing, underpins the spread of financial markets, and transforms the security structure, as the ability of states to monopolize the channels of media communication wither away.

These four sources of the overall power structure interact, and shape what Strange terms the 'secondary issue areas' of transport, trade, energy and welfare, where there is always an interaction of authority and market, and a transnational dimension containing other authorities. This structure is Strange's Cartesian synthesis, bringing together the world's political and economic systems into one. It contrasts singularly, she suggests, with the prevalent discussion in international political economy where states and markets relate one to another. This prevalent formulation she presents in the form of a simple equation: States (S) + Markets (M) = IPE, where states affect the production and distribution of wealth, and markets affect the distribution of power and wealth among states. In her definition of multiple authorities with power to allocate values and multiple markets in a pluralist world where politics reaches beyond states, her equation presents the two worlds of states and markets as one. Replace S, she suggests, with multiple authorities (An); the generic M with multiple markets (Mn), and add the variable mix of values, Vn. These values are allocated among social groups (Sn), understood as states, classes, generations, genders or multiple social groups. The alternative equation is thus: $An/Mn + Mn/An = Vn/Sn$.

These four structures cannot be dealt with in isolation one from another, but interact, so that changes, say, in the security structure, will interact with different changes in the other structures. These changes will affect the balance of power over outcomes between authorities and markets, and will have distributional implications in terms of who wins and loses. Only then is it possible to gauge the implications of structural changes for the secondary issue areas of trade or welfare.

Intermediary Conclusions

What intermediary conclusions may be drawn from this presentation of Strange's suggested approach to the world system? Let us answer the question in the light of the four related transformations, sketched in the introductory paragraph of this chapter. Strange's structural power approach definitely accounts for the transformation of the state system: for Strange, the United States, to use George Orwell's terms, is much more equal than any other animal in the world farmyard, definitely than any other member state of the affluent alliance or, for the foreseeable future, any coalition of them. The proliferation of states accompanying the world's fragmentation has multiplied the number of states whose claims to sovereignty are often, but far from always, fictional. The second transformation of the world system is the spread of 'market democracy'. Strange often indicates skepticism about claims that the nature of domestic regimes affects state behavior in the inter-state system. Nonetheless, 'market democracy' encapsulates the values of the affluent alliance, that in the course of the past 30 years have become nearly universal in scope. The third component of transformation is the emergence of the world market, recreated in Strange's view largely by the exercise of US power. In particular, the world credit system and money markets are stamped 'Made in the USA'. The fourth, and for Strange the most significant, component is the emergence of the corporation, and the internationalization of production. The bargains struck between states and corporations have created a 'new diplomacy', placing the United States at the hub of a transnational network of power. In every dimension of the power structure, the United States is pre-eminent, and therefore influences the balance of power between authorities and markets in a 'new medieval' world to affect outcomes that sooner or later tally with US values and interests. For Strange, the United States is the territorial center of a new and unprecedented non-territorial empire. This 'new medieval' world has a defective emperor, she suggests, and no pope. Given the peerless position she bestows on the United States, she could have argued from her position that the world has for the first time ever an emperor that anointed itself pope.

Perhaps the major paradox of Strange's approach is to seek to escape the clutch of state-centric realists, interdependence and regime theorists, or one-world society evangelists, but to always come back to presenting what realists would readily recognize as a unipolar world. The United States, she is saying, is not 'one among equals', but equal to none. Dominant values since the collapse of the Soviet Union may be arguably presented as some mix of liberal/social democrat/national/conservative ideas, familiar to US traditions, while the 'new medieval' world of many authorities and many markets is one where the United States most of the time – and definitely where the stakes are high – calls the shots, with a sharp eye to ensuring outcomes compatible with US values and interests. Simply, the US position at the summit of Strange's power structure allows the manifold manifestations of US power to condition a world to its own, often malevolent and short-term, interests. Her prayers, recommendations and fears flow from this. Her prayer is for the United States to change its ways and act in a less predatory, less destabilizing fashion; her recommendation is that, failing that, the United States be counterbalanced by a more cohesive Europe, and a more assertive Japan; her fears are that the present world system may experience, in new form, the disasters of the 1930s. Better then for the United States to act as world tyrant than for lawlessness to dominate as the 'new medieval' world takes on the familiar characteristics of the real medieval world, from which the Europeans emerged through the device of state sovereignties. If tyranny runs against the US grain then the alternative, at which she only hints, is that the states reclaim their (unequally) exercised sovereignties, and that the dispersion of authorities and markets which she records as a central feature of the last decades is brought to a halt or at least greatly curtailed. We are back in a different, more state-centric world of fragmented authority, one where the fundamentals of the politics of different sovereignties are unchanging.

In the last resort, Strange challenges us to be less optimistic of converting the world system into a laboratory for experiments for our own pet notions, for more democracy or more efficiency, without taking the complex realities of a diverse and unequal world into account. It is a plea to look beyond our blinkers, and above all not to be satisfied with just inheriting old and tried ideas unquestioningly. Strange was a rebel, but a conservative one.

References

Aron, R. (1962), *Paix et guerres entre les nations*, Paris: Calmann-Lévy.

Bull, H. (1997), *The Anarchical Society*, London: Macmillan.

Carr, E.H. (1939), *The Twenty Year's Crisis, 1919–1939*, London: Macmillan.

Cox, R. (1987), *Production, Power, and World Order*, New York: Columbia University Press.

Cox, R. (ed.) (1997), *The New Realism: Perspectives on Multilateralism and World Order*, New York: UN University Press.

Dahl, R.A. and C. Lindblom (1953), *Politics, Economics and Welfare*, New York: Harper.

Easton, D. (1965), *A Systems Analysis of Political Structure*, New York: Wiley.

Gilpin, R. (1987), *The Political Economy of International Relations*, Princeton, N.J.: Princeton University Press.

Keohane, R and J. Nye (1977), *Power and Interdependence*, Boston, MA.: Little Brown.

Keohane, R. (1984), *After Hegemony: Co-operation and Discord in the World Political Economy*, Princeton, N.J.: Princeton University Press.

Krasner, S. (1983), *International Regimes*, Ithaca, N.Y.: Cornell University Press.

Lasswell, H.D. (1950), *Politics: Who Gets What, When and How?*, New York: P. Smith.

Lindblom, C. (1977), *Politics and Markets: The World's Political-Economic Systems*, New York: Basic Books.

Morgenthau, H. (1967), *Politics Among Nations*, 4th edn., New York: Knopf.

Olson, M. (1982), *The Rise and Decline of Nations: Economic Growth, Stagflation and Social Rigidities*, New Haven: Yale University Press.

Strange, S. (1970), 'International Economics and International Relations: A Case of Mutual Neglect', *International Affairs*, 46(2), 304–15.

Strange, S. (1971), *Sterling and British Policy*, Oxford: Oxford University Press.

Strange, S. (1972), 'The Dollar Crisis', *International Affairs*, 48(2), 191–215.

Strange, S. (1976), *International Monetary Relations*, Oxford: Oxford University Press for The Royal Institute of International Affairs.

Strange, S. (1979), 'The Management of Surplus Capacity: Or How Does Theory Stand Up to Protectionism 1970s style?', *International Organisation*, 33(2), 303–35.

Strange, S. and R. Tooze (eds) (1981), *The International Politics of Surplus Capacity*, London: Allen & Unwin.

Strange, S. (1982), '*Cave! Hic Dragones*: A Critique of Regime Analysis', *International Organisation*, 36(2), 479–97.

Strange, S. (1984), *Paths to International Political Economy*, London: Allen & Unwin.

Strange, S. (1985a), 'Protectionism and World Politics', *International Organisation*, 39(2), 233–59.

Strange, S. (1985b), 'Interpretations of a Decade', in L. Tsoukalis, (ed.), *The Political Economy of International Money: In Search of a New Order*, London: Sage, pp.1–44.

Strange, S. (1986), *Casino Capitalism*, Oxford: Basil Blackwell.

Strange, S. (1987), 'The Persistent Myth of Lost Hegemony', *International Organisation*, 41(4), 551–74.

Strange, S. (1988a), *States and Markets: An Introduction to International Political Economy*, London: Pinter Publishers.

Strange, S. (1988b), 'The Future of the American Empire', *Journal of International Affairs*, 42(1), 1–17.

Strange, S. (1990), 'Finance, Information, and Power', *Review of International Studies*, 16(3), 259–74.

Strange, S. (1991a), 'Big Business and the State', *Millenium: Journal of International Studies*, 20(2), 245–50.

Stopford, J. and S. Strange (1991b), *Rival States, Rival Firms: Competition for World Market Shares*, Cambridge: Cambridge University Press.

Strange, S. (1994a), 'Who Governs? Networks of Power in World Society', *Hitotsubashi Journal of Law and Politics* (Special issue), 5–17.

Strange, S. (1994b), 'Wake up Krasner! The World has Changed', *Review of International Political Economy*, 1(2), 209–19.

Strange, S. (1995), 'The Defective State', *Deadalus*, 24(2), 55–74.

Strange, S. (1997) (2nd edition), *The Retreat of the State: The Diffusion of Power in the World Economy*, Cambridge: Cambridge University Press.

Strange, S. (1998a), 'Who are EU?' Ambiguities in the Concept of Competitiveness', *Journal of Common Market Studies*, 36(10), 101–14.

Strange, S. (1998b), *Mad Money*, Manchester: Manchester University Press.

Wallerstein, I. (1974), *The Politics of the World-Economy: The States, the Movements and the Civilisations*, New York: Academic Press.

Waltz, K. (1979), *Theory of International Politics*, New York: McGraw-Hill.

3 Knowledge and Structural Power in the International Political Economy

LYNN K. MYTELKA

Introduction

In *States and Markets*, first published in 1988 (1994a), Strange argued that 'there are two kinds of power exercised in a political economy – structural power and relational power', but that the former is more determinant 'in the competitive games now being played out in the world system between states and between economic enterprises' (Strange 1994a: 24). For students of political economy, 'it is not enough, therefore, to ask ... who has power. It is important to ask why they have it – what is the source of power' (ibid.: 23).

In this seminal work, Strange identified the 'knowledge structure' as one of the four bases of power in the international political economy. Its substantive content, however, remained ill-defined. Knowledge was conceptualized mainly in terms of the 'dominant' ideas and belief structures that historically gave power to and legitimized the authority of key actors in a political system. (ibid.: 121–30). Priests, potentates, politicians and scientific pundits were thus endowed, at various points in time, with the ability to 'change the range of choices open to others without apparently putting pressure directly on them' (ibid.: 31). To a lesser extent, knowledge was also linked to the accelerated flow of information made possible by the emergence of new information and communications technologies (ibid.: 132). The very fluidness of the concept of 'knowledge' led Strange, in this earlier work, to locate universities within the knowledge structure, but to embed transnational corporations (TNCs), key actors in today's system of knowledge production, solely within the 'production structure'.

The relationship of TNCs to the state, moreover, was only weakly articulated.

In *Rival States, Rival Firms* (Stopford and Strange 1991) and in her article, 'Wake up, Krasner. The world has changed' (1994b), Strange began to draw these two strands of power closer together. Though realists like Hedley Bull, Steven Krasner and Kenneth Waltz might see little difference between the international system of today and that of Machiavelli's time, accelerated technological change, she believed, was leading to a 'system of international production, organized, managed and planned by firms'. This she argued was bringing about 'a fundamental change in the economic base of the world of states, in the power and even possibly the legitimacy of the state' (Strange 1994b: 210).

Yet structural power derived from knowledge is less 'visible' than that based on finance or production. It is thus more difficult to identify the international rules and norms that shape the parameters within which it is exercised and to analyze the changing vectors of power through which these rules and norms are set. In much of the literature, therefore, knowledge is confounded with technology and/ or with information and its impact is perceived only when intermediated by production or trade.[1]

This chapter seeks to move beyond these initial efforts to link knowledge to structural power within the international system, by focusing upon the emergence of knowledge as a structural basis of power in its own right. The next two sections differentiate knowledge from information and technology and analyze the process through which knowledge increasingly has been privatized. The following section stresses the importance of knowledge and innovation in the competitiveness of firms and, by extension, of nations. It illustrates how the growing acceptance of this proposition was reflected in a more consensual relationship between TNCs and states and their collaboration in shaping global rules of competition during the 1980s and 1990s. This new relationship, it is argued in the concluding section, has become the basis for the creation of a structure of power in which knowledge figures centrally.

Understanding Knowledge

Technology is generally defined as the application of knowledge in production. Much of the earlier literature narrowed its scope to knowledge embodied in machinery and equipment and/or to knowledge that is codified in blueprints or books. The tacit knowledge that is required to operate production systems and their components and which is embodied in persons and in organizational structures was, most often, forgotten. So, too, was the new knowledge generated in the course of experiential and/or research activities and diffused through scientific publications, meetings or migration.

This simplification allowed technology to be assimilated to any other good or service that could be bought and sold in a market. Information, on the other hand, was regarded as freely accessible and non-rival, in the sense that many people could use that information at the same time without diminishing it. Information was thus characterized as a public good and its transfer was believed to be costless. Knowledge, too intangible to be measured, formed part of the residual in growth accounting (Abamovitz 1956).[2] Its acquisition was assumed to result from a quasi-automatic process of learning-by-doing (Arrow 1962). Over the next several decades, efforts focused unsuccessfully on reducing the residual by rendering knowledge more tangible. Labour was thus differentiated by skill level and industries classified by research and development (R&D) intensity.[3] Throughout, the underlying assumptions concerning knowledge as a public good remained unchallenged. Forgotten were the days when power lay in the hands of priestly classes and guilds that protected their knowledge of astronomy or smelting processes through oaths of secrecy. Forgotten also were the efforts by newly industrializing countries such as Great Britain to prevent the migration of persons whose knowledge of textile machinery and manufacturing processes might give rise to rival powers.

By the 1980s institutional economists had recognized that technology is not only embodied and codified but has a large tacit element to it. Tacit knowledge[4] refers to those aspects of technology that are embodied in the organizational routines and collective expertise or skills of individuals and teams. To the extent that this is the product of collective learning experiences within a given company and/or are derived from that company's interactions with actors in its proximate environment, the development of tacit knowledge provides the firm with proprietary knowledge advantages that are localized and firm-specific (Dosi 1988; Nelson and Winter 1982: 134; Teece 1988). As a consequence, firms that widen their opportunities for learning from many sources will have a particular advantage over those that do not.

Learning of this sort is also 'cumulative' in the sense that past learning experiences pave the way and condition the direction for future learning and technological undertaking. This can lead to a narrowing of the firm's field of vision and give rise to risk-averse behavior that reduces the innovativeness of the firm. But it can also be turned into a strategic advantage. This is because the cumulative and firm-specific nature of knowledge means that there are no quick fixes to the learning process, nor is it easy to 'leap-frog', as frequently assumed, into totally new areas of technology. Knowledge accumulation through learning is thus a lengthy process and requires conscious and sustained efforts by firms and governments. Both of these factors create major barriers to entry for new firms and slow down the process of catching up for economies that have built few knowledge bases from which to move ahead. Barriers such as these, that are inherent in the processes of learning and innovation, have been reinforced by new policies and practices. Only recently, however, have these become a focus of attention and analysis.

The Privatization of Knowledge

Although national patent legislation and the Convention of the Paris Union for the Protection of Industrial Property signed in 1883 began the process of privatizing knowledge, it took nearly a century before economists and political economists recognized that knowledge had become a vector of structural power in the international political economy. A number of changes brought this about, and have since reinforced this trend. Two of these stand out in particular, the role of TNCs in shaping the direction of technological change, and their growing ability to appropriate knowledge from sources around the world.

Underlying the power of TNCs in the knowledge structure were changes in both the policies of states and the practices of firms. Without pretending to be comprehensive, this section looks in particular at shifts in the locus of research and development activities over time, at the widening scope of intellectual property rights at national and international levels and at the reduced role of the state in maintaining alternatives to the TNC in the generation of and access to knowledge.

During the 19th century, the growing relationship of technological change to the profitability of firms within capitalist economies led to an important shift in the locus of research activities from independent non-profit laboratories, universities and individual inventors to in-house research and development facilities. A considerable amount of basic research thus came to be undertaken within private corporations (Freeman 1982). In the United States, in-house research rapidly became 'the dominant mode for supporting corporate America' (Teece 1988: 258). By the mid-1990s, R&D spending was highly concentrated in the OECD countries which accounted for some 90 per cent of total world R&D expenditures. Seven OECD countries accounted for 90 per cent of this, and the United States alone for 40 per cent (UNCTAD 1999: 199).

Even more importantly for the argument advanced here, R&D spending had become concentrated in a small number of large firms.

In the United States, for instance, just 50 firms (of a total of over 41,000) accounted for nearly half of industry-based R&D in 1996... In small developed countries, the level of concentration is even higher. In Switzerland, just three firms accounted for 81 percent of national R&D in the early 1980s and in the Netherlands, four for nearly 70 percent. (UNCTAD 1999: 199)

The ability to appropriate knowledge generated through in-house R&D was enhanced by the development of the patent system. Prior to the advent of patent legislation, knowledge shared some of the attributes of a public good. Knowledge, for example, could be used by many without diminishing its availability. This meant that knowledge could diffuse widely if it were made public, something that was not always the case where mercantilist thinking prevailed. The paradox of knowledge as a public good lay in the fact that, if new knowledge were to be freely accessible, investors would have little incentive to commit resources to producing it. Intellectual property rights provided one solution to this problem by transforming knowledge from a public into a private good. By the privatizing of knowledge, the knowledge becomes scarce and this enabled the patent holder to recoup their initial investment by exercising market power over the use of the knowledge and the price for its use.

In its initial conception, patent law granted a 'temporary' monopoly to an individual inventor on the assumption (a) that such monopolies were a necessary incentive for inventive activity and/or were compensation for this activity, (b) that patenting would ensure disclosure of an invention and thus provide sufficient incentives for its more rapid introduction into commercially beneficial industrial activities, and (c) 'that the monopoly costs to consumers or to other producers are smaller than the benefits that accrue from promoting inventive and investment activities through patents' (Vaitsos 1973: 72). Each of these assumptions, however, can be challenged today.

1   Most patents are held by transnational corporations, not by individual inventors. On a sector basis, in biotechnology, for example, the top five biotech firms, all based in the United States and Europe, control more than 95 per cent of the gene-related patents (UNDP 1999: 68).
2   As a result of changes in legislation governing the patentability of knowledge, patenting activity rose dramatically from the 1980s and the largest share of national patents was granted to 'foreigners in all countries but the US and Japan' (Rafiquzzaman and Whewell 1998: 4).
3   One consequence of the above is that the rents generated by the transformation of a quasi-public good into a private good do not

generate benefits in the form of increased inventive activity in the domestic economies of all but a very few countries where patenting activity by domestic firms takes place.

4   Access to patented knowledge has been further restricted by lengthening the patent life from 10 or 12 to 20 years (as under the Trade-related Aspects of Intellectual Property Rights – TRIPs – agreement). This, in many cases, exceeds the useful life of the patented product.

By significantly widening the scope of patent legislation to include both processes and products,[5] and by circumscribing the use of compulsory licensing, patents can substitute for local production and can significantly limit the diffusion of new technology. The latter occurs because these changes open opportunities to transform patents into import monopolies and/or to grant licenses only to affiliate firms. Throughout the 1990s, 70 per cent of global royalty and licensing payments were thus paid by affiliates to their parent firms (UNDP 1999: 68).

Whether as import monopolies or exclusive licenses, the cost of patented products reflects the premium made possible through the grant of a monopoly to the patent holder and in the former case corresponds as well to the higher cost of production in the industrialized countries. This has led to numerous knowledge-based conflicts during the 1990s. Initially, these were played out in national markets as large patent holders used their patents to block new entrants. DuPont, for example, refused to grant licenses for the production of chlorofluorocarbon (CFC) substitutes to Korean and Indian firms that sought to meet the phase-out requirements of ozone-depleting substances as required by the Montreal Protocol of 1987. Conflicts also arose over efforts by South Africa and Thailand to secure compulsory licenses for HIV drugs. Both countries were seriously affected by the AIDS pandemic and unable to afford the price of drugs produced in the United States. Attempts by a US and a Canadian company to produce a cheaper version of Zidovudine, known by its brand name, AZT, a monotherapy used in the treatment of HIV/AIDS, were halted following a lawsuit for patent infringement filed by Glaxo-Wellcome which held a monopoly on this drug.

Not all countries, however, were signatories of the Paris Convention and most developing countries were forceful opponents within the World Intellectual Property Organization (WIPO) to a further extension of the protection it offered. For those seeking greater protection the Uruguay round of trade negotiations was one way around WIPO. In this process American pharmaceutical companies and the office of the US Trade Representative (USTR) were the principal actors. The advisory committee on trade policy and negotiations, chaired jointly by Pfizer and IBM, was the forum for coordination between the US government and private sector firms (Ryan 1998: 104–5). When in 1986 the USTR insisted at Punta del Este that the protection of intellectual property rights figure on the agenda of the Uruguay Round 'few people at the USTR knew much about patents, copyrights, trade secrets, or trademarks…[B]y the time the Uruguay Round negotiators met in Montreal in 1990 to take stock of their efforts, the institutionalisation of intellectual property rights had become one of the highest trade-related priorities of the U.S. government' (ibid.: 1). Trade sanctions or their threat are increasingly being used to reinforce structural power in the knowledge sector.

In the late 1990s, although monotherapies were no longer state-of-the-art treatment for HIV/AIDs in the industrialized countries, where they have been replaced by a triple therapy, the latter was far too expensive for those infected by the disease in the developing world and the former continued to be effective in the prevention of mother-to-child transmission. It was in this period that a generic HIV drug developed in India in the early 1990s was forced off the market.[6] The Indian case illustrates the way in which trade sanctions are now being used to enforce intellectual property rights.

Unlike Canada and the USA, India had never signed the Paris Convention and its own legislation did not recognize product patents for pharmaceuticals. In 1991, Indian Cipla Laboratories initiated production of the antiretroviral, Zidovudine, under the brand name, Zidovir-100, and sold it at about one-quarter of the Glaxo-Wellcome price. It also began to export the drug to other developing countries. Then, in 1994, India signed the TRIPs agreement of the General Agreement on Tariffs and Trade (GATT) under which it was obliged to make changes to its patent laws to conform to the standards set in this agreement. These include both product patenting and an extension of patent lives to 20 years. A few years later, a coalition of parties in India's upper house prevented the passage of a government-sponsored bill intended to protect both products and processes. In July 1997, the United States accused India before the Dispute Settlement Panel of the WTO of having failed to extend patent protection to products in the pharmaceutical and agricultural chemical industries and alleged that US companies had suffered a loss of $500 million a year because of insufficient patent protection. The threat of sanctions led to a circumvention of normal democratic processes. To conform to its WTO obligations, the Indian government issued a presidential decree giving effect to these modifications.

The Montreal Protocol of 1987 exhibits yet a third way in which structural power based in the knowledge sector has affected international rule making, notably by enabling the United States to delay the introduction of international rules and thus create conditions favorable to the exercise of a monopoly on CFC substitutes by an American firm over a prolonged period.

In 1976, the US Academy of Science reported that evidence was accumulating to support the position that the ozone layer was being damaged by CFCs and other chemicals. It advocated the use of a precautionary principle: not to wait any further before taking action. A small number of large chemical companies, with DuPont at the head, opposed efforts to regulate CFCs during the 1980s or to ban them. The United States thus refused to have the issue brought up on the international agenda, despite growing pressure from countries in Europe. By the late 1980s, a hole had been found in the ozone layer and scientific evidence was quite conclusive that CFCs and similar chemicals were responsible. The chemical companies now turned their efforts to shaping the protocol itself and its phase-out periods. Much of this was done to ensure that a substitute would be available and would have been patented by the time the phase out was required. DuPont held those patents.

The Montreal Protocol also contained provisions for assistance to developing countries through the establishment of a Multilateral Fund, so that they could comply with the longer phase-out period that they were granted. The existence of the Fund widened the market for CFC substitutes and ensured a rapid payback for investment in R&D. The Montreal Protocol has been highly successful in reducing the global production and consumption of ozone-depleting substances. The rapid rise in such substances was halted and reversed in the 1990s and it is expected that by 2010 the ozone layer will have reconstituted itself. But the Montreal Protocol, in combination with the international system of intellectual property rights, has also been successful in securing monopoly conditions for TNCs from a small number of industrialized countries which refused to license production of CFC substitutes to manufacturers in developing countries such as Korea and India, where the high cost of importing these chemicals limited the widespread diffusion of an environmentally sound technology.

Despite the evident use of patent legislation as an instrument of market power during the 1970s and 1980s, under the Uruguay Round, the scope of patent legislation widened still further. Even more importantly, these new standards may now be enforced through trade sanctions.[7] The recently concluded Biosafety Protocol under the United Nations Convention on Biodiversity similarly shows the increased subordination of environmental and human health concerns to contractual trade obligations (Hutcheon 2000). In the process, the state's role in the provision of knowledge as a public good has been delegitimized and its dependence upon TNCs for knowledge production has increased. As global competition came to be based increasingly upon innovation, dependence upon the TNCs as a source of knowledge production rose still further.

Competing in the Knowledge Economy

During the 1980s and 1990s, production became more knowledge-intensive across a broad spectrum of industries, from agriculture, fishing and forestry to textiles, clothing and telecommunications (Mytelka 1987). Knowledge, in this sense, extends beyond the traditional research and development activities to include product design, process engineering, quality control, maintenance, marketing and management skills. Much of this involves tacit knowledge. Recent OECD statistics provide increased evidence of this trend. For the OECD as a whole, growth rates of physical investment over the years 1985–95 reached an annual average of 2.7 per cent, while investment in knowledge-based activities over the same period averaged 2.8 per cent (OECD 1999: 114).

Within the context of more knowledge-intensive production, firms began to compete not only on price but also on the basis of their ability to innovate. Continuous improvement in products, processes and managerial and organizational practices have thus become the leitmotifs of competitive firms. The entrenchment of an innovation-based mode of competition reduced product life cycles, accelerated the pace of technological change and raised the costs, risks and uncertainties of R&D.

Pressures now rose for market opening to amortize the rising costs of R&D over a wider range of markets. With liberalization and deregulation, innovation-based competition diffused rapidly around the globe. This has significantly altered the competitive conditions for firms and led to new roles for the state in supporting innovation by firms located within its territorial boundaries. For the firms, strategic partnering, accelerated mergers and acquisitions and the emergence of knowledge-based networked oligopolies are now key elements of their international corporate strategies. The latter emerged out of the globalization of knowledge-based competition that made it increasingly difficult to identify potential rivals in distant markets. Even more difficult to predict in this period of rapid technological change were one's competitors when these might emerge from other industries as a result of a technological discontinuity or through the combination of hitherto unrelated generic technologies. Digitalization and its impact on the boundaries of the information and telecommunications industries (IT) and genetic engineering leading to the merger of biotechnology in agriculture and pharmaceuticals into the new 'life sciences' industry are illustrative.

Knowledge-based networked oligopolies share several principal characteristics (Mytelka and Delapierre 1999). First, they involve collaboration in the generation and use of or control over the evolution of new knowledge. As a result, the new knowledge-based oligopolies are dynamic, seeking to organize, manage and monitor change, as opposed to rigidifying the status quo. Second, they are composed of networks of firms rather than of individual companies. Alliances thus form the basic structure and building-blocks of emerging global oligopolies. Third, their focus is less on creating static size barriers to entry than on shaping the future boundaries of an industry and the technological trajectories, standards and rules of competition within them which themselves are a source of dynamic entry barriers.

In the information and telecommunications industries of the 1990s, these new rules included the following:

- innovation-based competition with rapid movement down the performance/cost curve,
- equally rapid movement down the manufacturing learning curve in order to increase yields and volume to reduce costs,
- speed and flexibility in changing over to new product generations as the product life cycle shortened,
- increased use of mergers and acquisitions (M&As) to extend product variety, assure brand name recognition of products with the same basic functionality and gain market share in principal markets around the globe,
- increased use of strategic partnering to reduce the high costs and risks of R&D needed to maintain the pace of innovation, and shape the technological trajectory within an emerging industry or industry segment,
- efforts to maintain positions within the core group of firms in knowledge-based networked oligopolies through which the industry's future is increasingly shaped.

Through static (for example, scale, scope and price-based) and dynamic (knowledge and innovation-based) modes of competition, TNCs are thus creating new barriers to entry in local markets and heightening uncertainties for smaller local firms as they strategically switch between them. Through in-house R&D, linkages to research laboratories at home and abroad and increased strategic partnering activity, TNCs set the technological trajectories in many global industries and make critical decisions with respect to which new technologies are introduced onto the market, where, when and by whom.

Despite the structuring force of TNCs in the global economy, little is being done to strengthen competition. Indeed, the role of states thus far has been consensual and policies have been supportive. For Stopford and Strange (1991), this was to be expected since 'national' competitiveness measured in terms of international market shares, they argued, depended upon a collusive relationship between nation states and their TNCs. Thus, in both the United States and Europe, as Japanese firms in the information technology (IT) and automobile industries cut dramatically into the market share of their competitors, their presence triggered a new form of neomercantilist behavior, focused upon support for innovation and the development of rival R&D consortia.

The European Strategic Programme for Research and Development in Information Technology, ESPRIT, for example, provided funding for intra-European industrial cooperation in R&D with a view to strengthening the technological base of Europe's IT industry vis-à-vis its larger, more integrated Japanese and American competitors. As European firms encountered each other across multiple technology partnerships, opportunities for learning each other's strategies increased and so, too, did the incentives for collusion. During ESPRIT's first two phases (1983–92) Europe's 'Big 12' information technology firms were thus able to build the basis for a 'defensive oligopoly' through high rates of participation in this programme and their multiple linkages across the 561 R&D projects that were created in this period (Mytelka 1994). Similarly, Prometheus, an eight-year EUREKA programme, was designed to strengthen Europe's role in the growing automotive electronics market. It included all leading European-owned car companies and over 100 of their suppliers. Virtually absent from all these consortia were rival Japanese and US firms.

Research joint ventures in the United States exhibited similar characteristics (Vonortas 1999). Sematech, for example, was launched in 1987 primarily as a means to help stem the loss of market share by US semiconductor firms to their Japanese rivals. The US government supported this exclusive club of semiconductor firms and their suppliers with an annual grant of $100 million over eight years. In the automobile industry, the 'Initiative for a New Generation of Vehicles' launched by the Clinton administration in 1993, involved only the big-three US automobile manufacturers and their suppliers.

Many of these consortia were commercially successful, but to the surprise of earlier neomercantilism thinking in Europe, 'successful national champion firms, once launched, exhibited a tendency to behave like their international competitors' (Moran 1996: 427). Examples of this type of behavior multiplied over the 1990s in both Europe and North America,[8] yet this did not deter states from continuing to support 'local' TNCs through a variety of domestic and foreign policy initiatives aimed at strengthening the competitiveness of these firms vis-à-vis their foreign rivals.

The number of bilateral investment treaties (BITs) aimed at opening foreign markets to the investment of national firms thus grew over this period (UNCTAD 1999). At the same time, BITs have virtually eliminated earlier screening and authorization practices through which states had protected local firms against foreign TNCs. Their evolution thus illustrates a shift in the relationship between states and TNCs from one of confrontation with foreign TNCs to one of collaboration with TNCs headquartered both at home and abroad (Mytelka 2000b). So, too, do the efforts by industrialized countries to engage in bidding wars for foreign investment. These escalated dramatically over the course of the 1990s (Mytelka 1999) and there are no signs that belief in the need to attract foreign investors as a stimulus to knowledge generation and innovation is on the wane. A recent report by the French Planning Commission, for example, drew the conclusion that 'Multinational firms are increasingly globalizing their R&D activities... In this context, the objective of countries competing for such activities is to strengthen the attractiveness of their territories' (France 1999: résumé).

This has been reflected in changes in investment legislation. From the mid-1980s onwards, these have become overwhelmingly favorable to the TNC. In the period 1991–6, 34 per cent of the changes favorable to foreign direct investment (FDI) involved more incentives (UNCTAD 1997: 18) and competition through incentives intensified in 1998, when 45 per cent of the liberalizing measures involved increased incentives (UNCTAD 1999: 116).

Policies related to publicly funded R&D have been redesigned to promote the commercial development of publicly funded R&D and favor the private appropriation of the results of publicly funded research primarily through the patent system. The often cited US Bayh-Dole Act of 1980 had as an explicit policy objective 'to use the patent system to promote the utilization of inventions arising from federally supported research or development' (UNCTAD *et al.* 1998: 34). OECD data for the years 1981–97 show a steady decline in the share of R&D expenditures financed and undertaken by the state in the United States, Japan and the European Union (OECD 1999: 126–8). On a sectoral basis, the changes carried out over the 1980s and 1990s in biotechnology are revealing.

In the early 1980s, most crops and seeds were developed in the United States through public research and, to a lesser extent, farmers' cooperatives. Given the low barriers to entry, patents were rarely sought and saving and trading of seed was commonplace. This began to change with the advent of genetic engineering, but the rise in patenting activity accelerated when new legislation encouraged closer cooperation with the private sector, enabling companies to profit from products developed largely with public funds. The intellectual property of public and university research was increasingly passed over to private industry; the portion of public sector patents in bio-technology sold under exclusive license to the private sector rose from just 6 per cent in 1981 to more than 40 per cent by 1990 (UNDP 1999: 67).

Conclusions

> [K]nowledge is power and whoever is able to develop or acquire and to deny the access of others to a kind of knowledge respected and sought by others, and whoever can control the channels by which it is communicated to those given access to it, will exercise a very special kind of structural power. (Strange 1994a: 30)

This chapter has explored the changing relationship between states and firms in the creation of a structure of power in which knowledge figures centrally. Traditionally, the state has played a critical role in shaping the relationship between power and production in the inter-national economy.[9] Today, diplomacy operates increasingly within the parameters set by knowledge. Understanding the way in which the privatization of knowledge has contributed to the growing de-pendence of states upon firms for the generation and application of knowledge helps to explain the emergence of a consensual relation-ship between states and TNCs based on their contribution to the competitiveness of the nation. The close ties that states and minor TNCs maintained throughout the various international negotiating processes, in turn, have shaped the rules governing access to and control over knowledge.

Three critical changes, it was argued, have enhanced the role of knowledge as a vector for power and strengthened the position of TNCs relative to the state in shaping the strategic importance of know-ledge in the international political economy. These are the role now played by knowledge-intensive production and by innovation-based competition in global competitiveness, a shift in the locus of research and development activities over time and the widening scope of intel-lectual property rights at national and international levels. These changes have made possible the increased ability of TNCs to appropri-ate new knowledge and influence the future direction of technological change, and led to a decrease in the state's role in maintaining alterna-tives to the TNC in the generation of and access to knowledge.

The competitiveness of firms, the innovation literature argues, de-pends upon their embeddedness in a broader supportive institutional and organizational environment. Where this environment is lacking and where the mode of competition requires the firm to catch up and keep up with a rapidly moving technological frontier, serious obstacles to competitiveness for the sector and for the economy more broadly result. Countries thus face multiple problems: to stimulate innovative behavior in local firms at the same time as they attempt to attract innovative firms to locate activities with dynamic potential within the national territory and promote the outward investment that widens the scope of knowledge appropriation for local firms. Such policies are inherently contradictory.

Political economists stress the temporal dimension of events and interactions. Over time, therefore, as the historical context changes, so, too, will the vectors of power and their agents. In this connection, the close interrelationship between states and markets is taken as axiomatic. Markets are not self-regulating and their very existence is shaped by policies.[10] Without norms and rules, markets as we know them would not exist. The very ability of TNCs to emerge is itself a product of the interaction between states and markets,[11] an interaction that increasingly takes place in the sphere of national policy making and in international fora. From this perspective, the importance of size and the international spread of TNCs cannot be understood solely in financial or production terms[12] but must be seen to relate closely to the proprietary knowledge base which gives the TNC its structuring potential in the emerging world economy. It is in that context that the relationship between the state and TNCs has become pivotal in the international political economy.

This chapter has demonstrated how power derived from the knowledge structure increasingly shaped international rule making by the close of the 20th century. Like Strange's comments on the nature of change, it does not expect that these tendencies will inevitably be reproduced in the future. As Strange points out, the shift from 'state authority to market authority has been in large part the result of state policies. It was not that the TNCs stole or purloined power from the government of states. It was handed to them on a plate – and, moreover, for "reasons of state"' (Strange 1996: 44–5). We may not be able as yet to see how exactly this pendulum may swing back in the future from markets to some form of authority – not necessarily that of territorial states – but history does offer some reassurance that somehow, sometime, it probably will (Strange 1996: 45).

Notes

1   In *The Retreat of the State* (1996), for example, Chapter 4 on 'Politics and Production' emphasizes the role of TNCs in global production and policies such as the privatization of state-owned enterprises that reinforce the TNCs' power over production and trade.

2 Abramowitz (1956) found that barely half of the actual growth in output could be explained by the growth of inputs in terms of capital and labor. The residual was classified as unexplained total factor productivity.

3 For an excellent review of the earlier economic literature flowing from the initial work of Moses Abramowitz, see Nelson (1981). In a more recent article, Nelson has carried forward his critiques to deal with the 'new' growth theorists (Nelson 1998).

4 The concept of *tacit* knowledge was first introduced by Polanyi (1966) and later popularized by Nelson and Winter (1982) and others.

5 Today patent rights also cover life forms.

6 This case study is drawn from Carin Hakansta (1998).

7 In March 2000 the WTO found that Canada's patent regime violated the 20-year patent life of the TRIPs agreement since Canada did not accept this standard for patents granted prior to 1989, when Canada's patent laws extended patent protection for only 17 years. Canadian generic drug manufacturers were eagerly awaiting the expiry of such patents when the United States took the case to the WTO dispute settlement panel (Baxter 2000).

8 'Fiat rejected directives by the government of Italy to develop the Mezzogiorno and expanded production in Brazil. Michelin responded to French indicative planning by building plants outside France in a three-to-one ratio to those inside. Philips shifted production of electronics to Asia while parliamentarians in The Hague complained about unemployment in Amsterdam. Similarly, there was surprise and indignation in the United States Congress when the national participants in Sematech insisted on the right to deploy publicly-funded semiconductor technology in offshore sites' (Moran 1996: 427).

9 Adam Smith (1776) justified the British Navigation Acts, though they represented a deviation from his first principles of free trade, not only on the basis of the need to maintain a fleet for military purposes but because of their economic rivalry with another major seafaring power of the time, Holland. Alexander Hamilton (1791) was a leading early proponent of policies to protect domestic industry against competing imports.

10 See, for example, Polanyi's discussion of the self-regulating market (Polanyi 1944).

11 See, for example, the work of Hymer (1976) and Kindleberger (1969).

12 See Chapters 4 and 6 in this volume.

Bibliography

Abramovitz, M. (1956), 'Resources and Output Trends in the United States Since 1870', *American Economic Review*, 46, 5–23.

Abramovitz, M. (1986), 'Catching Up, Forging Ahead, and Falling Behind', *Journal of Economic History*, XLVI(2), June, 385–406.

Archibugi, D. and J. Michie (eds) (1997), *Technology, Globalisation and Economic Performance*, Cambridge: Cambridge University Press.

Arrow, K. (1962), 'The Economic Implications of Learning by Doing', *Review of Economic Studies*, 29, 155–73.

Baxter, J. (2000), 'World Trade Organization Patent Ruling Hurts Canada's Generic Drug Manufacturers', *Ottawa Citizen*, 4 March, p.1.

Biotechnology and Development Monitor (1998), 'Pharmaceuticals: The Role of Biotechnology and Patents', 34, (June), 13–15.

Cantwell, J. and O. Janne (1997), 'Technological Globalisation and Innovative Centres: The Role of Corporate Technological Leadership and Locational Hierarchy',

University of Reading, Department of Economics, Discussion Papers in International Investment and Management, Series B., Vol. X, No. 239.

Delapierre, M. and L.K. Mytelka (1998), 'Blurring Boundaries: New Inter-firm Relationships and the Emergence of Networked Knowledge-based Oligopolies', in M. Colombo (ed.), *The Changing Boundaries of the Firm, Explaining Evolving Inter-Firm Relations*, London: Routledge, pp.73–94.

Dosi, G. (1988), 'The Nature of the Innovative Process', in G. Dosi, C. Freeman, R. Nelson, G. Silverberg and L. Soete (eds), *Technical Change and Economic Theory*, London: Pinter Publishers, pp.221–38.

Dosi, G. and L. Orsenigo (1988), 'Coordination and Transformation: An Overview of Structures, Behaviours and Change in Evolutionary Environments', in G. Dosi, C. Freeman, R. Nelson, G. Silverberg and L. Soete (eds), *Technical Change and Economic Theory*, London: Pinter Publishers, pp.13–37.

Dunning, J.H. (1994), 'Multinational Enterprises and the Globalisation of Innovatory Capacity', *Research Policy*, 23, 67–88.

Duysters, G. and J. Hagedoorn (1995), 'Convergence and Divergence in the International Information Technology Industry', in J. Hagedoorn (ed.), *Technical Change and the World Economy: Convergence and Divergence in Technology Strategies*, Aldershot, UK and Brookfield, US: Edward Elgar, pp.205–34.

France, Commissariat Général du Plan (1999), *Recherche et innovation: la France dans la compétition mondiale*, rapport du group présidé par Bernard Majoie, Paris: La documentation Française.

Freeman, C. (1982), *The Economics of Industrial Innovation*, London: Pinter Publishers.

Freeman, C. and C. Perez (1988), 'Structural Crises of Adjustment: Business Cycles and Investment Behaviour', in G. Dosi, C. Freeman, R. Nelson, G. Silverberg and L. Soete (eds), *Technical Change and Economic Theory*, London: Pinter Publishers, pp.38–66.

Ganz-Brown, C. (1999), 'Patent Policies to Fine Tune Commercialization of Government-sponsored University Research', *Science and Public Policy*, December, 403–14.

Gereffi, G. (1997), 'The Reorganization of Production on a World Scale: States, Markets and Networks in the Apparel and Electronics Commodity Chains', in D. Campbell, A. Parisotto, A. Verma and A. Lateef (eds), *Regionalization and Labour Market Interdependence in East and Southeast Asia*, London: Macmillan/ILO, pp.43–91.

Gilpin, R. (1987), *The Political Economy of International Relations*, Princeton, NJ: Princeton University Press.

Hakansta, C. (1998), 'The Battle on Patents and AIDS Treatment', *Biotechnology and Development Monitor*, 343, March, 16–19.

Hamilton, A. (1791), *Report on Manufactures*.

Hart, J. and S. Kim (1997), 'Power in the Information Age', Indiana University, Indiana Centre for Global Business discussion paper no. 127, in J.V. Ciprut (ed.), *Of Fears and Foes: International Relations in an Evolving Global Political Economy*.

Hirst, P. and G. Thompson (1996), *Globalization in Question*, Cambridge: Polity Press.

Howells, J. and M. Wood (1993), *The Globalisation of Production and Technology*, Belhaven Press.

Hutcheon, M. (2000), 'Propositioning Nature, Negotiating International Environmental Regimes from The Convention on Biological Diversity to the Biosafety Talks', paper prepared for the International Studies Association meeting, Los Angeles, 15–18 March.

Hymer, S. (1976), *The International Operations of National Firms: A Study of Direct Foreign Investment*, Cambridge, Ma.: MIT University Press.

Lipson, C. (1985), *Standing Guard: Protecting Foreign Capital in the Nineteenth and Twentieth Centuries*, Berkeley: University of California Press.

Lundvall, B.-A. (ed.), *National Systems of Innovation*, London: Pinter Publishers.

Moran, Theodore (1996), 'Governments and Transnational Corporations', in *Transnational Corporations and World Development*, London: International Thomson Business Press, published by ITBP on behalf of UNCTAD, pp.418–47.

Moran, T.H. (1999), 'A New Paradigm: Foreign Direct Investment and Development', paper prepared for the AIB meeting, Charleston, November.

Mytekla, L.K. (1987), 'The Evolution of Knowledge Production Strategies within Multinational Firms', in J. Caporaso (ed.) 'A Changing International Division of Labour', *International Political Economy Yearbook*, 1, Boulder Co.: Lynne Reiner, pp.43–70.

Mytelka, L.K. (1994), 'Dancing with Wolves: Global Oligopolies and Strategic Partnerships' in J. Hagedoorn (ed.), *Technical Change and the World Economy – Convergence and Divergence in Technology Strategies*, Aldershot: Elgar, pp.182–204.

Mytelka, L.K. (1999), 'Locational Tournaments for FDI: Inward Investment into Europe in a Global World', in Neil Hood and Stephen Young (eds), *The Globalization of Multinational Enterprise Activity and Economic Development*, UK: Macmillan Press Ltd., pp.278–303.

Mytelka, L.K. (2000a), 'Mergers, Acquisitions and Inter-firm Technology Agreements in the Global Learning Economy', in D. Archibugi and B.-A. Lundvall (eds), *The Globalising Learning Economy*, Oxford: Oxford University Press, forthcoming.

Mytelka, L.K. (2000b), '"We the People": The Transformation of State–TNC relations at the turn of the Millennium', *Journal of International Management*, forthcoming.

Mytelka, Lynn K. and M. Delapierre (1999), 'Strategic Partnerships, Knowledge-Based Networked Oligopolies and the State', in C. Cutler, V. Haufler and T. Porter (eds), *Private Authority and International Affairs*, Binghamton, NY: SUNY University Press, pp.129–49.

Nelson, R. (1981), 'Research on Productivity Growth and Productivity Differentials: Dead Ends and New Departures', *Journal of Economic Literature*, 19, 1029–64.

Nelson, R. (ed.) (1993), *National Innovation Systems: A Comparative Analysis*, New York and Oxford: Oxford University Press.

Nelson, R. (1998), 'The Agenda for Growth Theory: A Different Point of View', *Cambridge Journal of Economics*, 22, 497–520.

Nelson R. and S. Winter (1982), *An Evolutionary Theory of Economic Change*, Cambridge, MA: Belknap Press of Harvard University Press.

OECD (1999), *OECD Science, Technology and Industry Scoreboard, Benchmarking Knowledge-based Economies*, Paris: OECD.

Penrose, E. (1951), *The Economics of the International Patent System*, Baltimore: Johns Hopkins University.

Polanyi, K. (1944), *The Great Transformation*, Boston: Beacon Press.

Rafiquzzaman, M. and L. Whewell (1998), 'Recent Jumps in Patenting Activities: Comparative Innovative Performance of Major Industrial Countries, Patterns and Explanations', Ottawa: Industry Canada, Working Paper No. 27, December.

Rosenberg, N. (1976), *Perspectives on Technology*, Cambridge: Cambridge University Press.

Ryan, M.P. (1998), *Knowledge Diplomacy: Global Competition and the Politics of Intellectual Property*, Washington, DC: Brookings Institution.

Smith, A. (1776), *An Inquiry into the Nature and Causes of the Wealth of Nations*, reprinted 1937, New York: Modern Library.

Stopford, J. and S. Strange (with J.S. Henley) (1991), *Rival States, Rival Firms: Competition for World Market Shares*, Cambridge: Cambridge University Press.

Strange, S. (1994a), *States and Markets*, 2nd edn, Cambridge: Cambridge University Press.

Strange, S. (1994b), 'Wake up, Krasner! The world *has* changed', *Review of International Political Economy*, 1(2), Summer, 209–19.

Strange, S. (1996), *The Retreat of the State: The Diffusion of Power in the World Economy*, Cambridge: Cambridge University Press.

Teece, D. (1988), 'Technological Change and the Nature of the Firm', in G. Dosi, C. Freeman, R. Nelson, G. Silverberg and L. Soete (eds), *Technical Change and Economic Theory*, London: Pinter Publishers, pp.256–81.

UNCTAD, *World Investment Report*, Geneva and New York: United Nations, various years.

UNCTAD, UNEP & DESA (1998), 'The role of publicly funded research and publicly owned technologies in the transfer and diffusion of environmentally sound technologies', background document for the International Expert Meeting on the Role of Publicly Funded Research and Publicly Owned Technologies in the Transfer and Diffusion of Environmentally Sound Technologies. Kyongju, Republic of Korea, 4–6 February.

UNDP (1999), *Human Development Report 1999*, New York: United Nations.

Vaitsos, C. (1973), 'Patents Revisited: Their Function in Developing Countries', in Charles Cooper (ed.), *Science, Technology and Development*, London: Frank Cass.

Vonortas, Nicolas (2000), 'Multimarket Contact and Inter-Firm Cooperation in R&D', *Journal of Evolutionary Economics*, forthcoming.

4 The Evolving Global Production Structure: Implications for International Political Economy

THOMAS C. LAWTON AND
KEVIN P. MICHAELS

Introduction

In the late 1980s, Strange first conceptualized power in the international system in terms of four interrelated structures: security, knowledge, finance and production.[1] She defined the production structure, the primary creator of wealth in the international system, as 'the sum of all arrangements determining what is produced, by whom, by what method and on what terms' (1988a: 62). The location of productive capacity, she contended, is far less important than the location of the people who make the key decisions on what is produced, where and how, and who designs, directs and manages to sell successfully on the world market. Viewing international wealth creation – and associated power – through this prism led Strange to some controversial conclusions about the international system. One of her conclusions was that US control over international production had increased despite a diminishing share of world trade; US hegemony was as strong as ever, only the will to exercise power had declined. She described the American Empire as a 'corporation empire' in which the culture and interests of corporations are sustained by an imperial bureaucracy of not only US government agencies but international organizations and regimes such as the OECD, IMF and GATT (1988b: 5).

Strange also highlighted the growing importance of international production sharing. In the mid-1980s, the volume of international production sharing exceeded the volume of international trade for the first time. The change is significant as it diminishes the power of states to control economic events. States retain considerable *negative* power to disrupt, manage and distort trade by controlling entry to the territory in which the national market functions. However, they cannot so easily control production that is aimed at a world market which does not necessarily take place within their frontiers (Stopford and Strange 1991: 14). This contention led to perhaps Strange's most controversial assertion: transnational corporations, controlling the vast majority of international production, had assumed a role alongside states as primary actors in the international system. Economic security had lost its national character: international firms and markets could now be considered as influential as national governments (Strange 1986: 296). As a result, states – with less capability of pursuing independent economic policies – had to master a new task: bargaining with, rather than directing, transnational corporations.

There have been significant changes in the nature of international production since Strange made these original arguments in the late 1980s. Among the changes are a surge in manufacturing and service exports, a shift in the composition of exports to high-technology goods, and the continued growth of international production sharing. These changes are driven in part by changes in the transnational corporation itself, where vertical integration is becoming less desirable, while 'horizontal specialization' on an international basis is becoming more common in scores of industries. Moreover, changes in technology are allowing TNCs to tightly integrate functions such as operations, logistics, and research and development on a global basis both *within* the firm and *between* firms – a trend that appears to be accelerating at the turn of the century with the onset of electronic commerce via the internet. Indeed, the impact of the internet on international production is and will be revolutionary for the foreseeable future.

These changes raise interesting questions for Strange's aforementioned assertions about the production structure. Is the concept of the production structure still valid? Have changes in international production increased or decreased US influence over the production structure? What issues do these changes raise for policy makers and IPE theorists? This chapter therefore has twin objectives: first, to describe some of the key changes in international production in the 1990s, and second, in light of these changes, to analyze the continuing relevance of the production structure for IPE theory and policy makers alike.

Changes in International Production

The past decade has witnessed many changes related to international production, caused by both political and technological factors. On the political side, the successful completion of the GATT Uruguay Round, the emergence of the World Trade Organisation and a general trend toward deregulation and privatization by governments around the world have created a favorable environment for global production and international trade. Technology has also shaped international production as a result of falling transport and communications costs, the onset of the internet and e-commerce, and the emergence of a new breed of service sector TNCs: global logistics suppliers. While the changes in international production are numerous, this chapter will highlight three trends with particular relevance for IPE: surging global trade, particularly in high-technology goods and services; disaggregation or 'explosion' of the production value chain, and the emergence of tightly integrated international production systems.

Surge in International Trade

The decade of the 1990s was characterized by significant growth in world trade in both goods and services. Merchandise exports averaged 7 per cent annual growth between 1990 and 1997, to reach $5.3 billion (Figure 4.1). Over the same period, exports of services grew at an 8 per cent annual rate to reach $1.3 trillion by 1997. Considering that world GDP averaged approximately 2 per cent growth over the same time frame, the record is impressive indeed (WTO 1998: pp.73–4).

The 1990s record of trade growth, on the heels of another strong decade of trade growth in the 1980s, led some commentators to proclaim a 'new era' in the world economy on the basis of globalization. While there has been a trend of growing trade since 1945, international trade is approximately the same share of the world economy as it was 100 years ago, prior to the two world wars (Henderson 1998: 34–67). Thus, while the current levels of international trade are not unprecedented, it is clear at the beginning of the 21st century that we are in a robust period of international trade growth. Despite this assertion, the authors of this chapter are not 'pop internationalists'![2]

Along with robust trade growth there has been a shift in the composition of trade favoring high-technology products, with a reduced contribution from basic materials and agricultural goods. A review of merchandise exports for the 1990–97 period (Table 4.1) is illustrative. The percentage of world exports attributed to agricultural products

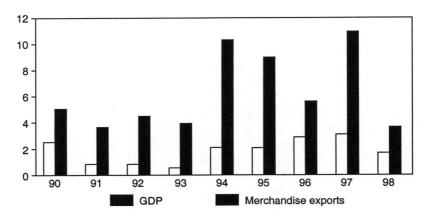

Source: World Trade Organization Press Release, 16 April 1999. Reproduced courtesy of the World Trade Organization.

Figure 4.1   Growth in the volume of world merchandise exports and GDP, 1990–98 (annual percentage change)

declined from 12.2 per cent to 10.8 per cent; mining products, similarly, shrank from a 14.3 per cent share of exports to 11.3 per cent. The 1990s were not a favorable decade for raw material trade. At the same time, the share of the office and telecommunications equipment sector as a percentage of exports grew from 8.8 per cent to 12.7 per cent, to reach $673 billion in 1997 – a substantial increase for a seven-year period and nearly identical to the decline in agricultural and mining products. The products making up this sector include computers and communications equipment, the basic building-blocks of the internet and the information economy. The contribution of other key sectors such as automotive, chemical and consumer goods to exports roughly held their own over the period, increasing at the same rate (7 per cent per annum) as overall merchandise export growth, but again significantly faster than world GDP growth. The data for service exports have by the WTO's admission, less precision than merchandise figures, but do highlight the declining contribution of transportation services as a result of falling real costs, from 28.4 per cent to 24.4 per cent, to overall international service trade from 1990 to 1997. In summary, while international trade grew at a robust pace in the 1990s, the composition of trade shifted away from raw materials to favor high-technology goods.

Table 4.1   Merchandise and service exports, 1990–7

Merchandise Exports Sector	Share World Merchandise Exports 1990 (%)	Share World Merchandise Exports 1997 (%)	Merchandise Export Value 1997 ($US bn)
Transportation equipment, machinery and parts	17.6	17.5	929
Computers, office and communications equipment and parts	8.8	12.7	673
Chemicals	8.7	9.2	490
Other semi-manufactures	7.8	7.5	399
Clothing	3.2	3.3	177
Textiles	3.1	2.9	155
Automotive products	9.4	9.3	496
Mining products	14.3	11.3	598
Agricultural products	12.2	10.9	580
Iron and steel	3.1	2.7	141
Other consumer goods	8.9	8.8	490
Miscellaneous	2.9	3.9	177
All merchandise	100	100	5 305
Service Exports Sector			
Transportation (air, sea, other)	28.4	24.4	320
Travel	33.1	32.8	430
Other commercial services	38.5	42.8	430
All services	100	100	1 180
Total merchandise and services			6 485

Source: World Trade Organization (1998). Reprinted courtesy of the World Trade Organization.

The Exploding Value Chain

A second important trend in international production is the growing physical separation of activities defining the *value chain* of the firm. As defined by Porter (1985: 36), the value chain is a collection of activities that are performed by the firm to design, produce, market, deliver, and support a product or service (see Figure 4.2). The configuration of a firm's value chain – the decisions relative to the technology, process and location, and whether to 'make or buy' for

The Value Chain

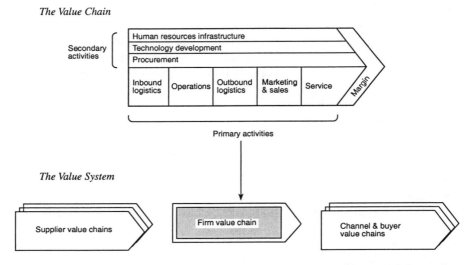

Source: Adapted with the permission of The Free Press, a division of Simon & Schuster, Inc., from *Competitive Advantage: Creating and Sustaining Superior Performance* by Michael E. Porter. Copyright © 1985, 1998 by Michael E. Porter.

Figure 4.2   Porter's value chain and value system

each of these activities – is the basis of competitive advantage. The value chain is, in turn, part of a larger value system that incorporates all value-added activities from raw materials to component and final assembly through buyer distribution channels.

For much of the 20th century, the value systems of many sectors were influenced by mass-production techniques pioneered by Henry Ford in the 1920s, which emphasized scale, standardization and vertical integration to increase automobile production productivity. The epitome of 'Fordist' production was the River Rouge (Michigan) production facility, which was colocated with a port and a steel foundry. Most value-added activities were confined to a single facility to improve coordination and reduce the transportation costs of intermediate goods.

A direct challenge to this production model emerged in the 1950s and 1960s from the Toyota Motor Company in Japan (Womack *et al.* 1990). In place of standard products with long production runs by a self-reliant vertically integrated firm, Toyota emphasized rapid product innovation, flexible production and just-in-time inventory systems. Rather than vertical integration, Toyota emphasized strong relations with suppliers clustered near final assembly facilities. The productivity advantages of the Toyota lean production approach were significant, as Toyota could produce an automobile with less than half the labor hours of its American and European competitors. The Toyota model continued to evolve with falling transportation and communications costs in the 1970s and 1980s and soon it became feasible to coordinate large, extended supply chains on a global basis.[3] This production model, which some scholars have dubbed 'post-Fordist', spread to other manufacturing sectors beyond the automotive and facilitated ever-greater movement of intermediate goods and components across national borders.[4]

The growing use of information technology in the 1990s brought further innovation to the post-Fordist model. The introduction of 'enterprise resource planning' (ERP) software improved intra-firm coordination between frequently disparate functions as conceptualized in Porter's value chain. Prior to ERP, key functions of the value chain, such as inbound logistics, operations, outbound logistics and marketing, frequently had separate organizations, with separate information systems that did not easily share information with each other. Each function was, in effect, in a 'silo' performing its own task but not optimizing overall operations. ERP created an 'electronic nervous system' to link each function together, improve decisions and increase overall productivity. Consider the impact on the operations and inbound logistics functions of a typical manufacturing firm. Historically, the operations (manufacturing) function demanded high inventory levels to ensure smooth production and avoid costly production shutdowns. At the same time, the inbound logistics function was focused on minimizing transportation costs. The result was excessive inventory levels that were replenished periodically in large batches by slow, inexpensive transportation alternatives. Enterprise resource planning broke down information barriers between 'functional silos' to shed light on the relationship between transportation costs, inventory levels and operations. In some cases, firms found that they could eliminate most inventories by shifting to faster, but more expensive, transportation alternatives (like air cargo) that replenished supply 'just in time'. Simply put, ERP allowed information to replace inventory.

Revolutionary advances in communications technology spurred further evolution of the production model in the late 1990s. The emergence of the internet as a low cost conduit for sharing vast quantities of data facilitated more and more information sharing between firms, extending the benefits of ERP from the *value chain* of an individual firm to the entire *value system* of firms and their suppliers and customers (see Figure 4.3). One of the early pioneers of this model was Dell Computer, which produced custom-made computers 'just in time' for orders received directly from the customer via telephone or the internet. As Dell received an order, it shared

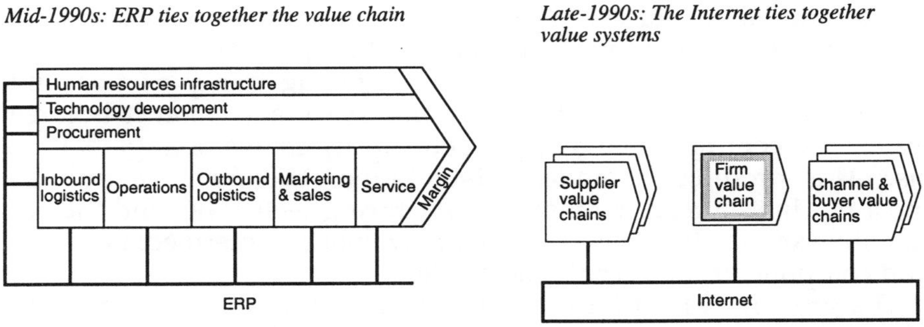

Mid-1990s: ERP ties together the value chain   *Late-1990s: The Internet ties together value systems*

Figure 4.3   Impact of ERP and the internet on value systems

production requirement information electronically with its suppliers worldwide for immediate delivery to a Dell production facility, where the computer was assembled and shipped directly to the customer within a week. The Dell model relied on 'demand side pull' rather than 'supply side push': no computer was produced unless there was corresponding demand in the marketplace. Thus the massive queues of inventory usually sitting idle within retail stores, distributors and factories were virtually eliminated. The productivity advantages of this production model were profound. Dell was able to operate with half the number of employees and one-tenth the inventory of its traditional computer competitors. Return on invested capital reached 195 per cent in 1999, compared to 10–20 per cent for traditional manufacturing firms.[5] Soon companies from around the world were flocking to Austin, Texas to understand the Dell production model, much as firms had flocked to Tokyo and River Rouge earlier in the century. The opportunity for productivity improvement was enormous; in the United States alone, the cost of goods in inventory of all value systems was nearly $1 trillion in 1997.[6] As the decade closed, the 'Dell Model' began to spread from high technology to traditional manufacturing sectors like automobile production. In late 1999, General Motors and Ford announced they were moving to electronic supply chain management systems similar to Dell Computer. If successful, the 'Dell Model' could be every bit as revolutionary to the production structure as Ford's vertical integration and Toyota's 'lean production' models were in earlier eras.

One major consequence of the 'exploding value chain' is the growth of trade in parts and components as distinct from finished products. A study by the World Bank (Yeats 1998) estimates that the share of parts and components accounts for some 30 per cent of world trade in manufactured products. Moreover, trade in components and parts is growing significantly faster than in finished products, highlighting the shift to international production systems. New types of value systems are emerging. In the transportation and machinery sector, for example, OECD countries were net exporters of parts and components (surplus of $77 billion in 1995), signifying the comparative advantage that many developed economies have in capital-intensive components, as well as the comparative advantage that many developing countries have in labor-intensive assembly operations. Over 40 per cent of the exports of manufactured goods from Mexico, for example, involve assembly operations using components manufactured abroad.

More Trade Controlled by TNC Networks

A third major international production trend is the growing influence of TNCs in international trade. With the number of TNCs increasing from 7000 in 1975 to 40 000 in 1995, and foreign affiliates of TNCs accounting for 25 per cent of world manufacturing output, an increasing proportion of world trade in manufactures is intra-firm, rather than international trade. In other words, it is trade that takes place between parts of the same firm but across national boundaries. Gilpin was one of the earliest writers in IPE to recognize the significance of this shift in trade patterns. He argued that:

> the result of this internationalisation of the production process has been the rapid expansion of intra-firm trade. A substantial fraction of global trade has become the import and export of components and intermediate goods rather than the trade of final products associated with more conventional trade theory. (1987: 238)

The current estimate is that about 30 per cent of world trade is intra-firm (Karliner 1997; WTO 1997). The upshot of this activity is that, unlike the kind of trade assumed in traditional international trade theory, intra-firm trade does not take place on an 'arm's length' basis. It is, therefore, subject not to external market prices but to the internal decisions of TNCs. Such trade may account for a very large share of a nation's exports and imports. Dicken has noted that more than 50 per cent of the total trade (exports and imports) of both the United States and Japan consists of trade conducted within TNCs, and as much as four-fifths of the United Kingdom's manufactured exports are flows within UK enterprises with foreign affiliates or within foreign controlled enterprises with operations in the United Kingdom (1992: 49). The economic power of TNCs is pervasive. Widening the prism beyond simply intra-firm trade, TNCs are involved in 70 per cent of world trade (Karliner 1997).

To summarize the trends in international production outlined in this section:

- International trade has increased significantly faster than world GDP over the last two decades, with the relative importance of high-technology goods increasing and the importance of agricultural and basic resources diminishing.
- The nature of production activities has changed to facilitate tightly integrated global supply chains as exemplified by the 'Dell Model'. As a result, parts and components account for a growing portion of trade.
- TNCs account for a growing share of world trade, with involvement in 70 per cent of trade activity and controlling one-third within their own networks.

Implications for Policy Makers

For policy makers, there are a number of important implications of the changing nature of international production. For one, the splintering of the value chain in many industries may herald the need for a new approach to industrial policy and wealth creation. Industrial policy, which traditionally has focused on particular industries or sectors, may now need to adopt a more *functional* approach (Lawton 1999). Returning to Porter's value chain, policy makers may need to focus on creating comparative advantage in particular *functions*, such as operations, logistics or research and development, rather than specific *industry sectors*, such as semiconductors or aerospace. This appears to be the conclusion reached by Taiwan, a state with considerable success in expanding wealth over the last three decades. The current blueprint for economic development calls for Taiwan to become an Asia-Pacific Regional Operations Center (APROC). Focusing on improving the removal of impediments to the free flow of goods, information, capital and personnel, Taiwan seeks to be the gateway to the Asian market for local firms and TNCs alike (CEPD 1997: 3–4). Among the goals are to dramatically increase the competitiveness of air and sea transportation, communications and financial services – the very linkages that tie value chains of firms together. Taiwan is betting that firms will locate their operations in countries where these support services are most competitive. This is a significant contrast with high-profile sectoral industrial policies of recent years such as Japan's fifth generation computer, the United States' flat panel display and Europe's semiconductor initiatives – endeavors that have all arguably failed. Taiwan's APROC objective acknowledges that 'picking winners' in an era of rapid technological change is an increasingly difficult and risky proposition.

A second implication of the changing production structure for policy makers, implicit in the Taiwan example, is the need to pay attention to infrastructure, particularly 'fast' infrastructure such as communications and air transportation. The changes in production outlined in this chapter, including the development of tightly integrated international value systems and the emergence of electronic commerce over the internet, point to greater importance for transportation and communications public policy.

Data volume over the internet is growing at an exponential pace – about 10 per cent *per month* – and will soon surpass voice traffic carried over the traditional communications infrastructure. Much of this growth is fueled by the globalization of production and the onset of electronic commerce. Moreover, if current trends continue, internet traffic will be one hundred times greater than traditional voice traffic before 2010. Increasingly, firms will rely on abundant and cheap communications services to develop new products and services, integrate their supply chains, and to simply remain competitive. This means that governments focused on economic growth must carefully craft telecommunications policies – including regulation, taxation and public ownership – that encourage the development of a state-of-the-art infrastructure to the greatest extent possible. The challenge for developing countries lacking capital for such a build-up will be especially acute. Increasingly, cooperation with telecommunications TNCs rather than protection of domestic suppliers will be required to develop this version of 'fast infrastructure' which is critical for economic development in an era of exploding value chains.

While the explosion of internet traffic has received headlines, another type of 'fast' infrastructure is gaining importance: air cargo. The changes in global production outlined in this chapter have contributed a 600 per cent increase in air cargo traffic between 1977 and 1997. As a result, in 1998 nearly 40 per cent of the world's merchandise trade by value moved by air cargo. In some Asian countries, the figure exceeds 60 per cent.[7] Airports are becoming magnets for economic activity, much like the historical role of maritime ports. Policy choices relative to air cargo service will therefore become more important than ever. Historically, the focus of governments, in negotiating air service agreements that regulate air travel between two countries, has been on passenger travel. The result has often been insufficient capacity or competition to adequately serve the needs of cargo customers. Another public policy issue deserving focus is the role of customs in a world of 'fast infrastructure'. Traditionally an unglamorous (and very often corrupt) government agency focused on revenue generation and policing, customs plays a growing role in facilitating the rapid movement of goods. Transparency, speed and 24-hour service are what TNCs require in an era where inventory levels are measured in hours rather than days or weeks. Policy makers that wish to attract TNC investment must now balance the security requirements of the country with the economic necessity of efficient customs procedures. Due in part to the emergence of 'fast infrastructure', comparative advantage has never been so mobile. Some regions are adept at wealth creation because their governments have learned how to gain advantage through time efficiencies. A good example of this phenomenon is Scotland, which has created a manufacturing center for high-technology goods, known as the 'Silicon Glen', in the past decade. According to a TNC executive with a computer facility in Scotland:

> Before, nobody was really producing in Scotland. Now, you can't afford not to go there. Why? Because they have constructed an infrastructure. If you go to Scotland everything is ready – the regulatory system, the tax environment, the transportation, the telecommunications – for you to set up your manufacturing facility as fast as you can. (Friedman 1999: 174)

This points to a paradox: in an era when the TNC may well be the single most important force creating global shifts of economic activity, political spaces are among the most important ways in which location-specific factors are packaged (Dicken 1992: 148–9) and 'fast' infrastructure will become an increasingly important location-specific factor.

A final implication for policy makers to consider is that the creation of public policy will become more complex as a result of changes in the production structure. A mixture of subnational actors, international institutions and TNCs now have a voice in many public policy decisions that were once the exclusive domain of state governments. Stopford and Strange (1991: 2) referred to this as 'new diplomacy': the concept that governments must bargain both with firms and with governments. This point is best illustrated with an example, again from Scotland. In early 1999, FedEx, a US-based air cargo TNC, decided that it wanted the right to fly direct cargo flights from Prestwick, in the heart of Scotland's computer industry, to Paris, its European air cargo hub. Frustrated that US–UK government negotiations for expanded European air traffic rights were stalled, FedEx took an unorthodox step and *unilaterally* applied to the British government for these rights. Traditionally, air traffic rights are handled by government-to-government negotiations, not by petitions from TNCs. FedEx indicated to the British government that, if not granted additional UK traffic rights to France, it might be forced to 'severely' scale back its transatlantic flights to Prestwick, a move that was sure to damage the operations of Scotland's computer industry. Interest groups on both sides of the issue quickly formed. Opposed to granting FedEx additional rights were a group of British air cargo carriers, who wanted concessions in the US market as a *quid pro quo*. Supporting FedEx were local government authorities, development agencies and scores of mainly US microelectronics and computer equipment firms from the Silicon Glen. A fierce public relations battle ensued, with one British executive accusing FedEx of trying to blackmail the British government. In late 1999, the British government announced that it would grant FedEx the air traffic rights it desired. FedEx even managed to upstage British carriers on their home turf when it was revealed that the FedEx chief executive officer met directly with the British deputy prime minister to advocate his position, while British carriers were only able to muster an audience with his junior transport minister.[8] While other factors, including domestic politics, may have played a role in the British government's decision, it appears that in this instance a coalition of subnational actors, a US air cargo TNC, and US computer and microelectronic TNCs were able to exert significant influence on British public policy formulation. Admittedly, this example is anecdotal, but it does illustrate the increasingly complex nature of public policy creation in an era of tightly integrated production systems. This may drive governments to create different types of institutions to ensure better coordination with subnational actors, TNCs and international organizations.

What does this mean for IPE Theory?

What do these trends in international production mean for Strange's perspective of the international system in particular and the study of IPE in general? First and foremost, Strange was a clairvoyant in anticipating (and interpreting) major changes in international production that are shaping the international system today. The empirical evidence indicates that the growth of global production sharing continues to gain momentum as a result of what we have termed 'the explosion of the value chain'. In the early 1990s, Stopford and Strange pointed to three factors that would drive greater production sharing: lower transport and information technology costs, provision of more sophisticated financial instruments, and new technologies that have altered the scale needed for efficient operation (1991: 35–7). A decade later, we live in a world increasingly tied together by the internet, a world where it is possible to outsource manufacturing and logistics to sophisticated global suppliers, a world where microprocessor designs are developed 24 hours per day by electronically transmitting designs between Asia, Europe and North America. Indeed, global production sharing is now much larger than foreign direct investment, the traditional focus of much IPE literature.

There is another critical consequence of the explosion of the value chain for IPE theory: it has facilitated what Bhagwati referred to as the 'splintering' of goods and services (1997: 437–8). For example, the inbound and outbound logistics functions, traditionally performed internally by manufacturing firms, are now often outsourced and purchased from highly capable outside suppliers. Logistics resides in the service sector, according to international economists. Thus, while the number of 'goods' produced in this example may not change, economic activity (and employment) appears to be declining in the manufacturing sector and increasing in the service (logistics) sector. Facilitating this phenomenon has been the emergence of global air cargo TNCs including DHL, FedEx, United Parcel Service and TNT. These firms have emerged to provide end-to-end logistics services and delivery anywhere in the world within 48 hours. After constructing global networks in the 1990s, all four TNCs now operate in more than 200 countries and, in 1998, DHL was named in a major survey by *Global Finance* magazine as the world's most global corporation.

Whilst the 'manufacturing matters' argument (Cohen and Zysman 1987) is still evoked by social scientists and by policy makers, it is getting harder to determine what exactly manufacturing is as the value chain explodes. As operations are disaggregated, the manufacturing process itself becomes fragmented. Identifying the manufacturing source of a product can be increasingly complicated in a world of outsourcing and strategic alliance networks. In its extreme form, it is even possible for a 'manufacturing' firm to be little more than a marketing and sales enterprise, having subcontracted all of its fabrication and assembly activities. This transformation of international production challenges traditional perspectives of international business, such as Vernon's product life cycle (1966), that view a product's value chain as a holistic entity to be transferred to another location as it matures. Vernon recognized that growth in demand for a product has locational implications (1966; 1974). As the need to be close to the customer base decreases and concerns over production costs increase, he argued that firms are likely to move production offshore. However, Vernon failed to consider that firm structure could be transformed in such a way as to render obsolete the need for the geographical colocation of value chain functions. This may in part be due to what Ietto-Gillies describes as Vernon's 'concentration on the product rather than the firm' (1992: 101). Consequently, Vernon and most other leading writers on international political economy and international business (for example, Buckley and Casson 1979; Dunning 1993) were unable to envisage the fundamental changes in the nature of international production that have occurred in the internet age.

Another key Strange assertion, that the United States maintains hegemony over the production structure, has also weathered the test of time. Focusing on the location of the decision makers who determine what is produced, when it is produced and the rules of engagement yields a very different perspective than simply the location of value-added activities or trade balances. Consider the domicile of the world's largest TNCs. Ranking the world's largest corporations by market capitalization – the value of publicly traded shares, which are a function of the value global investors place on current profitability and future earnings and growth potential – shows a commanding lead for US firms. In the *Financial Times* 1998 survey of the largest global corporations, the United States was home to nine of the top ten, 35 (70 per cent) of the top 50, and 244 (47 per cent) of the top 500 firms on the basis of market capitalization. In total, US firms make up 57 per cent (7.3 trillion) of the $12.7 trillion market capitalization of the largest 500 firms (Figure 4.4). In other words, the United States, with about one-quarter of the world's GDP, is home to three-fifths of the market value of the most significant TNCs – the primary wealth creators in the global economy.[9] The names of the top US TNCs are familiar to most people. These include Microsoft, General Electric, Exxon, Cisco Systems, Intel and IBM. In the world of international business, market capitalization (rather than turnover or number of employees) represents power – power to acquire other firms, raise capital or launch new product introductions. Global shareholders, at least by the close of 1998, had placed their votes, and they believed that more than half of the world's value creation would come from US-based TNCs.

While US TNCs are as potent as ever, the US government has also leveraged its power to shape the production structure. Key

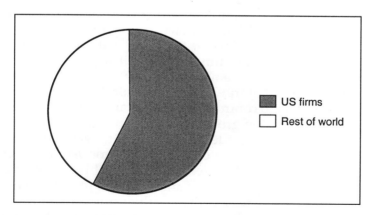

Source: Adapted from *Financial Times* Global 500 Survey, http://www.ft.com/ftsurveys/q3666.htm, 28 January 1999. Reproduced with the permission of *The Financial Times*, London.

Figure 4.4   Market capitalization of largest 500 global firms

provisions of the GATT Uruguay Round – from the inclusion of intellectual property protection to the General Agreement on Trade in Services – were included as a result of US insistence. Strange's perspective of international organizations as 'strategic instruments of national policies and interests' (1988b: 12) is not far from the mark, based on the Uruguay Round experience. The United States has also acted on a unilateral basis to pursue its national interests. A good example is the US conclusion of 'open skies' aviation treaties with over 30 countries in the 1990s, which removed capacity restrictions for international air transportation on a bilateral basis. Globally, competitive US TNCs such as American Airlines and FedEx were key beneficiaries of these bilateral aviation agreements. While the focus of this chapter is on TNCs and the changing nature of international production, it is clear that the US government is sometimes an indispensable partner for US TNCs in pursuing their interests.

Combining the strength of US TNCs with the US government, Strange's assertion that the holder of authority in the international production structure is the *international business civilization* consisting of public officials of some states, corporate managers, scientists, bankers and market players with headquarters 'in New York, Chicago, and Los Angeles' (1990: 262–5) remains highly relevant, perhaps more than ever as a result of changes in international production over the last decade.

Conclusion

The argument advanced in this chapter is that current trends in global production make Strange's production structure more relevant than ever for the study of International Political Economy. The emergence of the internet, combined with falling real transportation costs and a liberal trade environment, has allowed many TNCs to reconfigure their value systems and integrate operations on a truly global basis as never before. TNCs (particularly those based in the United States) appear to control a growing share of the world economy and, as evidenced by the growth of trade in intermediate goods, a growing share of world trade as well. In Strange's lexicon, TNCs have enhanced their influence on the global production structure as 'the people who make the key decisions on what is produced, where and how, and who designs, directs and manages to sell successfully'.

While TNCs have increased their influence over the production structure, we have not analyzed Strange's contention that TNCs have enhanced their power in the international system, that is, their ability to affect outcomes so that their preferences take precedence.[10] This is a highly complex issue that is beyond the scope of this chapter.

Undoubtedly, the growing economic clout of TNCs, as evidenced by the FedEx/Scotland example discussed earlier, does translate into significant influence over policy outcomes in many cases. What is clear is that TNCs and governments need each other more than ever. Furthermore, with the changes in international production structure that Strange first boldly described more than a decade ago, public policy creation will become an increasingly complex endeavor.

Notes

1   This approach has been extensively discussed in Chapters 1 and 2.
2   This term is take from Paul Krugman (1997) and refers to 'people who speak impressively about international trade [and competitiveness] while ignoring basic economics and misusing economic figures'.
3   For a discussion of Toyota's lean production approach, see Womack *et al.* (1990).
4   For a discussion of Post-Fordism, see R. Kaplinsky, in Eden (1993: 112).
5   Data from speech by Michael Dell to Detroit Economic Club, 1 November 1999.
6   See 'Colography Group Report Examines 20 Years of U.S. Air Cargo Deregulation', (http://www.colography.com.press/prnov97.htm), Colography Group, 22, 10 November, 1997.
7   According to the Colography Group, more than $2 trillion of world trade by value moved by air cargo in 1998. See 'Global Air Cargo Value, Tonnage Set All-Time Records in 1998', (http://www.colography.com/press/prWACTM98.html). An example of an Asian country dependent on air cargo is the Philippines, where 66 per cent of exports (by value) moved by air in 1998, according to the Philippine National Statistics Office.
8   The group of British air cargo carriers is known as the British Cargo Airline Alliance. For a discussion of the events surrounding this issue, refer to the *Journal of Commerce*, 13 April 1999 and 18 March 1999. Fedex subsequently decided to curtail services to/from Scotland.
9   The results of the 1998 Global 500 Financial Times Survey can be found at http://www.ft.com/ftsurveys/q3666.htm.
10 See Strange (1996: 17) for a discussion on power.

References

Bhagwati, J. (1997), in V.N. Balasubramanyam (ed.), *Jagdish Bhagwati: Writings on International Economics*, Oxford: Oxford University Press.
Buckley, P.J. and M. Casson (1979), 'A Theory of International Operations', *European Research in International Business*; reprinted in P.J. Buckley and P.N. Ghauri (1999), *The Internationalization of the Firm*, London: International Thomson Business Press.
CEPD (Taiwan Council for Economic Planning and Development) (1997), *The Plan for Developing Taiwan into an Asia-Pacific Regional Operations Center*, Taipei: Executive Yuan.
Cohen, S.S. and J. Zysman (1987), *Manufacturing Matters*, New York: Basic Books.
Dicken, P. (1992), *Global Shift: The Internationalization of Economic Activity*, (2nd edn), London: Paul Chapman Publishing.
Dunning, J.H. (1993), *The Globalization of Business*, London: Routledge.

Eden, L. and E.H. Potter (eds) (1993), *Multinationals in the Global Political Economy*, London, New York: Macmillan, St. Martin's Press.

Friedman, T.L. (1999), *The Lexus and the Olive Tree*, New York: Farrar, Straus, Giroux.

Gilpin, R. (1987), *The Political Economy of International Relations*, Princeton, NJ: Princeton University Press.

Henderson, D. (1998), *The Changing Fortunes of Economic Liberalism*, London: Institute of Economic Affairs.

Ietto-Gillies, G. (1992), *International Production: trends, theories, effects*, Cambridge: Polity Press.

Karliner, J. (1997), *The Corporate Planet: Ecology and Politics in the Age of Globalisation*, San Francisco: Sierra Club Books.

Krugman, P. (1997), *Pop Internationalism*, Cambridge, MA: MIT Press.

Lawton, T.C. (1999), *European Industrial Policy and Competitiveness: concepts and instruments*, Basingstoke: Macmillan Business.

Porter, M.E. (1985), *Competitive Advantage: Sustaining and Creating Superior Performance*, New York: The Free Press.

Stopford, J. and S. Strange (with John S. Henley) (1991), *Rival States, Rival Firms: Competition for World Market Shares*, Cambridge: Cambridge University Press.

Strange, S. (1986), 'Supranationals and the State', in J. Hall (ed.), *States in History*, Oxford: Oxford University Press.

Strange, S. (1988a), *States and Markets*, London: Pinter Publishers.

Strange, S. (1988b), 'The Future of the American Empire', *The Journal of International Affairs*, 42(1).

Strange, S. (1990), 'The Name of the Game', in N. Rizopoulos (ed.), *Sea Changes. American Foreign Policy in a World Transformed*, New York and London: Council of Foreign Relations Press.

Strange, S. (1996), *The Retreat of the State*, Cambridge: Cambridge University Press.

Vernon, R. (1966), 'International Investment and International Trade in the Product Cycle', *Quarterly Journal of Economics*, 80, 190–207.

Vernon, R. (1974), 'The Location of Economic Activity', in J.H. Dunning (ed.), *Economic Analysis and the Multinational Enterprise*, London: Allen & Unwin.

Womack, J.R., D.T. Jones and D. Roos (1990), *The Machine That Changed The World*, New York: Ranson Associates.

World Trade Organization (1997), *1997 World Trade Organization Annual Report, Vol. II*, Geneva: WTO.

World Trade Organization (1998), *1998 World Trade Organization Annual Report, Vol. II*, Geneva: WTO.

Yeats, A. (1998), 'Just How Big is Global Production Sharing?', World Bank, Policy Research Working Paper No. 1871, Washington, DC.

PART II
GLOBAL FINANCE
AND STATE POWER

5 Money Power: Shaping the Global Financial System

AMY C. VERDUN

Introduction

Any scholar interested in studying the International Political Economy (IPE) today would not think twice about placing considerable emphasis on the role of money and finance in order to understand what makes the world go around. A frequently quoted example is the fact that, for any single transaction in real goods, many thousands of financial transactions are registered. Speculative currency transactions and trade in equities are determining much of the registered value of currencies and firms, much more so than the 'real' economic fundamentals.

Though clear today, it has taken the discipline of IPE quite some time to fully appreciate the importance and the nature of the influence of money and finance. Susan Strange was an important advocate of the inclusion of these and related factors when studying IPE. As is noted in many other chapters in this volume, Strange emphasized the importance of looking at politics and economics simultaneously. Throughout her entire academic career Strange emphasized this relationship, and within this the importance of money and finance.

This chapter discusses the way in which works by Strange and others see the role of money and finance in the shaping of the contemporary global economy (the next two chapters, by Cohen and Underhill, respectively, further discuss this subject). This chapter considers the work Strange started in the late 1960s, through to her last book, *Mad Money*, published in 1998. The emphasis is on how Strange's analysis has influenced wider thinking in the IPE literature. Using the structural power framework, the chapter also emphasizes the relative role that various actors (including states) have had in the development of global economy.

The outline of this chapter is as follows. The next section discusses Strange's contribution to the IPE literature as put forward in her works in three decades of writing. It examines the relationship between politics and economics, money and power, and how her analyses have influenced the literature of International Relations (IR) and IPE. The third section examines how Strange's analyses on money and finance led to a reconceptualization of the role of actors, knowledge and elites. It will discuss the relationship between states and non-state actors, and the theoretical tools adopted to understand the power relationships between actors. The fourth section focuses more specifically on Strange's criticism on the study of international politics, using her study of money and finance. Strange was very critical about the way politics was problematized and studied. She was concerned with the way the framing of the subject of study had implications on redistribution of the costs and benefits of the political situation. Concerns were also about who ultimately would be taking responsibility for the 'outcome' of politics. The fifth section in turn criticizes Strange's approach of International Politics. It spells out how future generations of scholars can improve Strange's approach to IPE. Some of the fiercest criticisms of her work are that she did not empirically test her theoretical approach, nor did she provide empirically refutable hypotheses. The empirical evidence in her studies has also been criticized for being sketchy rather than substantial. Also, though she criticized the study of politics and the (lack of) responsibility taken by major actors (states, firms, international organizations, the world community) she did not describe an alternative plan that could correct these injustices. Ultimately, however, these matters were not her main concern. In a sense, to test rigorously her theoretical analyses would lead her to having to adopt a methodology that she was unwilling to accept. Strange, instead, wanted to provide her insights into the global political economy, and left it to future generations of scholars to take her ideas further.

The Political Economy of Money and Finance

Strange's interest in the study of currencies dates as far back as the 1950s and 1960s (Strange 1959; 1967). In the course of the 1970s, she started to fully develop her writing in this area. In these early years, the field of international studies was still much separated into 'international economics' and 'international relations'. The former was mainly dominated by economists and focused on international trade and international production. The study of money, monetary policy and finance was mainly done by economists and historians, and they typically stayed within the framework of their respective disciplines.

International Relations, by contrast, focused much more specifically on the role of states, security and world order. Money and financial matters did not feature highly on the research agenda of IR scholars, if at all.

Strange (1970; 1972a; 1972b) was one of the first scholars to call for a separate discipline of IPE to bridge the gap between international economics and IR (others were Baldwin 1971; Kindleberger 1970; Keohane and Nye 1972). After 20 years of relative tranquility in the monetary sphere, the mid-to-late 1960s and onwards showed that the stability of the monetary system and the value of national currencies were becoming more prominent issues in international politics. Indeed, by the middle of the 1970s, with the end of the Bretton Woods agreement and the oil crisis, inflation and currency fluctuations caused national governments major concerns. In addition, during this time period, the financial markets developed more rapidly. Decades of financial innovations as well as the integration and growth of financial markets have permanently changed international economic and political relations. This process still continues today.

Her study of the British pound sterling, the dollar and other international currencies led Strange to conclude that any analysis of currencies should look at both the political and the economic factors. In *Sterling and British Policy* (Strange 1971) she developed a theoretical framework explaining the use of international currencies including a typology of them: neutral currency, top currency, master currency and negotiated currency. She used this typology and her theoretical framework to answer the questions: when do countries decide to use a foreign currency, and what political consequences follow from this for both the issuing country and the country that uses the foreign currency? She concluded that the role and interest any given country will have in maintaining stability and an overall welfare of the international system depends on what type of currency its national currency is. Thus, here is where she had connected up the politics and the economics of international currencies.

In her next large study, *International Monetary Relations* (Strange 1976), this theoretical framework is further developed. In it she states that the period 1959–71 was characterized by a politicization of money, accelerating economic interdependence, the gradual erosion and abandonment of monetary arrangements, and continuing predominance of the United States. From this analysis she concludes that an IPE is emerging (Strange 1976: 356). The significance here of recognizing that there is an IPE is that the 'management or mismanagement' would be of concern not only to individual nation states but also to the international community. The economic interdependence means that the international community needs to speed up its response to potential conflicts. Finally, Strange was concerned about the fact that a new political framework would have to be set up to 'fill the vacuum' caused by the end of Bretton Woods. She envisaged that the United States would take the lead in these matters in consultation with its partners. But she was doubtful whether the US domestic politics would allow for much sharing of decision-making power.

During the 1980s, she further developed her thinking on the financial system. In the early 1980s her concern was still with the way the international monetary system was out of control. In various pieces she emphasized the importance of decisions and non-decisions by governments on the international financial system. Her sequel to the earlier studies on the 1960s was *Casino Capitalism*, that deals with the period 1970–85 (Strange 1986). It argues that the mismanagement of money and the lack of credit was the core of the problem in the 1970s and 1980s, *not* the rise of protectionism. In stating this she strongly attacks the economics discipline, and the politicians for having accepted that view. In her view the world 'disorder' was brought about by government decisions and non-decisions. She is concerned about the 'casino type' financial system because it affects everyone, though it affects some more than others. Those who are making the rules and those who are large players will typically be winners, and hardly ever among the greatest losers. By contrast, those who have to accept the rules and the results of the turbulent financial system (developing countries, ordinary people) are more at risk from it. She is also critical of the fact that no one seems to be taking responsibility for the well-being of the financial system. Moreover, financial stability would be needed to improve the chance of solving other issues in international politics as well (in the 1980s: cold war issues, debt crises and so on).

Her remedy is that the United States should assume a larger responsibility over the international financial system. In making decisions about monetary policy it should take the needs of the overall monetary system into consideration, rather than merely base it on domestic concerns. Though her analysis and the remedy are clear and she would continue to promote this medicine for a healthy financial system, Strange was skeptical about whether it would happen. She did not believe the US Congress would be capable and enlightened enough to assume its international responsibility and be able to reflect on matters beyond merely domestic ones. *Casino Capitalism* made an important contribution to the literature. It put in a strong claim for placing the international financial and monetary system at the core of the study of IPE. It also implicitly attacked the IR literature for not having taken this area of study seriously enough in its study of relations between nation state governments. Finally, it did the IPE literature a good service in drawing on a broad body of literature, including work by economic historians, monetarists, practitioners and, of course, IR scholars (realists and Marxists alike).

States and Markets, first published in 1988, in many ways offers the core of Strange's thinking on a number of theoretical issues. Previous chapters have discussed Strange's four dimensions (or structures) of power in IPE: security, finance, production and knowledge. This chapter focuses on the financial structure and, in the next section, on the knowledge structure. The financial structure has two core components: the power to create credit and the power to determine the exchange rates between the different currencies. The financial structure is defined as follows: 'the sum of all the arrangements governing the availability of credit plus all the factors determining the terms on which currencies are exchanged for one another' (Strange 1994: 90). The actors who influence the outcome of the financial structure clearly are national governments, but also bankers, stock exchange brokers and others. The analysis of the changes in the financial structure over the past decades, centuries, even millennia, is closed by emphasizing once again that the current situation is a mess. The largest four problems identified are debt management; supervision and control of banks; restoration of stability of debt and credibility of exchange rates between major currencies; and, finally, the bankruptcy of economic thought in a global financial structure (ibid.: 111). With regard to all these four problems, Strange emphasizes that the basic problem is *political* not *technical*. It is the lack of desire or willingness of the US government, or national governments collectively, to create rules or norms, or to transfer to international organizations these tasks. She is also concerned about the US dollar as bouncing up and down vis-à-vis other leading currencies, such as the yen and the D-mark. Finally, she is critical about the lack of political leadership by governments but also by the economics discipline that could theoretically inform governments what to do. This criticism on experts is connected to the argument made about the knowledge structure (see below). What we see in *States and Markets* is the culmination of her thinking on money and finance over a period of almost thirty years, including her broader analysis and theoretical framework on the role of power in IPE.

The second edition of *Casino Capitalism* announced a sequel. It would turn out to be Strange's last book: *Mad Money*. It discusses how the casino 'has gone mad ... wildly foolish to let the financial markets run so far ahead, so far beyond control of state and international authorities' (Strange 1998: 1). Again we see that Strange is deeply concerned about the consequences of the erratic financial system for the lives of ordinary people. Again she stresses the need for politicians to take responsibility. She identifies five important changes that have affected the global financial system. First are the technological changes that have made financial transactions faster and made available many financial innovations to purchase and sell.

The second is the dramatic increase in size and importance of markets. Third is the so-called 'end of banking': banks are no longer the main actors in international finance. Fourth is the emergence of Asia, in particular Japan and China. Fifth, and finally, are the changes in central banking supervision and control over the market. Her elaborate account of what happened in the 1980s and 1990s leads her to conclude the study on a cautious note. She stresses that finance determines much in the world economy. Related to this, financial mergers and other means to concentrate economic power have increased the power of those large corporations. As a result of these factors, national governments have less control over their economies and societies than before. This situation causes her to have two main concerns about the effects of this changed situation on world society. First is the effect this changed financial system has on 'moral contamination' – playing with the rules in such a way that a profit is made, even if the rules are not strictly obeyed (for example, insider trading). Another example of moral contamination is the bribery and corruption of politics, which she sees as having increased in recent years in relation to financial market growth. Her second main concern – as we see again – is the widening income gap between rich and poor, developed and underdeveloped, the resources available to the larger firms and business versus the ordinary people. Part of the story is the lack of access to credit of the latter and the abundance of it to the former.

Strange added to the IPE literature in an important way. When others were still focusing predominantly on the role of states (Gilpin 1987; Keohane 1984; Keohane and Nye 1977; Krasner 1983) or on domestic sources of state policies (Frieden 1991; Putnam 1988), Strange moved into the study of money and finance in order to understand what made the world go around. She successfully pleaded for economics to be integrated in the study of IR, or, more precisely, to advocate the creation of the study of IPE. As we shall see, just focusing on the importance of money and finance does not solve the classical IR questions; the problem remains, what then is the role of states, if the financial system has made the world more interdependent and if most of the individual nation state governments are deprived of many of their tools to influence the domestic economy? Also she did not convince the skeptics that the role of states was as limited as she led the reader to believe (Helleiner 1995; see also the chapters by Gilpin and Underhill in this volume). Let us now move to the knowledge structure and how experts, expertise and knowledge play a role in all this.

Knowledge and Finance

As has been mentioned, in order to fully grasp what was changing in the global economy, Strange introduced four sources of structural power. Strange's concept of the knowledge structure encompasses the role of knowledge, information, discourse and technocratic expertise, and the experts who have access to them. The knowledge structure 'determines what knowledge is discovered, how it is stored, and who communicates it by what means to whom and on what terms... . Power and authority are conferred on those occupying key decision-making positions in the knowledge structure – on those who are acknowledged by society to be possessed of the "right", desirable knowledge and engage in the acquisition of more of it' (Strange 1994: 121). Two examples of knowledge structures are medieval Christendom in Europe and the national scientific state. The recent technological innovations may well lead to a change in the knowledge structure, but only insofar as the elites and dominant groups and actors agree that the underlying beliefs systems are changing. The point to keep in mind here is that the concept of the knowledge structure is one that serves to explain power relations. It does not focus on the 'absolute' change in knowledge or information. A change in the knowledge structure can occur when a number of the powerful groups and actors start to move away from the commonly held belief systems under the existing knowledge structure. In the recent contemporary era an example of this is the retreat of the state: the idea that the national governments may be incapable but probably also not the legitimate and appropriate unit to deal with societal problems.

What the knowledge structure also points to is the way elites are formed. Interestingly, in this regard Strange makes a contribution to the IR/IPE literature in which other subfields of political science (such as policy studies and political theory) are much further advanced. She argues that groups that can self-identify as having the 'right' knowledge, the 'right education' the 'right ideas and belief systems' can signal these facts to one another. This type of reasoning was also found in the earlier work of Ruggie (1975) and later in the epistemic community literature (Haas 1992). Students of policy studies have also examined the role of experts and expertise and how it relates to politics. It is remarkable that a policy studies scholar such as Claudio Radaelli (1998) comes to similar conclusions to those of Strange. Radaelli points out that it is not necessarily having the information, knowledge or expertise that counts, but rather a mix of it and how the actor uses it politically. In *States and Markets*, Strange comes to a similar conclusion in her discussion of how the various structures come together to produce the overall power structure (Strange 1994: 130–35).

Returning to our specific study of money and finance, what concerns Strange in this regard is that a relatively small group of people (economists) with a roughly similar academic training (usually North American) determine the bulk of the political decisions to do with the financial system. Rarely do they consider the full range of implications that follow from their decisions. In fact, they often do not even consider their decisions to be determined by 'politics', but rather by technocratic motivations, or by economic reasoning. Yet, Strange points out, one needs to ask *cui bono* – who benefits. By not taking a political perspective on financial issues one fails to take responsibility for the redistributive outcomes of any given so-called 'technocratic' decision. Also the set of choices that these financial elites choose from are highly influenced by their training and their focus on what constitutes the 'problem' and what likely could be a 'solution' to this problem.[1] Thus this small specialized elite, who are thinking about these financial matters, are in part responsible for any unjust effect (in terms of costs and benefits) of the financial system on the various countries and the people who live in them. In criticizing the role of bankers and economists, Strange is in line with various other IPE scholars, mainstream (Pauly 1997) and more critical thinkers (Germain 1997). In fact she even is in line with former Federal Reserve officials themselves (Greider 1987). States have coopted these experts to help them make decisions that are predominantly the role of nation state governments. However, by letting experts deal with them in isolation from the political debates, they fail to consider their redistributive effects. As a result, a legitimacy problem emerges. Citizens are confiding in their governments to govern. Governments in turn let experts deal with issues, and in the end it is unclear who is to be held accountable for the outcome of this process.

Strange's Criticism of the Study of International Politics

Strange started off criticizing International Relations scholars for not including the role of economics, and criticizing Economics scholars for being too limited in their view of what constitutes an interesting problem to study. In subsequent years, she moved on to target the IR discipline's (in her view), overly obsessive preoccupation with states. Strange looked at it differently from the mainstream of the 1970s, 1980s and 1990s. States operate in a power structure together with others. These others can be actors (such as multinational firms) or structures (the four mentioned earlier). Thus states have to *share* the space of international politics with actors and they are embedded in and bound by structures.

However, by focusing in this way on the role of states, she also comes to a different conclusion as to what the 'problem' is that a student of international politics would want to address. Strange was concerned with the outcome of the whole interplay of actors and structures. The 'bottom line' for her was that the results of politics have an effect on the everyday life of ordinary citizens. She also stood up for the interests of poor and highly indebted developing countries. She stated that their situation was the unambiguous result of the decisions made by the wealthy industrialized countries. Thus her criticism on the study of IR was that it failed to ask the relevant questions about who benefits, and who should be carrying the responsibility. Strange had an answer to these questions. Those who are already in a 'powerful', 'influential' or well-off position will benefit, and those who are disadvantaged (lack access to credit, knowledge, decision making) will not benefit. Strange also had a solution to the problems. National governments, in particular the US government, should take responsibility over the overall well-being of the global economy, global security, rule of law (for trade and commerce) and environmental concerns. Strange advocated on many occasions that the United States should finally accept its responsibility. Yet, she remained skeptical that the US Congress was ready to take on its global responsibility.

Though this may appear contradictory, Strange was at the same time highly critical of the United States. What she disliked was the way in which the US students were trained. The career-oriented academic training that takes place in the United States was in her view reason for the kind of scholarship that American IR scholars produced. She disliked the more abstract methodologies that the US scholars were using: hypothesis theory testing, rational choice approaches and game theory, to name but a few. These were approaches that were more fashionable in the United States than in Europe. In her view, the political science literature had learnt the wrong lessons from economics: they were imitating the methods and concepts of liberal or neoclassical economists. In Strange's view, these approaches to the study of international politics close the researcher off from the real world (Strange 1994: 167). Of course, realizing that the United States was the dominant country, and that many of the leading persons in the world obtain their training in that country, she was also concerned that this trend would lead to academic research that she herself did not find rewarding (see also Verbeek in this volume). Thus, for more than one reason, Strange was disappointed in the United States. It is probably because the United States did not take on a role that she wanted it to take that she was so critical of that country.

Finally, Strange criticized the study of international politics for being too narrowly focused on states and too narrowly inspired by

IR literature. Strange had to move quite a distance to fully appreciate the importance of multinational companies, but ultimately, in *Rival States, Rival Firms*, in *Casino Capitalism* and in *Mad Money*, she shows that she has placed those actors in the same kind of category as states (although they have different powers). Strange criticized international politics for staying too much in the discourse of IR. She herself was continuously trying to cross the disciplinary boundaries and reading widely in the field of business, demography, economics, geography, history, psychology, sociology and so on. Her criticism again was that by just restricting one's view to the few debates in one's own discipline one may be able to 'do a better job' debating with one's peers, but has one really understood what is going on in the real world?

Criticism of Strange's Approach of International Politics

Though Strange has been a very influential academic in the field of IPE and has made important contributions to the literature of both IPE and IR, her work has not been received without criticism. The main points of concern can roughly be subdivided into two broad categories: (1) the rigorousness of her studies and her theories and (2) ambivalence about structure and agency including the role of the United States.

Let us turn to the first category. Various authors have stated that Strange's work is sketchy, not substantiated by hard evidence and cannot be rigorously tested. The same kind of criticism has been made about her theoretical approaches: they do not provide a clear basis from which one could easily derive testable hypotheses. What do scholars mean by this? In the previous paragraph this recent upswing in popularity of rational choice and game-theoretical models has already been mentioned. In recent years there has been a trend towards conducting political science research in such a way that one can quantify the results and make explicit statements about causal links among a limited number of variables. This methodology has been around for some time, but has increased in popularity in recent years (in fact in some academic departments in the United States 'battles' have been fought over what constitutes a sound research methodology). As was mentioned above, Strange was not keen on that type of research, and obviously tried to write her books for an audience different from those political science departments in the United States where the 'rigorous theory testing' people 'won the battle'. Why Strange never tried to appease those critics is a guess hard to make. It may have been her natural inclination. It could also have been that Strange came to the study of International Politics years before these battles were being fought in US schools. Another reason might have been that Strange came to academia at a later stage in life, having been a journalist for a number of years. One could argue that that shaped her writing style. However, regardless of these speculations as to why she did what she did, she personally believed that one was missing the point by framing research questions in such a way that they could be rigorously tested. In her view the world was dynamic and interactive. No model that could be tested by looking only at a few variables would be able, in her view, to describe adequately (let alone predict) the real world of international politics.

The second category of criticisms on Strange's work is perhaps more serious. Though she criticized the study of politics and the (lack of) responsibility taken by major actors (states, firms, elites, international organizations, the world community), she did not describe an alternative plan that could correct these injustices or imbalances. In particular, she was ambiguous about the role of the various actors, especially the role of states. What can they, and should they, do to correct things? As was mentioned above, Strange thought it was important that states get back in charge, and that the United States would take the lead. At the same time she had no confidence in the capacity of the United States to do this. She also emphasized that states were losing power, so how exactly they were to square that circle remained unclear. Related to this is a second ambiguity in her writings, which is related to the well-known structure/agency debate. Are actors free or determined? If it is one or the other, under what circumstances does that occur? Strange sees actors as pawns on a chessboard being able to make some moves but having to follow the rules of the game. Those who can determine the rules have the most power. However, none of them is ever in the position to fully set the rules. Yet, for a researcher wanting to use her theoretical approaches, it is a guessing game when an actor has the capacity to act independently, and when its actions are predetermined by the structure.

Though these concerns are serious in terms of moving on with her work and developing new research agendas, ultimately they were not her main concern. In a sense, to rigorously test these theoretical analyses would lead her to having to adopt a methodology that she was unwilling to accept: rigorous testing of theoretical propositions. In a sense, the second category of criticisms (the ambivalent role of the United States and states in general, and the structure/agency problem) is also a problem, mainly for those wanting to test and apply Strange's approach rigorously. All other students of IPE can just read her analyses and be inspired.

Conclusion

Based on her study of money and finance, Strange made a very important contribution to thinking about the international political economy. She was one of the advocates of establishing IPE as a distinct field of study and in doing so she firmly put IPE on the map, in particular the importance of studying money and finance. She developed various theoretical frameworks to understand the role of money and the role of power in IPE that made a major impact on the IPE literature.

Strange examined the role of money, the interaction between money, the financial systems, the role of states, non-state actors and the importance of the role of expertise. Her analyses show that the global financial system influences the realm of international politics in a very important way. Her oeuvre has shown convincingly that IR studies that only look at defense issues and the actions of national governments miss out on 'where the action is'. Clearly these realms are intertwined.

The recent changes in the global political economy have also had an impact on the overall relationships among countries and actors. They have also influenced what Strange has identified as being the four primary structures of the global political economy. This chapter has focused in particular on the financial and the knowledge structure.

Strange's style of writing is also distinct from that of various other scholars in the field. The pros and cons are clear. The advantage of her very clear and accessible writing style is that she makes the material she writes about interesting and comprehensible to almost any reader. The criticism, in particular from US scholars, is that she fails to incorporate the research methodology and social scientific approaches that make for rigorous testing of her theoretical frameworks. It is interesting that it is exactly this part of Strange's criticism of the United States that would make it impossible for her ever to have given in to those pressures. However, perhaps future scholars, Americans as well as scholars from the rest of the world, might want to take it upon themselves to embark on that research journey to deal with these matters, and in doing so, become 'neo-Strangians'.

Note

1   This is nicely illustrated in a case study of elite perceptions of Economic and Monetary Union (EMU) (Verdun, 2000). Monetary experts in trade unions, employers' organizations, ministries of finance and central banks in Britain, France and Germany all considered EMU desirable for a number of reasons. It is noteworthy that the discussion of EMU stayed firmly within the parameters of the economics debate.

Bibliography

Baldwin, D. (1971), 'Money and Power', *Journal of Politics*, 33, 578–614.

Frieden, J. (1991), 'Invested Interests; the Politics of National Economic Policies in a World of Global Finance', *International Organization*, 45(4), 425–51.

Germain, R. (1997), *The International Organization of Credit: States and Global Finance in the World Economy*, Cambridge: Cambridge University Press.

Gilpin, R. (1987), *The Political Economy of International Relations*, Princeton, NJ: Princeton University Press.

Greider, W. (1987), *Secrets of the Temple: How the Federal Reserve Runs the Country*, New York: Simon & Schuster.

Haas, P. (1992), 'Introduction: Epistemic Communities and International Policy Coordination', *International Organization*, 46(1), 1–35.

Helleiner, E. (1995), 'Explaining the Globalization of Financial Markets: Bringing States Back in', *Review of International Political Economy*, 2(2).

Keohane, R. (1984), *After Hegemony: Cooperation and Discord in the World Political Economy*, Princeton, NJ: Princeton University Press.

Keohane, R. and J. Nye (eds) (1972), *Transnational Relations and World Politics*, Cambridge, MA: Harvard University Press.

Keohane, R. and J. Nye (1977), *Power and Interdependence*, Boston and Toronto: Little, Brown and Co.

Kindleberger, C. (1970), *Power and Money: The Economics of International Politics and the Politics of International Economics*, New York: Basic Books.

Krasner, S. (1983), *International Regimes*, Ithaca and London: Cornell University Press.

Pauly, L. (1997), *Who Elected the Bankers? Surveillance and Control in the World Economy*, Ithaca: Cornell University Press.

Putnam, R. (1988), 'Diplomacy and Domestic Politics: The Logic of Two-level Games', *International Organization* 42(3), 427–61.

Radaelli, C. (1998), *Technocracy in the European Union*, New York: Longman.

Ruggie, J.G. (1975), 'International responses to technology: concepts and trends', *International Organization*, 29 (Summer), 557–84.

Stopford, J. and Strange, S. (with John S. Henley) (1991), *Rival States, Rival Firms: Competition for World Market Shares*, Cambridge: Cambridge University Press.

Strange, S. (1959), 'The Commonwealth and the Sterling Area', *Yearbook of World Affairs: 1959*, London: Stevens, pp.24–44.

Strange, S. (1967), *The Sterling Problem and the Six*, London: Chatham House.

Strange, S. (1970), 'International economics and international relations: a case of mutual neglect', *International Affairs*, 46(2), 304–15.

Strange, S. (1971), *Sterling and British Policy. A Political Study of An International Currency in Decline*, London, New York and Toronto: Oxford University Press.

Strange, S. (1972a), 'The Dollar Crisis 1971', *International Affairs*, 48(2), 191–215.

Strange, S. (1972b), 'International Economic Relations I: The Need for an Interdisciplinary Approach', in R. Morgan (ed.), *The Study of International Affairs: Essays in Honour of Kenneth Younger*, London: RIIA/Oxford University Press.

Strange, S. (1976), *International Monetary Relations*, in Andrew Shonfield (ed.), *International Economic Relations in the Western World 1959–71*, Volume 2, London, New York and Toronto: Oxford University Press.

Strange, S. (1986), *Casino Capitalism*, Manchester: Manchester University Press.

Strange, S. (1994), *States and Markets*, 2nd edn, London: Pinter Publishers.

Strange, S. (1998), *Mad Money*, Manchester: Manchester University Press.

Verdun, A. (2000), *European Responses to Globalization and Financial Market Integration: Perceptions of Economic and Monetary Union in Britain, France and Germany*, International Political Economy Series, Houndmills: Macmillan and New York: St Martin's Press.

6 Money and Power in World Politics

BENJAMIN J. COHEN

Introduction

The link between money and power in world politics was one of the most enduring themes in the work of Susan Strange. As she told a young American economist some third of a century ago, freshly arrived in London to write a book on the pound sterling, you cannot talk about international currency without considering the politics involved; a point she went on to demonstrate convincingly with her own magisterial study, *Sterling and British Policy* (Strange 1971b).[1] Strange well understood that money can be both a source and a target of power in international affairs; a point of contention as well as a means of possible cooperation. Issues of finance or currencies could not be relegated to the 'low politics' of technical economics alone. Money is inherently political, an integral part of the 'high politics' of diplomacy too. In her words: 'In international monetary relations, we have an issue-area that is self evidently part of the international political system' (Strange 1976: 20). A generation ago, such an assertion might have been considered controversial. That today the connection is taken for granted is a measure of Strange's lasting intellectual influence.

Yet questions remain, involving issues of both theory and praxis. What exactly is the nature of state power in monetary affairs, and how may it change over time? How does money influence the power of states, and vice versa? And what are the consequences of alternative distributions of monetary power for the management of global finance? Strange would be the first to admit that we still lack definitive answers to these critically important questions. The aim of the present chapter, using Strange's insights as a starting point, is to explore each question in turn, in hopes of developing a more coherent understanding of money's role in world politics. Issues of theory will be taken up first, then matters of monetary cooperation and governance.

For the purposes of this chapter, following Strange's lead, money will be understood to encompass all aspects of currency and financial relations – the processes and institutions of financial intermediation (mobilization of savings and allocation of credit) as well as the creation and management of money itself. As she wrote in *States and Markets*, 'The financial structure really has two inseparable aspects. It comprises not just the structures of the political economy through which credit is created but also the monetary system or systems which determine the relative values of the different moneys in which credit is denominated' (Strange 1994: 90). World politics, on the other hand, will be defined less expansively, to encompass here only relations between states or state-sponsored organizations (like the International Monetary Fund): the traditional stuff of international diplomacy. Admittedly, with the resurrection of global financial markets in recent decades, this fails to tell the whole story (Cohen 1996, 1998). As Strange herself stressed in much of her later work,[2] the politics of money has now expanded to include a multitude of private as well as public-sector actors. But so long as states remain the basic unit of formal governance throughout the world, inter-state relations clearly will continue to be a fundamental part of the story and well worth exploring on their own. The shifting balance of power between states and markets in monetary affairs, though relegated to the wings here, moves to center stage in the other two finance and money chapters of this volume (Chapters 5 and 7) by, respectively, Verdun and Underhill.

Strange Thoughts on Money

Money was literally the alpha and omega of Susan Strange's lifetime corpus of scholarship: the subject of her first book, *Sterling and British Policy* (Strange 1971b), as well as of her last, *Mad Money* (Strange 1998). In between came two other major financial studies: a detailed and comprehensive history of international monetary relations from 1959 to 1971, which appeared in 1976, and *Mad Money*'s noted predecessor, *Casino Capitalism*, published ten years later. Currency and financial issues also figured prominently in *States and Markets* (Strange 1994) and in several shorter papers (Strange 1971a; 1975; 1983b; 1985; 1990; Calleo and Strange 1984). The politics of money, it is safe to say, was never very far from her thoughts.

Not surprisingly, some of her thinking showed significant change over time, reflecting the evolution of real-world events as well as her own steep learning curve. Most noticeable was her gradual shift from the state-centric perspective of her early work to a greater emphasis on non-state actors, as capital markets revived and the pace of financial globalization accelerated (see also Lawton and Michaels, Chapter 4 of this volume). During the 1970s her principal emphasis was on inter-state relations and the diplomacy of monetary negotiations. In this respect she was no different from most other specialists at the time, who also treated governments as the main actors involved.[3] Market forces, insofar as they were considered at all, entered analysis as little more than a vexing constraint or complication for policy makers. More quickly than most others, however, she came to recognize the fundamental transformation being wrought by the reintegration of national financial markets and the rapid increase of cross-border capital mobility.[4] By 1986, in *Casino Capitalism*, she was already expressing concern about an international financial system in which the gamblers in the casino have got out of hand, almost beyond, it sometimes seems, the control of governments (Strange 1986: 21). By 1998, she was convinced that the casino had gone crazy. 'The financial markets,' she wrote in *Mad Money*, have 'run beyond the control of state and international authorities' (Strange 1998: 1).

In a more fundamental sense, however, her thinking was remarkably consistent, stressing key themes over and over again in a variety of analytical contexts. Four themes, in particular, stand out. First was the inherently political nature of money. 'No working politician,' Strange wrote, 'needs to be reminded of the political nature of monetary policy... Decisions concerning the management of money substantially affect other matters of great political sensitivity' (Calleo and Strange 1984: 91). More succinctly, 'the management of credit is *necessarily* highly political' (Strange 1985: 39, emphasis added). The basis of her view was historical, noting that, with the transition from primitive to developed financial structures, increased demands were placed on governments 'for the imposition of complex and precise rules to govern the operation of credit institutions and money markets' (Strange 1994: 97). The result, she felt, was an 'inseparability of money from politics' (Strange 1976: 20), not only at the domestic level but also, more to the point, at the international level where governance structures are so much more ambiguous. From the beginning, her scholarship was motivated by an almost missionary-like zeal to highlight the political element that she saw as 'the missing component in much current discussion of international financial and monetary issues' (Strange 1971a: 216). Monetary management, she insisted, was inevitably 'bound up, in large part, with what might be called the "foreign policy" of money' (Calleo and Strange 1984: 91).

A second theme, following logically from the first, was the connection of money to power, with the arrow of causation running in both directions. If money was inseparable from politics, so too was the politics of money inseparable from considerations of power, particularly at the international level, where 'relationships between states are *ultimately* decided by relative power' (Strange 1971b: 39, emphasis added). Power was both the cause and the effect of monetary outcomes.

In *Sterling and British Policy*, for example, Strange distinguished four types of international currency: top currencies, master currencies, negotiated currencies and neutral currencies (Strange 1971b; also 1971a). Power entered her analysis as both causal variable and consequence. Economic and political influence, she averred, was critical in determining what moneys would qualify for any of these roles: the 'power factor affecting an international currency', as she put it (Strange 1971b: 38). The power derived from an international currency, in turn, could also be used to exercise political leverage over others – and most likely would be. In her words: 'It is highly probable that any state economically strong enough to possess [an international currency] will also exert substantial power and influence. The rich usually do' (Strange 1971a: 222). The 'foreign policies' of money would inevitably reflect how much power each individual actor possesses. Likewise, the structure of the monetary system as a whole will reflect 'the general world balance of political and economic power ... the relative power of states' (Calleo and Strange 1984: 99).

A third theme, in turn, concerned that general world balance and what it might look like. Strange assumed that the distribution of power in monetary affairs would almost certainly be highly asymmetric, with a small number of states enjoying a disproportionately large share of influence. For her, there was no doubting 'the reality of the inequality of power' (Strange 1976: 20). The global system was bound to be distinctly hierarchical, with control concentrated for better or worse in a 'small oligarchy of monetarily important states' (ibid.: 22) – the 'affluent alliance', as she called it in her usual colorful fashion (ibid.: 23).

Hierarchy was an obvious feature of her early analysis of international currencies (Strange 1971a, 1971b). It was also evident in her later discussions of global monetary management, which always laid stress on the desirability of effective collective action by the most powerful nations. No reform of casino capitalism was possible, she contended, 'beyond the limits of what is conceivably acceptable to the chief governments of leading states' (Strange 1986: 149). Money has become mad because 'the political foundations for international financial cooperation are weaker today than they were in the 1970s and 1980s' (Strange 1998: 43). Hierarchy implied privilege, in her view, but also a measure of responsibility.

A final theme involved the United States, which Strange always regarded with a jaundiced mix of admiration and resentment (see also the contributions by Verbeek and Helleiner in Chapters 8 and 13, respectively, of this volume). America, she insisted, was clearly *primus inter pares*, even within the affluent alliance and even where others perceived hegemonic decline. The dollar was top currency – 'the choice of the market' (Strange 1971b: 5) – and the United States was 'lead player ... long accustomed to a dominant position' (Strange 1976: 43). Rumors of the demise of America's 'non-territorial empire ... the likes of which the world has never seen before' (Strange 1988: 13), particularly rampant in the 1970s and 1980s, were simply wrong, a 'myth of lost hegemony' (Strange 1987). Those who subscribed to the myth were misled by 'a rather narrow (and old-fashioned) understanding of power in world politics' (Strange 1985: 11). Even in the 1990s the United States remained 'the leading country of the world market economy' (Strange 1994: 115). In an age of increasingly mad money, only America retains the power, if anyone has, to reverse the process and tip the balance of power back again from market to state (Strange 1990: 266).

But for Strange there was a problem, the fact that America too often acts 'in exactly the opposite way to that of a responsible hegemon' (Strange 1994: 115), 'guided by its own rather narrow view of national interest' (Calleo and Strange 1984: 117). In principle, the United States should 'recognize its own true long-term national interest in exercising a wise hegemony over the world market economy' (Strange 1986:171). In practice, it is more likely that others will have 'no other alternative [but] to submit to a measure of tyranny by the most powerful and ruthless member of the affluent alliance' (1976: 358).

The Theory of Monetary Power

Three decades after her first book, these four themes of Strange's no longer seem particularly controversial. Indeed, it would be difficult to find any serious scholar today who would *not* agree that money is political; that power is both a cause and an effect of monetary outcomes; that the distribution of power in monetary affairs is distinctly unequal; and that the United States remains the most powerful of all states. Yet, as indicated, questions remain for further exploration. We begin at the level of theory. What do we mean by monetary power, where does it come from and how is it used?

The Meaning of Power

At its simplest, power in inter-state relations may be defined as the ability to control, or at least influence, the outcome of events. Two dimensions are important, internal and external. The internal dimension corresponds to the dictionary definition of power as a capacity for action. A state is powerful to the extent that it is insulated from outside influence or coercion in the formulation and implementation of policy. A common synonym for the internal dimension of power is 'autonomy'. The external dimension corresponds to the dictionary definition of power as a capacity to control the behavior of others; to enforce compliance. A state is also powerful to the extent that it can influence or coerce outsiders. Such influence need not be actively exercised; it need only be acknowledged by others, implicitly or explicitly, to be effective. It also need not be exercised with conscious intent; the behavior of others can be influenced simply as a by-product of 'powerful' acts (or potential acts). A common synonym for the external dimension of power is 'authority'.

Of most interest to students of international monetary affairs is the external dimension: the authority that one state can exert over others. Yet, apart from Strange herself, remarkably few scholars have even tried to explore monetary power in formal theoretical terms. In the contemporary era, Charles Kindleberger offered a few pioneering observations in his early publication on *Power and Money* (Kindleberger 1970); and a few years later I added some thoughts of my own in *Organizing the World's Money* (Cohen 1977). But as Jonathan Kirshner has written most recently, the topic is in fact 'a neglected area of study' (Kirshner 1995: 3). Theory calls for a reasonably parsimonious and well-specified set of propositions about behavior – statements that are both logically true and, at least in principle, empirically falsifiable. In that sense no true theory of monetary power may be said, as yet, to exist.

Kirshner's own effort, *Currency and Coercion* (Kirshner 1995), stands for now as the definitive work on the subject. But even his contribution, though praiseworthy, is not without limitations. Kirshner claims to present a general theory of monetary power – in his words, 'a general framework regarding the nature of monetary power, how it works, and when it will be successful' (ibid.: 20). In reality, however, his book offers less a theory than a handy taxonomy of many of the diverse ways that money can be used in inter-state relations as an instrument of coercion. Three broad categories of monetary power are distinguished: *currency manipulation*, referring to initiatives taken to affect the value and stability of target currencies; *monetary dependence*, involving efforts to create and exploit a sphere of influence; and *systemic disruption*, encompassing actions directed at specific international monetary systems or subsystems. Each category in turn is divided into several narrow subcategories, all bearing cleverly alliterative labels. Currency manipulation, for instance, may be protective, permissive, predatory or passive. Monetary dependence may be exploited through enforcement, expulsion, extraction or entrapment. Systemic disruption may be strategic or subversive.

Currency and Coercion is a goldmine of information. Kirshner provides a wealth of data in a wide range of historical case studies. But that is not the same thing as theory, which would offer us rigorous, abstract reasoning about either the sources or the uses of monetary power. A general theory would tell us something about the specific conditions that give rise to power in monetary affairs. It would also advance a coherent set of theses to explain when, how and why any given form of monetary power might be used in particular circumstances. *Currency and Coercion*, regrettably, does neither.

Nor, we must acknowledge, did Strange, however insightful her many contributions. Strange's approach too tended to the taxonomic: for instance, in her 'political theory of international currencies' (Strange 1971a, 1971b) with its four basic types: (1) top currency – the currency of the predominant state in the international system; (2) master currencies – currencies that emerge when an imperial power imposes use of its money on political dependencies; (3) negotiated currencies – what master currencies become when the dominance of the imperial power begins to wane; and (4) neutral currencies – currencies whose use originates in the strong economic position of the issuing state. Strange certainly did not ignore matters of either causation or consequence, but, beyond some cursory allusions to the broad 'power factor' behind international currencies, along with some brief comments on their potential leverage, little systematic detail is offered about, for example, what could determine shifts into or out of each category or about how and when each type might be used to an issuing country's advantage. In fact, there is not much here at all that would genuinely qualify as theory in the usual sense of the term.[5]

The same is also true of her most ambitious attempt to tackle the issue of power in the global economy, her landmark *States and Markets*, first published in 1988 (second edition, 1994). Traditional studies of world politics, the 'narrow (and old-fashioned) understanding of power' that Strange so vigorously criticized,[6] had mostly tended to identify power with tangible resources of one kind or another: territory, population, armed forces and the like. But in economic affairs, Strange correctly noted, what matters most is not physical endowments but rather structures and relationships: who depends on whom and for what. Hence power could be understood to operate at two levels, structural and relational. *Relational power*, echoing more conventional treatments in the IR literature, is the familiar 'power of A to get B to do something they would not otherwise do' (Strange 1994: 24). *Structural power*, the main theme stressed in this volume, is 'the power to shape and determine the structures of the global political economy ... the power to decide how things will be done, the power to shape frameworks within which states relate to each other' (ibid.: 24–5). Four key structures are identified: security, production, finance and knowledge. Of most direct relevance here of course is the financial structure: 'the sum of all the arrangements governing the availability of credit plus all factors determining the terms on which currencies are exchanged for each other' (ibid.: 90).

Strange's distinction between relational and structural power is critical, even inspired.[7] In the crudest terms, one refers to the ability to gain under the prevailing rules of the game, the other to the ability to gain by rewriting the rules of the game. Yet here too there is little that could genuinely be described as theory. Strange's discussion is essentially descriptive, offering a rich array of illustrations and historical narrative. What it lacks is a formal, systematic analysis of either the sources or determinants of use at either level of operation.

Towards a General Theory

Can we do better? Though space considerations prevent a more comprehensive treatment, a few suggestions are possible. Start with Strange's distinction between relational and structural power. In fact, the distinction was not new, having roots that go back to early theorizing by Robert Keohane and Joseph Nye about the implications of growing interdependence in the post-war world economy (Keohane and Nye 1973; 1977). States, Keohane and Nye noted, were becoming increasingly intertwined; hence each was becoming more and more dependent on others in all sorts of issue areas, economic or otherwise. Mutual dependence, however, was rarely symmetrical. Opportunities were therefore created for less dependent states to manipulate existing relationships to their own advantage. In the global system as a whole, Keohane and Nye concluded, it is possible 'to regard power as deriving from patterns of asymmetrical interdependence between actors in the issue-areas in which they are involved with one another' (Keohane and Nye 1973: 122). The basic question, in simplest terms, was: who needs whom more? Power could be understood to consist of a state's control over that for which others are dependent on it.[8]

In addition, Keohane and Nye suggested, interdependence between states has two important dimensions: *sensitivity* and *vulnerability*. Sensitivity interdependence involves the *responsiveness* of interrelationships – the degree to which conditions in one state are affected positively or negatively by events occurring elsewhere. Vulnerability interdependence involves the *reversibility* of interrelationships – the degree to which (in other words, the cost at which) a state is capable of overriding the effects of events occurring elsewhere. A state is 'sensitive' if it is unable to *avoid* outside influence within the existing framework of transactions and policies. A state is 'vulnerable' if it is unable to *reverse* the outside influence, except at very high cost to itself.

The sensitivity–vulnerability dichotomy has subsequently been criticized for a certain vagueness about the time scale involved. Plainly, the longer the period allowed for adjustment, the less clear is the difference between the two dimensions of interdependence. Yet the distinction retains analytical relevance because of its direct correspondence to the levels of relation and structure stressed by Strange. Sensitivity interdependence is clearly pertinent to analysis of state power at the relational level, where the transactional and policy framework is well established and generally accepted; while vulnerability interdependence is obviously of direct relevance to the structural level, to analysis of such questions as how governance frameworks are established and how they may be altered over time. In other words, they provide an opening for a more rigorous formulation of Strange's distinction between relational power and structural power.

Suppose then that we think of the monetary system as a vast web of asymmetrical interdependencies, all operating within an established framework of norms, rules and decision-making procedures. Power at the relational level may be understood to be a direct function of the degree of asymmetry in *specific* transactional relationships. The greater the asymmetry, the more incentive the less dependent state has to seek to extract advantage within the established framework (in game-theory terms, to seek its most preferred outcome within the existing payoff matrix). Power at the structural level may be understood to be a direct function of the *cumulative total* of asymmetrical relationships. The greater the number of asymmetries that favor one country, relative to those that disfavor it, the more structural power it will have; and the more structural power it enjoys, the more incentive it has to seek to extract advantage by favorably modifying the existing framework (in game-theory terms, to favorably restructure the payoff matrix).

The task of theory would then be twofold: to identify the key conditions that determine, first, when power at either level is or is not likely to be used (that is, when the incentive will or will not be acted upon); and second, when the use of power is or is not likely to be successful. Conditions may be both economic and political; they may also be domestic as well as international, cognitive as well as material – all making for a dense, indeed daunting, complexity. Any scholar talented enough to accomplish the task will deserve the title of the *next* Susan Strange.

Some Illustrations

A theory of monetary power formulated along these lines would have several advantages, not least the promise of greater understanding of the way states actually behave in the real world. As in most areas of social science, it would be foolhardy to aspire to anything so ambitious as a rigorous forecasting model, which is surely beyond our capacities. Social scientists, someone once quipped, were invented to make even weather forecasters look good. But it is not unrealistic to aspire to a higher degree of practical insight: greater sensitivity to the precise variables and factors that matter most in monetary affairs and to the way they relate and interact over time. Even if theory cannot clarify the future, it can surely help to clear the mind.

Another advantage of a theory formulated along these lines is that it can be constructed to build on, rather than reject or ignore, past contributions of Strange and others. Consider, for instance, Strange's taxonomy of international currencies: top, master, negotiated, and neutral currencies. Strange certainly was not the first scholar to note the element of hierarchy among the world's moneys, as she readily acknowledged. Economic historians had frequently remarked on the persistent tendency, in every epoch, for one or a small number of currencies to emerge as dominant in monetary relations: the Athenian drachma in the classical world, later the Byzantine gold solidus – the 'dollar of the Middle Ages', as one source put it (Lopez 1951) – the Florentine florin, the Venetian ducat, the Dutch guilder, the Spanish–Mexican silver peso, and of course, most recently, the pound sterling and US greenback.[9] In the modern era, elevated status was affirmed by such labels as 'key currencies'[10] or even 'dream currencies': the moneys that investors dream in (Brown 1978). But Strange was the first to *differentiate* systematically among the currencies at the peak of what has been called elsewhere the Currency Pyramid (Cohen 1998), calling attention to the fact that both causal factors and political consequences may vary significantly, depending on circumstances. In her own words:

> We should try to distinguish between the main types of situation, or sets of circumstances, in which a currency issued by one state comes to be used [by others].... All of them have political consequences... In some cases this pressure is strong and pervasive, in others it is weak, and intermittent. (Strange 1971b: 3–4)

An approach focusing on relational asymmetries would help accomplish Strange's objective. Her four currency categories, as well as the strength or weakness of pressures associated with each, can each be understood to result from distinctly different patterns of transactional and policy relationships. The challenge is to provide more systematic detail about what those relationships are.

Neutral currencies are perhaps the easiest to account for, being entirely economic in origin. Strange cited as examples the Swiss franc and the Deutschmark (now being replaced by the euro). Three asymmetries in particular have long been emphasized by economists as critical to encouraging widespread confidence in such currencies: (1) a proven track record of low inflation and (2) well developed banking or capital markets, both of which make a money attractive for store-of-value purposes; and (3) an economy that is large and well integrated into world markets, which makes the money attractive for medium-of-exchange purposes as well (Cohen 1998: 96–7). Add dominance of related networks of interdependencies (Strange's security, production and knowledge structures) and one national currency emerges as the top currency of its period. Master currencies require only one special form of asymmetry: a political dependency sanctioned by international law.

The approach can also be used to explain shifts into or out of each category, all of which are analyzable in terms of *changes* in any of those same economic or political asymmetries. Master currencies, for instance, morph into negotiated currencies when political dependency is terminated, resulting in a need to bargain diplomatically with users about the terms and conditions of use.[11] More generally, monetary specialists have addressed much attention to the problems posed for a top (or even neutral) currency as global circulation expands. Eventually, a significant 'overhang' of liabilities develops that will almost certainly erode the issuing country's insulation against outside influence as it grows increasingly dependent on the good will of foreign holders. The asymmetry will become even more pronounced to the extent that rival moneys begin to emerge as potential substitutes for the threatened currency. Theory need not be limited to comparative statics alone.

In similar fashion, consider Jonathan Kirshner's taxonomy of monetary power: currency manipulation, monetary dependence and systemic disruption. Though presented as if they were qualitatively different, the three categories really are distinguishable simply by the type and direction of asymmetries implied by each. Currency manipulation requires only an asymmetry of sensitivity in the single issue area of exchange rates. Economies that are relatively closed, rather than open, are less vulnerable to currency instability; so too are countries with payments surpluses rather than deficits, with large central bank reserves rather than small, or with external borrowing capacity that is substantial rather than limited. Monetary dependence requires any of the same conditions that create Strange's neutral, top or master currencies; while systemic disruption bears a family resemblance to her category of negotiated currency, where the tables have turned sufficiently to give some degree of leverage to the formerly dependent. The reversal of asymmetry may be political – the end of empire – or it may be economic, the result, for instance, of a growing overhang of liabilities. Thomas Schelling (1980) has written of the advantages to be derived from a strategy of 'rocking the boat', destabilizing behavior purposively designed to extract substantive concessions. Though they may be incapable of offering their own substitute for a dominant currency, smaller players may be able to use the threat of liquidation or withdrawal to gain valuable bargaining leverage. Such tactics, as Kirshner notes, have been a particular specialty of France over the years, both during the inter-war period, when its target was Britain's pound, and during the Bretton Woods era, when the dollar's 'exorbitant privilege' was at issue.[12]

In brief, we *can* do better. The keys to a more general theory are available. Will the next Susan Strange please stand up?

The Praxis of Monetary Power

Strange of course also had much to say about the *praxis* of monetary relations, focusing especially on issues of governance in the international monetary system. Scholars in the realist tradition of IR theory could readily identify with her emphasis on the role of power in this context. For her, control was naturally, if regrettably, concentrated in a small group of powerful nations in general and in one powerful country, the United States, in particular. If global management was unenlightened or inconsistent, it was mainly because the 'affluent alliance' failed to live up to its collective responsibilities. But this too leaves important questions unanswered. What precisely do we mean by governance in monetary affairs? Are the powerful necessarily irresponsible? And what is the proper way to understand America's role at the center of the monetary system?

The Meaning of Governance

Reduced to its essence, governance is about rules: how rules are made for the allocation of values in society and how they are implemented and enforced. Rules may be formally articulated in statutes or treaties outlining specific prescriptions or proscriptions for action. Or they may be expressed more informally, as implicit norms defining behavioral standards in terms of understood rights and obligations. Either way, what matters is that they exercise some degree of authority: some degree of influence over the behavior and decisions of actors. The rules of the game rule.

And who makes the rules? Power certainly figures prominently, as Strange insisted. A capacity for coercion is often the *sine qua non* for effective control of outcomes. But power *per se*, whether naked or cloaked, is by no means the only possible source of authority in social relations. In principle, the concept of authority falls somewhere between the contrasting modalities of coercion (the capacity for repressive violence) and persuasion (the capacity for reasoned elaboration) and is identical with neither. In the words of philosopher Hannah Arendt, 'If authority is to be defined at all, it must be in contradistinction to both coercion by force and persuasion by argument' (Arendt 1968). In practice, therefore, authority may arise from a variety of sources, not just power. These would also include tradition and charisma, the two alternative foundations stressed by Max Weber (1925); they might include as well religion, ideology or even mere intellectual convention. The key point is that authority, ultimately, is *socially constructed*, not handed down by the mighty but built up from our own ideas and experience. The strong undoubtedly have disproportionate influence, but only in the anarchy of the jungle do they exercise untrammeled dominion.

As a social construction, governance does not necessarily demand the tangible institutions of government. It may not even call for the presence of explicit actors, whether state-sponsored or private, to take responsibility for rule making and enforcement. To suffice, all that is really needed is a valid social consensus on relevant rights and values – a legitimate social institution, in short. As the political philosopher R.B. Friedman has written, the effectiveness of authority is derived from 'some mutually recognized normative relationship' (Friedman 1990: 71). Its legitimacy is based on historically and culturally conditioned expectations about what constitutes appropriate conduct. A practical distinction between societal orders based on formal design and organization (for example, the state) and more spontaneous orders that emerge naturally from the mutual accommodations of many diverse and autonomous agents has long been a staple feature of Western social philosophy, going back to Bernard Mandeville's *Fable of the Bees*, first published in 1714. The unplanned spontaneous model may be regarded as no less legitimate – no less *authoritative* – than the deliberately devised variety.

As a social institution, governance in an issue area like money thus may be founded on any one of four basic organizing principles. As written in Cohen (1977), these are:

1 *Automaticity*: a self-disciplining structure of rules and norms that are binding for all states.
2 *Supranationality*: a structure founded on collective adherence to the decisions of some autonomous international organization;

3   *Hegemony*: a structure organized around a single dominant country or a small group of dominant states with acknowledged leadership responsibilities (as well as privileges).
4   *Negotiation*: a structure of shared responsibilities and decision making.

Each of these four principles represents a theoretical limiting case. In practice, no single one among them has ever dominated monetary relations for long. Rather, as the global system has evolved, two or more principles have been pragmatically combined in various ways in search of an effective mode of governance. In the classical gold standard, for example, where every participating government was expected without question to buy and sell gold at a fixed price and to allow free import and export of gold, automaticity was clearly privileged, though not without elements of hegemony and negotiation as well. The system was distinctly hierarchical, with Britain at its peak, and there was also a considerable amount of cooperation among the major central banks. After World War I, by contrast, as the gold-standard 'rules of the game' were abandoned and Britain's financial dominance was gradually eroded, greater emphasis was placed on formal negotiation to maintain some degree of monetary stability – unsuccessfully, as it eventually turned out. Then came the Bretton Woods system, which was explicitly designed to combine automaticity, supranationality and cooperative negotiation in equal measure, but which in reality rested heavily on American hegemony. And then, finally, in the early 1970s, came the breakdown of Bretton Woods, which once again led to abandonment of many of the prevailing rules of the game, most importantly, the dollar's convertibility into gold and the par-value system of exchange rates. For many, including Strange, the result ever since has been 'an unstable and inequitable international monetary system' (Strange 1985:15) dominated by 'America's international hegemony' (Calleo and Strange 1984: 114).

Strange was undoubtedly right to stress the prominent role of power, especially structural power, in monetary governance. When it comes to relations among sovereign states, power is always a critical factor in shaping behavior. But she surely exaggerated in stressing *only* power as an effective source of authority, when it is clear that international relations have moved so far beyond the elemental law of the jungle. Strange tended to discount the role of social institutions in world politics. In her memorable *Cave! Hic Dragones* (Strange 1983a), she dismissed the notion of international regimes as little more than a 'passing fad' of American social scientists. Her preference was to think instead in terms of what she termed a 'network of bargains' (Strange 1994: 39): overt or tacit agreements that are 'the subject of a continued bargaining process' (1975: 219). But does this not seriously underestimate the degree of continuity in global structures? If the world truly were reinvented on a daily basis, the balance of power would naturally dominate, if not dictate, outcomes. In reality, however, Stephen Krasner's metaphor of tectonic plates (Krasner 1983) seems more apt: an image of much more stable social institutions, yielding to the pressures of power, if at all, only slowly and over considerable intervals of time. It is in those intervals that we see the force of other sources of authority.

In the durability of the International Monetary Fund (IMF), for example, we see the force of both automaticity and supranationality despite the many changes that have occurred since the 1960s. The US gold window may now be closed, exchange rates may no longer be pegged and, with re-emergence of global financial markets, deficit countries may no longer rely as heavily on the Fund as a source of international liquidity, yet the authority of the organization and of the many rules written into its Charter persist to ensure a measure of effective governance. Likewise, policy makers continue, for the most part, to respect commonly agreed standards of behavior, such as that states should not engage in mutually destructive competitive devaluations – demonstrating the force of learning as well. Admittedly, the quality of today's monetary management is hardly all it could be; and the leading states certainly exercise disproportionate influence over decision making, both within and outside the IMF. But that is not the same thing as the law of the jungle. Rule making and enforcement do not reduce to a simple equation of power.

The Challenge of Cooperation

Can the quality of today's monetary management be improved? Here, plainly, Strange was right to stress the central role of the most powerful. Reform of any kind requires leadership, and leadership comes most naturally to the strong. At issue is the challenge of cooperation: the ability of the 'affluent alliance' to mount effective collective action in the common interest. The question is why the leading financial powers find it so difficult to live up to their responsibilities.

For Strange the answer was, in simplest terms, selfishness: governments seek to exploit their power whenever possible in pursuit of narrow national interest. And there is no doubt more than a kernel of truth in that point of view. But in this regard too Strange surely was exaggerating when she stressed that *only* selfishness was a determining variable. The story is really much more complicated than that.

To begin with, even unalloyed selfishness does not necessarily assure uncooperative behavior, as any student of game theory would readily confirm. Monetary relations are a form of strategic interaction in which each player obviously does have an incentive to maximize payoffs at the expense of others. The logic of self-interest is clear. As Robert Axelrod (1984) has demonstrated, however, rational calculation will result in uncompromising selfishness only in single-play games where players need have no concern about longer-term consequences. In iterated games, by contrast, where the risk of costly retaliation by others is high, players have more incentive to cooperate to ensure higher cumulative gains. In Axelrod's words, 'The future can ... cast a shadow back upon the present and thereby affect the current strategic situation' (ibid.: 12). In monetary relations, where the 'shadow of the future' is particularly long, uncompromising selfishness may not pay at all.

Furthermore, not all games are the same. Recall Arthur Stein's distinction between 'dilemmas of common interests' and 'dilemmas of common aversions' (Stein 1990). The more challenging of the two are dilemmas of common interests, conflictual games, where reciprocal concessions must be made to avoid suboptimal ('Pareto-deficient') outcomes. Effective collective action in such situations may indeed be difficult to achieve or sustain. But many situations involve no more than dilemmas of common aversions, coordination games, where the issue is just to *avoid* a particular outcome and, hence, where the only question is how to establish a common focal point around which behavior may coalesce. Beyond agreeing to play by some standard set of rules (for example, driving on the right-hand side of the road), no compromise of underlying preferences is called for. The difference between the two classes of dilemma is reflected in the distinction economist Peter Kenen draws between two types of monetary cooperation, the 'policy-optimizing' approach, where governments seek to bargain their way from suboptimality to something closer to a Pareto optimum, and the 'regime-preserving' or 'public-goods' approach, where mutual adjustments are agreed for the sake of defending existing arrangements or institutions against the threat of economic or political shocks (Kenen 1988). The latter is clearly less demanding than the former.

Happily, many of the issues involved in monetary governance actually are more in the nature of coordination games, where 'regime preservation' rather than 'policy optimization' is at stake. Certainly, this is evident in the area of international banking regulation, as Ethan Kapstein has shown (Kapstein 1994). Every state shares a common interest in ensuring prudent behavior by banks, owing to their central role in the operation of the payments system. Likewise, at a broader macroeconomic level, experience testifies amply to the willingness of governments to act together effectively when broader collective goals appear at risk: for example, the Plaza Agreement of 1985, the joint response to the stock market crash of 1987, and the coordinated rescue packages mounted for Thailand and other Asian countries in 1997–8. Narrow self-interest clearly does not always dominate in the calculations of policy makers.

Indeed, much depends on what one means by cooperation. Consider, for example, the argument of Michael Webb (1995), who questions the view of Strange and others that policy coordination has weakened in recent years. Rather, he contends, it is the *form* of monetary cooperation that has changed. Earlier in the post-war period, collective action consisted largely of 'external' measures (for example, balance-of-payments financing and exchange rate co-ordination) designed to manage payments imbalances caused by incompatible national macroeconomic policies. Today, by contrast, cooperation encompasses the direct coordination of national monetary and fiscal policies themselves, policies that had previously been considered strictly 'internal'. What accounts for this shift in the form of cooperation? The explanation, Webb asserts, is to be found in the massive increase of capital mobility that has occurred in recent decades: Strange's mad money. Controversially, Webb contends that financial globalization has actually increased the degree of effective cooperation by making it virtually impossible for governments to pursue significantly divergent macroeconomic policies. This is a position diametrically opposed to Strange's more pessimistic interpretation.

Not that cooperation is therefore always assured. Even in coordination games, let alone conflictual games, discord is possible, as Richard Cooper (1975) long ago pointed out. Cooper listed five possible sources of disagreement among states on monetary issues: (1) different preferences regarding the distributional implications of alternative decisions; (2) different weights attached to alternative policy targets when compromises (tradeoffs) must be made among values; (3) different national economic circumstances, even when policy preferences are similar; (4) disagreement over the practical effectiveness of alternative instruments to achieve agreed objectives; and (5) uncertainty about the trustworthiness of other states. All five reduce the chances that cooperation will endure indefinitely and help account for the seemingly episodic quality of collective management efforts. Monetary cooperation, like passionate love, is self-evidently a good thing but difficult to sustain (Cohen 1993: 134). But that is not the same thing as attributing all failure to selfishness, a charge that borders on caricature (in love as well as in monetary affairs).

America's Role

Finally, there is the question of America's role in monetary affairs, to which Strange always attached absolutely vital importance. 'Nothing,' she wrote, 'happens unless the United States leads' (Strange

1983b: 179). Does this means that Strange fully subscribed to the familiar old theory of hegemonic stability?

Hegemonic stability theory, which originated in the writings of Charles Kindleberger (1973), Robert Gilpin (1975) and Stephen Krasner (1976), has long fascinated students of international political economy. Its central tenet, as summarized by Robert Keohane, is that 'hegemonic structures of power, dominated by a single country, are most conducive to the development of strong international regimes whose rules are relatively precise and well obeyed' (Keohane 1980: 132).[13] In other words, hegemony is critical to effective governance, whether in monetary relations or other dimensions of the world economy, and may even be necessary. Subsequent debate, ably surveyed by David Lake (1993), has focused in particular on the role of hegemony (or 'leadership,' as Lake prefers to label it) in 'producing' the 'international economic infrastructure' needed for stability. Following Kindleberger (1973), that infrastructure, a form of public good, is assumed to include a stable medium of exchange and store of value and adequate liquidity for both long-term development and short-term crisis management: essentially all the components of what Strange called the financial structure. Leadership, in turn, is assumed to be either benevolent or coercive. Lake explains the difference:

> When benevolent, the leader provides the international economic infrastructure unilaterally, or at least bears a disproportionate cost of providing the public good, and thereby gains relatively less than others. When coercive, the leader forces other, smaller states to contribute to the international economic infrastructure and, at an extreme, to bear the entire burden. (Lake 1993: 467)

Strange can be best understood as a regretful advocate of a coercive version of hegemonic stability theory. More than once she expressed the wish that America, with its unparalleled capabilities, would somehow find the will to live up to its leadership responsibilities. 'Reform must start with a change of mind in Washington,' she wrote in *Casino Capitalism* (Strange 1986: 170). The challenge is 'to see how to persuade people and politicians in the United States to use the hegemonic, structural power they still have in a more enlightened and consistent way' (Strange 1990: 274). But she was not hopeful.

The situation is quite the contrary in fact. America 'talked the talk' but didn't 'walk the walk'. In Strange's words: 'It is hard to see American liberalism in the twenty-five years after World War II as a genuine doctrine rather than as an ideology, that is, a doctrine to be used when it was convenient and fitted the current perception of the national interest and one to be overlooked and forgotten when it did not' (Strange 1987: 562). If Americans talked about the desirability of policy coordination, it was little more than 'an unconscious form of American imperialism ... a remedy that allows Americans to do as they please while others do as they are told' (Strange 1986: 153). All of Washington's financial initiatives 'have reflected a basic urge to dominate the monetary system so that external constraints may not limit the American political economy's expansive impulses, at home or abroad... . [Policy] results less in a dutiful management of the collective economic interest than in a nationalist exploitation of power' (Calleo and Strange 1984: 114).

Is America truly so irresponsible? Here, yet again, Strange surely exaggerated. That US policies are nationalistic is of course undeniable (Cohen 1980). In this respect America is no different from other countries, all of which act first and foremost out of an instinct for self-interest. But are US policies *only* nationalistic? Is American leadership *only* exploitative? The answers to those questions are not quite so simple.

Certainly, the nationalistic element of US policy is easy to see. Washington has always displayed a distinct preference for a maximum of autonomy in monetary affairs. Such a bias is also easy to understand, given America's overweening size and authority as well as its still relatively high degree of economic insularity. But for those very same reasons nationalism has never been the sole element of US policy, nor could it be. No country as influential as the United States can be wholly unmindful of the effects of its behavior on others. Structural power, in effect, cuts two ways: on the one hand, encouraging egoism in policy making, but, on the other hand, also discouraging inattention to possible systemic consequences. Washington needs no reminding of its capacity to subvert the world economy from which Americans presumably gain so much. As was written some two decades ago:

> A country still as large and powerful as the United States needs little incentive to avoid destabilizing behavior whenever possible. Its ability to disrupt is too evident; as American policy makers since John Connally have recognized, the nation's self-interest is too closely identified with stability of the overall system for them to try deliberately to act 'irresponsibly'.[14]

A conservative instinct for system preservation, therefore, is an everpresent element of US policy too and is also easy to see: for example, in the leading role Washington took in organizing costly financial assistance for Mexico in 1994–5 and for East Asian countries in 1997–8. The real issue is the *balance* between the elements of self-interest and system preservation in American behavior.

Admittedly, that balance has not been as consistent as one would like, not least because of the vagaries and rhythms of domestic US politics. It is also true that the balance has often tipped quite dramatically in the nationalist direction: for example, in 1971, when Richard Nixon closed the gold window, or in the early 1980s, when Ronald Reagan's supply-side experiment was launched. At times like these, American behavior has been anything but enlightened. But that is hardly the same thing as tyranny, *pace* Strange's disappointed scolding. It is one matter to seek to exercise autonomy when possible, quite another to exhibit a persistent, malign impulse to dominate and exploit others. In practice American hegemony has been, at worst, only intermittently coercive and certainly has not lacked for periods of benevolent generosity as well. To insist otherwise is also to border on caricature.

Conclusion

Susan Strange's contributions were monumental. Not only was she a pioneer in sensitizing us all to the intricate links between money and power in world politics, the 'political element' of money that had for so long been neglected, she also provided us with some key tools of analysis, including not least her critical distinction between relational and structural power in inter-state relations. Her early work highlighted in particular the reality of hierarchy in international monetary relations. Her later writing kept us alert to the difficult issues of cooperation and governance in global finance. Yet in the end she succeeded in raising more questions than she answered, at the levels of both theory and praxis. It is a tribute to her lasting influence that, for years to come, intellectual discourse in this core area of international political economy will most likely continue to be dominated by the research agenda she set.

Notes

1   The young economist was, of course, myself. My book, *The Future of Sterling as an International Currency* (Cohen 1971), was published the same year as Strange's *Sterling and British Policy* but with a much shorter half-life.
2   See, for example, Strange (1986; 1994 [1988]; 1996, 1998).
3   See, for example, my own contributions at the time (1971, 1977), which were also distinctly state-centric.
4   But not more quickly than all others. Modestly, I may claim to have made the point even earlier in a book, *Banks and the Balance of Payments*, published in 1981 (Cohen 1981), and in my contribution to the well-known volume on international regimes edited by Stephen Krasner, which appeared in 1983 (Cohen 1983). In both it was argued that, as a result of the revival of international finance, the international monetary system was becoming increasingly privatized, with implications that were then still barely understood.

5   I have chided Strange for this before. See Cohen, *Organizing the World's Money* (1977: 301, no. 36). Though Strange herself admitted as much in describing her approach as a taxonomy (Strange 1971a: 217) or a typology (Strange 1971b: 6), she in turn joshed me, in a review of my book published in *International Affairs* (55:1, January 1979), for my 'strong classroom – not to say, Germanic – habit of arranging everything in mnemonic lists for easy note taking'. Our relationship, though affectionate and mutually respectful, was not uncritical.

6   The quote is from Strange (1985: 11). See also Strange (1996: ch.2). The roots of Strange's non-traditional approach were first developed in her 1975 article on 'What is Economic Power, and Who Has It?' (Strange 1975).

7   Indeed, I had tried even earlier to make the same distinction, labeling the two levels 'process power' and 'structure power' (Cohen 1977: 53–7). But Strange's treatment was more fully developed.

8   In turn, Keohane and Nye owed an intellectual debt to the economist Albert Hirschman who, writing even earlier about Nazi Germany's trade policies before World War II, had ably demonstrated how 'the power to interrupt ... relations with any country, considered as an attribute of national sovereignty, is the root cause of the influence or power position which a country acquires in other countries' (Hirschman 1945: 16).

9   For more detail and references, see Cohen (1998: ch.2).

10   The term 'key currency' was originated after World War II by American economist John Williams. See, for example, Williams (1947).

11   The category of negotiated currency seems rather archaic today, decades after formal decolonization. But a British subject, writing at a time of rapid decline in the international status of the pound sterling, may be forgiven for having considered its inclusion topical.

12   For more detail on these two episodes of French 'systemic disruption,' see Kindleberger (1972) and Kirshner (1995: ch. 5). The term 'exorbitant privilege' was coined by Charles de Gaulle, president of France during the 1960s, who expressed particular resentment of America's capacity, owing to the dollar's universal acceptability, to run payments deficits 'without tears'.

13   Kindleberger put the point more succinctly in his famous aphorism that 'for the world economy to be stabilized, there has to be a stabilizer, one stabilizer' (Kindleberger 1973: 305).

14   Cohen (1980: 61). John Connally, treasury secretary in 1971, was instrumental in persuading Richard Nixon to terminate the dollar's gold convertibility.

References

Arendt, Hannah (1968), 'What is Authority?', *Between Past and Future: Eight Exercises in Political Thought*, New York: Viking Press, pp.91–141.

Axelrod, Robert (1984), *The Evolution of Cooperation*, New York: Basic Books.

Brown, Brendan (1978), *Money Hard and Soft: On the International Currency Markets*, New York: Wiley.

Calleo, David and Susan Strange (1984), 'Money and World Politics', in Susan Strange (ed.), *Paths to International Political Economy*, London: George Allen & Unwin, ch.6.

Cohen, Benjamin J. (1971), *The Future of Sterling as an International Currency*, London: Macmillan.

Cohen, Benjamin J. (1977), *Organizing the World's Money: The Political Economy of International Monetary Relations*, New York: Basic Books.

Cohen, Benjamin J. (1980), 'United States Monetary Policy and Economic National-
ism,' in Otto Hieronymi (ed.), *The New Economic Nationalism*, London: Macmillan,
ch.3.
Cohen, Benjamin J. (1981), *Banks and the Balance of Payments: Private Lending in the
International Adjustment Process*, Montclair, NJ: Allenheld, Osmun.
Cohen, Benjamin J. (1983), 'Balance-of-Payments Financing: Evolution of a Regime',
in Stephen D. Krasner (ed.), *International Regimes*, Ithaca, NY: Cornell University
Press, pp.315–36.
Cohen, Benjamin J. (1993), 'The Triad and the Unholy Trinity: Lessons for the
Pacific Region', in Richard Higgott, Richard Leaver and John Ravenhill (eds),
Pacific Economic Relations in the 1990s: Cooperation or Conflict?, Boulder, CO: Lynne
Rienner, pp.133–58.
Cohen, Benjamin J. (1996), 'Phoenix Risen: The Resurrection of Global Finance',
World Politics, 48(2), January, 268–96.
Cohen, Benjamin J. (1998), *The Geography of Money*, Ithaca, NY: Cornell University
Press.
Cooper, Richard N. (1975), 'Prolegomena to the Choice of an International Mon-
etary System', *International Organization*, 29, (Winter), 69–84.
Friedman, R.B. (1990), 'On the Concept of Authority in Political Philosophy', in
Joseph Raz (ed.), *Authority*, Oxford: Blackwell, ch.3.
Gilpin, Robert (1975), *U.S. Power and the Multinational Corporation: The Political
Economy of Foreign Direct Investment*, New York: Basic Books.
Hirschman, Albert O. (1945), *National Power and the Structure of Foreign Trade*, Berkeley:
University of California Press.
Kapstein, Ethan B. (1994), *Governing the Global Economy: International Finance and the
State*, Cambridge, MA: Harvard University Press.
Kenen, Peter B. (1988), *Managing Exchange Rates*, New York: Council on Foreign
Relations.
Keohane, Robert O. (1980), 'The Theory of Hegemonic Stability and Changes in
International Economic Regimes, 1967–1977', in Ole R. Holsti, Randolph M.
Siverson and Alexander L. George (eds), *Change in the International System*, Boul-
der, CO: Westview Press, pp.131–62.
Keohane, Robert O. and Joseph S. Nye, Jr. (1973), 'World Politics and the Inter-
national Economic System', in C. Fred Bergsten (ed.), *The Future of the Inter-
national Economic Order: An Agenda for Research*, Lexington, MA: D.C. Heath,
pp.115–79.
Keohane, Robert O. and Joseph S. Nye, Jr. (1977), *Power and Interdependence: World
Politics in Transition*, Boston: Little, Brown.
Kindleberger, Charles P. (1970), *Power and Money: The Politics of International Eco-
nomics and the Economics of International Politics*, New York: Basic Books.
Kindleberger, Charles P. (1972), 'The International Monetary Politics of a Near-
Great Power: Two French Episodes, 1926–1936 and 1960–1970', *Economic Notes*,
1(2–3), 30–44.
Kindleberger, Charles P. (1973), *The World in Depression, 1929–1939*, Berkeley and
Los Angeles: University of California Press.
Kirshner, Jonathan (1995), *Currency and Coercion: The Political Economy of Interna-
tional Monetary Power*, Princeton, NJ: Princeton University Press.
Krasner, Stephen D. (1976), 'State Power and the Structure of International Trade',
World Politics, 28(3), April, 317–43.
Krasner, Stephen D. (1983), 'Regimes and the Limits of Realism: Regimes as Au-
tonomous Variables', in Stephen D. Krasner (ed.), *International Regimes*, Ithaca,
NY: Cornell University Press, pp.355–68.
Lake, David A. (1993), 'Leadership, Hegemony and the International Economy:

Naked Emperor or Tattered Monarch with Potential?', *International Studies Quarterly*, 37(4) December, 459–89.

Lopez, Robert S. (1951), 'The Dollar of the Middle Ages', *Journal of Economic History*, 11(3), Summer, 209–34.

Schelling, Thomas C. (1980), *The Strategy of Conflict*, Cambridge, MA: Harvard University Press.

Stein, Arthur A. (1990), *Why Nations Cooperate: Circumstance and Choice in International Relations*, Ithaca, NY: Cornell University Press.

Strange, Susan (1971a), 'The Politics of International Currencies', *World Politics*, 23(2), January, 215–31.

Strange, Susan (1971b), *Sterling and British Policy: A Political Study of an International Currency in Decline*, London: Oxford University Press.

Strange, Susan (1975), 'What is Economic Power, and Who Has It?', *Economic Journal*, 30(2), Spring, 207–24.

Strange, Susan (1976), 'International Monetary Relations', in Andrew Shonfield (ed.), *International Economic Relations of the Western World, 1959–1971*, vol. 2, London: Oxford University Press, pp.18–359.

Strange, Susan (1983a), '*Cave! Hic Dragones*: A Critique of Regime Analysis', in Stephen D. Krasner (ed.), *International Regimes*, Ithaca, NY: Cornell University Press, pp.337–54.

Strange, Susan (1983b), 'The Credit Crisis: A European View', *SAIS Review*, Summer, 171–81.

Strange, Susan (1985), 'Interpretations of a Decade', in Loukas Tsoukalis (ed.), *The Political Economy of International Money: In Search of a New Order*, London: Sage Publications, ch.1.

Strange, Susan (1986), *Casino Capitalism*, Oxford: Blackwell.

Strange, Susan (1987), 'The Persistent Myth of Lost Hegemony', *International Organization*, 41(4), Autumn, 551–74.

Strange, Susan (1988), 'The Future of the American Empire', *Journal of International Affairs*, 42(1), Fall, 1–17.

Strange, Susan (1990), 'Finance, Information and Power', *Review of International Studies*, 16(3), July, 259–74.

Strange, Susan (1994), *States and Markets*, 2nd edn, London: Pinter Publishers.

Strange, Susan (1996), *The Retreat of the State: The Diffusion of Power in the World Economy*, Cambridge: Cambridge University Press.

Strange, Susan (1998), *Mad Money*, Manchester: Manchester University Press.

Webb, Michael C. (1995), *The Political Economy of Policy Coordination: International Adjustment Since 1945*, Ithaca, NY: Cornell University Press.

Weber, Max ([1925] 1947), *The Theory of Social and Economic Organization*, Glencoe, IL: Free Press.

Williams, John (1947), *Postwar Monetary Plans and Other Essays*, New York: Knopf.

7 Global Money and the Decline of State Power

GEOFFREY R.D. UNDERHILL

Introduction

The influence of Susan Strange on the contemporary discipline of International Political Economy has been pervasive. This was true even when her published work was largely in the specialized domain of international monetary relations. To a considerable extent because of her insights into the nature of the global economy and her insistence on integrating political and economic factors as part of the whole, there was considerable common ground to share with a range of scholars researching the global economy.

Strange's work was difficult to avoid, for a number of reasons. She argued that the world was changing, and something was happening to states. This in turn presented a challenge for theory. The economic dynamics of these developments were not part of some autonomous sphere of market forces, but were intimately related to the political dynamics, decisions and non-decisions, of states and the international system of states. Strange had more to say on this than most, because she had been among the first to recognize the importance of the changes which were taking place in the world political economy from the early 1960s onwards, particularly in the domain of financial markets (Strange 1976: ch.6). The world was not evolving as most scholars thought it was or should.

Firstly, she was drawing attention to the rapid pace and underlying dynamics of these changes in the context of a political economy approach. Secondly, Strange was asking awkward questions about how we should think about these changes, about what they implied for our theoretical efforts. Thirdly, her emphasis on politics and political interaction in the emergence of the global integration process, as opposed to structural economic explanations and other forms of determinism, fit well with others' research findings as they delved into the industrial adjustment process. Yet she did not by any means forget the importance of structural constraints and power in political interaction. Fourthly, she recognized the division between the domestic and international domains as a heuristic convenience for enhancing our specialized knowledge of certain aspects of reality, but not as anything to do with the real world as such. More often than not, this distinction got in the way of our understanding. Far too often it had to do with academic empire building and the system of intellectual disciples who riddled many universities and corrupted the purpose of scholarly enquiry. The domestic/international politics divide contributed to erecting disciplinary boundaries that few dared to transgress for fear that their own careers might be compromised. In this sense, and fifthly, she was one among those who reminded one repeatedly that most important for our understanding of the world around us was not the analysis of the pieces of the puzzle, though such specialized knowledge was an important precondition, but the ways in which the pieces – international, domestic, local; state, finance, industry *and theory* fit together.

So she wrote widely, including work on trade and industrial adjustment processes (Strange and Tooze 1981a; 1981b). The pragmatic purpose was to understand the world around us better so that something might be done about it. Humanity *might* (she was always skeptical on this point) come to devise better solutions if one had a better understanding in the first place. Otherwise, one was almost certain to get it wrong, and too often did.

Susan Strange thereby made it relatively easy for an emerging generation of scholars to make what seemed a natural progression from the study of the politics of either international or domestic economic issues, to political economy, international or otherwise. Much of what Strange advocated appeared if not self-evident, then at least a *prima facie* case for intellectual openness and skepticism about orthodoxies of various kinds. Most importantly, she forced one to think, indeed to *rethink*, all manner of things, by persistently asking the relevant and awkward questions which the majority of scholars conveniently left aside. Her work provided a solid and intellectually credible platform on which to stand and build. We are all political economists now.

This chapter is not alone in this volume in emphasizing the centrality of the global monetary and financial system to the work of Susan Strange (see Cohen and Verdun, among others, in this volume). It would be surprising if this were the case. Any analysis of her published work soon demonstrates the centrality of the international monetary system and the global financial order to her understanding of the intricacies of the international political economy. The insights she gained from years of empirical investigation into the system of credit creation and allocation, and international monetary order, underpinned her conception of international political economy as a field. For Strange, the monetary and financial order was the centerpiece of the global political economy, and what happened to the global monetary and financial system would have repercussions for the rest of the system. On this she was picking a fight with Marxists, among others, who insisted on the centrality of the means of production.

But the focus of this chapter is different from others in this part of the volume on 'Global Finance and State Power'. Cohen has focused on the link between understanding power in international relations and the global monetary system. Verdun has focused on Strange's analysis of how the structure of the financial system implies a set of embedded power relations underpinning the international system of states. These power relations affect the relative roles of state and non-state actors in the constitution of the international political economy, and Strange's arguments furthermore imply the need to challenge state-centric conceptions of international political economy.

The focus of the present chapter will be to carry forward the insights of Cohen and Verdun and to investigate how Strange's analysis of monetary and financial order, including the prominent role of non-state actors in the emergence of global financial markets, informed her understanding of the role of the state in an era of global economic integration. Strange saw changes in the monetary and financial order not just as important in themselves. She also saw them as integral to the transnationalization of production, presaging an increased role for global firms and other non-state actors in international political economy (Stopford and Strange 1991). The rise of global markets and non-state actors is intimately associated in Strange's work with the consequent erosion of state power in the global system. The reaches of the state are retreating in the face of the advancing tide of the market, like some atoll facing submersion in the face of global warming. The chapter will go on to challenge Strange's 'retreat of the state' thesis and to develop the theoretical implications of this challenge for our understanding of the global political economy and the state.

The central argument of the chapter can be summarized as follows. Strange has argued that structural changes in the global financial and monetary order have led to a wider pattern of changes in the global economic system, particularly market integration in the domain of production and trade. States and state policy (or lack thereof) have been integral to these developments, developments which have conferred increasing power on non-state actors, particularly firms and other market players, but also on private networks and systems of governance related to the growth of international markets (Strange

1994a: 14–16). These developments represent a 'retreat of the state', and states have been full participants in this process.

However, while Strange provided considerable empirical evidence for these trends, she never fully developed or clarified this argument about the diffusion of state authority in conceptual terms. The key to understanding this trend lies in the way in which we conceptualize states and markets. While Strange was a strong advocate of their essential interdependence, she never took the more radical step of considering the state and the market as part of the same essential ensemble of governance, or 'state-market condominium' (Underhill 2000a: 17). The public and private domains are much less distinct than the abstractions of much theorizing admit and state decision making was always heavily permeated by private interests (Underhill 2000b). In this sense there is no retreat of the state, but a changing balance of public and private authority within the state, hence a changing *form* of state embedded in structural market transformations, as opposed to a decline as such. This is an extrapolation, and not a refutation, of the arguments that Strange put forward throughout her long career. Despite Strange's persistent challenge to the discipline, there is a need to think yet more radically on this question of how we understand the role of the state in a global market context.

The Financial Structure and the Global Political Economy

As mentioned, Strange saw the system of credit creation and allocation, and the pattern of international monetary relations which that implied, as the most important underlying structural variable in the global political economy (Strange 1988: 88). This point was echoed in a systematic study by Germain (1997: 29, *passim*). In *Sterling and British Policy* (1971), Strange argued forcefully that the decline of the United Kingdom as a power was intimately bound up with the decline of sterling as the central currency in the global monetary and financial system. The United Kingdom suffered from a 'top currency syndrome' wherein policy makers continuously anticipated a role in the global financial structure and monetary system which was no longer appropriate or plausible. The City of London as a constituency and the Treasury/Bank of England complex drove a policy unnecessarily concerned with accommodating a continuing international role for sterling and for the City as a financial center.

The cost to the national economy was high in terms of managing reserves and the balance of payments as well as in terms of further problems with trade competitiveness (Strange 1971: 71, 328). British governments suffering from this ongoing 'top currency syndrome' repeatedly underestimated the freedom which the *decline* of sterling in fact conferred upon them in making policy. They did not realize they no longer had special responsibilities for international monetary order (ibid.: 336–7). There was no consequent need to hang on to overvalued exchange rates for the sake of the overall system and the Commonwealth remains of empire. Mistaken policy was inflicting great damage on any commonsense assessment of the national interest.

The centrality of the financial order was also highlighted by Strange's second major work, *International Monetary Relations* (Strange 1976). The book was an account of the decline of the post-war fixed exchange rate system usually identified with the Bretton Woods agreements and was perhaps her greatest work of scholarship. While Strange covered all the usual causes of the 1971 collapse in terms of exchange rate and balance of payments management, chapter six of *International Monetary Relations* contains important foundations of her future arguments about the centrality of the financial order to international monetary relations and the wider pattern of global order. This was her analysis of the Eurodollar market.

The rise of unregulated offshore capital markets introduced a growing element of short-term capital mobility to the global monetary system, which eventually overwhelmed the capacity of states to manage fixed exchange rates in relation to emerging balance of payments disequilibrium and differences in monetary policy objectives. The Euromarket had started as a good servant but soon transformed itself into a 'bad master' (ibid.: 176), having a largely negative effect on the capacity of governments to discharge their responsibilities in terms of either financial supervision or international monetary management (ibid.: 186). In this way, a market-based transformation of the global system of credit creation and allocation, pushed by the activities of non-state actors in the form of international banks, introduced a whole series of constraints on both national and international monetary management. Combined with the ever-expanding pool of dollars linked to the US deficit and domestic monetary laxity, the expansive growth of the offshore Eurodollar market undermined the fixed exchange rate system and introduced short-term capital mobility as a management problem in international monetary relations. This development was part of a wider pattern of growing and complex interdependence which reduced the general capacity of states to govern and rendered international cooperation simultaneously more necessary and politically more difficult; these constraints were asymmetrically distributed across the system of states (ibid.: 354–9): 'changes in the money markets ... were making increasingly obsolete the public sector adaptive policies so carefully devised at Bretton Woods and later revised and amended' (ibid.: 188). Of course, states, especially the United States and the UK authorities, had played a crucial role in the emergence of this 'market' phenomenon (ibid.: 179–84).

The international monetary system, then, is for Strange the infrastructure on which trade and production, in short the market, depend. The international monetary system is in turn shaped by the power to create and allocate credit, a power which 'is shared by governments and banks, (and much will depend therefore on the political and regulatory relation of one to the other)'. This ensemble was characterized by Strange as the 'financial structure' (Strange 1988: 90). In this sense, changes in the financial structure are likely to have a direct impact on the pattern of production and trade in the global economy by altering the options of firms in raising capital. In recent years, 'The balance has shifted from a financial structure which was predominantly state-based with some transnational links, to a predominantly global system in which some residual local differences ... persist as vestiges of a bygone age' (Stopford and Strange 1991: 41). 'The paradox is that this has not happened entirely by accident. The shift from state authority to market authority has been in large part the result of state policies' (Strange 1996: 44). As she insisted to the last, it is politics which is the key to understanding the pattern of change in the structures of international political economy. The array of structural forces were set free, not by markets in some sort of vacuum or 'by blind chance, but by the conscious decisions of governments, more especially the government of the United States' (Strange 2000: 85). 'Sometimes pushed by market forces, they still had freedom of choice, and by and large opted to give way, rather than resist. If this caused problems for them later, it was their own doing, their choice' (Strange 1998b: 18).

This transformation of the financial and monetary order has had implications for the global structure of production and of trade in goods and services. As capital has become more mobile, firms and markets have become more transnational, enhancing their power in relation to governments, which remain territorially based. The increase in capital mobility and the corresponding transnationalization of financial institutions, combined with technological changes which facilitated this process, was intimately related to changes in the global structure of production. Thanks to the liberalization of international finance, 'The old difficulties of raising money for investment in off-shore operations and moving it across exchanges vanished' (Strange 1994b). Aspiring or already global firms are no longer stuck with national capital markets, and can raise funds wherever they cost the least. Restrictions on a broad spectrum of investment decisions have been lifted. This has facilitated a rapid transnationalization of corporate production strategies and a commensurate increase in intra-firm and intra-industry trade, developments again associated with rapid technological change. Firms could fragment production processes and locate activities closer to markets or wherever production costs were most advantageous, spurring a rapid transformation of the international division of labor. From a system of national economies with a few multinational firms, the global political economy has become a system of ever more intense competition and thus ever more rapid adaptation of states and firms to the realities of the new 'triangular diplomacy' of state–state, firm–firm and state–firm (Stopford and Strange 1991: 19–23).

To summarize this section, Strange has argued cogently and consistently across a number of major works that changes in the global financial system, originating with the rise of the Eurodollar market, had a knock-on effect on the broader global political economy. In the first place the onset of short-term capital mobility overwhelmed the fixed exchange rate monetary system and undermined the capacity of states to regulate their financial sectors and manage relatively independent macroeconomic policies. Further wide-ranging liberalization of the financial system accentuated these developments in the 1980s and continued into the 1990s, enhancing greatly the volatility and uncertainty of the global economic climate for firms and states alike. These changes in the domain of money and finance were in turn associated with changes in the structure of production and trade. The trend towards global production strategies accelerated as both cause and consequence of rapid technological developments which facilitated the emergence of a global economy. States and firms alike found themselves in a more dynamic and competitive environment with (sometimes severely) asymmetrical consequences for different social constituencies and states in the system. This was the abiding image developed in Strange's seminal work, *Casino Capitalism* (Strange 1986), and to which she returned in her last work, *Mad Money* (Strange 1998a). It was the financial structure which was the key to understanding this brave new market world of ours which has earned the much-abused cliché, 'globalization'.

The Decline of State Power

Strange's argument concerning the nature of the global political economy did not stop with her analysis of the specific domains of finance, money, production or technology. She was also interested in the way the pieces of the puzzle fit together – what she called the four interlocking structures of the world economy: security, production, finance and knowledge (Strange 1988). In looking at the broader picture of global order, she went on to make equally persuasive arguments about the nature and role of the state in the emerging global system. This section will examine how Strange moved from an analysis of the underlying structures of political economy to an analysis of the implications of structural change for the complex patterns of political authority in the system of states in the last years of the 20th century and on into the new millennium.

The result of the shift to a more market-oriented and transnational economic order, propelled largely by global financial and monetary developments, is the diffusion of authority which once belonged firmly in the hands of states: 'The declining authority of states is reflected in a growing diffusion of authority to other institutions and associations, and to local and regional bodies, and in a growing asymmetry between the larger states with structural power and weaker ones without it' (Strange 1996: 4).

In the first place, as Stopford and Strange argued in 1991, states were manifestly less interested in the acquisition of territory than in the pursuit of wealth for the national economy: 'national choices of industrial policy and efficiency in economic management are beginning to override choices of foreign or defence policy as the primary influences on how resources are allocated' (Stopford and Strange 1991: 1). The traditional 'Westphalian' state was undergoing important transformations and our ideas about the state, for Strange, needed a corresponding adjustment (Strange 1994c). States now competed to attract capital and economic activity to further their economic development goals in international competition. The transnationalization of markets had placed ever-stronger cards in the hands of global firms. This accentuated the need for states to make themselves attractive to firms and thus dissipated their control over the levers of economic development. Once again asymmetry predominates: some states are manifestly better positioned than others to use their power and resources in this game of state–firm diplomacy which increasingly prevails over the traditional state–state variety. States are far from being pawns in this game, but the enhanced role of non-state actors, especially firms, is clearly analyzed by Stopford and Strange and further developed by Strange herself (Strange 1994b).

The enhanced role for firms is also highlighted by the new game of firm-to-firm diplomacy which Stopford and Strange pinpointed (see summary in Strange 1994b: 108–10). Capital mobility and transnationalization of production allows firms to develop their strategies more autonomously, yet intensified global competition pushes them to collaborate with each other and pool resources and innovations. This game of firm–firm diplomacy is intimately related to state–firm bargains and to the more traditional state–state diplomacy of international trade negotiations. The power exerted by the changing preferences of major multinational corporations as non-state actors was for Strange undeniable, and it was also undeniably altering the world of states themselves. A further effect was 'the dilution of the national identity of the business enterprise' (Strange 1998a: 181).[1]

These new realities cast ever-longer shadows of doubt on the validity of traditional realist and other state-centric approaches to international relations. Significant doubt was cast on a wide range of theories in economics, especially those of a liberal persuasion (Strange 2000: 85–6). As early as 1970, Strange had argued the need to overcome these theoretical shortcomings of economics and international relations by developing international political economy as a separate discipline (Strange 1970).

This increasing power of firms and therefore of market forces in the global political economy was a result of the structural changes in the financial and production structures, as well as in rapidly changing technologies (see previous section). The argument need not be repeated here; suffice it to say that money and finance were at the heart of any explanation proffered by Susan Strange. The real economy, sector after sector, 'dance[s] to the fast or slow rhythms of financial markets' (Strange 1998a: 180). Likewise with states: 'all run up against the limits set by international finance' (ibid.). The conclusion that Strange drew from these developments was that state power was being significantly circumscribed in an ongoing fashion. Sometimes this power had shifted upwards to institutions such as the European Union or other international instances, sometimes it had moved downwards to markets and local institutional bodies.

It was not just market actors, then, which had become the repositories of authority and power in the global political economy. Strange argued that the power of other non-state actors was increasing as well. International organizations such as the International Monetary Fund or the European Union were obvious candidates, with their legions of 'econocrats' (Strange 1996: ch.12). They become very much part of the fabric of global governance as states seek to overcome their own limitations through the delegation of power, but not necessarily the most important.[2] A range of private agents and networks, which had always been present, are emerging as important repositories of power and authority in the global economy. Private cartels controlling and manipulating markets, the power of the self-regulatory bodies of the professions, and even international mafias and criminal networks, had a role to play in this diffusion of authority (see Strange 1996: s.II). To a considerable extent, Strange's arguments lie behind the emerging recognition of the importance of non-state actors by other scholars (Cutler *et al.* 1999; Higgott *et al.* 2000).

This notion of power and authority residing in private as well as 'legitimate' public bodies implies that political authority is not just exercised by states, whatever international law or traditional political scientists may say. In fact, Strange's emphasis on non-state, especially private, actors requires a broadening of the traditional notion of politics to encompass not just what states or politicians in the formal political arena do, but a pervasive activity determining who gets what, when and how among a wide range of public and private actors in an increasingly transnational space (Strange 1996: ch.2).

States are not, then, the only important actors in either a domestic or international context. In fact, the distinction between the domain of international politics and the domain of domestic politics was a dubious one for Strange. Her challenge of this distinction was integral to her critique of traditional international relations scholars of the realist paradigm. Furthermore, political power is most often exercised in a quiet, almost unthinking way by those actors who have it, state and non-state alike, through structural as opposed to relational, or what some theorists call 'instrumental', power (Strange 1988: ch.2; see also Verdun in the present volume). Private non-state actors, such as bankers, exercise their authority through structural power, not a genuine ability to coerce others directly. They cannot compel states or other players to do things in the positive sense, but their control over the creation and allocation of credit constitutes power nonetheless by shaping the constraints on others, including states.

So if the state is in retreat, is it necessarily the case that non-state actors, especially market players, are advancing? Strange's arguments go a long way to support this conclusion. One possibility, she argued, was that authority had not gone anywhere: 'as power has become more dispersed, away from the sovereign state that was supposed to be the unit of analysis in international society, so some of the functions of authority are not being discharged by anybody. Power has evaporated, like steam' (Strange 1994a: 15). This situation yields the 'defective state' (Strange 1995) that could no longer fulfill the functions commonly assigned to it in the international system by the underlying assumptions of democratic governance. States had more and more difficulty smoothing out the economic cycle, affecting exchange rate determination, raising tax revenues from the corporate sector or satisfying the welfare demands of citizens (Strange 1994c: 213).

This issue of democratic legitimacy surfaced again and again throughout her work. It was an abiding concern in *Sterling and British Policy* (Strange 1971), was expressed strongly in *Casino Capitalism* (Strange 1986), to resurface in *Mad Money*. Structural change, the retreat of the state and the corresponding increase in power for non-state actors of various kinds has considerable implications for the future of democratic governance: 'not much remains of the accountability of market forces to political constraints' and hence 'the casting of a vote from time to time becomes a merely symbolic act. ... Moreover, none of the non-state authorities to which authority has shifted, is democratically governed' (Strange 1996: 197).

To this emerging crisis of the state, increased cooperation and institution building at the international level was not providing a viable solution. Part of the reason for this was once again the lack of democratic accountability in the international domain and the inability of states to develop alternative structures of governance, which ensure that democratic processes prevail. The result was an increasing sense of fundamental insecurity amongst many populations and constituencies in the international system (Strange 1994c: 216). Behind Strange's work lay an enduring uncertainty about the fragile legitimacy of the changing international (dis)order and almost certainly, as a colleague once put it, a fear of Armageddon, the most recent version of which was the 1930s and World War II. After all, she lived through it. This is what she called the 'clash between the legitimacy of the liberal economy and the legitimacy of the liberal polity' (ibid.).

The individuality and distinctiveness of particular national states and economic systems was also under threat from the process of global integration. Given that states were less able to make fundamental choices concerning key areas of policy and governance, it followed that they were less able to defend the specific values which history had, for better or for worse, conferred upon them. Opting for the world market is no longer an option, but an imperative for rich and poor alike. Yet let us not forget asymmetry: these imperatives are more powerful for the weaker, dependent societies and sociopolitical constituencies than for the dominant political economies of Europe and North America, especially the United States. This led Strange to postulate an ongoing and accelerating convergence of national economic models, a convergence towards the Anglo-Saxon style of capitalism (Strange 1997).

Yet Strange's version of convergence was different from most and contained more than a note of ambiguity, which is significant for the next section of this chapter. It was more sophisticated than many detractors would accept. For Strange, convergence and the retreat of the state were related phenomena, but were not the result of blind, structural economic forces of the market. The retreat of the state did not mean sovereignty at bay in the simplistic sense (Strange 1996: 46) or blind economic forces overwhelming a dysfunctional politics. In this way Strange took her political economy seriously: she never forgot her own insistence that the political and the economic domains could not meaningfully be prized apart. States have ceded power to non-state actors, but not for lack of choice. This was the significance of her account of 'non-decisions' in *Casino Capitalism* (1986), the (particularly American) non-decisions which led to the emergence of global financial integration as a structural force in the international system (Strange 1986: Introduction). Political decisions and non-decisions had set in motion the transnational market forces which were steadily emasculating state authority and capacity, and which risked undermining the legitimacy of the market system. 'The shift from state authority to market authority has been in large part the result of state policies' (Strange 1996: 44). Hers is an agent-centric explanation, not a determinist one.

New Forms of State and Market

Strange was perhaps best known for her book *States and Markets* (1988). This was her signature: she was a 'states and markets' person. Her challenge to scholars and policy makers to rethink their understanding of the relationship between the economic and the political domains (and therefore between their concrete embodiment as states and markets) was surely her most important contribution to the discipline. It is with this signature that she can be credited, with little exaggeration, as midwife of the discipline of international political economy in its contemporary manifestation. Modesty always led her to insist it was someone else, usually Charles Kindleberger,[3] but she was at the very least among the most explicit in issuing her call to arms (Strange 1970) to dismantle the academic apartheid between economics and political science/international relations.

Yet Strange was more interested in developing the *challenge* than in developing the theoretical case itself. She also was insistent that her challenge should rest on exhaustive empirical demonstration of her conceptual arguments, especially in her major works on the international monetary system.[4] There was often more than a hint of disdain for those who devoted themselves primarily to theoretical work: 'I am not generally regarded – nor would I wish to be – as a theorist in international relations. *Instead*, I devoted much time to analysing the global financial system and how it emerged' (Strange 2000: 83; emphasis added). In another article: 'I do find that most – not all – of my colleagues who teach international relations theory tend to suffer from some degree of myopia when it comes to the world around them' (Strange 1994c: 209).

The message was that theory was wont to go astray if not systematically related to empirical research and enquiry into the concrete nature of the world around us. This is a point which one can only welcome, and of course Strange was not by any means alone in making it. But it would not be unfair to point out the corollary: if one is to issue a challenge to theory, the conceptual points in question would be the stronger if rigorously developed in conceptual terms. It is in this regard that Strange was far more interested in *challenging* orthodoxy, in broadening the intellectual agenda, than in a systematic theoretical statement.

Strange *did* explore theory in considerable depth. Her work on power is widely recognized (see several of the contributions to this volume). *States and Markets* developed a model of interlocking structures in the global political economy, and also explored the role of values in theoretical enquiry (Strange 1988: ch.1). But if the relationship between states and markets was her signature, the hallmark of her work so to speak, then the absence of an explicit theoretical account of the relationship is the more interesting for its absence. There is no explicit theory of the state–market relationship, despite consistent and persuasive assertions backed by empirical evidence that the two were interdependent, inextricably intertwined.

As should be clear from the discussion in the previous section of this chapter, the state–market relationship is central to the 'retreat of the state' argument. The retreat of the state is the result of state decisions and non-decisions setting in motion the powerful, integrative market forces, which have diluted state authority and enhanced the authority of non-state actors. It was, as was argued above, very much an agent-centered explanation, which nonetheless had an important place for structural forces and structural power. But Strange never fully clarified in her theoretical work how this transformation took place. Her analysis suggests a series of unanswered questions: how could institutions which she recognized as being so jealous of their power in many respects (states) participate so fulsomely in their own, if partial, demise, at the hands of market forces and the non-state actors which constitute these forces? Was it foolishness? Myopia? Naïveté? How could states voluntarily give up their power over so crucial a domain as monetary and financial policy, especially when it was such a hard-won historical battle to gain the prerogative in the first place (Schwartz 2000)? Furthermore, if the state could voluntarily give up its power, why could it not get it back, a scenario she appears to judge as highly implausible? Did states, through decisions and non-decisions alike, dissipate their authority once and for all, like light and matter down a black hole? Indeed, if states retreat from some domains of activity, does this necessarily make them weaker? If state agents could alter the structure, is this irrevocable, and how is the ongoing process of structural change driven once states have given up much of their capacity to affect the system? Where does the politics go if not to a nether world where states have little in terms of functions to perform?

For Strange this problem would have been more one of finesse than of urgency. Yet there is a conceptual point at stake here which is central to the whole state–market debate, and thus to international political economy as a discipline. That states participated in their own retreat and emasculation, a process fraught with danger for the legitimacy of the global system, remained for Strange a paradox. Her contribution was to force us to grapple with the implications of this transformation, not to explain precisely *how* states and markets were integral to each other. But her account of this development presumes a close relationship between the power of non-state actors in the market and the outcome (or 'non-outcome', to emphasize once again the role of non-decision making) of the policy process. In other words, she assumes, but did not develop a theory of, a close relationship between states and non-state actors, particularly those in the market. This is in many ways common sense, but the precise nature of the relationship is crucial to theoretical debates in IPE. To what degree are states autonomous actors in the global system? How beholden to capital is the state in a recognizably capitalist system? Is a liberal–pluralist model, or a Marxist model, or a realist model of state most appropriate for our study of international political economy? There is a need to be clear about what one means by state, and what one means by market.

Strange's starting point in the early 1970s (Strange 1970) was that both disciplines in her firing line, international relations and international economics, assumed a real separation between, and a separate set of explanatory variables for, the economic and political domains. She insisted in contrast that the two were part of the same puzzle. So the behavior of states cannot be separated from their key constituencies of non-state market actors, whether these are becoming more transnational, and thus independent, or not.

Somehow states are related to, embedded in, the social and economic constituencies which they seek to manage, and Strange was not of course unaware of this. In several works she emphasized the importance, not just of understanding the 'national' interest of states, but of understanding in *whose* interest the national interest had been defined and constructed: 'who decides what policies are in the national interest?' (Strange 1998b: 18). Society, with its complexity, diversity and asymmetrical power relationships, was present in her theoretical landscape without being explicitly explained: 'History gives us many examples of states choosing policies supposedly in the national interest, but which in fact were chosen to serve the interests of social, political, or economic elites, and burdened society with high costs and risks' (ibid: 18–19). Strange even argued in a well-known exchange with Stephen Krasner (1994c: 215), yet without further developing the point herself, that society-based approaches to IPE were likely to flourish and state-centric approaches likely to atrophy for lack of relevance.

The problem here is that Strange, for all her radical advocacy of the imperative of integrating international economics and international relations in a new, broader discipline of international political economy, still treated the state and the market as two separate, if interdependent, entities. There was in her work, as in most scholarly analysis of the global political economy across a range of perspectives (for example, Gilpin 1986; Boyer and Drache 1996; Schwartz 2000), an epic struggle between the state and the market. Either the state or the market was in control, depending on one's perspective (for example, Strange 1996 and various, versus Kapstein 1994). As long as the system is portrayed as a tug-of-war between the two, then they may be interdependent but not genuinely part of the same dynamics or *political* economy.

Yet we need to take our Polanyi (1944) and the notion of political economy seriously: he argues that the market makes no sense without the state, that indeed the market was structured and enforced by the state. The idea of a separate economic domain without politics was a stark utopia, which failed, resulting in surely the greatest human tragedy of the modern period, the Depression and World War II.

This means that there is still one more and crucial conceptual step to take in order to move beyond the tug-of-war position of state–market dichotomy. The concept of states and markets as separate entities is an often-useful abstraction, but we need to remind ourselves that states and markets are not separate *things* as such. They are part of the same integrated ensemble of governance, a state–market *condominium* (Underhill 1997a), and should be thought of as such. This can be demonstrated empirically through case material, whether it be on global financial markets or international trade (ibid.; Underhill 1998). The private interests of the market are integrated into the state, asymmetrically in accordance with their structural power and organizational capacity, through their close relationship to state institutions in the policy decision-making process and in the ongoing pattern of regulatory governance of market society. This is particularly prevalent in financial market governance (Underhill 1997b). What we tend to consider state prerogatives are often delegated to self-regulatory associations of private interests anyway, demonstrating that 'public' responsibilities can be exercised by private bodies in many instances, just as private interests can appropriate public institutions for their own particularistic purposes.

The adjustment process and structure of economic interaction in the political economy is managed simultaneously through the process of economic competition among firms, on the one hand, and the policy and regulatory processes mediated by the institutions of the state, on the other. This is clearly visible in corporatist systems in Western Europe, where even labor is integrated into both state policy processes and the strategic decision making of firms, or in the close

integration of private firms/associations into the system of bureaucratic management which characterizes the economic development
process in Japan. The point is less obvious to observers of Anglo-
Saxon political economies where the independence of the private
sector appears more marked than in other societies. But the considerable evidence of 'regulatory capture' of the agencies of governance in
the US economy should indicate the need to avoid the stereotypes
developed in, particularly, the economics literature. A market without institutions and governance, including some form of judicial
authority or arbitration, is inconceivable. If we all admit that 'perfect
competition' is an abstraction from a messy, more prosaic reality of
various forms of second best market fixing, we can begin to see more
clearly the reality of the political economy: if the state does not rig
the market, private interests will. That the state exists in symbiosis
with private interests explains how private interests are an integral
part of the pattern of market governance even in so-called 'strong
state' systems like France (Underhill 1998: chs 2–3).

In this sense, the regulatory and policy-making institutions of the
state are one element of the market, one set of institutions, through
which governance operates. The structures of the market are constituted as much and simultaneously by the political processes of the
state and the political resources of the various constituencies involved in the policy process as by the process of economic competition
itself; likewise the political and regulatory process is as much part of
the strategies of firms as the game of investment and marketing
(Underhill 1998: 18–25; *passim*). The preferences of market agents and
other constituencies of market society are integrated into the institutions of the state through policy and regulatory processes at domestic
and international levels of analysis, depending on their individual
organizational capacities/coherence, and of course power. The incentives and constraints of state policy and regulation are in turn
part of the landscape of firm decision making, conferring advantages
on some and costs on others, just as some are more capable of affecting the policy outcome than others.

Of course this conceptualization of states and markets appears
counterintuitive in our era of global integration increasingly dominated by private sector market processes. The case also appears
difficult to support in view of the existence of multiple sovereignties
in the global economy. Our contemporary experience of modern capitalism and the prevalence of economic modes of analysis engrave on
our intellects the idea of the state–market dichotomy. Yet it is precisely against this sort of orthodoxy that Strange taught us to rebel.
Adam Smith is useful here: he pointed out that the very public responsibilities of generating and distributing wealth are better
accomplished through a free interaction of private economic agents

(see discussion in Underhill 2000). Public goals could be accomplished by private agents, and (more worrisomely in Smith's opinion) *vice versa*. This, however, does not render the economy any less political: one can delegate or fragment authority and decision-making power, but one cannot depoliticize the system as such. It remains an ensemble of governance.

There is also nothing surprising in the idea that a transnational market structure, or indeed any market, should have multiple institutional nodes exercising authority in different ways and even with different functions. There is nothing necessarily coherent about the institutions and preferences of the state in this regard, any more than we would expect coherence across a system of multiple sovereignties. The federal state analogy is useful here. Therefore we should not misconceive the identifiable institutional/organizational structures of the state as a separate phenomenon external to the dynamics of the market. The phenomenon of multiple sovereignties does not detract from this view, it simply means that the market is structured by multiple sovereignties, legal fictions all, rather than one single institutionalized locus of authority. Again, anyone who lives in a federal state or indeed the European Union should be comfortable with this assertion.

So what can we make of this in relation to Strange's retreat of the state argument? It may be argued that the notion of a state–market condominium as an integrated ensemble of governance makes the retreat of the state argument much more tenable and comprehensible, while altering it in crucial ways. It provides answers to the questions posed earlier in this section: how could states do this to themselves? How could they emasculate their capacity to govern crucial aspects of the social whole? Why would they retreat, and can they ever get their power back again?

If the process of market structuration is as much a phenomenon of the policy and regulatory processes of the state as it is of the process of competition among firms, then it is not difficult to understand the role of 'non-state' private interests, integrated into the complex institutional fabric of the state, in driving the process of global integration. In this sense Strange is perfectly correct to identify the role of states in propelling the integration process forward. As the pattern of material interests in national political economies has become more transnational, so the state has changed. The state has become far more a facilitator of global market processes than a protector of domestic market structures and interests; witness the acceleration of trade liberalization from the 1980s (Milner 1988; Destler and Odell 1987). The pattern of political authority becomes more transnational in symbiosis with the transformation of the market. The state has progressively delegated a number of tasks either to private bodies or to institutions of international cooperation, though it maintains its functions in terms of domestic political legitimacy and all the tensions that entails.

In this sense what we have seen is not so much a *retreat* of the state, but a transformation of the state in symbiosis with the transformation of economic structures. We have changing forms of state emphasizing different functions over others, not an emasculation as such. This is akin to Jayasuriya's argument concerning the transformation of sovereignty: there has been a steady transnationalization of the institutions of governance of the global political economy (Jayasuriya 1999). There may be a retreat of the state from particular activities and functions, but if one properly understands the dynamics of the state–market condominium, it should be clear that the form and functions of the state will continue to evolve, as indeed they have in the past. This also implies that the state could claw back (at a cost!) its authority should political and market circumstances make this likely, just as the state in the inter-war period wrested authority over the market from private actors following the collapse of laissez-faire and the crisis of legitimacy spawned by the Depression. World War II strengthened this trend as market activity became organized around the function of community survival (expansion in the case of the aggressors) as opposed to private opulence. It is worth pointing out that this period from the Depression to the 1970s, the period of national economic management, was relatively exceptional in historical terms (Schwartz 2000). In many respects we have returned to the more limited role for states, which was the norm under 19th-century laissez-faire, albeit with enhanced public welfare functions. The question is not why is the state in retreat, but how long is this form of state–market condominium sustainable in the face of the increased volatility of the global financial markets? That was a question which was also central to the work of Susan Strange.

Conclusion

Strange argued cogently that the process of financial globalization had considerable implications for the nature of political authority in the political economy. From this, and from her observations concerning the changing nature of technology and the transnationalization of production, she postulated that the state was in retreat in the face of market forces and other forms of non-state authority in the global system. She rightly observed that this was as much a political process as a market phenomenon. This observation challenged all of us to think more innovatively about the relationship between states and markets. Yet Strange herself never went on to develop a theoretical account of this state–market relationship, leading her to the somewhat misleading conclusion that the state as such was in retreat. Despite her insistence on their essential interdependence, she still portrayed a tension between the dynamics of markets and the dynamics of states. However, if we reconceptualize the state–market relationship as a condominium, an integrated ensemble of governance, as opposed to two separate *things* with separate *dynamics*, a clearer picture emerges. This is one of changing, indeed transnationalizing, patterns of political authority in symbiosis with the changing structure of the market. Political authority and the market remain inseparable, as Strange insisted, but there is a changing balance of public and private authority which is reflected not in a retreat as such, but in the changing *forms* of state over time.

Notes

1 This thesis is hotly contested by others: see, for example, Pauly and Reich (1997).
2 Strange long remained skeptical about the potential of international organizations.
3 Whose own immense contribution I am not trying to diminish in any way. Susan was just more direct in challenging others to rethink both international relations and international economics as disciplines.
4 Though this emphasis on in-depth empirical research was perhaps less evident in her later years.

References

Boyer, Robert and Daniel Drache (1996), *States against Markets: the Limits of Globalization*, London: Routledge.
Cutler, A. Claire, Virginia Haufler and Tony Porter (eds) (1999), *Private Authority and International Affairs*, Albany: State University of New York Press.
Destler, I.M and John Odell (1987), *Anti-Protection: Changing Forces in United States Trade Politics*, Washington, DC: Institute for International Economics.
Germain, Randall D. (1997), *The International Organization of Credit: States and Global Finance in the World Economy*, Cambridge: Cambridge University Press.
Gilpin, Robert (1986), *The Political Economy of International Relations*, Princeton, NJ: Princeton University Press.
Higgott, Richard, Geoffrey R.D. Underhill and Andreas Bieler (eds) (2000), *Nonstate Actors and Authority in the Global System*, London: Routledge.
Jayasuriya, Kanishka (1999), 'Globalization, Law and the Transformation of Sovereignty: the Emergence of Global Regulatory Governance', *Indiana Journal of Legal Studies*, 6(2), Spring, 425–55.
Kapstein, Ethan B. (1994), *Governing the Global Economy: International Finance and the State*, Cambridge MA: Harvard University Press.
Milner, Helen (1988), *Resisting Protectionism: Global Industries and the Politics of International Trade*, Princeton, NJ: Princeton University Press.

Pauly, Louis W. and Simon Reich (1997), 'National Structures and Multinational Corporate Behaviour: Enduring Differences in the Age of Globalization', *International Organization*, 51(1), Winter, 1–30.

Polanyi, Karl (1944), *The Great Transformation*, Boston: Beacon Press.

Schwartz, Herman M. (2000), *States versus Markets: History, Geography and the Development of the International Political Economy*, 2nd edn, London: Macmillan.

Stopford, John and Susan Strange (with J.S. Hanley) (1991), *Rival States, Rival Firms: Competition for World Market Shares*, Cambridge: Cambridge University Press.

Strange, Susan (1970), 'International Economics and International Relations: a Case of Mutual Neglect', *International Affairs*, 46(2), April, 304–15.

Strange, Susan (1971), *Sterling and British Policy: A Political Study of an International Currency in Decline*, Oxford: Oxford University Press.

Strange, Susan (1976), *International Monetary Relations*, in Andrew Shonfield (ed.), *International Economic Relations in the Western World 1959–71*, Oxford University Press.

Strange, Susan (1986), *Casino Capitalism*, Oxford: Blackwell.

Strange, Susan (1988), *States and Markets: An Introduction to International Political Economy*, London: Pinter.

Strange, Susan (1994a), 'Who Governs? Networks of Power in World Society', *Hitotsubashi Journal of Law and Politics*, special issue, June, 5–17.

Strange, Susan (1994b), 'Rethinking Structural Change in the International Political Economy: States, Firms and Diplomacy', in R. Stubbs and G.R.D. Underhill (eds), *Political Economy and the Changing Global Order*, Basingstoke: Macmillan, pp.103–15.

Strange, Susan (1994c), 'Wake up Krasner! The world *has* changed', *Review of International Political Economy*, 1(2), Summer, 209–20.

Strange, Susan (1995), 'The Defective State', *Daedelus*, 24(2), Spring, 55–74.

Strange, Susan (1996), *The Retreat of the State: the Diffusion of Power in the World Economy*, Cambridge: Cambridge University Press.

Strange, Susan (1997), 'The Future of Global Capitalism; or will Divergence Persist Forever?', in Colin Crouch and Wolfgang Streeck (eds), *The Political Economy of Modern Capitalism: Mapping Convergence and Diversity*, London: Sage, pp.183–91.

Strange, Susan (1998a), *Mad Money*, Manchester: Manchester University Press.

Strange, Susan (1998b) 'What Theory? The Theory in *Mad Money*', CSGR Working Paper no. 18/98, University of Warwick, December.

Strange, Susan (2000), 'World Order, Non-State Actors and the Global Casino: the Retreat of the State?', in R. Stubbs and G.R.D. Underhill (ed.), *Political Economy and the Changing Global Order*, 2nd edn, Oxford: Oxford University Press, pp.82–90.

Strange, Susan and Roger Tooze (1981a), 'The International Politics of Surplus Capacity, or how does Theory Stand up to Protectionism 1970s Style?', *International Organization*, 33(3), Summer.

Strange, Susan and Roger Tooze (eds) (1981b), *The Politics of International Surplus Capacity*, London: Allen & Unwin.

Stubbs, Richard and Geoffrey R.D. Underhill (eds) (1994), *Political Economy and the Changing Global Order*, Basingstoke: Macmillan.

Stubbs, Richard and Geoffrey R.D. Underhill (eds) (2000), *Political Economy and the Changing Global Order*, 2nd edn, Oxford: Oxford University Press.

Underhill, Geoffrey R.D. (1997a), 'Transnationalising the State in Global Financial Markets: Co-operative Regulatory Regimes, Domestic Political Authority and Conceptual Models of the State', unpublished paper presented to the annual workshops of the European Consortium for Political Research, Berne, Switzerland, 27 February–4 March 1997.

Underhill, Geoffrey R.D. (1997b), 'Private Markets and Public Responsibilities in a

Global System: Conflict and Co-operation in Transnational Banking and Securities Regulation', in G.R.D. Underhill (ed.), *The New World Order in International Finance*, London: Macmillan, pp.17–49.

Underhill, Geoffrey R.D. (1998), *Industrial Crisis and the Open Economy: Politics, Global Trade and the Textile Industry in the Global Economy*, London: Macmillan.

Underhill, Geoffrey R.D. (2000a), 'Conceptualizing the Changing Global Order', in R. Stubbs and G.R.D. Underhill (eds), Political Economy and the Changing Global Order, 2nd edn, Oxford: Oxford University Press, pp.3–24.

Underhill, Geoffrey R.D. (2000b), 'The Public Good versus Private Interests in the Global Financial and Monetary System', *International Comparative and Corporate Law Journal*, 2(3), London: Institute for Advanced Legal Studies.

PART III
CRITICAL PERSPECTIVES ON INTERNATIONAL RELATIONS

8 Criticizing US Method and Thought in International Relations: Why a Trans-Atlantic Divide Narrows IR's Research Subject

BERTJAN VERBEEK[1]

Introduction

The research question guiding this chapter is whether the current debate regarding the nature of international relations in general, and international political economy in particular, is related to different views of various academic communities, roughly along an American/non-American cleavage. Such a divide is thought to exist, corresponding approximately with a divide between (predominantly American) rationalists and (predominantly European) constructivists. It will be argued that any claim about American intellectual hegemony obscures the main issue at stake: are international politics and international economics related, but clearly distinct, spheres, or do they constitute one integrated research subject? The answer to this ontological question sets limits on the theoretical approaches available. This chapter argues in favor of the second perspective and suggests that the work of Strange is one of the few examples, albeit an imperfect one, of such a perspective presently available in the discipline. The chapter is structured as follows. The next section considers the place of knowledge in the power structures of world politics. In the third section, we investigate the claim that the academic community studying international relations is divided by an

American/non-American cleavage. Next, the chapter shows how such a debate obfuscated the ontological and epistemological questions underlying our object of study. In the fifth section it is argued that our object of study requires a perspective which truly integrates (inter)national politics and (inter)national economics. As of now, only a few such integrated perspectives are at hand. This chapter claims that Strange offers one such integrated perspective. From the analysis presented below it follows, first of all, that rationalist (rational choice) and constructivist approaches need not be mutually exclusive avenues to knowledge about international affairs, and second, that IR scholars need to debate whether their research subject is constituted by the political aspects of international economic relations or by the international political economy.

Knowledge as a Dimension of Structural Power

This volume focuses on the nature of power in international politics and the international economy. Knowledge is an important source of power. In several other chapters it has been argued that the notion of structural power has been one of Strange's major contributions to the study of international affairs. Structural power refers to the power to shape and determine the structures of, as Strange preferred to call it, 'the world political economy', in which all actors, domestic as well as transnational, have to operate. Structural power should be distinguished from relational power, which refers to the more familiar notion of power developed by Robert Dahl, the ability of A to get B to do things he or she would not otherwise have done (Strange 1988: 24–5; Dahl 1976). Phrased in simple terms, one could compare it to a game of cards. Structural power is the power to dictate the rules of the game, whereas relational power refers to the maximum number of points a player can gain in the game, if she plays her hand well.[2] As mentioned in previous chapters, structural power can be conceived of as the interplay between four dimensions:[3] security, production, finance, and knowledge. Each dimension offers sources of structural power (Strange 1988: 24–9). Many contributions to this volume deal with finance and production as sources of structural power and with the question of whether changes in these dimensions over the last 20 years have resulted in changes in the traditional concentration of structural power in a few states (or even one).

The knowledge dimension of structural power, however, merits a discussion of its own. It is defined by Strange as the determination of 'what knowledge is discovered, how it is stored, and who communicates it by what means and on what terms' (ibid.: 117).[4] Technology is an important part of the knowledge dimension. Indeed, in her later work, Strange argued that technological change might be the instigator of fundamental shifts within the other three dimensions of structural power (Strange 1998a: 22–42). Technological development, however, is not a sufficient condition of furthering shifts in the dimensions of structural power. Such shifts can only come about because of a change in the belief systems that underpin the political–economic arrangements that are acceptable to a society (Strange 1988: 123; 1998a: 69, 182).

The ability to affect perceptions and beliefs is thus a crucial part of the knowledge dimension of structural power. Since the rise of the modern state system, this ability has been traditionally concentrated in the hands of the state through its system of education. As long as structural power was concentrated in the hands of one state, like the United States after World War II, this hegemon derived part of its power from its control over what is commonly accepted as knowledge (Strange 1987). Indeed, she argued that 'there can be little doubt that power [in the knowledge dimension] lies with American universities and American professional associations' (Strange 1995a: 65). This observation warrants two questions: first, to what extent has the study of international relations in general, and international political economy in particular, traditionally been dominated by American hegemony in the knowledge dimension of structural power? Second, to what extent have alleged fundamental changes in the 'world political economy' affected the knowledge dimension of structural power and, subsequently, the study of international relations and international political economy?

An American/Non-American Cleavage?

If knowledge is a source of structural power, intellectual hegemony in the field of international relations should be found in the United States until at least the end of the 1980s. The end of the cold war would change the security configuration, and globalization would become a popular concept. Similarly, the post-cold war world can be expected to pose a challenge to such a presumed American intellectual hegemony in the discipline. Strange is very clear about American leadership in the study of international relations and the effects it has had. According to her, American academics are characterized by a belief that it is possible to formulate a general theory of international relations and that the best road to this objective is the imitation of concepts and methods developed by (classical) economics. The result is a discipline that focuses on how the rational behavior of states results in interactions that produce or maintain equilibria (Strange 1995b: 164; 1998b: 215–16). This dominant perspective among

American scholars of international affairs is intimately intertwined
with the policy needs of the American government. Robert Cox once
distinguished 'problem-posing theory' from 'problem-solving theory'. Whereas the former aims at a critical analysis of the values that
are implicit in international relations research, the latter takes such
values for granted and offers solutions to theoretical and empirical
puzzles within the accepted system of values (Cox 1981; 1987). Strange
considers mainstream international relations theory a clear example
of 'problem-solving theory': academic interests change parallel to
changes in political attention in the United States. To her, the rise of
international regime theory is intimately related to the perceived
policy need to maintain international order despite the alleged breakdown of American hegemony in the 1970s and 1980s. The
disappearance of regime theory[5] from the academic agenda reflects
the reduced policy need for it in the post-cold war world in which
the United States is the single major state actor in world politics
(Strange 1995b: 159–60; 1996: xiii–xiv).[6]

Strange's analysis raises two questions. First, is the discipline of
international relations characterized by an American hegemony and,
second, if so, does it result in a dominant view on the discipline? The
latter question can be better understood in terms of the knowledge
dimension of structural power: does American hegemony produce
one overarching perspective that is imposed on diverging views that
creep up outside the United States? Or is American hegemony exercised more subtly, because non-American scholars imitate the
dominant perspective? Ole Waever has recently investigated the claim
that the discipline of International Relations is dominated by Americans and by a certain type of scholarship (Waever, 1998). His analysis
of the contents of eight leading journals in international relations
(four American and four European) reveals that six of them contain a
majority of American and Canadian authors (ibid.: 696–701). Moreover, a closer inspection of four such journals (two American and
two European) suggests that rational choice, emphasizing interests
and power, is the metatheoretical orientation of the majority of the
articles. Constructivism, which focuses, among other things, on shared
norms and values, surfaced in European rather than American journals (ibid.: 701–3). Waever thus argues that the theoretical profile of
the discipline is now largely colored by a relatively small group of
American authors who write in a few journals, notably *International
Organization* and *International Studies Quarterly*. He thus corroborates
Strange's hunch that rational choice-oriented Americans dominate
the field (cf. Biersteker 1993; Hodgson 1994). Waever and Strange
also concur on the explanation for this situation: Americans ultimately search for a general theory of international behavior and
believe that the economists' approach of logical deduction and parsi-

mony is the main avenue to that goal. Europeans, on the contrary, supposedly have a more historical approach to research in which complexity is valued more highly than parsimony (cf. Rittberger 1995; Keohane 1995). As a matter of fact, Waever explains the growth of popularity of rational choice by the slow 'de-Europeanization' of American international relations, as demography reduces the number of American IR scholars who received (part of) their training in Europe, or from European-educated teachers (Strange 1998b: 215–16; Waever 1998: 689). This overall picture of the current state of the IR discipline nicely fits in with the emerging consensus that the main debate in the field today is not between (neo)realism and (neo)liberalism, but rather between rationalism and constructivism (Katzenstein *et al.* 1998).

This convenient juxtaposition of American rationalism and European constructivism is highly disturbing, for three reasons. First of all, it is highly misleading to speak of an American/European divide. Waever's analysis clearly shows that many Americans adhere to the 'European constructivists' camp' and that many Europeans share the rationalist principles of the 'American intellectual hegemon'. What is truly puzzling is why the majority of the academic IR community seem to judge *International Organization* and *International Studies Quarterly* their most important intellectual guidance. Whatever the solution to this mystery of intellectual hegemony, it is certainly the case that many topics did not become legitimate in mainstream IR until they received the blessing from authors in these journals. One major example of this phenomenon is the reception of the importance of beliefs to the study of world politics. In the subdiscipline of foreign policy analysis the crucial importance of beliefs systems of policy makers has been common sense since Alexander George's refinement of the so-called operational code (George 1969). The 1970s witnessed increased collaboration with cognitive psychologists and attention to processes of perception and misperception (Jervis 1976). This resulted virtually in a field of specialization (cf. Rosati 1995). Yet belief systems did not receive due attention in the major journals until much later, when the explanation of the specific contents of certain international environmental regimes required the incorporation of opinions and values of the members of so-called 'epistemic communities' (for example, Haas 1989). The incorporation of belief systems into accepted IR frameworks did not occur until the publication of a book by authors who publish regularly in *International Organization* (Goldstein and Keohane 1993). The accumulation of knowledge was thus lagging behind by at least two decades thanks to the hierarchy among the discipline's journals. Similar stories could be told regarding attention to the relationship between international and domestic politics, and the acceptance of constructivist arguments.

Secondly, identifying geographic entities with academic orientations makes it attractive to disregard certain arguments on the ground that they come from certain countries or cultures and thus would be the mouthpiece of certain interests or positions of some cultures that should easily be traded in for the position of another. Of course, Waever (1998) and Biersteker (1993) are correct in arguing that academic positions always reflect the occurrence of real events and that there is a close connection between a culture's particular values and outlook and the analytical angles their academic communities take. It is quite natural that American scholars have been concerned with theories of cycles of hegemonic leadership and with international cooperation in the absence of such leadership, given the relative position in the international system of the United States. However, just as it would be wrong to consider the creation of academic knowledge to happen completely in an independent fashion according to its own rules, it would also be wrong to reduce academic knowledge simply to being no more than the reflection of a country's interests or value system.[7] For IR theory that means that the constructivists and the rationalists try to convey certain key arguments that are general claims and thus merit attention whether or not they can be traced back to interests and values. As will be shown below, the seemingly neat overlap between American/rationalist and European/constructivist hinders us in appreciating the academic issues they want to address and in seeing that they need not be that much apart at all.

Finally, and most importantly, the American/European divide blinds us to the main question facing the IR discipline at present: what is the nature of world politics today? The discussion between rationalists and constructivists has created a smokescreen around several important issues. The debate that is being conducted today focuses on the question of rationality, and the related issues of theory building and parsimony. Constructivists accuse rationalists of sacrificing the complexity of the real world for the sake of building parsimonious theories by assuming the rational, utility-maximizing behavior of actors. In particular, rationalists thus allegedly miss the mechanism by which preferences of actors are chosen (or constructed, as constructivists would say) in the first place. Furthermore, their emphasis on interests should make them overlook the origins of norms and values in international relations other than as the logical (that is, interest-driven) choice of the most powerful states. Rationalists, on the other hand, argue that constructivists pay little attention to the importance of theory building and tend to stick to limited case studies of the formation of norms and preferences, and thus make it more difficult to reach findings that produce cumulative knowledge.

This bickering is highly unfortunate. First of all, it has led to the portrayal of rationalists as scholars who are interested in the behavior of monolithic states in an anarchic system only. Even though many a neorealist may limit her research to that topic, there is no *a priori* reason why a rationalist approach can be applied to such situations only. It is perfectly possible to 'break up the billiard ball state' and analyze the impact of domestic actors and still follow rationalist recipes (Hollis and Smith 1991): Allison's models of governmental politics and organizational process (Allison 1971) can easily be re-phrased in rationalist terms (see, for example, Welch 1998; Bendor and Hammond 1992). The impact of domestic politics on the behavior of states can be analyzed in a similar fashion (for example, Bueno de Mesquita and Lalman 1992). Nevertheless, constructivists have a point when they criticize rationalists for paying little attention to prefer-ence formation and perceptions (Wendt 1992; see, for an exception, Wu and Bueno de Mesquita 1994).

It is here that constructivists and rationalists should reach out for each other. Rationalists should be aware that, although preferences may be considered as given for the purpose of explaining a conflict between diverging preferences of various states, the formation of preferences is a social phenomenon in its own right. It may well be that so-called 'critical constructivists' are right in emphasizing that preferences are social constructs (Weldes 1998: 218). Nevertheless, if a rationalist has decided that his research question investigates the relative success with which a state imposes its preference on other states in the context of, for instance, an international organization's conference, she need not worry about where that specific preference came from. A constructivist could challenge her findings if he dem-onstrates that the 'winning preference' was not so much the imposed preference of one state, but that the 'winning preference' won the day because of a transnational coalition of various actors built around one out of many possible preferences, thus circumventing the prefer-ence of the powerful state. This, however, requires the constructivist to develop a notion of why some rather than other preferences win the day. This attention to power mechanisms has until now been absent in most constructivist writing. This is where constructivists may profit from the power politics reasoning in the rationalist camp. Similarly, a rationalist may profit from a constructivist's insight, for instance, if he wants to explain the specific contents of an interna-tional regime, which requires reference to the process of preference formation. All in all, rationalists and constructivists simply pose, at times, different, mutually incompatible, and at other times, more similar, compatible questions. They do not, however, necessarily present two irreconcilable perspectives on international relations.

The popular identification of a rationalist epistemology with an ontology that puts emphasis on monolithic states in an anarchic international system has additional unfortunate consequences. It is true that, in practice, authors who have adopted such an ontology have monopolized the rationalist perspective in IR theory. They have thus managed to incorporate empirical domains that they had been accused of not being able to analyze, especially international economic relations and long-term cooperation between states. The major key to this success has been the international regimes literature, the majority of which adopts a rationalist perspective (Verbeek 1993). This is unfortunate for a number of reasons. First, its emphasis on agreements in the sphere of international trade has produced a bias in favor of long-term cooperation, simply because such material issues make Pareto-optimal outcomes possible more easily: side payments and exchanges are easier in domains that can ultimately be expressed in terms of money. It is much more difficult to reach agreements on relatively immaterial matters such as security (Rittberger 1990) or the environment (Young 1994). Rationalism has thus made the real world look more cooperative and has neglected the role of conflict (cf. Coser 1956). Secondly, rationalism has nurtured an academic community that focuses on states, while it is in principle capable of approaching non-state actors as well. It is to be regretted that only a few rationalist accounts exist of the behavior of non-state actors, such as international organizations, (for example, Nicholson 1998), multinational corporations (cf. Pauly and Reich 1997: esp. 2–3) and non-governmental organizations (for example, Reinalda and Verbeek 2000) in international relations. By their unnecessary neglect of non-state actors (and emphasis on states), rationalists have thus reinforced the position of those IR scholars who traditionally emphasize security relations between states and those IPE scholars who focus on the (state) politics of international economic relations. They have thus silenced the debate on 'what the world out there looks like'. Because the debate between rationalists and constructivists has focused on epistemology, it has rendered invisible the ontological debate.

The Real Issue: The Ontology of International Relations

Paradoxically, IR scholars pay little attention to the ontological question of what the world looks like. Although it seems as if they have written about nothing else since the end of the cold war and the arrival of globalization, IR scholars seldom touch on the question of whether the changes in the real world should affect their fundamental outlook on the world. It is true that few people nowadays adhere to strict realist principles only. They would be hesitant to argue that territorial security still is the primal concern of international affairs today and that the game of balance of power between states structures all other international interactions.[8] Rather, most scholars emphasize the increased importance of issues other than security, such as economics, the environment, migration, human rights and so on. In addition, they argue that states should not be the exclusive focus of IR studies (cf. Krause and Williams 1997). Instead, they hold that more attention should be paid to multinational corporations, non-governmental and international organizations, international media, finance traders and so on. Most scholars would therefore heartily agree that international political economy nowadays is an important field of study. It might even be the central concern of IR studies today, because it potentially touches most of the 'new issues' mentioned above. Ontologically speaking, a shift can be observed towards leaving behind the narrow conception of IR as the security *problématique* of sovereign states in favor of international political economy. This emerging consensus, however, has not yet resulted in agreement on what constitutes the *problématique* of international political economy.

The problem of International Political Economy as the study of international affairs is that few scholars have tried to define explicitly what the *core business* of the discipline should be. This has resulted in a situation in which two views are implicitly put forward. On the one hand, we find studies that insist that politics and economics are related, but remain two distinct empirical spheres. They imply that maximum possible integration is to analyze one sphere with tools from the other. On the other hand, we find studies claiming that politics and economics are part of the same empirical sphere, indeed the *political economy*. These argue that the subject should be approached as a whole. So far, the former studies have had the upper hand.

Mainstream IPE regards politics and economics as two related, but distinct, empirical domains. This position finds its best expression in the work of Robert Gilpin (1975; 1987) who conceives of economics as the domain of absolute gains, while he defines politics as the realm of relative gains. The former is the world of 'the way wealth is created'. The latter is the realm of power, which is always a relative matter: 'one actor's gain in power is by necessity another's loss' (Gilpin 1975: 34). In this view, politics and economics are related exactly because wealth creation is instrumental in power creation. Although it may thus be important to understand various dimensions of wealth creation, such as technology, transaction costs or consumer behavior, in the end it all serves the purpose of understanding power relations. In addition, authors in this tradition argue that, in the short and middle term, states should be the dominant actors in this perspective. The most important reason they put forward is that states set the conditions of economic behavior, not only within their territories but also, through conflict or cooperation, in the international economy. In the long term, however, changes in economic conditions may affect the power base of states and thus upset the power distribution between states (Gilpin 1975: 33–43; 1987: 8–24). In principle, this conception of international political economy allows for the analysis of the impact of economics on politics and vice versa, yet, in practice, it has led to an emphasis by IPE scholars on the short-term implications of economic processes for the power positions of states and the methods employed by states to keep control of the effects on their power position.

This is embodied in two streams of literature. On the one hand, we find those studies of international regimes and governance systems that argue that states are the most important actors within such forms of cooperation and that the extent of their cooperation can be explained by considerations of relative power. States will not agree to regimes, or refuse to implement them, if they judge that other states will gain, or have gained, more from such cooperation than them. Such studies, on the whole, stick to the state as a unitary utility-maximizing actor (see, especially, Grieco 1990; Krasner 1991). On the other hand, we find those studies that reject the unitary character of the state and take into consideration the impact of domestic institutions and actors on a state's behavior. Such institutions and actors include electoral systems, interest group politics and policy networks. Nevertheless, these studies too focus on explaining the behavior of states in the international economy. This is why Strange has argued that IPE no longer aims at the integrated analysis of political and economic phenomena. Rather, it has developed into the political analysis of international economic relations. In particular, IPE scholars narrow down their research to analyzing foreign economic policy. This has two consequences. First, they miss the impact of systemic variables, such as structural power, in the 'world political economy'. Second, they tend to follow the foreign economic policy agendas of governments (Strange 1995b: 164–5). In other words, they are prone to being 'problem-solving' rather than 'problem-posing'. Ironically, scholars who approach the interface between (international) politics and (international) economics *ontologically* as the 'Politics of International Economic Relations' increasingly adopt an *epistemology* that is borrowed from economics: rational choice. This causes a lot of confusion, and the wrath of Strange in her presidential address to the 1995 meeting of the International Studies Association (Strange 1995c). The two positions (a political ontology coupled with an economical epistemology) need not be Siamese twins, as will be argued in the next section.

The Need for an Integrated Perspective on Politics and Economics

Is there a need for an integrated perspective on politics and economics? Put differently, would it not be enough to concentrate on the *politics* of international economic relations only? Obviously, in the final analysis, everyone is free to formulate the research question he wants. If most IR scholars decide that those subjects that interest them most are the ways states hammer out trade bargains among themselves or how domestic pressure group politics affects such bargaining, then they should take on these questions, yet at least two reasons stand out for attempting to go beyond such a conception of the discipline. First of all, it would mean concentrating our efforts on short-term, maybe middle-term, developments only: the conclusion of regimes, their implementation, the impact of institutions on actors' preference formation, as well as on their compliance with international agreements, and so on. What we would miss, however, would be the long-term perspective. This long-term perspective was already present in Gilpin's original conception of the international political economy, when he correctly argued that long-term economic developments will affect the power base of states (Gilpin 1975: 37). At the time, he deducted from this observation that states would therefore seek to control long-term economic developments.[9] The last decade's debate on economic globalization suggests that such long-term control has become increasingly difficult. It therefore seems safe to conclude that the long-term interaction patterns of the political and economic realm should no longer be approached exclusively from the perspective of political dominance.

The second reason for leaving behind the current practice of the politics of international economic relations is the identification of politics with the state. Now we reach an important cleavage dividing the discipline, not just of IR or IPE, but rather of political science in general. Even though most scholars would probably agree that politics is about power, the majority of them would relate power to the state or government (and its institutions). Most political scientists – be they German, French, Dutch, British, American or otherwise – have been educated to analyze political behavior in the context of the state. Those IR scholars who practice the politics of international economic relations will therefore have a bias in analyzing phenomena that relate to the behavior of states or to domestic actors trying to affect the state. A conception of international political economy which wants to go beyond the politics of international economic behavior should therefore give up its bias towards locating power processes in the state (or inter-state interaction) (cf. Strange 1995d).

This need for a reconception of the empirical domain of the discipline has been widely recognized, and has even resulted in the founding of a journal explicitly aimed at such a reconception (*Review of International Political Economy*). Its founding editors sadly remark that few attempts have been made so far. Testable theories based on such reconceptions are even harder to find (Editorial 1994; Krasner 1994). Strange is one of the few scholars who, already in her early writings (Strange 1970), attempted to reconceive the discipline.[10] Strange included the long-term perspective in her conception. She also moved away from the bias towards the state.

To Strange, the long-term perspective is captured in her concept of structural power. Structural power ensures that some actors have the ability to set the rules of the game in the world political economy. The dominance of one or a few actors in organizing the production of welfare, financing it as well as defending it and having access to the most relevant knowledge, explains why things basically do not alter over a long period of time. Changes in these four dimensions of structural power will bring about alterations in this power to dictate the game. Strange also moved away from a bias towards the state. Well into the 1980s, she claimed that structural power continued to reside in one state, the United States (Strange 1987; 1988). In her later work, she argued that structural power had been fragmented. States in general, and the United States in particular, may have maintained structural power in the security, and possibly the knowledge, dimensions, they had certainly lost it in the production and finance dimensions. These new possessors of structural power are hard to individualize. Rather, structural power is now concentrated in the hands of many actors, especially multinational corporations (especially large accountancy and insurance firms), the financial markets and transnational criminal organizations (Strange 1996).

This description of structural changes is founded on a wholly different conception of politics and, in consequence, the relation between politics and economics. Following Harold Lasswell (1950), Strange holds that politics is about the distribution of power, about 'who gets what, when, how?' By implication, the study of politics, or international relations for that matter, is not about what states do, but rather about who affects the distribution of wealth, justice, security and freedom (Strange 1988). Any actor, be they the Sicilian Mafia, or the United States government, can affect that distribution. At the same time, however, she urges us not to forget that such distribution is strongly influenced by the way structural power conditions the game and its possible outcomes.

Strange's contribution to a new international political economy does not only lie in her long-term concept of structural power and refusal to focus instantly on the state. As important is her claim that the four dimensions of structural power are always part of any international phenomenon that we may want to explain, as well as her claim that no *a priori* hierarchy exists between these four dimensions (ibid.). The idea that structural power is an integrated whole based on the four dimensions of security, production, finance and knowledge is Strange's solution to integrating the spheres of (inter)national politics and (inter)national economics. This requires each student of international political economy to systematically assess how a specific combination of these four dimensions structures the interactions that eventually determine the specific distribution of fundamental values in a given issue area.

At the same time, she leaves an important puzzle unresolved. Even though no *a priori* reason may exist to assume a hierarchy between the four dimensions of structural power, it may well be that such a hierarchy characterizes the real world. Strange suggests as much in her own empirical work. She clearly considers processes in the knowledge structure to be the cause of fundamental transformations in the other dimensions of structural power. Technological changes, combined with shifts in the belief systems of policy makers, producers and consumers, clearly alter the balance in the security, production and finance dimensions. Over the last 20 years, technological innovations in communication (satellites, fax and the internet) and transport (roll-on–roll-off ships, containers) have lowered transactions and contributed thus to the development of what we now call economic and financial globalization. At the same time, they affected the security dimension of structural power. Fast communication and new transport logistics affected the existing balance of power in security relations (Strange 1996; 1998a). At the same time, Strange's work also gives ammunition to those realists who would claim that the distinction between high politics and low politics is still relevant today. For one thing, many technological changes, such as the internet, have been the product of the arms race in the security dimension. In addition, they would say, Strange herself shows how shifts in who possesses power in the finance structure in the 1980s and 1990s have been dependent on shifts in security relations. She argues that the increased weight of German finance (and the still relatively minor weight of Japanese finance) can be explained by the context of the security dimension: the United States lost structural power to Germany because Germany needed the United States less for its security after the end of the cold war. Japan, however, is still dependent on the United States for its security, and therefore the United States has maintained its grip on Japanese finance (Strange, 1998a: esp. 60–77).

On the one hand, we could relax and say that this illustrates precisely the interrelationship between the various dimensions of structural power. On the other hand, however, we should be alarmed. Empirical research will have to show the precise nature of dependencies among these four dimensions. It would be unfortunate if the important concept of structural power were to fade away into history, just as complex interdependence did in the 1970s. Complex interdependence also meant the development of a new concept of power, yet it was never followed up by research aimed at investigating these so-called 'asymmetrical relationships'. Rather, complex interdependence developed into a pluralist notion in which everything seemed related to everything else (Keohane and Nye 1977; 1987; Verbeek 1993). The concept of structural power risks a similar fate if it is invoked obliquely. Even Strange has not always been clear in her empirical analyses of relational power (1988; 1996) on how relational power relations were nested exactly in structural power conditions.[11]

Now we get to the crux of the matter. Accepting the possibility that, next to the hierarchy between structural and relational power, further hierarchies may exist within the relationship between the four dimensions of structural power implies that we need to develop Strange's conception of international relations (her ontology) into testable theories. The problem here, however, is twofold: first, Strange herself did not contribute extensively to theory development on the basis of her ontology; second, she rejected much existing theorizing because she identified it with an ontology she rejected (the politics of international economic relations) and with an epistemology she rejected (economics-borrowed rational choice). How can this be put right?

The adoption of ontology that has as its point of departure an integrated perspective on international political economy does not preclude any epistemological position at all.[12] It does imply that politics is about the how and what of the distribution of material and immaterial goods and that the relevance of state actors is, in the end, an empirical question. Within that context, it is up to the researcher to decide which variables at which levels of analysis he needs to include in his research. If he wants to stick to the neorealist research program, he is perfectly happy to investigate the extent to which the security structure affects outcomes in the world political economy. If he wants to examine a country's trade policies, he is perfectly happy to adopt either a discourse analysis or a rational choice approach to the position of the various actors, as long as the research design is geared towards *explaining* trade policies (rather than describing many possible policy positions without accounting for the victory of one over another). There is no need for constructivists to be afraid of a rational choice approach. The advantage of the thought experiment of reasoning *as if* actors behave rationally is that it promotes the formulation of relatively simple, but clearly testable, propositions. These tests can next lead us to what cannot be explained by these simple propositions. These lacunae can then be filled by insights provided with tools from constructivists. That is precisely why students of rational choice need not be afraid of constructivists either. They may help them in explaining the contents of policies, because constructivists know a lot about preference formation. They may help them in explaining why actors do not always behave in the way the 'as if' assumption of rationality would have predicted. They may help them in explaining why some actors are norm- rather than interest-driven. Strange was wrong to be critical of theorists. Her perspective on international relations badly needs them, if sound links are to be established between her grand vision and her empirical observations.

Conclusions

The main conclusion of this chapter must be that it is wrong and useless to ponder much over an American/non-American cleavage in the discipline of International Relations. The discussion about such a cleavage too easily identifies North American academic research with rationalism (rational choice) and non-American academic research with constructivism. This twist to the debate offers a smokescreen that obscures the real issue at stake. The question should not be rationalist or constructivist, but rather what is the empirical domain of our discipline today. It has been argued above that the dominant view, the politics of international economic relations, ignores long-term developments and has a tendency to focus on state behavior. An integrated perspective is needed, which combines rather than isolates the political and economical sphere. Susan Strange has been one of few IR scholars who have constructed such an integrated perspective, yet her approach still requires us to think through and apply its theoretical and methodological consequences. This chapter argues that this requires a pragmatic approach to the way research should be conducted, which recognizes that rationalist and constructivist positions are often complementary rather than mutually exclusive.

Notes

1   I would like to thank Markus Haverland, Mirjam Kars, Robin Kells, Robert H. Lieshout, Anna van der Vleuten, Femke van Esch, Amy Verdun and Anton Weenink for their critical suggestions.
2   Strange is not unique in developing a notion of structural power. An example is Stephen Krasner's concept of *meta-power* (Krasner 1985).
3   Strange talks of four 'structures' of structural power. This may lead to

confusion (cf. Cox 1996). Therefore the term 'dimension of structural power' is preferred here.

4   The notion of control over beliefs and perceptions has long been a subject of discussion in political science, for instance in Steven Lukes's concept of 'the third face of power' (Lukes 1974) and Robert Cox's idea of ideological power (Cox 1987). Cf. Strange (1996: 23–5).

5   For a more optimistic assessment of the current state of international regime theory, see Hansenclever *et al.* (1996).

6   This reproach, of course, rings a familiar bell to those who participated in the debate raging in the 1960s and 1970s regarding the implicit values realism was alleged to espouse: a Western perspective on international affairs; change-averse, as the status quo was the best possible world; ignorant of issues of distributing wealth; the possibility of sacrificing the interests of small states, even their territorial integrity, for the sake of international order, that is the order reflecting the interests of the dominant state and so on (cf. Vasquez 1983).

7   Cf. the discussion in the history of political philosophy on whether a philosopher's text only conveys the meaning which can be understood from the plain text or reflects the political interests of the author and the events during which it was written (Skinner 1978).

8   Mearsheimer (1994) is one such author. One could find them as well among theorists of cycles of hegemonic leadership.

9   Of course, Gilpin later elaborated on the long term perspective in his study of cycles of hegemonic leadership (Gilpin 1981).

10   Robert Cox (esp. 1987) is another example of such a scholar.

11   In my view, this can be explained by Strange's lack of clarity surrounding the question whether structural power is just another, yet qualitatively different, source of power for actors or whether structural power is a systemic property, constraining and enabling actors. If the latter is the case, Strange may, ironically enough, be quite close to structural realism.

12   Possibly, it precludes the position of those postmodern critical constructivists who come close to claiming that intersubjectivity does not exist.

References

Allison, Graham T. (1971), *Essence of Decision. Explaining the Cuban Missile Crisis*, Boston, MA: Little, Brown.

Bendor, Jonathan and Thomas H. Hammond (1992), 'Rethinking Allison's Models', *American Political Science Review*, 86(2), 301–22.

Biersteker, Thomas J. (1993), 'Evolving Perspectives on International Political Economy: Twentieth-Century Contexts and Discontinuities', *International Political Science Review*, 14(1), 7–33.

Bueno de Mesquita, Bruce and David Lalman (1992), *War and Reason: Domestic and International Imperatives*, New Haven, CT: Yale University Press.

Coser, Lewis (1956), *The Functions of Social Conflict*, New York: The Free Press.

Cox, Robert (1981), 'Social Forces, States, and World Orders: Beyond International Relations Theory', *Millennium. Journal of International Issues*, 10(2), 126–55.

Cox, Robert (1987), *Production, Power, and World Order*, New York: Columbia University Press.

Cox, Robert (1996), '"Take Six Eggs": Theory, Finance and the Real Economy in the Work of Susan Strange', in Robert Cox, with Timothy J. Sinclair (eds), *Approaches to World Order*, Cambridge: Cambridge University Press, pp.174–88.

Dahl, Robert A. (1976), *Modern Political Analysis*, Englewood Cliffs, NJ: Prentice-Hall.

Editorial (1994), 'Forum for Heterodox International Political Economy', *Review of International Political Economy*, 1(1), 1–12.

George, Alexander L. (1969), 'The "Operational Code": A Neglected Approach to the Study of Political Leaders and Decision-Making', *International Studies Quarterly*, 13(2), 190–222.

Gilpin, Robert (1975), *U.S. Power and the Multinational Corporation. The Political Economy of Foreign Direct Investment*, New York: Basic Books.

Gilpin, Robert (1981), *War and Change in World Politics*, Cambridge: Cambridge University Press.

Gilpin, Robert, with the assistance of Jean M. Gilpin (1987), *The Political Economy of International Relations*, Princeton, NJ: Princeton University Press.

Goldstein, Judith and Robert O. Keohane (eds) (1993), *Ideas and Foreign Policy: Beliefs, Institutions, and Political Change*, Ithaca, NY: Cornell University Press.

Grieco, Joseph M. (1990), *Cooperation among Nations. Europe, America, and Non-Tariff Barriers to Trade*, Ithaca, NY: Cornell University Press.

Haas, Peter M. (1989), 'Do Regimes Matter? Epistemic Communities and Mediterranean Pollution Control', *International Organization*, 43(3), 377–403.

Hansenclever, Andreas, Peter Mayer and Volker Rittberger (1996), 'Interests, Power, Knowledge: The Study of International Regimes', *Mershon International Studies Review*, 40, Supplement 2, 177–228.

Hodgson, Geoffrey M. (1994), 'Some Remarks on "Economic Imperialism" and International Political Economy', *Review of International Political Economy*, 1(1), 21–8.

Hollis, Martin and Steve Smith (1991), *Explaining and Understanding International Relations*, Oxford: Clarendon.

Jervis, Robert (1976), *Perception and Misperception in International Politics*, Princeton, NJ: Princeton University Press.

Katzenstein, Peter J., Robert O. Keohane and Stephen D. Krasner (1998), 'International Organization and the Study of World Politics', *International Organization*, 52(4), 645–85.

Keohane, Robert O. (1995), 'The Analysis of International Regimes: Towards a European–American Research Programme', in Volker Rittberger, with the assistance of Peter Mayer (eds), *Regime Theory and International Relations*, Oxford: Clarendon, pp.23–45.

Keohane, Robert O. and Joseph S. Nye, Jr. (1977), *Power and Interdependence. World Politics in Transition*, Boston, MA: Little, Brown.

Keohane, Robert O. and Joseph S. Nye, Jr. (1987), '*Power and Interdependence* Revisited', *International Organization*, 41(4), 725–53.

Krasner, Stephen D. (1985), *Structural Conflict. The Third World against Global Liberalism*, Berkeley: University of California Press.

Krasner, Stephen D. (1991), 'Global Communications and Nation Power: Life on the Pareto Frontier', *World Politics*, 49(3), 336–66.

Krasner, Stephen D. (1994), 'International Political Economy: Abiding Discord', *Review of International Political Economy*, 1(1), 13–19.

Krause, Keith and Michael C. Williams (eds) (1997), *Critical Security Studies. Concepts and Cases*, London: UCL Press.

Lasswell, Harold D. (1950), *Politics: Who Gets What, When, How?*, New York: P. Smith.

Lukes, Steven (1974), *Power: A Radical View*, London: Macmillan.

Mearsheimer, John J. (1994), 'The False Promise of International Institutions', *International Security*, 15(1), 5–56.

Nicholson, Michael (1998), 'A Rational Choice Analysis of International Organizations: How UNEP helped to bring about the Mediterranean Action Plan', in Bob Reinalda and Bertjan Verbeek (eds), *Autonomous Policy Making by International Organizations*, London: Routledge, pp.79–90.

Pauly, Louis and Simon Reich (1997), 'National Structures and Multinational Corporate behavior: Enduring Differences in the Age of Globalization', *International Organization*, 51(1), 1–30.

Reinalda, Bob and Bertjan Verbeek (2000), 'A Theory of NGO influence', in Bas Arts and Bob Reinalda (eds), *NGOs and World Politics*, Nijmegen: Nijmegen University Press.

Rittberger, Volker (1990), *International Regimes in East–West Relations*, London: Pinter Publishers.

Rittberger, Volker (1995), 'Research on International Regimes in Germany: The Adaptive Internalization of an American Social Science Concept', in Volker Rittberger, with the assistance of Peter Mayer (eds), *Regime Theory and International Relations*, Oxford: Clarendon, pp.3–22.

Rosati, Jerel A. (1995), 'A Cognitive Approach to the Study of Foreign Policy', in Laura Neack, Patrick J. Haney and Jeanne A. Hey (eds), *Foreign Policy Analysis. Continuity and Change in Its Second Generation*, Englewood Cliffs, NJ: Prentice-Hall, pp.49–70.

Skinner, Quentin (1978), *The Foundations of Modern Political Thought. Volume I*, Cambridge: Cambridge University Press.

Strange, Susan (1970), 'International Economics and International Relations. A Case of Mutual Neglect', *International Affairs*, 46(2), 304–15.

Strange, Susan (1987), 'The Persistent Myth of Lost Hegemony', *International Organization*, 41(4), 551–74.

Strange, Susan (1988), *States and Markets. An Introduction to International Political Economy*, London: Pinter Publishers.

Strange, Susan (1995a), 'The Defective State', *Daedalus*, 24(2), 55–74.

Strange, Susan (1995b), 'Political Economy and International Relations', in Ken Booth and Steve Smith (eds), *International Relations Theory Today*, University Park: Pennsylvania State University Press, pp.154–74.

Strange, Susan (1995c), 'ISA as a Microcosm', *International Studies Quarterly*, 39(3), 289–95.

Strange, Susan (1995d), 'The Limits of Politics', *Government and Opposition*, 30(3), 291–311.

Strange, Susan (1996), *The Retreat of the State. The Diffusion of Power in the World Economy*, Cambridge: Cambridge University Press.

Strange, Susan (1998a), *Mad Money*, Manchester: Manchester University Press.

Strange, Susan (1998b), 'Why do International Organizations Never Die?', in Bob Reinalda and Bertjan Verbeek (eds), *Autonomous Policy Making by International Organizations*, London: Routledge, pp.213–20.

Vasquez, John A. (1983), *The Power of Power Politics: A Critique*, New Brunswick, NJ: Rutgers University Press.

Verbeek, Bertjan (1993), 'Beyond the Challenge of Neorealism. An Agenda for International Political Economy', in Roger Morgan, Jochen Lorentzen, Anna Leander and Stefano Guzzini (eds), *New Diplomacy in the Post Cold-War World*, London: Macmillan, pp.90–97.

Waever, Ole (1998), 'The Sociology of a Not So International Discipline: American and European Developments in International Relations', *International Organization*, 52(4), 687–727.

Welch, David A. (1998), 'A Positive Science of Bureaucratic Politics?', in Eric Stern and Bertjan Verbeek (eds), 'Whither the Study of Governmental Politics in Foreign Policymaking? A Symposium', *Mershon International Studies Review*, 42, Supplement 2, 210–16.

Weldes, Jutta (1998), 'Bureaucratic Politics: A Critical Constructivist Assessment', in Eric Stern and Bertjan Verbeek (eds), *Mershon International Studies Review*, 42, 216–25.

Wendt, Alexander (1992), 'Anarchy is What States make of It. The Social Construction of Power Politics', *International Organization*, 46, 391–425.

Wu, Samuel S.G. and Bruce Bueno de Mesquita (1994), 'Assessing the Dispute in the South China Sea: A Model of China's Security Decision Making', *International Studies Quarterly*, 38(3), 379–403.

Young, Oran (1994), *International Governance. Protecting the Environment in a Stateless Society*, Ithaca, NY: Cornell University Press.

9 Theorizing the 'No-Man's-Land' Between Politics and Economics

A. CLAIRE CUTLER

Introduction

It seems entirely appropriate to say at the very onset that this chapter is inspired by a puzzle. The puzzle stems from a sense of *déjà vu* experienced when perusing recent international political economy literature in search of inspiration for this analysis of Susan Strange and critical theory. Inspiration was found in a special issue of *New Political Economy*, where the guest editors wrote of a 'renaissance' in the field of international political economy that they associate more generally with 'the proliferation and global diffusion of ideas of, and about, globalisation and the centrality to such ideas of claims about the international or global political economy' (Hay and Marsh 1999: 5). Of course, and here begins the puzzle, the special issue is entitled *Putting the 'P' Back into IPE*. The editors explain that by putting the 'P' back into IPE they do not mean that politics has been absent from IPE. Rather, they suggest the need for a 'new political economy' that reformulates what 'the political' means. This requires moving away from neorealist, statist, economistic and deterministic formulations and extending the parameters of what is regarded as political activity, including for example the activities of multinational corporations, nongovernmental organizations and global social movements. Their goal is not simply greater analytical and theoretical clarity, although these are most certainly some of the consequences of this 'new political economy'. Rather, the ultimate goal is a very practical one, albeit with profound normative implications. The goal is to undermine and to displace the overwhelming sense of the inevitability of globalization. 'The real challenge for new international political economists, and the real need for a new international political economy, is to expose and demystify this seemingly inexorable logic [of globalization] and to restore again the capacity to think that things might be different' (ibid.: 19). To this end, the contributors invite readers to challenge the adequacy of purely economic analysis of globalization (Higgott 1999) and the orthodoxy of separations between economics and politics (Burnham 1999) and domestic and international politics (Cerny 1999).

Now, to continue with the puzzle, Strange, who has been described as 'a great international relations theorist' (Palan 1999: 121) and who, in a 'path-breaking initiative', (Brown 1999: 532) 'was almost single-handedly responsible for creating "international political economy" and turning it into one of the two or three central fields within international studies in Britain' (ibid., 1999: 531), spent much of her academic career writing about both the 'P' and the 'E' in IPE. Indeed, in articles written 30 years ago, she wrote of the absence of 'a substantial literature on the theory of international political economy' and the need to fill the 'gap' between international relations and international economics (Strange 1970: 309). This gap was caused by the acceleration of the international economic system and its outdistancing and outgrowing the international system of states. She argued that states simply could not keep up with the 'disturbance effects' of international economics on domestic employment, prices, interest rates or monetary reserves. Nor could they attend properly to the 'hindrance effects' when the effectiveness of national policy instruments are undermined by contradictory international economic developments. Finally, states, she argued, were facing new types of international conflicts stemming from increasing inter-state competition and the resulting coincidental damage to the international economic interests of other states. Moreover, the gap between economics and politics extended to their study and to the deepening of analytical distinctions between the study of international economics and the study of international politics (ibid.: 307).

Strange called for a 'radical desegregation' and dismantling of artificial disciplinary barriers separating international economics, politics and law: 'These barriers need to be overthrown, broken up, and done away with' (Strange 1972: 63). Indeed, 'the idea of "economic relations" as a discrete, discernible, and definable sphere of human activity – and therefore as a separable segment of international studies – is an absurdity' and a form of academic apartheid (ibid.: 65). She continued, in strikingly contemporary terms, to describe the impossibility of the concept of purely 'economic relations' by illustrating the embeddedness of economic activity in social, political and legal frameworks:

An 'economic activity' may be held to embrace consuming; producing or processing; buying or selling; broking; and borrowing or lending ...

each of these activities brings at least two parties into an economic relationship. But it is seldom if ever a *purely* economic relationship. ... Every economic activity only exists in a social framework of law and custom, in a particular political order and in a particular social structure... It is even more true of the economic relations between states. States are never complete strangers to one another, linked only by an economic bargain, as individuals may sometimes be (if rarely) ... behind each economic bargain struck with another state there lies a complex web of historical association, political and strategic conflict or co-operation, and social and cultural sympathy or antipathy. No practicing policy-maker would ever pretend for a moment that this web had no influence on the pattern and development of international economic relations. (ibid.: 65–6)

Now for the puzzle. How is it that 30 years later the now well-established field of International Political Economy can be claiming a theoretical, analytical and practical renaissance that involves repoliticizing IPE, challenging disciplinary, analytical and theoretical distinctions between economics and politics, between domestic and international relations and between other separations that, due to reasons of space are not mentioned at length here (like the public and private spheres)? One way of responding to this puzzle is to say that students of IPE have not learned very much in the past 30 years, notwithstanding Strange's exhortations. However, this response, while amusing, is banal and obscures deeper ideological and professional obstacles that are at work in shaping the self-images of the discipline of international relations (Steve Smith 1995; Kahler 1997). This chapter contends that the key to the puzzle lies not only in resolving the analytical, theoretical and practical challenges posed three decades ago by Strange and rearticulated today by proponents of new political economy; it also requires facing the more profound normative challenge embedded in the new political economy. Once one acknowledges the capacity for human agency to change the world, it becomes incumbent on one to consider how to do so. A review of Strange's work as a critical thinker suggests that the puzzle is best framed in the form of a paradox. However, before framing the paradox it will be helpful to consider the nature and role of critical theory for, as will become apparent, this paradox lies at the heart of her contribution as a critical thinker.

Critical Theory in International Relations

We might begin with the now familiar distinction Robert Cox makes between critical theory and problem-solving theory.[1] Problem-solving theory 'takes the world as it finds it, with the prevailing social and power relationships and the institutions into which they are organized, as the given framework for action' (Cox 1981: 88). It is instrumental in its goal of improving the workings of institutions, but does not call into question the patterns or purposes of these institutions and relations. In contrast, critical theory 'stands apart from the prevailing order of the world and asks how that order came about' (ibid.). Unlike problem-solving theory, critical theory 'does not take institutions and social power relations for granted but calls them into question by concerning itself with their origins and how and whether they might be in the process of changing. It is directed toward an appraisal of the very framework for action, or problematic, which problem-solving theory accepts as its parameters' (ibid.). There are several dimensions of critical theory that differentiate it from problem-solving theory. The first is its inherent normativity in the sense of its concern with ethics and morality in international relations. While normative international relation theory encompasses 'that body of work which addresses the moral dimensions of international relations and the wider questions of meaning and interpretation generated by the discipline' (Brown 1992: 3), it also encompasses theories designed to promote social, political and economic change. As Cox notes, 'Theory is always *for* someone and *for* some purpose. All theories have a perspective. Perspectives derive from a position in time and space' (Cox 1981: 87). All theories either explicitly or implicitly embrace values and promote purposes and interests and the goal of critical theory is to lay these bare in order to 'allow for a normative choice in favor of a social and political order different from the prevailing order' (ibid.: 90; see also Hazel Smith 1996). Thus, related to the normativity of critical theory is its transformative and emancipatory potential. Critical theory assists in identifying alternatives to the existing world order that promote the values and goals of human emancipation. Mark Neufeld associates emancipatory theory with the assistance of 'those poorly served by present social and political arrangements, through which the disadvantaged can empower themselves to effect radical social change' (Neufeld 1995: 20).[2] Andrew Linklater frames critical theory in terms of 'theory committed to the reduction or eradication of constraints on human autonomy' (Linklater 1986: 308).[3]

In addition to its normative and emancipatory dimensions, critical theory is characterized by its historicity. 'Critical theory is theory of history in the sense of being concerned not just with the past but with a continuing process of historical change. Problem-solving theory is nonhistorical or ahistorical, since it, in effect, posits a continuing present (the permanence of the institutions and power relations which constitute its parameters)' (Cox 1981: 89). Thus Cox argues that neorealism, his prototype for problem-solving theory, is not historical theory even when engaged in historical analysis. This is because it uses history to illustrate the continuity of structural anarchy as the defining characteristic of politics. Neorealism uses history as 'a quarry providing materials with which to illustrate variations on always recurrent themes. The mode of thought ceases to be historical even though the materials used are derived from history. Moreover this mode of reasoning dictates that, with respect to essentials, the future will always be like the past' (ibid.: 92).[4] In contrast, critical theory 'does not envisage any general or universally valid laws which can be explained by the development of appropriate, generally applicable theories… One cannot … speak of "laws" in any generally valid sense transcending historical eras, nor of structures as outside of or prior to history' (Cox 1985: 53).

Moreover, the stuff of history for critical theory is both material and non-material. It is found in the structures that constitute our productive or material and institutional worlds, as well as our non-material or ideational worlds. The 'framework for action' for critical theory is constituted by certain combinations of ideational and material conditions and institutions which take the form of specific historic structures or blocs (Cox 1981: 97). We may thus study human history in terms of the emergence and decline of historic blocs comprising historically specific material, institutional and ideational forces.[5]

For Cox, historical materialism is a 'foremost source of critical theory' (ibid.: 95), an integral element of which is its focus on historical change as a dialectical process. The dialectic operates as a system of logic, meaning the search for truth through the exploration of contradictions. It also operates historically, in that the 'dialectic is the potential for alternative forms of development arising from the confrontation of opposed social forces in any concrete historical situation' (ibid.). Significantly, it is the dialectic that opens up the potential for transformation in the human condition, thus completing the link between historical materialism and emancipation.[6]

Today many students of historical materialism and critical theory are centrally concerned with identifying potential sources of transformation in international relations. As mentioned above, new political economy takes as its point of departure the pressing need to challenge the apparent inexorable process of the globalization of what Stephen Gill refers to as 'neoliberal discipline' and 'market civilization' (Gill 1995a). Gill identifies a 'new constitutionalism' in the 'locking-in' of market policies through the use of legal and juridical forms and processes that entrench neoliberalism as the global constitutional norm (Gill 1998).[7] He is concerned first and foremost with the way in which the new constitutionalism is affecting a restructuring of the global political economy by insulating dominant economic forces, such as leading economic states and transnational business enterprises, from public accountability and democratic rule (ibid.: 23).[8] Globalized productive and financial relations are eroding the foundations of democracy and further marginalizing the underprivileged, underemployed and unemployed, and the weaker elements of society. The expansion of private processes of adjudication and dispute resolution are reinscribing elitist forms of authority and rule, contributing to the erosion of democratic institutions and deepening the disjuncture between local and transnational economic and social forces (Cutler 2000a; 2000b; 1995).

These processes are strengthening and deepening the hold of private corporate power over both global and national political economies by expanding the authority of private systems of governance and regulation (see Cutler *et al.* 1999). Moreover, the adherence to distinctions between economics and politics, and between national and transnational/global political economies, obscures these processes by removing what are conventionally regarded as 'economic matters' from the sphere of 'politics'. All the while, there is a growing sense of inevitability, coupled in some cases with feelings of impotence and panic stemming from a recognition that we are, indeed, being increasingly 'locked-in'. Many people are looking for sources of human intervention and opposition and are raising the vexing problem of the capacity of human agency to engage in emancipatory and transformative politics (Gill 1995b; Rupert 1997; Rupert and Smith 2000; Strange 1994b; Giddens 1994; Chin and Mittelman 1997).

Strange was acutely aware of the practical challenges posed by the acceleration of economic activity and technological advance and the increasing inability of states to manage global disturbances and effects. Although she regarded the term 'globalization' to be 'loose and woolly', she argued that certain aspects of globalization can be documented and studied with a view to determining how globalization might be stopped (Strange 1998a: 704). These aspects include the globalization of markets and production that produce governance problems for states, the transnationalization and loss of national control over the identity and operations of multinational corporations, and a shift in the balance of power, away from governments and labor, toward capital. Strange finds evidence of all three, notwithstanding the contrary views of many critics of the globalization thesis. She summarizes the political consequences of globalization as 'the shift in power from states to markets; the increased asymmetries of state power; and the gap in government' (Strange 1995b: 296). Moreover, she finds the first consequence to be most significant as a political economist because 'if true, it suggests a much wider definition of politics and a larger concept of what should be researched and studied by those interested in politics than is conventionally perceived' (ibid.: 296–7). However, she has little faith in the abilities of the present structures of 'global governance' to avert or manage the loss of state control and authority, which threatens to undermine democratic controls on executives and regulatory controls on business interests (Strange 1996: 198). Neither international organizations nor international regimes are able to provide effective governance (Strange 1996; 1983). However, for a time it appeared that she continued to have faith in the ability of states, especially powerful ones like the United States, to govern effectively, but their failure to do so eluded her (see Strange 1988: 242–3; Cox 1992). She later even lost faith in the governance abilities of states, observing that there is 'no opposition' capable of rendering state and proliferating non-state authorities accountable (Strange 1996: 198). As a result she concluded that the Westphalian system of rule 'has been an abject failure' (Strange 1999: 345.) The Westphalian system or, as she refers to it with her characteristic humor, the 'Westfailure system', is premised upon the attribution of sole political authority and the monopoly of the legitimate use of violence to territorially defined states (Strange 1999). The failure of the state system is threefold: it is failing nature in its inability to avert environmental damage that threatens survival of all that is living; it is failing capitalism in its inability to regulate financial markets and institutions; and it is failing world society by allowing the development of a growing gap between a transnational capitalist class and the 'have-nots' in the world. These are strong denunciations of the Westphalian model of rule and are more characteristic of critical approaches to IPE than of the dominant neorealist approaches, suggesting that her work is most appropriately considered within a critical stream.[9] However, as we turn to consider her contribution as a critical thinker or theorist, it will become apparent that at least part of the reason why she was unable to explain failures in state governance was that she never fully accepted her own advice to develop an integrated understanding of international politics and economics. Indeed, it will be argued that, paradoxically, Strange reproduced the separation between economics and politics in her analysis of the global political economy. As a consequence, she remained in the 'no-man's land' (Strange 1996: 67) between economics and politics where she was either unable or unwilling to take the steps involved in developing a critical understanding of human agency and of transformative and emancipatory politics.

Strange as a Critical Thinker or a Critical Theorist?

We must begin by first acknowledging the difficulty of treating Strange as a political theorist, given her disinclination towards pure theory divorced from empirical research and her reluctance to consider herself as a 'theorist' (see Brown 1999: 532; Strange 1998; Palan 1999: 122). She considered herself very much an empiricist, eclectic in both her disciplinary inspirations and her theoretical inclinations (Strange 1991; and see Palan 1999). However, recognizing the difficulty of categorizing her work in any definitive way, we might consider the extent to which she shares any common ground with critical theory, as above conceived.

To begin, critical theory was differentiated from problem-solving theory, the former being transformative and emancipatory in purpose. Strange was clearly a problem solver, but she was more. She was very much concerned with understanding outcomes and finding solutions to problems plaguing the global political economy. However, she did so with very little deference to conventional wisdom in the field, pushing beyond analytical, theoretical and disciplinary boundaries. The practical policy implications of her analysis of monetary relations came across clearly in two of her earlier works, *Sterling and British Policy* (1971) and *International Monetary Relations* (1976), as too did the view that economists had little relevant understanding of the subject given their narrow disciplinary and methodological orientations (see also Chapters 5, 6 and 7 in the present volume). The conviction that the conventional approaches to IPE, whether either narrowly economistic or narrow in their definition of politics, were incapable of providing useful understanding of global economic processes and problems was a central theme in her work right to the end. She recently noted that the 'questions should always begin by asking: "By what political and economic processes, and thanks to what political and economic structures, did this outcome come about?" After causes come consequences: Who benefitted? Who paid? Who carried the risks? Who enjoyed new opportunities?' (Strange 1995a: 172). However, she argued that the focus of enquiry should not be exclusively state-centered, but involves an extension to the limits of politics and a broadening of the concept of power

> so that it includes structural as well as relational power, the power to influence the ideas of others, their access to credit, their prospects of security, their chances of a better material life as consumers. These two changes mean that when we look for causes, we shall look beyond states to markets and market operators, and to non-state authorities over them. And when we look at consequences again, we shall look beyond states to associations of people other than 'nations': to classes, generations, genders, even species. (Ibid.)

The alternative focus on markets had taken shape in several works, including *The International Politics of Surplus Capacity*, edited with

Roger Tooze (1981) and *States and Markets* (1988). The focus on non-state authority was to shift somewhat, most recently from markets to firms in *Rival States, Rival Firms,* with John Stopford (1991), *The Retreat of the State* (1996), *Casino Capitalism* (1997) and *Mad Money* (1998). Consistently, throughout these works Strange engages in problem solving, but with a difference. In rejecting what she referred to as the American PIER (Politics of International Economic Relations) approach,[10] which confines IPE to the study of the politics of economic relations of states and governments, she was keenly aware of the normative dimensions and implications. Broader definitions of 'power' and 'politics' required nothing less than 'going back to the beginning' and starting with 'moral philosophy' and fundamental values relating to the justice of outcomes or their consistency with autonomy and freedom of choice (Strange 1995a: 171; 1988: 19). However, there is some ambiguity in her recognition of the moral dimensions of her engagement. In *The Retreat of the State*, she recognizes 'a new absence of absolutes' and concludes that, in the present world of 'multiple' and 'diffuse' authority, 'our individual consciences are our only guide' (Strange 1996: 199). This is certainly no manifesto for transformative and emancipatory action.

While ambiguity over Strange's commitment to transformative and emancipatory politics limits our ability to regard her as a critical theorist, there certainly is a historicity to her work. It is evident in the detailed historical analysis of monetary relations and policy in her earliest works and continued to be evident in subsequent work. In *States and Markets*, she rejects the possibility of developing 'an all-embracing theory' (Strange 1988: 16) and that there is one 'correct' interpretation of history (ibid.: 18), but she tells us that we need history in order to understand causes in the global political economy. She notes that '[c]onsequences today – for states, for corporations, for individuals – imply causes yesterday. There is no way that contemporary international political economy can be understood without making some effort to dig back to its roots, to peer behind the curtain of passing time into what went before' (ibid.). In *The Retreat of the State*, she reiterates that 'history is a good guide' to understanding transformations in the world economy (Strange 1996: 193). However, her history is not that of historical materialism or dialectical processes of change, although she shares much with the work of Robert Cox and draws greatly upon his work, particularly in her latter years.[11] Like Cox she theorized the international political economy as comprising dominant structures. But where Cox identified production, knowledge and institutional structures, Strange identified four structures: including financial, production, knowledge and security structures (Cox 1981; Strange 1988). Moreover, she gave primacy, at least until late in her life, to financial structures.[12] As Cox comments, the ontology of world order presented in *States and Markets* distanced Strange from the Marxist emphasis on production and accumulation and related power in the world economy to the ability to create and have access to credit (Cox 1992: 175). Indeed, Strange regarded her formulation as separating her from Marxists and Cox (1988: 26). Thus her work focused throughout the years on money, finance and markets – the exchange foundations of capitalism.

While her vision of theory, the nature of her recourse to history and her ontology of international relations do not suggest a great affinity with critical theory, there is one remaining and very central way in which her work does engage critical theory. This relates to her efforts to redefine politics by integrating the disciplines of economics and politics. Like many Marxists or historical materialists, Strange rejected the separation between economics and politics (Wood 1981; Cox 1981: 86). Indeed, she made a lifelong quest of exposing the political foundations of economics and the economic foundations of politics. Her solution was to integrate the two disciplines. However, curiously and paradoxically, she never succeeded in doing so. This is because she missed the crucial insight provided by historical materialism that the spheres are not in fact functionally separate. Rather, their separation is theoretical and analytical: the separation is an artificial construct created by capitalism and liberal political economy to insulate the political aspects of economic distribution from societal and democratic controls. The work of Ellen Meiksins Wood has been drawn on before (Cutler, 1997; 1999) to make this point in other contexts, but it bears repeating:

> The differentiation of the economic and the political in capitalism is, more precisely, a differentiation of political functions themselves and their separate allocation to the private economic sphere of the state. This allocation reflects the separation of political functions immediately concerned with extraction and appropriation of surplus labor from those with a more general communal purpose ... the differentiation of the economic is in fact a differentiation within the political sphere. (Wood 1981: 82)[13]

Thus the solution does not lie in adding economics to politics and mixing, or vice versa. Rather, the solution lies in recognizing the embeddedness of both in material and non-material structures of power. The solution lies in recognizing the embeddedness of markets in social and productive relations involving states, non-state actors, labor and capital. The reason why the gap in the governance of money and financial markets eluded Strange was that she continued to reproduce markets as distinct from politics – as impersonal and disembodied entities – as distinct from states, non-state actors, governments and politics. The belief that 'the impersonal forces of world markets, integrated over the postwar period by private enterprise in finance, industry and trade more than by the cooperative decisions of governments, are now more powerful than the states to whom ultimate political authority over society and economy is supposed to belong' and that markets are the 'masters over the governments of states' (Strange 1996: 4) removes human agency from the picture and feeds directly into theories of the inevitable and inexorable nature of globalization. Belief in markets as impersonal entities neglects the crucial fact that markets are composed of people and business associations that are ultimately constituted by human beings. This tends to remove the human element from market relations: markets simply exist as powerful, depersonalized entities, whose links to structures of production, power and influence remain obscure. It also strengthens the neoliberal tendency to regard market forces as the most natural, neutral, efficient, consensual and just mechanisms for determining 'who gets what' on a global scale (Cutler 1995). As Peter Burnham notes, 'markets are fetishised as discrete, technical, economic arenas and the overwhelming tendency is to view them in terms of trade, finance and the application of new technology' (Burnham 1999: 38). As a result, labor markets are neglected and viewed as external to the politics of economic adjustment and restructuring. Burnham associates this tendency with liberal and realist analysis of IPE, as well as with critical theorists like Cox, who, he argues, 'separate social reality into rigid categories and look for external linkages between artificially disaggregated phenomena' (ibid.: 39). Ultimately, this view tends to 'fail to grasp the complex organic set of social relations which is the global economy' (ibid.: 40).[14]

The belief that states have lost authority to impersonal markets reproduces the very separation between economics and politics that Strange tried to displace and obscures the extent to which the present system is undergoing profound transformation. Notwithstanding the erosion of state authority, capitalism is stronger than ever and is now making possible the emergence of new forms and locations of authority (Cutler 1999; 2000a; 2000b). But the focus on the exchange foundations of capitalism to account for the erosion of state authority obscures the transformation in authority relations governing a 'new capitalism' based upon prior transnational productive relations. Strange recognized that productive structures are foundational, regarding them as the 'real' economy, while money and finance were the 'symbolic' economy (see Strange 1988; Cox 1992). However, the recognition of a distinction between the 'real' and the 'symbolic' was not internalized in her work. There is some indication in her latest works that she was beginning to put a face to the impersonal market. This was the face of production, the firm and the transnational corporation. But the focus on depersonalized market forces persisted.

The focus on firms took shape in *Rival States, Rival Firms*, but was more fully developed in *The Retreat of the State*. She increasingly focused on firms and later on transnational production and the growth of a global 'business civilization' (Strange 1994b). In one of her last pieces she developed a historical analysis of the contemporary global political economy that attempted to illustrate the symbiotic nature of the development of capitalism and of the state system (see Strange 1999). However, once again she characterized capitalism as an exchange system (in terms of the role states came to play in the creation and management of credit) and asked 'what is to be done?' about the contemporary failures of management. Unfortunately, her response only tentatively took up Cox's invitation to address the issue of transnational production and business (Cox 1992: 186). She alluded to the insights of sociologists who 'tend to think in terms of social classes and social movements' and appealed to the insights of those who find evidence of the existence of a 'transnational capitalist class' (Strange 1999: 352–3). Strange concluded with references to the works of Robert Cox and 'the reconstitution of civil societies and political authorities on a global scale building a system of global governance from the bottom up' (ibid.: 354).[15] However, the solution to the problem of global governance eluded her. The persistence of the distinction between economics and politics blocked the ability to personalize, denaturalize and demystify market relations and to conceptualize markets as rooted and embedded in prior and constitutive relations of production.

Conclusions

This review of the critical aspects of Strange's thought suggests that, while she was indeed a very critical thinker, she was not a critical theorist. Had she more time she might well have taken up the challenge of critical theory more directly, although it is doubtful that she would ever have styled herself as a 'critical theorist'. Notwithstanding her concern that theory be informed by practice and practice by theory, developing an understanding of the analytical, theoretical and ideological unity of economics and politics eluded her and was arrested by the very distincton she sought to displace. This is instructive for students of IPE, for it illustrates the durability of the dominant self-images of the discipline of international relations, which are crafted and, seemingly, endlessly reproduced through ideological, professional, political and disciplinary means (Smith 1995; Kahler 1997). The challenge remains one of understanding the ideological and political interests served by the dominant modes of theorizing and to displace them. Strange contributed immeasurably to understanding the political implications of the nexus between economics and politics. This is no mean achievement. It remains for the rest of us to displace this separation analytically, theoretically, ideologically and practically.

Notes

1   Cox (1981). For good introductions to critical theory in international relations, see Brown (1992: ch.8), Linklater (1990; 1992), and Halliday (1994).
2   Neufeld identifies three defining characteristics of emancipatory theory. The first is 'theoretical reflexivity' and an 'on-going process of "theoretical reflection on the process of theorizing itself"', the second involves accepting 'the constitutive and non-reductive power of human consciousness in dialectical interaction with the natural environment', the third is 'its engagement in social criticism in support of practical political activity oriented toward social transformation' (Neufeld 1995: 20).
3   See also Linklater (1986; 1990; 1992).
4   A perfect illustration of this tendency in neorealism may be found in a wonderful piece by Stephen Krasner (1993) that engages in detailed historical examination of the Peace of Westphalia only to conclude that not much has changed since then. (See also Krasner 1994; 1997.) Cox (1985: 53) makes this same criticism of the work of Kenneth Waltz which, 'despite his wide historical learning', 'is fundamentally unhistorical'.
5   For more on historic blocs, see Robert Cox (1987) and Stephen Gill (1993).
6   Hazel Smith shows that the relationship between historical materialism and emancipatory practice is considerably more complex than is suggested here. She observes that historical materialist theory and emancipatory practice are 'mutually constitutive'when viewed in the context of the methodology of historical materialism and the political purposes of Marxism (Smith 1996: 195).
7   See also Cutler on the entrenchment of neoliberal discipline through the globalization of private international legal norms and practices (Cutler 1995; 1997; 1999; 2000a; 2000b).
8   See also William Scheuerman (1999) for a good analysis of the problematic relationship between the global rule of law and democracy.
9   This is particularly evident in the rebuttal she wrote to Krasner's analysis of the continuing relevance of neorealism and the Westphalian system (Strange 1994a), discussed above in note 4, where Strange implored him to 'wake up' and recognize structural changes in the world that severely compromise neorealism's explanatory capabilities and shed doubt on the continuing relevance of Westphalian assumptions of rule. For more on critical approaches to the Westphalian system, see Cutler (2001).
10   She associated the PIER approach most closely with Robert Gilpin (1987) and Joan Spero (1990).
11   References to other historical sociologists, such as Michael Mann (1986), also appear in her work.
12   But see Chapter 10 by Roger Tooze in the present volume for an insightful analysis of the significance of the knowledge structure to her thinking.
13   See Cutler (1997; 1999).
14   See Cutler, (2000b) for a similar analysis of the way in which liberal and radical theorists utilize distinctions between economics and politics to depoliticize international economic law.

15   Strange here quotes Cox from Cox (ed.) (1997: 34).

References

Brown, Chris (1992), *International Relations Theory: New Normative Approaches*, New York: Columbia University Press.

Brown, Chris (1999), 'Susan Strange – a critical appreciation', *Review of International Studies*, **25**, 531–5.

Burnham, Peter (1999), 'The Politics of Economic Management in the 1990s', *New Political Economy*, 4(1), 37–54.

Cerny, Philip, G. (1999), 'Globalising the Political and Politicising the Global: Concluding Reflections on International Political Economy as a Vocation', *New Political Economy*, 4(1), 147–62.

Chin, Christine and James Mittelman (1997), 'Conceptualising Resistance to Globalisation', *New Political Economy*, 2(1), 23–37.

Cox, Robert (1981), 'Social forces, states and world orders: beyond international relations theory', reprinted in Robert W. Cox with Timothy J. Sinclair (1996), *Approaches to World Order*, Cambridge: Cambridge University Press, pp.85–123.

Cox, Robert (1985), 'Realism, positivism, and historicism', reprinted in R.W. Cox with T.J. Sinclair (1996), *Approaches to World Order*, Cambridge: Cambridge University Press, pp.49–59.

Cox, Robert (1987), *Production, Power and World Order; Social Forces in the Making of History*, New York: Columbia University Press.

Cox, Robert (1992), '"Take six eggs": theory, finance and the real economy in the work of Susan Strange', reprinted in R.W. Cox with T.J. Sinclair (1996), *Approaches to World Order*, Cambridge: Cambridge University Press, pp.174–88.

Cox Robert (ed.) (1997), *The New Realism: Perspectives on Multilateralism and World Order*, Basingstoke: Macmillan; New York: St. Martin's Press; Tokyo: United Nations Press.

Cutler, A. Claire (1995), 'Global Capitalism and Liberal Myths: Dispute Resolution in Private International Trade Relations', *Millennium; Journal of International Studies*, 24(1), 377–97.

Cutler, A. Claire (1997), 'Artifice, ideology and paradox: the public/private distinction in international law', *Review of International Political Economy*, 4(2), 261–85.

Cutler, A. Claire (1999), 'Locating Authority in the Global Political Economy', *International Studies Quarterly*, 43, 59–81.

Cutler, A. Claire (2000a), 'Globalization, Law and Transnational Corporations: The Deepening of Market Discipline', in Theodore Cohn, Stephen McBride and David Wiseman (eds), *Power in the Global Era*, London: Macmillan.

Cutler, A. Claire (2000b), 'Historical Materialism, Globalization and Law: Competing Conceptions of Property', in Mark Rupert and Hazel Smith (eds), *The Point is to Change the World; Socialism Through Globalization?*, London: Routledge.

Cutler, A. Claire (2001), 'Critical Reflections on Westphalian Assumptions of International Law and Organization: A Crisis of Legitimacy', *Review of International Studies*.

Cutler, A.C., Virginia Haufler and Tony Porter (eds) (1999), *Private Authority and International Affairs*, New York; SUNY Press.

Giddens, Anthony (1994), *Beyond Left and Right: The Future of Radical Politics*, Stanford: Stanford University Press.

Gill, Stephen (ed.) (1993), *Gramsci, Historical Materialism and International Relations*, Cambridge: Cambridge University Press.

Gill, Stephen (1995a), 'Globalisation, Market Civilisation and Disciplinary Neoliberalism', *Millennium; Journal of International Studies*, 24(1), 399–423.

Gill, Stephen (1995b), 'Theorizing the Interregnum: The Double Movement and Global Politics in the 1990s', in Björn Hettne (ed.), *International Political Economy: Understanding Global Disorder*, Halifax: Fernwood Publishing, pp.65–99.

Gill, Stephen (1998), 'New Constitutionalism, Democratisation and Global Political Economy', *Pacifica Review*, 10(1), February, 23–38.

Gilpin, Robert (1987), *The Political Economy of International Relations*, Princeton, NJ: Princeton University Press.

Halliday, Fred (1994), *Rethinking International Relations*, Vancouver: University of British Columbia Press.

Hay, Colin and David Marsh (1999), 'Introduction; Towards a New (International) Political Economy?', *New Political Economy*, 4(1), 5–22.

Higgott, Richard (1999), 'Economics, Politics and (International) Political Economy: The Need for a Balanced Diet in an Era of Globalisation', *New Political Economy*, 4(1), 23–36.

Kahler, Miles (1997), 'Inventing International Relations: International Relations Theory After 1945', in M.W. Doyle and G.J. Ikenberry (eds), *New Thinking in International Relations Theory*, Boulder, CO: Westview Press, pp.20–53.

Krasner, Stephen, D. (1993), 'Westphalia and All That', in Judith Goldstein and Robert O. Keohane (eds), *Ideas and Foreign Policy*, Ithaca: Cornell University Press, pp.235–64.

Krasner, Stephen, D. (1994), 'International political economy: abiding discord', *Review of International Political Economy*, 1(1), 13–20.

Krasner, Stephen, D. (1997), 'Pervasive Not Perverse: Semi-Sovereigns as the Global Norm', *Cornell International Law Journal*, 30(3), 651–80.

Linklater, Andrew (1986), 'Realism, Marxism and Critical Theory', *Review of international Studies*, 12(4), 301–12.

Linklater, Andrew (1990), *Beyond Realism and Marxism: Critical Theory and International Relations*, New York: St Martin's Press.

Linklater, Andrew (1992), 'The Question of the Next Stage in International Relations Theory; A Critical–Theoretical Point of View', *Millennium; Journal of International Studies*, 21(1), 77–98.

Mann, Michael (1986), *The Sources of Social Power Volume I: A History of Power from the Beginning to A.D. 1760*, Cambridge: Cambridge University Press.

Neufeld, Mark (1995), *The Restructuring of International Relations Theory*, Cambridge: Cambridge University Press.

Palan, Ronen (1999), 'Susan Strange 1923–1998: a great international relations theorist', *Review of International Political Economy*, 6(2), 121–32.

Rupert, Mark (1997), 'Globalisation and American Common Sense: Struggling to Make Sense of a Post-Hegemonic World', *New Political Economy*, 2(1), 105–16.

Rupert, Mark and Hazel Smith (eds) (2000), *The Point is to Change the World: Socialism Through Globalization?*, London: Routledge.

Scheuerman, William, E. (1999), 'Economic Globalization and the Rule of Law', *Constellations: An International Journal of Critical and Democratic Theory*, 6(1), 3–25.

Smith, Hazel (1996), 'The silence of the academics; international social theory, historical materialism and political values', *Review of International Studies*, 22, 191–212.

Smith, Steve (1995), 'The Self-Images of a Discipline: A Geneaology of International Relations Theory', in Ken Booth and Steve Smith (eds), *International Relations Theory Today*, University Park: Pennsylvania University Press.

Spero, Joan (1990), *The Politics of International Economic Relations*, 4th edn, New York: St. Martin's Press.

Stopford, John and Susan Strange (with John Henley) (1991), *Rival States, Rival*

Firms; Competition for World Market Shares, Cambridge: Cambridge University Press.

Strange, Susan (1970), 'International Economics and International Relations: A Case of Mutual Neglect', *International Affairs*, 46(2), 304–15.

Strange, Susan (1971), *Sterling and British Policy: A Political Study of an International Currency in Decline*, London and New York: Oxford University Press.

Strange, Susan (1972), 'International Economic Relations I: the Need for an Interdisciplinary Approach', in Roger Morgam (ed.), *The Study of International Affairs: Essays in Honour of Kenneth Young*, London: Royal Institute of International Affairs, Oxford University Press, pp.63–84.

Strange, Susan (1976), *International Monetary Relations*, in Andrew Shonfield (ed.), *International Economic Relations in the Western World 1959–71*, Volume 2, London and New York: Oxford University Press.

Strange, Susan (1983), '*Cave! Hic Dragones:* a critique of regime analysis', in Stephen D. Krasner (ed.), *International Regimes*, Ithaca; Cornell University Press, pp.337–54.

Strange, Susan (1988), *States and Markets*, 2nd edn, London and New York: Pinter Publishing.

Strange, Susan (1991), 'An Eclectic Approach', in Craig N. Murphy and Roger Tooze (eds), *The New International Political Economy*, Boulder, CO: Lynne Rienner, pp.33–49.

Strange, Susan (1994a), 'Wake up, Krasner! The world *has* changed', *Review of International Political Economy*, 1(2), 209–19.

Strange, Susan (1994b), 'Global Government and Global Opposition', *Politics in an Interdependent World: Essays Presented to Ghita Ionescu*, Aldershot, UK and Brookfield, US: Edward Elgar.

Strange, Susan (1995a), 'Political Economy and International Relations', in Ken Booth and Steve Smith (eds), *International Relations Theory Today*, University Park: Pennsylvania University Press, pp.154–74.

Strange, Susan (1995b), 'The Limits of Politics', *Government and Opposition*, 30(3), 291–311.

Strange, Susan (1996), *The Retreat of the State*, Cambridge: Cambridge University Press.

Strange, Susan (1997), *Casino Capitalism*, Manchester: Manchester University Press.

Strange, Susan (1998a), 'Globaloney?', *Review of International Political Economy*, 5(4), 704–20.

Strange, Susan (1998b), *Mad Money*, Manchester: Manchester University Press.

Strange, Susan (1999), 'The Westfailure system', *Review of International Studies*, 25(3), 345–54.

Strange, Susan and Roger Tooze (eds) (1981), *The International Politics of Surplus Capacity; Competition for market shares in the world recession*, London: George Allen & Unwin.

Wood, Ellen Meiksins (1981), 'The separation of the economic and the political in capitalism', *New Left Review*, 127, 66–95; reprinted in E.M. Wood (1995), *Democracy Against Capitalism: Renewing historical materialism*, Cambridge: Cambridge University Press.

10 Ideology, Knowledge and Power in International Relations and International Political Economy

ROGER TOOZE

Introduction

This chapter attempts to develop a critical analysis of ideas, ideology and knowledge in the global political economy (GPE). It seeks to review the way we think about the nature of ideology and knowledge by situating them within a critical political economy of knowledge, and, from this revised conception, it illustrates the necessary role of 'neoliberal ideology' in constructing and maintaining the current configuration of power in the GPE. Within this broad conceptualization of knowledge and ideology, three further specific arguments are interwoven in the overall analysis: one, that any understanding of the three spheres of contemporary structural transformation that this book is concerned with (see Chapter 1) will be limited and inadequate if that understanding remains grounded in the metatheoretical parameters of what has been constructed as 'mainstream' International Relations (IR) and International Political Economy (IPE);[1] two, that an adequate understanding of structures of IPE must necessarily include the structures of intersubjective meaning as an integral part of 'objective' reality; three, clearly related, that Strange's development of a 'new realist ontology of global political economy' is thus a necessary but not sufficient framework for an adequate understanding of this structural transformation.

The analysis builds upon and interprets the arguments of previous chapters within the context of critical perspectives on IR/IPE. It supports, augments and modifies the case made by Claire Cutler,[2] although we use a different starting point and focus on different questions, partly drawn from Robert Cox's 'critical political economy' (Cox 1995). Our interpretation of Cutler's important argument is this: that despite her critical intentions, and perhaps because of them, the problems and issues of IR/IPE that Strange first identified and described and then tried to explain and resolve were eventually made more resistant to her own analysis by the clearly unintended and hidden, but nevertheless real, meta-theoretically constructed separation of 'politics' and 'economics' in her work. Despite her best intentions and efforts to (re)integrate 'politics' and 'economics', her work did not ultimately succeed in doing this, although it demonstrated beyond all question that such a reintegration is necessary.

We will take the above argument a step further and attempt to show, as part of a critical discussion of ideology and knowledge in IR/IPE, that what we call Strange's 'project of radical ontology' was ultimately frustrated, not only by the reproduction of this separation, but also by two related significant and equally hidden metatheoretical aspects of her work. Given the importance of Strange's work in the identification and articulation of structures of IPE, in particular what she called 'the knowledge structure' (Strange 1988), it is indeed ironic that it is precisely her view of knowledge and ideology, grounded in her fundamental but nonetheless gradually evolving empiricism, that together construct such a fundamental barrier to the achievement of her intellectual and political goals.

Essentially, then, this part of our argument comes down to the simple point that Strange's development of a radical 'realist' ontology[3] in the long run demanded more than her epistemological practice allowed her to deliver. However, as has already been suggested, here Strange is far from alone in being confounded by the apparently hidden and embedded precepts of what has become constructed as mainstream methodology and epistemology (Tooze and Murphy 1996; MacLean 2000). Despite the new-found mainstream (but clearly still marginalized) legitimacy of reflectivist or constructivist approaches (Keohane 1989; Walt 1998), the majority of scholars, writers and practitioners in IR/IPE still work within a 'traditional social science' view of knowledge production. This view, in a mutually supportive relationship with a variety of state-centered ontologies, prevents them from understanding the totality of power in the global political economy, particularly structural power and the nature of authority.

The Social Context of IR/IPE Knowledge

Concepts such as 'knowledge' and 'ideology' do not have meaning outside society and, as such, come to us as part of the historically constituted social reality that we have to deal with. Their past formulations and theorizations contribute to constructing their meaning today, particularly by the reproduction of specific meaning through the actual social and political practice of everyday life. In order, then, to think about knowledge and ideology in a way that attempts to take account of these historically prior definitional and theoretical commitments, that is those meanings of knowledge and ideology that are themselves already part of the existing discourse, we need to consider the process of knowledge production itself. One of the key questions is whether the production of knowledge, including, of course, academic knowledge, is subject to, and is part of, the same social, political and economic forces as those political economic entities that we claim to have knowledge of. If so, then the process of knowledge production is itself a 'political economy' in the way that Stephen Gill has suggested: 'perspectives in a political economy should be considered as part of global political economy, that is, a part of the ontological object of analysis for political economists and students of international relations' (Gill 1994: 85).

Consequently, taking Strange seriously, as Cutler is absolutely right to do, as a 'critical thinker' means, as Strange probably intended, stepping outside the parameters of the conventional and dominant practices of International Relations and International Political Economy. Unless the critique itself is located primarily within the metatheoretical frame of what is accepted as the mainstream view, any attempt to evaluate this critique by using only the criteria of the mainstream is flawed. It is flawed because (a) it places the critique within a set of assumptions that the critique does not accept in the first place; and (b) it misrecognizes the nature of that critique by not acknowledging the consequences of prior philosophical and methodological commitments for political economy. Hence, evaluating critical work, such as Strange's, means using a wider, more inclusive conception of politics, and IR/IPE, and using the conception of a political economy of knowledge itself. Moreover, it necessarily means questioning existing methodology by and through the articulation of a methodology from within critical thought (see, for example, Morrow 1994). The core of such a critical methodology is the reflexivity of social inquiry: that is, that knowledge and theory should be able to explain its own existence and form (McCarthy 1993).

However, this does not mean throwing out of all the evaluative criteria of conventional IR/IPE, but situating the knowledge-producing practices of conventional IR/IPE within the wider structure and practice of the social production of knowledge (Sayer 1992; Morrow 1994). This means that we need to think of 'IPE', both the academic study and the global system of political economy, not as something existing outside our theories and concepts, but 'IPE' as already constructed by as well as analyzed with our theories. In this instance the opening up of our way of thinking about IPE and the structures made visible by Strange have now become part of the existing theorization of IPE. And the existing theorization itself then becomes the basis for critique – a critique, amongst others, of Strange's work. In this sense Strange's theoretical contribution to IPE is now both an instrument and an object of critique.

This is not to say that an evaluation of Strange's work that operates within conventional (epistemological) parameters is not valuable or not appropriate, for example, as ably demonstrated by Cohen's thought-provoking analysis in Chapter 6 of this volume.[4] However, it is to say that the scope for the evaluation of and reflection upon Strange's work is narrowed and limited by confining that evaluation within the parameters of the dominant practices of IR/IPE (and economics) as part of conventional social science. Furthermore, this limitation has important consequences for our understanding and our construction of global political economy.

The parameters of conventional social science, as manifest in IR/IPE, are derived from a particular conception of how we know what we know – a particular conception of the process of producing legitimate social knowledge based on a specific view of 'science'. This conception is almost always presented as a 'given', determined by the supposedly fixed and objective nature of science. However, as science is itself social practice, this is not the case. Given the social production of science, the practices of producing 'social' science, that is social knowledge legitimated by and through the methodology of science, necessarily incorporates the same social forces as its exemplar. Indeed, the process we construct and use for producing legitimate knowledge is politics, and is thus a necessary part of any discussion of power. As Bourdieu succinctly points out, 'The theory of knowledge is a dimension of political theory because the specifically symbolic power to impose the principles of the construction of reality – in particular, social reality – is a major dimension of political power' (1977: 165). As we have suggested, in the practice of most mainstream IR/IPE the knowledge basis of 'theory' is assumed as given, as decided by the community of science, and, hence, as something outside the concern of politics, something unacknowledged that is there to be built upon, most often without any question. Here, 'theory' has a precise function, and 'theoretical debate' does not normally involve the interrogation of the knowledge base of theory. This practice can give the appearance of much 'theoretical' diversity, but most of the diversity will be within a specific conception of producing legitimate knowledge, carried on presumably unaware of (or, perhaps, in denial of) the implications for the understanding of power in IPE (Murphy and Tooze 1991).

The 'Standard' Parameters of IPE Knowledge Production

The specific view of science that is now embedded in mainstream IR/IPE as that producing legitimate knowledge is based on the notion of a 'scientific research program'. This is derived from the work of the philosopher of science, Imre Lakatos (1970), in an exchange of views with Karl Popper over the status of Thomas Kuhn's 'normal science'. A modified 'Lakatosian' research program founded on the methodological separation of scholars from their social context has since that time been constructed as the metatheoretical framework by and for the mainstream of IR/IPE academics. As part of the actual if unintended construction of this legitimating framework, both Robert Keohane (1989) and Stephen Krasner (1996) clearly demonstrate what does and what should constitute legitimate knowledge in IR/IPE. Although both are very important in establishing the parameters for the evaluation of theory, this chapter focuses more on Krasner, as his was a specific attempt within a critical context to evaluate theory of IPE.

Keohane comprehensively demonstrates a set of 'criteria for the evaluation of theoretical work in international politics' (1989: 36–8) through the use of the conception of a 'scientific research program' modified to take account of the difficulty of applying Lakatos' strict 'scientific' (hard?) criteria to the 'softer' world of social reality.[5] Krasner later emphasizes the necessity (and exclusiveness) of the conception of a 'scientific research program' as the criteria by which to judge the 'success' of approaches to IPE. He states that 'the success of different approaches to IPE has been determined primarily by their ability to generate a progressive research program' (1996: 122), where 'progressive' means 'the discovery of new facts (other than the anomalous facts that they were designed to explain)' (Keohane 1989: 37).

Parenthetically, it is intriguing that these defining, and disciplining, statements seem to have forgotten David Easton's crucial remark, in a volume widely regarded by American political scientists as forming part of the founding basis of their own 'scientific' study of politics, that 'A fact is but a peculiar ordering of reality according to a theoretic interest' (Easton 1953, cited in Rosen and Jones 1977: 167). That is, what is 'a fact' is itself theory/concept-dependent, and therefore evaluating a theory/approach on the basis of 'the discovery of new facts' is not a sufficient or appropriate sole criterion of evaluation of 'progress' in the theory of IPE. Indeed, if our goal is to try to understand the totality of power in GPE, limiting ourselves to this criterion is assuming a level of simplicity of access to 'reality' that does not exist.

In these 'progressive research programs' legitimate knowledge is exclusively knowledge that conforms to the rules of the 'Western Rationalistic Tradition'. That is, '[I]nternational political economy is deeply embedded in the standard epistemological methodology of the social sciences which, stripped to its bare bones, simply means stating a proposition and testing it against external evidence' (Krasner 1996: 108–9). This being the case, 'theories have fallen from favour either because they did not conform with [*sic*] empirical evidence or because they could not be formulated in ways that were, in principle testable' (ibid.: 122). If 'empirical evidence' is itself theory-dependent, and 'testability' means only testing against a quantifiable material reality, then what are we to make of this statement?

Two important claims are being made above. First, the statement that IPE is 'deeply embedded in the standard epistemological methodology' is one of confident assertion of a claim to universal practice: IPE is (identical to) the 'standard epistemological methodology' and vice versa. No question! Moreover, it is a universalizing statement which delegitimizes and marginalizes other approaches constructed within 'non-standard' epistemology as 'prescientific, ideological, self-interested or the like' by promoting the notion of the standard epistemology offering a 'view from nowhere with all its rights and privileges' (McCarthy 1993: 135). Second, 'testing ... against external evidence' is fundamentally unproblematic because of the assumed accessibility of 'reality', in the form of 'empirical evidence'. The ready accessibility of 'reality' comes partly because of the presumed separation of subject and object of testing, and partly because of the pre-existing commitments to forms of empiricism that are embedded in the contemporary practice of IR/IPE (MacLean 2000). There are many discussions of the 'technical' problems of such a standard methodology, the nature of evidence, the dependability of statistics, the problem of questionnaires, and so on. Keohane himself even includes 'reflectivist' approaches in the domain of theory in his discussion of ideas and foreign policy, although he does not seem to be able to resolve the problems of integrating 'ideas' into instrumental rationalist analysis (Goldstein and Keohane 1993). However, in the mainstream these discussions of IR/IPE take the actual possibility of 'testing' against a known, or knowable, unproblematic and non-theoretic external reality as given, as common sense, as unquestioned and, as Krasner seeks to demonstrate in the last few pages of his chapter (1996: 122–5), even as unquestionable.

The way that Krasner demonstrates the unassailable status of the 'standard epistemological methodology' in his 1996 chapter is important and deserves a close analysis. The rhetorical and logical devices he uses are frequently also used by those who want to defend the 'unquestionability' of the version of positivism that mainstream IR/IPE uses. After basing his analysis of the accomplishments of international political economy only on those works that fit within his asserted articulation of what constitutes legitimate knowledge in IPE, and hence implicitly making the two claims discussed above, in his 'Conclusion' Krasner deals with other methodologies. He correctly identifies the principal difference between his 'standard' epistemology and other possible or actually challenging epistemologies as the separation of subject and object. He then lumps together all non-positivist, or post-positivist epistemologies as 'those versions of post-modernism that reject any separation between the student and object of study' (Krasner 1996: 122). Later in the 'Conclusion' he asserts in regard to 'those variants of post-modernism that reject the Western Rationalistic Tradition' that 'for these post-modernists there are many analytic categories each of which contains its own truth. *Testing can never be definitive and is often entirely irrelevant* (ibid. 124, emphasis added).

Krasner then moves to argue that, given the admitted weakness of the (positivist) findings of IPE, maybe the answer is to 'throw it all up' and 'adopt a post-modern stance' as 'it would be more fun if it were not necessary to muck through all that messy and ambiguous data' (ibid.). Finally, for our purposes, he turns to the core argument of enlightenment positivist knowledge, that 'to embrace post-modernism would be to strip social science of the most important contribution that it can make to the betterment of human society: that contribution is to discipline power with truth' (ibid.: 124–5).

It is important not to be understood as arguing in support of the relativism that marks forms of postmodernism by the act of arguing against Krasner, as that would be falling into the precise political trap set, but Krasner's argumentation is both clever and flawed. The logical moves of this argument are as follows:

- identify the only legitimate epistemology as a specific version of the western rationalist tradition (WRT);
- identify and label *all* non-legitimate (that is, the rest of) epistemology as 'postmodern';
- characterize 'postmodernism' in a way that emphasizes extreme versions in order to maximize the threat to the positivist correspondence theory of truth;
- this clearly results in the rejection of any and all non-WRT epistemology and, hence, reciprocal confirmation of the one true epistemology.

Krasner then adds to the force of this argument with two further moves that, by prior definition, both seek to delegitimize all non-standard epistemology:

- the claim that for 'postmodernism' testing against reality is, anyway, irrelevant and not 'definitive', as it is in the 'standard epistemology';
- finally, assert that only positivism can 'discipline power with truth' and suggest to the reader that the alternative is 'Hitler's Germany, Stalin's Soviet Union, Mao's China' or at the very least a nihilistic society which 'hardly moves society towards peace and justice'.

Critical Theory and the 'Standard Epistemological Methodology'

This argument and its rhetorical moves give the appearance of logical, consistent, rational thought. It is, however, a mixture of assertion and claim, a rhetorical mixing up of certain linguistic devices with other statements that need demonstration. Moreover, the whole argument is framed as a statement of power – the power to define what is legitimate social knowledge. Furthermore, the acceptance of Krasner's argument has very significant implications for academic IPE as well as the social construction of global political economy itself.

There are many grounds to contest and, arguably modify Krasner's case, but for the purposes of the argument in this chapter the following should suffice. First, WRT is not the only methodology possible and, even if it were, it is neither fixed nor undisputed (in particular, see Feyerabend 1993). Problematizing methodology clearly demonstrates the political significance of epistemology.

Second, the defining of the contemporary methodological universe as 'WRT versus postmodernism' is an attempt to predefine and to limit the domain of contestation by constructing the *doxa* in such a way as to predefine both the orthodoxy and the heterodoxy in a way that the orthodoxy has to 'win' (Bourdieu 1977: 165–72). This definition effectively removes from consideration any other approach. Specifically, it denies any space/legitimacy for any form of 'critical theory' or 'critical realism'.

Third, the characterization of 'postmodern' is simplistic, too narrow and deliberately negatively skewed. Fourth, for the 'standard epistemological methodology' testing does *not* produce definitive knowledge, it produces contingent knowledge (see the essays in Lakatos and Musgrave 1970; Feyerabend 1993). The process of 'testing' is itself a defining mode, but only in the sense of a specific notion of empiricism (Morrow 1994; MacLean 2000).

Fifth, Krasner may be right about 'disciplining power with truth' in the abstract, but just because a social process has the claimed capability to produce 'truth' it does not mean those who produce knowledge will use it. Where were the mainstream IR/IPE analyses of the Pinochet regime in Chile? Where are the mainstream IR/IPE analyses of world poverty today (Tooze and Murphy 1996)?

By not allowing space for 'critical realism', or other forms of critical theory, as acknowledged 'opposition' to the 'standard epistemological methodology', Krasner reproduces the impossibility of a resolution to what Morrow refers to as 'the standoff between empiricism and subjectivism as the only choices' (1994: 77), which is represented by the opposition between positivism and postmodern relativism. Critical theory does not resolve this polarization, but rejects its formulation in the first place, by redefining the relations between epistemology and ontology. For critical theory epistemology 'cannot be based on some pure scientific method that is [itself] based on logic and empirical data: the methodologies of the sciences are many, and empirical evidence is always available for strong competing views'. Crucially, 'epistemological and methodological pragmatism does not necessarily require ontological scepticism – the suggestion that we cannot confidently posit realities independent of our consciousness' (ibid.). The possibility of ontological realism, that is that we can posit realities that exist independent of our consciousness, removes the framing methodological opposition that defines, limits and handicaps the mainstream debate outlined by Krasner.

Thus critical theory may give us a way forward for IR/IPE, which does not result in the kind of narrow evaluation carried out by Krasner (1996) and does result in the possibility of human emancipation, although it is important to note that critical theory still has, in itself and in its relation to IR/IPE, many problems (see Jones 2000). What is significant for the arguments of this chapter is that critical theory in its insistence on reflexive knowledge, on the social production of knowledge, leads to the necessary inclusion of meaning and language in our conception of social reality through the rejection of the separation of subject and object. Ideas and ideology are thus part of the totality of social life, in reciprocal relationships with a constructed material environment. This means that a theory of IR/IPE which does not take account of non-material, ideational aspects of power, through the concept of intersubjective meaning, only deals with a part of the structure of power. That is the part of the structure made accessible and meaningful by the empirical methodology that is used (MacLean 2000). The other parts of power structures remain invisible, hidden and unrecognized, although not unconstructed. Intersubjective meanings are thus an integral part of the necessary basis for the analysis of structures of GPE.

Hence the almost unconscious assumptions made by those in the mainstream in their everyday practice of research and thinking about the way that social life is constructed, including the way that their own knowledge is attained and what this knowledge means, configures that knowledge so as to misrecognize the nature and extent of power in the GPE.[6] A key aspect of this misrecognition is that it is a misrecognition of the arbitrariness of structures in the GPE, and the nature of the social construction and legitimation of these structures. Misrecognition has serious political implications, in that the very concepts and theory of IR/IPE play a key part in constituting the structure of power in the GPE, because 'the social world is itself constructed in part by the very ideas that researchers employ to understand it' (McCarthy 1993: 137). By misrecognizing the structure of power, and then by promulgating analyses based upon this misrecognition, IR/IPE theory as produced through the 'standard epistemological methodology' is instrumental in helping to reproduce and reinforce existing structures of power. This is because existing structures of power are themselves already constructed by and through social, including academic, adherence to a specific set of 'principles of the construction of reality' (Bourdieu 1977: 165). In general, 'systems of domination … are maintained not only through the appropriation, control and allocation of essential material requirements by the dominant class, race or gender, but also through the reproduction of particular systems of meanings which support them' (Sayer 1992: 35). That is, mainstream IR/IPE theory in this sense is deeply conservative in its acceptance of 'what is', no matter what the intended purpose, or declared interests, the theory sets out to serve. As MacLean (2000) clearly shows, the generic roots of this, and other, crucial misrecognitions partly lie in the historical commitment to empiricist philosophy embedded in the methodology of mainstream IR/IPE.

Critical theory, then, of whatever mode,[7] necessarily questions or problematizes the actual production of knowledge. 'One of the first tasks of critical theory is to challenge the privileged "non- position" of social-scientific knowledge by analyzing the modes of its production, the role it plays in society, the interests it serves, and the historical processes through which it came to power' (McCarthy 1993: 135–6). By recognising (academic) knowledge as a social product and by demanding that such knowledge should be reflexive, critical theory constructs a different set of questions for the evaluation of knowledge. More specifically, it constructs a different set of questions for the evaluation of that formal type of knowledge we call 'theory', and, in the process of doing this, critical theory necessarily changes our conception of what we understand and what we describe as 'theory'.

One of the few scholars to attempt an analysis of IR/IPE theory other than as purely intellectual product has been Tom Biersteker in his important, but predictably often overlooked, article on 'Evolving Perspectives on International Political Economy' (Biersteker 1993). Here Biersteker argues that theories of IPE 'are contingent upon, and reflect substantial portions of, the context in which they were formulated'. Moreover, 'theory is context bounded and emerges either consciously or unconsciously in the service of (or driven by) particular interests' (ibid.: 7). For Biersteker 'context' ordinarily has at least three different components: intertextual, social and individual. Over time, 'the direction of theoretical research tends to be the outgrowth of the dialectical relationship between theory and social context, combined with the nature of the reaction of a given theoretical undertaking to its predecessor (given the intertextual nature of theoretical reflection)' (ibid.: 8).

Biersteker's emphasis on the importance of intertextuality as a context for theory is a necessary and significant step forward. For example, a recognition of the intertextual context is particularly important for understanding the development of Strange's work, as many of her theoretical innovations and interventions were clearly in direct response to both the theoretical and policy claims of US scholars. However, although Biersteker unequivocally states that theory 'is socially constructed, and the investigators and their intellectual tools are part of the social context of their investigation and reporting' (ibid.), he does not then explore the necessary methodological implications of his statement. He is content to follow through his provocative and stimulating meta-analysis of perspectives on IPE within the otherwise unmodified framework of the 'standard' methodology, without a consideration of the actual criteria and conditions for the development of the reflexive IPE that would seem to be indicated by his own analysis.

Here Biersteker is in a similar position to Strange: he is not conforming strictly to the established social rules for the production and content of knowledge (as applying his own analysis to his article will demonstrate). If 'theory' is a social product it has purpose (embedded at many levels) and is subject to the same social forces as other social products. As in any social group, individual contributions are judged by their conformity to the norms of group production. As we have seen within IR/IPE the promulgation of an exclusively legitimate methodology effectively defines the framework of legitimate knowledge production within the group. The function of the upholders of this framework is one that Robert Cox calls 'gatekeeping', as they control admission to the 'group'. 'Once properly endorsed with the unwritten certification of the invisible network, then you may be considered for publication in the recognized journals and find peer reviewers from among members of the group for your longer manuscripts' (Cox 1996: 178). Certainly, there should be room for critique from both within and without any such 'group', but it is important to recognize the social process of 'gatekeeping' as consistent with realms of action in other domains of political economy.

Knowledge and Ideology in IR/IPE

Knowledge

So what does the foregoing analysis mean for our analysis of contemporary structural transformation? It means simply that the mainstream theory (that dominant practice of IR/IPE that constructs theory using the 'standard epistemological methodology') does not adequately recognize or specify the nature of structures or power, nor can it adequately recognize or specify globalization (Germain 2000). This is because the particular set of 'principles of the construction of reality' used by the dominant group for the production of knowledge is not able to recognize the centrality of intersubjective meanings, and hence language and meaning, to the construction of power. Neither, of course, does it recognize the reflexivity of knowledge, specifically the reflexivity and context boundedness of academic knowledge of the global political economy. Attempts to 'add' or integrate ideas and ideology to the 'standard epistemological methodology' are highly problematic, and are probably doomed to failure. As Ruggie has pointed out in regard to this aspect of the mainstream position:

> Krasner is one of the few contemporary realists to take seriously the relationship between power and norms. We can agree with much of what Krasner has to say about the efficacy of norms, principles of legitimacy, and movements of thought – indeed, he even invokes hermeneutics. And yet, in the end, we remain perplexed at how he reconciles this position with his fervent commitment to logical positivism. (Ruggie 1998: 98, footnote 5)

Ruggie is not the only one to 'remain perplexed' at the seeming inability of mainstream thinkers to make sense of their own methodological commitments![8] One of the ways to understand this problem is through a consideration of how we analyze 'knowledge'.

We now seem to hear every day about the importance of the knowledge economy to economic growth and life enhancing technological developments. We are surrounded by evidence of the activities of the knowledge economy and we use every day the technologies of the knowledge economy. Moreover, our society is constructed and is being reconstructed according to the imperatives of an ideology of technical rationalism in which technical–rational knowledge has attained the very highest legitimacy (Habermas 1972). It is rather surprising then to realize that IR and, in particular, IPE have had, with a few exceptions, very little to say directly about the international political economy of knowledge as a whole as a specific theoretical and practical concern. It was, of course, Strange who set out an ontology of IPE that identified and gave ontological status to the 'knowledge structure', most formally in *States and Markets* (Strange 1988/1994).

In *States and Markets*, Strange proposes a theory of IPE based on a radically different ontology than that of the mainstream, and indeed different from that normally seen as 'radical' itself (see Cox 1996). She later developed this into what she called a 'new realist ontology', where 'the essence of realism ... is the acknowledgement that outcomes, even in matters of trade and finance, cannot be properly analysed ... in disregard of the distribution of power' (Strange 1997: 4). As mentioned in previous chapters, the basis of her ontology was the articulation within the totality of IPE of four interrelated but ontologically separable structures of power: security, finance, production and knowledge. The interactions between and within the four structures produce the global political economy. Each of these four has a different distribution of power, that for security not necessarily being the same as that for finance. And within each structure entities, notably not just states, wield structural power by constructing the framework (norms, rules, imperatives) within and by which power is exercised.

In identifying the knowledge structure as one of her four 'primary structures' of IPE, Strange was able to place the analysis of the power of beliefs and ideas in IPE within this structure. Power derived from the knowledge structure 'comprehends what is believed (and the moral conclusions and principles derived from those beliefs); what is known and perceived as understood; and the channels by which beliefs, ideas and knowledge are communicated – including some people and excluding others' (Strange 1994: 119). She thus identifies and defines a knowledge structure in the following way: 'a knowledge structure determines what knowledge is discovered, how it is stored, and who communicates it by what means to whom and on what terms' (ibid.: 121). As Mytelka emphasized in Chapter 3 of the present volume, this definition explicitly recognizes the production, possession, control, communication and, above all, the legitimization of knowledge as a prime structure of political economy – one that is as important for the distribution and realization of power as any of the other three structures in her frame of analysis. Within the knowledge structure, Strange has a particular notion of the relationship of belief systems to structures of power which seems very close to the critical conception of the relationship between materiality and systems of meaning (Sayer 1992: 35). For Strange, 'structural analysis suggests that technological changes do not necessarily change power structures. *They do so only if accompanied by changes in the basic belief systems which underpin or support the political and economic arrangements acceptable to society'* (Strange 1994: 127, emphasis added). In other words, power is constructed and maintained not by material means alone but with necessary supportive 'belief systems' or 'systems of meaning' or, even, 'ideology' (Bauman 1999). However, and crucially, Strange differs from Sayer, and the critical realists, by not wanting to recognize the reflexive nature of knowledge and the consequences that this might have for her own analysis as well as her analysis of GPE.

Although she was very aware of the philosophical problems of her attempts to analyze the knowledge structure (Strange 1994: 136; Palan: 1999), Strange thought that what the student of IPE

> is more immediately concerned with is the nature of power exercised through a knowledge structure, whether past, present or future; with whether the centres of such power are presently undergoing significant change; and with what the 'cui bono' consequences are for states, classes, corporations and other groups. (Strange 1994: 136)

Hence the knowledge structure is here, and in analyses that follow (Strange 1996a; 1997; 1998), defined by Strange objectively, and by default, as she has no other way of acknowledging ideas and belief systems within the confines of the epistemology she uses, although, as pointed out, she clearly recognizes and includes the significance of human values and belief systems in her conception of this structure.

The problem is how we then understand and analyze these values and belief systems as integral elements of the knowledge structure when, as this chapter argues, they are constituted, and take their meaning and power, intersubjectively. This epistemological problem is heightened by Strange's insistence on the theoretical and ontological equivalence of each of the four primary structures. By not giving any of the four primary structures of the world political economy logical or causative priority over the others, Strange maintains her open, empirical approach of not predetermining analytical outcomes. However, in so doing she produces a major theoretical conundrum: is the knowledge structure prior or not to the security, production and finance structures (May 1996: 184–6; Ellehoj 1993)?[9]

Defined purely as an 'objective' structure, there is a strong argument that only knowledge allows the other structures to function *qua* structure, but this depends upon making certain assumptions about the nature of political economy, so that it is still possible to argue a functional and causal equivalence, as Strange indeed does (Strange 1994; 1996b). However, if the knowledge structure has an acknowledged intersubjective element, or can only be fully comprehended intersubjectively, then a purely objective conceptualization is not sufficient, and, more important, the knowledge structure is then necessarily prior to security, production and finance. By defining the knowledge structure in the way she has, although totally consistent with her broad approach, Strange has as a result underestimated the consequences, both for her own analysis and for political economy, of some of the philosophical debates she rightly identifies but does not pursue (see Palan 1999). Her 'new realist ontology', based upon primary structures, is indeed a necessary step forward for IPE, but it seems not to be sufficient.

The problem with discussing 'knowledge' as a primary component of political economy is that knowledge is only known, understood and acted upon, and therefore generated/created, stored, transmitted and controlled, via the medium of language. Language is necessary for ideas, values and belief systems – all elements of knowledge but all treated as 'subjective' by the prevailing epistemological orthodoxy. And language, as social construct, presumes intersubjectivity to achieve meaning (Taylor 1985). Because language not only enables knowledge of political economy, but *is* knowledge of political economy, as meaning, any conception of such knowledge that is based upon only the recognition of 'objective' elements (that is, does not include language and indeed other 'subjective' elements), as argued in the previous section, can only ever be partial. And partiality leads to a misrecognition of structures in GPE.

The argument here is that a knowledge structure as part of a radical ontology and conceptualized and constructed on the basis of Strange's epistemology is a highly significant theoretical innovation in IPE. However, because of the problems and limitations of that epistemology she not only risks creating significant logical and empirical contradictions in her analysis, but she also risks missing some of the most significant elements of power that her new and expanded ontology of IPE should help recognize. However, these are not the only implications brought about through the limitations and problems of Strange's operational epistemology. Perhaps even more worthy of comment is the limitation on the possibility of reconstructing IPE on the basis of a synthesis between economics and politics. The achievement of such a synthesis remained one of Strange's most fundamental aims for the whole of her academic life, but our argument here is that she could not have reached such a synthesis, to her own satisfaction, on the basis of the methodology she used throughout that academic life.

Ideology

In writing about knowledge and belief systems, Strange did occasionally use the concept of ideology. She used the label 'ideology' as a critique of other work, often the analyses of US scholars, where she thought that specific interests were directing theory and analysis. For example, 'ideas and ideologies... have often served to veil the conflict between special and national interests. In the period covered by *Mad Money*, the concealing ideology has been that of liberal economics and, specifically, monetarism and supply-side economic logic'.[10] Here, 'ideology' is something constructed to hide the 'reality' of knowledge and interests, as in the dominant usage of the post-1945 era it is a cloak to obscure the truth. In the prevailing knowledge context of this era, 'ideology' is revealed as 'ideology' by the claimed ability of rationalist social science to 'discipline power with truth' (Krasner 1996: 125). 'Ideology' in this sense stands in the way of the truth, distorts the truth, in the interests of those who have power. Of course, the assumption here is that we have an unassailable method to attain truth in society. If not, then all knowledge can be ideological as there is no basis for distinction, or ideology becomes the condition of knowledge before science (Bauman 1999: 126–8).

These and other instances reveal the problems that Strange (and many others more in the mainstream of social science) had and have in incorporating the notion of ideology into an analysis of post-cold war IR and IPE.

In a thoughtful and revealing discussion of contemporary politics, Zygmunt Bauman suggests that, while ideology has had a number of socially constructed meanings over historical time – an 'essentially contested concept' in an 'essentially contested reality' – we now live in a world constructed in such a way that it is 'no more essentially contested' (ibid.: 109–31). Bauman traces the changes in the intersubjective meanings of ideology from when it was first used towards the end of the 18th century. There is no space here to comment on or offer further interpretation of the historical argument he makes, except to say that it makes much sense as a basis for a critical reconstruction of politics and political economy.

Locating the concept of ideology within a critical analysis challenges the basic conditions of the social science, post-1945 construction of the meaning of ideology. Given that all systems of social power are maintained both materially and through 'the reproduction of particular systems of meaning which support them' (Sayer 1992: 35), ideology is an integral part of the formation of social reality: all social reality. In this sense ideology does not distort 'real' or 'objective' social reality, as the IR 'cold war' usage suggests, but becomes part of the construction of a particular system of intersubjective meaning. It is thus essential to the construction of power in providing the necessary legitimating functions, the belief systems and the sense of future possibilities that human beings in complex relationships require.

From this critical conception of ideology it is clear that the process of neoliberal globalization has gone hand-in-hand with the construction of enabling and supporting intersubjective meanings. The apparent triumph of neoliberal ideology in recent years is, however, the result of a long historical process in which the basic concepts of social life have been defined and constructed in certain ways (see Polanyi 1957). In this historical process even the unquestioned meanings of deeply embedded core social practices, such as what constitutes economic activity, become changed to fit particular interests, but are kept in the realm of what Bourdieu calls 'doxa', where 'the natural and social worlds appear as self-evident' (Bourdieu 1977: 164; also see MacLean 2000). Hence the purpose of neoliberal ideology is the construction of a sense of reality that the present social structure of global capitalism and the distribution of wealth and power engendered by that social structure is, and should be, natural. That is that the global capitalist society is not the product of power and arbitrariness, but of normal and natural processes that have to be accepted.

In this context, the summary argument that Bauman makes regarding neoliberal ideology needs emphasizing here:

> The point of similarity between the neo-liberal world-view and a typical 'classic' ideology is that both serve as a priori frames for all future discourse, setting what is seen apart from what goes unnoticed, awarding or denying relevance, determining the logic of reasoning and the evaluation of results. What, however, makes the neo-liberal world view sharply different from other ideologies – indeed, a phenomenon of a separate class – is precisely the absence of questioning; its surrender to what is seen as the implacable and irreversible logic of social reality. (Bauman 1999: 127)

In the 'natural' processes of globalization the political goal is to achieve a 'self-evident' structure of (global) society in which there is as near as possible a 'quasi-perfect correspondence between the objective order and the subjective principles of organization'. In order to achieve this, those who wield power must capture the 'instruments of knowledge of the social world', as these are

> political instruments which contribute to the reproduction of the social world by producing immediate adherence to the world, seen as self-evident and undisputed, of which they are the product and of which they reproduce the structures in a transformed form. (Bourdieu 1977: 164)

Hence the importance of not allowing epistemology (one of the key 'instruments of knowledge of the social world') to be defined as 'given', as outside the parameters of what we in academic IPE should question.

As Strange argued in the last lines of her last piece of writing, 'although academic debate by itself rarely changes the basic ideas ... that at any time dominate the knowledge structure, academic debate when it takes place against a background of growing disillusion, of doubt and uncertainty can act as a catalyst to action'.[11] One can only hope that, as in so many other aspects of IPE, she is right.

Notes

1   For brevity, the combined theory and practice of both IR and IPE will be referred to as 'IR/IPE'. This does not mean either that IR fully encompasses IPE, or that they are equivalent. Nor does it denote any specific relationship other than that the mainstream and much of the heterodox academic study of what we now call IPE was originally developed from within IR. The relationship between IR and IPE is rightly contested, as part of the developments that this chapter considers.

2   See Chapter 9 of the present volume.

3   Although much of her work, particularly after 1988, included some ontological questioning, the most comprehensive statement of her thoughts on this is Susan Strange (1997).

4   Although there are some serious problems with Cohen's analysis which principally stem from his notion of what constitutes 'theory', particularly in contrast to Strange's arguments against the possibility of a 'general theory'. See Ronen Palan's excellent analysis of Strange's theoretical position (Palan 1999).

5   This move by Keohane always seemed simply to move the locus of the question of positivist understanding to another 'theoretical' place without resolving any of the problems. For a later critique of Keohane's argument, see Walker (1989).

6   See John MacLean's pathbreaking analysis of the philosophical cage of empiricism and its political implications in MacLean (2000).

7   There is much available literature on the various modes of critical thought and its relation to IR/IPE. One of the clearest statements is Rengger and Hoffman (1992) and the most comprehensive attempt yet to address the promise and problems of critical theory and world politics is Jones (2000).

8   An attempt has been made to consider these problems in depth in Roger Tooze, *Reflections on International Political Economy: Theory, Knowledge and Power*, Manchester: Manchester University Press (forthcoming).

9   May (1996) considers this at length, and Ellehoj (1993) sets out a framework where knowledge becomes the foundational primary structure.

10   This quote comes from a manuscript that Susan Strange was finalizing on her death, entitled 'Finance in Politics: An Epilogue to Mad Money'. It will be published by Manchester University Press in the second edition of *Mad Money*.

11   This is the last sentence of 'Finance in Politics'; see note 10 above.

References

Bauman, Z. (1999), *In Search of Politics*, Cambridge: Polity Press.

Biersteker, T.J. (1993), 'Evolving Perspectives on International Political Economy: Twentieth Century Contexts and Discontinuities', *International Political Science Review*, 14(1), 7–33.

Bourdieu, P. (1977), *Outline of a Theory of Practice*, (trans. R. Nice), Cambridge: Cambridge University Press.

Cox, R.W. (1995), 'Critical Political Economy', in B. Hettne, (ed.), *International Political Economy: Understanding Global Disorder*, London: Zed Books.

Cox, R.W. (1996), '"Take Six Eggs": theory, finance and the real economy in the work of Susan Strange', in R.W. Cox, with T. Sinclair, *Approaches to World Order*, Cambridge: Cambridge University Press.

Ellehoj, P. (1993), 'Deux et machina: The Process of International Economic Cooperation', in R. Morgan *et al.* (eds), *New Diplomacy in the Post-Cold War World: Essays for Susan Strange*, London: Macmillan.

Feyerabend, P. (1993), *Against Method*, 3rd edn, London:Verso.

Germain, R.D. (ed.) (2000), *Globalization and its Critics: Perspectives from Political Economy*, London: Macmillan/PERC.

Gill, S. (1994), 'Knowledge, Politics and the Neo-Liberal Political Economy', in R. Stubbs and G. Underhill (eds), *Political Economy and the Changing Global Order*, London: Macmillan.

Goldstein J. and R.O. Keohane (eds) (1993), *Ideas and Foreign Policy: Beliefs, Institutions and Political Change*, Ithaca: Cornell University Press.

Habermas, J. (1972), *Knowledge and Human Interests*, London: Heinemann.

Jones, R.W. (ed.) (2000), *Critical Theory and World Politics*, Boulder, CO.: Lynne Rienner.

Keohane, R.O. (1989), *International Institutions and State Power*, London: Westview.

Krasner, S. (1996), 'The accomplishments of international political economy', in S. Smith, K. Booth and M. Zalewski (eds), *International Theory: positivism and beyond*, Cambridge: Cambridge University Press.

Lakatos, I. (1970), 'Falsification and the Methodology of Scientific Research Programmes', in I. Lakatos and A. Musgrave (eds), *Criticism and the Growth of Knowledge*, Cambridge: Cambridge University Press.

Lakatos, I. and A. Musgrave (eds) (1970), *Criticism and the Growth of Knowledge*, Cambridge : Cambridge University Press.

MacLean, J. (2000), 'Philosophical Roots of Globalization and Philosophical Routes to Globalization', in R.D. Germain (ed.), *Globalization and its Critics*, London: Macmillan/PERC.

May, C. (1996), 'Strange Fruit: Susan Strange's Theory of Structural Power in the International Political Economy', *Global Society*, 10(2), 167–89.

McCarthy, T. (1993), 'The Idea of a Critical Theory and its Relation to Philosophy', in S. Benhabib, W. Bonß, and J. McCole (eds), *On Max Horkheimer: New Perspectives*, Cambridge, MA: MIT Press.

Morrow, R. (with D.D. Brown) (1994), *Critical Theory and Methodology*, London: Sage.

Murphy, C.N. and R. Tooze (eds) (1991), *The New International Political Economy*, Boulder, CO: Lynne Rienner.

Neufeld, M. (1995), *The Restructuring of International Relations Theory*, Cambridge: Cambridge University Press.

Palan, R. (1999), 'Susan Strange 1923–1998: a great international relations theorist', *Review of International Political Economy*, 6(2), 121–32.

Polanyi, K. (1957), *The Great Transformation: the political and economic origins of our time*, Boston: Beacon Press.

Rengger, N. and M. Hoffman (1992), 'Modernity, Postmodernism and International Relations', in J. Doherty, E. Graham and M. Malek (eds), *Postmodernism and the Social Sciences*, London: Macmillan.

Rosen, S.J. and W.S. Jones (1977), *The Logic of International Relations*, New York: Winthrop Publications.

Ruggie, J.G. (1998), *Constructing the World Polity*, London: Routledge.

Sayer, A. (1992), *Method in Social Science: A Realist Approach*, 2nd edn, London: Routledge.

Strange, S. ([1988]/1994), *States and Markets: An Introduction to International Political Economy*, London: Pinter Publishers.

Strange, S. (1996a), 'A Reply to Chris May', *Global Society*, 10(3), 303–5.

Strange, S. (1996b), *The Retreat of the State: the Diffusion of Power in the World Economy*, Cambridge: Cambridge University Press.

Strange, S. (1997), 'Territory, State, Authority and Economy: a new realist ontology of global political economy', in Robert W. Cox (ed.), *The New Realism*, London: Macmillan, pp.3–19.

Strange, S. (1998), 'International Political Economy: Beyond Economics and International Relations', *Economies et Sociétés, Relations économiques internationales*, Serie P, no.4, 5–26.

Taylor, C. (1985), *Philosophy and the Human Sciences: Philosophical Papers 2*, Cambridge: Cambridge University Press.

Tooze, R. and C. Murphy (1996), 'The Epistemology of Poverty and the Poverty of Epistemology in IPE: Mystery, Blindness and Invisibility', *Millennium; Journal of International Studies*, 25(3), Winter, 681–707.

Walker, R.B.J. (1989), 'History and Structure in the Theory of I.R.', *Millennium; Journal of International Studies*, 18(2), Summer, 163–83.

Walt, S.M. (1998), 'International Relations: One World, Many Theories', *Foreign Policy*, Spring.

PART IV
STATE POWER AND
GLOBAL HEGEMONY

11 The Retreat of the State?

ROBERT GILPIN

Introduction

Shortly before her death, I wrote to Susan Strange and expressed my deep intellectual debt to her. When I was a junior professor, I attended a seminar she was presenting at the London School of Economics, where she introduced me to the importance of what we now call 'multinational' or 'transnational' corporations. This fascinating experience was the beginning of my first encounter with what later became known as 'international political economy'. A few years later, Strange's 'International Economics and International Relations: A Case of Mutual Neglect' (1970) and *Sterling and British Policy* (1971) opened up another new intellectual world to me; whereas the former was a pioneering argument for the importance of international political economy, the latter is a classic study in the field. Throughout my career, Strange's writings have been a source of inspiration. Even though she and I frequently disagreed, I have always considered her a truly outstanding scholar in international relations.

Strange was the most outspoken critic of regime theory (1982: 479–97). According to her, regime theory was at best a passing fad, and at worst a polemical device designed to legitimate America's continuing domination of the world economy. Strange and other critics alleged that such international regimes as those governing trade and monetary affairs had been economically, politically and ideologically biased in America's favor, that these regimes were put in place by American power, reflected American interests, and were not (as American regime theorists have argued) politically and economically neutral. Strange charged that many of the fundamental problems afflicting the world economy actually resulted from ill-conceived and predatory American economic policies rather than simply being symptoms of American economic decline.

'Strange's foremost example of American culpability was the huge American demand in the 1980s and 1990s for international capital to finance America's federal budget and trade/payments deficit' (1982). Through use of what she referred to as 'structural power' (such as America's military, financial and technological power), she alleged that the United States continued to run the world economy during that period and made a mess of it. Strange and other critics also alleged that the regime of the dollar as the key international currency had permitted the United States to behave irresponsibly. More generally, Strange and other foreign critics charged that the American discipline of international political economy, and regime theory in particular, have been little more than efforts to defend America's continuing desire to reign economically and politically over the rest of the world.

In *The Retreat of the State* (1996), Strange admonished fellow scholars in the field of international political economy to broaden their analytic horizon and pay more attention to non-state actors. As she convincingly argued, the state (or rather the nation state) is changing and may in certain ways be declining. However, the diminished role of the state in international economic affairs does not lead to the conclusion that the state has become as helpless in the face of inexorable market forces as her book implied. Her corrective to the traditional canon of international political economy is important, but it is overstated and based on a misreading of the economic role of the state both in the contemporary era and in the past. Despite the increasing importance of the market, the ability of states, especially strong ones, to control or at least to moderate the economic forces besetting them continues to be a significant factor in the outcomes of 'political economic' activities.

The Retreat of the State represented a significant change in Strange's intellectual orientation. Her earlier writings on international political economy gave primacy to the state or at least equal prominence to the role of states and of the market. Later in her life, this balance changed and she began to emphasize the increasing importance of the market and of transnational actors relative to that of the state and its policies. The more market-oriented Strange who wrote *The Retreat of the State* could not possibly have written the incisive criticisms in the 1980s of the irresponsible behavior of one state (the United States) and its negative consequences for the international economy. In contrast to her earlier and correct position that both state and market are necessary to political economy, Strange argued in *The Retreat of the State* that an historic shift had taken place from the central role of the state in the international system to a system where power is dispersed among a number of actors. These include multinational corporations (MNCs), international organizations (IOs) and non-governmental organizations (NGOs). This theme is set forth most clearly in *The Retreat of the State* where Strange summarized the argument of the book:

> The argument put forward is that the impersonal forces of world markets, integrated over the postwar period more by private enterprise in finance, industry and trade than by the cooperative decisions of government, are now more powerful than the states to whom ultimate political authority over society and economy is supposed to belong. (1996: 4)

Strange 'got it right' in her earlier and more state-centric writings, but her later more 'market-oriented' writings significantly overstated the retreat in the economic role of the state. Yet 'retreat' is an ambiguous term and can have quite different meanings.

This chapter assesses Strange's argument that states have been largely stripped of their ability to carry out their traditional economic functions, including management of the overall economy, provision of social insurance and regulation of business activities. Economic globalization and the increasing integration of national economies by trade, international finance and the activities of multinational corporations have certainly constrained the ability of states to carry out their economic functions. However, these constraints are much less binding than Strange and many others have argued. The state has not lost its economic autonomy and it does continue to have considerable latitude in the formulation and implementation of economic policies. More attention should be given to the important state functions of establishing the legal framework for economic activities and managing the national economy through the use of macroeconomic policy.

The Globalization Thesis

Although Strange did not employ the term 'globalization' and in fact scorned its use, her argument that markets have largely superseded national governments in the realm of economic affairs rests on the belief that states have become tightly integrated into a global economy over which they had little or no control.[1] Proponents of the globalization thesis assert that a quantum change in human affairs has taken place as the flow of goods, services and investment across national borders has expanded from a trickle to a flood. Political, economic and social activities are alleged to have become worldwide in scope, and interactions among states and societies are believed to have eradicated the importance of national borders. As global integrative processes widen and deepen, it is asserted that markets have become the most important mechanism determining both domestic and international affairs. A number of scholars, including Strange herself, have argued that in this highly integrated global economy the nation state has become an anachronism.

Although the term 'globalization' is now used very broadly, economic globalization has entailed only a few key developments in trade, finance and foreign direct investment by multinational corporations. Since the end of World War II, international trade has greatly expanded and has become a much more important factor in both domestic and international economic affairs. Whereas the volume of international commerce had grown by only five-tenths of one per cent annually between 1913 and 1948, it grew at an annual rate of 7 per cent from 1948 to 1973. International trade in fact has grown much more rapidly than global economic output. Throughout the postwar era, trade has grown from 7 per cent to 21 per cent of total world income, while the value of world trade has increased from $57 billion in 1947 to $6 trillion in the 1990s. In addition to the great expansion of merchandise trade (goods), trade in services (banking, information and so on) has also significantly increased during the decades of the 1970s and 1980s. With this immense expansion of world trade, international competition also greatly increased. Consumers and export sectors within individual nations benefit from increased openness, but many businesses find themselves competing against more efficient foreign firms. During the 1980s and 1990s, trade competition became even more intense as a growing number of industrializing economies shifted from an import-substitution to an export-led growth strategy. Nevertheless, it is important to recognize that, even today, the major competitors for almost all American firms remain other American firms.

Underlying the expansion of global trade have been a number of developments. Since World War II, trade barriers have declined significantly as a result of successive rounds of trade negotiations. For example, over the past half-century, average tariff levels of the United States and other industrialized countries have dropped from about 40 per cent to only 6 per cent, and barriers to trade in services have also been lowered. In addition, since the late 1970s deregulation and privatization have further opened national economies to imports. Technological advances in communications and transportation have reduced costs and thus significantly encouraged trade expansion. Taking advantage of these economic and technological changes, more and more businesses have expanded their horizons to include international markets. Despite these developments, most trade still takes place among the three advanced industrialized economies (the United States, Western Europe and Japan) plus a few emerging markets in East Asia,

Latin America and elsewhere. Most of the less developed world in fact is excluded, except as exporters of food and raw materials.

Since the mid-1970s, the removal of capital controls, creation of new financial instruments and technological advances in communications have contributed to a more highly integrated international financial system.[2] The volume of the trade in foreign exchange (buying and selling national currencies) in the late 1990s reached approximately $1.5 trillion per day, an eightfold increase since 1986. Meanwhile, the global volume of exports (goods and services) for all of 1997 was $6.6 trillion or *only* $25 billion per day! In addition, the amount of investment capital seeking higher returns has grown enormously; by the mid-1990s, mutual funds, pension funds and the like totaled $20 trillion, ten times the 1980 figure. The significance of these huge investments is greatly magnified by the fact that foreign investments are frequently leveraged, that is, they are investments made with borrowed funds. Finally, derivatives or repackaged securities and other financial assets play an important role in international finance. Valued at $360 trillion (larger than the value of the entire global economy), they have contributed to the complexity and also the instability of the international economy.

This financial revolution has linked national economies closely to one another, significantly increased the capital available for developing countries, and accelerated economic development, particularly in the case of the East Asian emerging markets. However, as a large portion of these financial flows has been short-term, highly volatile and speculative, international finance has become the most vulnerable and unstable aspect of the global capitalist economy. The immense scale, velocity and speculative nature of financial movements across national borders have made governments more vulnerable to sudden shifts in these movements. Governments can therefore easily fall prey to currency speculators and to large 'hedge' or speculative funds, as happened in the 1992 European financial crisis, the punishing 1994–5 collapse of the Mexican peso and the devastating East Asian financial crisis in the late 1990s. Although, for some, financial globalization exemplifies the healthy and beneficial triumph of global capitalism, for Strange and others the international financial system was 'out of control' and in need of improved regulation.

The term 'globalization' itself came into popular usage in the second half of the 1980s in connection with the huge surge of foreign direct investment (FDI) by multinational corporations (MNCs). Foreign direct investment expanded significantly, increasing much more rapidly than either world trade or economic output. Throughout much of the 1990s, FDI outflows from the major industrialized countries to industrializing countries rose by approximately 15 per cent annually until the cumulative value of FDI amounted to hundreds of billions of dollars in the late 1990s. However, the largest fraction of FDI has been directed to the industrialized countries themselves, especially the United States and Western Europe, and the greatest portion of this investment has been in such high-tech industries as automobiles and information technology.

It is important to look at several noteworthy aspects of MNC activities. Despite much talk of corporate globalization, FDI is actually highly concentrated and unevenly distributed around the globe. Most FDI is directed to the United States, China and Western Europe because firms are attracted to large or potentially large markets. FDI in less developed countries, with a few notable exceptions, has been modest. In addition to several Latin American countries, and particularly the Brazilian and Mexican automobile sectors, most FDI in developing countries has been placed in the emerging markets of East and Southeast Asia. By far the largest recipient among the developing economies has been China. When one speaks of corporate globalization it should be appreciated that only a very few countries are deeply involved. It must also be appreciated that MNCs are the product of the culture and national policies of their home society; they have not transcended the world of nation states. There are and very likely always will be fundamental differences among American, Japanese and European firms that reflect their distinctive national origins.

Economic globalization has been driven by political, economic and technological developments. The compression of time and space by advances in communications and transportation and the emergence of the information economy have greatly reduced the costs of international commerce and, largely under American leadership, both the industrialized and industrializing economies have initiated decreases in trade and investment barriers. Eight rounds of multilateral trade negotiations under the General Agreement on Tariffs and Trade (GATT) have significantly decreased trade barriers. Since the mid-1980s, Latin American, Pacific Asian and other developing countries have introduced important reforms to reduce their trade, financial and other economic barriers. More and more firms are pursuing global economic strategies to take advantage of these developments.

The elimination of capital controls and the movement toward a global financial system, accompanied by the removal of barriers to FDI, have also accelerated the movement toward both global and regional integration of services and manufacturing. In both industrialized and industrializing economies the spread of pro-market thinking has strongly influenced economic policy and led to a reduction of the role of the state in the economy. The collapse of the Soviet command economy, failure of the Third World's import-substitution strategy and the growing belief in the United States and other industrialized economies that the welfare state has become a major obstacle to economic growth have encouraged acceptance of unrestricted markets as the solution to the economic ills of modern society. Sweeping reforms have led to deregulation, privatization and more open national economies.

These impressive and significant developments have led proponents of the globalization thesis to argue that the nation state is finished as an economic actor, and a number of books proclaim the death or at least the decline of the state. Although the role of the state has been diminished by these developments, the state continues to be a powerful actor in economic affairs, and in some instances its importance has been actually increasing. In order to assess these two opposed views on the role of the state in the contemporary world, the next section will discuss the ability of the state to manage the national economy through its use of macroeconomic policy. If, as is probable, the state still has an important function in managing the modern economy, then the idea that the economic role of the state has become obsolete is highly questionable.

The Effectiveness of Macroeconomic Policy

One of the most important functions of the modern state has been the overall management of the national economy. Since the end of World War II, and especially with the acceptance in the early postwar era of Keynesian economics, national governments in the advanced industrialized economies have been held responsible for the general performance of the economy. The state's task has been to promote national economic stability and to maneuver the economy between the undesirable conditions of recession and inflation. Through the employment of macroeconomic policies, the state has been able to control, at least to some extent, the troubling vicissitudes of the market. At least in the case of the United States and some other countries, the national executive has used fiscal policy, mainly in the form of government spending, to promote full employment. The American central bank and other central banks have expanded or contracted the national money supply to steer the economy between recession and inflation. Although many other factors are involved in the success or failure of national economies, central banks have gained a prominence in guiding the economy between the equally dangerous shoals of inflation and recession.

In *The Retreat of the State,* Strange did not devote much attention to the issue of macroeconomic policy. However, her argument that the power of the state over economic affairs had significantly declined implies that national governments could no longer manage their economies. Assuming that this is a fair inference from her book, an examination of the efficacy of macroeconomic policy in today's global economy provides a means of testing Strange's 'retreat of the state' thesis. It is true that macroeconomic policy has become more complicated in the highly integrated world economy of the 21st century; however, macroeconomic policy still does work and can achieve its goals at least as well as it ever could. What better example than the Federal Reserve's very successful management of the American economy in the mid-to-late 1990s! Moreover, the principal constraints on macroeconomic policy today, as in the past, are to be found at the domestic rather than at the international level.

Macroeconomic policy consists of two basic tools for managing a national economy: fiscal and monetary policies. The principal instruments of fiscal policy are taxation and government expenditures. Through lowering or raising taxes and/or increasing or decreasing federal expenditures, the federal government (Congress and the executive) can affect the national level of economic activities. Whereas a federal budget deficit (spending more than tax receipts) will stimulate the economy, a budget surplus (spending less than tax receipts) will decrease economic activities. Monetary policy works through determining the size and velocity of a nation's money supply. In the American case, the Federal Reserve can stimulate or depress the level of economic activities by increasing or restricting the supply of dollars available to consumers and producers. The principal method employed by the Federal Reserve to achieve this goal is its determination of the national level of interest rates; whereas a low interest rate stimulates economic growth, a high rate depresses it. The interaction of fiscal and monetary policies is complex and shall be discussed only briefly.

The globalization thesis argues that the effectiveness of both fiscal and monetary policies has been severely undermined by the integration of national financial systems and that new financial instruments such as derivatives, along with advances in the information economy, have greatly increased the size and velocity of international financial flows. Fiscal policy, some argue further, has been seriously constrained by the need of national governments to please the owners of international capital. If, for example, a government were to implement economic policies or take other actions upsetting to international lenders, many allege that the latter could punish the former through raising interest rates and/or refusing to finance the former's budget deficit. Therefore, some reach the conclusion that the threat that international capital can pose does limit the autonomy of individual states. Some also argue that a government's ability to raise taxes has been undercut by the increased international mobility of multinational firms; if one government raises taxes, it is alleged, MNCs can shift production and other activities overseas. For all these reasons, many conclude that the governmental ability to use taxation to manage the economy and achieve other public policy goals has been diminished.

Furthermore, arguments have been made that the effectiveness of monetary policy has been significantly reduced by the increased importance of international financial flows. If, for example, a central bank lowers interest rates to stimulate the economy, investors will transfer their capital to other economies with higher interest rates and thus negate the intended stimulus of lower rates. By the same token, if a central bank increases interest rates in order to slow the economy, investment capital will flow into the economy and counter the intended deflationary effects of higher rates and stimulate economic activities. In all these ways, economic globalization is believed to have undermined the efficacy of fiscal and monetary policy. In brief, some consider national governments no longer able to manage their economies.

The contention that macroeconomic policy has become ineffective in a globalized economy can be placed in proper perspective by considering what economists call the 'trilemma' or 'irreconcilable trinity' of economic policy.[3] Every nation is confronted by an inevitable tradeoff among three desirable goals of economic policy: fixed exchange rates, national autonomy in macroeconomic policy and international capital mobility. A nation might want a stable exchange rate in order to reduce economic uncertainty and stabilize the economy. Or it might desire discretionary monetary policy in order to promote economic growth and steer the economy between recession and inflation. Or a government might want freedom of capital movements to facilitate the conduct of trade, foreign investment and other international business activities. Unfortunately, a government cannot achieve all three of these goals simultaneously. It can have at most two, but not all three, of these objectives. For example, choosing a fixed and stable exchange rate, along with some latitude for independent monetary policies, would mean forgoing freedom of capital movements because international capital flows could undermine both fixed exchange rate stability and independent monetary policies. On the other hand, a country might choose pursuit of macroeconomic policies to promote economic growth, but it then would have to sacrifice either a fixed exchange rate or freedom of capital movement.

This analysis tells us that, although economic globalization does constrain government policy options, it does not impose a financial straitjacket on national macroeconomic policies. Whether an individual nation does or does not have the capacity for an independent macroeconomic policy is itself a policy choice. If a nation wants to have the capability to pursue an independent macroeconomic policy, it can achieve that goal by abandoning either fixed exchange rates or capital mobility. Different countries do in fact prefer to emphasize one or another of these three desired goals. The United States, for example, prefers independent monetary policy and freedom of capital movements and thereby sacrifices fixed exchange rates; the members of the European Economic and Monetary Union (EMU), on the other hand, prefer relatively fixed exchange rates and have initiated creation of a common currency to achieve this goal. Some other countries, such as China, that place a high value on macroeconomic independence, have imposed controls on capital movements. Domestic economic interests also have different preferences. Whereas export businesses have a strong interest in the exchange rate, domestic-oriented businesses place a higher priority on national policy autonomy. Investors prefer freedom of capital movements, whereas labor tends to be opposed to such movement, unless of course it means inward rather than outward investment. In short, economic globalization in itself does not prevent a nation from managing its economy through use of fiscal and monetary policies.

To evaluate whether or not national monetary policy continues to be effective in an age of economic globalization, one must first consider how monetary policy is used by a nation's central bank to manage the overall economy. Although central banks operate differently around the world, an examination of how the American Federal Reserve (the Fed) steers the American economy is instructive and reveals that, at least in the American case, globalization has had only minimal effects.

Through its power to increase or decrease the number of dollars in the economy, the Fed is able to steer the overall economy. The level of national economic activity is strongly influenced by the size of the nation's money supply. An increase in the money supply stimulates economic activities; a decrease in the money supply slows down economic activity. The Fed has three basic instruments to determine the nation's supply of money. The first directly affects the money supply; the other tools work indirectly through the banking system. Of the three techniques, the first to be discussed below is by far the most important.

The Fed's primary tool for overall management of the economy is changing the federal funds rate, which is the interest rate that one bank charges another to borrow money. The principal means employed is to open market operations carried through the Federal Reserve Bank of New York Open Market Desk. Through the sale or purchase of US government securities, the Fed can influence the overall level of national economic activity. If, for example, the Fed wants to raise the funds rate in order to slow the economy, it sells US government securities to commercial banks. The effect of this action is to take money or liquidity out of the banking system and hence out of the economy. If, on the other hand, the Fed wants to lower rates in order to stimulate the economy, it uses dollars to purchase securities from banks and increases the money or liquidity in the economy.

The Fed can also change the discount rate when it changes the funds rate. The discount rate is the interest rate on loans that the Fed makes directly to the nation's commerical banks. The discount rate is usually set equal to or a half-point below the funds rate. The Fed, for example, loans money to banks whose reserves fall below the Fed's reserve requirements (see below); this may happen if a bank has made too many loans or is experiencing too many withdrawals. By lending to private banks and increasing the reserves of those banks, the Fed enables banks to make more loans and, thereby, increase the nation's money supply. By raising or lowering the discount rate on its loans to banks, the Fed influences the reserves of those banks and hence the total amount of loans that banks can make. Whereas raising the discount rate decreases loans and money creation, the lowering of the discount rate increases loans and money creation. These changes in turn have a powerful influence on the overall level of economic activity.

Another tool that the Fed has available is its authority to determine the reserve requirements of the nation's banks. Reserve requirements specify the minimal size of the monetary reserves that a bank must hold against deposits subject to withdrawal. Reserve requirements thus determine the amount of money that a bank is permitted to lend and, thereby, how much money the bank can place in circulation. Through raising or lowering reserve requirements, the Fed sets a limit on how much money the nation's banks can inject into the economy. However, this method of changing the money supply is used infrequently because changed reserve requirements can be very disruptive to the banking system.

Globalization has had an impact on each of these policy instruments. The effectiveness of open market operations has probably been somewhat reduced by the growth of the international financial market. The purchase or sale of US bonds by foreigners can affect the national money supply; in the late 1990s, it was estimated that approximately $150 billion were held overseas by foreigners. Yet this number is dwarfed by the $8 trillion American economy. Also the American financial system (like that of other industrialized countries) exhibits a 'home bias', that is to say, most individuals keep their financial assets in their own economy. It is possible, however, that central banks in smaller and weaker economies find that their ability to manage the money supply has been decreased, as was exemplified by the 1997 Asian financial crisis.

The continuing power of the Fed over national banks and the money supply through raising or lowering the funds and/or discount rate has been challenged by the development of the credit card and other new forms of money. These credit instruments have decreased, at least somewhat, the effectiveness of the Fed's use of the discount rate to control the economy. Still more problematic for the Fed is the increasing use of e-money in internet commerce. In effect, these developments mean that the monopoly once held by the Fed and the banking system over the creation of money is being diluted. Through use of a credit card or participation in e-commerce, an individual or business can create money. Yet, at some point, e-money and other novel forms of money must be converted into 'real' or legal tender, and at that point the Fed still retains control of the creation of real money. Thus, although the monetary system has become much more complex, the Fed still has the ultimate control over the monetary system and, through it, the overall economy.

Although the power of the Fed and other central banks over the economy has been somewhat diminished by globalization, as long as cash remains the ultimate means of exchange and the settlement of accounts, central banks can still retain a substantial control over the money supply and hence of the economy. In fact, even if everyone switched to electronic means of payment but credit issuers still settled their balances with merchants through the banking system (as happens with credit cards now), central banks would still retain overall control. However, one day, e-money could displace other forms of money. If and when this develops, financial settlements could be carried out without going through commercial banks and as a consequence central banks would lose their ability to control the economy through the setting of interest rates. The result of this development would be what Friedrich Hayek has called the 'denationalization' of money, yet it would seem reasonable to believe that some public agency would still be needed to control inflation and monitor the integrity of the computer system used for payments settlements.[4]

With respect to the matter of reserve requirements, intense competition among international banks may have induced central banks to reduce reserve requirements in order to make the banking industry more competitive. Japanese banks, for example, have long been permitted by the Japanese government to keep much smaller reserves than is the case for American banks. One of the major purposes of the Basle Agreement, named after the Swiss city where the International Bank for Settlements is located, was to make reserve requirements more uniform throughout the world. Rumor has it that this agreement was engineered by the Fed to decrease the international competitiveness of Japanese and other foreign banks vis-à-vis American international banks. Whatever the underlying motive, the Agreement has been termed a response to financial globalization, and uniform international reserve requirements largely re-established their effectiveness as instruments of policy.

The principal constraints on macroeconomic policy are found at the domestic rather than at the international level. In a domestic economy isolated from the international economy, the major constraint on fiscal policy is the cost of borrowing. If a national government were to use deficit spending to stimulate its economy, the resulting budget deficit would have to be financed by domestic lenders. However, an upper limit is placed on government borrowing because, as the budget deficit and the costs of servicing the deficit rise, bond purchasers become more and more fearful that the government may default on its debt and/or use monetary policy to inflate the money supply and thus reduce the real value of the debt. The increased risk as debt rises causes lenders to stop lending and/ or to charge higher and higher interest rates; this then discourages further borrowing by the government. Also another important constraint on monetary policy in a domestic economy is the threat of inflation; this threat places an upper limit on the ability of a central bank to stimulate the economy through increasing the money supply and/or lowering the interest rate. At some point, the threat of inflation will discourage economic activity. In short, there are important limits on macroeconomic policy that have nothing whatsoever to do with the international economy – and these domestic constraints existed long before anyone had heard the term 'globalization'.

Economic globalization has made the task of managing an economy both easier and at the same time also more difficult; furthermore, globalization has greatly increased the risks to an economy from imprudent economic policies. On the one hand, globalization has enabled governments to borrow more freely; the United States in the 1980s and 1990s borrowed heavily from Japanese and other foreign investors in order to finance a federal budget deficit and a high rate of economic growth. However, this debt-financed growth strategy, as Strange pointed out in *Casino Capitalism* (1986) and again in *Mad Money* (1998), is extraordinarily risky, potentially damaging to the international economy, and cannot continue forever; fearing the collapse of the dollar, investors could one day flee dollar-denominated assets for safer assets denominated in other currencies. The consequences of such flight could be devastating for the United States and for the rest of the world economy. Thus, although economic globalization has increased the latitude of governments to pursue expansionary economic policies through borrowing excessively abroad, such serious financial crises of the post-war era as the Mexican crisis in 1994–5, the 1997 East Asian financial crisis, and the disturbing collapse of the Russian ruble in August 1998 demonstrate the huge and widespread risks associated with this practice.

Economic globalization and the greater openness of domestic economies have also modified the rules of economic policy.[5] As demonstrated by the Fleming–Mundell model of open macroeconomics, the choice of either fiscal or monetary policy to manage an economy has quite different consequences in an open economy than is the case in a closed economy. At the beginning of the 21st century, for example, if governments wish to support a fixed exchange rate, they must rely more on fiscal than on monetary policy than would be the case in a closed economy. If, on the other hand, the government chooses to let the currency float, it will need to depend more on monetary than on fiscal policy. In short, the increasing openness of national economies has made the exercise of macroeconomic policy more complex and difficult. This situation does not mean, however, that a national government can no longer guide the economy around the dangerous shoals of inflation and depression, but it does mean that the risk of shipwreck has grown.

The Need for a Historical Perspective

The globalization thesis lacks a historical perspective. Those individuals who argue that globalization has severely limited economic sovereignty appear to believe that governments once possessed unlimited national autonomy and freedom in economic matters. Their reasoning appears to assume that nation states in the past enjoyed an unrestricted ability to determine economic policy and manage their economies, that governments were free because they were not subordinate to or encumbered by transnational market forces. As proponents of the globalization thesis contrast economic policy in the modern era to this imagined past, they conclude that nation states have, for the first time ever, become constrained by the increased integration of national economies through trade, financial flows and the activities of multinational firms. In effect, having assumed that states once had complete economic freedom, these individuals misperceive the reality of the fundamental relationship between the state and the economy. When viewed from a more accurate historical perspective, the relationship of state and market in the modern era is neither particularly startling nor revolutionary.

In the decades prior to World War I, national governments had, in fact, little effective control over their economies. Under the classical gold standard of fixed exchange rates, governments were more tightly bound by what economic historian Barry Eichengreen has called 'golden fetters' than they were in the late 20th century world of flexible exchange rates. Moreover, as Nobel Laureate Arthur Lewis has observed, prior to World War I the economic agenda of governments everywhere was limited to little more than the efforts of central banks to maintain the value of their currencies at par with sterling. Also, as John Maynard Keynes pointed out in *The Economic Consequences of the Peace* (1919), national economic policy had not concerned itself with the welfare of the 'lower orders' of society. However, this relatively minor and highly constrained role of the state in the economy began to change dramatically with World War I, the Great Depression, and other economic and political developments.

Throughout the 20th century, the relationship of state and market changed as governments harnessed their economies for 'total war' and to meet their citizens' rising economic expectations; the great wars of the 20th century, the Great Depression and the immense economic demands of the cold war greatly elevated the state's role in the economy. During the three periods of intense concern about national security, governments fashioned new tools to manage their economies and began to exercise historically unprecedented control over their economies. The Great Depression, the rise of organized labor and the huge sacrifices imposed on national societies by World War II led Western governments after 1945 to expand their activities to guarantee full employment and the economic welfare of their citizens. In addition, the perceived success of the Communist experiment encouraged Western governments to help Keynes's 'lower orders'. After World War II, governments in every advanced economy assumed the responsibility to promote full employment, provide social insurance and achieve an ever-rising national standard of living.

Nevertheless, even after World War II, the role of Western governments in managing the economy remained fairly limited; in fact, economists themselves exaggerated the ability of governments (with their advice, of course) to use Keynesian techniques to manage and 'fine-tune' their economies (Berger and Dore 1996). Although high rates of economic and productivity growth were required to fulfill the rising and exaggerated expectations of Western populations, these rates declined significantly after 1973 in both the United States and Western Europe. Economists could not explain the drop in economic and productivity growth, nor could they advise governments how to reverse this downward trend. Although American economic and productivity growth rose again in the late 1990s, there is intense controversy about the role of government economic policy in this reversal. In effect, constraints on the effectiveness of macroeconomic policy have been due more to the limited ability of governments to manage the economy than to economic globalization.

Conclusion

The world at the opening of the 21st century is witnessing what Strange has labeled 'the retreat of the state'. However, this development can be overstated and a historical perspective is called for. Beginning with World War I, the role of the state in the economy experienced an enormous expansion, a development that, since the early 1980s, has slowed as retrenchment of the economic power of the 'warfare/welfare' state has begun. Yet the state continues to have a significant role in contemporary economies; it is not retreating in the sense of becoming eviscerated and becoming a hollow shell that will soon be thrown into the dustbin of history. Insofar as a retreat of the state has taken place in Western societies, this development reflects a significant change in international politics and economic ideology more than it does the constraining effects of economic globalization. In the United States and elsewhere, the end of the cold war and the triumph of a conservative anti-statist economic ideology associated with Margaret Thatcher and Ronald Reagan have resulted in an onslaught against the interventionist state. These political and ideological developments have forced the state to retreat to the more modest role that it had possessed in the late 19th century (Desch 1986). However, this development was not made inevitable by inexorable economic forces, and a more economically and politically insecure world would lead to a resurgence of state power.

Notes

1   The literature on economic globalization has become enormous. The most ency-clopedic work is David Held, Anthony McGrew, David Goldblatt and Jonathan Perraton, *Global Transformations: Politics, Economics and Culture* (Stanford: Stanford University Press, 1999).
2   An excellent discussion of this development is Benjamin J. Cohen, *The Geography of Money* (Cohen 1998).
3   The trilemma is set forth in Robert A. Mundell, *International Economics* (Mundell 1968).
4   'A Survey of the World Economy', *The Economist*, 25 September, 1999, p.42.
5   This and other discussions in this chapter are based in part on *The Economist*, 20 September, 1987, special 'Survey on the World Economy: The Future of the State'.

References

Berger, S. and R. Dore (1996), *National Diversity and Global Capitalism*, Ithaca: Cornell University Press.
Burtless, G., R.E. Lawrence, R.E. Litan and R.J. Shapiro (1998), *Globaphobia: Confronting Fears About Open Trade*, Washington D.C.: The Brookings Institution.

Cohen, B.J. (1998), *The Geography of Money*, Ithaca: Cornell University Press.
Desch, M. (1996), 'War and Strong States, Peace and Weak States', *International Organization*, 50(2): 237–68.
Doremus, P.N., W.W. Keller, L.W. Pauly and S. Reich (1998), *The Myth of the Global Corporation*, Princeton: Princeton University Press.
The Economist (20 September 1987), special 'Survey on the World Economy: The Future of the State'.
The Economist (25 September 1999), 'A Survey of the World Economy'.
Eichengreen, B. (1992), *Golden Fetters: The Gold Standard and the Great Depression, 1919–39*, New York: Oxford University Press.
Gilpin, R. (2000), *Global Political Economy: The New International Economic Order*, Princeton: Princeton University Press, forthcoming.
Held, D., A. McGrew, D. Goldblatt and J. Perraton (1999), *Global Transformations: Politics, Economics and Culture*, Stanford: Stanford University Press.
Keynes, J.M. (1919), *The Economic Consequences of the Peace*, London: Macmillan.
Lewis, W.A. (1978), *The Evolution of the International Economic Order*, Princeton: Princeton University Press.
Mundell, R.A. (1968), *International Economics*, New York: Macmillan.
Strange, S. (1970), 'International Economics and International Relations: A Case of Mutual Neglect', *International Affairs*, 46(2), 304–15.
Strange, S. (1971), *Sterling and British Policy*, London: Oxford University Press.
Strange, S. (1982), 'Cave! Hic Dragones: A Critique of Regime Analysis', *International Organization*, 36: 479–97.
Strange, S. (1986), *Casino Capitalism*, New York: Basil Blackwell.
Strange, S. (1996), *The Retreat of the State: The Diffusion of Power in the World Economy*, Cambridge: Cambridge University Press.
Strange, S. (1998), *Mad Money*, Manchester: Manchester University Press.
Yoffie, D.B. and B. Gomes-Casseres (1994), *International Trade and Competition: Cases and Notes in Strategy and Management*, 2nd edn, New York: McGraw Hill.

12 Strange's Oscillating Realism: Opposing the Ideal – and the Apparent

STEFANO GUZZINI[1]

Introduction

Writing about the relationship between Susan Strange and realism is like trying to make two moving targets meet. This is because there are nearly as many forms of realism as there are realists. Moreover, Strange consistently shifted the direction of her scholarly and non-scholarly work. Hence, if this chapter claims that Strange can be well understood as a realist, this has to be a realism of sorts.

This chapter argues that Strange's version of realism has been systematically oscillating between two poles: opposing the ideal and the apparent. This oscillation, which can also be found in E.H. Carr, produced perhaps her most important conceptual contribution, namely 'structural power'. At the same time, it is responsible for two important internal tensions in her work: it clashes with her encompassing materialist position with which she wanted IR to become IPE and, eventually, it renders her views on (political) agency incoherent.

The Two Poles of Strange's Realism

Strange's realism displays a central duality. Traditionally, the discipline of international relations conceives of realism in opposition to idealism, to utopian thinking. Without wanting to deconstruct the long lists of dichotomies that have been spurred by this distinction (see Walker 1987; 1993) or the fictitious presentation of inter-war debates as idealist (for this critique, see Schmidt 1998), this chapter will show that Strange fits rather well with some of the central tenets of realism, so understood. She did not spare her criticism of those fellow realists who did not seem to appreciate what she considered to be major shifts in the nature of global affairs. Strange, the anti-idealist realist, was the champion of a power-materialist discipline of IPE, which subsumes, if not swallows, classical IR and its more narrow-minded scholars, as she would see them. However, political theory distinguishes a second facet of realism, understood in opposition to yet another phenomenon: the real is the opposite of the apparent (see the characteristically astute discussion in Bobbio 1996 [1969]: XIV–XVII). This facet has frequently been the main motivation of Strange's work, in particular when she scorns the self-celebration of the 'American Century'.

This double heritage of political realism, opposing both the ideal and the apparent, is ripe with tensions. Realism as anti-idealism is status quo-oriented. It relies on the entire panoply of arguments so beautifully summarized by Alfred Hirschman in his *The Rhetoric of Reaction* (Hirschman 1991). According to the *futility* thesis, any attempt at change is condemned to be without any real effect. The *perversity* thesis would argue that, far from changing for the better, such policies only add new problems to the already existing ones. The central *jeopardy* thesis says that purposeful attempts at social change will only undermine the already achieved. The best is the enemy of the good, and so on. Anti-apparent realism, however, is an attitude more akin to the political theories of suspicion. It looks at what is hidden behind the smokescreen of current ideologies, putting the allegedly self-evident into the limelight of criticism. With the other form of realism, it shares a reluctance to treat beautiful ideas as what they claim to be. But it is much more sensitive to their ideological use, revolutionary as well as conservative. Whereas the anti-ideal defends the status quo, the anti-apparent questions it. It wants to unmask existing power relations.

International Relations (IR) has known many scholars who have shifted back and forth between these two conceptions of realism, often without noticing it. The most obvious example, perhaps, is E.H. Carr's (1946) *The Twenty Years' Crisis*. In the initial chapters, he sets up a typology of realism as opposed to utopia and argues for a discipline of IR, which now has to settle down, and get rid of its early history of hopes and wishes, as necessary as they had been to launch the discipline. Yet, at the same time, Carr takes visible delight from bashing his fellow Britons who, in the name of liberalism, were so amazingly blind as to believe that what was good for Britain was good for the world. The famous critique of the apparent 'harmony of interests' strikes the reader as obviously realist; but it is a realism of a very different kind. Far from defending the real against a utopia that will never come, it unmasks a utopia dressed up as real. Being aware of the historical character of any ideology, Carr later logically delves into the study of history, indeed into the history of change *par excellence*, the history of revolutions. For the same reason, he relies on Karl Mannheim's (1936) historical sociology of knowledge (for a trenchant exposition of the intellectual origins and internal inconsistencies of Carr, and the usually one-sided reception, see Jones 1998). It comes as no surprise, then, that many radical writers, such as, for instance Robert Cox (1986 [1981]), see themselves in the tradition of the realist Carr.

Strange's realism does not feel comfortable with either strand for too long, being no absolute defender of prudence misunderstood as immobility, and no proponent of change illuminated by the grand vision. It is as if her work reversed its direction whenever it risked getting too close to one pole. Again, this oscillation is necessary for such a type of realism. As Carr had remarked a long time ago, '[t]he impossibility of being a consistent and thorough-going realist [understood as anti-ideal] is one of the most certain and most curious lessons of political science' (Carr 1946: 89). The anti-ideal position, if reified, becomes itself an ideology that needs to be undermined.

By the same token, this double realist inspiration does not in itself provide a framework for understanding the world – a theory, as it were; realism so understood is merely an attitude towards the world (for this argument, see also Gilpin 1986 [1984]: 104–5, referring back to Rosecrance). Consequently, Strange's work is torn by internal tensions that she was at pains to reunite.

Yet perhaps it is exactly the tension and intellectual challenge of this oscillation which inspired some of her most important conceptual particularities, many of which are important contributions to both IPE and realist thought. As the next section will attempt to show, anti-ideal realism is the source for her wider materialist conception of politics as expressed by the necessary shift from IR to IPE. In order to make this argument, Strange develops a new approach to power, including prominently 'structural power', perhaps one of the more important contributions to IPE and realism. At the same time, her discontent with the present 'ungovernance' of the international system, and the role the United State plays therein, introduces her anti-apparent realism. She criticizes the present ruling of the global political economy, which comes in the disguise of a necessity, to which we cannot but adapt. For her, such a view is nothing but a new version of an apparent 'harmony of interests' embodied by the international business civilization. Instead, she sees it as a global order, which the collectivity of states, and in particular the United States, chooses not to control.

This oscillating reliance on the two sides of realism produces two internal tensions, as the third section will try to show. On the one hand, her structuralist understanding of power includes a structure – knowledge – which basically contradicts her realist materialism. On the other hand, her assessment of the diffusion of power eventually clashes with her very critique of US policies.

The Necessity for a Realist to be a Political Economist: Taking Power Materialism Seriously

While studying the politics of a currency and the decline of a former global actor, Strange (1971) commenced a long series of publications that examine the interrelationship between power and finance. This is the one continuous inspiration for her research. She drew two lessons, that might appear obvious today but were quite contentious to many of her colleagues in IR at the time, particularly to realists.

The first lesson was that international politics could not be reduced to what states do. As well as in her later study on the Bretton Woods system (1976), state policies, even if nicely designed and with all the best intentions, have 'realistically' to take into account the force of private actors, such as firms. To put it more generally, they have to cope with market forces. In her career, Strange made no secret of her contempt for the British Foreign Office which was still too much attached to a view of the world long since obsolete. The insistence on a classical definition of international statecraft, classical war and classical diplomacy could not, according to her, produce anything but political blindness in world affairs.

Her academic colleagues in IR were not spared either. Exasperated by her own collaboration with Schwarzenberger at University College London, she insisted that if IR did not incorporate political economy, it was doomed to produce useless analysis. She never shared the strategic focus of many of her colleagues during the cold war. Whereas, in her earlier work, she maintained a focus on the state system, even that focus would give way to the triangular diplomacy between states and firms in her co-authored *Rival States and Rival Firms* (1991).

The second lesson, more directed against economists – whether politicians or academics – was that the driving force in international economics was not trade, but finance and production. In fact, in her world view, the most important factor in the political economy was the control of capital (credits and production). With the need to keep good ratings on stock and debt markets and the need to hedge against currency rate fluctuations, capital markets of all sorts became the driving forces of modern capitalism. Trade, despite its prominence in mainly US studies, was largely a secondary indicator following these more profound forces. In a move similar to her critique of IR security spe-

cialists, Strange criticized the discipline of economics as basically irrelevant. Instead of abstract modeling, her approach to political economy
was always more historical and progressively shifted to insights from
political geographers, and business and banking economists.

As a result, her approach can be said to be very critical of realism.
Ever since Waltz's *Theory of International Politics* (1979) was used to
redefine the agenda in IR, Strange's type of analysis appeared fundamentally at odds with contemporary realism. Confronted with a crisis
of the realist school, Waltz resurrected a disciplinary wall, which
defined the subject-matter (international politics, not foreign policy),
a method (based on an analogy with neoclassical economics) and a
specific approach (systemic realism, or outside-in, based on the balance of power, as the only theory of IR). His success exasperated all
those who had been trying to open up the research agenda.

Yet if some scholars were exasperated by what realism had done to
the discipline of IR, some realists were increasingly wary of what the
discipline of IR had done to realism. Hence some realists who wanted
to open up the research agenda, rather than to move it to other
disciplines, opposed Waltz's narrow definition of both IR and realism. Although doing so in a different vein, Robert Gilpin also tried to
shift realists away from the classical security agenda. The works of
both Gilpin and Strange stand out as attempts to break loose of the
neorealist straitjacket imposed on international research (see also
Guzzini 1998: chapter 11). As such, they are not much interested in
reproducing the paradigmatic distinction between domestic and international politics, so cherished by neorealists. Nor are they interested
in keeping politics apart from economics. Indeed, all the disciplinary
walls so meticulously erected by Waltz would come tumbling down.
A realist IPE in the vein of Strange and Gilpin is a critique of the role
realism, both old and new, played in defining a narrow agenda for
research – and for politics.

At the same time, this move, as critical as it became to much of the
traditional realists who populated IR in Strange's early career, is a
move that does not fit the classical realism–idealism divide. Strange
did not criticize realism for its cyclical vision of history, for its obsession with conflict, for its emphasis on power and hierarchy. Instead,
she criticized it *for not taking these issues seriously enough*; that is, for
assuming a very static environment, as if the historical development
of capitalism had no effect on power politics. The history of conflict
might repeat itself, but not its nature.

In fact, Strange argues for a revision of realism, in which its basic
power materialism is redefined. Matter matters, but not only the
strategic one. The control of finance, that is currency, capital and
credit, is the matter of the day. As a good realist, she will admit that
the security structure is predominant 'in the last resort' (1988), but

for the time being we have to deal with the other ones. Her IPE, similar to Gilpin's version, is one possible but logical outcome of an attempt to update realism in an age of the welfare state and global capitalism. Behind the apparent materialism of the balance of power lurks a more encompassing one in a realist political economy.

Being both a critique of disciplinary realism and a renewal of realist materialism, it comes as no surprise that her approach centers on the old realist obsession with the concept of power. But given her understanding of what moves global politics – her redefinition of politics itself – she has to develop a view on power that differed from the classical realists. For her, power is more diffused both in its sources and effects. In order to better apprehend its present sources, she conceptualizes international hierarchy as the effect of the interrelation of four power structures: security, finance, production and knowledge. The control of these basic resources – arms, credit, capital and technology/culture – defines who is top dog or under dog in international affairs. Obviously, these power resources are not limited to state agents. In fact, firms might be prominent in the last three, many states irrelevant in all. The second part of her concept of power, the diffusion of power effects, is based upon the increasing globalization of politics. Here, Strange is essentially concerned with the effects of actions which, whether intended or not, crucially affect others. It is this second aspect that eventually produces tensions in her realism, moving from the anti-ideal to the anti-apparent.

A Critique of the Apparent Decline of US Power: Taking Soft Power and the Diffusion of Power Seriously – Eventually

The basic tension in Strange's approach can be summarized as follows: how is it that in a world in which power is increasingly diffused and the capacity to control events is said to evaporate, some actors are still criticized for being basically responsible for the situation and able but not willing to resolve it? The answer lies in a shift from the anti-ideal critique of our view of the world, stressing its base on material power redefined, to the anti-apparent critique of the top dogs, the 'international business civilisation' with its headquarters in the United States (Strange 1990: 260–65), that makes us believe that not much can be changed (Gramscian undertones are not fortuitous). Yet this shift produces internal tensions: to uphold the anti-apparent critique of the United States, Strange has to rely on a concept of structural power whose two ingredients, the diffusion of the sources of power, including ideas, and the diffusion of its effects, contradict both her anti-ideal materialism and eventually her critique of the United States itself.

The Idealist Streak in Soft Power

As long as Strange does not refer to the diffusion of power, there is not much of a tension. Hence her earlier critique of regime theory (1982) argues that international organizations, allegedly important in these international regimes, have no impact whatsoever. This, as she says herself, is the clearly (anti-ideal) realist streak in her argument.

But then an anti-apparent realist part creeps in. For her, the new focus on regimes and IOs should not blind us to the 'non-territorial empire' of the United States (ibid.: 482). In this piece, Strange basically argues that the United States is setting the research agenda, and that it has a vested interest in presenting the world run by regimes. Furthermore, she argues that regime theory is biased in assuming that everyone wants regimes, and more of them. This point is perhaps better phrased when she refers to 'order' as being the main aim of some states and not of others. This recalls Carr's typical realist criticism of the apparent harmony of interest in the status quo. Moreover, it is overly state-centric, leaving out important bargains and distributional issues below and across state frontiers.

The basic tension starts to develop when her critique of US policies, that is policies by a state, clashes with a world view which is less and less statist. The solution, or at least so it seems, lies again in the reconceptualization of power: the US empire is non-territorial, its power is structural. Hence one could have the cake and eat it: the United States is still *at* the center of world power, its policies could make a difference – and yet all this is part of a more diffused international power structure. But does it work?

The debate about the decline of US power in the aftermath of the Vietnam War, a debate that took on a political economy spin in the 1980s, provided Strange with a welcome foil for developing her thoughts on the changed nature of international power and politics. According to her, far from being a symptom of US decline, the demise of Bretton Woods was a testimony to US might: the United States was able to destroy the most important international regime on its own conditions – and got away with it (Strange 1986). In other words, although not necessarily controlling all outcomes, the United States still controlled the rules of the game and could bend them in its favor. This is a conscious choice. This part of her concept of structural power could be called 'indirect institutional power' (Guzzini 1993).

A second aspect of structural power is conceptually more daring. It insists on the study of unintended effects as part of power analysis. Instead of taking them as a kind of fatal mishappening, the anti-apparent realist rebels and argues that such effects are perfectly conscious by now. Moreover, those effects that are important for the international power structure are the result of the actions of only a few international actors. Their place in the respective power structures is such as to systematically (structurally) affect others. Perhaps it would be better therefore to refer to this part of her concept of structural power as 'non-epistemic power', as Morriss (1987) does, or as 'non-intentional power' (Guzzini 1993).

To have used the concept of power as a hinge for her critique of the United States is not fortuitous. Here Strange plays with a central characteristic of the concept of power. Power is a concept which has a variety of purposes (Morriss 1987: 37–42). To mention two: power is used in practical contexts in which we are interested in what we can do to others and what others can do to us. It is also important in moral/legal contexts where it functions as an indicator of effective responsibility: if actors could not have carried out an act (if they had not the capacity to do so), they cannot be found guilty for it. The first indicates the realm of action, power as an indicator of politics as the 'art of the possible'; the second assesses possible blame. By limiting the practical context to only those actions with which we intend to affect others, we rule out any moral judgments on those actions that affect others, whether intended or not.

Hence, to have redefined power is necessary for a realist of the anti-apparent inspiration. Leaving out non-intentional power mobilizes a status quo research bias and blinds us to the tacit power of the strong. It is useful to look at power from the side of the power holder and not, as non-intentional power does, from the perspective of the actors affected by it.

This reconceptualization, meant both to attack US power and policy and to display a vision of a diffused power system in international relations, does run into trouble, however. It eventually must relax the materialist understanding of power. This becomes visible when Strange likens her critique of the US decline debate to Joseph Nye's *Bound to Lead* (1990a). The similarities are remarkable indeed. In a later article, Nye (1990b) specifies why he sees no decline in US power. First, rather than having any other country picking up US power, the world is characterized by a 'general diffusion of power' (Nye 1990b: 155). Second, given the rise of political interdependence and modern technology, power is becoming 'less transferable [from one issue area to another], less coercive, and less tangible' (ibid.: 167). In such circumstances, it turns out to be a cost-efficient strategy to get other actors to do what you want them to do, not by ordering or imposing (command power), but by getting them to want what you want (co-optive or soft power). For the latter, increasingly important, form of power, intangible resources are crucial, such as cultural attraction, ideology and international institutions. Here the United States is by far the most influential actor, whose power is growing rather than receding. This combines well with Strange's understanding of the knowledge structure, which is not only about technology, but also about belief systems, ideologies, fashions and ideals (Strange 1988). This concept smuggles the issue of culture into her political economy approach.

Consequently, her critique of the US decline school produces some tensions with her critique of the apparent continuity of the classical IR agenda, as mentioned above. In the first critique, she argues for a thoroughly materialist account of international affairs. In the second, she makes an important concession to less materialist conceptions of politics. The knowledge structure has two components, technology/ know-how and culture. Whereas the first can be accounted for, the second looks like an idealist cuckoo in the realist nest.

For a realist, the use of language and ideology is no problem, as long as it can be shown that actors are in control of it: ideas are factors of power when they are manipulated by actors. Strange does see the ideological use of much US theorizing that systematically tends to shift blame abroad. If the US government could not keep its house in order, and had to leave Bretton Woods, it was because of the USSR/cold war (in Vietnam), the US government's generosity towards its allies, the liquidity problem of the international monetary system, the oil shocks, and so on: 'American theorising has thus become an elaborate ideology to resist sharing American monetary power' (Calleo and Strange 1984: 114).

Unfortunately for a coherent realism, Strange does not assume that the ideology embedded in the business civilization, or the advantages occurring to English-speaking countries by the use of their mother tongue and their cultural products, are necessarily manipulated or channeled in a specific direction: they have a life of their own (they form a structure). Denying their existence and importance for the worldwide hierarchy would be 'unrealistic' for the anti-apparent realist, even if its account is at odds with the materialism underlying Strange's anti-ideal realism. The implication is candidly spelled out by Nye: 'when ideals are an important source of power, the classic distinction between *realpolitik* and liberalism becomes blurred' (Nye 1990b: 170).

'Ungovernance' by the Non-territorial Empire as a Critique of the United States: Taking the Diffusion of Power Seriously

This subsection explores the second part of the tension between the diffusion of power on the one hand, and the critique of US action on the other. Whereas we discussed earlier the mismatch of soft power and materialism, we now refer to the mismatch between the increasing non-territoriality of power, its diffusion – if not evaporation –

and US control and responsibility. This section claims that Strange's concept of power cannot really overcome the tension. It is a tension that builds up gradually in her work when she refocuses away from US control and onto international 'ungovernance'. The tension subsists later in another source of strain: her Keynesian urge for international regulation and her realist pessimism that anything like this will actually happen (see Leander's discussion in Chapter 18 of the present volume).

The initial motivation of Strange is her drive to demystify US decline, that is to question the only apparent truth. One of Strange's best known articles on the 'myth of lost hegemony' has a very symptomatic title (1987). Her demystification aims at the real existing *Pax Americana* as the best of all possible worlds, or, a slightly weaker claim, as a world which could not have been avoided – ordained, as it were, 'by God or History' (Strange 1974/5: 215).

She uses her concept of structural power to reveal the hidden might and responsibility of the United States. This is already visible in her famous analysis in *Casino Capitalism*, where she shows that a series of decisions and non-decisions by the US government (mainly) were responsible for the present system, whether intended or not. Finally, she alludes to the fact that it suits the US government to keep it as it is, a statement made more strongly in *Mad Money* (Strange 1998).

She is most explicit in later pieces, where she dissects the power of the United States to set the rules of the games to be played in the four basic power structures. Starting with the production structure, she argues that, although TNCs control the largest part, this does not mean that the United States has lost control over the world economy. Most TNCs are based in the United States. The others, wanting to be profitable worldwide, have to conduct business on US territory. It follows that the structural power of the United States is not to be measured in US GNP but 'as the total value of goods and services produced by large companies responsive to policy decisions taken by the US government' (Strange 1989: 167). The same applies to the financial structure, where the United States has lost power to the banks or to the foreign exchange markets, but can take it back: 'As the experience of the Roosevelt administration in 1930s showed clearly, bankers like everyone else (even insider traders) are subject to the law, and the law can be changed to bring them back under the control of the states' (ibid.: 168). 'In every important respect, the United States still has the predominant power to shape frameworks and thus to influence outcomes. This implies that it can draw the limits within which others can choose from a restricted list of options, the restrictions being in large part a result of US decisions' (ibid.: 169). Put more bluntly, 'it is the world economy that is the anvil and the United States the hammer, in Lenin's apposite metaphor' (ibid.). As a result, power, no longer being territorially defined, is still concentrated in the United States, which is the core of the non-territorial empire. Its capital is Washington, but its control over people (not over land) extends to all aspects of its 'international business civilization'.

Given this assessment, it is obvious that Strange believes some new form of international regulation has to be found. Since she does not much trust international institutions, she keeps her faith, somewhat ironically, with the United States itself, which, would be the most benign hegemon (ibid.: 173). Her critique of the United States's structural power is meant to make the country conscious of, responsible about and thus responsive to the effects of their action: the usual excuses will not do. But this faith is also the result of her realist inclinations that not much will be done without getting the consent of the powerful. If the United States is indeed as powerful as she describes, then all depends on it. Therefore she does not fail to lambaste, provoke and ridicule US policies so as to provoke directional change.

In her last writings, this assessment starts to be undermined by her own vision that all governments, including the US, have lost control over the world economy. It is not at all sure that she would repeat the confident assessment of US power after 1989. It might have been the choice of the United States, and not some technical necessity, to 'lift the lid' of globalization, but it is not clear that the process can subsequently be reversed.

This analysis finally produces a typical realist dead-end: the optimism of the will is persistently checked by the pessimism of the intellect. Strange's inclinations cannot envisage any other solution than one guided by the most powerful actors, and yet she says this will not be forthcoming. Although she maintains her attack on US unilateralism, she is then at a loss to conceive of any solution to the general problem of ungovernance. Her realist inclinations cannot conceive of regimes or world governments as solutions – and she offers little other alternative to this classical dichotomy. Strange's entire approach leads her repeatedly to ask for a recreation of the Keynesian control over the world economy, in particular its finance (1989: 175–6; 1996: 194), a move her realist vision of IR cannot conceive of happening.

As a result, her concept of structural power has played a trick on her argument. At the start, it allowed her to unravel US influence where it might not necessarily be seen. But insisting on the diffusion of power inevitably led to an analysis, where also the control of the still most powerful state can no longer be assumed to guarantee world stewardship. Far from resolving the problem, the concept of structural power embodies it. Once controlling for its two facets, however, it can be fruitfully used to analyze social hierarchy and control in the global political economy. It opens up one promising track for analysis in IPE.

Epilogue: Retreat or Reform of Realism?

This chapter has argued that Strange's version of realism can be best understood as oscillating between a (conservative) opposition to the ideal and a (critical) opposition to the apparent. This oscillation pushed her to make perhaps her most important conceptual contribution – structural power. At the same time, it forced her into internal tensions concerning her underlying materialism and her views on (political) agency.

After presenting the two types of realism, Bobbio proceeds by saying that there is a third one, attempting a synthesis of the first two. Such a realism would scorn both the catechism of the utopian and the cynicism of the reactionary. Indeed, realism can be understood as the attempt to steer through a middle-ground between the realm of necessity and the realm of freedom (Berki 1981). As such, 'real' realism, one not confounded with any of the poles, would necessarily come mainly as a negative attitude, always reversing direction, speedily oscillating (see also Griffiths 1992). Strange might seem to fit this bill. While doing so, she makes an achievement of no small proportion by rescuing a more credible, 'realistic' version of realism through a structural analysis of power which goes beyond any other realist writings – and which can be fruitfully used also by non-realists.

But, at the same time, this realism can produce a very stale, if not sterile, political agenda. It gives discussions this priggish taste so typical of the realist scholar who 'has always been there already' – not by moving forward, but by shifting to the right and left. The one solution perhaps best suited to keeping this type of 'real' realism alive was proposed a long time ago by the realist who had struggled most with this double heritage of realism, E.H. Carr. His idea was not to oscillate between the two poles at any single point in time, depending on which audience one chose to address. Instead, he oscillated between the poles over time, meeting head-on the truth of the day, whether reactionary or revolutionary (Carr 1961: 177). In *Mad Money*, her political testament, Strange may have come closest to this (temporarily) one-sided stance when she knew that her oscillation could no longer continue.

Note

1 I would like to thank Anna Leander, Tom Lawton and Amy Verdun for helpful comments on an earlier draft. All disclaimers apply.

References

Berki, R.N. (1981), *On Political Realism*, London: Dent & Sons.
Bobbio, Norberto ([1969] 1996), *Saggi sulla scienza politica in Italia*, Roma-Bari: Editori Laterza.
Calleo, David and Susan Strange (1984), 'Money and World Politics', in Susan Strange (ed.), *Paths to International Political Economy*, London: George Allen & Unwin, pp.91–125.
Carr, Edward Heller (1946), *The Twenty Years' Crisis: An Introduction to the Study of International Relations*, London: Macmillan.
Carr, Edward Heller (1961), *What is History?*, London: Penguin.
Cox, Robert W. ([1981] 1986), 'Social Forces, States and World Orders: Beyond International Relations Theory (+ Postscript 1985)', in Robert O. Keohane (ed.), *Neorealism and its Critiques*, New York: Columbia University Press, pp.204–54.
Gilpin, Robert ([1984] 1986), 'The Richness of the Realist Tradition', in Robert O. Keohane (ed.), *Neorealism and its Critics*, New York: Columbia University Press, pp.301–21.
Griffiths, Martin (1992), *Realism, Idealism and International Politics: A Reinterpretation*, London and New York: Routledge.
Guzzini, Stefano (1993), 'Structural power: the limits of neorealist power analysis', *International Organization*, 47(3), Summer, 443–78.
Guzzini, Stefano (1998), *Realism in International Relations and International Political Economy: the continuing story of a death foretold*, London and New York: Routledge.
Hirschman, Alfred (1991), *The Rhetoric of Reaction: perversity, futility, jeopardy*, Cambridge, MA: Belknap Press of Harvard University Press.
Jones, Charles (1998), *E.H. Carr and International Relations: A duty to lie*, Cambridge: Cambridge University Press.
Mannheim, Karl (1936), *Ideology and Utopia*, New York: Harvest Books.
Morriss, Peter (1987), *Power: A philosophical analysis*, Manchester: Manchester University Press.
Nye, Joseph S. jr. (1990a), *Bound to Lead: The Changing Nature of American Power*, New York: Basic Books.
Nye, Joseph S., jr. (1990b), 'Soft Power', *Foreign Policy*, 80, Fall, 153–71.
Schmidt, Brian C. (1998), *The Political Discourse of Anarchy: A Disciplinary History of International Relations*, Albany: State of New York University Press.
Stopford, John and Susan Strange (with John Henley) (1991), *Rival States and Rival Firms: Competition for World Market Shares*, Cambridge: Cambridge University Press.
Strange, Susan (1971), *Sterling and British Policy*, London: Oxford University Press.
Strange, Susan (1974/5), 'What is economic power and who has it?', *International Journal*, 30, 207–24.
Strange, Susan (1976), 'International Monetary Relations', in Andrew Shonfield (ed.), *International Economic Relations of the Western World, 1959–71*, Volume 2, London: Oxford University Press.
Strange, Susan (1982), '*Cave! Hic Dragones*: A Critique of Regime Analysis', *International Organization*, 36(2), Spring, 479–96.

Strange, Susan (1986), *Casino Capitalism*, London: Basil Blackwell.
Strange, Susan (1987), 'The persistent myth of lost hegemony', *International Organization*, 41(4), Autumn, 551–74.
Strange, Susan (1988), *States and Markets: An Introduction to International Political Economy*, New York: Basil Blackwell.
Strange, Susan (1989), 'Toward a Theory of Transnational Empire', in Ernst-Otto Czempiel and James Rosenau (eds), *Global Changes and Theoretical Challenges: Approaches to World Politics for the 1990s*, Lexington, MA: D.C. Heath, pp.161–76.
Strange, Susan (1990), 'The Name of the Game', in N. Rizopoulos (ed.), *Sea-Changes: American Foreign Policy in a World Transformed*, New York: Council on Foreign Relations Press, pp.238–74.
Strange, Susan (1996), *The Retreat of the State: the diffusion of power in the world economy*, Cambridge: Cambridge University Press.
Strange, Susan (1998) *Mad Money*, Manchester: Manchester University Press.
Walker, R.B.J. (1987), 'Realism, Change and International Political Theory', *International Studies Quarterly*, 31 (1), March, 65–86.
Walker, R.B.J. (1993) *Inside/Outside: International relations as political theory*, Cambridge: Cambridge University Press.
Waltz, Kenneth N. (1979), *Theory of International Politics*, Reading, MA: Addison-Wesley.

13 Still an Extraordinary Power, but for how much Longer? The United States in World Finance

ERIC HELLEINER

Introduction

As Verbeek discusses in Chapter 8 of the present volume, Strange was often known as a leading critic of 'American' academic approaches to the study of International Political Economy. During the 1980s, she focused much of her criticism on the 'hegemonic stability theory' (HST), a theory that dominated US International Political Economy (IPE) scholarship during this period. Put simply, the theory asserted that a hegemonic leader was needed for a stable, open international economy to exist. The popularity of the theory stemmed from the fact that it offered a clear explanation – declining American hegemony – for the growing instability of the global economy since the early 1970s.

Strange's principal criticism of American discussions of the HST was often misunderstood. She did not focus her critique on the underlying theoretical claim that a hegemonic leader was important for the stability of an open, global economy. Indeed, much of her writing in this period finished with a plea for strong and consistent American leadership as the solution to global economic troubles, especially global financial instability. Instead, Strange criticized the way in which many American scholars used the HST to interpret the growing global economic instability since the early 1970s. In her view, many American scholars overstated the extent of the decline of American hegemonic power. What had changed since the early 1970s, she argued, was not the capability of the United States to lead, but rather its *willingness* to act as a responsible and benevolent leader (see especially Strange 1986; 1987).

This short chapter begins by highlighting the accuracy of Strange's view about the endurance of US hegemony in global finance in light of developments during the 1990s. Throughout the 1980s, many US scholars argued that Japan was severely eroding US power in global finance as it emerged as the world's largest creditor and the size of its financial institutions and markets quickly surpassed that of their American counterparts. This dramatic shift of power, they argued, was setting the stage for increasing global financial stability in the 1990s (for example, Gilpin 1987; Murphy 1989). With her insistence on America's enduring power in global finance, Strange stood quite alone in criticizing this widely held view of Japan's financial clout by the late 1980s (Strange 1990). A decade later, however, it is Strange's analysis of the limits of Japanese power, rather than the popular view she criticized, that has stood the test of time. By the late 1990s, it was hard to deny that the United States had remained, as Strange (1982) put it, 'still an extraordinary power' in world finance.

If developments in the 1990s confirmed Strange's view, should we then assume that the United States will remain without serious rivals in world finance for the foreseeable future? In the second section of this chapter, it is argued that this assumption would be incorrect. The section begins by outlining how the project of accelerating regional financial and monetary integration in Europe will bring greater European power in global finance in the coming years and goes on to highlight how, as Strange anticipated, frustration with the poor quality of American financial leadership has become an important motivation for the project of accelerating Europe's financial and monetary integration over the last two decades. Although she appealed for the United States to adopt a more enlightened style of leadership, Strange recognized that its failure to do so might encourage Europe and Japan to seek to constrain, or insulate themselves from, the influence of US financial power over time. After highlighting the accuracy of this prediction in the European case, I also note briefly how it may also be coming true in the Japanese case. The consequence of a pattern of US international financial policy making since the early 1970s thus will likely be an erosion of American financial hegemony over the medium term. In this way, Strange's analysis of the trajectory of American hegemony appears to be doubly correct.

The Limits of Japan's Financial Challenge

Throughout the 1980s, many US scholars argued that American financial power was rapidly eroding in the face of a challenge from

Japan. One reason for this view was the enormous outflow from Japan of long-term capital at that time. Each year during the late 1980s, Japan was exporting close to $100 billion in long-term capital. These movements of capital quickly earned it the title of world's largest creditor (as well as the world's largest aid donor), a development that was particularly striking because it coincided with America's descent into debtor status for the first time in the post-1945 period.

The growing international prominence of Japan's private financial institutions and markets also appeared to demonstrate Japan's newfound financial power. By 1989, for example, Japanese banks had come to acquire 40 per cent of all international bank assets, a share larger than that of any other national group of banks. The big four Japanese securities firms also found themselves consistently among the top ranks of Eurobond underwriters in the late 1980s, and Japanese financial institutions also came to dominate rankings of the size of the world's largest financial institutions as measured by market capitalization in this period. Similarly, the Tokyo Stock Exchange came to account for a larger share of world stock market capitalization than the New York market in this period and Tokyo's share of international banking activity surpassed that of New York. Turnover in Tokyo's bond and foreign exchange markets also began to equal that in New York markets during the late 1980s (Helleiner 1989; 1992).

In light of these dramatic developments, it is not surprising that so many analysts argued that Japan was suddenly challenging the United States for the position of hegemonic leader in world finance. Susan Strange, however, remained a skeptic. At the center of her argument was the distinction between 'relational power' and 'structural power'. She acknowledged that Japan, by virtue of its creditor status, was acquiring 'relational power'; that is, power to influence directly the behavior of others. But she believed that the more enduring and significant form of power in the modern global financial system was 'structural power', which she defined as the power to indirectly influence others by controlling the structures within which they must operate. In the global financial system, she argued, the United States still held key structural power, for several reasons.

First, the United States continued to issue the currency – the US dollar – in which most international transactions took place. Strange argued that the enduring pre-eminence of the dollar as a world currency not only eased America's ability to finance external payments deficits, giving it power in global macroeconomic diplomacy, it also ensured that the United States was the key lender-of-last-resort in international financial markets. Despite Japan's growing prominence, Strange highlighted how the yen was used very little at the international level in the 1980s. Even the Japanese themselves relied heavily on the US dollar in their international transactions in both trade and finance. Indeed, the bulk of their assets held abroad were denominated in this foreign currency, a quite unprecedented and vulnerable situation for the world's largest creditor.

Strange also called attention to the continued importance of US financial institutions, especially to the prominent role played by US financial markets in the global financial system. Although some Japanese markets and institutions may have surpassed their American counterparts in size by the late 1980s, Strange argued that American markets and institutions remained the 'market leaders' in global finance, driving innovation and change. International investors continued to find North American markets particularly attractive because of their openness, minimal regulation and depth. The continued centrality of these markets and institutions to world finance, argued Strange, gave US policy makers an indirect, structural form of power. Not only did it enhance America's ability to attract footloose global funds, but it also ensured that US regulatory moves had important international implications.

Strange argued that the final source of structural power for the United States in global finance was its unequalled influence in the International Monetary Fund (IMF) and World Bank. This influence stemmed from its dominant voting share and the veto power that this share gave it over major decisions. Insofar as these institutions remained at the center of the architecture of the global financial system, US influence within them gave the United States power to influence the structures within which others were forced to operate.

The Bursting of Japan's Financial Bubble

Although Strange's opinions were very much a minority voice by the late 1980s, two financial crises in the 1990s have proved how insightful they were. The first crisis was the spectacular asset deflation in Japan in the early 1990s, a development that forced all observers to re-evaluate their assessment of Japan's financial power. Symbolizing this deflation was the drop in the Nikkei index of the Tokyo Stock Exchange by over one half between late 1989 and late 1992. Real estate prices also collapsed by a similar magnitude in most major Japanese urban centers over the same period. The immediate cause of these developments was the tightening of Japanese monetary policy by Bank of Japan Governor Yashushi Mieno after his appointment to the post in December 1989. Mieno's move, however, only accelerated the inevitable collapse of a speculative financial 'bubble' that had emerged in the Japanese financial system in the late 1980s. The combination of low interest rates and a rapidly growing money supply in this period had inflated the value of financial assets – particularly stocks and real estate – to artificially high levels. These inflated values were then brought back down to earth by Mieno's changed policy course (Wood 1992).

The bursting of this financial bubble had several important implications for Japan's international financial influence. Most obviously, it revealed that key features of Japan's financial power in the late 1980s had been based on the unrealistic asset prices. The enormous degree of market capitalization of the Tokyo Stock Exchange, for example, had been a product of the bubble and was now reduced to a level well below that of New York. Similarly, the huge capital base of Japanese financial institutions in the late 1980s suddenly contracted in the face of falling share prices and property values at home. Indeed, the financial collapse in Japan led many foreign bankers to worry about the soundness of the previously all-powerful Japanese financial institutions and to begin as early as 1992 to charge risk premiums to the latter in international banking markets (*The Economist* 1992). As a result of their difficulties at home, many Japanese financial institutions also began reducing their overseas operations after a decade of rapid international expansion. Japanese banks' share of new credits to non-banks in international markets fell from 46 per cent in the 1985–9 period to 5 per cent in the 1989–mid-1991 period, while their share of international bank assets dropped to less than 30 per cent by mid-1992, the lowest level since 1986 (Wagstyl 1992; Waters 1992). The declining position of Japanese financial institutions in international rankings after 1989 also made it clear that their prominence had not been achieved through any kind of superiority in financial skills. Instead, it had been based primarily on their privileged access to Japanese customers and enormous domestic funds during the bubble years. As one official in Japan's Ministry of Finance diplomatically put it, 'probably the international activities of Japanese banks were above the capabilities they had at the time' (quoted in Martin 1992).

The bubble's collapse also revealed important weaknesses in the international competitiveness of Japan's financial markets, a point Strange had been highlighting. The retreat of Japanese investors and institutions from the international arena revealed the extent to which Tokyo's international financial markets had been dependent on their business. The volume of turnover in Tokyo's foreign exchange market, for example, fell well behind that of New York by 1992, after almost surpassing the latter only three years earlier.[1] The bursting of the bubble also brought to light some dubious practices in Japan's domestic financial markets, such as loss compensation schemes in securities markets and fraudulent bank loans. The seemingly close links between the Ministry of Finance and some of the institutions involved also called attention to the absence of a strong, independent regulator of Japan's financial markets (Wood 1992). These developments, along with the broader collapse in the size of Japanese domestic markets, led many to re-evaluate Tokyo's prospects as an international financial center. While 32 per cent of foreign financiers surveyed by the Japan Centre for International Finance in 1989 believed that Tokyo would surpass New York and London as the world's leading financial center within five years, this figure had dropped to 6 per cent by the time of the 1992 survey (Terazono 1993). In a separate report published in early 1993, prominent foreign and Japanese bankers complained in particular about the lack of transparency in Japanese financial market practices and decision making, as well as the absence of diversified financial instruments. Indeed, the report noted that, of 25 financial instruments widely available in Europe and the United States, only 12 were present in Japanese financial markets (Thompson 1993a).

In addition to changing Japan's capital flows and the international standing of its financial markets and institutions, the entire bubble episode revealed an even more serious weakness in Japan's financial challenge in the late 1980s: its failure to develop the yen as an international currency. The central factor behind the Bank of Japan's loose monetary policy in the late 1980s that produced the bubble was the country's continuing external dependence on the US dollar. After the major industrial nations agreed in 1985 to encourage the dollar to depreciate, the Bank of Japan had actively sought to smooth the dollar's path downwards by dropping Japanese interest rates and boosting Japanese growth through an expansionary monetary policy. Japan was especially vulnerable to fluctuations in the dollar's value because most Japanese external assets were denominated in dollars and because the vast bulk of Japan's trade was conducted in dollars. When the 1987 stock market crash seemed to signal the fragility of the US external financial position, Japanese officials felt it difficult to reverse their defence of the dollar despite the fact that this defence was clearly encouraging an asset inflation in Japan (Kazuhide 1991). It was not until Mieno's decisive action that the subordination of Japanese monetary policy to the external goal of supporting the dollar was finally ended. Ironically, it was thus a major weakness – Japan's dependence on the dollar – that encouraged the bubble that produced much of Japan's alleged financial strength in the late 1980s. Only with Mieno's independent stance was the bubble burst and the fictitious nature of that strength exposed.

Japan and the Asian Financial Crisis

The second financial crisis to reveal the underlying weaknesses of Japan's 'structural power' in global finance was the 1997–8 East Asian financial crisis. If the bursting of Japan's financial bubble in the early 1990s highlighted its continued dependence on the dollar and the weak international position of its markets and institutions, this crisis called attention to the significance of Japan's lack of power within the IMF.

This crisis was obviously devastating for the many East Asian countries it directly affected, but it also affected Japan. Not only was a large portion of the loans outstanding to crisis-afflicted countries owed to Japanese banks, but also Japan's broader economic ties to the region guaranteed that its economy would be affected by the crisis. Given the high stakes, one would have expected Japanese policy makers to take a strong leadership role in managing the crisis. In fact, the United States played the leading role, but only because of its control of the IMF.

The US leadership role was particularly striking in light of some important differences of opinion between US and Japanese policy makers on the question of how the crisis should be managed. US officials blamed the crisis primarily on domestic mismanagement and 'crony' forms of capitalism in the crisis-affected countries. The solution, prescribed by the IMF, was for these countries to introduce tough macroeconomic austerity programs and extensive microeconomic restructuring programs designed to deregulate markets along more neoliberal lines. In this way, the crisis was used to bring East Asian countries more in line with American conceptions of the proper role of the state in economic life.

By contrast, Japanese officials were more inclined to assign some blame for the crisis to large speculative flows of international finance. Consequently, they were more sympathetic to those who argued for the use of capital controls and other interventionist practices which were more in keeping with the traditions of the East Asian 'developmental state' model. They also supported more accommodating international financial support with fewer conditions.

Because of its control of the IMF, the US approach won the day. Japanese officials were forced to recognize that they could have more influence only if they were willing to launch a serious challenge to the political architecture of international finance that enabled the United States to dominate the agenda. Given the high stakes involved for Japan, it is perhaps not surprising that Japanese officials did in fact contemplate such a challenge for a brief moment. At several points in the second half of 1997, they floated an idea of creating an Asian Monetary Fund with approximately $100 billion under its control. The money would have come mostly from Japan itself, but several other Asian countries, such as China, Hong Kong, Taiwan and Singapore, also pledged funds (Wade and Veneroso 1998). This body could have acted as a kind of mini-IMF, helping to bail out East Asian countries on more accommodating terms than the IMF was offering. It was, in other words, a proposal designed to break US control of the official financial architecture in the region (Godement 1999: 46).

Not surprisingly, the proposal found considerable support among policy makers in East Asia, but US Treasury Secretary Rubin and his deputy Larry Summers were 'lividly opposed' to it (Pempel 1999: 230). US officials recognized the potential threat to their influence in the region and their control of the public architecture of global finance via their influence in the IMF. More generally, Chalmers Johnson argues:

> The Americans instantaneously objected, correctly sensing that Japan was about to try its hand at long promised but never delivered international leadership. If the Japanese had succeeded, they would have slipped the leash of the US Cold War system. Moreover, they would have started using their surplus capital to help countries in Asia rather than continuing to send it to the world's number-one debtor nation, the United States. (Quoted in Godement 1999: 47)

In the face of this strong US opposition, the Japanese government quickly and quietly dropped the idea. This decision signaled its yielding to US structural power in global finance.

Will the United States' Financial Dominance Last?

Developments in the 1990s thus confirmed Strange's view that the Japanese challenge to US financial power was overstated. They may also have begun to confirm a second prediction she made. Although Strange appealed for the United States to adopt more enlightened policies, she argued that the increasingly exploitative and inconsistent nature of its financial leadership since the early 1970s might encourage Europe and Japan to begin to try to constrain, or insulate themselves from, US hegemonic influence over time. This section explains how this motivation has indeed acted as one of the incentives behind the European Union's moves towards closer financial and monetary integration in recent years, and goes on to describe how frustration with US leadership has also recently begun to encourage Japanese financial policy makers to carve out a more independent and autonomous position within world finance. Both of these developments suggest that American financial dominance is likely to give way to a more pluralistic world financial order in the coming years.

Europe's Challenge to US Financial Power

While developments in Japan had posed an immediate and visible challenge to American dominance of world finance in the late 1980s, two European initiatives in this period have turned out to pose a more important threat over the medium term. The first was the June 1988 decision by the European Council to liberalize capital controls across the European Community within two years (Greece, Spain, Portugal and Ireland were given a slightly longer time frame). This effort – part of the broader European project to complete the single market by 1992 – was designed to create a unified European financial space that would allow European financial markets to rival those in the United States and Japan. As then-European Commission President Jacques Delors put it, financial liberalization would give 'our financial centers the opportunity to be among the most important in the world' and 'it is this that gives us our say in the world with the Americans and Japanese on debt, on financial flows' (quoted in Helleiner 1994: 161).

A number of statistics were produced around this time to highlight the relative size and potential influence of European financial markets. If unified, for example, the European government debt market would be slightly larger than the US Treasury bond market. Similarly, European bank deposits in 1989 were one and a half times the size of those in the United States (*The Economist* 1991; Stevenson 1989: 5). There is no doubt that markets of this size should give Europe some 'structural power' in global finance. As the US Chamber of Commerce noted, the size of a unified European banking market would give the European Union considerable clout in negotiations over international banking regulations (Dunne 1992). At the same time, however, this newfound structural power can easily be overstated by these aggregate statistics. Europe's financial markets are highly decentralized and, as Fred Bergsten (1997: 88) notes, there 'will be no central government borrower like the US Treasury to provide a fulcrum for the market'. Moreover, as we saw in the Japanese case, large size does not always ensure that the markets will be 'market leaders'. Indeed, within Europe, only London's financial markets pose a serious challenge to the 'leadership' of US markets in terms of their innovative quality and depth.

The second and more dramatic European initiative was the 1988 decision to establish the Delors Committee, whose mandate was to begin active and detailed discussions on how Europe could move towards economic and monetary union (EMU). These discussions led to the commitment made by EC governments at Maastricht in December 1991 to move toward EMU in a three stage process, culminating in the creation of a common currency and central bank, beginning in 1999. The EMU project has important implications for US financial power.

To begin with, it will likely help to break down some of the fragmentation of Europe's financial markets and accelerate their integration. Second, the creation of a common central bank will give Europe a more unified voice in international macroeconomic diplomacy. It might even encourage more unified European voting stances in the IMF, where EU countries already hold a larger collective voting share than the United States (Pauly 1992). Indeed, Henning (1997) notes that some could even ask – incorrectly in his view – whether a consolidated European quota will require a relocation of the Fund (since its Articles of Agreement require that it be located in the territory of its member with the largest quota).

Most important, the creation of a single European currency may seriously challenge the dollar's central global role over the medium term. Already, when taken together in 1995, the share of world trade denominated in European currencies was 31 per cent versus 51 per cent for the dollar. Using figures from September 1997, George Tavlas (1998) notes that the share of international bond offerings denominated in European currencies was quite close (41.9 per cent) to that denominated in dollars (45.1 per cent). The European Commission (1990: 182) also noted that the euro would be a particularly attractive currency to international investors because it will be backed by a conservative central bank dedicated to price stability, and because it would be able to be held in unified European money markets that would be 'the largest in the world'.

As already noted, the Commission likely overstates this last point, since Europe's money markets are fragmented. Indeed, the deepest and most innovative money markets for international investors in Europe remain those in London, a financial center which is not even part of the common currency zone at this point. But, interestingly, Britain's lack of participation in EMU has not stopped euro money markets from emerging in London. Indeed, the Bank of England had already begun actively promoting what were then ecu-based financial markets in London as far back as the late 1980s through regulatory changes and the issuance of Treasury paper denominated in the European currency (Plenderleith 1991; Corrigan 1992).

The European Commission (1990: 183) noted one final way in which EMU may threaten the dollar's position. It observed that, with no more intra-EC foreign exchange intervention necessary, an estimated $230 billion of the total $400 billion of foreign exchange reserves of EC member states would no longer be needed, the majority of which was held in dollars. If these excess reserves were sold suddenly, Pauly (1992: 108) predicted that the result would be 'destabilizing in the extreme' for the dollar.

European Frustration with US Financial Leadership

If the project of integrating Europe monetarily and financially is likely to pose a challenge to US financial power in the coming years, to what extent is this challenge an intentional one? Certainly, many of the goals underlying this project have nothing to do with this objective. Instead, they relate to various intraregional and even domestic objectives within the member countries of the EU. At the same time, however, it is important not to neglect the role of this external goal entirely.

Delors' hope that the 1988 liberalization of capital movement would enable European financial markets to challenge their American counterparts more directly has already been quoted. Similarly, throughout the late 1980s and 1990s, support for EMU was driven in part by the explicit goal of challenging US financial power. For example, in outlining the official rationale for EMU in its 'One Market, One Money' report, the European Commission (1990: 194) praised the way EMU would constrain US power and bring greater 'symmetry' to the global financial order. Similarly, Henning (1998: 563–5) notes how Europeans were often driven to support EMU at key moments in this period by a desire to reduce Europe's dependence on the dollar and enhance European financial power vis-à-vis the United States. Indeed, he observes more generally that the various initiatives to strengthen European monetary cooperation since the early 1970s have almost always been driven at least partly by these objectives.

What has been the motivation for challenging US financial power? Interestingly, European policy makers have been driven by a frustration similar to that expressed by Strange with the quality of US financial leadership since the early 1970s. Recall that Strange's key objective in highlighting the enduring hegemonic power of the United States in global finance was to put forward an alternative explanation of the growing instability in the global financial system since the early 1970s. Strange argued that instability had been caused, not by declining US hegemony, but by the inability of the United States to act as a responsible leader throughout this period.

She was particularly critical of its macroeconomic policies which, she argued, were increasingly characterized by inconsistency, unilateralism and efforts to shift adjustment burdens onto foreigners. This pattern of policy making, in turn, also prevented the United States from providing a stable world currency as it had done in the era of the Bretton Woods system. Moreover, instead of being a reliable lender to the world, the United States became one of the world's largest debtors in this period in order to finance its fiscal and trade deficits. Finally, Strange also criticized the United States for a series of crucial 'non-decisions' that encouraged the growth of unregulated global financial markets. From Strange's perspective, these patterns in US behavior signaled a shift from the kind of benevolent, far-sighted US leadership of the post-war period to a more exploitative and inconsistent style of leadership.

In highlighting how global instability stemmed from poor US leadership rather than declining US power, Strange's goal was not to alienate US policy makers: quite the opposite; her objective was to convince American policy makers to assume a more responsible leadership role in global finance. US leadership, she argued, was the key to restoring a stable global financial order. But Strange also seemed increasingly pessimistic about the prospects for this kind of leadership emerging from the United States. She was particularly concerned about the way US policy makers seemed to be swayed more by short-term domestic considerations than by a long-term commitment to a stable world economy. A key source of the trouble, she argued, was the US Constitution's separation of powers, which 'has tended to make policymakers in Washington ever mindful of the capacity of powerful lobbies and interest groups operating upon or within Congress to distort, frustrate, or even reverse strategies adopted by the White House towards the outside world' (Strange 1987: 572).

In a context where appropriate US leadership was not forthcoming, Strange anticipated that governments in Europe and Japan might feel increasingly compelled to constrain the arbitrary use of US hegemonic power as a way of insulating themselves from its effects. In her words, these governments might seek ways to cultivate their own financial power as a means of trying to 'nudge' the United States towards less unilateralist behavior (Strange 1986: 167, 186–9). As Henning (1998) points out, this has indeed been one of the main motivations of European policy makers in their efforts to promote closer monetary cooperation since the early 1970s. It has also been a particularly prominent motivation for EMU. As the European Commission (1990: 191) notes diplomatically, a key benefit of EMU is that it would force the United States to become 'more conscious of the limits of independent policy-making'. In words very similar to those used by Strange, the Commission (ibid.: 195) continues: 'Although the presence of a hegemon may be beneficial as long as it remains the anchor of the system, it is no longer so when it ceases to provide stability.'

Japanese Frustration with US Leadership

To what extent will Japan also be encouraged for the same reason to challenge US financial power more overtly in the coming years? Certainly, the experience of the bubble economy and the more recent Asian financial crisis have led to a growing interest in Japan in adopting a more assertive and independent stance in global finance. To begin with, the way in which the bubble's collapse had revealed the underlying lack of competitiveness of Japanese financial markets has encouraged reform in this area. In 1996, Japan announced a set of far-reaching initiatives to liberalize Japan's financial markets which were designed explicitly to help Tokyo regain its position as a leading financial center (for example, Nakamoto 1998).

The experience of the bubble economy also led to considerable discussion among Japanese policy makers of the need to reduce their dependence on the dollar. This sentiment in fact began during the bubble era. Frustrated by their constrained monetary position in that period, prominent Japanese financial officials and politicians began to call publicly for the first time for a move away from a dollar-based international financial order (Helleiner 1992: 435). By the early 1990s, the desire for greater financial independence from the United States had become widespread (Leadbeater 1992).

Particularly prominent were calls for the yen to be used more extensively in trade and finance within the East Asian region. Its use in the region had in fact already begun to grow during the bubble years. One reason was that the Bank of Japan began to promote the building of a liquid short-term money market in Japan. The absence of such a market in which foreigners could hold yen-denominated assets had been a key cause of the extremely limited internationalization of the yen. The Bank of Japan had traditionally opposed the growth of money markets on the grounds that such markets would hurt its ability to control monetary policy through regulatory means. Its externally constrained low interest rate policy in the late 1980s, however, encouraged it to see such a market in a somewhat more positive light. A monetary policy involving active intervention in liquid money markets promised an alternative way of influencing Japan's monetary situation (Sender 1992: 84; *The Economist* 1989). Although the Bank of Japan's initiatives to construct a money market in the late 1980s were limited, they marked an important first step in a process that was crucial if Japan was to promote the yen as an international currency.

The more important factor promoting increased use of the yen in East Asia during the bubble years was Japan's enormous wealth and its soaring currency during the late 1980s. These prompted very large Japanese investment and aid flows into the East Asian region, which in turn produced large new yen-denominated liabilities for East Asian countries such as Indonesia, the Philippines, Malaysia, Thailand and South Korea. Indeed, for these countries, the yen's share of total external liabilities began to surpass that of the dollar in the late 1980s, a change that encouraged the central banks of these countries to accumulate greater yen holdings in their official reserves

(Tavlas and Ozeki 1991: 45). Japanese capital outflows into East Asia in the late 1980s also encouraged a greater use of the yen in Japan's trade. Not only did these capital flows spur greater trade with East Asia, where the yen is used more actively (approximately 50 per cent of Japan's exports to Asia are denominated in yen, according to Cohen 1998), but Japanese investment also often consisted of Japanese firms locating offshore in order to export yen-denominated products back to Japan (Thompson 1993b).

The yen's growing international use in the region in this period, alongside the frustration with dollar dependence, prompted the Japanese government to begin to take a more active interest in regional financial leadership. In early 1991, for example, the Bank of Japan organized and hosted a meeting of central bankers from Thailand, Malaysia, Indonesia, the Philippines, Singapore, Australia, New Zealand and South Korea. This meeting was designed to become an annual event and, according to one journalist at the time, 'what the Bank of Japan has in mind ultimately is developing something akin to an Asian version of the European-dominated Bank for International Settlements (BIS) in Basel, Switzerland' (Rowley 1991: 42). Interestingly, these meetings excluded the United States, making them one of the few regional economic groupings to do so and demonstrating Japan's new efforts to carve out a financial policy that was more independent of the United States. These meetings were followed by the more concrete step in 1996 of Japan signing agreements with nine countries to lend their central banks yen in order to stabilize exchange rates (Cohen 1998).

In some ways, it is surprising that these moves did not lead Japan to take a more decisive regional leadership role during the 1997–8 Asian crisis. To be sure, its proposal to create an Asian Monetary Fund was in keeping with the leadership role that Japan had begun to cultivate slowly in the region. But as we have seen, Japanese policy makers chose not to push the proposal very actively in the face of strong American opposition. Interestingly, however, this setback and the unilateral American handling of the Asian crisis seemed to strengthen the determination of Japanese policy makers to acquire a larger financial leadership role in the region by late 1998. In October of that year, Japan announced a $30 billion assistance package – the Miyazawa Plan – for East Asian countries affected by the crisis. The assistance pointedly did not include the kinds of tough neoliberal conditions that were attached to IMF assistance. Included among the recipients, for example, was Malaysia, which had introduced capital controls in defiance of US and IMF advice only a month earlier. Indeed, important Japanese financial policy makers, such as vice-finance minister for international affairs Eisuke Sakakibara (1999), made it clear that this aid to Malaysia signaled that 'Tokyo was not necessarily opposed to the control on capital outflows to avert a crisis'.

This effort to carve out an independent Japanese leadership role likely frustrated US officials, just as the Asian Monetary Fund proposal had a year earlier. Indeed, as P.K. Basu (the director of Crédit Suisse First Boston in Singapore) noted, the Miyazawa Plan was 'de facto' the Asian Monetary Fund proposal put forward without the proposal for institutional reform (*Business Times* 1999). This time around, however, Japanese policy makers stuck to their position more forcefully. Sakakibara reports that he extracted a compromise this time from Larry Summers, who, as deputy Treasury Secretary, was leading efforts to rescue Brazil from its financial crisis at the time. In exchange for a promise that Japan would not join European countries in opposing the US plan for the Brazilian rescue, the United States agreed not to oppose Japan's rescue plan for Malaysia and other Asian countries (Sakakibara 1999).

An interesting feature of the Miyazawa Plan was Japan's offer to guarantee yen-denominated bond issues from some East Asian countries that have been having trouble borrowing on world capital markets (Malaysia was the first country to take up this offer, in December 1998). The offer is designed not just to restore these countries' creditworthiness, but also to encourage the issuance of more yen-denominated bonds in the region. The determination of Japanese officials to encourage the internationalization of the yen in the post-crisis era has also been signaled by several other recent moves. These include the withdrawal of a withholding tax on government securities, the abolition of a securities transaction tax, and the creation of a deeper yen debt market by broadening of the range of short-term government securities issued. There have also been some prominent calls within the Japanese government for Japan's Overseas Development Agency loans to be repaid in yen, as well as Japan's oil imports (Nakamoto 1999; Sender 1999).

Once again, the experience of the Asian crisis has played a role in prompting this growing desire among Japanese policy makers to promote the internationalization of the yen. As Nakamoto (1999) notes, '[m]any LDP politicians believe over-reliance on the US dollar was partly responsible for the Asian currency turmoil'. When the dollar appreciated by roughly 50 per cent vis-à-vis the yen between 1995 and 1997, many countries in Asia whose currencies were pegged to the dollar experienced growing balance of payments problems. Their trade with Japan had grown considerably since the late 1980s and this exchange rate change encouraged larger imports from, and fewer exports to, Japan. The crisis revealed, in other words, the need to ensure that growing intraregional trade was matched by increasingly close exchange rate management within the region. This, in turn, required that the dollar's role in the region be diminished.

In sum, Japan's experience with US unilateral leadership during the bubble economy period and the 1997–8 Asian financial crisis has encouraged it to consider cultivating a more assertive and independent position in global finance. As has been true of European policy makers, Japanese officials have become particularly interested in cultivating closer integration within their own region as a way of insulating themselves from the effects of US dominance. Whether this initiative will be as successful as that in Europe remains to be seen.

Conclusion

This chapter has tried to highlight two ways in which Strange's analysis of American hegemony has been proved correct during the 1990s. First, her insistence during the 1980s that US scholars were overstating the decline of US financial hegemony in the face of the Japanese challenge turned out to be remarkably accurate. Two events in particular – the bursting of Japan's financial bubble in the early 1990s and the handling of the 1997–8 Asian crisis – revealed the underlying weaknesses in Japan's challenge. As Strange put it in the early 1980s, the United States remained the only 'extraordinary' power in the world financial order during the 1990s.

Equally prescient has been Strange's anticipation of growing reactions against US financial leadership over time. In Strange's view, the source of global financial instability since the early 1970s has not been the decline of US power but the poor quality of US leadership. Two solutions have thus presented themselves to European and Japanese policy makers over this period. The first option, taken up by Strange with vigor throughout the 1980s, has been to try to persuade the United States to change its ways and adopt a more enlightened and consistent form of leadership. As this strategy has been less than successful, however, foreign governments have increasingly turned to a second option anticipated by Strange: the cultivation of independent financial power with which to insulate themselves from, and constrain, US behavior. This option has been pursued in a more extensive way in Europe, but it also appears to be increasingly on the political agenda in Japan. The implication of its implementation in both contexts is that, over the medium term, we will move from a hegemonic financial order to a more decentralized one characterized by more of a balance of power between the United States, Japan and Europe.

Whether this latter scenario might produce greater global financial stability is an issue that Strange did not address in depth. Some other observers who share Strange's assessment of the quality of American leadership since the early 1970s have suggested that it would. David Calleo (1987: ch.8), in particular, has argued that a world monetary order based on more 'pluralistic' or 'balance of power' principles may be more likely to produce stability over time than one based on hegemony. His reasoning is straightforward: a hegemonic power is inevitably tempted to exploit its dominant position in global finance over time to serve its own interests rather than the interests of the stability of the system. In his words, 'unchecked power corrupts its holder and leads to overextension, unnatural dependence, exploitation, instability and desperate resistance' (ibid.: 137).[2] In this way, Calleo directly challenged the assumptions of the hegemonic stability theory. Interestingly, some prominent European policy makers have advanced a similar critique in defending the way EMU might lead to a more pluralistic world financial order. Jacques Delors, for example, argued in 1993 that EMU would make the EU 'strong enough to force the United States and Japan to play by rules which would ensure much greater monetary stability around the world' (quoted in Henning 1998: 565).

Strange herself, however, did not appear to put forward such a direct challenge of the hegemonic stability theory. Indeed, she did not seem to show much enthusiasm for a monetary order based on 'pluralistic' principles. To be sure, she agreed with Calleo's criticism of the way the United States used its financial power from the early 1970s. But as a long-standing observer of international relations, she did not believe that significant international economic cooperation between the leading powers in a more decentralized order could be terribly effective. Indeed, in *Mad Money*, she noted that the prospects for such cooperation seemed less favorable than they had been a decade earlier. For this reason, she seemed to view a pluralistic order only as a second-best solution.

Perhaps another reason why she did not take up Calleo's argument more actively was her growing conviction in the 1990s that the debates about the hegemonic stability theory were diverting analysts from a more important trend: the diminishing power of *all* states vis-à-vis global financial markets. In this context, Strange argued that debates about hegemony and the distribution of power *between* states were missing the point. As she put it in *Mad Money*:

> For us in the 1990s, it seems to many experts that Kindleberger was right: the system does need management or 'governance' when things start to go wrong. Yet these days, no single hegemonic leader is strong or rich enough to fill the role unaided. Instead, we may have to pin our hopes to the chances of a collective leadership as a substitute for a national hegemon. (Strange 1998: 55)

Whether the decline of American power will increase or diminish the chances of this collective leadership emerging is a question that will need to be answered in the coming years.

Notes

1   Between 1989 and 1992, daily turnover in the New York market grew from $129 to $192 billion, while that in Tokyo grew from $115 to $126 billion (Blitz 1993).
2   Moreover, Calleo (1976, 1987) directly challenges Kindleberger's analysis of the inter-war years to suggest that the instability in that period was a product not of the absence of a hegemonic leader but rather of the exploitative efforts of Britain to use its position of financial dominance to serve its interests.

Bibliography

Bergsten, C. Fred (1997), 'The Dollar and the Euro', *Foreign Affairs*, 76(4), July/ August, 83–95.
Blitz, James (1993), 'All Change in Foreign Exchanges', *Financial Times*, 2 April.
Business Times (1999), 'Asian Fund, Single Currency May Be Inevitable', *Business Times* (Malaysia), 14 July.
Calleo, David (1976), 'The Historiography of the Interwar Period: Reconsiderations', in B. Rowland (ed.), *Balance of Power or Hegemony: The Interwar Monetary System*, New York: New York University Press.
Calleo, David (1987), *Beyond American Hegemony*, New York: Basic Books.
Cohen, Benjamin (1998), *The Geography of Money*, Ithaca: Cornell University Press.
Corrigan, Tracy (1992), 'London Increases Share of Ecu Banking Market', *Financial Times*, 11 February.
Dunne, Nancy (1992), 'Europe Will Be "Richest Market in World"', *Financial Times*, 2 January.
The Economist (1989), 'Opening the Door to Japan's Short-term Money Markets', 9 April.
The Economist (1991), 'A Fistful of ECUs', 13 July.
The Economist (1992), 'Japan's Monetary Implosion', 31 October.
European Commission (1990), 'One Market, One Money', *European Economy*, 44.
Gilpin, Robert (1987), *The Political Economy of International Relations*, Princeton, NJ: Princeton University Press.
Godement, François (1999), *The Downsizing of Asia*, London: Routledge.
Helleiner, Eric (1989), 'Money and Influence: Japanese Power in the International Monetary and Financial System', *Millennium; Journal of International Studies*, 18, 343–58.
Helleiner, Eric (1992), 'Japan and the Changing Global Financial Order', *International Journal*, 47, 420–44.
Helleiner, Eric (1994), *States and the Reemergence of Global Finance*, Ithaca: Cornell University Press.
Henning, C. Randall (1997), *Cooperating with Europe's Monetary Union*, Washington, DC: Institute for International Economics.
Henning, C. Randall (1998), 'Systemic Conflict and Regional Monetary Integration: The Case of Europe', *International Organization*, 52(3), 537–73.
Kazuhide, Uekusa (1991), 'The Making and Breaking of a Bubble Economy', *Japan Echo*, 18(4), 23–7.

Leadbeater, Charles (1992), 'Japan Learns Lessons from a Burst Bubble', *Financial Times*, 26 October.
Martin, Peter (1992), 'Ghosts of the Decade Past', *Financial Times*, 29 May.
Murphy, R. Taggart (1989), 'Power Without Purpose: The Crisis of Japan's Global Financial Dominance', *Harvard Business Review*, March–April, 71–83.
Nakamoto, Michiyo (1998), 'Decision to Opt for Big Bang Came as a Surprise', *Financial Times*, 26 March.
Nakamoto, Michiyo (1999), 'Japanese PM in Call to Boost Profile of Yen', *Financial Times*, 4 January.
Pauly, Louis (1992), 'The Politics of European Monetary Union: National Strategies, International Implications', *International Journal*, 47.
Pempel, T.J. (1999), 'Conclusion', in T.J. Pempel (ed.), *The Politics of the Asian Economic Crisis*, Ithaca: Cornell University Press.
Plenderleith, Ian (1991), 'Briefing: Ecu Instruments', *Euromoney*, August, 56–8.
Rowley, A. (1991), 'Shy Bloc Builder', *Far Eastern Economic Review*, 14 February.
Sakakibara, Eisuke (1999), 'Mr. Yen Managing Crises: International Intervention Averted Global Depression', *The Yomiuri Shimbun*, 6 August.
Sender, Henny (1992), 'BoJ Bashing – and Boosting', *Institutional Investor* (International Edition), September.
Sender, Henny (1999), 'Japan Wants Yen to Go Global', *Globe and Mail*, 7 January.
Stevenson, Merril (1989), 'In the Balance: A Survey of Europe's Capital Markets', *The Economist*, 16 December.
Strange, Susan (1982), 'Still an Extraordinary Power: America's Role in a Global Monetary System', in R. Lombra and W. Witte (eds), *The Political Economy of Domestic and International Monetary Policy*, Ames, Iowa: Iowa State University.
Strange, Susan (1986), *Casino Capitalism*, Oxford: Blackwell.
Strange, Susan (1987), 'The Persistent Myth of Lost Hegemony', *International Organization*, 41(4), 551–74.
Strange, Susan (1990), 'Finance, Information and Power', *Review of International Studies*, 16, 259–74
Strange, Susan (1998), *Mad Money*, Ann Arbor: University of Michigan Press.
Tavlas, George (1998), 'The International Use of Currencies: The US Dollar and the Euro', *Finance and Development*, 35(2), 46–9.
Tavlas, George and Yuzuru Ozeki (1991), 'The Japanese Yen as an International Currency', unpublished paper, Washington: International Monetary Fund.
Terazono, Emiko (1993), 'Interest in Japan as Financial Centre Wanes', *Financial Times*, 30 March.
Thompson, Robert (1993a), 'New Plea to Japan to Reform Markets', *Financial Times*, 5 February.
Thompson, Robert (1993b), 'The Yen's Role in East Asia', *Financial Times*, 26 May.
Wade, Robert and Frank Veneroso (1998), 'The Resources Lie Within', *The Economist*, 7 November.
Wagstyl, Stefan (1992), 'Shock Waves Around the World', *Financial Times*, April 10
Waters, Richard (1992), 'Japanese Banks Step Up Pace of International Withdrawal', *Financial Times*, 13 November.
Wood, Christopher (1992), *The Bubble Economy*, New York: Atlantic Monthly.

14 The United States and World Trade: Hegemony by Proxy?

JUDITH GOLDSTEIN

Introduction

In 1982, Susan Strange participated in the writing of a volume whose purpose was to understand the cause and effect of the proliferation of international institutions in the post-World War II period. Arguing against the mainstream, she suggested that the concept of an international regime was 'negative in its influence, obfuscating and confusing instead of clarifying and illuminating, and distorting by concealing bias instead of revealing and removing it' (1982). Strange's criticism of the use of the concept derived from a perception that regime analysis was in her words, 'vague, faddish, static, held a value bias, and was, overly state centered'. Behind all these criticisms was one theme: American academics failed to understand the foolishness of an explanation of international organizations independent of US interests and power.

This chapter takes up Strange's challenge to put American power and interests at the center of an analysis of international institutions. Its empirical focus is commercial policy and the role of the United States in the creation and evolution of the General Agreement on Tariffs and Trade (GATT), now called the World Trade Organization (WTO). The chapter argues that the GATT regime served a dual purpose. Not only did it promote an international policy of trade liberalization but also its rules and norms promoted a preference for that policy within the United States. Faced with an institutional bias toward protection, US leaders sought to use the regime to assure the mobilization of domestic groups with an interest in trade openness. That political purpose has been undermined by the new WTO. Its structure, while serving the needs of the United States to deal with commitment problems associated with the end of the cold war, is far less helpful to American leaders seeking to preserve support for open trade. The result has been an increase in the politicization of trade policy in the United States and a decline in support for both the trade regime and its purposes.

To show this changing relationship between international rules and domestic political purpose, this chapter is divided into four parts. First, a short theoretical beginning outlines US politics and explains why US leaders thought it necessary to create an international organization in order to liberalize trade. Second, we examine the origins of the GATT and America's role in its form and scope. Third, we look at the WTO and ask to what extent the new regime reflects changes in America's power and interest. Part four offers concluding remarks.

US Commercial Policy

Liberal trade policies are difficult to maintain, especially in democratic polities. The general problem is straightforward. Although free trade is a policy in which the majority reaps gains as a result of the more efficient use of resources, a trade barrier is a good whose benefits are concentrated. In the absence of some institutional solution, the existence of diffuse costs and concentrated benefits will lead trade policy to suffer an 'Olsonian' fate.[1] There will be an underprovision of the free trade 'good' because those who are hurt by high prices (consumers) have less of an incentive to mobilize to defend open trade than do those who reap a concentrated benefit from a trade barrier. Winegrowers in France, autoworkers in the United States and rice producers in Japan are organized and articulate defenders of pro-protection policies that protect their interests; if their governments want to pursue liberal trade, they must find others to articulate an opposing interest.[2]

This underprovision of free trade is no better evidenced than in the United States. The American Constitution grants the right to set tariffs to Congress. Given the small size of its electoral units, especially in the House of Representatives, the problem of maintaining a pro-free trade coalition in the United States is formidable. As districts increase in size, leaders are more willing to think about the 'general' good, basically because they are able to make tradeoffs between competing groups with crosscutting interests. Thus the US President with the largest constituency has historically been more willing to support free trade than has Congress. Among congressional representatives, the Senate is more free trade-oriented than is the House. With very small districts, House members have greater difficulty ignoring organized groups in their districts. Even though a majority may exist that will benefit from trade liberalization, it is more likely that the voice of import-competing groups will determine the votes of these representatives. The outcome is a log-roll in which all interests are accommodated; the cost is a suboptimal collective policy.[3]

Given this institutional bias, it is not surprising that high barriers to trade characterized the first hundred years of US economic history. But while trade barriers may have been functional for the United States in its early years, they became increasingly inefficient as the United States industrialized. As American manufactures, agriculture and banking sectors expanded, it became evident that American trade policy was out of step with the needs of the country. Trade needed to expand. American exports required access to foreign markets; consumption of imported goods was a requisite for the repayment of foreign debt. The structure of American institutions, however, made it difficult for policy to change in line with the new needs of the nation. The problem was that the Constitution granted Congress, and in particular the House of Representatives, primary responsibility for tariff policy. As suggested above, small congressional constituencies, the organization of congressional committees and House rules that encouraged log rolling made it near impossible to either lower tariffs unilaterally or agree to reciprocal reductions.[4]

The early 1930s ushered in a new era of trade policy making. The epic event was the passage of the Reciprocal Trade Agreements Act of 1934 (RTAA). The legislation amended the 1930 Smoot–Hawley Tariff Act, the last tariff schedule to be set unilaterally by Congress, to allow the President to negotiate reciprocal trade agreements with foreign governments. In exchange for increased access to foreign markets, the President was authorized to reduce US duties up to a pre-set amount. No specific duties were established. More importantly, agreements that did not exceed the specified reduction level did not have to return for legislative approval under the treaty provision of the Constitution. In short, delegation had two key components: the right to negotiate the reciprocal reduction of the tariff schedule and the ability to enforce an agreement not supported by a large congressional majority.[5]

Delegation changed the relationship between the two branches of the US government. This shift was a necessary prerequisite to the opening of the US economy. Given the distribution of public attitudes on trade liberalization in the United States during the 1930s, finding a majority in congress to support a trade treaty was extremely difficult, if not impossible. Delegation was an institutional innovation or 'fix' that created such a majority. Delegation was not an absolution of power by Congress, as is sometimes said; Congress gave the President authority for limited periods, forcing re-authorization at regular intervals. Rather, delegation was merely a method for the restructuring of social support for trade openness at both the congressional and executive levels.[6]

Trade policy making changed after 1934 in two specific ways. First, after 1934 the President crafted agreements that were immune from being 'picked apart' by pro-protection groups. These agreements were bundled: access to the US market was predicated on reciprocal access to new markets. Congress was able to give presidents the power to negotiate these agreements because they and their constituents operated behind a 'veil of ignorance' of exactly which industries in their districts would or would not be in the final trade 'bundle'. The effect of this uncertainty was a change in the incentives of groups to mobilize. Before 1934, the cost and benefits of organizing, that is, the probability of some gain as a result of expending the costs to overcome collective action problems, favored those who were anti-trade. After 1934, the probability of a particular industry finding itself in the final 'bundle' declined, thus lessening the incentive of anti-trade groups to expend the costs of organizing. This effect was compounded by an increase in the cost of organizing, a result of the shift in the locus of policy setting to the executive branch. Where pre-1934 groups only had to have a presence in their district, they now needed to organize on the national level. On the other hand, export industries, with little reason to organize to stop pro-protection groups in the old system, now had an interest in the process of tariff setting. While exporters had no incentive to organize before 1934, a result of the unilateral process of congressional tariff setting, they now found that policy had a direct implication for their access to new markets.[7] Thus, even without a change in underlying preferences, the shift in rules of tariff setting changed the organization of group politics in the United States. This shift explains the ability of the United States to find support for lower tariffs in the years after the Great Depression.[8]

This initial change in institutional structures created a majority in support of tariff negotiations. However, after 1974, a second institutional fix was devised in response to the expansion of the international trade agenda from tariffs to non-tariffs (NTBs). As world tariff levels declined, other aspects of nations' trading practices – from procurement practices to subsidies – became the major impediments to world trade. While Congress had agreed to pre-approve tariff reductions, thereby allowing the President to negotiate tariff treaties, such a procedure was impractical for NTBs. The nature of international agreements now entailed a treaty's explicit return to the legislature for approval of changes in domestic law. Although the general political problem was the same, that is, anti-trade groups would have asymmetrical power to veto legislation, the solution of prestipulating the President's authority was now impractical.

The institutional fix was again an ex ante commitment, not to specified reductions but rather, to a 'closed' vote. Under the system known as 'fast track', the President would negotiate concessions in consultation with relevant congressional committees. Then, at least 90 days in advance, he would give notice of intent to enter into a non-tariff barrier agreement. Both Houses of Congress would be required to act within 60 days of his submitting the implementing legislation. In return for consultation, Congress would vote under a closed rule: no changes would be allowed either in committee or on the floor.

American leadership in the creation of an open trading regime would have been impossible without these two institutional fixes, both of which granted agenda power to the President, facilitating the creation of a majority in favor of trade liberalization. The shift in institutions did not allow Congress and/or the President to 'hide' from powerful groups. Rather, liberalization of the American market reflected the existence of an electoral majority in favor of an open trade policy. Agenda control and/or fast track can manipulate but not change the preferences of the legislature: Congress repeatedly renewed the trade program because presidents used their negotiating authority to make agreements that bundled export gains with import losses so as to keep 51 per cent of Congress in the coalition. Thus open trade was possible not because delegation allowed the President to ignore preferences but, rather, because the President 'bundled' international and domestic tariffs so as to change preferences. The innovation of the period was not delegation alone but the ability to conclude agreements that made members of Congress willing to trade off the political risk of opening their home market for the political benefit of increased access to foreign markets. At heart, American openness is a function of pro-trade preferences, sustainable only to the extent that there are positive feedback effects from international trade on the American economy. The American political system retains its pro-protection institutional bias. Trade policy making remains precarious and occurs in the shadow of the economic effects of the world economy. Leaders need to be wary of the mobilization of anti-trade groups and are not insulated, as is the case in some political systems, against social resistance.

Both the existence of the GATT and the particular rules and norms that came to characterize the regime can be understood as an extension of America's institutional problem. As suggested in the next section, the United States promoted a set of regulations, a form of negotiation and a system of exceptions, all to facilitate electoral support within the United States. In a fundamental way, the United States created an institution that could solve the problems facing leaders at home in the 1950s through the 1970s. The unintended result of these earlier fixes, however, was a set of new trade-related issues in the 1990s that threatens to undercut support for the trade regime at the beginning of the new millennium.

Creating the GATT

Strange's critique of regime theory was leveled at explanations of international institutions that excluded consideration of national power. Reviewing conventional explanations for the existence of the trading regime, Strange's critique could not be more prescient. The dominant explanations for the existence of the GATT/WTO regime are systemic.[9] Such analyses assume that trade relations are akin to the strategic interaction of the 'prisoner's dilemma'. States eschew cooperation out of fear of opportunistic behavior by their trading partners. States prefer cooperation but such a policy is not pursued because opening up your borders to trade, in the absence of some commitment mechanism, invites opportunistic behavior on the part of your trading partners. Regimes arise in response to this dilemma in order to provide information about both the intentions and behavior of other states. As Strange noted, there is little need for power in explanations in which states join regimes out of self-interest. Rather, the system is stable because self-interested actors prefer to cooperate, no matter the distributional consequences, as long as the time horizon of interaction is sufficiently long.[10]

There are at least two problems with an analysis of the contemporary trade regime that fails to incorporate the relative power and interests of the United States both at the creation of the regime and in subsequent years. First, such approaches implicitly assume states have single-peaked and fixed preferences that are maximized through international cooperation. Such an assumption excludes the heart of the trade policy-setting process in the United States. Constructing support for free trade is an ongoing process; to assume support and then model rational behavior based on that support is a misrepresentation of the political situation. Further, not only are preferences not single-peaked, but they are not fixed. Preferences over trade policy are effected by exogenous events, such as the state of the world economy. America's commitment to open trade cannot be dissociated from trade's economic effects. Groups mobilize as a result of economic variables, such as the trade balance or changes in the trading behavior of other countries. As well, preferences can shift as a result of endogenous phenomena, such as the growth of environmental movement. In short, the preferences American central decision makers project to the world will change, depending upon these and other factors.

Second, and related, without consideration of US preferences, there is no explanation for the particular set of rules and norms that characterize the trade regime. Neoinstitutional analysis says little about the choice over a particular form of cooperation, even though it is acknowledged that cooperation can occur in multiple settings.[11] Yet rules are consequential. The explanation for the choice of the particular set of rules and norms that constitute the trade regime is found not only in America's ability to effect a particular outcome due to power but also within the domestic polity where choices over rules are made.

The GATT was the creation of the United States. To understand its form, analysis should begin with the preferences of US decision makers and the strategies they selected as a means to gain domestic support for these preferences. The GATT was created to spur trade but its supporters understood, unlike the theoretical case for free trade or the example of the British opening in the 19th century, that the United States would not be able to unilaterally open up its shores to foreign goods. Not only did the United States face a recalcitrant Congress but also, in the post-World War II years, leaders could not easily trade off social welfare goals with the promise of aggregate economic prosperity. Thus American leaders faced a domestic dilemma. Given the inter-war experience, members of the US Department of State concluded in the early 1940s that the American market could not remain closed. Such a policy was associated with depression and war. Yet political support for openness was precarious. Openness would require not just delegation to the President, but some delegation to an international agent. Thus planners may not have spoken with one voice on exactly what the US role would be in worldwide trade liberalization, but they agreed that some form of multilateral international organization would be helpful both to maintain order in commercial markets and to assure America's participation in the process of liberalization.[12]

The State Department's first effort to create a trade regime failed. The International Trading Organization (ITO) charter, ratified in the fall of 1947 in Havana, was an organization whose purpose was to be the regulation of multiple aspects of commerce, from trade to foreign direct investment. The organization was a compromise between the American and British notions of the scope of the trading regime. The US plan was more modest, reflecting the limited mandate given to the US President in the original 1934 legislature. The British sought an organization that could facilitate a number of goals, such as a full employment economy, not just expanded trade. From the start, the planned organization met with resistance at home. A wide array of groups organized against aspects of its mandate and the process of approval became bogged down in Congress.[13] While waiting for congressional approval, the United States moved to carry out the mandate of tariff reduction granted to them in the last renewal of the RTAA in 1946. Calling together delegates of nations to meet in Geneva, the United States orchestrated, under UN guidance, the first set of multilateral trade talks. While politicians continued to argue about the ITO, an agreement was concluded that not only led to a lowering of tariffs but also codified what came to be known as the GATT.

The GATT itself was a 'thin' set of rules based on one norm: specific reciprocity. Many commentators argue that diffuse reciprocity as it was manifest in most-favored-nation (MFN) status to all members was the defining element of the regime.[14] Clearly, the use of MFN was an important mechanism for the expansion of trade to new nations throughout the decades. MFN increased the volume and direction of trade relations by granting countries access to markets otherwise denied.[15] However, a far more important element of the regime was a simpler norm of 'tit-for-tat' that operated both at the time of signing new agreements and at moments when countries reneged on a promise. Tariff negotiations were based on a principle of all key suppliers giving exactly as much access to their own market as they gained through another country's concession. These gains and losses were moneterized and the GATT secretariat facilitated the accounting mechanism. Similarly, when a country, for whatever reason, took back its concession, trading partners needed to be equally compensated.

Why such a norm? Following on the logic of American politics suggested above, it fit with the needs of American leaders. Reciprocal agreements bundled together the interests of import-competing producers with those of exporters, therefore expanding the coalition by including the interests of groups who benefitted from expanded trade. Similarly, retaliation was targeted at group mobilization at the time of national reneging on an agreement. Retaliation's purpose was to mobilize those who most benefitted from free trade (exporters) in order to pressure the government to adhere to the rules of the regime. Its function was to counter the weight of rent-seeking import-competing groups. Reciprocity and retaliation were two sides of the same coin, joined by the notion of 'equal gain, equal loss'.[16] Nations opened up borders when given a similar amount of access to another market; when countries reneged, for whatever reason, the losing country needed to be made 'whole'. The deals were based on value and not specific products, allowing countries to move their tariff schedules in line with the changing power of domestic groups.

Where MFN allowed nations to have a 'free ride', specific reciprocity at both the times of negotiation and ex post reneging explicitly eschewed any asymmetry of concessions. All concessions were based on an even bargain among the principal suppliers; if governments defected and broke an agreement, they either made an equal concession or were punished with an 'equal' amount of retaliation (calculated on the basis of the amount of trade to be gained or lost). Although the procedures for negotiating trade barrier reductions changed over time, the fundamental norm was entrenched in the regime, even though it stands in contraposition to neoclassical economic ideas. All members of the GATT benefitted from 'specific reciprocity' between the major trading partners through the rule of MFN, but an agreement did not occur if major trading partners did not offer a concession: there may have been a free ride for the tertiary trading partners, but never for those countries that accounted for the bulk of trade in a product.

The inculcation of reciprocity was not the only element of the GATT structure that was created to be a convenience for US elected officials. Most basically, the structure of the GATT as a political and not a technical undertaking reflected US interests.[17] Liberalization would occur in the shadow of politics; therefore countries should be exempted from liberalization if necessary, given the power of particular groups. The regime was 'thin'. GATT had dubious standing in international law, its focus was narrow and it was filled with exceptions and loopholes. The organization mirrored the fluidity of domestic politics. US decision makers did not want to be constrained by a set of explicit rules and/or a large secretariat filled with individuals providing purely technical interpretations of these rules.

The politicization of the GATT for domestic reasons explains the odd set of rules and exceptions incorporated into the agreement. Rather than being inchoate, they are tied together by considerations of US domestic preferences. For example, the existence of Article 19, the escape clause, is directly associated with congressional preferences. In 1946, the United States had included a similar safeguard in its trade treaty with Mexico, allowing the United States to rescind a tariff agreement under specific conditions. Once given the escape clause, Congress demanded that negotiators in Geneva include just such a clause in all future treaties. The result was the generalization of this demand into GATT rules.

According to Article 19 of the GATT, countries could escape their bound tariff concessions due either to serious injury of a producer, a result of some change in circumstance or some unforeseen development. The mechanism, however, by which a country decided whether such a 'change in circumstance' had occurred was domestic, and not international.[18] Thus the burden of proof that the use of Article 19 was unjustified was placed on the complainant, not the country invoking the clause.[19] This allowed the United States freedom to respond, when and if necessary, to changed economic circumstances that forced a political response with no fear of an international veto.

The escape clause is one of two key mechanisms by which nations could get out of GATT tariff agreements. The other mechanism is stipulated in Article 28 and again illustrates the 'political' and not technical nature of the original regime. In writing the GATT rules, member countries understood that agreements were not immutable. Rather, the contract between two countries to lower their trade barriers was just a contract: under specific conditions, countries could re-examine the agreement and decide to alter its terms. Thus, according to Article 28, nations could revisit their agreements in light of their economic affects. Nations were allowed to change tariffs every three years during what was called the 'open season', in between these set periods under rules governing 'out of season' changes and/ or they could use Article 28(5) to change the structure of their tariffs at other times, as long as the general tariff level remained the same. In principle, Article 28 was to cover cases in which either negotiators misperceived the effects of an agreement or change of circumstance forced them to protect some industry. In practice, the provisions were rarely used. The constraint on changing your schedule was that the overall level of concession needed to be stable, that is, governments could alter their schedules, but they needed to swap one group's protection for the next. Given that this swap needed to occur in the absence of benefits from a larger set of negotiations, few democratic governments were able to utilize the safeguard, given group pressures. If on the other hand a country chose not to make a counterconcession and just raised its tariff level, it faced retaliation. Such a strategy would have leaders under pressure from exporters, who faced a loss of access to some market. The result was that safeguard provisions were used only rarely and agreements were not breached. The stability in the GATT regime was not a result of tight rules. Rather, it was stable because safeguard provisions, like tariff negotiations, had specific effects on the mobilization of domestic groups within member countries.[20]

US influence was also apparent in the scope of the GATT regime. Although not so intended, US action circumscribed the GATT to the reduction of barriers mainly in manufactured products. Given US comparative advantage in agriculture, the omission of liberalization of trade in farm products in early negotiations is anomalous. The exclusion of agriculture, however, reflects then-current US domestic farm programs. In the Agricultural Adjustment Act (AAA) of 1933, the United States legislated a system of price supports for certain agricultural products that were tied to domestic price levels. When negotiators went to Geneva, Congress made it clear that the United States was not to enter into any agreement that would undermine that policy. The results were a set of exceptions for agricultural trade: quantitative restrictions were permitted under Article XI; certain farm subsidies were excepted from the general prohibition under Article XVI and export subsidies on agricultural products were tolerated under Article XVI.[21]

Take, for example, Article XI, explicitly drafted by American ITO negotiators. According to GATT rules, countries are allowed quantitative restrictions when 'necessary to the enforcement of governmental measures'. In particular, countries could use this measure if they maintained production controls. Since the United States was the only country with such production controls, they were the only nation at its writing who benefitted from this exemption.[22] Even with this exception, the US policy became inconsistent with GATT rules when Section 22 of the AAA was passed. With this authority, Congress could place import restrictions on any agricultural product, even if that product was not subject to governmental production controls. When the United States imposed such quotas on a range of products including cotton, wheat, peanuts and dairy, it demanded a new waiver, allowing these actions. The GATT parties responded by giving the waiver, timed to encourage the reauthorization of negotiating authority that passed Congress in 1955.

It is ironic to note that, although it was American pressure that led to the exceptions for farm products, it was the Europeans who ultimately built an agricultural policy incorporating all these exceptions. The Common Agricultural Policy (CAP) was never illegal by GATT standards, at least according to the specifics of law. In creating the CAP, Europeans were careful to remain consistent with the agricultural exceptions fostered by the United States, including that for export subsidies. The irony is that by the 1960s, the United States realized that it had made a strategic mistake in supporting agricultural exceptionalism. As manufactures increasingly had access to foreign markets, the lack of admittance for farm products, the most competitive in the world, began to hurt the US balance of trade. But while the United States could have gotten any set of rules in the 1940s, its power was far less by the 1970s; the United States now had great difficulty finding partners willing to negotiate over agricultural products. Having allowed their farm sectors to develop under a protective wall, both EU members and Japan were confronted with powerful farm interests, making it difficult for any government to increase farm trade. Thus, even with significant pressure from the United States to open up markets, these countries made few concessions. Only in hindsight is it apparent that the United States should have forced agricultural trade onto the GATT agenda. At the time, Congress asserted that the only (and best) method to maintain high farm prices and thus a vibrant farm sector was through its particularistic policies, and not through international trade.

In sum, at its creation, the GATT was an international organization that could not have been better suited for the American political system. The GATT was multilateral yet the United States exercised control by its right to veto any decision by the contracting parties. The rule of consensus voting, explicitly granting an equal vote to all parties, also assured the United States that no decision could be rendered that was unwelcome 'back home'. All GATT members had MFN status and pledged non-discrimination in its trading relationship, yet reciprocity mandated an equal gain for opening up the US market. The GATT was full of political loopholes and safeguards. Not only could the United States escape its obligations, if necessary, but there was no fear of obligations being expanded to future members. Existing members who for any reason did not accept an accession agreement could abstain from granting full MFN status to those who joined later under Article 35.[23] Consistent with American power, the GATT secretariat was created with few powers and had no means, other than through collecting and disseminating information, to force countries to change some egregious practice. The central authority that could have existed, in the form of the dispute settlement procedures (DSP), was disabled from the start. Under the GATT, a government could veto the creation of a panel to adjudicate a dispute as well as any decision made by a panel that was created that was contrary to their interests.[24] This is not to say that nations did not ever use the dispute procedures but, rather, that they were a convenience, a means to deal with recalcitrant groups through the intentional tying of one's hands. In addition, the agreement provided numerous means for reneging on a tariff agreement, either through compensation or through changes in the tariff schedule. In comparison to the other international institutions created in the same era, the GATT was weaker, more democratic, more member-driven and less technical. Where the International Monetary Fund developed into a cohesive and explicit technical organization, the GATT remained an essentially political agency.

If the GATT was so weak, why did the United States support its creation? American central decision makers needed two things that could only be garnered through international cooperation. First, if the President was to retain his negotiating authority, he needed to craft agreements that were as inclusive as possible. Bilateral agreements were not going to be sufficient; a majority in favor of trade liberalization could be found only if more nations were at the table. Second, the problem of social resistance loomed large in light of previous tariff history. Delegation to the executive solved part of the problem of finding a majority in favor of trade liberalization. However, delegation did not mean that presidents could ignore organized resistance. Rather, that resistance needed to be balanced by mobilizing groups in favor of continued openness to counter pro-protection interests. This was impossible in the absence of the GATT, or some similar organization. Through international delegation, US leaders were able to effect a change in domestic trade politics. By 'tying their hands' through international delegation, they shifted the choice set of domestic groups. Increasing trade brought wealth and the creation of interests in economic openness, thereby sustaining the liberalization program over time.

The Evolution of the GATT into the WTO

Few analysts dispute that the GATT accomplished its core mission. Trade expanded dramatically in the years following its creation and regime membership stood at 135 in 2000. Membership in the GATT facilitated the process of tariff reduction in the United States begun with the delegation of negotiating authority to the President in 1934. As shown in Table 14.1, joining the GATT was part of a tariff reduction strategy the United States had embarked upon before the first Geneva Round of trade talks.

Table 14.1   US tariff reduction by trade rounds, 1934–79 (per cent)

GATT Round	Cut in all duties	Remaining duties (as share of 1930 tariffs)
Pre-GATT	33.2	66.8
Geneva, 1947	21.1	52.7
Annecy, 1949	1.9	51.7
Torguay, 1950–51	3.0	50.1
Geneva, 1955–6	2.5	48.9
Dillon, 1961–2	2.4	47.7
Kennedy, 1964–7	36.0	30.5
Tokyo, 1974–9	29.6	21.2

Source: Reproduced with permission from *The Trading System After the Uruguay Round* by John Whalley and Colleen Hamilton. Copyright © Institute for International Economics, 1996. All rights reserved.

Even before beginning the Uruguay Round of trade talks, the United States had accomplished a considerable reduction in rates, something that would have been politically unimaginable 100 years earlier. While the 1950s were years of relatively limited success in trade talks, the earlier period and the Kennedy and Tokyo Rounds were extremely successful. Still, the power of groups in the United States is evident in the last column. When the United States entered the Uruguay Round, duties, at about 21 per cent of those found in the 1930 Act, still protected segments of the workforce. Thus, in the period of GATT's tenure, world markets expanded dramatically, a result of the increase in both the breadth as well as the depth of trade relations governed by GATT rules.

The direction of the regime shifted over its existence, due to changes both in membership and trade issues. While the early trade rounds focused on lowering barriers to trade, later rounds focused on expanding the amount of trade covered by GATT rules. Indicative of this shift, the most dramatic outcomes from the last set of trade negotiations, the Uruguay Round, were not the formal reduction of trade barriers but the inclusion of textiles and agriculture in the regime (by changing barriers to tariffs) and the expansion of the GATT regime into new areas, such as services and intellectual property (GATS and TRIPS). Unlike in earlier rounds, this expansion in breadth did not facilitate bargaining, and more items on the table did not lead to a greater range of deals. Rather, the Uruguay Round's organization into 15 specific negotiating groups made it more and not less difficult to come to agreements across issue areas. Early rounds were akin to clubs. Deals were struck among a small group of like-minded representatives, all of whom accepted reciprocity as the basis for dealing with each other. The Uruguay Round eschewed this negotiating structure. Although some private negotiations occurred, far more time was spent in formal settings, with delegates giving prepared speeches but offering few concessions. The demand for more transparency was met by more open meetings and more press coverage; the effect was that delegates became wary of saying anything that would get them into trouble at home.[25]

The other dramatic change in the regime was its slow but consistent move toward being more formal, technical and 'legal'. The result of this movement, born in the Uruguay Round, was the rebirth of the organization itself into the WTO. Two aspects of the agreement to restructure the trade regime are key. First, the new regime includes previously signed agreements that were quasi-institutionalized in the GATT structure. These include 'grey' area agreements such as those in textiles, as well as more specific codes adopted since the Tokyo Round (1974–9) on a range of trade issues from technical barriers to anti-dumping. Joining the WTO was a 'single undertaking', meaning that all countries signed on to these preceding agreements, even if they were not an original party. The intent was to simplify and therefore regularize aspects of trade relations; the effect was an expansion of the scope of the regime, although without any increase in the size or funding of the secretariat.

This expansion of the scope of the WTO was only consequential because of a second change in the regime, that is, the change in dispute settlement procedures. Without a change in sanctioning authority, the expansion of GATT rules would have gone unnoticed. Under the new regime, nations can now demand that a panel be constituted to decide whether or not a nation is violating a WTO rule. In the past, the rule violator could veto both the formation of such a panel and, if a panel was established, the adoption of the report by the GATT members. Neither the power to undermine the creation of a panel nor the right to veto a report exists with the new WTO. The dispute procedures were expanded even beyond ad hoc panels to include a permanent appellate court with new legal standing. As with the GATT, nations retain a range of options, including ignoring a finding of wrongdoing by a panel or the appellate court. In theory, when a ruling is made in favor of the complainant, nations are supposed to change the egregious practice or, at minimum, compensate the trading partner for loss of trade. If they do not, retaliation is authorized by the WTO. In practice, however, since retaliation is meaningless for most small countries, the system is most effective when the parties are the major trading nations.[26] Still, small countries have far more authority than would be expected from a 'realist' perspective.

A recent review by Robert Hudec takes up the question of whether or not the new regime grants weaker countries more power than would be expected from a conventional model of international politics. His evaluation is based on cases adjudicated in the first 33 years of the DSP.[27] Using the predicted number of cases that would have occurred had the rate in the last 14 years of the GATT remained consistent, Hudec shows a significant rise in the number of disputes processed under the WTO. This 60 per cent increase in cases under the WTO suggests that more countries are using the DSP in the WTO than they did under the GATT regime. One explanation for the increase could be that the system works better: countries are now more confident that the powerful nations will not undermine the process and deny them an equal hearing. Hudec argues against this explanation, suggesting instead that the increase in cases merely represents the expansion of obligations undertaken during the Uruguay Round. He defends his position by looking at the types of cases that have led to panels. Of the 98 cases, 43 per cent of the increase can be attributable to a failure to meet a new obligation, almost all of them brought by the United States.[28] Further, the expansion of cases against developing nations is also due to the change in the breadth of the regime. Since all nations are now obligated by the 'single undertaking' as part of their membership to the WTO, they are now subject to a whole host of new rules. If we include these new 'developing country' cases, the data suggest that almost all of the growth in cases can be attributed to the expansion of rule coverage.

Hudec's notion that the significant change in the WTO was not the 'binding' of the powerful, but the expansion of the breadth of countries and products covered by WTO rules, is also suggested by a review of defendants and complainants before and after the WTO was created (see Table 14.2). Where the notion of more binding would suggest a rise in the number of cases brought by the developing countries, the data reveals that, rather than being the complainants, the poorer countries are more often the defendants.

Table 14.2   Use of dispute settlement procedures since 1980
             (percentage)

Country	Complainant		Defendant	
	GATT (1980–1994)	WTO (1995–1998)	GATT (1980–1994)	WTO (1995–1998)
United States	26	32	36	21
EU	19	22	28	20
Other developed	25	16	22	20
Developing countries	31	31	13	39

Source: Hudec (1999: 22 and 24). Reproduced courtesy of the Minnesota Journal of Global Trade, Inc., Minneapolis, Minnesota.

Although the data show that there has been no significant change in the number of cases brought against the United States in the DSP, the perception of such change looms large among interest groups in the United States. At the heart of criticism is the legal standing of the organization and whether or not international rulings will lead to changes in domestic laws. The GATT agreement explicitly regulated products and not process: the rules of trade extended only to goods leaving one market and entering the next. As suggested above, this more concise definition of the regime's purpose was consistent with American interests at the close of World War II. At that time, leaders had no interest in trade being a tool of a domestic policy, such as full employment, and thus defended a more circumscribed agenda. The result is that production and/or labor standards are not under the control of the organization and that the use of commercial policy to target production practice by member countries could be construed as a barrier to trade. Thus rulings from panels that higher US environmental standards in gasoline usage and fishing methods could not be invoked so as to exclude a foreign product from its market were consistent with America's earlier interpretation of the regime's purpose. These rulings, however, led environmental groups to argue that international law was being used to violate democratic procedures. If the United States wants to set high standards for labor, the environment or human rights, argue representatives of these groups, no international agency should force a change in those laws.

The issue of the regulation of 'process versus product' is not the only substantial change in the underlying rules and norms of the regime. Equally fundamental is a shift in the use of reciprocity, in particular, in cases when a nation reneges on an agreement under a safeguard clause. Under the GATT, the threat of retaliation was a means to activate export groups. Countries could renege but they needed either to offer an alternative concession or to accept retaliation. The result was that concessions were extremely stable.[29] WTO rules are not governed by this norm of specific reciprocity. Under the WTO, both compensation and/or retaliation are waived for the first three years of a safeguard action. The logic of the change was that it encourages nations to follow the rules. Nations could invoke a safeguard for a justified and technical reason and not worry about retaliation.[30] Consistent with the increase in use of court-like settings to handle disputes, this change in rule suggests a shift toward a more legalistic and technical regime.

Protecting countries from retaliation, especially from countries with larger markets, can also be explained by a shift in power within the trade regime. The centralization of authority in countries that contributed large markets for each other's goods has eroded. Most notably, the WTO changed the system of voting rules and replaced the old consensus rule, granting the United States a veto, with a series of different rules. Unanimity is now limited to cases of amendments to general principles, such as MFN treatment. Otherwise, a three-quarters majority vote is needed for an interpretation of a provision or a waiver of a member's obligations and a two-thirds majority for amendments relating to issues other than general principles. Unlike a weighted voting system, such as is found in the IMF, decision making may appear to be more democratic. It is far more complex. As was the case in the deadlock over the new director general and the inability to get a consensus on a new trade round in Seattle in 1999, multiple coalitions exist, not all of which include the major powers.

These changes may be partially explained by a shift in the size and composition of the trade regime. The GATT encouraged small countries to 'free ride' on the concessions offered by the larger nations but offered them few opportunities to participate in decision making.

Such a tradeoff was acceptable when the regime's focus was on fixed barriers to trade, such as tariffs or quotas. The expansion of the regime into new goods and new areas also brought the trade practices of a larger number of countries under scrutiny. Smaller and less developed nations faced greater obligations than in earlier times. The response was more voice in decision making.

The GATT system of decision making has been described as a system of consensus building through the creation of concentric groups.[31] The more influential countries, those with a greater share of world trade, were at the center, making choices that would then spread out to larger groups, after consensus was reached among them. The system built a consensus at the cost of representation of the majority of members. The appeal of more formal votes to the majority of nations is better representation. The problem with the democratization of the regime, however, may be a loss of support by the major powers, in particular the United States.

The evolution of the regime is not only a reflection of changes in membership, agenda and scope. The United States participated in and encouraged these changes. In part, the explanation may be found in the more general shift in the 1990s toward the legalization of a number of aspects of international politics.[32] This general shift has numerous explanations, including changing perceptions of American interests by key leaders in the United States. Where international trade in the 1950s, for example, was the purview of economists, it is far more likely today to find lawyers dominating negotiations and interpretation of rules and rule violations. But lawyers alone cannot explain trade legalization. As suggested below, trade legalization may be one more manifestation of American power in the post-cold war years where the principal problem facing the United States is the inability to make a credible commitment to abide by its agreements.[33]

The WTO Structure and the Future of the Trade Regime

From the point of view of systemic theories of international organizations, the formalization and legalization of the trade regime is logical and progressive. Logic suggests that increased monitoring and formalization of rules will decrease opportunism. The result should be more cooperation and compliance. Such analysis, however, ignores an important part of the history of the regime. The United States did not only support the GATT out of fear of opportunism. Rather, the GATT was a means to create and maintain a majority in support of trade liberalization at home. The GATT facilitated larger and more diverse bargains, it allowed the United States to give particularistic protection when necessary for political reasons and its voting system granted the United States veto power. The result was that US central decision makers found it convenient to support the GATT; trade expanded and domestic conflicts, deriving from distributional problems resulting from trade liberalization, were finessed.

If the GATT structure was as well suited to the needs of US domestic politics as is suggested above, why did the United States advocate the creation of the WTO? Changes in the GATT structure could not have occurred without the agreement of the three major actors in the negotiations, the United States the EU and Japan. All supported the modification in institutional design, although each for a different set of reasons. Japan and the EU believed that the new procedures would constrain the United States from using unilateral means to force them to open up their markets, such as occurred in Section 301 cases. The United States, comparatively, saw itself to be more often in compliance with WTO rules than its trading partners. This led the United States to support strengthened dispute settlement procedures as a means to both legitimate American claims that others were 'cheating' and as an additional tool for the expansion of markets abroad.

Underlying these changes is a fundamental American problem. In the post-cold war period, the United States has emerged as the sole military leader. This pre-eminence is less clear in the world economy where the United States and her products face significant competition both at home and abroad. Competition exists not only as a result of the successful integration of the European economies but because of emerging economies in Asia and elsewhere.

The effect of military hegemony is that the United States has a significant commitment problem. In the face of a communist threat, America's allies had reason to believe that the United States would live up to its commitments, both economic and military. Without that threat, America's interests are less defined. The result is a lack of confidence in American commercial policy. One answer, implicitly advocated by a powerful group of trade lawyers, is the formalization and legalization of agreements, thereby enmeshing the United States in a set of reputational and crosscutting agreements that are more costly to break. Thus the decision to 'self-bind', much in the fashion observed above in the WTO.

Unfortunately this solution of increasing the degree to which the United States 'binds' itself works only to the extent that military and economic hegemony coexist. As the United States faces increasing competition, the inability to renege on agreements will become increasingly constraining on leaders at home. The GATT succeeded because of its political nature. The triumph of the 'technical' over the 'political' aspects of the regime, however, may make it increasingly difficult for American leaders to find support for free trade. US trade politics is characterized by a powerful 'baptist and bootlegger' coalition of the left and right. Environmental and human rights groups are in a coalition with labor and isolationist interests. This coalition was spurred by exogenous changes, such as the growing trade imbalance, but, as well, controversy over the North American Free Trade Agreement (NAFTA) and the creation of the WTO prompted public attention. Politicians such as Ross Perot and Pat Buchanan gained support by campaigning on anti-trade platforms. The ability of the coalition to organize against trade liberalization was witnessed on numerous occasions, including the fight over NAFTA, passage of the WTO's implementing legislation, the rejection of fast-track legislation and the 1999 Seattle ministerial meeting of the WTO.[34]

This politicization of trade has made it increasingly difficult for the United States to find a majority in support of the regime's purposes. While the old GATT served to assure that the United States held pro-trade preferences by mobilizing groups whose interest lay with trade expansion, the new structures appear to mobilize anti-trade groups. This has occurred for three reasons. First, through the DSP, the WTO gives non-Americans oversight over aspects of US trade policy, fostering claims that compliance with the WTO is an endorsement of a 'race to the bottom'. Second, due to changes in the GATT voting system, the WTO policies no longer mirror the interests of the more powerful members. The GATT demanded consensus to make policy decisions; the WTO has adopted a range of voting procedures that make it more difficult for the United States to veto any policy that is not in its interest. In short, while the GATT system mirrored underlying power relations, the new WTO does not. The result is the perception of a loss of sovereignty and the mobilization of groups on the right. Third, reciprocity encouraged export groups to counter the weight of rent-seeking import-sensitive industries. Since the new rules allow nations to renege without compensation, they have less of an incentive to organize to counter producer groups seeking closure of the American market. The result is less voice for those who benefit from liberal trade.

This chapter began with the simple observation that American power in the post-World War II years led to the creation of a trade regime that suited the needs of domestic political leaders. Maintaining a pro-free trade foreign policy is difficult in the United States, given domestic institutional arrangements. The GATT facilitated a 'fix' of this institutional problem by mobilizing a pro-free trade constituency. As a result of changing power relations, the new WTO no longer mirrors the domestic political needs of American central decision makers. Such a shift may have been inevitable with the demise of the Soviet Union but it has had unintended consequences for domestic politics.

America's allegiance to the trade regime is far more tenuous than at any earlier time. The trade regime was a success because it served a double purpose; not only did the regime expand international commerce, but it facilitated the building of free trade coalitions in member countries. In this way, the regime not only reflected the underlying preferences of its most powerful member but it played an important role in sustaining and expanding a particular set of trade preferences. Although the WTO is still in its infancy, proponents should be wary of the WTO undercutting its basis of support. Trade politics is essentially about politics, not technical rules. The new WTO may be better suited than was the GATT to solve the host of systemic problems associated with international trade policy. However, such solutions are without value if member countries are not committed and interested in free trade.

Notes

1   Mancur Olson (1971).
2   For an exposition of the role of export groups, see Michael Gilligan (1997). For an expansion of this general argument, see Goldstein (1998).
3   The textbook example is offered by E.E. Schattshneider (1935) of the 1929–30 Smoot–Hawley Tariff. No one wanted a huge tariff height but each representative wanted something for his constituents. The result was high tariffs and a rapid decline in trade.
4   For a more in depth development of this argument, see Judith Goldstein (1998).
5   For a more detailed analysis of trade delegation, see Destler (1995) and Goldstein (1993).
6   For an analysis of how the trade process influenced the creation of support for liberal trade, see Bailey *et al.* (1997).
7   See Gilligan (1997).
8   It is also key that the US economy did very well by opening up its borders. Congress regularly renewed trade authority to the President because at least 51 per cent of the districts benefitted from tariff reductions.
9   For the best exposition of the neoinstitutional explanation for international organizations, see Keohane (1984).
10 See Axelrod (1981).
11 Cooperation is a multiple equilibrium situation, that is, there is no way of knowing, ex ante, about any particular way in which nations will decide to maintain the regime.
12 See Goldstein (1993).
13 Odell and Eichengreen (1998) argue that the ITO could have been approved if Truman had desired; the more traditional view is that there were too many groups arrayed against the agreement and Truman did not have the resource to push it through. See Krueger (1998).
14 Keohane (1986).
15 The incorporation of both specific and diffuse reciprocity is one of the many unusual features of the GATT regime. Given that the bedrock value of free trade suggests that unilateral free trade was superior to closure, one would imagine that only the MFN versions of reciprocity would have characterized the organization. In the absence of political constraints, this may have been the case. The use of specific reciprocity was necessary in order to garner support at

home for trade agreements. Over time, the political necessity became elevated to an article of faith that trade agreements (and punishments for trade infractions) should always be 'balanced'.

16 This argument is developed in Goldstein and Martin (2000).
17 Jackson (1998) makes this distinction in his work on the dispute settlement system. The distinction is applicable to other parts of the GATT system as well.
18 See Goldstein (1993) for the domestic mechanisms for gaining escape clause relief, and Goldstein and Martin (2000) for variation in use across GATT members.
19 This doctrine was elaborated in a dispute between the United States and Czechoslovakia in which the United States argued that is was not their legal responsibility to defend their action. See Dam (1970: 102–3).
20 See Goldstein and Martin (2000) for data on use of Article 28.
21 See Dam (1970: 257–73).
22 Ibid.: 259–60.
23 Invoked by the United States in 1971 against Romania and 1973 against Hungary. Of all the accession agreements, the largest number of countries invoked Article 35 in respect of Japan.
24 See Hudec (1993).
25 There are a number of histories of the Uruguay Round. For an overview, see Whalley and Hamilton (1996) and Secchi (1997).
26 This is not to say that the large countries ignore panel rulings that are brought by smaller countries. However, if the ruling is against a powerful domestic constituency or is politically difficult for decision makers at home, a nation may find it inconvenient to comply, especially if there is no threat of retaliation. During the GATT, even with the ability to veto decisions, countries usually complied with panel decisions.
27 Hudec (1999: 16).
28 Ibid.: 19.
29 See Goldstein and Martin (2000).
30 Krueger (1998).
31 See Blackhurst (1998) on GATT/WTO decision-making procedures.
32 See the special issue of *International Organization* (2000).
33 See Abbot and Snidal (2000).
34 US participation in the WTO has a five-year sunset provision. Congress has mandated that the government prove that the United States has benefitted from membership as prefatory to renewal. Part of that process includes the United States Trade Representative (USTR) reporting on the wins and losses from the DSP.

Bibliography

Abbott, Kenneth W. and Duncan Snidal (2000), 'Toward a Theory of International Legalization', *International Organization*, forthcoming.
Axelrod, Robert (1981), 'The Emergence of Cooperation among Egoists', *American Political Science Review*, 25, 306–18.
Bailey, Michael, Judith Goldstein and Barry Weingast (1997), 'The Institutional Roots of American Trade Policy: Politics, Coalitions and International Trade', *World Politics*, 49(3), April, 309–38.
Baldwin, Robert (1998), 'Imposing Multilateral Discipline on Administered Protection', in Anne Krueger (ed.), *The WTO as an International Organization*, Chicago: University of Chicago Press.

Blackhurst, Richard (1998), 'The Capacity of the WTO to Fulfill Its Mandate', in Anne Krueger (ed.), *The WTO as an International Organization*, Chicago: University of Chicago Press.

Dam, Kenneth (1970), *The GATT: Law and the International Economic Organization*, Chicago: University of Chicago Press.

Destler, I.M. (1995), *American Trade Politics*, 3rd edn, Washington, DC: Institute for International Economics.

Downs, George W. and David M. Rocke (1995), *Optimal Imperfection? Domestic Uncertainty and Institutions in International Relations*, Princeton, NJ: Princeton University Press.

Evans, John (1971), *The Kennedy Round in American Trade Policy*, Cambridge, MA: Harvard University Press.

Gilligan, Michael J. (1997), *Empowering Exporters: Reciprocity, Delegation, and Collective Action in American Trade Policy*, Ann Arbor: University of Michigan Press.

Goldstein, Judith (1993), *Ideas, Interests, and American Trade Policy*, Ithaca, NY: Cornell University Press.

Goldstein, Judith (1998), 'International Institutions and Domestic Politics: GATT, WTO and the Liberalization of International Trade', in Anne Krueger (ed.), *The WTO as an International Organization*, Chicago: University of Chicago Press.

Goldstein, Judith and Lisa Martin (2000), 'Legalization, Trade Liberalization, and Domestic Politcs: A Cautionary Note', forthcoming.

Hudec, Robert E. (1993), *Enforcing International Trade Law: The Evolution of the Modern GATT Legal System*, Salem, NH: Butterworth Legal Publishers.

Hudec, Robert E. (1999), 'The New WTO Dispute Settlement Procedure', *Minnesota Journal of Global Trade*, 8(1), Winter.

International Organization (2000), 'Special Issue on *Legalization and World Politics: Perspectives from Law and Political Science*', forthcoming.

Jackson, John H. (1998), *The World Trade Organization: Constitution and Jurisprudence*, London: Royal Institute for International Affairs.

Keesing, Donald B. (1998), *Improving Trade Policy Reviews in the World Trade Organization*, Washington, DC: Institute for International Economics.

Keohane, Robert O. (1984), *After Hegemony: Discord and Collaboration in the World Political Economy*, Princeton, NJ: Princeton University Press.

Keohane, Robert O. (1986), 'Reciprocity in International Relations', *International Organization*, 40(1), Winter, 1–27.

Krasner, Steven (ed.) (1983), *International Regimes*, Ithaca, NY: Cornell University Press.

Krueger, Anne (ed.) (1998), *The WTO as an International Organization*, Chicago: University of Chicago Press.

Milner, Helen V. (1988), *Resisting Protectionism: Global Industries and the Politics of International Trade*, Princeton, NJ: Princeton University Press.

Odell, John and Barry Eichengreen (1998), 'The United States, the ITO and the WTO: Exit Options, Agency Slack and Presidential Leadership', in Anne Krueger (ed), *The WTO as an International Organization*, Chicago: University of Chicago Press.

Olson, Mancur. (1971), *The Logic of Collective Action*, New York: Schocken Books.

Sassoon, Enrico (1997), 'Objectives and Results of the Uruguay Round', in R. Faini and E. Grilli (eds), *Multilateralism and Regionalism after the Uruguay Round*, London: Macmillan.

Schattschneider, E.E. (1935), *Politics, Pressures and the Tariff: A Study of Free Private Enterprise in Pressure Politics, as Shown in the 1929–30 Revision of the Tariff*, Englewood Cliffs, NJ: Prentice-Hall.

Schott, Jeffrey (1994), *The Uruguay Round*, Washington, DC: Institute for International Economics.

Secchi, Carlo (1997), 'The Political Economy of the Uruguay Round: Groups, Strategies, Interests and Results', in R. Faini and E. Grilli (eds), *Multilateralism and Regionalism after the Uruguay Round*, London: Macmillan.

Shonfield, Andrew (1976), *Politics and Trade*, London: Oxford University Press.

Strange, S. (1982), 'The Politics of Economics: A Sectoral Analysis', in W.F. Hanrieder (ed.), *Economic Issues and the Atlantic Community*, New York: Praeger.

Whalley, John and Colleen Hamilton (1996), *The Trading System after the Uruguay Round*, Washington, DC: Institute for International Economics.

Winham, Gilbert (1986), *International Trade and the Tokyo Round Negotiation*, Princeton, NJ: Princeton University Press.

PART V
PARTITIONING THE
GLOBAL ECONOMY

15 European Competitiveness and Enlargement: Is There Anyone in Charge?

JULIE PELLEGRIN

Introduction

Playing on the words of Robert Reich in his renowned 1990 treatise on US competitiveness,[1] Strange titled her 1998 keynote *Journal of Common Market Studies* lecture (and corresponding journal article) 'Who are EU?' She took up the point made by Reich on the ambiguity of the concept of competitiveness and applied it to the case of Europe: promoting 'European competitiveness' is fine, but whose competitiveness are we talking about exactly?

The question is topical, as European competitiveness – or the lack of it – is a sensitive and widely debated issue. Following Reich, Strange argues that 'European competitiveness' applies to European societies rather than European firms. But, contrary to him, Strange goes deeper into the understanding of the forces at work in the world economy that shape the framework of constraints and opportunities within which firms and policy makers take their decisions. By identifying the accelerating pace of technological change and its associated increasing costs as a decisive factor pushing firms into international production, Strange suggests the right policy objective to be adopted in an era of global change: policy makers should be more concerned with the competitive conditions of their society than with the competitiveness of their national firms abroad, the aim being to attract foreign firms, which bring with them jobs for the local workforce as well as access to markets, capital and technology. She thus reviews a set of possible policies to achieve this goal, and mentions – quite briefly – the eastern enlargement of the European Union (EU): by making available larger markets, enlargement makes Europe an attractive place for firms in continuous search of new markets (Strange 1998: 111).

This chapter takes the question of the impact of enlargement on European competitiveness as an opportunity to apply, combine and discuss some of Strange's theses on production, power and knowledge in a fast-changing world economy. It maintains that enlargement has the potential for radically altering the bases of competitiveness in Europe, not only because wider markets make Europe a more attractive place to do business, but also because it represents an unprecedented opportunity to engage Europe-wide processes of industrial and corporate restructuring. Even though the latter is a feature neglected by Strange (1998), the question she raises (whose competitiveness does enlargement strengthen?), the conclusions she reaches (improving 'structural competitiveness') and the reason she puts forward and develops elsewhere ('global competition') all have a salience that transcends the point she makes about enlargement in her article. This chapter will try to show how some of Strange's theses can acquire a 'power of predictability' that she herself has sometimes not fully envisaged: Strange power, indeed!

The central argument of the chapter is that the process of EU enlargement is taking place at a quite specific time in the history of international competition, characterized by the increasing knowledge content of competitiveness. Who is taking advantage of enlargement to strengthen their competitiveness in this context? Is it firms, sectors or countries? If so, which ones: German firms, EU or Central and Eastern European countries (CEECs)? There are risks that, rather than enabling CEECs to catch up and become knowledge-based economies, corporate integration could further entrench development differentials between the EU and CEECs and confine the latter to low wage specialization patterns. This would make Europe a rather unattractive place to do business, and 'European competitiveness' would not improve as a result.

CEECs therefore need to be very careful to avoid the risks and reap the benefits of the presence of foreign firms in their economies. Production networks deserve particular attention as they play a crucial role in the context of the transformed conditions of international competition. This is the conclusion Strange reaches, but here it is applied to the EU's eastern neighbors and extended, beyond foreign direct investment carried out by multinationals, to 'international production networks'. Overall, the chapter illustrates power asymmetries between states, as well as a growing imbalance in the respective capacities of states and firms, as the former depend more on the latter for their access to knowledge.

This chapter is based on empirical data and demonstrates how Strange's theses dig deeply into 'reality'. First, the characteristics of the new framework of constraints and opportunities that has emerged since the fall of the Berlin wall are reviewed. Next, the analysis centers on a particularly relevant, if neglected, aspect of the development of East–West interdependence: outward processing traffic. Finally, some important policy implications are inferred and a wider insight is given into the system of market management emerging in an enlarged Europe. The ultimate objective of the chapter is to illustrate one of the great strengths of Strange's thinking: asking the right questions, providing effective conceptual tools to think about them … and leaving each of us free to find our own answers (Strange 1988).

Enlargement and Competitiveness: Potential and Risk

Eastern enlargement of the EU has considerable potential to alter the bases of competitiveness in Europe. This is an argument that is all too often neglected, if not ignored, but which could give a decisive turn to negotiations between the EU and prospective member states to the east. Exactly how and why could this happen?

The reason why enlargement could have a much wider impact on Europe's competitiveness than Strange (1998) suggests, is in fact developed at length in her 1991 jointly authored book, *Rival States, Rival Firms*. The accelerating pace of technological changes forces firms into international production, by inciting them to secure market shares and adopt new production methods (Strange 1991: 42). The eastern enlargement of the EU is very timely in both respects.

The following sections elaborate briefly on the potential offered by the enlargement process, on the new requirements of international competition, and on whether anyone is taking advantage of the new European framework of constraint and opportunity.

New Opportunities

At first sight, the opening up of CEECs offers at least two sets of opportunities. On the one hand, the liberalization of economic transactions between East and West makes new markets available; on the other hand, it brings together economies characterized by large wage differentials which, associated with proximity, offer EU firms an alternative production base in their immediate vicinity. This combination of larger markets and lower production costs has – *prima facie* – tremendous potential for enhancing trade, investment and growth across Europe. Enlargement would enable Western firms to realize economies of scale and scope, as well as to relocate those segments of their production process which are no longer competitively produced in their domestic economies. At the same time, the process is expected to offer CEECs' firms much-needed access to markets, capital and technology.

However, these new opportunities are not as obvious as it might seem. First, their economic significance is contested. The individual markets made available by the opening up of CEECs are somewhat limited in size, the only exception being Poland. Another factor limiting the attractiveness of CEECs as consumer markets is the low level of per capita income, even though they have potential in terms of growth that is of interest to would-be investors. Also the evolution of wages in CEECs appears to be following a generally upward trend and, despite remarkable increases since 1991, relatively low absolute levels of labor productivity partially counteract the low labor costs.

More fundamentally, the process brings together countries with significantly different levels of development, posing the question of the terms of their economic interdependence. Not only is real GDP per head in CEECs 32 per cent of the EU average,[2] but there are also considerable disparities among CEECs. While incomes in the Czech Republic, Hungary, Poland, Slovakia and Slovenia were between one-third and two-thirds of the EU average, the rest were below one-third of the EU average in 1995 (Grabbe and Hughes 1997).

Overall, not much can be said about the prospects of East–West integration on this basis alone. One of Strange's constant concerns was to bring the conditions at work in the world economy into the analysis:[3] the way in which the potential presented by enlargement will actually be seized upon depends in fact on the transformed conditions of competitiveness in the world economy.

New International Context

The opening up of CEECs is taking place at a quite specific time in the history of international competition: 'global competition' is characterized by the increasing *volatility* of conditions with which firms and states are confronted (Stopford and Strange 1991: 4). This uncertainty is due to the accelerating pace of technological changes, or, put another way, to a 'changing relationship of knowledge to production' in the context of the overhaul of the old Fordist model of mass production and consumption (Mytelka 1991). This leads firms to internationalize and adopt 'new forms of production' (NFP), enabling producers to 'supply the market with new products and services, and to produce old ones by new processes' (Stopford and Strange 1991: 34).

The development of NFP in the 1980s was marked by 'the diminishing significance of low labour costs and access to raw material as a source of competitive advantage, and the increasing importance of quality production methods and proximity to markets'.[4] Firms' competitiveness increasingly includes 'soft' elements such as the ability to compete on delivery, to differentiate products – and to do this rapidly. As pointed out in *Rival States, Rival Firms*, it is, in this context, no longer enough to rely on low costs to be successful on world markets. The fact that technological competitiveness develops at the expense of cost competitiveness requires special attention to the conditions promoting a process of continuous innovation within firms and economies (Ernst *et al.* 1998). If competition is more knowledge-based, it does not mean, however, that costs are no longer relevant. On the contrary, minimum costs are taken for granted. Thus quality and costs are still necessary conditions to compete; but 'knowledge' now makes the difference.

To comply with the requirements of the increasing knowledge content of production and in order to face uncertainty, firms need to be as flexible as possible. For this they increasingly resort to non-equity forms of inter-firm agreements and establish 'new forms of investment' (Stopford and Strange 1991: 38). An 'organizational response' to globalization, international production networks (IPN) are woven throughout the world economy, mainly at the instigation of multinational corporations (MNCs). They can have many different forms, but they are characterized by a common trend towards the de-integration of the production chain (see Chapter 4 of the present volume for further details). This applies at all levels, from outsourcing at an upstream stage to mergers and acquisitions, and other forms of strategic partnering further down the production chain. This is to reduce the costs of new investments either by passing the cost burden on to local suppliers, or by pooling resources. For developing or emerging countries, this practice of de-integrating the production chain offers local firms multiple opportunities for linking with IPN (Stopford and Strange 1991: 39, 86).

It is important to understand that, in an era of global competition, IPN are privileged instruments for the promotion of local innovative capabilities. Innovation is defined as a socially and institutionally embedded interactive process that involves a large range of actors linked through networks (Lundvall 1988). Interactions and linkages between 'users' and 'producers' of technology enable the exchange and diffusion of the decisive tacit component of knowledge on which firms' competitiveness is based.[5] 'Innovation' should not be taken here in too technicist a sense, nor should it be measured (only) in terms of research and development (R&D) intensity. Rather, the emphasis is to be placed on the ability of firms to *learn* processes and practices that are new to them. In Stopford and Strange's words: 'though much attention has been focused on technological breakthroughs (...), change can also be created in small steps as firms find new ways of upgrading efficiencies' (Stopford and Strange 1991: 71).[6]

Also 'networks' should be taken here in a broad sense to encompass not only internalized transactions within firms, but also, and especially, non-equity forms of cooperation, as these are particularly favorable to the learning process depicted above. The pervasive generalization of MNCs' activities already depicted in *States and Markets* (Strange 1994: 76) suggests that the latter are major 'network organizers'.[7] The recourse to international linkages is particularly imperative for CEECs, as the latter have to substitute for domestic linkages, which were severely disrupted by the demise of the planned economy and the subsequent vacuum in the system of innovation (Radosevic 2000). What is more, they have to do this quickly as the enlargement process is already at an advanced stage, leaving them very little time to build technological capabilities on their own. Finally, the fact that CEECs are latecomers among latecomers makes the imperative internationalization process even more difficult for them, as competition to be included in the IPN has never been fiercer.

Asymmetries and Divergences

The eastern enlargement of the EU offers an unprecedented opportunity to establish new forms of production in line with a redefinition of the terms of international competition as outlined above. However, it is not entirely clear whether this potential is being seized, and to whom the benefits – if any – of liberalization are *in fact* accruing. 'Cui bono?' as Strange would ask: whose competitiveness does enlargement strengthen?

The risk is that, rather than allowing CEECs to catch up and become competitive economies, enlargement actually confines CEECs in low wage specialization patterns of the least dynamic sort, particularly unsuited to the requirements of 'global competition'. If development differentials are entrenched without fostering growth dynamics on the regional scale, it is the European level of competitiveness as a whole – measured not so much by the performance of EU firms abroad as by the capacity of an enlarged Europe to provide a favorable framework to encourage business – which is at stake. Do we have evidence that enlargement is not a zero-sum game benefitting some, at the expense of others, or on the contrary that it helps establish knowledge-based economies in CEECs?

In this respect, there is a worrying increase in divergence between member states and candidate countries, among candidate countries themselves and, within the latter, between sectors where foreign penetration is high and sectors dominated by national firms. In all this, EU policies are not entirely blameless.

A number of indicators show that integration through trade and foreign direct investment (FDI) is uneven. CEECs have been very successful in reorienting their trade relations towards Western Europe and, in 1994, the EU had become the most important market for CEEC exports, accounting for over half of the total. However, just four CEECs account for over three-quarters of total imports and exports with the EU, while the other CEECs fall far behind; the four are, in decreasing order, Poland (30 per cent of total trade with the EU), the Czech Republic (20 per cent), Hungary (16 per cent) and Slovenia (10 per cent).

Patterns of FDI are also very uneven. Two 'tiers' can be roughly identified, with the first four countries taking around 80 per cent of FDI in the region. What is more, levels of FDI are generally considered to be low compared to expectations and to other regional experiences.[8]

There is controversy over the contribution made by integration through trade and investment in the CEECs' catching up. There are many debates and uncertainties concerning the question as to whether the structure of CEECs' foreign trade is moving as a whole towards more elaborate products, as well as considerable methodological difficulties. A number of studies testify to the fact that CEECs are not locked into traditional specialization patterns and are also developing new capacities. In particular, there are encouraging signs in favor of the strengthening of the technological content of CEECs' trade.[9] Of specific concern, however, is the fact that all these studies note to some extent the increasing disparities throughout the region with respect to the ability of CEECs' export structure to shift in favor of more capital- and skill-intensive products.

As to the role of FDI, here again, evidence is mixed. Beyond expectations concerning inflows of capital,[10] local firms count on FDI to get access to market and technology. However, FDI to CEECs has been generally documented as taking place for market access reasons (Meyer 1998; Widmaier and Potratz 1999: 19). MNCs commit relatively large amounts of FDI with the main aim of securing market shares of what is expected to be a fast growing regional market. Although, at the beginning of the transition process, FDI mostly consisted of joint ventures, since 1993 the establishment of greenfield plants has become the preferred form of involvement. The implications for the possibility of spillover are problematic. The traditional view has it that greenfields create more value (activities with higher knowledge and R&D content) and can involve new suppliers. On the other hand, greenfields are more likely to operate either in isolation or in 'enclaves' consisting of domestic suppliers who followed their customers (Benacek *et al.* 1999). Overall, FDI in CEECs appears to be a game of big players more concerned with first mover advantage than with the effective spillover of knowledge and techniques to their local partners. As a result, FDI has met with severe criticism and some disillusionment followed high expectations.

It is worth stressing that, in all the aspects of economic presence in CEECs, Germany always figures pre-eminently, and is often responsible for *overwhelming* proportions (Hughes 1996). For virtually all of the CEECs, Germany is the single most important EU trading partner. Overall, Germany accounts for about half of total EU exports to and imports from CEECs. German firms are the largest foreign direct investors in Hungary, while it is in the Czech Republic that the German presence is the most important (30 per cent of the stocks of FDI in 1995). In Poland, German firms are the main alliance partners for local Polish firms and they are third in terms of total amount of invested capital. A distinctive feature of the German involvement in CEECs is subcontracting activities and non-equity links. Germans make far more use of subcontracting activities than their counterparts from other EU countries. For example, Germans have 2.5 times more 'outward processing traffic' (OPT – see below) in CEECs than other EU firms. What is more, the involvement of German firms in CEECs is characterized by a preference for outward processing traffic, as opposed to FDI,[11] which might denote a deep restructuring of the German industrial basis involving the crucially important 'Mittelstand' or small and medium-sized business sector.

Overall, corporate integration does not seem to be helping to reduce the gaps between the EU and CEECs. Integration is uneven both quantitatively and qualitatively and there is no general evidence that CEECs as a whole are gaining from increased integration with the EU. This is not to say that 'the liberalization of East–West trade relations has been (…) more beneficial to the West than it has been to the East' (Black 1997: 69). Even if the rates of growth are quite impressive, trade with CEECs is still marginal and accounts for less than 10 per cent of total extra-EU trade. In addition, Western corporate strategies are more market-oriented than efficiency-driven, and improved competitiveness is not their main underlying rationale.

Even worse, EU policies tend to contribute to further entrenching the differentials (Baldwin 1994; Messerlin 1993). As Grabbe and Hughes (1997) put it, 'investors show the same preferences as the EU and NATO in terms of [CEECs'] relative progress'. Thus, to the question 'who benefits?', the only partial exception – at least quantitatively – is perhaps German firms. Otherwise, in general terms and despite the great potential represented by the opening up of CEECs, levels of competitiveness in Europe do not appear, until now, to have been altered in any decisive way (Zysman and Schwartz 1998).

Conditions for Strengthened European Competitiveness: Evidence from 'Outward Processing Traffic'

The above broad picture of corporate integration presents some evidence gathered in the literature on East–West corporate integration based on aggregate trade and FDI data. As pointed out in Stopford and Strange (1991), there are several reasons why this is only partially satisfactory. First, aggregate figures might lose much of their significance in the face of the variability of corporate strategies. More fundamentally, it is striking to note that studies on economic integration continue to focus on either trade or FDI (the two being only rarely connected). This is despite the fact that, as Lawton and Michaels illustrate in Chapter 4, the tendency towards the de-integration of firms' value-added chain brings about a growing proportion of intra-firm trade that is not recorded as such in trade or in FDI data. In this respect, FDI figures 'hide more than they reveal' (Stopford and Strange 1991: 18): if we are looking for evidence that enlargement strengthens European competitiveness in an era of global competition, it might well be that we are simply looking at the wrong indicators.

A possible alternative is given by the unduly neglected data on outward processing traffic (OPT). The OPT arrangement is a specific custom regime which grants preferential trade access[12] to CEECs' exports to the EU. These are actually *re*-exports, which were preceded by imports of material sent by EU producers to CEECs in order to be processed there. Although imperfect, OPT data provide an indication of intra-firm trade; they trace what Stopford and Strange name 'dependent exports', that is, exports undertaken at the instigation of foreign firms (ibid.: 1991: 39).

That OPT data have been the object of such neglect[13] is all the more unjustified given that OPT represents an important share of CEECs' total trade and that its mechanisms, designed by EU policy makers, entail important consequences for the terms under which East–West economic interdependence develops. OPT data suggest that market access is not the only reason inciting EU firms to do business in CEECs. Some corporate restructuring is in fact going on, and – of specific relevance here – EU policies have been instrumental in promoting this process. Fundamentally, OPT data offer evidence on the formation of IPN which are expected to make a crucial contribution to the establishment of knowledge-based economies in CEECs. OPT is therefore at the same time a test case to assess whether and under what conditions enlargement is capable of enhancing competitiveness in Europe. OPT is particularly relevant to understanding the EU approach concerning the way in which enlargement is, or is not, expected to have an impact on competitiveness.

A Brief Quantitative Overview

OPT 'temporary' trade accounted for a non-negligible proportion of CEECs' foreign trade and is an important factor contributing to the past and present trade performances of CEECs. In 1997, the arrangement is estimated by local sources to have accounted for 26 per cent of both Hungarian and Czech exports to the EU,[14] a figure roughly confirmed by UN sources which also include Poland[15] (UNECE 1997). Even lower, EUROSTAT, data display quite high proportions of approximately 10 per cent for the three countries in 1997. In 1993–4 (a peak), around 20 per cent of Polish and Hungarian exports to the EU and 12 per cent of Czech exports to the EU were in fact *re*-exports after processing of material 'temporarily' imported from the EU.

Interestingly enough, the proportions of OPT are particularly high in sectors which are the most dynamic in CEECs' foreign trade structure: textile and clothing – T&C – (with outstanding proportions in the Polish case which go up to 80 per cent of total exports to the EU) and electrical machinery (around 20 per cent of Czech exports to the EU in 1997, and 11 per cent of the Hungarian ones, after a peak of over 30 per cent in both countries in 1993). Reflecting the German domination in CEEC trade flows, CEECs' OPT activities are mainly undertaken at the instigation of German firms. In 1995, for example, the German share of total EU OPT engaged in CEECs reached the impressive proportion of 75 per cent.

Mechanisms

It is in a very literal sense that the OPT regime influences the distribution of the gains resulting from trade liberalization and the terms under which East–West economic integration develops. Since it is foreign partners who source the inputs and who also market the outputs, local CEEC producers are deprived of their market power at both ends of the production chain. This implies that CEECs' comparative and local firms competitive advantages are exploited, not directly by local firms, but indirectly by their EU partners. In particular, local firms are forced into partnerships with EU firms when they are unable to leverage their competitive advantage within EU markets because of traditional protectionist measures established by the EU. In that case, OPT is indeed the only option if locally competitive firms from CEECs want to access EU markets. In other words, the recourse to OPT is made all the more imperative when local firms are competitive and trade protection measures are particularly binding. The OPT mechanisms are thus a clever way of transforming potentially rival patterns of specialization into complementary ones (Zysman and Schwartz 1998) in such a way that the interests of EU producers are preserved (Ellison 1999: 268). Overall, these mechanisms tie CEEC firms into vertical production chains controlled by EU firms, and promote the vertical division of labor on the regional scale.

What is worrying about OPT is that, in the face of the very low entry and exit costs that the arrangement offers to foreign firms, local partners are being cut off, for quite some time, from upstream and downstream linkages. This impairs their chances of recovering their independence and of being able to take over production on their own if their foreign partners decide to withdraw from their arrangements. Alternatively, but with an equally detrimental effect, foreign partners may actually stay committed to their local partners and lock the latter into the low end of their production chain, thus perpetuating a specialization pattern based on low wages. In short, the OPT mechanisms tend to promote the 'maquiladorization' of CEECs (Ellingstad 1997).

The question is, if the EU (that is, the German partners), takes advantage of the flexibility characterizing the arrangement to put an end to its commitment, does this mean that between 10 and 25 per cent of the foreign trade of these CEECs is at risk?

OPT Developments

In fact, it appears that EU firms remain committed to their local partners. Although wages have been rising throughout CEECs, no massive withdrawal has been documented: OPT does not appear to be a volatile business subject to cyclical downturns and wage increases.

There is mixed evidence as to whether the arrangement contributes to the locking of local firms into low wage specialization patterns, or whether it helps facilitate a process of upgrading. There are some signs of the upgrading of the OPT product structure with moves towards more value-added goods which are accompanied by geographical shifts (Eichengreen and Kohl 1998). EU producers are to some extent 're-relocating' eastwards their lower value-added processing activities, especially in T&C and footwear. In the first tier of CEECs (in particular in the Czech Republic and Hungary), instead, they keep higher value-added activities in T&C, and engage OPT in higher value-added sectors like machinery and equipment (UNECE 1997). Thus, although there is no evidence at firm level that local firms upgrade their position in the production chain of their partners, at country level, OPT seems to follow and contribute to the formation of different tiers in Europe.

Overall, and until now, the best one can say about the contribution of OPT to the dynamics of regional integration is that, rather than being detrimental, the arrangement has been a good second best. Either because they were too competitive or because they were too weak, local firms had no real alternative to OPT. In the end, the instrument has proved to be extremely helpful in reorienting CEECs' foreign trade.

A Retrograde Policy Instrument?

The measure was devised on the model of a US measure,[16] at a time when the international crisis triggered (or accelerated) the decline of traditional sectors in developed countries, eroding their competitiveness and putting employment at risk. In this context, the OPT measure was expected to enable the relocation of EU firms' production activities abroad, while keeping the process under close political monitoring so as to minimize adverse consequences for domestic employment levels. As a matter of fact, the preferential treatment extended to re-imports into the Single European Market is granted to EU producers only if the latter respect many different stringent conditions concerning the level of the production kept at home. At the same time, as shown above, the OPT mechanisms help protect against imports from competitive CEEC firms. OPT is thus a measure reconciling the often contradictory objectives of promoting EU firms' competitiveness while preserving employment. It also reveals the clear exploitative attitude of the EU in its relations to CEECs.

It is worth stressing, however, that the OPT legislation is not necessarily the result of a deliberate intent on the part of the EU. A look at the decision-making process that led to the adoption of the text reveals no real centralization of competence at the Community level because the positions of the different actors involved were, and still are, highly diverging. For example, in the T&C sector, national authorities have managed to preserve part of their traditional prerogatives by fixing quotas. As to the other sectors, they are subject to the Common External Tariff, so that centralization of competence is in principle easier. In fact, national authorities had considerable autonomy as far as the application of the regulation was concerned. German firms, in particular, enjoyed a very liberal interpretation of the Community legislation by German authorities.

Overall, the arrangement placed in the hands of the Commission a powerful instrument of industrial policy to promote the competitiveness of EU firms. However, the potential was not seized. The OPT developments have been the arbitrary outcome of the exacerbation of the workings of EU procedures rather than the design of a self-determined body devising an industrial policy with precise contours.

The Use Firms Make of the OPT

'Look at the firm level,' Strange would suggest. Indeed, even though the arrangement contains such intrinsic discriminating mechanisms, what is important in the end is what firms actually make of it. There is evidence in this respect that OPT does not necessarily entrench heterogeneity in Europe. Who exactly takes advantage of the measure?

It is not in the least paradoxical that, symmetrical to the very 'dependency' bias of the OPT mechanism, the arrangement presents some outstanding potential to fulfill many of the requirements associated with the changing terms of international competition. What was presented as a threat (the facility with which foreign partners can withdraw from their commitment) becomes, in the new context of international competition, a decisive asset: flexibility. Combined with proximity, this offers an opportunity to apply new production methods like 'just in time'. Hence what can be considered in a traditional perspective to be precarious relations become assets in the new context of transformed competition conditions. This turns OPT relations into partnerships that are no less durable.

Whether the potential is seized as such, that is, as assets to conform to the new requirements of competitiveness, depends to a large extent on the motives underlying the strategies engaged by foreign partners. OPT can develop at the instigation of firms rationalizing their strategies on the regional scale – efficiency seeking – or correspond to survival strategies carried out by companies which relocate their activities in order to lower costs.

Some could find motives for concern in the overwhelming majority of OPT in CEECs carried out by German firms. This is especially true if German companies use OPT to exploit CEECs' cheap labor, and transform neighboring countries into Germany's economic backyard. In fact, OPT can also be used by German firms as a vehicle to implement new production methods and carry out significant transfers of knowledge to local firms. German firms would then be 'network organizers', the main instigators of production networks that appear to be so important in the establishment of knowledge-based economies. In the end, however, the outcome depends on the capacity of local firms to take advantage of OPT to learn from their partnerships. The importance of the learning process that can be triggered by OPT helps relativize excessive fears of 'Germanization'.

Put bluntly, the OPT measure appears to have been designed by EU policy makers to enhance the competitiveness of EU firms at the expense of CEECs' firms. However, the above developments tell a slightly different tale. While the arrangement has the potential to perpetuate differentials in an enlarged Europe, the measure can also present an opportunity for both EU (German) and local firms to implement 'new forms of production'. Hence, alongside a 'traditional' interpretation of OPT as an old-fashioned vehicle for carrying out workbench activities, one might find scope for optimism as OPT can become an unexpected instrument to help comply with the requirements of global competition.

Everything depends on the use *individual* firms make of the measure, with two series of determining factors yielding a large number of possible combinations: the motive of foreign partners and the ability of local firms to take advantage of their OPT partnership. This is clearly relevant as far as policy making is concerned.

Who is in Charge of Competitiveness in an Enlarged Europe?

The OPT experience is useful for gaining some interesting insight into policies aimed at enhancing 'European competitiveness'. Beyond that, it provides insights into the actual influence that political authorities retain over economic developments.

Economic Policies

It takes little for OPT either to relegate local firms to a position of true structural dependency or to promote the development of local firms' capabilities. Much depends on whether local firms are ready to learn. This occurs, not by deploying radically new technical competencies, but, more simply, by adding new and improving old practices, and by keeping up with the latest technical developments. This has a general validity concerning the role of IPN in strategies for CEEC development (Lorentzen 1998).

A first implication is that focusing policy attention on how to attract FDI is simply not enough. Confronted with the example of developed countries that trigger incentive 'tournaments' to maximize inward investments, countries with a lower degree of attractiveness are understandably worried about being left out of this global game (Myant 1999; Mytelka 1999). However, attracting FDI cannot be an objective *per se*. As illustrated in *Rival States, Rival Firms*, host states have to engage in partnership-style relations with foreign firms so that the 'two parties can cooperate to promote their mutual interests' (Stopford and Strange 1991: 95).

In this respect, given the potentially crucial contribution of international linkages to the process of building up knowledge-based economies in 'latecomers', the attention should shift away from narrowly defined FDI, towards IPN in general. Measures and programmes adopted especially in Hungary and more belatedly in the Czech Republic, aiming at promoting backward linkages between MNCs and local firms, are a step in the right direction.

More fundamentally, CEECs' policy makers need to foster the 'structural competitiveness' of their economies (ibid.: 63), as this is the *sine qua non* condition for making the most of the presence of foreign firms. Although entering into IPNs is instrumental to learning, it is also imperative that countries make efforts to facilitate this learning process on a local basis if their firms are to benefit from their partnerships with foreign firms. Thus CEEC governments should engage in 'sustained investments in building an educated society' (ibid.: 13) as 'their role in fostering education and R&D assumes a far greater proportion than hitherto in conditioning their success in attracting those foreign firms who might assist in achieving national aims' (ibid.: 56).

On the Governance of the Economy in an Enlarged Europe

Strange's theses on the changing locus of the exercise of power help appreciate the ultimate relevance of the OPT experience: an illustration of the new mechanisms of economic governance in an enlarged Europe at a time of global competition.

The OPT measure was initially adopted with the clear exploitative attitude that traditionally characterized the EU's approach towards CEECs. Yet there have been many unexpected developments: for instance, the fact that there was no effective centralization of competence at the EU level, that it is German firms who have massively taken advantage of the measure and that the latter can use the arrangement to apply new forms of production and become 'network organizers' in CEECs. All of these factors are relevant in understanding who has authority over economic matters.

First, the fact that OPT competence was not transferred to the Community illustrates a failure to transpose a system of governance at the EU level which applies at the national level, that is, the centralization of competence in a single political authority over a territorially defined constituency. The latter is simply outdated in the context of the growing interconnectedness of the world economy.

What is more, influence over OPT developments is shared, not only between states, but also increasingly between states and firms. The different EU governments have indeed chosen to be more or less active in taking advantage of the measure to effectively exercise control over national firms. As to CEECs, they have even less influence over the outcome, as their role is reduced to acting as 'good landlords' (Strange 1998: 113). This uneven degree of control takes place in a general context of diminishing leverage of political authorities over economic matters. The fact that the outcome of OPT partnerships can vary so widely from firm to firm suggests that the OPT policy measure takes its full significance at firm level: firms are *empowered* by policy makers in the determination of the OPT outcome. This experience thus testifies to the 'diffusion' of power in economic matters in general, and to the fact that it is market actors in particular who benefit most from this diffusion. In other words, it illustrates a shift in the privileged locus of the exercise of power away from the traditional political arena and towards the market.

Finally, German firms that control their local OPT partners' production chains are powerful simply 'by being there' (Strange 1996: 26). Crucially, they are powerful because they possess the *knowledge* that is going to be decisive for the development of local firms and economies. The power German firms thus exercise in CEECs is more 'diffuse', more 'impersonal'. In one word, it is more 'structural' (Strange 1994; 1996).

In this respect, the analysis of knowledge that Strange pioneered in *States and Markets* (1988/1994) appears to be visionary. She was indeed among the first to consider knowledge as a source of power, convinced that this was an area likely to be characterized by the fastest and the most far-reaching changes. She was also very aware of the overlap with the production structure. In her words: 'the impact (...) these technological changes in the knowledge structure have had on the production structure (...) have centralized power in the big transnational corporations' (Strange 1994: 133). She perhaps did not know at the time how right she was, as it was some years later that the 'knowledge-based' economy captured the attention of the academic community (see Mytelka's arguments in Chapter 3 of the present volume). Strange's analyses invite us to concentrate on one fundamental development in the world economy: the fact that, by occupying an increasingly dominant position in the control over knowledge formation, market actors are bound to enjoy an ever-growing share of authority in the international political economy.

Conclusion

How can enlargement strengthen 'European competitiveness'? Strange asks the right question, and provides useful conceptual tools for elaborating the answers. The reason why the one achieved in this chapter departs from the line she briefly suggests in her 1998 *Journal of Common Market Studies* article has to do with the very strong emphasis that she places on the search for new markets as a motor driving firms abroad. This view quite rightly ensures that she plays down the importance attached elsewhere to labor costs. But it also somehow deflects her attention away from the repercussions that technological innovation has on the very production process itself. Thus, even though *Rival States, Rival Firms* provides a convincing invitation to pay more attention to 'new forms of production' and 'new forms of investment', the importance of international production in general and production networks in particular, as vehicles for transferring *knowledge* and thus for exercising structural power, is not really explored.

However, quite interestingly, it is Strange who actually gives us the means for disagreeing with her and for complementing her analyses. In this sense, the framework of analysis she proposes is particularly heuristic, not only because the notions she defines are extremely pertinent in accounting for many different situations, but also because her contribution is simply more than the sum of her arguments. There are links between the different issues she raises, such as the connection between production and knowledge structures, which open up new promising areas for research.

In the end, all this is possible because of Strange's deep understanding of the dramatic changes at work in the world economy. Her conceptual vision will endure for some time to come, despite the accelerating rate of the changes that she was amongst the very first to identify and emphasize.

Notes

1　Reich (1990).
2　On a PPP (purchasing power parity) basis.
3　See Stopford and Strange (1991: 8) for example.
4　Porter (1990), quoted in Martin (1998).
5　There is a public element of knowledge, which is codifiable, and a tacit component, which is non-tradable and firm-specific. The latter corresponds to the 'technological capabilities' of a firm. See Ernst *et al.* (1998).
6　See also the definition of innovation in Ernst *et al.* (1998: 13): it is 'a process by which firms master and implement the design and the production of goods and services that are new to them irrespective of whether or not they are new to their competitors – domestic or foreign'.
7　Network organizers are generally considered to be domestic firms, domestic business groups, design institutes, foreign trade organizations and so on. To include foreign firms is contrary to a fundamental assumption generally adopted in the literature on National Innovation Systems according to which 'agglomeration economies' are strongly favored by proximity and are supposed to develop best in a national context.
8　This is not necessarily so if FDI figures are measured against population and GDP. For example, with respect to FDI per head, Hungary comes just after France, Spain and the UK, and is ahead of Portugal.
9　This is broadly confirmed by 'unconventional' trade studies that trace the changing technological basis of CEECs' trade (Hotopp and Radosevic, 1999). See also Freudenberg and Lemoine (1999), UNECE (1997).
10　FDI is expected to make up for a notorious lack of domestic capital, thus easing

budgetary constraints, reducing debt burdens and providing cash receipts for privatization (see the Hungarian case in particular).

11   In Hungary, for example, the German share in EU OPT is 80 per cent, whereas the German share in FDI ranges between 40 and 45 per cent.

12   This 'preferential access' consists of a reduction and sometimes a suspension of tariff and/or access to additional quantitative restrictions, that is, specific OPT quotas.

13   There are some exceptions: Eichengreen and Kohl (1998), Graziani, in Zysman and Schwartz (1998), Lemoine, in Zysman and Schwartz (1998), UNECE (1995), Schmidt and Naujosk (1994).

14   Respectively, the Kopint Datorg and Czech Statistical Office (CSU).

15   According to the Economic Bulletin for Europe, proportions of OPT in total Hungarian, Czech and Polish exports to the EU amount to 21–25 per cent (UNECE, 1997).

16   There are many texts regulating the OPT regime in the EU. One of the first regulations is in Council Directive of 18 December 1975, in OJ L 24, 30.1.76. Another important text is Council Regulation 636/82, 16 March 1982, OJ L 76, 20.3.82. For the United States, the respective legislations are Items 806.30 and 807.00 of the old US Tariff Schedule, now HTS US 9802.00.600 and 902.00.800.

References

Baldwin, R.E. (1994), *Towards an Integrated Europe*, London: Centre for Economic Policy Research.

Benacek, V., M. Gronicki, D. Holland and M. Sass (1999), 'The Determinants and Impact of Foreign Direct Investment in Central and Eastern Europe', mimeo.

Black, S.W. (1997), *Europe's Economy Looks East*, Cambridge: Cambridge University Press.

Eichengreen, B. and R. Kohl (1998), 'The external sector and development in Eastern Europe: The determinants of differential performance', *Journal of International Relations and Development*, 1(1–2) July.

Ellingstad, M. (1997), 'The Maquiladora Syndrome: Central European Prospects', *Europe–Asia Studies*, 49(1).

Ellison, D.L. (1999), 'The Eastern Enlargement: A New or Multi-Speed Europe?', in B. Widmaier and W. Potratz, W. (eds), (1999), *Framework for Industrial Policy in Central Eastern Europe*, Aldershot: Ashgate.

Ernst, D., T. Ganiatsos and L. Mytelka (1998), 'Technological capabilities in the context of export-led growth: a conceptual framework', in D. Ernst, T. Ganiatsos and L. Mytelka (eds), *Technological Capabilities and Export Success in Asia*, London: Routledge.

Freudenberg, M. and F. Lemoine (1999), 'Central and Eastern European Countries in the International Division of Labour in Europe', CEPII Documents de Travail, No. 5, April.

Grabbe, H. and K. Hughes (1997), 'The implications of eastward enlargement for EU integration, convergence and competitiveness', paper presented at a TSER Workshop, 'Technology, Economic Integration and Social Cohesion', MERIT, Naples, November.

Hotopp, U. and S. Radosevic (1999), 'The Product Structure of Central and Eastern European Trade: the emerging patterns of change and learning', *MOST-MOCT*, 2.

Hughes, K. (1996), 'European enlargement, competitiveness and integration', in K. Hughes (ed.), *Competitiveness, Subsidiarity and Industrial Policy*, London: Routledge.

Lorentzen, J. (1998), 'Foreign Capital, Central Europe's Catch-up, and EU Enlargement: Policy Issues and Analytical Problems', *Journal of International Relations and Development*, 1(1–2) July.

Lundvall, B.A. (1988), 'Innovation as an interactive process: from user–producer interaction to the national system of innovation', in G. Dosi, C. Freeman, R. Nelson, G. Silverberg and L. Soete, (eds) *Technical Change and Economic Theory*, London: Pinter Publishers.

Martin, R. (1998), 'Central and Eastern Europe and the International Economy: The Limits to Globalisation', *Europe–Asia Studies*, 50(1).

Messerlin, P.A. (1993), 'The EC and Central Europe: The missed rendez-vous of 1992?', *Economics of Transition*, 1(1), 89–109.

Meyer, K. (1998), *Direct Investment in Economies in Transition*, Cheltenham: Edward Elgar.

Myant, M. (1999), 'The Tigers of Tomorrow? Structural Change and Economic Growth in East–Central Europe', in M. Myant (ed.), *Industrial Competitiveness in East–Central Europe*, Cheltenham, UK and Lyme, US: Edward Elgar.

Mytelka, L.K. (1991), 'Crisis, technological change and the strategic alliance', *Strategic Partnerships – States, Firms and International Competition*, London: Pinter Publishers.

Mytelka, L.K. (1999), 'Locational Tournament for Foreign Direct Investments: inward investments into Europe in a global world economy', in N. Hood and S. Young (eds), *The Globalization of Multinational Enterprise Activity and Economic Development*, London: Macmillan.

Porter, M. (1990), *The Competitive Advantage of Nations*, London: Macmillan.

Radosevic, S. (2000), 'Transformation of science and technology systems into systems of innovation in central and eastern Europe: the emerging patterns of recombination, path-dependency and change', *Structural Change and Economic Dynamics*, forthcoming.

Reich, R.B. (1990), 'Who is US?', *Harvard Business Review*, 68(1), 53–64.

Schmidt, K.D. and P. Naujoks (1994), 'Outward Processing in Central and Eastern European Transition Countries: Issues and Results from German Statistics', Kiel Working Papers 631, The Kiel Institute of World Economics.

Stopford, J. and S. Strange (with J.S. Henley) (1991), *Rival States, Rival Firms – Competition for World Market Shares*, Cambridge: Cambridge University Press.

Strange, S. (1991), 'An eclectic approach', in C.N. Murphy and R. Tooze (eds), *The New International Political Economy*, Boulder, CO: Lynne Rienner.

Strange, S., ([1988] 1994), *States and Markets*, London: Pinter Publishers.

Strange, S. (1996), *The Retreat of the State – The Diffusion of Power in the World Economy*, Cambridge: Cambridge University Press.

Strange, S. (1998), 'Who are EU – Ambiguities in the concept of competitiveness', *Journal of Common Market Studies*, 36(1), 101–14.

UNECE (1997), 'Outward Processing Trade between the European Union and the Associated Countries of Eastern Europe: the Case of Textile and Clothing', *Economic Bulletin for Europe*, 47.

Widmaier, B. and W. Potratz (1999), *Framework for Industrial Policy in Central Eastern Europe*, Aldershot: Ashgate.

Zysman, J. and A. Schwartz (1998), 'Reunifying Europe in an Emerging World Economy: Economic Heterogeneity, New Industrial Options and Political Choices', *Journal of Common Market Studies*, 36(3), September.

16 The Dynamics of Paralysis: Japan in the Global Era

JEAN-PIERRE LEHMANN

Introduction

A combination of external forces and internal decay caused the paralytic stagnation and economic morass that has afflicted Japan since the early 1990s. Fundamentally, Japan has failed to respond to the challenges and stimulus of globalization. As the world economy opened and expanded, Japan retrenched. The fact that Japan should experience decline is not surprising – all nations and economies at some stage do decline. What has been extraordinary has been both the *speed* and the *degree* with which Japan fell from the dizzying heights of apparent world champion to the pits of the world's sickest – and alarmingly so – industrial economy. Japan is the 'Ottoman Empire' of the 21st century world economy.

To understand the failure of the Japanese political economy to integrate into the new era of the international political economy, an analysis of the recurrent shifts in the country's politicoeconomic systems seems especially useful.

In short, for over a century Japan embarked on a quest to 'catch up' with the West, whether as an imperial power in the late 19th century, as a military invader in the mid-20th century, or as an economic dynamo since the 1950s. The paradox is that Japan proceeded to fail, immediately after it had seemingly quite brilliantly succeeded. If the 1990s were Japan's lost decade, immediately before, in the 1980s, the country seemed supreme and, indeed, invincible.

1989

In 1989, Emperor Hirohito of Japan died and the Nikkei index reached an unprecedented, indeed hitherto unimaginable peak, almost touching the 40 000 mark.[1] Virtually all the world's leaders came to pay their respects at Hirohito's funeral, yet here was a man whose passive complicity in Japan's policy of warfare and the atrocities that characterized it is beyond dispute.[2] So why was everyone there, paying their 'respects' to a man who many would argue should have been shunned by the international community?

Part of the reason was that the cold war was not yet over. Hirohito died in January; the Berlin wall was not brought down until November, 11 months later. From the outbreak of the cold war – and the communist takeover in China in 1949 and the 'hot' wars in Korea and Vietnam – Japan had been a key US rook on the international chessboard. Not only did that explain why George Bush should be present at the funeral, but also why pawns of the Western cold war camp such as the Zairian president, Mobutu Sese Seko, should be there. Hirohito owed his survival, indeed rehabilitation and international respectability, to cold war politics.[3]

Another important part of the reason everyone was there had to do of course with Japan's astonishing wealth. Japan's economic reconstruction in the 1950s led to the 'economic miracle' of the 1960s. It showed considerable resiliency through the difficult 1970s, emerging in the 1980s as an economic superpower.[4] In the course of the 1980s, Japan's economy grew at such speed and so massively that it was confidently predicted in many quarters that it was only a matter of a short time before its GNP would surpass that of the United States. Its unceasingly growing trade surplus seemed to demonstrate the devastating competitiveness of Japanese products.

The massive appreciation of the yen against the dollar following the September 1985 Hotel Plaza Accord in New York, whereby the exchange rate halved, from 240 to 120, in a matter of two years, gave further impetus and image to a Japanese economic giant. The Japanese edge appeared increasingly also in its technological prowess, especially in electronics, leading alarmed American academics and policy makers to proclaim that it was gaining leadership over the United States: in the words of the title of the most influential book on this subject, the United States and Japan had 'traded places'.[5]

Whereas the United States had hitherto perceived Japan as a passive and quite docile partner, with only relatively minor grievances over trade issues (textiles, steel, television sets), by the 1980s, as Japan's economic might grew and its trade surplus – especially with the United States – bulged, a far more pugilistic American policy began to emerge. What was termed the 'revisionist' American thesis about the relationship with Japan (more crudely described as 'Japan bashing') emphasized the need for Japan to change, but that this could only be achieved by exerting forceful external pressure. The Japanese term *gaiatsu* (outside pressure) became part of international trade vocabulary. Throughout the Reagan, Bush and early Clinton administrations, a trade war between Japan and the United States loomed ever more threateningly on the horizon. The question of Europe's role in this fray was raised and debated: should Europe join the United States in breaking down Japanese barriers, or should it adopt a more neutral, albeit constructive, position? Strange (1995), alarmed by the escalation of the US–Japan battle, argued not only that Europe should not join in the attack, but also, in line with her more general perception of the state of international economic affairs, that firms and other non-state actors should take a firmer initiative. The US–Japan trade battle was more a reflection of an increasingly obsolescent mercantilist competition between nation states.[6]

The trade battle notwithstanding, it was also during the 1980s that Japanese foreign investment took off like a series of rockets, the most vivid illustrations of which included the acquisition of Columbia Studios in Hollywood, of the Rockefeller Centre and other prime American (and European) real estate, of vast tracks of Hawaii and the Australian Gold Coast, and so on. It was also in the late 1980s that Japan emerged as the world's leading nation in absolute terms of overseas aid.

It can therefore be argued that the international community flocked to Hirohito's funeral because of the perception that Japan was the emergent global economic hegemon.

In 1989, Japan stood at the pinnacle of its post-war power. It seemed invincible, headed for an uninterrupted course of ascendancy, reflecting a remarkable historical pattern dating back at least a century giving Japan the aura of 'success'. Japan, it was believed, had been and would continue to be a highly successful nation, a model among nations not only of the developing world, but indeed of the West as well. Ezra Vogel's famous book, *Japan as Number One: Lessons for America*, published in 1979, served as a gospel for the 1980s.

Ten years later, how things had changed. The 1990s, in the starkest possible contrast with the previous decade, were not good for Japan. From the pinnacle of power, it has now been wallowing for virtually a decade in the mire of its industrial impotence. The concern today is not that the Japanese economy will take over the planet, but that it risks sinking and taking the planet with it. Many volumes have been written over the decades explaining Japan's rise as an economic power; the literature on Japan's decline, its causes and future trends, is (for obvious reasons) more recent.[7]

The focus and contention here are as follows: Japan's success through various stages of world history arose from its ability to adjust to successive 'paradigm shifts'. This reflected Japan's policies and goals as a nation state in the conventional framework of international relations and international politics. In the course of the 'paradigm shifts' that have evolved in recent decades, however, and especially in the critical changes that have occurred in the international political economy following the end of the cold war, analyzed in successive works of Strange,[8] Japan has failed. In a nutshell: whereas Japan understood, indeed mastered, the rules of the game of the international political economy during the phases of nationalism, its failure in the 1990s arose from not understanding and hence not succeeding in the new environment of globalism.

Japan has failed mainly because its elites have not understood the changes. That in turn may be due to the fact that the changes occurring in the global environment render the Japanese elites – the country's leaders of the administration, industry and politics – and their ideologies obsolete. Strange was quite popular in Japan, but Japan's policy makers (and probably most of its policy thinkers) could not really understand her, just as they still fail to understand the current forces driving the external environment. The title of this chapter is 'The Dynamics of Paralysis'; it could have been given a more Pirandello-like twist, for example: 'Japan's Leading Actors in Search of a New Paradigm'.

Historical Dynamics of Success

Japan's success in the modern age dates back to the Meiji Restoration of 1868. However, before that Japan was in fact quite remarkably successful as a feudal society in which were laid the foundations for pre-modernization.

Paradigmatic Shift I: the Edo Edifice[9]

Following almost a century of endemic civil wars and the beginnings of relations with the West, by the early to mid-17th century Japan had cut itself off from the outside world through a strict policy of isolation. Thus was inaugurated the Edo era (1603–1867), named after the city (renamed Tokyo – capital of the East – in 1872) where the Tokugawa shogunal dynasty established its capital. Whereas many countries in Asia (and elsewhere) found themselves colonized during this period (for example, the Philippines, Indonesia) or evolved in such a manner as to be unprepared for the great turbulent challenges that the era of industrialization and imperialism would bring, as in China and Korea, Japan stood apart.

One of the considerable achievements of the Edo edifice was to develop a sense of national identity. A good deal of the higher learning that took place, especially during the era's last century, involved the study of ancient texts regarding the 'historical' (that is, mythological) origins of Japan. This, among other things, led to the rebirth of the cult of the emperor. In time, this national identity served as ideal material for developing a national, indeed nationalistic, ideology and sense of national uniqueness.

There were many negative aspects. Peasants were brutally exploited; for more than a century-and-a-half the population was kept constant (at about 30 million), by means including the regular use of (mainly female) infanticide; the status of women deteriorated considerably as the samurai imposed their phallocratic warrior values on society at large. The Tokugawa also succeeded, on the whole, in maintaining strict ideological and political orthodoxy. The regime was both feudal and totalitarian, the latter aspect represented, *inter alia*, by a vast network of secret police and spies. Furthermore, although a good deal of Western technology was imported into Japan, the country's closed-door policy prevented it from engaging in philosophical or political discourse with the outside world.

When, in the mid-19th century, Japan was integrated into the Western world economic system, it possessed considerable advantages compared to other non-Western – and indeed many Western – countries. It had a quite advanced domestic economy, a well-developed infrastructure, a powerful and extensive national administrative apparatus, considerable technological know-how and a strong sense of national identity.

In its special millennium edition, *The Economist* aptly summarized the impact of Japan's extended period of exclusion and aloofness:

> the Japanese paid a heavy price for their centuries of self-imposed isolation. They missed out on the intellectual tempest that struck the West, bringing it the industrial revolution and such notions as individual rights and social justice. Japan has paid dearly ever since, as it struggled to catch up with western ways of thinking. Even now, this is one reason why it still lacks the confidence to make a moral, intellectual and political contribution to world affairs to match its economic one.[10]

Paradigmatic Shift II: the Meiji Model[11]

By the late 19th/early 20th centuries, Japan had emerged as a strong nation and as an industrialized power. Perhaps the greatest success of the Meiji leaders was in bringing about the developmentalist state, a state where economic development occurs, not as an end in itself, but as a means to an end, the end of nationalism and national power. The Meiji economic architecture, comprising powerful administrative guidance from the technocratic bureaucracy, a limited number of oligopolistic industrial conglomerates (*zaibatsu*) with close ties to the administration, a financial system controlled by the state and geared to support industry, and a trade policy aimed at exporting goods and importing technology, proved to be highly successful, solid and truly innovative. The Meiji model became the Japanese model. Japan was the first – and for quite some time the only – non-Western nation to have undergone a successful industrial revolution. By the beginning of the 20th century, Japanese industry in diverse sectors was actively and successfully competing in world markets.

Japan as a country industrialized, but society remained in many respects 'feudal'. There was a significant increase in national wealth, albeit highly unevenly distributed, though general living standards improved throughout most of the country. In the course of the Meiji years (1868–1912) the population doubled. However, no cosmopolitan capitalist bourgeoisie emerged. There were the oligarchs – primarily the upper echelons of the civil bureaucracy and the military – who retained political power, and the oligopolists – the scions of the *zaibatsu* families, Mitsui, Iwasaki and so on and their chief retainers – who retained economic power. The two were closely connected by both formal and informal means. The rest of Japanese society was mobilized and manipulated to serve the interests of the establishment.

Meiji Japan had many slogans. *Fukoku-kyohei* (rich nation–strong army) was the most pervasive and the most indicative of the Meiji ethos. 'If you can't beat them, join them' might also have served to encapsulate the thrust of Japan's foreign and imperial policy. Joining the Western club, or so it was perceived, required not only industrial power, but also colonial power. By no means was this the only motivation for Japanese imperialism, but it was politically an important one. Fairly soon after the establishment of Japan's modern state, therefore, it set about carving out for itself an empire. Japan did not have the military or naval range to launch out on distant shores, as did the Western European empires (with the exception of Britain's colonization of Ireland), hence it concentrated on its neighbors instead. It was also of course the case that, by the time Japan joined in on the act, most territories on distant shores had already been seized.

An important measure of the success of the Meiji model is the fact that the world's most powerful nation at the time, the United Kingdom, established a special relationship with Japan, including an alliance that lasted from 1902 to 1922. It became a pattern in Japan's paradigmatic shifts that it succeeded in closely allying itself with the successive dominant powers. Also, as was to be the case in the post-

World War II period in its relationship with the United States, Japan allied itself with Britain without adopting the British liberal ideology or system. It was a fundamentally Bismarckian Japan that allied itself with Britain against Germany in World War I.[12]

Paradigmatic Shift III: 'Fascism' and Opportunism

The end of the 1914–18 war brought Japan the status of a great power and an increase in its sphere of influence in China. Japan was not totally immune from the wave of liberalism that swept the West in the 1920s. Lessons were to be drawn from World War I. The 'democracies' had emerged victorious. Three imperial despotic regimes – Russia, Austria–Hungary and the Ottoman Empire – lay in ruins. Thus, as in the 1870s, the door of liberalism opened again to Japan and beckoned it forth. For a while, an illusion of liberalism did sweep through the country. However, while there were some concrete developments, such as the extension of full male suffrage in 1926, no real fundamental reform of the state apparatus or any significant questioning of the dominant ideology occurred.

In the 1930s, with the Japanese economy, like others, ravaged by the Great Depression, Japan again had a number of options. Liberalism (possibly in a New Deal-type guise), socialism and fascism were the main models operative in the world at the time. Japan chose the fascist road – albeit one it traveled in its own way. In fact, Japan had no option apart from the fascist model. Opting for the liberal model would have required a bourgeois revolution in both social structure and culture (or ideology) that the establishment would simply not countenance. As to socialism, combating it, in Japan as in other countries, was one of the justifications for fascism.

When World War II was over, Japanese intellectuals and Western experts sought to analyze what had happened in Japan. It had been allied with Nazi Germany and Fascist Italy yet, in many fundamental respects, the Japanese political system and behavior of the 1930s and early 1940s differed from those in Germany and Italy or, for that matter, in Spain, Portugal and Argentina. Whereas in these countries the fascist regimes represented a radical break with the past, proclaiming a new era and aura, such as a third Reich to last a thousand years, in Japan the emphasis was on continuity and conservation. There was no *führer*, *duce* or *caudillo* figure, something that would have caused tension with the emperor system. There was the emperor, but he had been around for some time and in no way could be presented – in fact, quite the contrary – as a populist figure. Nor was there any mass political party such as the Nazis in Germany or even the *falange* in Spain. In discarding the common Western political nomenclature of fascism as inapplicable to Japan, a number of experts drew the conclusion that what had occurred in the country during this period should perhaps simply be defined as 'Japanism'.[13]

Again, even moderate steps towards reform were seen by the establishment to be impossible, as the whole edifice of the emperor system risked collapsing. Far better to divert domestic antagonisms by engaging in foreign exploits. It was more than just convenient that one of the great European powers, Germany, was in the process of dressing up primitive and brutal instincts with the rhetoric of vision, ideology, indeed millenarianism. This provided Japan with the opportunity of emulating that great power and to devise its own version of a vision, subsequently codified as 'the eight corners of the world under one roof'.

Japan's ideal scenario was to win the war and to establish a sizeable empire in China and Southeast Asia. The second-best scenario was to obtain a negotiated settlement, leaving Japan with perhaps not quite so huge an empire, but an extensive sphere of influence throughout most of Asia nonetheless. The disaster scenario was to lose the war and be relegated to the status of a minor power. The undreamed-of scenario was to lose the war and win the peace. Yet that is what happened.

Paradigmatic Shift IV: the Economic Miracle

What the Japanese had not been able to do, the Americans did for them. The period of the American Occupation witnessed a series of reforms that had the most important result of significantly strengthening Japan's industrial structure and socioeconomic infrastructure. Parasitic elements, such as absentee landlords and the nobility (with the notable exception of the imperial family), were discarded.

The same fate awaited the military. With the armed forces removed from positions of power, Japan's potential for belligerency was virtually eliminated by the inclusion of an article (Article 9) in the new Constitution that forbade the country to exercise the sovereign right to go to war. The hitherto martial Japan stood militarily crippled, but by no means defenceless. The Americans extended to the Japanese probably the best defence deal ever: they would unilaterally protect Japan, without any need whatsoever of any form of Japanese reciprocity. Thus Japan was able to keep its military expenditure to a minimum, while basking in the knowledge that the American nuclear umbrella protected it.

Japan acquired its 'democracy' not – as has been the case with virtually all nations that have gained democracy – by the efforts and struggle of its own people, but as a gift from outside, that is from the United States. In fact, although the Americans did in the early stages of the Occupation set about putting in place not only thorough economic reforms, but social and political ones as well, the *realpolitik* of the cold war soon resulted in the latter being jettisoned or at least very significantly toned down.[14]

A significant economic force of continuity between pre- and post-war Japan was in the transformation of the *zaibatsu* into what came to be known as the *keiretsu*. The American Occupation authorities had sought to dismantle the conglomerates as a means of bringing about economic democracy and liberalism to the country. In the years immediately following the Occupation, however, the main pre-war groups (Mitsui, Mitsubishi, Sumitomo) reassembled and a few new ones were formed. The Japanese economy thus retained its highly and tightly oligopolistic nature.

Perhaps the most blatant characteristic of continuity in the economic realm between pre- and post-war Japan was in the sustained – indeed enhanced – power of the central bureaucracy. The Ministry of Finance and the Ministry of International Trade and Industry (MITI) throughout most of the post-war decades had an iron grip on the nation's economy. This bureaucratic power over the economy was reflected in the quite militantly mercantilist orientation of Japan's economic ideology. Turning liberal economic theory on its head, the Japanese economic dogma held that imports were bad, exports were good, and the same, indeed even more so, applied to foreign direct investments: outward good, inward no good.[15]

The post-war Japanese establishment consisted of three powerful pillars: the national bureaucracy, the oligopolistic *keiretsu* and the ruling party that was formed in 1955 (through the merger of two pre-war political parties), the Liberal Democratic Party. The LDP held a monopoly on government for the next four decades. Between these three pillars, that came to be referred to as the 'iron triangle', both formal and informal interrelationships existed. This constituted what in the West was known as 'Japan, Inc.'[16]

Japan, Inc. was highly successful in many ways. It was especially skillful and successful in exploiting its relationship with the United States. As the United States's main ally in the Pacific and as its 'democratic' bulwark against communism, from the latter part of the Occupation years and in ensuing decades considerable favors were lavished on the Japanese.[17] A highly favorable exchange rate (360 yen to the dollar) was fixed as a means of facilitating Japanese exports. The American market was opened wide, while the Japanese were permitted to maintain a closed market in order to protect 'infant' and other special interest sectors, which ultimately came to mean virtually everything. The Americans transferred a good deal of technology to boost Japanese productivity, industrial development and competitiveness.[18]

Beyond the special favors gained from the United States, the Japanese 'model' proved very successful in other respects. Perhaps the greatest Japanese industrial achievement lay in the rapid and solid developments in production technology in a number of specific fields, primarily linked to electronics, optical instruments, office and factory automation, and transport equipment. Japan also experienced considerable gains in education. Building on the foundations laid in the Meiji era in primary education, Japan saw perhaps more than in any other country a massive expansion and enhancement of secondary education. Already by the 1960s, Japan had the world's most educated workforce. Thrift, hard work and discipline were some of the more noticeable achievements of Japanese post-war society. The wealth generated by the rapid rise of the GNP was, unlike the situation in pre-war Japan, reasonably equitably distributed. By the 1970s, Japan had become a 'middle-class' society.[19]

These are all significant achievements. The Japanese establishment was able effectively to mobilize resources to obtain quite spectacular economic ends. The bulk of Japanese society benefitted materially from these developments. Many foreign observers looked upon Japanese economic management and society with admiration,[20] while others, not necessarily admirers, nevertheless felt that the Japanese system was bound to win and hence maintaining – or regaining – competitiveness dictated that it be transferred and adopted.[21]

In reality, while Japan was the country that had most benefitted from the open liberal international economy that the West had sought to construct on the ashes of World War II, Japan itself was not an open, liberal or internationally oriented (except in promoting exports) economy. In the 50-plus years after the war, Japanese society failed in many crucial respects to live up to some of the more positive developments that characterized other industrialized postmodern countries and even some developing countries.[22]

Thus, while postmodern liberal societies were characterized by pluralism, with distinct and diverse actors emerging in the public policy process, such as consumer groups, regional groupings, non-government organizations (NGOs), corporations, trade unions, pensioners, the media and so on, a similar trend did not occur in Japan. Until the early 1990s, the establishment remained both tightly cohesive and highly exclusive. The Japanese economy was clearly constructed to serve the interests of producers, not those of consumers. This was secured and repeatedly re-enforced by protectionist and oligopolistic policies and practices. A comparable situation applied to the labor market, which was rigidly organized to suit the interests of large corporations. Graduates were recruited from high schools or universities for 'lifetime employment' in the major corporations. The objective was under no circumstances to seek the employee's individual development, let alone empowerment, but for the corporation to have its exclusive pool of malleable human resources. The fact that the labor market lacked intercorporate mobility was due, not necessarily so much to workers' 'loyalty', but to the fact that Japanese company employees typically lack individual skills. Their strength is derived from collective mass and the corporations they serve, their connections, contacts and so on. Without these they have nothing particular to offer to the market.[23]

There was no incremental 'retreat of the state' (Strange 1996). The state retained its power over all aspects of the national economy. Nor was there, therefore, any separation, whether in reality or even conceptually between the state and the market. Japanese corporations did not gain the autonomy that has tended to characterize most industrialized countries. Nor were the few foreign companies that managed to establish a position in the Japanese market perceived as anything else than foreign, the only possible exception being IBM Japan. The greatest difficulty faced by foreign firms in Japan was to recruit high-calibre graduates. For young Japanese graduates, especially from elite institutions, working for a Japanese company was *de rigueur*. There were no laws against working for foreign companies, but it was seen as unpatriotic and heavily frowned upon.

While foreign investors were not welcome in Japan, Japanese companies operating abroad retained their nationalist, indeed xenophobic ethos. Strange, who was generally quite sympathetic towards Japan, writing about Japanese corporate human resource management practices in their foreign operations, commented that 'their exclusivist, not to say racist, habits of restricting senior management positions to Japanese and keeping out the indigenous workforce may prove a handicap in the long run' (1992: 13). By no means is Japanese corporate discrimination limited to Westerners.[24] Ronnie Chan, a prominent 'overseas Chinese' entrepreneur, has provided a quite blistering attack on Japanese practices and policies in Asia:

> Japan's foreign direct investment is of limited benefit. ... unlike the US and Europe, Japanese companies are widely known to be reluctant to transfer technology and management know-how...Rigorous management localisation plans, so common in most western companies, are almost unheard of in Japanese companies. Few Japanese foreign operations are headed by a native person...Besides structural impediments to foreign trade and investment, Japan is also notorious for its social and cultural barriers. Contrast Japanese and western department stores and one sees that the former carries far fewer Chinese, Thai or Malaysian products.[25]

One of the issues that Chan's comments bring to the fore is the absence on the part of Japan of a regional commitment, regional integration or regional solidarity. There are no Korean cars on Japanese streets, as there are no Koreans in senior positions in Japanese companies, or Korean deans of faculties in prestigious Japanese universities, or Korean editors of Japanese papers, and so on. There are successful Korean entrepreneurs, for example Masayoshi Son, the chairman and founder of Softbank. To succeed, however, they need to found their own companies as they would not stand much chance of success in traditional Japanese companies. The same general point applies to Chinese, Filipinos, Thais, Indonesians, Malaysians and so on. As a former colonial power, Japan has exhibited none of the openness that former Western colonial powers have extended to their erstwhile colonial subjects. In Britain, for example, not only the Irish but Indians and West Indians are to be found in senior positions in British corporations, liberal professions, educational institutions and so on.[26]

Chan also identifies the language problem. Indeed, it is one of the paradoxes that, while Japan is the world's second biggest economy and it is the Asian country which has (or should have) the closest ties and affinities with the West, it is also a country where the international language, English, is least spoken, including by the elites.[27] The English language issue also illustrates the point that, even by the beginning of the 21st century, Japan still has not seen the emergence of a liberal cosmopolitan bourgeoisie. There are very strong networks inside Japan among Japanese, but very few Japanese possess strong international networks. Japanese tend to be conspicuous by their absence in major international gatherings. When they do attend, given their poor linguistic capabilities, they tend to contribute and understand little. Between the outside world and Japan, therefore, information and knowledge flows are lacking. For this reason, among others, as *The Economist* noted,[28] Japan has not contributed morally, intellectually or politically to world affairs in a manner commensurate with its economic power.

That, however, would not be counted as a failure by the post-war establishment. That was not their goal. The goal was to achieve economic power. National greatness was calculated solely in terms of GNP.[29] To that end, the establishment needed to remain cohesive and single-mindedly determined. So far as possible – even while respecting democratic appearances – dissent had to be stifled.[30] A liberal cosmopolitan bourgeoisie that might have a conflict of loyalties between universal principles and international obligations and Japanese mercantilist interests would clearly not fit into the paradigm. For the same reason, Japanese firms needed to remain exclusive. Allowing foreigners into positions of senior management, even in foreign subsidiaries, risked diluting the establishment's cohesion and determination. While there are, therefore, many Japanese corporations with activities abroad, none, with the possible exception of Sony – which has gone further than any Japanese company in appointing foreigners to senior positions, including two who sit on the Sony main board – can fit the description of a 'multinational' company.

Another dimension on which Japan stands out in contrast with other industrialized and even with many developing countries is in the virtual absence of civil society. There are Japanese branches of western NGOs, such as Amnesty International or the World Wildlife Fund, but they tend to be both highly sedate and minority affairs. With the exception of Peace Boat, there are no internationally oriented Japanese NGOs: there has been no Japanese institution that has made a contribution to global humanitarian issues (such as Médecins sans Frontières or Oxfam), ecological issues (for example, Friends of the Earth) and so forth. A 'Japanese non-governmental organization' in fact comes across as an oxymoron.

Japan's fourth paradigmatic shift was resoundingly successful on the basis of its own terms and goals. It was therefore not surprising that the funeral of former Emperor Hirohito should have drawn such an international crowd of VIPs. Two or three years after the funeral, however, the world began to change rapidly: there was a global paradigm shift, but Japan failed to adjust. Hence the paralysis that has plagued the country for the last decade.

Japan's Globalization Quagmire

As was stated in the introduction to this chapter, a combination of external forces and internal decay caused the paralytic stagnation and economic morass that has afflicted Japan since the early 1990s. The internal decay was brought about partly by the excesses of the bubble economy in the second half of the 1980s that resulted in massive bad debts for banks, other financial institutions and many manufacturing firms. The post-bubble drama was aggravated, however, by the sclerotic, indeed rotten condition and disintegration of the post-war structure. As successful as the structure established by the architects of the post-war Japanese economy had been for several decades, eventually – as with any regime that lasts too long – it became decrepit through its own corruption, incestuousness and lack of innovation. By the late 1980s, Japan was a society dominated by reactionary old men – and in many respects the situation still remains the same. Change was by definition a force to be resisted. The absence of viable actors outside the establishment·meant there was no legitimacy of heterodoxy, of constructive criticism or alternative power structure.

This situation rapidly proved to hold true in the political domain. The LDP split up and lost its stranglehold on political power in 1993.

Three non-LDP prime ministers took power in rapid succession, although two of them had previously been members of the LDP. Initially, Ichiro Ozawa emerged as the main 'opposition' behind-the-scenes figure, though he is himself an ex-LDP party machine man *par excellence*, long associated with one of the murkiest LDP political bosses, Shin Kanemaru. Within four years, the LDP was back in power, albeit in coalition. The brief expulsion of the LDP had not, in fact, resulted in political pluralism (or even the formation of a two-party structure), mainly because there had never been any genuine political fragmentation or alternative forms of real political legitimacy to the LDP. There are a host of parties in Japan, but in reality there are far fewer options – real choices for voters –than are to be found, not only, in older democracies, but even in new ones such as Korea and Taiwan.

There has indeed been a systemic breakdown in Japan. The LDP, even if still in power, no longer has the monopoly it enjoyed for most of the post-war decades. The bureaucracy has lost most of its reputation and legitimacy, and a good deal of its clout. The Ministry of Finance in particular has become a target of criticism – even ridicule – resulting from its egregious errors and repeated failure to resolve Japan's financial catastrophe.

The hitherto seemingly invincible Japanese firms that were going to conquer the planet have had persistently poor results. There have been widespread bankruptcies. Some of the most established Japanese enterprises, such as the mighty securities firm Yamaichi, the prestigious Long Term Credit Bank (LTCB) and the country's second-ranking car maker, Nissan, have fallen and have, ironically, had to be rescued by foreigners. Quite apart from the spectacular failures, perhaps more important is the fact that there have been hardly any companies that have been able to boast even remotely sterling performances. Toyota is doing OK but its profits come exclusively from the American market. Sony is trying to move from being a manufacturer to being a provider of systems, solutions and software, but the transition is painful and not yet assured. Indeed, the performance of Japanese industry throughout virtually all sectors can be described as ranging from abysmal to mediocre. It is in the corporate sector that the fall from grace has perhaps been the most astonishing and humiliating.

The ailments of the Japanese economy at the macro level, primarily due to the travails of the financial sector and the decline of private consumption,[31] should normally only tangentially affect the corporate sector. For example, while the US economy was doing poorly through the 1980s, firms in Silicon Valley and many in finance were actively innovating and booming along. The same phenomenon could be seen in Sweden and Switzerland, where macroeconomic stagnation did not prevent firms such as Asea-Brown-Boveri (ABB), Astra, Novartis, Nestlé and others from remaining highly profitable and dynamic global corporate actors. The fact, however, that in Japan the stagnation of the economy and the paralysis of government should so adversely affect private corporations underlies the point stressed earlier, namely that in Japan the separation between state and market has not yet – or certainly has not yet fully – occurred.[32]

The acute financial difficulties in which Japanese firms have found themselves have had a number of critical repercussions. Although widespread and extensive layoffs have not occurred, the structure and nature of the labor market have nevertheless been permanently altered. The lifetime employment guarantee is past history. This in turn will have a considerable impact on the nature of the Japanese corporation. It, too, is destined to change. Financial difficulties, coupled with government reforms resulting in (theoretically) greater transparency, for example in accounting standards, are forcing firms to abandon the unprofitable cross-shareholdings they held in their respective sister *keiretsu* firms. That and the merger of a number of the major banks effectively mean that the *keiretsu*, too, are also rapidly becoming history.[33]

While internal decay is causing systemic disintegration, equally forceful have been the external pressures. The collapse of the Berlin wall heralded globalization at a geopolitical level, while the eventual completion of the Uruguay Round and the establishment of the World Trade Organisation (WTO) provided the geoeconomic framework for globalization. The exponential developments in the information and communications revolution have intensified and accelerated the process. Globalization is practically a force unto its own, something that frightens many people, notably the demonstrators at the WTO ministerial meeting in November/December 1999 in Seattle. As described by Stopford and Strange (1991), the new era presented a new paradigm whereby firms compete for global market share and governments compete for global investment share. Countries no longer compete on how aggressive they are – for example, in fostering industrial policies or promoting mercantilist trade policies – but on how attractive they are to investors, both domestic and foreign.

A key repercussion of this process has been the massive global corporate restructuring that has occurred, is occurring and will continue to occur. Japanese firms, by virtue of their highly parochial (that is, non-global) nature have not been able to participate in this dynamic process, nor is it clear that they actually understand it. Thus in the gigantic present-day global battlefield, Japanese firms are not prominent players or, in many cases, may not be players at all. Though strong Japanese firms in traditional sectors do remain, such as Canon in office equipment, Honda and Toyota in transportation equipment or Sony in consumer electronics, no Japanese firm has emerged as a global player either in services or in cutting-edge information technology (or, for that matter, biotechnology).

The late 1990s saw a fairly dramatic reversal of the pattern that had characterized the Japanese economy hitherto. Japan, subsequently copied by a number of other East Asian countries, notably Korea, practiced what Daniel Yergin has labeled the compete out/protect in model.[34] This, as pointed out earlier, applied both to goods and to investments. The huge gap between outward and inward direct investments set Japan totally apart from the norm among the world's industrialized and industrializing economies (with the exception of Korea). Although the flow of outward investments still surpasses the inward investment flow on a quantitative basis (albeit by significantly less than in the past), on the qualitative front the very late 1990s have seen some very dramatic developments that would have been unimaginable only a couple of years earlier.

The only dynamic element operating in Japan at present is the increasing foreign presence and influence. Foreign companies, including GE Capital, Ripplewood and Axa, have made significant inroads into the Japanese financial services sector through acquisitions. Along with Citibank, Merrill Lynch and some others, it is now these foreign players who are the major movers and shakers. Cable & Wireless won a significant victory against NTT in making an acquisition in telecommunications. Ford has upped its share in Japan's fourth major auto manufacturer, Mazda, and has taken over management control. Quite amazing has been the acquisition of Japan's second-biggest car maker, Nissan, by Renault. Until that transaction was carried out, Renault had had no presence at all in Japan. The disarray and decline of Japanese industry has opened up considerable opportunities for foreign companies – at last – to establish a presence in the Japanese market.[35]

The level of activity of merger and acquisition (M&A) in Japan, it should be emphasized, is still very low when compared to M&A in the Western economies. However, compared to what had previously occurred in Japan, the change is revolutionary. It is revolutionary not only because of the numbers, but also because of the power and innovation that the foreign executives of the companies making the acquisitions are bringing to Japanese industrial society.

Foreign companies are beginning to have a much greater impact on the Japanese market. In contrast to the ineffectiveness, indecisiveness and advanced age of most Japanese captains of industry, foreign managers come across as effective, dynamic and young. Yet whether these developments are actually influencing Japanese corporations is not clear. What is clear is that the old guard – the ageing Japanese captains of industry and their lieutenants in waiting – are resisting and probably will continue to resist both rejuvenation and internationalization. Resistance to radical change can also be expected from those younger cadres that are locked into, and therefore have vested interests in, the system. For example, the fact that Japanese senior executives are generally incapable of communicating in English means that overseas subsidiaries of Japanese companies need to maintain (and remunerate) vast cohorts of Japanese managers. In many cases their role consists of little more than acting as transmission agents (interpreters) between the Japanese head office and the foreign subsidiary. Thus, alongside the formal organizational chart, most overseas subsidiaries of Japanese companies have a parallel structure. At the European headquarters of Toyota, for example, these individuals are known as 'division coordinators' (DC): the accounting department might, for example, have a Belgian general manager, but he or she will be 'shadowed' by a Japanese DC specifically and exclusively appointed to that particular task. The Japanese who hold these positions are expatriates sent from head office. The costs, of course, are astronomical.

Masao Yukawa, formerly board member of Mitsubishi Corporation, was one of the few Japanese writers to show a clear grasp of what globalization is about. He has argued that 'Japanese companies are ill-prepared for globalisation' and that 'there is no doubt that Japan must change to accommodate this global economy'.[36] In the paradigm of global competitiveness, corporations that win will be those that are able to attract the best managers, irrespective of their national, ethnic or religious origins. To date these lessons do not appear to have been learned – possibly not even considered – by Japanese companies. They retain their exclusivist policies and practices.

Japan at the beginning of the 21st century is decaying on the inside and being shaken up from outside. It is, as stated in the introduction, the 'Ottoman Empire' of the 21st century world economy'.[37] The combination of internal decay and external pressures has also led Japanese and other commentators to compare the contemporary scene with that at the end of the Edo era on the eve of the Meiji Restoration. The Ottoman Empire collapsed and caused global havoc. The Edo regime also collapsed, but in so doing gave way to one of the most dynamic societies of the 19th century. Will that Japanese precedent be repeated? Or will Japan go the way of the Ottoman Empire?

Some Perspectives for a New Paradigm for Japan

Japan's condition is serious. It is serious for Japan, serious for Asia and serious for the world economy. So far, calamities have been avoided mainly because, throughout the decade that Japan has been languishing, the extraordinarily dynamic performance of the US economy has provided the world economy – and especially the post-crisis East Asian economies – with the locomotive it needs. An American economic downturn would have a negative effect on the whole of the world economy, but especially on East Asia, all of whose economies depend heavily on exports and all of whose export sectors depend heavily on the American market. An ailing Japan would simply not be in a position to take up the economic slack.[38] A deteriorating economic environment in East Asia will significantly increase geopolitical risks in a region that contains the world's most potentially explosive powder kegs.

Furthermore, a sclerotic and paralytic Japan will not be in a position to deal intelligently and forcefully with the growing challenge that the People's Republic of China will increasingly pose. For centuries, indeed millennia, China was the dominant power in East Asia. From the latter part of the 19th century the balance of power between China and Japan shifted, with Japan gaining ascendancy. That transformation, however, involved three wars and millions killed and maimed. The possible frictions arising as a result of growing Chinese power and declining Japanese power are many and deep.[39] The current political and economic state in which Japan finds itself hardly bodes well for the future challenges that lie ahead.

It has become a *mantra* in the Western press that Japan is changing. That it is changing is certain. What it is changing to is the question. It is not yet at all clear that an answer is being formulated, let alone emerging. Japan has experienced a systemic breakdown. But no new system is in place. There are at present no architects or engineers, just tinkerers. Although the Japanese public is clearly distressed by the old men who continue to dominate the scene, there are no young men or women thrusting themselves forward. This is one big difference from the late Edo and early Meiji eras, when the reins of power were grasped by forceful and courageous individuals in their late twenties and thirties. In Japan of today, the young seem too overwhelmed by their superiors. The gerontocratic state looks as though it will last some years yet.

A new positive paradigm for Japan, therefore, would require rejuvenation. Furthermore, while, as has been noted, there is destruction occurring in the Japanese political economy, at this stage there is no evidence that it would justify being described as 'creative destruction'. Although restructuring has begun to occur in an increasing number of Japanese companies, what has been lacking has been innovation. This applies both at the individual corporate level and at the broader macroeconomic level.

As one means of moving forward more confidently into the 21st century, one critical step would have been to confront the 20th century with greater courage and with the determination to seek the truth. All societies harbor myths,[40] but Japan is, as so often, an extreme case.[41] All societies seek to avoid confronting unpleasantness. The case of Switzerland being forced to demystify its role and accept some very brutal realities regarding its behaviour in World War II is one of many recent examples.[42] In France, only under President Chirac was an admission finally made that the Vichy government – and not just the Nazi occupiers – were responsible for the deportation of French Jews. There are many Western examples the Japanese could learn from in embarking on this painful road. A joint Korean–Japanese commission on seeking the truth on the 'comfort women' forced by the Japanese government into prostitution during World War II would be an example. The Japanese could also invite Chinese academics to participate in an in-depth inquiry on slave labor camps, or the Nanjing massacre, or the experimentation of chemical warfare carried out on Chinese civilians.

The refusal to accept that the primary aim of social science is to seek after the truth is something that causes a very deep divide between the intellectual communities of Japan and the West, and indeed all non-totalitarian societies.[43] In order to pass that particular threshold, an absolute *sine qua non* will be to address the question of the emperor's role during the war and indeed to subject the entire imperial institution to the rigors of scientific historical inquiry.[44] Japan's emancipation into the 21st century, and the beginnings of seeking a paradigm that would correspond to the kind of moral and political standpoint that it should be prepared to adopt, require abolishing all taboos and especially such morally and politically dangerous taboos as a sacrosanct imperial institution.

Another critical step will be for Japan to assume its regional responsibilities and to develop a sense of regional commitment and solidarity. It is true that Japan is the biggest dispenser of aid in the region and that a number of regional initiatives have occasionally been formulated, the latest version being the so-called 'Miyazawa Plan' for regional reconstruction. Japanese aid and other initiatives, however, have all been arm's-length exercises, involving no significant engagement and no sacrifice.[45] As Yukawa would put it, Japanese initiatives in Asia have been in the 'numerator' category, not in the 'denominator'. To achieve genuine regionalization, Japanese policy makers would need to heed the earlier remarks of Ronnie Chan. Japan should learn to interpret regionalization as a two-way process. Only then can Japan claim Asian regional credentials. And only once that has been achieved can Japan seriously pursue its new paradigm.

A *leitmotiv* throughout the historical periods described here has been the absence in Japan of the emergence of a cosmopolitan liberal bourgeoisie. A cosmopolitan liberal bourgeois can be highly patriotic, though not of the 'my country right or wrong' variety. Adherence to universal principles of morality and internationalism would create the kind of conflict of loyalties that ultimately causes progress and enlightenment in societies. Far more Japanese need to learn to be fluent in English – that is an absolute requisite in the globalization age.[46] Making the effort to learn English will also provide outsiders with evidence that the Japanese are genuinely committed to communicating. More Japanese need to study abroad and more efforts need to be directed at attracting foreign students. Japanese universities and other educational institutions should internationalize by appointing foreigners in career track positions, as professors, deans and even presidents of universities.

It is also absolutely necessary for Japanese companies to cease engaging in exclusivist human resource practices. Not only, as Strange contended, will this 'prove a handicap in the long run', but the question will arise – certainly, should arise – in global markets whether such behavior can any longer be tolerated. Here again, therefore, when Japanese companies will be becoming and seen to be becoming genuinely multinational, another important dimension to the new paradigm will become visible.

The efforts of many policy makers and policy thinkers in the West have been directed at getting Japan to open its markets and to play by the rules and spirit of an open liberal international economy.[47] For that goal to be achieved, however, Japan needs to become an open liberal international society. If that does emerge as the new Japanese paradigm, if Japan does succeed in making a paradigmatic shift in tune with the global paradigm, then Japan's contribution to the international political economy in the 21st century will be significant and constructive. If that shift is not brought about, if Japan persists in its exclusivist practices, then the outlook not only for Japan, but for East Asia and for the global community will be bleak.

Notes

1   In the course of the 1990s it fell to below 13 000, but has since risen and is to be found hovering at about 18 000, still less than half its previous value.
2   In the immediate post-war years, both Japanese and American establishment scholars sought to remold the emperor as a likeable liberal, a victim of the militarists. David Bergamini's *Japan's Imperial Conspiracy* (1971) was the first major effort by a Western scholar to assess critically the role of Hirohito in the decades preceding the war and during the war. As the title implies, Bergamini found the emperor guilty of active connivance in the build up to the war and in its activities, including the atrocities. The Bergamini thesis remains controversial. Though the earlier view of the emperor as hapless victim is rejected, the degree of his involvement, whether passive or active, remains a matter of conjecture and dispute for many commentators. John Dower, one of the most

outstanding contemporary historians of modern Japan, has provided a suc-
cinct appraisal. When Hirohito died, Dower expressed 'regret that the Shôwa
Emperor [Hirohito] did not use his immense power and prestige to attempt to
check the rising tide of Japanese militarism and repression that culminated in
the China and Pacific wars, or to press for an earlier end to World War II in
Asia'.

This, of course, is the most sensitive issue of all where the emperor is concerned. Indeed, in many circles, both in Japan and the West, any intimation of
imperial war responsibility is virtually taboo. Yet, after all the disarming arguments concerning the emperor's conservative understanding of 'constitutional
monarchy' and the like have been presented, the fact remains that, prior to
1945, Emperor Hirohito was a young, vigorous, well-informed monarch who
possessed real power, often made his preferences known, and actively allowed
himself to be turned into the central icon of Japanese ultranationalism. We will
never know exactly what he did or did not do between 1926 and 1945. In light
of the death and destruction that was unleashed in his name, beginning in the
1930s, however, it does not seem inappropriate to wish that he had been more
forceful in working for peace (John Dower, *Japan in War and Peace: Essays on
History, Culture and Race*, 1993, p.351). See also Ben-Ami Shillony, *Politics and
Culture in Wartime Japan*, 1981, pp.36–44).

After the abortive coup d'état of Lieutenant Tejero in Spain in February 1981,
some six years after the death of Franco, one fully appreciated the fact that the
courage and tenacity of King Juan Carlos in refusing to make any compromise
at all with the putschists was instrumental in the coup's failure and the preservation – indeed strengthening – of democracy in Spain. The suggestion was
made to a number of Japanese historians and also to some journalists that they
should write articles contrasting Juan Carlos' attitude in 1981 with Emperor
Hirohito's failure to make a public condemnation of the young officers who
carried out a coup d'état in Japan in February 1936. The coup was ultimately
quashed, but only as a means for officers of superior ranks to take control of
the government and thereby both impose more repression domestically and
accelerate the road to war. (See Ben-Ami Shillony, *Revolt in Japan: The Young
Officers and the February 26, 1936 Incident*, 1973.)

3   For a fascinating analysis of the rehabilitation of the Emperor by MacArthur
and for the impact of US policy during the Occupation on the development of
Japanese politics and society, see John Dower, *Embracing Defeat: Japan in the
Wake of World War Two*, 1999.

4   The term 'economic superpower' in reference to Japan was first coined by
Hermann Kahn, founder of the Hudson Institute, in *Japan: the Emergence of an
Economic Superpower* (1972). Kahn's book appeared the year before the first oil
crisis. This caused a retardation in Japan's economic ascendancy and the implementation of ultimately quite successful industrial adjustments. The economic
superpower status was eventually gained in the 1980s.

5   Clyde Prestowitz, *Trading Places: How America Allowed Japan to Take the Lead*
(1988).

6   Susan Strange, 'European Business in Japan: a Policy Crossroads?', *Journal of
Common Market Studies*, 33(1) (1995): 1–25.

7   Bill Emmott, now editor of *The Economist*, was one of the very few to buck the
trend of writing about the sources of Japanese success and power, focusing
instead on its weaknesses and internal contradictions, in a highly incisive and
prescient book, published the year of the Japanese apogee, 1989, *The Sun Also
Sets: Why Japan Will Not be Number One*. Jean-Pierre Lehmann, 'La paralysie
japonaise: causes et conséquences pour l'économie mondiale – un rôle pour
l'Europe', *Politique Etrangère*, hiver 1998/1999, assessed the Japanese malaise

from a broad range of perspectives, including the political, economic, moral, social, cultural, historical and geopolitical dimensions.

8   The works of Susan Strange that are the most relevant to the discussion in this chapter are *States and Markets*, 1988; 'States, firms and diplomacy', *International Affairs*, 68(I) (1992): 1–15; *The Retreat of the State: the Diffusion of Power in the World Economy*, 1996; and with John Stopford, *Rival States, Rival Firms: competition for world market shares*, 1991.

9   On the developments and dynamics of the Edo and Meiji eras and their legacies in the construction of contemporary Japan, see Jean-Pierre Lehmann, *The Roots of Modern Japan*, 1982.

10   'Japan and the world: Go home – 1639', *The Economist*, Millennium Special Edition, 1 January 2000.

11   See note 9.

12   This of course did not set Japan apart: World War I's alliances included a number of strange ideological bedfellows, not the least of which was Republican France with Tsarist Russia.

13   See, for example, Ivan Morris (ed.), *Japan 1931–1945: Militarism, Fascism, Japanism?*, 1967.

14   See John Dower, *Embracing Defeat*, 1999.

15   Throughout the 1980s, as Japan's trade surplus ballooned and ballooned, most of the focus of policy makers and academics was on the country's trade barriers. Dennis Encarnation, in *Rivals beyond Trade: America versus Japan in Global Competition*, 1992, was one of the first to draw attention to the much more significant fact that, more than goods being kept out of the Japanese market, it was the hostility to inward investments – in contrast to booming Japanese foreign direct investments in Western markets, the US in particular – that was responsible for creating a most unlevel playing field. See also, Jean-Pierre Lehmann, 'Japan 20: the West 1 – Reversing the Scorecard', *Business Strategy Review*, 4(2) (Summer 1993).

16   While there have been quite a number of Western critiques of the Japanese economy, most works in English by Japanese economists on the Japanese economy are more in the nature of encomiums. An important exception, and a truly excellent analysis, is that by Shigeto Tsuru, *Japan's Capitalism: Creative Defeat and Beyond*, 1992. As to the policy process and the exercise of power in Japan, see Karel van Wolferen, *The Enigma of Japanese Power*, 1989.

17   Special attention was focused on maintaining the LDP in power, including the use of secret funds doled out by the CIA to assist LDP politicians in winning elections and in living in the style to which they were fast becoming accustomed! See John Dower *Japan in War and Peace* (1993) and *Embracing Defeat* (1999) and also Walter LaFeber, *The Clash: US–Japanese Relations Throughout History*, 1997.

18   Tsuru, *Japan's Capitalism*, is especially fascinating to read on the contribution of American Occupation policy to Japan's subsequent economic development (see chapter 1, 'The defeat and the Occupation reform' and chapter 2, 'The road to recovery'); this is partly because his analysis is complemented by personal recollections, as he was involved in policy circles at the time.

19   A recent study, however, would appear to show that the Japanese government's claims about the society's egalitarianism have been somewhat exaggerated. See Douglas Ostrom, *Rich and Poor in Japan: How Wide is the Gap?*, 1999.

20   Foreign admirers through the 1960s, 1970s and 1980s, were able to witness the considerable changes that occurred. It was in the second half of the 1980s that one became critical. Having gained considerable economic victories, by the second half of the 1980s it seemed that Japan should evolve into a more responsible international citizen. It should be less self-centered. From having been

probably the greatest beneficiary of the open international economy, it was now time for Japan to become a benefactor. It was frustrating that the country seemed incapable of acting – indeed even of seeing – beyond its own very narrowly defined national interests.

21 People who argued along such lines in the United States included Clyde Prestowitz (*Trading Places*), James Fallows (*Looking at the Sun: the Rise of the New East Asian Economic and Political System*, 1994) and Laura d'Andrea Tyson (*Who's Bashing Whom? Trade Conflict in High Technology Industries*, 1992). Tyson served as President Clinton's first national economic council chairperson. A number of Europeans were also in favor of emulating the Japanese model, notably the former French Minister of Finance, Christian Sautter (see *Japon: le Prix de la Puissance*, 1973; *La France dans le Miroir Japonais*, 1996; and, with Claude Meyer, *La Puissance Financière du Japon*, 1996). Conrad Seitz, *éminence grise* of former German Foreign Minister Genscher, expressed a similar view in his publication, *Die japanisch-amerikanische Herausforderung: Deutschlands Hochtechnologie-Industrien kämpfen ums Überleben*, 1991.

22 For an analysis of postmodern society, see Robert Cooper, *The Post-Modern State and the World Order*, 1997.

23 A Japanese journalist friend commented that, when Drexel's collapsed in the late 1980s, at a time when he was serving as correspondent in New York, he was impressed by the speed with which Drexel professionals (apart from those who went to jail!) were able to move into other companies or form their own, and thereby continuously bring innovation to the marketplace. On the other hand, as he pointed out, when Yamaichi Securities collapsed, very few of the professionals had any individual skills and hence had no innovations to contribute. Eventually, they were 'taken over' *en bloc* by Merrill Lynch.

24 Strange noted that, 'In Brazil, some Japanese firms reportedly would not consider even Brazilian Japanese as foremen. They were perceived as having "gone native".' Brazilian Japanese who came to find work in Japan during the 1980s were subjected to considerable discrimination.

25 Ronnie Chan, 'The Asian myths', *Financial Times*, 24 June 1999.

26 This is not to deny that there are also acute problems of racism in Western societies from which many suffer. The situation in Japan, however, is quite *sui generis* in the degree to which foreigners, including fellow Asians, even those born in Japan, are excluded.

27 Japanese newspapers recently reported that, among Asian countries, in TOEFL (English as foreign language) tests, Japan's score was the second worst, only ahead of North Korea!

28 See note 10.

29 Shigeto Tsuru, *Japan's Capitalism*, comments on this point quite forcefully and frequently. See also Chalmers Johnson, *MITI and the Japanese Miracle: the Growth of Industrial Policy, 1925–1975*, 1982.

30 On this subject, see Masao Miyoshi, *Off Center: Power and Culture Relations between Japan and the United States*, 1991.

31 One of the most incisive and persistent critics of the Japanese economy has been Paul Krugman. Both published and non-published articles on his views, critiques and remedies for the Japanese economy can be found in his personal website, http://web.mit.edu/krugman/www/.

32 Jean-Pierre Lehmann and Dominique Turpin, 'Global Leadership: Dilemmas and Challenges for Japanese Management' (in Japanese), *Keidanren Monthly*, April 1999.

33 For an overview of transformations occurring in Japanese industry, see 'Restoration in progress – A survey of business in Japan', *The Economist*, 27 November 1999.

34   Daniel Yergin and Joseph Stanislaw, *The Commanding Heights: the Battle between Government and the Market Place that is Remaking the Modern World*, 1998.

35   In 1999, total inbound M&A amounted to $24.2 billion, a threefold increase on the previous year; foreign M&A amounted to 32 per cent of total M&A in Japan, which itself also registered a 300 per cent increase on the previous year. See Paul Abrahams, 'Foreign investors surging into Japan', *Financial Times*, 10 December 1999, and Naoko Nakamae, 'Japanese M&A activity hits high of $78bn', *Financial Times*, 30 December 1999.

36   Masao Yukawa, 'Japan's Enemy is Japan', *The Washington Quarterly* (Winter 1999): 14.

37   See, for example, Roger Buckley, 'Japan remains the sick economy of the industrialised world', *International Herald Tribune*, 28 December 1999.

38   See Peter Montagnon, 'The Future of Asia: Catching the next wave', *Financial Times*, 28 December 1999.

39   For the links between economics and security in East Asia, see Jean-Pierre Lehmann, 'Economic Interdependence and Security in the Asia–Pacific', in David Dickens (ed.), *No Better Alternative: Towards Comprehensive and Cooperative Security in the Asian Pacific*, Centre for Strategic Studies, Wellington, New Zealand, 1997 and Paul Dibb, David Hale and Peter Prince, 'Asia's Insecurity', *Survival*, 41(3) (Autumn 1999).

40   For an extremely interesting analysis of the uses of history as myth and the uses of myth as history, see Robert Gildea, *The Past in French History*, 1994. Among the studies on myths in Japanese consciousness, see Peter Dale, *The Myth of Japanese Uniqueness*, 1986.

41   The Japanese penchant for economizing with the truth can assume quite astonishing proportions. In a recent study by the OECD and the Luxembourg Income Study Group aimed at analyzing and comparing income distribution among OECD countries, the Japanese government 'refused to provide data on income distribution that would allow meaningful comparisons', presumably as these might expose the myth of Japan's egalitarian reputation. See Gillian Tett, 'A myth may mask the reality of life in Japan', *Financial Times*, 5 January 2000.

42   See Pierre Hazan, *Le Mal Suisse*, 1998.

43   When Robert Cole, a distinguished industrial sociologist and Japan specialist, published an article demonstrating that Japanese automotive and automotive parts companies in the United States were actively practising anti-black discriminatory recruitment policies, he was violently attacked by many Japanese, including not only those in the companies themselves, but also by the media and by academics. He was told that, even if what he wrote was true, as a 'friend of Japan' he should have refrained from bringing this matter to light – that is, from telling the truth! See Robert Cole and Donald Deskins, 'Racial Factors in Site Location and Employment Patterns of Japanese Auto Firms in America', *California Management Review*, 31(1) (Fall 1988).

44   The current state of affairs is ludicrous. As John Dower (*Japan in War and Peace*, p.352) laments, 'even after Japan's surrender, the mystique of the unbroken imperial line has prevented the Japanese from doing serious archaeological research on their own ancient past. ... This is a delicate matter indeed, for what is at issue here are the great tumuli that date from around the fourth century and have remained unexcavated to the present day. ... Although recent scholarship suggests that the earliest and largest tombs may belong to a different royal lineage that preceded the current imperial family, this is too heretical for most Japanese antiquarians to contemplate. Thus, the hundreds of ancient tumuli designated as belonging to the present imperial family remain closed.'

45   On Japanese aid policy, see Bruce Koppel and Robert Orr (eds), *Japan's Foreign Aid: Power and Policy in the New Era*, 1993.

46   The problem of English in Japan is by no means one that only Westerners complain about. English is the *lingua franca* also in Asia and, for example, the official language of ASEAN. Japanese inability to communicate in English is an impediment to closer relations and more direct communication with 'fellow Asians'.

47   See, for example, the works of Edward J. Lincoln: *Japan's Unequal Trade*, 1990; *Japan's New Global Role*, 1994; *Troubled Times: US–Japan Trade Relations in the 1990s*, 1999.

References

Bergamini, D. (1971), *Japan's Imperial Conspiracy*, London: Heinemann.

Cole, R. and D. Deskins (1988), 'Racial Factors in Site Location and Employment Patterns of Japanese Auto Firms in America', *California Management Review*, 31(1), Fall.

Cooper, R. (1997), *The Post-Modern State and the World Order*, London: Demos.

Dale, P. (1986), *The Myth of Japanese Uniqueness*, London: Croom Helm.

D'Andrea Tyson, L. (1992), *Who's Bashing Whom? Trade Conflict in High Technology Industries*, Washington D.C.: Institute for International Economics.

Dibb, P., D. Hale and P. Prince (1999), 'Asia's Insecurity', *Survival*, 41(3), Autumn.

Dower, J. (1993), *Japan in War and Peace: Essays on History, Culture and Race*, New York: New Press.

Dower, J. (1999) (ed.), *Embracing Defeat: Japan in the Wake of World War Two*, New York: W.W. Norton.

Emmott, B. (1989), *The Sun Also Sets: Why Japan Will Not be Number One*, London: Simon and Schuster.

Encarnation, D.J. (1992), *Rivals Beyond Trade: America versus Japan in Global Competition*, Ithaca: Cornell University Press.

Fallows, J. (1994), *Looking at the Sun: the Rise of the New East Asian Economic and Political System*, New York: Pantheon Books.

Gildea, R. (1994), *The Past in French History*, New Haven: Yale University Press.

Hazan, P. (1998), *Le Mal Suisse*, Paris: Stock.

Johnson, C. (1982), *MITI and the Japanese Miracle: the Growth of Industrial Policy, 1925–1975*, Stanford: Stanford University Press.

Kahn, H. (1972), *Japan: the Emergence of an Economic Superpower*, London: Penguin.

Koppel, B. and R. Orr (1993) (eds), *Japan's Foreign Aid: Power and Policy in a New Era*, Boulder: Westview Press.

LaFeber, W. (1997), *The Clash: US-Japanese Relations Throughout History*, New York: W.W. Norton.

Lehmann, J.P. (1982), *The Roots of Modern Japan*, London: Macmillan.

Lehmann, J.P. (1993), 'Japan 20: the West 1 – Reversing the Scorecard', *Business Strategy Review*, 4(2), Summer.

Lehmann, J.P. (1997), 'Economic Interdependence and Security in the Asia-Pacific', in D. Dickens (ed.), *No Better Alternative: Towards Comprehensive and Cooperative Security in the Asian Pacific*, Wellington, New Zealand: Centre for Strategic Studies.

Lehmann, J.P. (1998–9), 'La paralysie japonaise: causes et conséquences pour l'économie mondiale – un rôle pour l'Europe', *Politique Etangère*, Hiver.

Lehmann, J.P. and D. Turpin (1999), 'Global Leadership: Dilemmas and Challenges for Japanese Management' (in Japanese), *Keidanren Monthly*, April.

Lincoln, E.J. (1990), *Japan's Unequal Trade*, Washington D.C.: The Brookings Institution.

Lincoln, E.J. (1994), *Japan's New Global Role*, Washington D.C.: The Brookings Institution.

Lincoln, E.J. (1999), *Troubled Times: US-Japan Trade Relations in the 1990s*, Washington D.C.: Brookings Institution.

Miyoshi, M. (1991), *Off Center: Power and Culture Relations between Japan and the United States*, Cambridge, MA.: Harvard University Press.

Morris, I. (1967) (ed.), *Japan 1931–1945: Militarism, Fascism, Japanism?*, Boston: D.C. Heath & Co.

Ostrom, D. (1999), *Rich and Poor in Japan: How Wide is the Gap?*, Washington D.C.: Japan Economic Institute.

Prestowitz, C. (1988), *Trading Places: How America Allowed Japan to Take the Lead*, New York: Basic Books.

Sautter, C. (1973), *Japon: le Prix de la Puissance*, Paris: Le Seuil.

Sautter, C. (1996), *La France au Miroir du Japon: croissance ou declin*, Paris: Editions O. Jacob.

Sautter, C. and C. Meyer (1996), *La Puissance Financieère du Japon*, Paris: Plon.

Seitz, C. (1991), *Die japanisch-amerikanische Herausforderung: Deutschlands Hochtechnologie-Industrien kämpfen ums Überleben*, Bonn: Aktueil.

Shillony, B.A. (1973), *Revolt in Japan: The Young Officers and the February 26, 1936 Incident*, Princeton, N.J.: Princeton University Press.

Shillony, B.A. (1981), *Politics and Culture in Wartime Japan*, Oxford: Clarendon.

Stopford, J. and S. Strange (1991), *Rival States, Rival Firms: Competition for World Market Shares*, Cambridge: Cambridge University Press.

Strange, S. (1988), *States and Markets*, London: Pinter Publishers.

Strange, S. (1992), 'States, firms and diplomacy', *International Affairs*, 68(1), 1–15.

Strange, S. (1995), 'European Business in Japan. A Policy Cross-roads?', *Journal of Common Market Studies*, 33(1): 1–25.

Strange, S. (1996), *The Retreat of the State. The Diffusion of Power in the World Economy*, Cambridge: Cambridge University Press.

Tsuru, S. (1992), *Japan's Capitalism: Creative Defeat and Beyond*, New York: Cambridge University Press.

Van Wolferen, K. (1989), *The Enigma of Japanese Power*, London: Macmillan.

Vogel, E. (1979), *Japan as Number One: Lessons for America*, Cambridge, MA.: Harvard University Press.

Yergin, D. and J. Stanislaw (1998), *The Commanding Heights: the Battle between Government and the Market Place that is Remaking the Modern World*, New York: Simon & Schuster.

Yukawa, M. (1999), 'Japan's Enemy is Japan', *The Washington Quarterly*, Winter.

17 Regional Blocks and International Relations: Economic Groupings or Political Hegemons?

ALFRED TOVIAS

Introduction

Several years ago this author predicted that the success of the Uruguay Round would not mean that the move towards the consolidation of trading blocks would be stopped, only that the move would be slower. A scenario of confrontation would rapidly develop if any of the two existing or potential trading blocks (the EC/EEA and the US/NAFTA[1]) should, first, lose interest in the multilateral process of negotiation; second, become an entity which systematically excludes would-be candidates from joining in new initiatives; third, maintain or increase the average level of protection against non-members; fourth, resort to bilateral reciprocity for the granting of trade concessions; fifth, impose unilaterally retaliatory measures and resort to threats; or sixth, discriminate against foreign producers within the block.

Unfortunately, conditions four and five materialized in the late 1990s and clearly the fiasco of the Seattle meeting of November–December 1999, which was to launch a new round of multilateral trade negotiations (MTN), called the Millennium Round, signifies a loss of interest in multilateral negotiations.[2] Not surprisingly, the Seattle flop has led many countries to look for regional alternatives, once again. It is very revealing that Japan, which until Seattle had always rejected the bilateral discriminatory route to trade liberalization, is for the first time seriously considering the possibility of negotiating free trade agreements (FTAs) with Singapore, South Korea and Mexico.[3] It can be expected as well that the United States will

pursue the idea of extending NAFTA to all of the western hemisphere with greater vigor.[4]

The end of the cold war might have something to do with the
present state of affairs. The end of the bipolar ideological struggle
has allowed governments to shift their attention to the economic
dimension of international relations. Trade policy issues have replaced 'high foreign policy' issues on the diplomats' agendas. Foreign
ministers, who in the past might have been happy to leave these
issues to their colleagues presiding over Ministries of Trade, remind
everybody that trade policy is foreign policy. The depoliticization of
trade policy, an outcome of the creation of the GATT (General Agreement on Tariffs and Trade) and the adoption of the unconditional
version of the most–favored–nation principle after World War II,
seems to have come to an end.

Or was there a depoliticization at all? Strange would have said no
– a position shared in this chapter. In an unpublished paper written
in 1990,[5] she argued that politics and political institutions had always determined the character of trade policies and the choice of
trade partners, and that politics would continue to have a big influence on both the content of trade and the direction of trade flows.
She gave as typical illustrations of what she meant in the post-1945
trade order the examples of East–West and of French–African trade
patterns. Moreover, she argued that the EC was a political entity.
Regarding the early EC trade deals with Central and Eastern Europe
after 1988, they were more guided by emotions than by economic
considerations, a translation of the relief felt by the fall of the Berlin
wall.

In the same vein, it is well accepted among Europeanists that the
EC never followed the doctrine of separating trade from politics,
since that would have implied neutralizing its main foreign policy
instrument (and until recently its sole one) and its primary means of
influencing events in the world. The United States, the world's other
economic superpower, refused to enter into bilateral deals until the
early 1980s. Then, for different economic and strategic reasons, it
decided to negotiate a free trade agreement with Israel, signed in
1985. This first departure of the United States from the previous
doctrine of strictly adhering to multilateralism would become a precedent for other preferential deals. Numerous reasons existed to push
the United States in that direction. One was 'EC-1992', plans put
forward by the EC Commission in 1985 to complete the EC's Internal
Market by December 1992. By 1988, everybody in Washington was
speaking about 'Fortress Europe'. It is commonly accepted that one
of the US responses was to sign an FTA with Canada in 1989. At the
same time, the Uruguay Round negotiations that had started in 1986
were stalling and the US government thought that the regional av-

enue could offer the possibility of cutting deals with 'like-minded' countries on GATT-plus issues (investment regimes, environmental and labor standards), something unthinkable at the time at the multi-lateral level.[6]

This chapter will analyze whether the move towards exclusive trade deals, that is, discriminatory trade agreements between sovereign states mostly on a regional basis, can be interpreted as a move either towards 'benign regionalism' understood here as the consolidation of natural economically grounded groupings, or rather towards 'aggressive regionalism', defined here as the creation of continental trading blocks led by regional hegemons with the explicit or implicit aim of increasing bargaining power vis-à-vis the rest of the world. The existing literature on IPE is a very poor guide in this respect. A survey made for this chapter shows that there is no clear definition of what a trade block is, nor indication of which trade blocks exist at present. Spero identifies the EC as the world's largest trading block, and then compares it with the United States or Japan, which are themselves considered as trading blocks (1992: 77). The same applies to Frieden and Lake (1991: 367). Both studies fail to identify preferential trade agreements between the EC and non-member countries as creating a larger trading block of which the EC would be the block's hub. The 1988 US–Canada free trade agreement is described as a reinforcement of the multilateral regime and a model for future GATT agreements on investment and services, although potentially a departure from the US post-war policy of multilateralism in international trade (Spero 1992: 85). On the other hand, Gilpin refers both to the EC and the US trade agreements with countries in their own peripheries as emerging regional blocs (1987: 397). Over the last three decades, well established IPE scholars (for example, Gilpin 1987; Krasner 1976), have predicted at different points in time that the erosion of US hegemony tended to give rise to protectionist economic blocs, but the available evidence is ambiguous to say the least, according to Mansfield and Milner (1997: 10).

This move towards trading blocks was again predicted in anticipation of the failure of the Uruguay Round (Spero 1992) . The common feature in all these studies is that none of them bothers to define the concept. Others do not refer to trading blocks at all, but to 'bilateralism' as a way to overcome the problem of 'free riding' inherent to the GATT-based post-1945 trade regime based on the unconditional form of the most-favored-nation clause. Keohane speaks of 'cooperative protectionism', instead of using the term 'bilateralism' (1984: 38).

Strange (1991) also asked the question of whether trading blocks were actually emerging in the early 1990s. She was clearly very skeptical. She argued that multinational corporations and more generally international firms were not interested in the establishment of trading blocks and therefore would not push states in that direction and let them use discriminatory commercial policy for political ends, something that could ruin business. She argued as well that the only real regional economic blocks are those based on particular monetary regimes, allowing for exchange controls and ultimately the possibility of declaring the currency used in the region inconvertible. That had been the case in the past for the sterling area. She recognized that the financial structure that ties a colonial currency to an imperial one and that unites its banking system to that of a dominant country could exert a powerful influence on trade flows (Strange 1988: 170), but trading blocks *per se*, not linked to currency union or currency boards, could not emerge because on balance internationally minded firms would oppose their formation and, after all, she always reminded us, it is firms that trade, not states.

After this survey of the IPE literature, one has the clear feeling that much remains to be done to clarify once and for all the nature and purpose of regionalism and of regional trading blocks and to set them apart from other creatures. Strange's question remains: are trading blocks virtual or for real? Thus this chapter is organized in the following way. The second and third sections deal with the question of whether the regionalization of world trade is a reality and examine the distinction to be made between the regionalization of world trade and regionalism in trade. We also study the concept of 're- gional trading blocks'. Particular attention is devoted in the fourth section to the issue of relative economic size of the partners, in particular the situation of smaller countries in a regional trading block. The chapter goes on in the fifth section to show that there are large differences between customs unions (CUs) and free trade areas (FTAs) in terms of their potential influence on international (economic) relations. Following this analysis, the question arises in the sixth section as to which regional trading blocks exist, if any. We proceed from there in the seventh section to illustrate how the concept of open regionalism espoused by the United States is at odds with the concept of trading blocks. Finally, the chapter looks into the scant empirical evidence that trading blocks are emerging and becoming actors in international affairs.

The Regionalization of World Trade

Kol (1995) makes a useful distinction between block formation which refers to regionalism among countries that are members of a *formal* agreement on free trade and further economic integration and regionalization which relates to the relative concentration of trade among countries bound not by a formal agreement but by informal cohesion such as geographical proximity. The latter has been called by Krugman (1991) a 'natural trading block'. It is a structural feature. In other words, much of existing bilateral trade among countries is linked to a series of proximity or neighborhood factors such as geographic distance, cultural links, common language, similarity of tastes, standards of living, ways of life (consumption patterns) or political systems. Modern trade theories since Linder (1961) have emphasized these factors, as opposed to the neoclassical trade model that emphasized relative factor endowments (for example, capital/labor ratios, land/labor ratios). Linked to the existence of many economies of scale to be reaped in modern industrial production, this gives rise to intra-industry trade and to trade in heterogeneous products. Models linking geography and trade offer new explanations for the concentration of economic activity, such as proximity to inputs, localized pecuniary and non-pecuniary externalities and market size effects in scale-sensitive industries. From this analysis, some commentators arrive at the conclusion that clusters will only develop in the center (the largest and more diversified country or countries). However, others show offsetting forces benefitting the peripheries such as lower trade costs, search for improved market access, proximity to certain specific inputs and sometimes redistribution policies in different forms (such as military aid). We should observe that this can exist in parallel to and independent of the existence of formal trade agreements. In other words, there can be regionalization without regionalism or trading blocks and vice versa (see later).

That there is a tendency towards the regionalization of international trade in large areas of the world does not seem to be much in dispute among the experts. Freudenberg *et al.* (1998) have calculated relative trade intensity indexes for almost every country in the world, showing empirically that countries trade more intensively with others in their own region, although this is not a universal phenomenon.[7] We observe it in the Euro-African region in particular and somewhat in the western hemisphere, but much less so in Asia. An exception to the rule are petroleum-producing countries.

The evidence would therefore indicate that the much heralded 'death of distance' has not yet had a significant impact on trade patterns. If we look over the period 1980–94, relative trade intensities indexes have been increasing in the case of Europe, increasing but at a slower pace in the western hemisphere and decreasing in Asia. Other experts say that regionalization as such has been accompanied in Asia by a general opening of national economies. This would tend to obscure the 'natural' regional tendencies for Asia as well.

When seeking the long-term reasons for regionalization, it appears that the conclusion of regional trade agreements is only one of many factors explaining regionalization and in fact the correlation can only be clearly traced in the case of the EC and possibly in the case of the EC–EFTA (European Free Trade Association) 1972 agreements. On the other hand, as Ethier (1997) observes, a less known, less obvious fact is non-discriminatory trade liberalization, which makes geographic distance more important relative to trade barriers over time. This might therefore be expected to cause a country's trade pattern to become more regional. Therefore regionalization might be at least in part a direct result of the success of multilateral liberalization engineered through the GATT!

Regionalism in Trade and Regional Trading Blocks

Before speaking about regional trading blocks, we will first define regionalism in trade as the idea that countries *should* preferentially promote trade with countries of the same region rather than with any other country in the world. This is done for a variety of reasons, including political, cultural, defensive and, last but not least, economic.[8]

If the reason is economic, it is normally to maximize – beyond what occurs spontaneously (namely the regionalization) – the benefits from trade and specialization. Governments can help engineer this process by concluding 'negative integration agreements',[9] which we would relabel 'barrier-smashing' agreements. These aim at facilitating trade among countries of the same region and would include the agreement to construct a bridge between Denmark and Sweden and the construction of the Eurotunnel between Britain and France. However, economists have long since shown that these agreements can end up diminishing the welfare of the countries involved because of the existence of trade diversion. Second, it is also clear that these regional agreements are not signed with the aim of improving the economic lot of countries outside the region. If the countries involved in the agreement have sufficient weight in world trade, the trade diversion will lead to an improvement of the terms of trade of the signatories of the discriminatory trade agreement vis-à-vis non-members.

The non-economic reasons for trade regionalism include, first, to gain privileged access to strategic resources (such as energy); second, to artificially develop the dependence of other countries of the region on your own markets or own resources; and third, security and other political motives (such as the political stabilization or the democratization of the partner).

To sum up, regionalism in trade is defined here as a political movement towards the creation or expansion of preferential regional trade agreements, that is, regionalism is inherently preferential. Therefore the concept much in fashion nowadays of 'open regionalism' (see later) should never be used if by that one refers to the creation of non-preferential trade agreements, as it is then a contradiction in terms.

The creation of a regional trading block goes well beyond the conclusion of regional preferential trade agreements to attain objectives such as those indicated above. Here there is an additional objective, namely to actively influence international trade relations with non-members and, more generally, international relations. Note that there is no pejorative connotation ascribed to the term. It does not describe a protectionistic or egocentric group of states. It is value-neutral. As indicated above, negative integration agreements can have positive terms-of-trade effects for the members, but they are unintended. In order to manipulate the terms of trade with non-members or to be able to extract other economic or non-economic concessions, members must first unify or coordinate their foreign economic policies and instruments. This is why CUs are seen as obvious trading blocks, provided they have enough muscle at the international level. Here relative economic size vis-à-vis non-members plays a role. It might be that the creation of the CU does not have terms-of-trade effects because the creation of a larger unit does not detract from the fact that the latter continues to be small compared to other rival trading units. The CU between Switzerland and Liechtenstein does not help both countries to improve their terms of trade vis-à-vis non-member countries. On the other hand, the original six members of the EC could expect that joining in a CU would make a difference, in terms of the higher leverage achieved in MTNs, for example.

So the idea here is that the creation of regional trading blocks may allow countries to achieve extraregional objectives that they could not attain on their own. Theoreticians stress that, to reap the benefits of the enlarged leverage obtained through union, trading blocks should be more protective than their individual members: that is, all things being equal. The block may conduct a strategic trade policy, whereas the individual member of the club may not. Of course the outcome of the block's moves depends on who it has facing it. If it is another block of similar size, the final outcome of the strategic game may be unpredictable, because of the risks of retaliation. But if 'the other' is not a block but a small country, then the outcome of a trade war seems clear-cut. The worst-case scenario for the small country of course is if the different trading blocks conspire against it (in the military domain this corresponds to the situation of Poland in 1939). This is what countries like Korea and Taiwan seem to fear since the creation of both the EEA and NAFTA. Let us now turn to the situation in small countries.

Small Countries and Regional Trading Blocks

Regional integration agreements (RIAs), as they are called now, have been in fashion since the early 1990s because theoreticians have proved fairly recently and quite explicitly that in most cases they are likely to improve the economic welfare of member countries. Not only inter-industry specialization but also intra-industry specialization is likely to happen on a wider scale if agreements are reached on a regional basis. Also there will be a better exploitation of national and international scale economies.

Many experts argue that, for small countries that neighbor an advanced developed economic powerhouse (such as the EU or the United States), these agreements help strengthen domestic policy reform, give a sense of security to the population and insure that market access to the large market of the neighbor will never be at risk. Whalley and Perroni (1999) insist on this insurance argument: countries have more confidence nowadays in an FTA commitment than in an MFN commitment in the case of a global trade war. This implies that, in such a case, members of an FTA or a CU would exempt each other from retaliation. They make the point that this is a valuable concession by a large country (such as the United States). Not surprisingly, they come to the conclusion that the economically smaller countries (like Canada) will have to offer side-payments to the regional hegemon in the form of non-trade concessions. They show, for instance, that, in a global trade war with no RIAs[10] and with everyone setting its optimal tariff, the EU would set tariffs in the range of 900 to 1000 per cent and the United States would settle around 500 per cent, the difference reflecting a different degree of openness between the two economies. Mexico, Canada or Japan, with less retaliatory power, would impose lesser tariffs. This illustrates the point that these agreements are shaped more by the small countries as an insurance against retaliation in a trade war than to gain new concessions. The authors also make the obvious point that the United States would be better off with a CU instead of an FTA because US tariffs are higher than Canada's for instance; therefore Canada would have to join in the retaliatory efforts of the United States by raising protection much beyond its current levels with an FTA-type agreement. They make the final point that the value of RIAs to large countries rises as the risk of global trade conflicts rises, since large countries can extract increasingly larger insurance premia from the smaller parties joining in the discriminatory scheme.

What seems clear is that small countries in RIAs tend to gain even more than the larger ones (in economic terms). Moreover, staying outside any discriminatory arrangement places the small state in the underdog position, with the danger of one or several trading entities conspiring against it. This is why economists traditionally insist(ed) that most-favored-nation treatment (that is, non-discrimination) is the best international regime for small countries. In a world of large regional trading blocks with no MFN treatment, there is no question that small trading countries would have to enter into one block (no matter which) rather than remain non-aligned. Of course, if allowed, small countries should try to enter more than one block. However, there may be limits to such a strategy. For a small country, the basic issues are, first, whether new or existing blocks remain relatively open or not; second, whether they are open to new membership or at least associate membership, even to countries which do not belong to the region; and third, whether membership in one club does not preclude simultaneously joining other clubs. For example, it is not clear if membership in the European Economic Area (EEA) is compatible with participation in NAFTA because, to some extent, EEA regulations are of a supranational character. For instance, Brussels decides on large mergers involving the non-EC members of the EEA, such as Norway.

If emerging blocks remain fairly open, there is not much point in entering a specific block. If one of them is inward-looking while others are not, it is an open question as to whether the small country would gain more by trying to enter the inward-looking block than by not entering. Unless the inward-looking block has a lot of leverage on the rest of the world, including on the other blocks, entering may not only lead to losses from trade diversion, but also put in jeopardy access to the other blocks.

Of course there is a price to pay for belonging to a specific trade block. First, there is the inherent cost of trade diversion in favor of the preferred trade partner. That includes of course an economic cost, because third-country imports are replaced by more expensive imports from the preferred partner. There is a political cost, because you not only discriminate 'in favor of some country' but by definition also 'against other countries'. Apart from the cost of trade diversion, an additional disadvantage of being in a block for a small country is that exporters do not try to adjust to world standards but rather to the block standards. This is what happened to Australia in the 1950s and 1960s, with very bad results. The same applies to Eastern European members of the ex-COMECON. Thus, if allowed, small countries should try to enter or to be closely associated with more than one block.

As far as the large country or regional hegemon is concerned, its gains can only stem from a few sources (Tovias 1978: 256). These are, first, political influence gained through the artificial increase of foreign trade with smaller satellite countries in its periphery; second, terms-of-trade gains through optimal discrimination against non-members;[11] and third, more influence over multilateral trade negotiations in the international arena.

Customs Unions versus Free Trade Areas

In some sense, customs unions are 'FTA-plus'. They seem to add 'barrier-smashing agreements' (see above) and the unification of tariff rates. But in fact they go much beyond that, with large political implications. First, it is not the unification of tariff rates that is important but rather the unification of tariff policies. The creation of a CU implies the partial unification of trade policies, since tariffs still play a central role in the latter. Second, members of a CU must agree on what to do with tariff revenues cashed at the border of the union: either redistribute or create a common purse. If the latter, then members will have to decide jointly what to do with the revenue: there is a common budget to manage. Third, no rules of origin are needed, since the tariff to be applied on a given product at any of the entry points to the CU is the same and thus there is no reason for any private agent to import the product through an entry point where the tariff applied is lowest, as could be the case in a free trade area. To prevent this from happening (something called in the jargon 'trade deflection'), the partners to a free trade area have to introduce rules of origin in their bilateral trade.

In contrast, an FTA only requires the unification of policies regarding the definition and cumulation of origin. There is no common tariff, therefore there is no common commercial policy. Free trade areas are not the same as free trade. They do not even guarantee the duty-free passage of all goods from one partner country to the other. Therefore, tariff borders among member countries must not only be maintained: they are actually reinforced by new non-tariff barriers (NTBs), namely certificates of origin.

Both CUs and FTAs lead to trade creation and trade diversion. If trade diversion is substantial, it might influence world prices of goods imported by the partners (see above). Observe that, both in a CU and in an FTA, each member country can veto the enlargement of the agreement to new members. In general, the member countries lose their freedom of action in both cases regarding the agreement itself, which contains binding obligations.

All things being equal, FTAs tend to be less trade-diverting than CUs, because low-country tariffs do not raise their external tariff on non-members after the FTA is created. In the specific case of FTAs, a shifting effect discovered by Shibata (1967) takes place, which means net trade diversion is likely to be less damaging for the group as a whole than in a CU, after provision is made for capacity expansion in the low-tariff country.[12] Dynamic effects are also less dramatic. For instance, investment diversion is likely to be less marked. On the whole, then, third countries should, all other things being equal, be less offended or made anxious by the creation of an FTA than by the creation of a CU.

Regarding trade policy, the members of a CU negotiate their common tariff as a block in international trade negotiations, unlike the case in an FTA. However, FTA members tend to shadow their positions, as for example EFTA did during the Kennedy and Tokyo Rounds of the GATT. Let us take tariffs on inputs and intermediary products as an example. They affect the prices of final products produced by member states and sold in other member states. Assume Sweden and Finland have an FTA agreement. If Sweden reduced the tariff on imported leather, Finland would have to consider doing the same. Also if, as a result of MTNs, the gap between the members' tariffs vis-à-vis non members increases by much (because the low-tariff country has diminished its own tariffs), the high-tariff country will see shifting effects increase, trade diversion increase and welfare diminish. Also the larger the gap, the greater the temptation to smugglers to deflect trade. The high-tariff country will subsequently be forced to diminish its own tariffs as well. Thus, although bargaining power in MTNs is clearly greater for CUs than for FTAs, it so happens that FTA members are obliged to harmonize their positions somewhat. Although this appears to constrain them, it actually gives them the possibility to raise their individual bargaining power vis-à-vis non-members and therefore improve their terms of trade in trade with non-members. In another realm, common rules of origin can be modified and manipulated in such a way as to improve the terms of trade or attract investment to the FTA artificially (Cooper 1999: 231–2).

In bilateral trade policy, FTA partners keep their entire freedom to negotiate their own deals with particular countries of interest to them but not to other member countries. They also remain free to cut the tariff on a unilateral basis, unlike the situation in CUs. Here the example of Israel is revealing. The FTAs signed by Israel with the EC, the United States and EFTA led in the 1980s to so much trade diversion against the rest of the world (mainly Asian-originating imports), with huge real costs to the Israeli economy, that the Israeli government decided to implement drastic unilateral tariff cuts over the period 1991 to 2000. Another important but separate point: even if one of the partners to the FTA is a hegemon, international trade law as embodied in the WTO does not allow the latter to impose its trade policy on the smaller members of the FTA. This is of course not the case in an asymmetrical customs union, where the small member must in fact adjust to the trade policy of the large member. For instance, in the Treaty creating the 1996 customs union between the EC and Turkey, there is no legal obligation imposed on the European Commission – when negotiating a new trade agreement with a third country – to even consult Turkey.[13]

Which Regional Trade Blocks Exist?

The European Community

Here we have an entity that goes well beyond a CU. Commercial policy regarding imports of products is decided on a supranational basis, with practically no role left to the individual governments. This refers to the important (former) Article 113, already included in the 1957 Treaty of Rome (which has become Article 133 in the new treaties) and providing for such a common policy after the transitional period for the creation of a CU (which was in place by July 1968). Regarding trade in services, according to a ruling by the European Court of Justice in 1994, both individual member countries and EC institutions have joint responsibility. The latter have acknowledged the exclusive competence of the Community regarding the cross-border direct supply of services (analogous to trade in goods) but not for the other modes of supply such as consumption abroad, commercial presence and the presence of natural persons. In some cases, member states have been particularly reluctant to give the Commission any role whatsoever, for example in negotiation of aviation agreements with third countries such as the United States. Export policies are not yet totally unified, for example in the domain of export controls and arms exports. Since January 1999, 11 of the 15 member states have created an Economic and Monetary Union (EMU). This means that one of the most important non-tariff barriers in their mutual trade, namely the exchange rate, has been eliminated. This should increase trade interdependence among them even more and therefore increase the cohesion of this subgroup of 11 countries. The exchange rate of the euro can in theory become an instrument of the EMU's trade policy in the future. Observe that exchange rate policy is to be determined by the 11 governments, not by the European Central Bank or by the European Commission.

The EC can be characterized, by and large, as a regional trade block, both benign and aggressive. It is benign if we take into account that, after each enlargement, it has not increased overall protection against outsiders, as theory predicted should happen. Neither has the completion of the Single Market led to Fortress Europe. But the Community sometimes has behaved aggressively when using trade sanctions to modify policies of targeted countries such as

South Africa, Libya or Israel. Its weight in international trade is so colossal that nobody can ignore it. Moreover, it is also an important actor in global trade relations, with a full-fledged unified import policy on almost any item and quite a unified export policy. This allows the EC to negotiate in MTNs or bilaterally to conclude trade agreements or impose trade sanctions; in other words, to use carrots and sticks in relations with third countries. It is interesting, however, to note that, for the moment at least, exchange rate policy is not fully unified at the EC level: some EC members remain outside the monetary union, and therefore cannot as such be used by the EC in the conduct of its foreign policies, since it is not responsible for exchange rate policy. Only the political representatives of the 11 participating states can use foreign exchange rate policy as an instrument of foreign policy.

The European Economic Area (EEA)

The EEA includes the 15 EC members, plus Iceland, Liechtenstein and Norway. It creates a single market for goods, services, capital and labor among EEA members. It is a multilateral, not a bilateral, agreement between the EC and the other three countries. Could one speak of the EEA as a trading block? One might be tempted to answer negatively. To begin with, there are no elements of a common trade policy. There is not even a Common Customs Tariff for the member countries and in theory Norway, for instance, is free to conclude FTA agreements with any non-EEA member country. However, as explained above, the latter must shadow the EC's trade policies, not only regarding tariffs but also regarding NTBs – or at least take them into account when adopting a position. This includes not only trade in goods but also trade in services. Insofar as a change in the EC's trade policy is frequently a result of the deepening of the Single Market (for example, in the domain of health or environmental standards), the non-EC members of the EEA have some influence through their participation in the decision shaping, if not in the decision making (for instance, in the domain of hormone-fed beef). Curzon (1997: 199) states emphatically that EFTA countries in the EEA would not be free to negotiate on services or capital movements with third countries. Concerning the negotiation of mutual recognition agreements with third countries of certification and tests, the EEA Treaty states clearly that EFTA countries must conform to the format used by the EC in previous negotiations with third countries. In a trade war between the EC and the United States, Norway would almost certainly align itself with the EC, but this would put Norway in an unenviable position. Yet the EC cannot automatically count on the backing of Norway in WTO negotiations or when its DSM (dispute-settlement mechanism) is invoked or activated by a non EEA-member country, such as the United States. For instance, in the banana dispute, Norway could remain aloof and of course was not one of the countries the United States retaliated against. To illustrate this point further, it appears that Norway will probably align itself with the United States and against the EC on fishing issues when raised in future multilateral trade negotiations.

The Customs Unions between the EC and Turkey, Malta and Cyprus

Cyprus, Malta and Turkey have a CU with the EC, and thus are already part of the EC trade block. They have transferred tariff setting to Brussels, as well as the possibility of cutting preferential trade deals with non member countries. According to Pelkmans and Brenton (1999), Turkey already applies the EC's regulations on rules for imports, for administering quotas, against dumping and concerning new trade remedies (1999: 98). It has also negotiated MFA-type arrangements with the main clothing suppliers of the EC. By 2001, Turkey must have adopted the EC agreements with all Mediterranean non-member countries and adopt the EC's Generalized System of Preferences scheme benefitting developing countries. Intellectual property and competition policies must conform to the EC's *acquis communautaire*. At least in theory, Cyprus, Malta and Turkey should be consulted by the Commission when the latter intends to devise a particular trade policy in the WTO or a new trade policy relative to particular countries or group of countries (for example Mediterranean countries, Russia or Ukraine) . However, as distinct from the EEA case, there is no mention in the respective CU agreements that the three CU partners of the EC will participate in the decision shaping regarding these issues.

The EC and Bilateral FTAs with CEEC and Mediterranean Countries

One might ask whether the hub-and-spoke structure put in place in the 1990s by the EC and its two peripheries amounts to the creation of a new trading block at the world level. In other words, is the EC's bargaining power in MTN at the WTO increased by this structure relative to the United States and Japan? The answer is ambiguous. On the affirmative side, it might be said that those spokes which are going to become member countries of the EC in the future and are therefore going to adopt the EC's *acquis communautaire* in external relations in a matter of years, are de facto members of the EC trade block. For instance, Hungary, an important agricultural exporter and until 1999 a member of the Cairns Group, has had to withdraw from this club at the request of the EC. This will increase the relative leverage of the EC in agricultural negotiations in the context of the WTO.

On the other hand, all the other spokes can theoretically cut their own deals with non-member countries and form new free trade areas either with countries that are on the EC's periphery (the other spokes) or with other hubs. This is what Israel has been practicing, for instance. Members of the Euro-Mediterranean Partnership are therefore not part of the EC's trading block in the sense of a strategic trade alliance. It should be stressed that the concept of 'partnership' was invented by the EC, precisely to make a distinction from actual 'membership'. Therefore the EC should not count on them in case of need.

The North American Free Agreement (NAFTA)[14]

Is NAFTA a trade block and was it ever intended to be a trading block? No but perhaps yes in some respects. NAFTA is a FTA between three countries, therefore not a hub-and-spoke deal. Each of the three members can maintain in principle its independent trade policy vis-à-vis non-members. There is no strategic trade alliance between NAFTA members. None of the three members has ever mentioned the possibility of upgrading NAFTA into a NACU (North American Customs Union). Structurally, however, NAFTA is dominated by a hegemonic partner, the United States, in the sense that, and conforming with what was said in our theoretical discussion, Canada and Mexico must pay close attention to US trade policies vis-à-vis non-members. But the United States cannot impose its ideas on the two smaller partners. An example of this would be if NAFTA were enlarged to incorporate other states, whether they are in the western hemisphere or not. The United States must, as any other member, use the dispute settlement procedures in the agreement should a conflict arise with the other two members, thus renouncing unilateral action. The United States frequently stresses that NAFTA is an example of open regionalism, which, as explained below, is at odds with the concept of regional trading blocks. More generally, the concept of market-driven regionalism that is so desirable in the United States seems at odds with the concept of trading blocks as being active in international affairs. Moreover, the lack of legal personality of NAFTA implies that it has no voice in the WTO – a clear difference from the EC situation. In some respects, one may consider NAFTA to be a regional trade block. For instance, given NAFTA's size, any agreed change between the parties regarding the definition and cumulation of rules of origin can influence the three countries' bargaining power in MTNs. The same goes for changes in the domestic content rules of the investment part of the agreement. It is important to note that NAFTA is a comprehensive trade and

investment agreement, extending to agriculture, industry and services. Again, in a trade war between the United States and the EU, it
seems that Canada and Mexico could not remain neutral, unless they
had previously cut their own free trade deals with the EC.[15] A trade
conflict opposing the United States and developing countries would
probably place Mexico in a difficult position. In such a case, the
United States could probably not count on Mexico's support.

MERCOSUR

The customs union to be formed by Argentina, Brazil, Paraguay and
Uruguay has some of the features of a regional trade block. It does not
contemplate that member countries will pool fiscal revenue derived
from the Common Customs Tariff or that there will be a Common
Commercial Policy. The move towards the establishment of the CU
started in 1995. However, at the time of writing, the Common Customs
Tariff is still not in place and the press has reported many delays and
backtracking in the programme for the dismantling of trade barriers
among member states. This is mainly an outcome of the financial crisis
and devaluation of the Brazilian currency, which has led to a massive
Argentinian bilateral deficit. This has made life difficult for the Argentinian authorities and led to strain in relations with Brazil. In any case,
it is unlikely that the potential buying power of the block is such as to
have much influence on the terms of trade of MERCOSUR. However,
the fact that the EU has approached MERCOSUR to explore the possibility of an agreement as a preventive measure in case the idea of the
FTA of the Americas develops shows that MERCOSUR can play strategically with the few cards it has at hand.

Open Regionalism and Regional Trading Blocks

The concept of open regionalism seems to be the exact opposite of
the concept of regional trade blocks, but there are many definitions
of open regionalism, according to the meaning given to the term
'open'. Alternatives include (1) 'open' taken as non-preferential, (2)
'open' in terms of new membership, (3) 'open' taken as GATT-
compatible, and (4) 'open' in terms of subjects covered.

Clearly, trading blocks as defined in this paper do not conform to
the first[16] and last definitions, but are compatible with 'weak' versions of the second and third definitions, of open regionalism. First,
all of the six possible examples examined above (the EU, the EEA,
the EC customs unions with Turkey, Malta and Cyprus, the Europe
Agreements and the EU–Mediterranean association agreements,
NAFTA and MERCOSUR) are in principle open to membership for

more countries in the same region but not to countries outside the region. Second, all six versions conform to Articles 24 of GATT 1994, the article on integration agreements as amended during the Uruguay Round. Although any WTO member can nowadays use the DSM to challenge the conformity of these entities to WTO rules, it seems highly unlikely that the agreements would be challenged *in toto*, but rather some of its aspects (such as is currently the case regarding the new banana regime devised by the EC in tandem with the Single Market programme).

Are the Different Regional Trading Blocks Effective in Influencing International Relations?

The answer to the above question is clear-cut: only the EC (pillar one of the European Union) is acting as a trading block and as such has become a long standing actor in international relations, a role acknowledged now by friends and foes of the EU and by most IPE scholars. Although the customs union involving the EC, Cyprus, Malta and Turkey could have acted as a trading block, in theory with more leverage than the EC itself, it has not. In the particular case of Turkey, this is probably due more to the circumstances surrounding the creation of this particular CU in 1996, and what followed after, than to anything else. In other words, the row between Turkey and the EU regarding the latter's refusal, until December 1999, to consider Turkey as a candidate for membership, has clearly had paralyzing effects on the potential for external action of the CU. This situation could change in the near future. Turning to NAFTA, it is not an entity which currently has an influence on international affairs, unless we factor in the systemic effect expected from the US government at the time of the creation of NAFTA as such: showing other important players that the United States had an alternative to the Uruguay Round. For some experts, NAFTA was in fact a bargaining ploy to counter regionalism in Europe and re-energize the Uruguay Round at a time when it was in the doldrums. Much the same can be said of MERCOSUR. Apart from its creation, which was considered by some, particularly in Brazil, as necessary to act as counterweight to the creation of NAFTA, there has not been much external action by MERCOSUR apart from the above-mentioned contacts with the EU.

Conclusion

There is no question that, beyond the quite obvious regionalization of world trade, there is a substantial move towards trade regionalism. This commenced more than four decades ago with the creation of the European Economic Community in 1957, but intensified from the mid-1980s (particularly with the creation of NAFTA, the EEA and MERCOSUR). If one argues about the existence of regional trading blocks, we conclude that there is really only one – the EC and its custom union partners – and that this will in all likelihood remain the case for the foreseeable future. This is not astonishing. The reason is that it is difficult for a group of sovereign states to form such a block. We mentioned at the outset the emphasis placed by Strange (1991) on the notion that it is firms that trade, not states, and firms have to compete hard for world market shares. A large national market share is not enough. This fact was realized a long time ago by all individual EC member countries' firms, not only those in small countries. They pushed, along with other interested parties, for the Single Market programme and also for multilateral trade liberalization. More generally, firms have to open the gates over which governments of territorial states preside as gatekeepers. So firms tend naturally to dislike gatekeepers, and that includes regional trading blocks, following Strange's logic, because the gates of the block stand in their way. The point being made here is that regional trading blocks are political animals whose formation must be explained by the will of those behind their formation. These are sovereign states, intending to influence international relations, including – but not exclusively – international economic relations, by negotiating as a block. There is nothing inherently wrong with this purpose. There is nothing 'aggressive' about this and therefore the term 'aggressive regionalism' should be rejected because it is value-loaded, while the term 'regional trading block' is value-neutral.

The present wave of trade regionalism (sometimes identified as 'The New Regionalism'), starting more than a decade ago, cannot be interpreted as a move towards the creation of trading blocks. The former is business-driven and is based on the idea that discriminatory trading arrangements between a developed and a developing country do cause inward direct investment into the developing country, either from multinational corporations of non-member countries or from those of the developed country involved in the deal. Not surprisingly, then, the agreements contemplated under the umbrella of the New Regionalism must be and are actually loosely structured (and that includes NAFTA).[17] Some would speak about 'benign regionalism', but we would reject the term, as we reject the term 'aggressive regionalism', because both are value-laden terms. In any case, in the New Regionalism, the associated countries do not aspire to negotiate as a block, nor at the WTO or in bilateral negotiations with the EC, for that matter. The point made here is that a free trade area is *not* a political animal and a customs union is not always so.

However, the latter at least has the potential to become one. For instance, the US bargaining power vis-à-vis the EC or Japan has barely increased as a result of the creation of NAFTA. On the other hand, the European countries' bargaining power in the GATT or elsewhere has increased through the creation and successive enlargements of the original EC and through the conclusion of CUs with Turkey, Malta and Cyprus. Although Strange might not have agreed entirely with our thesis at the time, she probably would now identify the EMU group as a trading block, in view of her insistence on linking trade and monetary matters in the definition of economic blocks. In her 1990 paper, she senses, however, that, although a larger free trading area linking the EC with Central and Eastern European countries is desirable, far outweighing any marginal negative effect it may have in slowing progress towards integration between the EC member states this would be good news for the United States and Japan. Why? Because a looser but larger EC would surely be less easy to turn into a 'Fortress Europe'. But the bad news for the United States and Japan, she predicted, would be that the EC, if it did indeed become the core of a much larger European Economic Space, would be in a much stronger bargaining position in negotiations with Japan and the United States. She argued this even before the signing of the Maastricht Treaty or the creation of a monetary union. In fact, this chapter modifies somewhat Strange's concepts, showing that only countries which are part of the customs territory of the EC (as is the case of Turkey, Malta and Cyprus and will be the case for any of the applicant countries becoming EC members) are truly part of the block, but not others in the EC's periphery such as Norway or the EC's Euro-Med partners.

Notes

1   In this chapter we will use the term 'EC' when referring to what is now currently known as the European Union, rather than the term 'EU', because the subject is related to trade policy which is a matter handled by member countries in the first pillar of the EU and is supranational. EEA is the European Economic Area including the 15 EC members, Iceland, Liechtenstein and Norway. NAFTA is the North American Free Trade Agreement.

2   For an overview of what the Seattle meeting was supposed to achieve, see *The World Trade Brief* (London: Agenda Publishing), November 1999. For an analysis of what went wrong see Bayne (2000).

3   *International Herald Tribune*, 17 December 1999. The Japanese government has been reluctant to envisage a 'sphere of influence' policy for Southeast Asia over the years, the main reason being the fear of being accused of neocolonialism by their potential satellites and former enemies from World War II. Obviously, this trauma is disappearing as time passes.

4   *The Economist*, 11 December 1999.

5   See Strange (1990).
6   Kahler (1995: 82); Mayer (1998: 339).
7   For an early analysis on this subject, see Lorenz (1991).
8   This definition, underlining a policy choice by national decision makers, contrasts clearly with others underlining the natural forces of proximity, income and intra-firm trade.
9   So called by Jan Tinbergen, the first Nobel Prize laureate in Economics. See Tinbergen (1965: 76).
10 Assuming here that the EU is a large country.
11 General equilibrium models, such as the ones presented by Kemp (1969) or Caves (1974), yield similar results.
12 A shifting effect occurs when the producers in the low-tariff member of the FTA realize it is worthwhile shifting all their sales to the high-tariff country, where prices paid by consumers are obviously higher; meanwhile, consumers in the low-tariff country will replace locally protected supplies by third-country imports on which they will pay the (low) tariff. See Curzon (1997: 182–4), for a diagrammatic analysis of the effect.
13 Public officials in the European Commission stated to this author that it tries to inform Turkey on an informal basis. Only regarding standard legislation (for example, in the domain of customs) is the Commission obliged by Article 55 of the CU agreement to consult Turkey before a final decision is reached at the EC's Council of Ministers.
14 See Bonser (1991), Cooper (1999), Porter (2000) or Whalley (1992) for analysis on the genesis of NAFTA.
15 This is now the case between Mexico and the EC, as they concluded a free trade agreement in January 2000. See *The Economist*, 29 January 2000.
16 This is why APEC (Association of Pacific Exporting Countries) does not deserve particular attention in the preceding section. See Bollard and Mayes (1992).
17 See Bowles (1999).

Bibliography

Bayne, N. (2000), 'Why Did Seattle Fail? Globalization and the Politics of Trade', *Government and Opposition*, 35(2), Spring, 131–51.
Bollard, A. and D. Mayes (1992), 'Regionalism and the Pacific Rim', *Journal of Common Market Studies*, 30(2), 195–210.
Bonser, C.F. (ed.) (1991), *Toward a North American Common Market – Problems and Prospects for a New Economic Community*, Boulder, CO: Westview Press.
Bowles, P. (1999), 'Regionalism and Development After(?) the Global Financial Crises', paper presented at the CSGR 3rd Annual Conference, University of Warwick, 16–18 September.
Caves, R. (1974), 'The Economics of Reciprocity', in W. Sellekaerts (ed.), *International Trade and Finance: Essays in Honour of Jan Tinbergen*, London: Macmillan.
Cooper, A. (1999), 'NAFTA and the politics of regional trade', in B. Hocking and S. McGuire (eds), *Trade Politics*, London: Routledge, pp.229–45.
Curzon, V. (1997), 'The European Free Trade Association' in A. El-Agraa, *et al.* (eds), *Economic Integration Worldwide*, London: Macmillan, pp.175–202.
Ethier, W. (1997), 'The new regionalism', unpublished paper, April.
Freudenberg, M., G. Gaulier and D. Unal-Kesenci (1998), *La régionalisation du commerce international: Une évaluation par les intensités relatives bilatérales*, Paris: CEPII.

Frieden, J. and D. Lake (1991), *International Political Economy*, 2nd edn, New York: St. Martins Press.

Gilpin, R. (1987), *The Political Economy of International Relations*, Princeton, NJ: Princeton University Press.

Kahler, M. (1995), *International Institutions and The Political Economy of Integration*, Washington, DC: Brookings Institution.

Kemp, M. (1969), *A Contribution to the General Equilibrium Theory of Preferential Trading*, Amsterdam: North-Holland.

Keohane, R. (1984), 'The World Political Economy and the Crisis of Embedded Liberalism', in J. Goldthorpe (ed.), *Order and Conflict in Contemporary Capitalism: Studies in the Political Economy of Western European Nations*, Oxford: Clarendon.

Kol, J. (1995), *Block Formation, Fragmentation and Stability in the World Economy*, The Hague: Scientific Council for Government Policies.

Krasner, S. (1976), 'State Power and the Structure of International Trade', *World Politics*, 28, 317–47.

Krugman, P. (1991), 'Is Bilateralism Bad?', in E. Helpman and A. Razin (eds), *International Trade and Trade Policy*, Cambridge, MA: MIT Press, pp.9–23.

Linder, S. (1961), *An Essay on Trade and Transformation*, New York: Wiley and Sons.

Lorenz, D. (1991), 'Regionalisation versus Regionalism – Problems of Change in the World Economy', *Intereconomics*, 26(1), 3–10.

Mansfield, E. and H. Milner (eds) (1997), *The Political Economy of Regionalism*, New York: Columbia University Press.

Mayer, F. (1998), *Interpreting NAFTA*, New York: Columbia University Press.

Pelkmans, J. and Brenton, P. (1999), 'Bilateral Trade Agreements with the EU: Driving Forces and Effects', in O. Memedovic, A. Kuyvenhoven and W. Molle, *Multilateralism and Regionalism in the Post-Uruguay Era. What Role for the EU?*, Dordrecht, Kluwer, pp.87–120.

Porter, T. (2000), 'The North American Free Trade Agreement', in R. Stubbs and G. Underhill (eds), *Political Economy and the Changing Global Order*, 2nd edn, Oxford: Oxford University Press, pp.245–53.

Shibata, H. (1972), 'A Theory of Free Trade Areas', in P. Robson (ed.), *International Economic Integration*, Harmondsworth: Penguin Books, pp.68–87.

Spero, J. (1992), *The Politics of International Economic Relations*, 4th edn, London: Routledge.

Strange, S. (1985), 'Protectionism – why not?' *The World Today*, 41(8–9), 148–50.

Strange, S. (1988), *States and Markets*, New York: Blackwell.

Strange, S. (1990), 'Trade Policies of the European Community', Florence, EUI, unpublished paper.

Strange, S. (1991), 'Are Trade Blocs Emerging Now?', paper prepared for the International Political Science Association World Congress in Buenos Aires, July.

Tinbergen, J. (1965), *International Economic Integration*, 2nd edn, Amsterdam: Elsevier.

Tovias, A. (1978), 'Differential Country Size as an Incentive to the Proliferation of Trading Blocs', *Journal of Common Market Studies*, 16(3), March, 246–66.

Whalley, J. (1992), 'CUSTA and NAFTA: Can WHAFTA Be Far Behind?', *Journal of Common Market Studies*, 30(2), 125–42.

Whalley, J. and C. Perroni (1999), 'The New Regionalism: Trade Liberalization or Insurance?', paper presented at the CSGR 3rd Annual Conference, University of Warwick, September.

18 Strange Looks on Developing Countries: A Neglected Kaleidoscope of Questions

ANNA LEANDER[1]

Introduction

The relevance of Strange's work to developing countries is often overlooked. This owes more to the lack of interest and the selective reading of most commentators than to the absence of arguments and threads of thought regarding developing countries in Strange's writings. One of her major books (*Rival States, Rival Firms*), deals mainly with structural change in international production and its implications for developing countries. The book is based on case studies of Kenya, Malaysia and Brazil. In Strange's thinking about international finance, the 'debt problem' and its effects for developing countries as well as for the international financial system figure prominently. Most significantly, one of her fundamental questions was always *cui bono*? In answering it, she invariably refers to developing countries. In other words, although Strange was no doubt most interested in overall international structural change, it is not necessary to dig out the odd footnote to find ideas about developing countries and how to study them.

The aim of this chapter is to bring out this generally overlooked aspect of Strange's work. It proceeds by drawing attention to the pillars around which Strange's approach evolves. It begins by underlining the crucial and growing importance of international structures (second section) and, in particular, international financial structures (third section) for the analysis of developing countries. It develops

Strange's claims that it is increasingly difficult to opt out of the international system, that development is increasingly asymmetrical and that, consequently, questions of international regulation become increasingly salient. The chapter then follows Strange in arguing that private actors (fourth section), as opposed to states, governments and policy makers (fifth section), are central for understanding developing countries. I develop the argument that private actors have been empowered by recent structural shifts and that, although the state is very important, state capacity has been severely circumscribed. Each section further argues that it is important to move beyond general arguments and trends, and to understand variations and nuances in the effects of trends and applicability of arguments. In short, the chapter argues that Strange's approach opens an interesting and rich kaleidoscope of questions. However, it also points to areas where the analysis and the answers would have been more convincing and richer if Strange had developed more explicit links with existing literature on developing countries.

Dependency Today: the Overarching Theme

> Opting out of the world market economy is no longer an option. That is what dependency means today (Strange 1994: 215).

An overarching theme in Strange's work is the priority of international structures, yet she is no friend of dependency. On the contrary, 'dependency is an antique bed due for the junkyard' (Stopford and Strange 1991: 228). Contrary to dependency scholars, as she reads them,[2] Strange thinks that the influence of international structures can be positive as well as negative and that there is no escape from it. Strategies of self-reliance are no longer viable. Instead, developing countries have to use the opportunities opened by recent structural changes in the international economy. Their very unequal ability to do this (for internal or external reasons) explains the growing disparity among developing countries. It also points to the significance of international economic regulation as the only possible way of improving the fate of developing countries on the whole.

Strange insists, as dependency scholars or Hirschman (1980: v–xii) would, that the economy has to be thought of in structural or systemic terms. The rules of the game advantage and empower some actors as opposed to others. They make it possible for some states, but not for others, to pursue the 'national' economic policies they want, set the agenda in international institutions, and ignore the effects their policies have on others. The implication is that, first, states can gain and lose power through the structural effects of the international system;

second, these systemic effects can be instrumentalized; and third states have unequal capacity to influence, and assume responsibility for, order and disorder in the international system. The refusal of scholars to recognize this political nature of the international economy is something Strange consistently criticized.

Strange further insists that recent changes in the international political economy have made it more necessary than ever to give priority to international structures in the analysis of developing countries. Technological change and politics (of public and private actors) have led to a change in the way the economy works. They have made the rapidly growing internationalization of production and finance possible. Moreover, they have resulted in an increasingly technology-intensive production where profit margins are squeezed. In these conditions, strategic alliances have become crucial to reduce costs and risks or to extend market shares. Similarly, finance and financial strategies have become increasingly important both to firms and to states. These processes further accelerate the process of internationalization. The result is that the rules of the game in national economies and the direction of change are determined by 'international' structures:

> We [Stopford and Strange] tried to explain how and why it was that some national institutions were better able than others to help firms respond promptly and effectively to these new challenges. But we also tried to explain that the need to respond at all was due to structural changes in the whole world market economy. (Strange 1997: 184)

Strange pinpoints some crucial implications of these changes for developing countries. The first is that development is increasingly difficult and unequal. More successful developing countries manage to take advantage of the new opportunities: they attract foreign-owned firms keen to lower costs and capture market shares, play investors off against each other and make better use of them. They have access to international financial markets at reasonable costs and enjoy investor confidence. By contrast, the poorest countries find themselves trapped in a vicious circle where their underdevelopment is aggravated by their incapacity to attract investors and finance because of their underdevelopment. While more successful countries have the stable institutions and international clout necessary to deal with international instability and crisis, the poorest ones end up as pariahs in the international economy. Moreover, the asymmetry between rich and poor countries tends to increase. Poor countries face increasing barriers to entry into the world markets, are increasingly vulnerable to international financial markets, have an ever-weaker influence over the way the international economy is governed and often (partly as a consequence) have very weak states.

A second effect of structural change is that withdrawal is no longer an option. A country, or a group of individuals, cannot simply decide that they do not want to participate in the international economy and thereby free themselves from its influence. Or, more correctly, the price of doing so is exceedingly high. The reason is, first, that there are considerable advantages to openness. The altered nature of technology and competition has made reliance on foreign-owned firms for market access, technology and job creation a *sine qua non* of development. Moreover, access to international financial markets as a source of credit and profits is increasingly important both for firms and for public institutions. Second, public and private institutions (including the IMF, WTO, other governments, foreign and local business, rating agencies and hedge funds) pressurize countries to open up to international trade, direct investment and finance. Heavy penalties, such as the closing down of financial and trade markets, the absence of investors, lowered credit ratings and pressure on currencies, usually face countries who do not comply. Consequently, although openness may not bring development, forgoing openness amounts to forgoing development. For Strange, it is therefore not surprising that most countries chose to 'liberalize' and see strategies of self-reliance as neither adequate nor realistic.

Third, since the economic and political fate of developing countries is increasingly decided by international factors, it is crucial to think about international regulation (Strange 1995: 72). For Strange, the key characteristic of present international regulation is 'ungovernance': an increasing number of issues remain unregulated. The existing regulation tends to express the interest of dominant states and private actors. It is not the outcome of a formal political process. Central issues never get onto the agenda of international organizations and, if they do, the IOs have little chance of arriving at and implementing decisions that do not reflect the interests of dominant actors. Clearly, some governments, the US in particular, bear more responsibility for, and have benefitted more from, this state of affairs than others. There is growing asymmetry 'between states whose domestic policies have an impact on societies and economies other than their own, and states which have no such power and were more likely to suffer and have to adapt to the domestic policies of the more powerful governments' (Strange 1998a: 706). Partly because of this, Strange is skeptical about the prospects of international regulation. The 'assumption is that Africa does not matter because no important economic interests are greatly affected' (1998b: 116). But an even greater obstacle may be that in many cases regulation would require the collaboration, if not the control, of private actors.

A final significant implication of Strange's analysis is that it questions the tendency to think about developmental successes and failures *exclusively* in terms of state strategies and responsibilities. In many cases:

> failure to manage the national economy, to maintain employment and sustain economic growth, to avoid imbalances of payments with other states, to control the rate of interest and the exchange rate is not a matter of technical incompetence, nor moral turpitude nor political maladroitness. It is neither in any direct sense their fault, nor the fault of others. None of these failures can be blamed on other countries or on other governments. They are, simply, the victims of the market. (Strange 1996: 14)

This is not to say that governments are relieved of responsibility or that no institutions and policies are better than others. The point is a different one, namely that the capacity of the state to achieve its goals needs to be placed in perspective.

The following sections develop central aspects of this general caveat. However, it is useful to first point out that it is directly tied to some of the most heated and central debates about developing countries today. Moreover, linking up to these debates would be a good way of refining the arguments and answering the questions emerging from the general caveat.

First, the debate about the nature of Strange's structural shifts is far from closed and much remains to be done to refine and develop our understanding of them. Many authors contest that they exist at all. Some argue that the world is no more integrated than before World War II (Hirst and Thompson 1996). Others claim that the present trend is merely a 'return' to normal (Mann 1997) or that it is simply vastly overstated (Wade 1996). Strange would be the first to recognize that, because of the complexity and dynamism involved in the changes she describes, the areas of 'significant ignorance' have become larger rather than smaller and that, in order to understand the processes under way, continued research is badly needed. However, to make the argument convincing, a more refined and detailed analysis is required. Strange points out that arguments based on existing statistics are often inadequate because they fail to capture the shifts or because they misinterpret the data available (Strange 1998b). However, this is an insufficient reason for not trying to do better. Linking up more extensively with existing writing on the subject would be an obvious start.

Second, further specifying what is meant by 'no opt out' and how much scope for variation remains seems very important. North Korean style autarky may neither be attractive nor feasible. Everyone will agree. However, restricting capital account openness, and to a certain extent foreign direct investment and trade may well be viable (Amsden 1990; Wade and Veneroso 1998). Such nuances are crucial and are intensely debated. Linking up Strange's work with this issue would be an excellent way of refining and strengthening our understanding of the extent to which opting out is really precluded and, how much leeway there is for states and their citizens to decide on a particular kind of society, reflecting a particular mix of values.

Finally, Strange's work tends to assume rather than elaborate on the mechanisms by which structural shifts affect developing countries. Clearly, again this is an area that is replete with work. Indeed, the question of how international and national structures are articulated has haunted not only dependency scholars[3] and their present-day heirs, but also most political economy work on developing countries. Linking up with this is a precondition to advance the usefulness of Strange's approach for analyzing how and why asymmetries in development are linked to the (non-)regulation in specific areas of the international economy. Strange would most likely have started to develop this linkage through examining how the governance of international finance affects development.

Involuntary Losers in the International Casino: the Implications of Structural Change

The aspect of international structural change that Strange worked the most on is that of finance. She writes that: 'my personal conviction ... is that it is *the* prime issue of international politics and economics' (1998c: 18). This also holds for developing countries. Due to structural shifts, the organization and distribution of finance are increasingly decided internationally. That is to say, developing countries are increasingly touched by the highly political effects of the international financial structure. This is nowhere more visible than in the so-called 'debt problem'.

Financial Structures and Development

> 'The great difference between an ordinary casino which you can go into or stay away from, and the global casino of high finance, is that in the latter we are all involuntarily engaged in the day's play' (Strange 1986: 2).

This also applies to developing countries. It is a mistake to think that a country is unaffected by global finance just because its financial markets are barely emerging, its foreign debt is low, or because its citizens live a life which seems far removed from the life of financial operators who channel trillions of dollars through globally integrated, deterritorialized capital markets. Such countries are not observers who, from a safe distance, watch fortunes being made and destroyed. They are involved, and more vulnerable to international financial structures than most of their rich counterparts.

The links of developing countries to international finance have a number of implications: (a) their exchange rates (if their currencies are convertible), their interest rates (if the capital account is open) and more generally the terms on which they can raise credit are directly tied to the overall system. For instance, a decision by the United States to raise interest rates will alter the relative attractiveness of their currency, of their government bonds and of the shares their firms' trade on the market; (b) they are affected by the increasing volatility and instability inherent in the international system. A crisis in Mexico will affect Turkey, Argentina or Malaysia even if there is no perceptible change in policies and no change of economic 'fundamentals'; (c) their 'internal' institutions are shaped by the empowering and disempowering effects of the international financial structure. Private, mobile, capital holders are strengthened (see also Frieden 1991). They can raise and earn money internationally. They can escape the (ever weakening) grip of the state that can neither force them to pay taxes nor control their doings. For example, an adequate explanation of the Korean state's loss of control over its *chaebols* (industrial groupings) should include (among other things, of course) the effects of opening up to international financial markets in the 1990s (Amsden and Euh 1993).

Strange would argue that international financial structures have particularly strong and skewed effects on the poor and on institutionally weak developing countries: their decisions about interest rate changes do not matter and they are unlikely to be consulted about the interest rate changes in countries where it does matter. Instability and crisis originating elsewhere is also more likely to touch them: financial market actors are likely to be less confident about the prospects of their economies and financial markets and hence more likely not to engage themselves and keep the option of quick withdrawal open. Finally, the impact of financial structures on national institutions is likely to be all the more dramatic as poor and underdeveloped countries are likely to have the weakest national institutions (firms, banks, states, political parties, organized interest groups and civil society). In Strange's view, developing countries are not only involuntary players, but also recurring losers.

So why do developing countries not leave the system? The answer refers back to the claim, that because of structural change, opting out is no longer an alternative, or at least it is increasingly less of an option. Production is ever more technology-intensive. Low wages are no longer enough. Investing in technology becomes all the more important. This creates incentives for the opening up to international finance as one way of raising capital. Moreover, development increasingly depends on buying international technology and know-how or cooperating with firms that possess these. In return, these firms demand a promising business. This usually includes operating under liberal policies on finance. Local business usually supports their demand since they, too, increasingly have to compete on international terms. Furthermore, access to the markets of developed countries, also crucial for development, is often conditional on opening the country's own economy, including the service sector (banking and finance included, as reflected in the General Agreement on Trade in Services (GATS)). Finally, international financial institutions, private and public, demand the opening up of financial markets as a counterpart for confidence and further extension of credits (though there is no guarantee that liberalizing will be enough). Consequently, the offer of opening up to international finance is one that most countries cannot and do not want to refuse.

Developing countries tend to be caught in the uncomfortable situation of playing a game, which certainly offers some gains but in which, on the whole, they are recurring losers. Leaving it is neither more attractive than staying in nor likely to be feasible.

The Politics of Debt

The skewed impact of the international financial structures is nowhere more visible than in the impact of international debt. Overall, the debtors have borne the costs of the 'debt problem', including when this problem was largely caused by the non-regulation of international credit. However, the effects of this have been very unequal. While some newly industrializing countries (NICs) have managed to use international private finance to their advantage, the poorest debtor countries have fallen into a debt trap.

In contrast with the manner in which lending within national economies is handled, the international debt problem is dealt with in an ad hoc, case-by-case fashion. In most national economies legal procedures regulate bankruptcy and forbid usury and private enforcement of debt repayment. In the international system, no overarching authority could impose such regulations. No agreement is in sight on what the content of an international bankruptcy and lending system would be. Nor is there much enthusiasm for the creation of such a system. Strange argues that it would damage the illusion of sovereignty (1998c: 98): 'Pragmatically, creditor governments since 1945 have followed the same strategy [as Palmerston in 1848] of leaving undecided what punitive measures would or would not be applied against foreign defaulters on transnational obligations' (ibid.: 99).

'Pragmatically' clearly means that who takes what share of the cost, and what kind of 'punishment' is imposed on the debtor, is a matter of what is feasible in view of the relative ability and influence of the creditors and debtors. This, in turn, to a large extent reflects the empowering and disempowering effects of international financial structures.

Indeed, the debt crisis closely mirrors the system effects of international finance. Developing countries have borne the costs of debt problems that were often not home-grown. Strange considers issues like imprudent lending, developed country trade and investment policies, US interest rate and exchange rate shifts, contagion effects and the increasing volatility and instability of international finance to have been crucial ingredients in the recent debt crises (1982, 1994, 1997). Nevertheless, repayment has been the rule. Rescheduling, debt swaps, write-downs and so forth have not been designed to provide developing countries with the equivalent of a bankruptcy option. Rather, these alternatives have been created to uphold the illusion that a debt crisis is solved and that there is no threat to the overall system. Similarly, to the extent that the debt burden has been borne by creditors, it has been shifted from private to public ones, reflecting the growing strength of private actors. Whereas part of the costs of the 1982 Mexican crisis ultimately fell on private bankers (through the bank contributions to the 1983 rescue package and the 1989 Brady Plan), in 1997 the United States took the lead in getting other governments, the World Bank and the Asian Development Bank to put up most of the funds (Strange 1998c).

The ever more stringent and far-reaching (structural) IMF adjustment programs are perhaps the clearest illustration of the weak position of the debtors. These programs do not reflect the priorities of the debtor. The IMF 'rescue packages do work as antidotes to the virus that could attack the global financial system. They do not necessarily cure the carrier of the virus – the indebted country' (ibid.: 111). Moreover, they may be perceived to wreak long-term development. Thus, in Mexico, 'a spontaneous protest movement grew rapidly. It called itself *El Barzon*, referring to the strap that held an ox under the yoke – as Mexicans felt themselves held in the yoke of foreign debt (Strange 1998c: 99). Finally, and by implication, there is an obvious risk that debtors are forced to follow whatever economic theory is the fashion of the day, often to their detriment. Thus, 'while the IMF's empire may be growing, it would be wise as an institution to beware the hubris of its own experts' (Strange 1998b: 112).

However, it would be misleading to place all developing countries in one basket. The increasing disintermediation of international finance and the corresponding growing importance of private actors have affected countries very unequally. Thus Strange argues that, 'unlike in the 1980s, there was no general "debt crisis" in the 1990s' (ibid.: 121). While many NICs rely extensively on the 'more mobile, less vulnerable insurance and pension fund managers and other portfolio investors' for international credit,[4] the poorest countries receive virtually no private funds. Private creditors have 'lost confidence'. Public, notably multilateral, creditors have stepped in to take their place, often with the aim of allowing private creditors to leave without losses. By following this strategy,

> the Bank and the Fund actually created a debt trap even worse than the one they purported to remedy. What happened was that multilateral organisations in the aftermath of the debt crisis of the 1980s lent debtor governments new money to pay off or reschedule private or bilateral debt. But the terms on which this money was lent were much harsher and the sanctions against non-payment much stricter than for the debts they took over. Then between 1986–88 the IMF started withdrawing funds from debtor countries, exacerbating the effect of commercial withdrawal. Similarly, the World Bank started taking more money from the debtors than it lent them for old and new projects. (Strange 1998c: 106)

The result is bleak development prospects. In the 1990s, the amount the poorest African debtors spent on servicing their debts to multilateral institutions was higher than the amount they spent on health, basic nutrition and education (1998b: 114). The foundering of political initiatives[5] to deal with the situation again illustrates the very unequal say of countries when it comes to regulating international debt. The initiatives have been allowed to founder on the apparently insurmountable definitional issues (which countries, what conditions, which cost-sharing arrangements) and of course the fear of futility (these initiatives would not solve the problem) and perversity (moral hazard).

In sum, development is shaped by international finance. The provision of credit is crucial for investment and hence for growth.[6] Also the terms on which credit is given are increasingly determined internationally. For Strange, this cannot be accounted for once other factors have been considered (for example, the institutional setting and the strength of the state or factors of production endowment and the nature and distribution of capital). International finance *shapes* these factors. These general claims leave plenty of room for elaboration and, again, could fruitfully be tied into existing debates.

An obvious place to start is to develop in more detail how and why in given cases international financial structures have (or have not) shaped developmental paths, institutions and state policies. It is true that the literature on this issue is rather scant.[7] However, linking up with what there is would seem like a promising starting-point.

Indeed, precisely because of the very unequal and varied effects of changes in international finance, it seems very important to specify the mechanisms of this influence and to develop a far more precise understanding of what any one country can do to control these mechanisms. The detailed case studies go some way in this direction.

Second, on the issue of debt, the most pressing issue is what can be done to regulate international finance in a way that is slightly less disadvantageous to the citizens of developing countries. On this issue there is an enormous amount of (usually specialized economic) work of which Strange is very critical. Evaluating work on the prospects of 'our international guardians' in regulating international finance, she first points to the 'sudden enthusiasm for self-regulation [which stems from the fact that] large internationally active banks found that regulators were often uninformed and wasted everybody's time'. Strange provides little in terms of solutions. She even seems to find it difficult to think about the issue. As so often, Strange the Keynesian political economist advocating international regulation is blocked by Strange the international realist who thinks that such regulation is impossible. She therefore limits her aspiration to stating the problem correctly. A crucial part of the problem is the privatization of power.

The Privatization of Power: the Changing Hierarchy of Actors

Strange argues that it has become imperative to study the role of private, non-state actors in shaping the fate of developing countries. These actors may always have been more important than was thought. Be this as it may, as a result of structural change, private actors are now absolutely central. As stressed above, private actors play a central role in deciding who gets credits on what terms and governments continuously bargain (or wish they were in a situation to bargain) with them. But they also play a central role in most other areas of international political economy. If politics is not only about what states do and international politics not only about security, taking private actors seriously becomes unavoidable. This point is illustrated below through the elaboration of the link between structural change and the evolving role of two private actors in developing countries: firms and organized crime.[8]

The Role of Private Firms: on the Politics of Production

For Strange, one of the key changes of the past two decades has been the globalization of production and the related change in relations between developing countries and foreign investors. Strange believed that development prospects, as well as internal institutions and 'state capacity', are now largely shaped by firms and that firms therefore have to be at the heart of any serious analysis and explanation of economic development.

This evolution is due to the internationalization of production. It is not only possible but also necessary for firms to compete according to international standards. This does not mean that firms produce or sell everything everywhere, nor has it erased national imprints from their strategies, internal structure and management/ownership. The argument is that, as markets are increasingly integrated, firms are forced to compete on international terms, even in their home markets (1998b). They rival each other for international market shares. Finally, their production and marketing networks are extended as they strive to lower costs and obtain greater flexibility.

Simultaneously, a 'new dependency' is emerging. Firms possess the technology and know-how needed for development. The marketing and production networks of multinationals are often the *sine qua non* of market access. Consequently, it is harder than ever for poor countries to be truly independent of the capitalist world economy.

> But dependency is no longer equated with the relegation of local labour to menial tasks in the fields or the mines (…) The foreign firm has not only proved that it can be an engine of growth – in incomes, in jobs, in exports, in skills – it is also perceived as such. (Strange 1996: 49)

According to Strange, the change at the level of private firms and in their strategies explains why so many countries have developed rapidly over the past two decades despite the predictions of 'most economists, most governments and most bureaucracies' to the contrary. Thus Strange argues that firms,

> and not government aid programmes, were going to accelerate the modernisation of developing countries. Sometimes it has been done by the sale of patent rights, more often by the licensing of patented technology, by joint ventures with local firms, and by strategic alliance in which the TNC offers quick dependable market access through its established brand name or through its distribution networks of dealers and retailers. (ibid.: 59).

The opportunities may not be sufficient to narrow the North–South gap. For instance, Strange believes that it is virtually impossible for the South to get a foothold in the service sector that is increasingly important for economic growth.

Strange argues that foreign-owned firms set the parameters for 'internal' politics of development and shape 'national' institutions.

Two examples will be used to illustrate the point: labor relations and taxation. Labor costs are plainly visible and easily compared and, consequently, important in determining foreign investment location. The mushrooming of 'export processing zones' which exist precisely because they allow foreign-owned firms to avoid national regulations (including taxes and labor market rules) is one of many illustrations of how developing countries have rushed to accommodate the (often unarticulated), demands of foreign firms. However, governments also adjust internal labor relations. Foreign firms usually look at militant and politicized unions as a threat to the stability of their own operations and to the political stability of a country in general. Consequently, 'most states tend to oscillate between exclusionary, repressive policies, and attempts to incorporate the labour movement in the official political and administrative structure' (Stopford and Strange 1991: 198). Overall, Strange believes that, de facto, a growing share of labor relations is regulated by firms and not by the state, and therefore 'firms just like states can be conceived as social institutions for the co-ordination of potentially conflicting interests' (Strange 1996: 60).

Second, it has often been argued that globalization makes it more difficult to raise taxes. Firms can threaten to relocate their production and/or make their investments elsewhere if the costs are too high. Taxation is a cost that is easily visible and manageable and therefore subject to bargaining. The consequence is that governments courting firms (local and foreign) find it difficult to impose, not only corporate taxation, but, more generally, any tax that will increase the costs of firms. This, of course, also concerns social contributions and income taxes which will show up as part of the real wage in the firms' calculations. A second, less well understood, aspect of the tax issue is the role of firms as 'tax-gathering organisations' (ibid.). Firms gather 'taxes' when they receive exemptions from tax payments in various forms and thereby are allowed to distribute internally and internationally the gains from taxes. Internationally, firms often get tax exemptions for costs they have had abroad (for example, for the payment of royalties, import duties, legal costs and even bribes) and this is a way of distributing the money of taxpayers in one country to the government in another one. Similarly, firms distribute tax income on the national level when they are exempted from paying taxes on the fringe benefits of their employees (most concerned are owners and managers) or on charitable donations (funding a private school or university or a newspaper). Obviously, both 'national' and foreign-owned firms in a country engage in this kind of redistribution. It could be added that the increasing clout of top-level management puts pressure on countries to allow this kind of indirect tax redistribution, since income payment on top salaries and deduction possibilities for fringe benefits become major factors determining location (Strange 1996).

The Mafias: on the International Politics of Diffusing Authority

> Like transnational enterprises, organised criminal gangs – mafias, for short – have been around for a long time. Neither is a new phenomenon. Yet in both cases, what is new is their number; the expanding extent of their transnational operations; and the degree to which their authority in world society, and in the world economy, rivals and encroaches upon that of governments. (Strange 1996: 110)

These are the opening lines of a chapter on the role of organized crime in world politics. The general thrust is that, as Mafias become internationalized, the balance that existed in many places between states and Mafias is unsettled, to the advantage of the latter. For many countries, the new authority acquired by organized crime is profoundly reshaping the (non-)possibilities of development and growth. Organized crime becomes the political authority which decides what is done where and on what conditions. More than a state, it is organized crime that determines the path of economic development. This may apply to rich as well as to poor countries. However, the process has often gone further in poor countries, where organized crime is openly at war with the state and/or threatening to take it over from within. Cases in point are Colombia, Sudan, Afghanistan and Russia. The point that Strange makes is that accounts of development have to remain open enough to leave space for this influence where it counts and to see that organized crime is not a national phenomenon. Even if we talk about the Russian, Ukrainian, Colombian or Italian Mafia, the success of these organizations is intimately linked to structural shifts in the international political economy.

Organized crime has thrived off the magic of the international market. International demand for the goods and services provided by organized crime has grown rapidly. Drugs are part of the story.[9] However, as Strange points out, only 40 per cent of money laundering done through international banks is thought to come from drug deals. The rest is accounted for by the profits from other kinds of illegal trading – in arms and nuclear material for instance – and tax evasion (1998b: 124). On the supply side, structural shifts have made alternative activities relatively less profitable. Thus Strange does not hesitate to draw a direct link between the fact that 'developed countries had steadfastly refused UNCTAD pleas to apply the principles of agricultural support and protection that they used at home to support and protect export crops produced by developing countries' and the fact that many farmers turned to growing illegal crops instead (Strange 1998d: 15). Of course, precisely how the link between supply and demand works is bound to depend on what particular good or service any Mafia provides. It is possible to contrast drugs with trade in arms or paramilitary services. Strange's point is that, more often than not, today, supply and demand are no longer determined exclusively, or even mainly, within the confines of the nation state.

In addition to this, the increasing clout of organized crime in development is attributable to the operation and (non-)regulation of the international financial system. This system makes it possible to launder dirty money with relative ease. Using transnational banking services and the rapidly growing numbers of international tax havens has provided organized crime with an easy escape route from national controls on the origin of funds, and correspondingly weakened the grip of states. Thus Strange points out that it is no coincidence that major tax havens are situated at the crossroads of the principal routes of the illegal narcotics trade or close to major financial centers (see also Palan 1998). Moreover, she argues that there have so far only been feeble attempts at regulation, partly because banks resist regulation which would make them act as 'policemen'. For all 'clean' business, clients need to trust the bankers' confidentiality. A bank reporting suspicious funds would merely lose its clients to more tight-lipped banks.[10] Attempts to regulate also remain feeble because many states and state officials have an obvious self-interest in preserving the role of transnational banks in facilitating and blurring the traces of white-collar crime and tax evasion. Last, but not least, the assumption is that the state is still dealing with professionals who have integrity of a special kind:

> The ideational sources of the permissiveness [of the international banking system] lie in the ambivalence of capitalist systems toward the 'learned professions'. This permissiveness allowed bankers and accountants to share with priests the privileges of client confidentiality. Banks and tax havens have exploited this privilege, and in doing so have punched a big hole in the governance system of international finance. (Strange 1998d: 15)

This section has shown that private actors (Mafias and firms) play an increasing role in determining development and that the reason for this is largely structural change in international political economy. However, it is clear from both examples that, by repeatedly trying to drive home this argument, Strange is raising as many questions as she answers.

There is an obvious need to ask questions about and clarify exactly the nature of private actor influence in different countries and different sectors, as well as what allows us to explain the differences. In part this makes it necessary to develop links between work on developing countries and specialized work on private actors. This is the sense of Strange's repeated call for an integration of business and management theories. Of course, the integration is already extensive. In fact, there is considerable work on different private actors, including international ones, in or in relation to developing countries. Strange herself draws on this work, particularly in *Rival States, Rival Firms*.

Moreover, the argument raises fundamental questions about politics. Strange points to the obvious question of the extent to which private firms can fill functions formerly filled by the state (education, health care and taxation for example)? More generally, the evolving role of private actors raises the question (dear to scholars in institutional economics and comparative political economy) of what happens to corporatist relationships and more broadly to state autonomy and the range of policy options in a context where private, often foreign, actors play a growing role (Evans 1995; 1997). This issue brings us to the last section of this chapter.

The Paradox of Defective States: on the Primacy of Understanding the State

> I am not arguing that states themselves are obsolete. Collectively they are still the most influential and therefore critical source of authority in the world system. But they are increasingly becoming hollow, or defective, institutions. To outward appearances unchanged, the inner core of their authority in society and over economic transactions within their defined territorial borders is seriously impaired. They are like old trees, hollow in the middle, showing signs of weakness and vulnerability to storm, drought, or disease, yet continuing to grow leaves, new shoots, and branches. Some are clearly more defective in terms of their ability to play their roles in society, further advanced in decrepitude, than others. (Strange 1995: 57)

The role of the state in developing countries is not neglected in the literature. It is poorly understood, according to Strange. Claims to sovereignty and authority over the economy and society are taken at face value. As a result, we do not understand the problems facing developing countries, nor do we seriously discuss potential solutions. Yet sovereignty claims ring increasingly hollow and this is particularly true of developing country states. This is *not* the same as saying that the state has no role to play in development. On the contrary, the state has a crucial role to play. The implication is rather that the issue of how well the state *can* play this role deserves serious attention.

The general argument that state authority is increasingly problematic, particularly in developing countries, flows directly from the arguments that have been presented above. But it may be useful to draw together the parts of the argument at this point. The developmental path, the nature of national institutions and politics, and the growth prospects of developing countries are increasingly determined at the international level, by international finance and by private actors. As a group, developing countries have lost out in this process to states who benefit from the working of the system and who (partly as a consequence) have an influence over how it is (not) regulated, as exemplified by the debt problem. To paraphrase Strange (1996: 189): power has (a) shifted upwards from weak states to stronger ones with global or regional reach beyond their frontiers; (b) shifted sideways from states to markets and thus to non-state authorities deriving power from their market shares; and (c) has evaporated, in that no one is exercising it. The last point bears repeating: the loss of authority is not zero-sum: 'What some have lost, others have not gained. The diffusion of authority away from national governments has left a yawning hole of non-authority. Ungovernance it might be called' (ibid.: 14). The result is that many, perhaps most, societies have to be content with the mere appearance of autonomy, with a facade of statehood.

The claim that the state as an institution has been weakened does not imply that the state does not matter. Strange, paradoxically perhaps, believes the contrary to be true. For developing countries, it is absolutely crucial to have well functioning states. Strange is convinced that markets will not, on their own, distribute resources to further development. She therefore believes that 'small poor countries cannot afford the luxury of letting market forces determine outcomes' (Stopford and Strange 1991: 8). An effective state is a precondition for attracting foreign-owned firms and creditors and for making good use of their presence.

Strange would hasten to add that the nature of effective state intervention has changed, too: it is no longer about governing business (or markets) and bargaining, it is about offering business collaboration, stability and favorable conditions.[11] Consequently, for Strange, the increasingly troubled nature of state authority in many developing countries seriously impairs development; it hampers the emergence of effective national and international economic regulation. It may even engender a vicious circle whereby the weakness of state authority deters creditors and foreign investors and leaves private actors (Mafias, terrorists, tax-evaders) unchecked, which in turn further weakens state authority. Moreover, the weakness of state authority makes arriving at effective regulation unlikely and arduous. It increases the problems of developing countries in facing the 'opposing phalanx of rich, aid-giving industrialised countries who either stonewall their demands for more aid or for preferential trading arrangements, or fob them off with empty symbolic gestures' (ibid.: 52). The lack of economic and political credibility in many developing countries curtails their ability to propose, let alone impose, regulation and reform proposals. Moreover, it makes implementation of any international regulation that can be agreed upon increasingly difficult as governments lose their grip on the private sector that is often the object of these regulations (Strange 1996: 190; 1998b: 141).

Strange points to two possible escape routes from this situation: one is that of state alliances where Japan and Europe would ally behind, initiate and impose regulation, with developing country support wherever possible. The second escape route is that of 'negarchy' or, in other words, the limitation and constraining of arbitrary authority, by non-compliance (Strange 1996: 197). However, it is most likely that neither road will be taken.

The picture that Strange paints of the state's role in development is discomforting. She is both telling us that the state has a central (albeit changed) role to play in development and that it is decreasingly (albeit unequally) capable of filling this role. On the one hand, Strange the Keynesian would seem to be on the side of those 'statist' or 'institutionalist' writers who argue that the state has a central role to play since markets will not on their own bring development. On the other hand, Strange the IPE scholar finds the idea most 'statists' have of the state's role in the economy anachronistic. It ignores the extent to which economies are tied to world markets and policies have to be correspondingly adjusted. The strategies Strange advocates for developing countries are close to neoliberal ones, in that she persistently points to the virtues of openness to trade and foreign direct investment, even if she (like many liberals) is very critical of the claim that openness to short-term financial flows is good or necessary. Strange is also critical of statists for thinking of the capacity of the state to carry out policies as determined by national institutions. Not that she would appreciate it if her work became a foil, justifying or distracting attention away from corrupt practices with the shallow excuse that it is all the fault of the international system. However, avoiding Scylla is no reason to steer straight into Charybdis. For Strange, the 'Asian exceptionalism' is tied not only (or even mainly) to a set of national institutions and a form of embeddedness but to a specific historical period where cold war politics determined the conditions on which these economies received market access, foreign direct investments and finance. With the end of the cold war, this exceptionalism comes to an end, as does the Asian 'state-led' miracle (ibid.: 7).

Discomforting as it may be, this argument suggests a number of very important questions. A first set concerns the extent to which the state in general, as well as the state in given developing countries, has actually become 'defective' and hollow. Indeed, Strange insists that the loss of state control over social, economic and political life is very unequal; while some are increasingly akin to no-go grey zones, others have lost control in the same way as developed countries have lost control. For any one country it matters what kind of loss of control one is talking about. It matters for what policies are realistically part of the options from which the state can choose and it matters for the prospects that any kind of policy will be effective.

This points directly to a second set of questions: what development strategies are feasible? Developing countries today are being pushed to adopt strategies which have never been tried before and which even those advocating them are not adopting. They are asked to allow foreign owned firms and banks to control the bulk of their economy and to have the state act essentially as a 'host for firms' (Stopford and Strange 1991). The question is of course whether this unorthodox strategy has any chance of working and what its long-term political implications are.

Finally, there is the issue of what happens to democratic politics in a world where private, often foreign, actors make a very significant share of the decisions and where the state makes it an absolute priority to cater for business needs (Held 1991). Authors in IPE have argued that the result is likely to be a more authoritarian or restricted form of democracy (Evans 1997, Gill 1997). However, Strange partly dodges the issue. According to her, we feel uneasy about this for personal reasons. We share 'Pinocchio's problem' of what to do once the strings which provided certainties about our political identity and loyalties are cut and we have to decide for ourselves:

> If indeed, we have now, not a system of global governance by any stretch of the imagination, but rather a ramshackle assembly of conflicting sources of authority, we too have Pinocchio's problem. Where do allegiance, loyalty, identity lie? Not always, obviously, in the same direction. Sometimes with the government of a state, or with a social movement operating across territorial frontiers. Sometimes with a family or a generation, sometimes with fellow members of an occupation or a profession. (Strange 1996)

However, we probably also feel uneasy about this because the 'ramshackle assembly of conflicting sources of authority' makes it uncertain how much it matters in the first place where our allegiance lies, if democratic institutions can be established or sustained and how influential democratic policies can be. The key question is whether or not democracy can survive the reshuffling of authority and identity tied to globalization.[12]

Conclusion

This chapter has argued, with Strange, that structural shifts have made international structures, the politics of finance, the privatization of power and the problematic nature of state authority an indispensable part of any serious analysis of developing countries today. The chapter also underlined that Strange's argument that overall trends matter for developing countries leaves us with important and interesting questions about precisely how they matter, why they matter so differently and how their influence could be made more equitable.

Strange herself could certainly have done more to provide answers. The issue of how international structures interact with national ones is prominent in much work on developing countries, ranging from that of liberal economists to the present-day heirs of dependency scholars, passing by the work of so-called 'constructivists'. Similarly, there is extensive writing on why some institutions, countries and social groups are empowered and disempowered by international changes and why they are better at dealing with them. Finally, on the issue of reform prospects, there is extensive work in 'liberal' and institutionalist approaches in international relations (the fundamental issue of when conflict is possible) as well as in economics.

So why does Strange not do more to provide answers and to link up with this work more extensively? A specific answer is that her contradictory convictions and interests often prevented her from doing so. Strange the Keynesian political economist believed that international economic regulation was absolutely necessary, yet was prevented by Strange the realist international relations scholar from seriously believing that such regulation was a possibility worth thinking about. 'Keynesian Strange' was convinced that (international and/or national) state regulation of the economy is a necessity. Yet 'British Strange' put her faith in civil society and looked at bureaucracies with distaste. Consequently, she oscillated between a plea for self-regulation and a plea for (top-down) structural reform. Finally, 'Strange the scholar', who fought for the establishment of *international* political economy, found it very hard to engage with the work in comparative sociology or political economy which could have provided the details and nuances for her arguments.

More generally, there are obvious limits to the theoretical and empirical terrain that any researcher can cover and integrate. Strange's real contribution is an incisive empirical analysis, striking formulations, and an open-ended, though coherent, approach which allows her to develop our understanding of general trends and our capacity to raise questions. Indeed, Strange's unrelenting, often sweeping, academic theory bashing is not to be taken at face value. She has both a critical and a constructive theoretical project. She spent much of her long academic life criticizing the normative and practical implications of 'bad theory' (Guzzini *et al.* 1993). Moreover, Strange was inordinately consistent about which ingredients of theory are indispensable. She even provides an 'anti-textbook' (1988) that spells out her approach.

This approach is applicable also to developing countries and many of Strange's arguments are about developing countries. The many open questions and overly general arguments should be considered as an invitation to further research. They should certainly not serve as an excuse for continuing to neglect Strange's work on developing countries.

Notes

1 I would like to thank the participants in the IRES departmental seminar at the Central European University, Doro Bohle, Amy Verdun, Tom Lawton and, especially, Stefano Guzzini for their comments. Obviously, they do not share the responsibility for the results.

2 In fact, many – if not most – (ex-)dependency scholars would have no difficulties with the following non-deterministic claims and would draw similar conclusions.

3 Palma (1980) sees this as the key point of dependency.

4 Strange cites an estimate by Michel Aglietta to the effect that 90 per cent of the Mexican debt in the 1995 crisis was owed to non-official investors, including the holders of *tesobonos*, foreign fund managers and non-banks (1998c: 104).

5 Including the Brady initiative of 1992 to allow the poorest debtors to reschedule their debts and the IMF/World Bank initiative of 1996 to write off part of the debt.

6 Strange is obviously not alone in stressing the central role of finance in development. Classical economics underlines the importance of insufficient savings and therefore insufficient possibilities to invest. Historians (for example, Braudel 1979; Gerschenkron 1966) point out the increasing importance of controlling and channeling finance in conditions of late development.

7 The bulk of literature on finance and development is focused on more narrow questions such as why countries liberalize when they do (see Haggard *et al.* 1993: 3, fn.2 for a list of exceptions).

8 The choice could clearly have been different: Strange also writes about firms and business in specific sectors (shipping, insurance and telecoms, for instance), about 'econocrats', and about accountants as significant private actors. Also she refers to – but has not developed – the role of NGOs, the media and the international sports clubs in shaping international politics.

9 Strange quotes figures according to which the heroin market recorded a twentyfold increase and the cocaine market a fiftyfold increase between the mid-1970s and mid-1990s (1998c: 128).

10   Strange argues that one way around this difficulty would be to establish the equivalent of bond rating agencies (Standard & Poor, Moody's) for banks and to (somehow) make them reward the cleanest banks (1998c: 131).
11   In this she joins the many authors who write about the altered role of the state as a result of international shifts (for example, Cerny 1988; Dunning 1991; Evans 1995: ch.8).
12   Bauman, Beck and Fukuyama in a *Zeit* series (nos 46–9, 1999) on the future of democracy.

References

Amsden, Alice (1990), 'Third World Industrialization: 'Global Fordism' or a New Model?', *New Left Review*, 182, 5–31.

Amsden, Alice H. and Yoon-Dae Euh (1993), 'South Korea's Financial Reforms: Good-bye Financial Repression (Maybe, Hello New Institutional Restraints)', *World Development*, 21, 379–90.

Braudel, Fernand (1979), *Civilization matérielle, économie et capitalisme XVe–XVIIIe siècle*, Paris: Armand Colin.

Cerny, Philip G. (1988), *The Changing Architecture of Politics. Structure, Agency and the Future of the State*, London: Sage Publications.

Dunning, John H. (1991), 'Governments and Multinational Enterprises: From Confrontation to Co-operation?', *Millennium; Journal of International Studies*, 20(2), 225–45.

Evans, Peter (1995), *Embedded Autonomy: States and Industrial Transformation*, Princeton, NJ: Princeton University Press.

Evans, Peter (ed.) (1997), *State–Society Synergy: Government and Social Capital in Development*, Berkeley: International and Area Studies Research Series 94.

Frieden, Jeffrey (1991), 'Invested interests: the politics of national economic policies in a world of global finance', *International Organization*, 45, 425–51.

Gerschenkron, Alexander (1966), *Economic Backwardness in Historical Perpective. A book of Essays*, Cambridge, MA: Harvard University Press.

Gill, Stephen (1997), 'An Emu or an Ostrich? EMU and Neo-Liberal Economic Integration. Limits and Alternatives', in Petri Minkkinen and Heikki Patomäki (eds), *The Politics of Economic and Monetary Union*, Helsinki: The Finnish Institute of International Affairs, pp.205–28.

Guzzini, Stefano, Anna Leander, Jochen Lorentzen and Roger Morgan (1993), 'New Ideas for a Strange World: Melanges pour Susan', in Roger Morgan, Jochen Lorentzen, Anna Leander, and Stefano Guzzini (eds), *New Diplomacy in the Post Cold War World*, London: Macmillan, pp.3–25.

Haggard, Stephan, Chung H. Lee and Sylvia Maxfiled (eds) (1993), *The Politics of Finance in Developing Countries*, Ithaca: Cornell University Press.

Held, David (1991), 'Democracy, the Nation State and the Global System', in David Held (ed.), *Political Theory Today*, Stanford: Stanford University Press.

Hirschman, Albert O. (1980), *National Power and the Structure of Foreign Trade*, Berkeley: University of California Press.

Hirst, Paul Q. and Grahame Thompson (1996), *Globalization in Question: The international economy and the possibilities of governance*, Cambridge: Blackwell.

Mann, Michael (1997), 'Has Globalization Ended the Rise and Rise of the Nation-State?', *Review of International Political Economy*, 4, 472–96.

Palan, Ronen (1998), 'Trying to Have Your Cake and Eating It: How and Why the State System Has Created Offshore', *International Studies Quarterly*, 42, 625–44.

Palma, Gabriel (1980), 'Dependency and Development: A Critical Overview', in

Dudley Seers (ed.) (1991), *Dependency Theory: A Critical Reassessment*, London: Pinter Publishers, pp.20–73.

Stopford, John M. and Susan Strange (with J.S. Henley) (1991), *Rival States, Rival Firms, Competition for World Market Shares*, Cambridge: Cambridge University Press.

Strange, Susan (1986), *Casino Capitalism*, Oxford: Basil Blackwell.

Strange, Susan (1988), *States and Markets. An Introduction to International Political Economy*, Oxford and New York: Basil Blackwell.

Strange, Susan (1994), 'Wake up Krasner! The world *has* changed', *Review of International Political Economy*, 1, 209–19.

Strange, Susan (1995b), 'The Defective State', *Daedalus*, 24(2) Spring, 55–74.

Strange, Susan (1996), *The Retreat of the State: The Diffusion of Power in the World Economy*, Cambridge: Cambridge University Press.

Strange, Susan (1997), 'The Future of Global Capitalism; or Will Divergence Persist Forever?', in Colin Crouch and Wolfgang Streeck (eds), *The Political Economy of Modern Capitalism*, London: Sage, pp.182–92.

Strange, Susan (1998a), 'Globaloney? (Review Essay)', *Review of International Political Economy*, 5, 704–20.

Strange, Susan (1998b), *Mad Money*, Manchester: Manchester University Press.

Strange, Susan (1998c), 'The New World of Debt', *New Left Review*, 230, 91–114.

Strange, Susan (1998d), 'What Theory? The Theory in Mad Money', Centre for the Study of Globalization and Regionalism, working paper .

Wade, Robert and Frank Veneroso (1998), 'The East Asian Crash and the Wall Street–IMF Complex', *New Left Review*, 228.

PART VI
EMERGING AGENDAS

19 The Doubtful Handshake: From International to Comparative Political Economy?

G.P.E. WALZENBACH

Introduction

The work of Susan Strange as a pathbreaking contribution to the field of international political economy has been generally acknowledged. Surprisingly, given her concern with power relationships, comparative political economists have not taken on board these insights to the same extent. This has more to do with disciplinary sensitivities than with fundamental epistemological differences, in particular, as far as the role of institutions is concerned. Nevertheless, it is possible to reconcile a broadly defined institutionalist perspective with the argument about structural power. In making this point, however, a refinement of the state retreat hypothesis would have to be accepted. The latter follows from tracing the comparative dimension in Strange's work. Her recommendation to compare rather than to contrast in order to identify common trends in any political economy is a reminder of the need to establish a proper balance in analytical terms.

Therefore this chapter argues that the separation between international and comparative political economy has been an artificial one: firstly, as far as the focus of analysis is concerned, because of the increasing role played by non-state authorities; secondly, with regard to the method of analysis, because of an overriding concern with the distribution of values in society. For the same reasons, an explicit synthesis – or handshake – between the two remains doubtful. It would be more fruitful to investigate potential organizational alternatives in existing polities.

Institutions and Structural Power

As Strange's work offers an alternative theory of power, she can ignore neither the role of the state nor that of institutions. Consequently, her definition of international political economy leaves a significant role for institutions when analyzing social, political and economic arrangements affecting the global systems of production, exchange and distribution. These arrangements are 'the result of human decisions taken in the context of man-made institutions' (Strange 1994: 18). As mentioned earlier in this volume, the concept of structural power implies that state action is rooted in four fundamental structures: knowledge, security, production and finance. Furthermore, it assumes that human beings seek to provide basic values such as wealth, freedom and justice through social organization (ibid.: 17). Frequently, however, political systems will fail to realize these demands and, especially in times of globalization, a power shift from states to firms will undermine the proper functioning of democratic institutions (Palan 1999: 127–9).

In *The Retreat of the State*, Strange (1996: 197) did emphasize this legitimacy problem of a market economy. In a situation where authority is increasingly diffused, the accountability of market forces to political constraints has become less relevant. In turn, the traditional tasks of state institutions – delivering public services and redistributing income – are under threat. Despite considerable variation in this process, the specific research questions of comparative political scientists appear to be misplaced. As Strange (1997: 182) was convinced about the convergence of capitalist production and exchange to a common pattern, why should one want to know which of the diverse forms of capitalism are more likely to succeed in competition with others or what national institutions would affect the outcome of this particular competition? Instead, it was the speed with which states have to adapt to changing circumstances that would require explanation in the current stage of capitalism. Though she did come up with answers concerning the question why some national institutions were better in helping firms respond to new international challenges, other themes were considered more important: Why did governments have to become active at all, and how were changes in the world economy brought about? Not surprisingly, her answer did rest on policy decisions and corporate strategies taken by those with structural power rather than those with relational power (Strange 1996).

In any relationship there is always one party that determines the surrounding structure within which interactions take place. Thus structural power imposes 'a bias on the freedom of choice' (Strange 1994: 31). In the present world economy, for example, power is unequally distributed among states and a dominant state will almost naturally try to bias economic activity towards the same pattern. In practice, the structural power of the United States to change the options open to other governments, to foreign banks and trading corporations has vastly increased as a consequence of internationalized markets (Strange 1990a: 266).

From an institutionalist perspective, this notion of structural power is found wanting. We learn that 'it is derived in part from coercive force and in part from wealth' and that it 'is not confined to states and those who seize the power of government', but little is said about the dynamics of power relationships and how relational power is ultimately translated into structural power (Strange 1994: 33–4). At best there are similarities with Marxist accounts. Only a particular class is in the position to change the mode of production leading to adaptations in the institutional superstructure. From the structural power of the capitalist class over production follows logically the ability 'to consolidate and defend its social and political power, establishing constitutions, setting up political institutions and laying down legal and administrative processes and precedents that make it hard for others to challenge or upset' (ibid.: 29). In other words, a whole political system can be designed upon the capitalist template of society.

In institutional terms, it is more helpful to include notions of political and economic power even if it is difficult to draw a clear line between the two. In Strange's own account, economic power is subordinated to political power as it is manifest in the control over the state apparatus. Even in the case of private corporations and state enterprises with their own internal procedures and hierarchies of authority, decision making is essentially political rather than purely economic. In both environments the leadership can use power resources to compel obedience or conformity to their preferences from others (ibid.: 25–6).

The study of politics as well as economics has neglected the structural power argument. In fact, most comparative political scientists could gain new insights by taking on board this fundamental concept. In national political systems, for example, law can institutionalize and legitimize power derived both from coercive force, from the unequal distribution of wealth and from a general consensus about national aspirations. Likewise, the creation of economic markets is regularly the result of deliberate political decisions leading to institutional differences across sectors and time (ibid.: 37).

The doubts that Strange has expressed on the usefulness of a distinction between politics and economics are shared by a number of institutionalist writers. Hall (1997: 175) puts emphasis on the mediating role of institutional arrangements in his review of the role of power in political economy. The analysis should focus on the question of how institutions distribute power and resources across social groups and how the material interests of those groups are affected by particular economic policies. In the specific context of industrial relations, Pontusson (1995: 125) favors a conception of trade unions and business associations as both political and economic institutions. Most prominently, Lindblom (1977: 8) stated that 'in all political systems of the world, much of politics is economics, and most of economics is also politics'. Given such similarities, is it possible to reconcile the argument about structural power with institutionalist thinking?

A potential answer rests with the three central claims of historical institutionalism. According to this approach, institutions determine, firstly, the capacity of governments to legislate and implement policies; secondly, the strategies of political or economic actors by virtue of the opportunities and constraints they provide; and thirdly, the distribution of power among all these actors. Despite a dominant role of institutional arrangements, attention is also given to a set of other variables. Most importantly, the distribution of power among key actors becomes relevant in the context of a political situation specified by interest constellations and individual strategies.

There is, therefore, a growing awareness that a set of underlying structures shape the configuration and operation of political as well as economic institutions. In the long run it is the systemic power of capital that is defining and redefining the interests of a whole set of collective actors. In particular, when analyzing institutional change, both structural power relations and different interest constellations are of crucial importance. In a further step, institutions in themselves could be interpreted as a kind of structure constraining the action of individuals operating within them (Pontusson 1995: 120–25). Thus markets likewise could be considered institutions, which limit, for example, the choice open to firms and governments in international trade when trying to gain an export contract.

Unlike many other scholars, Strange (1996: 126) never saw the nation state as the exclusive unit of analysis and underlined the relevance of sectoral differences. Institutionalism, of course, can accommodate such an extended focus by including organizational arrangements tied to certain production structures rather than to centralized governmental agencies. And the same holds true if in a respective analysis firms are among the major actors in an issue area of international relations.

It is not necessary to concur with Drucker (1995: 140) who praises the modern large corporation as 'the representative social institution of society' in order to verify this claim. At least (neo-)institutionalism does encompass the nature of inter- and intra-firm relations when it identifies a distinctive set of sanctions and incentives rooted in a particular industrial relations system or the organizational features of capital. As a consequence, corporate enterprises seeking policies supportive of their long-term strategies will adapt to these constraints and opportunities cumulating in a particular pattern of aggregate economic performance (Hall 1997: 181). Thus structural variables have entered an institutional analysis. It remains to be seen whether they are the causal factors standing behind the convergence or divergence of capitalist production patterns across a large number of industrialized countries.

Comparative Political Economy

The previous section pointed to the possibility of integrating institutionalist reasoning into Strange's work. Frequently, however, her criticism was geared towards the dominance of comparative approaches overstating, as she thought, the role of national policies in the evolution of modern capitalism. On the one hand, comparative political scientists tend to overlook sectoral differences stemming from market forces, on the other, the differences they record are relatively insignificant given the common forces of structural change in the world economy (Strange 1995: 310).

In *States and Markets*, Strange (1994: 9) left it to the reader what to think, even if that meant interpreting the world political economy from a strictly national point of view. Since part of the lesson was to learn an appreciation of the ways in which different societies have ordered their political economy, the nexus between authority and market could depend on the value systems of particular countries (ibid.: 4–5). Clearly, whether a comparative or international political economist, the rationale for analysis can satisfy both: 'different societies (or the same societies at different times), while producing some of each of the four values, nevertheless give a different order of priority to each of them' (ibid.: 17). It is the mix of wealth, security, freedom and justice that distinguishes societies from each other.

In addition, a comparative approach should be in a position to provide answers to the question of why all industrialized states have adopted broadly similar system-sustaining policies and institutions at about the same time in the development of their political economy. Recall Strange's dictum: 'it always seemed to me that comparative social scientists are misnamed; they do not compare nearly as much as they contrast' (Strange 1997: 183). Rather than being a rejection of comparative approaches as such, this statement can be seen as a request to restore a proper balance. Surely, one of the purposes of comparative analysis is to 'demonstrate that certain relationships among variables hold true in a wide variety of settings' (Peters 1998: 26). Apart from differences, similarities and consistency, common causal factors and identical categorizations should receive equal attention. Thus political economists can still be committed to comparison as a method of analysis, but not necessarily to the proposition that cross-national variations are more important than common trends (Pontusson 1995: 129).

It is in this area that the overlap between comparative and international political economy is most obvious. When Palan (1999: 128), for example, qualifies states broadly as 'political processes' taking place in a variety of (sub)systems, he defines international political economy in terms of 'diversity represented by different societies'. His thoughts run contrary to the reductionism inherent in realist assumptions about international relations, but they match those in the comparative camp of political economy. For them the insight that societies are different and change over time can be taken for granted. Thus international political economy understood as an extended version of comparative political economy requires the development of theories from empirical observation rather than from a single overriding principle. At the same time, it cautions comparativists against the trend to identify as many 'models of national capitalism' as there are nations.

Strange (1998c: 107) herself was too much a pragmatist to give up the comparative dimension in political economy completely. The many problems of capitalist societies were acknowledged without presenting a deterministic argument in theoretical terms. While globalization and the imperatives of competition for market shares do affect the choice of national and common policy options, there remains room for maneuver in the European context to make societies productive and secure in this century. Though in basic agreement with a large number of writers who see the international political economy characterized by a new 'global' game, the tactical moves and strategies devised by individual states were still of interest (Strange 1998b). The globalization process continues to depend on the ability of states to (re)direct capital and trade flows as well as production facilities between national spaces (Palan 1999: 129).

At the same time, the criticism of comparative institutionalism helped to discover three new trends that occur under internationalized market conditions (Strange 1997: 187–8):

- the autonomy and the ability of governments to manage their national economies according to their own will has generally declined;
- the growth in transnational regulation of capitalist behavior

supplants national regulation and is eroding national differences;

- the loss of identity between the location of the firm's headquarters and its behavior in the world economy leads to the denationalization of the firm.

As a consequence, firms and enterprises had to gain center stage in the work of political economists. Admittedly, many of these private actors continued to appear with a strictly national affiliation on international markets but their behavior became much more responsive to multiple governments and not just to the government of their country of origin.

In addition, Strange qualified the findings of comparative political economists in an important way. She was not content with the view that 'multinational' is just a misnomer for enterprises which remain essentially national in character by maintaining their roots with society. By contrast, her argument was that these entities 'in their conduct' would not continue forever to be distinguished from each other by their national origins. In other words, 'change, though slow, is away from the home base, not towards it' (Strange 1998c: 105). Due to the way these enterprises are run and managed, convergence towards a new hybrid form of the transnational corporation is taking place. The latter replaces Vernon's preferred terminology of the 'multinational enterprise' with a view to establishing consistency with Strange's own core assumption of American global reach in a world with a growing asymmetry of regulatory power among the governments of capitalist countries (Vernon 1973).

Therefore the work reviewed here does not challenge the comparative method *per se*. Rather it presents a forceful demand to be aware of the various dimensions to be covered by proper comparative research. With regard to the role of firms, this meant to observe differences and similarities that 'are as likely to be related to the sector and the kind of business they are in as they are to their nationality' (Strange 1998c: 104). As noted before, even with calibrated instruments of comparison the state has to come back in at some stage: now transnational firms 'compete against one another for market shares in a number of *national* markets' (Strange 1996: 188, emphasis added).

After all, Strange conceived only the work in comparative politics that is exclusively state-based as being misplaced. Obviously, it made little sense to compare the policies of two host states in general, if their organizational structures are not always the most important independent variable in explaining the special relationship between firms and government. If this analytical tool is too blunt an instrument for her specific research question, maybe it can be refined through a twofold notion of authority. While intersectoral comparisons within national economies reveal that there are sectors greatly constrained by the traditional intervention of state authority, there are other sectors where state authority has been replaced. The very nature of these substitutes – banks, professions, Mafias, econocrats – suggests ample room for novel forms of comparative analysis.

Moreover, despite the common factors of capital mobility and technological change, divergent factors in the operation of capitalist production carry equal weight when comparing sectors of the economy (Strange 1997: 187). In fact, once the assumptions about the role of institutions affecting competing enterprises are modified, the differences between largely oligopolistic and highly competitive sectors become even more striking.

It was also by way of comparison that a whole set of conclusions became possible in Strange's work on international finance. One could think, for example, of her comparative typology of currencies in order to come to grips with the decline of sterling in the post-war period (Strange 1976: 1–40). Later she noted a big difference between the financial power exercised by the United States and that exercised by Japan, which in turn led to the finding about the special role information plays in the global financial structure. As she explained in her own words: 'what I am *comparing* is the structural power to extend or restrict the range of options open to others, with the relational power which Japan exercises' in the field of international finance (Strange 1990a: 259, emphasis added). Indeed, *Mad Money* is full of 'the everyday stuff of comparative politics and political economy' presenting the enormous variation in the financial regulatory systems of the United States, France, Germany and Japan (Strange 1998a: 140).

In Strange's early work, the potential of taxonomies and typologies for comparative purposes is exploited to the full. Long before mainly American scholars indulged in regime analysis as a possibility for structured comparison of diverse issue areas, and the return of Haas (1990) to a sophisticated typology to understand the causes of change in international organizations, her exceptional piece on the International Monetary Fund formed part of a comparison of the decision-making process in half a dozen UN specialized agencies (Strange 1974). It turned out that the course of international institutions was determined by the reactions of powerful governments to developments in the international political economy. As in other forms of comparison – across time, countries and political systems, firms and sectors – two closely related themes did inevitably emerge: the relative priority given to the central values of a society and the decisions leading to the realization of a particular mix of these values (Strange 1994: 23).

Retreat of the State

The critical reflection on the role of the state follows logically from the concern with institutionalized power relationships and comparative political economy. According to Strange's line of reasoning, a relocation of state power has already become a matter of fact: it had moved from states to markets and to 'non-state authorities' deriving power from market shares. The extension of this argument, however, with a view to postulating a general retreat of the state did run into difficulties. These shortcomings are present in two related propositions, namely that power had 'evaporated', in that no one was exercising it, and that it had shifted 'upward' from weak states to stronger ones with global or regional reach beyond their frontiers (Strange 1996: 189). Neither of the two does necessarily imply state retreat.

To be fair, Strange never lost sight of the more fundamental problem of governmental responsibilities, especially when it came to the regulation of financial markets. A relatively unregulated financial system, while increasing the degree of freedom for national residents to shift wealth out of the country, would create a paradoxical situation. National governments with their increased vulnerability to balance of payment deficits are held politically responsible, rather than the entrepreneurs who created the problem in the first place. This is all the more worrying as nation states no longer control what takes place in their territorial space. Common to all of them is the need to compete for the investments of transnational corporations by presenting profitable locations for business. As a consequence the forces of globalization would make the state into a 'landlord for the enterprises inhabiting the national territory' and governments into 'handmaidens of firms' (Strange 1998c: 113).

In making this point, Strange found herself in good company. First of all, she extrapolated Lindblom's assertion on the 'privileged position of business', which saw American private enterprises in a position to put additional pressure on political leaders by threatening to move their capital and investments elsewhere (Lindblom 1977). Like others, she also asked questions about the capacity of governments to regulate increasingly international markets and was convinced that their operation would shift the interests of firms away from traditional regulatory regimes and modes of production (Hall 1997: 187). Moreover, Strange took side with those who favored the systemic power of capital, embedded in the structures of capitalism, as the most obvious explanation for the dominant role that business actors have come to assume (Pontusson 1995: 142). At least temporarily, following the logic of accumulation, enterprises would be forced to seek additional markets rather than simply moving to other ones, and state agencies and business enter into a symbiosis, where in 'return for state support, the firm more readily adapts its strategies to accommodate national political (including economic security) goals' (Stopford and Strange 1991: 234). In practice, foreign policy interests could merge with industrial policy to create a 'new diplomacy' aimed at obtaining the value-added within the respective home territory (Strange 1992: 7).

However, some ambiguity remains in all of this when the role of the state in policy formulation and decision making is taken seriously (Müller and Wright 1994). True, when firms gain additional power, demands for changes in terms of policies could soon be followed up by more substantial reforms as regards institutional frameworks. But knowing the complexity of the policy-making process in any advanced industrialized country, would this amount to a situation where international capital has gained control over public policy? From a historical perspective it seems impossible to determine whether Keynesian macroeconomic policies have reached the point of no return and whether the alleged trend of declining state autonomy is indeed irreversible.

Strange (1990a: 262–3) did not negate the responsibility of national governments to assume new liability for the activities of banks within their jurisdiction which had acted according to their global reach. Once again in her forte – the politics of finance – she was most clear about how these developments came about. Most importantly, for the purposes of this section, they followed conscious policy decisions by governments, especially on the regulation of financial markets and banking institutions. Even though induced by a capitalist (pro-market) production structure organized so as to encourage and reward technical innovation, the latter was still the creation of politically determined laws and administrative decisions. One has to think here, for example, of the policy decision to allow the development of London as an alternative location for American banks dealing in Eurodollars or changes in the Japanese financial system triggered by market responses to direct US government pressures (Strange 1990a: 268).

Given such insights, it is hard to see why all governments ultimately are forced to adjust the order of political priorities – their agendas and policy targets – in pursuit of world market shares. At best, changes in firm–government relations can provide one of many causal factors for the observed convergence of reform programs across nations (Berger 1996). Therefore it seems sensible to refine the argument and to distinguish 'external' from 'internal' state retreat. In the case of the former, state autonomy is eroded in a number of international arenas and policy sectors. By contrast, 'internal' state retreat refers to a situation where governments still retain a nodal decision-making position in certain policy areas, albeit more constrained through a network of domestic bargains (Müller and Wright 1994: 7–8).

In empirical terms, the acceptance of this modification could do much for establishing greater consistency and continuity in Strange's work. In the same way as leading politicians find it hard to admit their reduced capacity to manage national economies because of globalized market conditions, they have difficulties in changing internal constraints in the form of government spending programs entrenched in industrial societies (Castles 1998: 322; Garrett 1998: 11). Since governments will be held responsible externally to foreign creditors and trade partners and internally to their voters and domestic interest groups, the net effect has been a containment of the rise in state expenditures rather than any dramatic reduction. Most evidently in policy areas that have been traditionally neglected by writers on international political economy, the 'Rhine model' with its economic and social superiority, might be here to stay in the short to medium term (Albert 1993: 168). In the not too distant future, capitalist systems will have to adjust not only to technological change and stronger competition, but likewise to population ageing and fertility decline, the latter, more likely, resulting in the growth of expenditure rather than in its decline.

Other advantages of a refinement in the state retreat hypothesis show themselves when analyzing international institutions as one set of actors in the international arena. On the one hand, Strange (1996: 171) depicts 'econocrats' in their exercise of authority as essentially system-preserving. The political activities taking place in specific institutional contexts would reinforce the authority of governments as participants in existing regimes of trade, finance and investment. Again, the United States serves as the prime example, with its efforts to liberalize international capital movements by putting pressure on its allies through the International Monetary Fund. In the case of the European Union, on the other hand, national governments seem to worry more about their national influence and continue to implement policies that are highly competitive with one another. The member states would really prefer a vacuum of power to some of the key policy areas mentioned in the treaties.

Ultimately, Strange (1996: 179) concluded that, if the state has lost significant political authority, it is unlikely to be 'upwards' to a supranational institution. Thus she underestimated the potential of international institutions to become independent· third parties by pretending their capacity to solve the transformed 'Lindblom problem', that is the regulation of competition among states that collude with the private sector (Walzenbach 1998: 60). If the external dimension of the argument about state retreat is explicitly acknowledged, both of the two aforementioned examples could be accommodated within the same concept. The econocrats will strive to use the pressure emerging from their constituency for their own purposes, presenting another threat to state autonomy.

A Synthesis of Comparative Politics and International Relations?

In recent years, an attempt has been made to synthesize comparative politics and international relations as a methodological response to the phenomenon of globalization (Keohane and Milner 1996b: 257). The burden is put on those studying international relations theory that are asked to introduce a 'systematic analysis of domestic politics' into their field (Milner 1998). Frequently, this request is justified because of a generally accepted prevalence of institutions as means of preference aggregation at the domestic and international level.[1]

At first sight, Strange (1995: 310) could not agree more: the separation of international relations from domestic political relations had been a 'totally artificial' one. As always, she showed some sympathy for the breaking down of barriers between disciplines.[2] However, as this section will show, her proposals on how to turn this proposition into reality and how to organize a respective analysis distinguished her work from that of other scholars (Strange 1994: 14–39). As one of her lasting achievements, she showed the overriding importance of the following four elements in a 'realist' approach to social science research.

1   The analytical method of political economy can be applied regardless of the academic divide between comparative government and international relations. Whether the research design is exclusively comparative or includes a single global economic system with simultaneously coexisting national societies, the focus must remain the same: each time an answer will rest with the way a set of different values is allocated.

2   The sources of superior structural power can be found at all levels. In fact, they are even 'the same in very small human groups' such as families and village communities. As a consequence the analysis of the political economist has to watch out for the motives – control over security, production, credit and knowledge – standing behind the exercise of authority.

3   The world is but a network of bargains and some bargains are more important than others. The most fundamental of all bargains is that between authority and the market. Another important bargain is that between the governments of states that in turn relies on the durability of domestic bargains. These sets of bar-

gains are liable to change over time and hence require sustained analysis.[3]

4   The analysis of transnational relations is as important as the analysis of intergovernmental relations. There is a common trend towards 'transnational substitutes' and 'functional equivalents' of the nation state. This is most evident in relations across national frontiers, between social and political groups or economic enterprises, or between any of these and the government of another state.[4]

In the context of a specific research project, this set of guidelines meant also a particular sequencing of analysis. With Strange's ambition to understand the dynamic of domestic and international politics as one, the comparison of national systems of financial regulation became the logical starting-point before moving on to the role of international institutions (Strange 1998a: 140).

In contrast to this bottom-up approach, Hall (1997: 178) summarizes the work of political economists who all tend to see changes in the international economy as the driving force behind politics. Only in a second step is this kind of economic reductionism given up, by attributing importance to producer-group politics and electoral coalitions at the domestic level. Despite contrasting views as to how increasing flows of goods and capital across national boundaries will affect the policies and institutions of the industrialized nations in detail, various accounts are brought together as part of a common top-down perspective.[5]

Along similar lines, Keohane and Milner argue that domestic politics in countries around the world should show signs of the impact of the world economy. In their account, a new consensus has already accepted that 'we can no longer understand politics within countries without comprehending the nature of the linkages between national economies and the world economy, and changes in such linkages' (1996a: 3). Strongly influenced by the thinking of economists, they refer to internationalization as 'the processes generated by underlying shifts in transaction costs that produce observable flows of goods, services, and capital' and explain changes in economic policies as well as political institutions with changes in relative prices (ibid.: 4).[6] In this analytical framework, changing value systems on the part of political actors are not a central concern and potential effects in the distribution of power and wealth can be neglected.

At least authors such as March and Olsen (1998: 963) have tried to establish a proper balance between domestic and international politics when they identify spillover processes operating in both directions. However, this balance is only achieved this time by separating (domestic) democratic factors from (international) individualistic factors of competitive self-interest. At any rate, the Strange-type approach had to go beyond such forms of reductionism as it incorporated the strict demand to expand the reach of politics.

Through the emphasis on transnational rather than international relations, Strange could observe asymmetrical patterns in state–market relationships and still operate with a kind of governmental dominance in the last instance. As put in her own words, 'the relationship across frontiers with some governments will be far more important in determining the outcomes in political economy than will relations with other governments' (Strange 1994: 21). The consequences of the biased exercise of state authority were described in dramatic terms: voters in most countries are denied the option to create jobs, countercyclical Keynesian demand management is impossible and a large part of the electorate prefers to abstain from political life. Much worse, modern democracies are apt to decline as voters become frustrated with constitutional government once they realize 'that their government is at the mercy of the US' (Strange 1996: 197).

Surely, this was an exaggerated scenario, to be matched only by the simplicity of the remedy. As the US President and Congress still hold the power to reverse the process, they could tip the balance of power back again from market to state. Nevertheless, as became clear from individual case studies, some of these points did carry a grain of truth (Strange 1990b: 270). For example, in the management of foreign debt, powerful states can exercise their authority indirectly through the bureaucracies of international organizations. Thus cooperation in these issue areas was possible only with the countries of the United States' choosing (Strange 1996: 193). Most clearly, American structural power could be exercised through a particular financial structure combined with large-scale capital flows from other countries to the United States (Strange 1990a: 268). For American politicians this could sometimes mean the conscious neglect of the US budget deficit or the prevention of Keynesian solutions on a worldwide scale (Scharpf 1987: 319–23).

For Strange (1987; 1990a: 268), a combination of domestic and international politics would not change a central theme in political economy, that is 'how to persuade people and politicians in the US to use the hegemonic, structural power they still have in a more enlightened and consistent way'.[7] Crises in the world economy would be initiated by political factors and hence could only be solved politically in the form of enlightened US leadership (Strange 1998a: 184–5). In response, the American-type synthesis did also identify political pressures emanating from the international system, but identified US influence on increased internationalization only as a correlated factor (Keohane and Milner 1996b: 255–6). Keeping in mind Strange's proposals on how to conduct research, the handshake between domestic and international politics remains doubtful, for it has always been hard 'to separate the two sides of the coin' (Strange 1998a: 44). The tools for analysis have to come from political economy – the discipline that never cherished a respective distinction in the first place.

Alternatives to Global Governance

Perhaps the most interesting contribution of Strange has been to reintroduce the distinction between state and non-state authority as the *problématique* around which political analysis should develop. As becomes clear from the most prominent case, the governance of firms, non-state authorities are not democratically governed. Though for reasons of efficiency and effectiveness not all forms of authority need to have a broad support base, the increasing diffusion of authority upwards and sideways from the state to other states and to non-state authorities results in a general lack of accountability and an unprecedented democratic deficit (Strange 1996: 197).

Note that this analysis does not rely on an argument where 'international integration' does result in convergent policies and institutions across nations that eventually undermine democratic nation states (Hall 1997: 195). In normative terms it concurs with the view expressed by Dahl (1990: 52) according to which 'democratic authority requires a variety of forms'. But in the current phase of capitalist development, traditional mechanisms of mutual adjustment among different forms of authority to solve problems have become inadequate. Now responsibility is excessively fragmented and the corresponding number of actors too large to know where to look for action (Lindblom 1977: 345).[8]

In this context, Strange mentioned three alternatives, each mutually compatible and inspired by a comprehensive understanding of politics as an exchange process of binding decisions for support (Deutsch 1968: 42). Hence her early preference to describe a network of bargained situations, with state authority retaining a nodal decision-making position, rather than to resort to terminology that already assumes an existing 'system of global governance'. It is an open question as to whether transnational movements and coalition of governments can establish functional equivalence to fully developed political systems (Strange 1996: 198). Although convinced that 'we have to invent a new kind of polity', she only sporadically gave some tentative hints as to what precise form such alternatives could acquire (ibid.: 190).[9] Certainly, it would be a question of the relative values shared by society. The first model that could tip the balance towards more equity, more stability and the quality of economic growth foresaw a reformed 'participatory capitalism' with widely shared decision-making powers at the subnational level of towns and provinces.

This demand for radical devolution cannot be integrated smoothly into the conceptions of others sharing the same cause-and-effect relationship as regards markets and dispersed authority. Crouch and Streeck (1997: 17), for example, posit that democratic sovereignty over the economy can be restored if it is internationally shared, that is, 'if the reach of what used to be "domestic" political institutions is expanded to match an expanding market', thus taking precisely an opposite direction in search of a solution. The notion of 'embedded neoliberalism', on the other hand, creates the impression that practical solutions do exist. At the regional level of the European Union, the free market has been already embedded 'in a regulatory framework which fosters both competitive business and social consensus' (Rhodes and Apeldoorn 1997: 184–5). Yet the large number of non-state authorities, inside as well as outside Europe, should caution against rash conclusions.

The future is bright, as far as new stimulating research is concerned, if Strange's second alternative is taken into account. Not only do states have the authority to allocate values, but the firm as a political institution can do just the same (Strange 1995: 309). Here the demand to redefine politics and to extend the limits of politics can have far-reaching consequences. It revives long-standing debates on means to restrain the capability of 'multinational enterprises' to exercise flexibility and choice across national and regional boundaries. So far the idea of creating an international organization with the task to devise respective ground rules has not progressed sufficiently. An internationally operating firm would still find it hard to accept such an institution taking part in the majority of its allocative decisions (Vernon 1973: 270). Given the Strange-type realism, a threat of considerable unilateral state action, in cases where firms do not justify their key decisions, would equally be an option only for the most powerful states. Rather than highlighting potential gains from intergovernmental cooperation, the more promising path is to be found in changes within non-state authorities themselves.

If the large 'corporation is in fact a private government', more should be learnt about its internal distribution of power (Vogel 1987: 405). Then, if the transnational enterprise is more than a specific organizational form, can it be sufficient, in terms of 'industrial citizenship', to simply convince workers that they have an equal stake in the prosperity of their firms (Drucker 1995: 208)? Obviously, extending the criterion of procedural democracy to the government of firms would amount to the imposition of an internal control mechanism to ensure that corporate decisions are influenced by those most heavily affected by them. But would worker management and worker ownership, as advocated by Dahl (1990: 115), be a solution to the efficiency–fairness tradeoff acceptable to society as a whole? Probably pragmatism will once more carry the day. In fact, with regard to the big American multinational corporations, it has already been noted that they are more closely related to the socially conscious Rhine model than to an Anglo-American model of highly flexible capitalism (Albert 1993: 208). In the not too distant future, a firm's dependency on the stock market or the distribution of its share capital might turn out to be a valid indicator for substitutive forms of democratic legitimacy.

At the same time, developments on the part of state authorities should not be neglected. Strange (1995: 297) agreed with those scholars who saw changes in markets undermining traditional systems of democratic government. Of course, this could go hand-in-hand with a strengthening of executive power vis-à-vis societal interests. In order to free business from its traditional constraints, political actors in this specific arena had to reassure their leadership in relation to some of their closest collaborators: legislatures and interest groups. Consequently, country-specific studies concluding that 'neither total control by the state nor total retreat of the state was a panacea' could underline the ambiguous effects of dispersed state authority (Schmidt 1996: 439).

The third and final alternative goes back to *Casino Capitalism*. At the time of its publication in 1986, a return to national economies – nationally regulated and managed – appeared to be the only viable solution, 'since international decision-making was beyond the capacity of nationally accountable governments' (Strange 1986: 189). Though this type of 'controlled disintegration' or 'decentralised decision-making' was conceived as a drastic remedy, it should remind executive actors facing pressures from the globalized market economy of options still to be pursued nationally (Scharpf 1997). A number of scholars have now begun to stress the continuing latitude of national governments to make political choices (Berger 1996; Gourevitch 1996: 259; Hall 1997: 188). In these interpretations, political entrepreneurship has maintained an important role in national systems. Politicians will continue to secure their re-election by intervening in the economy.[10] Under certain circumstances, economic shocks might lead to political crises that in turn create new opportunities for domestic policy solutions (Keohane and Milner 1996a: 16). While domestic institutions link international and domestic politics by channeling the strategies of political leaders, their policies can still make a difference (Keohane and Milner 1996b: 255).

All of this points to a redefinition of unilateralism as a response to globalization. In order to go beyond merely 'defensive strategies', this would have to entail an increased flexibility and openness of national projects that are initiated by executive government. The established structures of domestic polities need to incorporate more rather than less diversity in the form of sectoral coalitions, substitutive forms of democracy and devolution. For future societies this kind of selective specialization seems to be the most promising alternative of all.

Conclusion

The institutionalist perspective taken in this contribution helped to identify the comparative dimension in the work of Susan Strange. Seen from this angle, her arguments about the rise of transnational corporations, the retreat of the state and the reallocation of authority under internationalized market conditions become less extreme. Indeed, one can see the clear intention behind the use of trenchant scenarios to alert the reader to the existing shortcomings of orthodox thinking found in much of the literature on comparative politics *and* international relations. From this follows also a good deal of skepticism as to the possibility and, in fact, necessity to combine these two subdisciplines of political science into one new paradigm. There are, at least in rudimentary form, alternatives to global governance that do warrant the somehow different and more cross-cutting analytical tools of political economy.

Therefore Strange should be remembered as a distinguished political economist, first of all, because she advocated an extension of politics into areas traditionally dominated by economists. In terms of method, this implied the recourse to a number of analytical tools – structural power, network of bargains, non-state authority – rather than pushing any one of them to the highest sophistication. She did so with excellent results. With relatively minor modifications, her contributions can be utilized for theoretically informed empirical research on a wide range of issues. The concepts she used and the themes she chose invariably reflected a sense of both promising research agendas and practical relevance. Taken together, this should be good news for comparativists and specialists in international relations alike.

Notes

1   Strange (1996: 69) agreed with the Putnam model insofar as the overall likelihood that a bargain will be struck at the international level depends on the balance of political forces within the participating countries.

2   Indeed, this was a fundamental requirement if one would want to expand rather than to narrow the analysis.
3   Thus the identification of the partners in the key bargains becomes 'an essential stage in the analysis of a *dynamic* situation' (Strange 1994: 40, emphasis added).
4   Other types of non-state authorities – banks, religious associations, universities and scientific communities – can also become participants in transnational politics.
5   The causal chain is clear. The story of globalization starts with shifting material interests of key economic groups because of similar economic pressures (Hall 1997: 189).
6   More specifically, domestic institutions can also block or distort these relative price signals from the international economy (Keohane and Milner 1996b: 254).
7   An answer to this question would have to rely on traditional instruments of political science and comparative government.
8   Ideally, this would require a recombination of economic (and political) institutions at various spatial levels. Boyer and Hollingsworth (1997: 468) have redefined the notion of 'nestedness' to describe this situation.
9   According to March and Olsen (1998: 947) only 'local processes of growth, adaptation, elaboration, conflict, and competition within and among political units' could lead to such new political orders.
10   In seminars Strange frequently stressed the special responsibility politicians have with regard to their electorates. Given this important constraint, some of the findings of policy analysis would be in need of modification.

References

Albert, M. (1993), *Capitalism against Capitalism*, London: Whurr Publishers.

Berger, S. (1996), 'Introduction', in S. Berger and R. Dore (eds), *National Diversity and Global Capitalism*, Ithaca and London: Cornell University Press, pp.1–25.

Boyer, R. and J.R. Hollingsworth (1997), 'From National Embeddedness to Spatial and Institutional Nestedness', in R. Boyer and J.R. Hollingsworth (eds), *Contemporary Capitalism*, Cambridge: Cambridge University Press, pp.433–84.

Castles, F.G. (1998), *Comparative Public Policy*, Cheltenham, UK and Lyme, US: Edward Elgar.

Crouch, C. and W. Streeck (1997), 'Introduction: The Future of Capitalist Diversity', in C. Crouch and W. Streeck (eds), *The Political Economy of Modern Capitalism*, London: Sage, pp.1–18.

Dahl, R.A. ([1970] 1990), *After the Revolution?*, New Haven and London: Yale University Press.

Deutsch, K.W. (1968), *The Analysis of International Relations*, Englewood Cliffs, NJ: Prentice-Hall.

Drucker, P.F. ([1946] 1995), *The Concept of the Corporation*, London: Transaction Publishers.

Garrett, G. (1998), *Partisan Politics in the Global Economy*, Cambridge: Cambridge University Press.

Gourevitch, P.A. (1996), 'The Macropolitics of Microinstitutional Differences in the Analysis of Comparative Capitalism', in S. Berger and R. Dore (eds), *National Diversity and Global Capitalism*, Ithaca and London: Cornell University Press, pp.239–59.

Haas, E.B. (1990), *When Knowledge is Power*, Berkeley: University of California Press.

Hall, P.A. (1997), 'The role of interests, institutions and ideas in the comparative political economy of the industrialised nations', in M.I. Lichbach and A.S. Zuckerman (eds), *Comparative Politics*, Cambridge: Cambridge University Press, pp.174–207.

Keohane, R.O. and H. Milner (1996a), 'Internationalization and Domestic Politics: An Introduction', in R.O. Keohane and H. Milner (eds), *Internationalization and Domestic Politics*, Cambridge: Cambridge University Press, pp.3–24.

Keohane, R.O. and H. Milner (1996b), 'Internationalization and Domestic Politics: A Conclusion', in R.O. Keohane and H. Milner (eds), *Internationalization and Domestic Politics*, Cambridge: Cambridge University Press, pp.243–58.

Lindblom, C.E. (1977), *Politics and Markets*, New York: Basic Books.

March, J.G. and J.P. Olsen (1998), 'The Institutional Dynamics of International Political Orders', *International Organization*, 52(4), 943–69.

Milner, H. (1998), 'Rationalizing Politics: The Emerging Synthesis of International, American and Comparative Politics', *International Organization*, 52(4), 759–86.

Müller, W. and V. Wright (1994), 'Reshaping the State in Western Europe: The Limits to Retreat', *West European Politics*, 17(3), 1–11.

Palan, R. (1999), 'Susan Strange 1923–1998: A Great International Relations Theorist', *Review of International Political Economy*, 6(2), 121–32.

Peters, Guy B. (1998), *Comparative Politics*, London: Macmillan.

Pontusson, J. (1995), 'From Comparative Public Policy to Political Economy', *Comparative Political Studies*, 28(1), 117–47.

Rhodes, M. and B. van Apeldoorn (1997), 'Capitalism versus Capitalism in Western Europe', in M. Rhodes, P. Heywood and V. Wright (eds), *Developments in West European Politics*, London: Macmillan, pp.171–89.

Scharpf, F.W. (1987), *Sozialdemokratische Krisenpolitik in Europa*, 2. Auflage, Frankfurt am Main: Campus.

Scharpf, F.W. (1997), 'Combating Unemployment in Continental Europe', *RSC Policy Papers*, 97(3), Florence: European University Institute.

Schmidt, V.A. (1996), *From State to Market?*, Cambridge: Cambridge University Press.

Stopford, J. and S. Strange (with J.S. Henley) (1991), *Rival States, Rival Firms*, Cambridge: Cambridge University Press.

Strange, S. (1974), 'IMF: Monetary Managers', in: R.W. Cox and H.K. Jacobson (eds), *The Anatomy of Influence*, London: Yale University Press, pp.263–97.

Strange, S. (1976), *Sterling and British Policy*, London: Oxford University Press.

Strange, S. (1986), *Casino Capitalism*, Oxford: Blackwell.

Strange, S. (1987), 'The Persistent Myth of Lost Hegemony', *International Organization*, 41(4), 551–74.

Strange, S. (1990a), 'Finance, Information and Power', *Review of International Studies*, 16, 259–74.

Strange, S. (1990b), 'The Name of the Game', in N. Rizopoulos (ed.), *Sea Changes*, New York: Council on Foreign Relations Press, pp.238–73.

Strange, S. (1992), 'States, Firms and Diplomacy', *International Affairs*, 68(1), 1–15.

Strange, S. (1994), *States and Markets*, 2nd edn, London: Pinter Publishers.

Strange, S. (1995), 'The Limits of Politics', *Government and Opposition*, 30(3), 291–311.

Strange, S. (1996), *The Retreat of the State*, Cambridge: Cambridge University Press.

Strange, S. (1997), 'The Future of Global Capitalism; or Will Divergence Persist Forever?', in C. Crouch and W. Streeck (eds), *The Political Economy of Modern Capitalism*, London: Sage, pp.182–91.

Strange, S. (1998a), *Mad Money*, Manchester: Manchester University Press.

Strange, S. (1998b), 'Globaloney?', *Review of International Political Economy*, 5(4), 704–20.

Strange, S. (1998c), 'Who are EU? Ambiguities in the Concept of Competitiveness', *Journal of Common Market Studies*, 36(1), 101–14.

Vernon, R. (1973), *Sovereignty at Bay*, Harmondsworth: Penguin Books.

Vogel, D. (1987), 'Political Science and the Study of Corporate Power: A Dissent from the New Conventional Wisdom', *British Journal of Political Science*, 17(4), 385–408.

Walzenbach, G. (1998), *Co-ordination in Context: Institutional Choices to Promote Exports*, Aldershot: Ashgate.

20 Going Beyond States and Markets to Civil Societies?

TIMOTHY M. SHAW, SANDRA J. MACLEAN AND MARIA NZOMO

Introduction

Susan Strange is remembered for encouraging us to go beyond states as the primary actor in international relations and bring in companies. As she and others have argued, the competition between states is no longer for territory but for shares in the world market for goods and services. Yet, at the beginning of the new millennium, it has become apparent that international relations and international political economy are not solely determined by states and markets. Rather, they are functions of complex, often paradoxical,[1] arrangements among the trinity of state, business and civil society. Therefore, in this chapter, we argue that we should go beyond the outdated and misleading orthodoxies of both realism and international political economy by bringing in civil societies. This involves focusing on how non-governmental organizations (NGOs) and other elements in civil society seek to maximize their global activity and visibility.

While privileging civil society is our primary purpose, we also suggest that, at the dawn of the 21st century, we should focus more on South as well as North and treat the meso-/regional level of relations more seriously. Moreover, informed by contemporary informal and illegal exchange, we should go beyond legitimate and official trade and finance to examine the burgeoning worlds of black markets, drugs, gangs/mafias, money laundering, private security and so forth. Taken together, this group of issues is compatible with Strange's legendary non-traditional perspective: she would enjoy such analyses and debates whether or not they were entirely compatible with her own iconoclastic approach. We are confident, however, that such extensions of 'Strange power' are indeed consistent with her realistic if not realist view of international relations in the late 20th century. Indeed, they expand upon a theme she introduced in one of her last publications (1999): the failure of 'Westfailianism'[2] to sustain a capitalist system that was protective of the planet or its people.

This chapter spans a set of overlapping debates, from globalization to governance, with relevance to the interrelated fields of international relations and international political economy and development studies (Dickson 1997; Dunn and Shaw 2000; Shaw 1997) (see final section below). In particular, extending 'Strange power' to include civil society means that notions of 'governance', at all levels 'from local to global' (Stiles 2000), become more inclusive and sustainable, yet also more disputed and challenging. Governance at the turn of the millennium means more than government, but rather the involvement on a continuous basis of non-state actors like companies and NGOs in inducing as well as identifying and responding to the policy challenges confronting governments. Moreover, governance no longer refers only to processes contained within national boundaries. Instead, it involves interactions among the triad of state, business and society actors at all levels from local through national and regional to global, As Held *et al.* put it, our new era has seen layers of governance spread within and across political boundaries (1999b: 487).

Governance for the 21st Century: Bringing in Civil Society

The multi-layer, multi-actor governance systems that are emerging at the beginning of the 21st century are evolving at least partly in response to new forms and greater levels of insecurity within and across societies. To paraphrase Strange, changing patterns of governance reflect the social failure of Westphalianism (1999: 345). To find remedies in this new security environment for the deteriorating socioeconomic conditions, looming threats to the environment and the growing alienation of people from their states, she argued that 'we have to escape and resist the state-centrism inherent in the analysis of conventional international relations' (ibid.: 354). In this 'epitaph', Strange refers positively to Robert Cox's work on civil society as the means of resistance to the failing state system, to which we refer below.

At the start of the 2000s, such remonstrations now resonate within an ever-widening circle of scholars across various disciplines and ideological perspectives. Yet, at the beginning of the 1990s, even after the end of the cold war, Strange's voice was one of the few to warn of the security problems inherent in the changes taking place in the global political economy. At that time, with typical prescience, she argued that 'the name of the game' of international relations was being radically altered as preoccupations shifted from control of territory to control of market shares. Indeed, corporate power had become so excessive, she insisted, that, in order to re-establish an effective balance between state and market, 'the task of the 1990s' was 'to devise a wholly new system of government for the business civilization of the next century' (Strange 1990).

If there was a limitation in Strange's views on governance for the new millennium, it was that she focused too narrowly on state–market relations (especially those of the North) and paid too little heed to the efforts or responsibilities of civil societies. Yet, implicitly, her argument was based on concerns about social justice and providing new governance institutions for a changing civilization. However, as indicated by an article she wrote toward the end of the 1990s and of her life, Strange was beginning 'to bring in civil society' more explicitly, noting, in particular, that an emerging global civil society is not to be dismissed lightly (Strange 1999: 352).

We can only speculate as to what advances Strange's clear thinking might have provided had she been granted the time to hone her ideas on civil society and incorporate them in her recommendations for emerging systems of governance. Nevertheless, although now bereft of her insight, the project that she had embarked upon has been taken up by several other capable scholars from various disciplines – sociology and political philosophy as well as economics, international political economy and international relations – representative of the growing awareness among scholars of the dislocations of power caused by globalization and the need for a new 'social contract' among governments, businesses and citizens, sociologists. Held *et al.* argue:

> The emerging shape of governance means that we need to stop thinking of state power as something that is indivisible and territorially exclusive. [And, while it] makes more sense to speak about the transformation of state power than the end of the state [we must] re-form our existing territorially defined democratic institutions and practices so that politics can continue to address human aspirations and needs. (1999b: 495)

Overall, the challenge is to provide systems of governance among our aforementioned trinity of actor types that protect human dignity and security, or, as indicated by the UNDP's tenth anniversary edition of its annual *Human Development Report*, the problem is how to advance and then realise 'globalisation with a human face' (1999: 1). The UNDP response emphasizes a range of possible forms of governance, which are no longer just 'good' or 'democratic' but also associated with several issues such as global/island/ocean peace building and so on, all of which privilege 'human development': 'National and global governance have to be reinvented with human development and equity at their core' (ibid.: 7).

Any such reinventions are likely to proceed unevenly, evolving out of intense political struggle. Therefore the optimism of Held and others such as Archibugi, Galtung and Falk (Holden 2000), who see hopeful prospects in the 'changing contours of political community' for extending the institutional base for democracy beyond national borders, may be somewhat premature. Their concept of a 'cosmopolitan democracy' depends upon the establishment of a layered form of governance that would reflect and accommodate the multiple identities and needs of people who share interests and loyalties across as well as within circumscribed geographical boundaries. Yet, as Cox (1999: 133) observes, the democratizing elements within this emerging transnational civil society are not particularly strong or well-organized. Moreover, there are various covert, often quite malignant, informal actors who operate outside or on the margins of legitimate systems of governance. Such anti-democratic, even anarchical, forces contradict any idealistic notions about the extent to which democratizing propensities exist within the non-state sector.

Yet we would argue that the highly symbolic *fin-de-siècle* débâcle of the 'battle for Seattle'[3] suggested that institutions like the WTO, let alone the Multilateral Agreement on Investment (MAI) cannot take civil society for granted. A state and corporate consensus is no longer enough. In the 21st century, all three 'sides' or points of our governance 'triangle' will have to be legitimate participants if there is to be any possibility of realizing sustainable human development and security; that is, civil society as well as state and firms coexisting, even cooperating, in a democratic political culture (UNDP 1999: 12).

The prospects of defining, agreeing and sustaining such three-sided governance architecture have improved with the increasing skepticism expressed among senior World Bank officials about the efficacy of orthodox structural adjustment prescriptions (Court 1999). By the end of the 20th century, the easy hegemony of 'neoliberalism' had surely peaked, as symbolized by the cautions advanced by disparate analysts from George Soros to Gerry Helleiner.[4] So just ahead of the millennium, the Bank under James Wolfensohn and Joseph Stiglitz began to move back towards a somewhat more Keynesian perspective to connect the simultaneous phenomena of 'globalization' and 'localization' (World Bank 1999/2000: iii and 4): a 'Comprehensive Development Framework' (ibid.: 21).

Bringing in Civil Society: Rival States, Rival Firms, Rival NGOs

Our primary thesis is that we cannot understand, let alone contribute to, contemporary world politics without bringing in 'civil society': the myriad roles of non-state, non-corporate actors, outside as well as inside national territories (Aulakh and Schechter 2000; Murphy 2000; Van Rooy 1999).

Just as recognizing the role of companies in international relations meant analyzing firm–firm as well as state–state and firm–state relations (Strange 1994: 108), so including civil societies in our purview means treating a trio of actor types in 'international relations': civil society–civil society as well as civil society–firm and civil society–state. Such a formulation lends greater reality and policy relevance to any analysis of contemporary global politics, such as debates over landmines, ozone depletion, the WTO or the MAI (Keck and Sikkink 1998, Lipschutz 1996; Wapner 1996). As the latest World Bank *World Development Report 1999/2000* indicates:

> *Processes are just as important as policies.* Sustained development requires institutions of good governance that embody transparent and participatory processes and that encompass partnerships and other arrangements among the government, the private sector, non-governmental organizations (NGOs), and other elements of civil society. (1999/2000: 14)

Our 'triangle' of state–company–civil society relations is somewhat different, then, from that advanced by Strange in the 1990s, as her notion of 'diplomacy' consisted of firms dealing with both home and foreign governments as well as with other firms (Strange 1994: 108; 2000: 85). To be sure, theoretical distinctions between this trinity of actor types is harder to sustain in practice given overlaps of individuals, institutions, ideologies and so forth: the apparent autonomy between states, companies and civil societies declines, even disappears, when actual relations are investigated. Nevertheless, despite the tendency towards collaboration and cooptation, such distinctions remain valid, as indicated by distinct corporate and civil society as well as state and regional positions over, say, biodiversity, global warming, genetically modified foods and so on (Aulakh and Schechter 2000; Lindberg and Sverrisson 1997; Van Rooy 1999).

Nowhere is this redefinition and rearrangement further advanced than in Africa. In the first 40 years of post-colonial formal independence, the state in Africa has gone from appropriating near-monopolistic powers over both economy and society to an equally precipitous liberalization and privatization of both as well as the polity. Civil society, primarily in the shape of myriad, heterogeneous NGOs, has become crucial to the continent's basic needs in terms of the provision of education, health and other services. Africa is itself heterogeneous, so in the new century we need to distinguish between 'collapsed' or 'failed' states (for example, Liberia, Sierra Leone, Somalia) and 'developmental' regimes (for example, Botswana, Mauritius, Uganda). In all cases, private investment and management has become central, whether formally (as in Botswana) or informally (as in Somalia). Furthermore, human security as well as human development is increasingly a function of private organizations: whether formal and legal security companies or less legal and more controversial mercenary organizations, mafias and so on (see below). Africa has examples of (relatively) successful cases of reform, transition and reconstruction (for example, Ghana, Mozambique, South Africa, Uganda) and of unsuccessful attempts at peace building (for example, Angola, the Democratic Republic of the Congo (DRC), Sudan). The problematic process of democratization is apparent in post-Abacha Nigeria, and the possibilities for a proliferation of fragmenting states most immediate in the DRC and Somalia. Local to regional governance in the continent increasingly includes a range of non-state actors. Whether renaissance or anarchy will endure remains an open question (Shaw and Nyang'oro 2000).

Nevertheless, bringing in civil society permits a more comprehensive notion of 'governance', appropriate to the new millennium. A growing awareness of the 'triangular' configuration of the governance complex as well as the importance of a strong civil society within that nexus is evident in Africa. At the grassroots, organizations such as the National Constitutional Assembly (NCA) in Zimbabwe are mobilizing to demand input into legislative processes. Others, such as the regional organization, MWENGO, are attempting to forge transnational links among NGOs to address issues of governance and globalization. Many, both individually and collectively, are putting pressure on (or more rarely, working with) governments to promote human security issues of environment, health and human rights and others (MacLean *et al.* 2000). Beyond the grassroots, there is also considerable interest in various research institutes to document as well as promote these new energies in civil society. An example is the UNDP/CODESRIA 15-country programme that has the ambitious research and dissemination mandate to analyze economic, social and political trends in order to propose 'participatory intervention methods and approaches for strengthening civil society and governments' (Nzomo 2000).

Towards the Globalization of Political Economy: beyond 'Mad Money'

Strange advocated bringing firms back into international relations. In addition to further extending the field to civil society, we argue that it now needs to become more global by including distinctive forms of states and firms (as well as civil societies) in the 'South' as well as the 'North'. To be sure, definitions of and distinctions between North and South are becoming more problematic, particularly given the 'Asian miracle' (then 'flu') along with the proliferation of Southern diasporas in the North (Court 1999; Shaw 1997). To be fair, Strange herself, in the first half of the 1990s, identified diverse responses to 'globalizations' and 'conditionalities' among Brazil, Kenya and Malaysia (Strange 1994: 109–10).

Nevertheless, very unequal patterns of basic needs, technology and vulnerability persist, particularly given the incidence and impact of two decades under the hegemony of neoliberalism, leading to a proliferation of 'structural adjustment' conditionalities. In the post-cold war era, tensions are most frequent between the more and less developed countries. Therefore, for reasons of pragmatism as well as principle, inequalities need to be reduced rather than encouraged. As the UNDP suggests: 'The opportunities and benefits of globalization need to be shared much more widely' (1999: 2). Otherwise, human security will become ever more problematic in the North as well as South. The interconnectedness of new security issues in both North and South is especially apparent in a range of new threats, from 'fundamentalist terrorists' to migrations and viruses. Perhaps their most familiar form in the 1990s was 'internal' conflicts in the South which 'spilled over' to both immediate regions and the North in terms of a range of peace-keeping expectations, refugee flows and reconstruction programs (Shaw and MacLean 1999; Shaw *et al.* 1998). Increasingly expensive 'externalities' related to exponential inequalities both between and within states, exacerbated if not caused by structural adjustment conditionalities.

In particular, picking up on one of Strange's primary concerns, the UNDP is bothered that new information and communications technologies are not only driving globalization but also exacerbating inequalities: 'polarizing the world into the connected and the isolated' (UNDP 1999: 5). Likewise, the World Bank post-structural adjustment seeks to balance divergent pressures towards globalization and localization though technological and other connections:

> This report does not praise or condemn *globalization and localization*. Rather, it sees them as *phenomena that no development agenda can afford to ignore*. While national governments remain central to the

development effort, globalization and localization require that they engage in essential institution-building at both the supra- and subnational levels in order to capture the benefits of growth in the 21st century. (World Bank 1999/2000: 4–5, emphases added)

Regional arrangements may mitigate some of the more gross differences, but regional corridors or triangles and hubs-and-spokes tend to replicate global hierarchies on a local level.

Beyond 'Casino Capitalism' to 'Narco-Diplomacy'?

The dynamic growth of global capitalism has been accompanied by an even more dramatic expansion of the international black market (Naylor 1999). Informal and illegal trade in alcohol, diamonds, drugs, gold, guns, oil and so forth now constitutes at least 10 per cent of global trade. This is more evident in some countries and regions than others, but present in all. It has spawned its own money-laundering nexus – a distinctive form of foreign direct investment. This in turn has led to a 1990s variety of imperial interventions: 'ugly American' agents of the FRB/FBI positioned in the central banks of suspect or sanctioned countries. Moreover, it has become more global, as Eastern European mafias have joined those already established in Asia, North America and Western Europe: a particular subset of diasporic communities (Shaw 2000b).

Just as global corporations dwarf many countries in size, so would a range of other non-state actors, from global NGOs to transnational mafias (ibid.). The latter have established their own global 'strategic alliances' to facilitate their international activities (Beere and Naylor 1999). They have developed their own technologies of telecommunications (for example, cell-phones, global positioning and the internet) and coercion (for example, AK47s and remote-controlled bombs) to advance their market share or 'rent'. Like states and companies, they continuously struggle for market share, being ready to move into new sectors as opportunities arise (second-hand and/or stolen vehicles from Western to Eastern Europe, French beer to Britain, and so on). Their considerable resources can keep civil wars going as well as finance private armies. They are adroit at 'geopolitics', taking advantage of well-located island and land-locked states to smuggle particular commodities or technologies, whether containers or trains or airfreight. Such adroitness has led to new forms of inter-state cooperation in regional seas, such as 'shipriders' from the Caribbean on US Coastguard patrols around Florida.

Strange implored us to bring in firms, but some of these 'firms' are national and/or sectoral 'branches' of transnational organized crime syndicates! Clearly, Strange was aware of this, observing with her usual understated irony that 'a lot of rascals get away with too much loot' (1990: 266). Yet her solutions to the growing levels of corruption and associated insecurities were based on the overly optimistic assumptions that revising relations between states and markets was sufficient and that global financial instability could be restored through the re-establishment of American hegemony (albeit with an enlightened internationalist profile). Although she was certainly not alone in arguing that the end of the cold war provided 'a wonderful and unexpected opportunity' to bring the world out of the 'particularly dangerous wood' that existed at the beginning of the 1990s, there was insufficient consideration given to where the impetus for the necessary changes would come from. As Strange herself noted: 'structural change ... has driven the developing countries into the arms of the TNCs and ... the same structural change has driven the TNCs into the arms of developing countries' governments' (1991: 248). In short, the salient feature of the globalized political economy is that 'big business and the state' are complicit in supporting the interests of transnational capital. Hence the most likely source of change is from within the disadvantaged sector of civil society: the site of counterhegemonic forces.

Scholars who employ a Gramscian historical materialist perspective have elaborated representations of civil society as the site of such resistance. Foremost among them is Robert Cox who draws on Gramsci's concept of civil society as the realm of both continuity and transformation in governance structures and processes. According to this view, during periods of 'hegemony', civil society is characterized by a preponderance of social and cultural practices and attitudes that reinforce the dominant ideology. Always at least latent in civil society, however, and emerging during periods of stress to challenge the prevailing order, are counterforces: potent sources of social and political change. In short, 'civil society is both shaper and shaped, an agent of stabilization and reproduction, and potential agent of transformation' (Cox 1999: 5). Although Gramsci's concept of civil society was developed in the early 20th century for the particular circumstances of Italy, Cox has exposed the similarities between the social and political upheavals associated with the system change occurring in that country at that time and those that are currently destabilizing the international system that has been in existence since the 1600s.

Consistent with Gramsci's understanding of the role that civil society played in governance in his time and place is the realization that the instability in our present-day structures of governance may originate from or be reproduced in civil society. Hence civil society is a space in which competing ideas and interests may coexist, compete or clash. In certain cases, the contestation is anything but 'civil', to the extent even that it may be inappropriate to consider some of the antagonists to be part of civil society, but rather as 'uncivil' elements of greater society who operate outside the boundaries of institution-alized social order. In the present transformation in order, the state's responsiveness has been transferred from the domestic constituency to global capital, thereby opening up a vacuum or void for govern-ance which has allowed such groups to be more assertive and opportunistic. As they are often more directly and lucratively con-nected to global market forces, many reactionary, criminal or other malevolent forces have tended to move into the available space more decisively than have democratic or developmentalist elements in civil society.

As already indicated, various conservative, illegal and terrorist groups exist and often associate in a covert world that is beyond the surveillance and regulatory capabilities of formal governance insti-tutions, yet the formal and informal worlds occasionally overlap: 'the covert world penetrates the visible authorities in government and corporations' (Cox 1999: 14). This can occur in operations rang-ing from diamond smuggling in Africa to aeronautics sales deals in Europe and North America. As a consequence, where more socially responsible forces in civil society have emerged, they are frequently displaced, coopted or otherwise weakened by stronger powers. In Cox's words:

> promotion of civil society has been coopted by forces beyond the propagation of neoliberal economics as a way of defusing and channeling potential protest. Consequently, civil society, in its dual form of class based organizations and social activism, has a latent but not very fully realized potential for social and political transforma-tion. The covert world, in the form of organized crime, drug cartels, and political corruption, is rife in these countries (which have had a decline in both state authority and effectiveness in regulating the mar-ket). The decline in state authority is not matched by a development of civil society. (1999: 23)

New Regionalisms: beyond 'the Retreat of the State'?

Both the retreat of the old state and resilience of new forms of gov-ernance are apparent at the intermediate, meso-level: a rather heterogeneous range of 'regional' relations and institutions. The 'new regionalisms' perspective (Boas, Marchand and Shaw 1999) goes be-yond formal, inter-state economic (and strategic) structures such as the EU (or NATO) to examine a range of informal as well as formal, non-state and state arrangements, which may or may not be similar in scale or scope.

In particular, this novel approach looks at flexible forms of regional governance involving all the trio of actors types indicated above, companies and civil societies as well as states, which may be based on shared culture, ecology, ethnicity, history, (in)security and peace building. Such regional architectures may embrace just some parts of, rather than all of, states as participants. They are increasingly structured in terms of 'corridors' or 'triangles' in which mutual interests of the trio of actor types – companies and civil societies as well as states at all levels, especially the local – can be advanced. If the former are found most frequently in (landlocked) southern Africa, the latter tend to predominate in (archipelagic) Southeast Asia. However, they can also serve to advance corporate rather than community interests when such forms are transmuted into hubs and spokes.

The meso-level has become particularly engaged in post-bipolar strategic issues in Africa and elsewhere in the South, from the apparent domestic conflicts in, say, Angola, Liberia, Mozambique, Sierra Leone and Somalia to a variety of peace-keeping/peace-building responses, with profound regional dimensions. Each of these involves not just states, but also private sectors and civil societies, notably NGOs, albeit in variable proportions as conflicts proceed (Shaw *et al.* 1998). Informal sectors can keep conflicts alive through regional exchanges as well as private security arrangements, just as regional states may seek to contain such conflicts through their own peace-keeping forces (Shaw 2000b).

Overall, regional approaches to governance may enhance opportunities for human development and security. However, as we argued in the previous section, new coalitions are being formed among state, businesses, civil societies and non-civil elements that operate in the grey areas between formal and formal political and economic systems. Many of these combinations have a regional character or at least regional dimensions. Therefore, while agreeing in principle with the World Bank's assertion that 'an alliance among the government, NGOs, local firms and multinational corporations can go far to foster cooperation towards common goals' (1999/2000: 71) – whether in national or regional contexts – we recognize that such beneficial arrangements may be unrealistic for some situations. Regulation of international finance from above, as Strange argued, in response to pressures from below, is a necessary component in any strategy to move us back from 'the brink of global anarchy'.

From 'Rival States, Rival Firms' to Rival Paradigms

In her characteristically straightforward way, Strange asserted that 'so much IR theory is irrelevant and uninteresting', not only 'dull reading' but also 'largely irrelevant to the dominant political issues of the day' (2000: 83) This chapter and the entire collection in this volume point towards both better reading and more relevant analysis: beyond rival states and firms to rival paradigms relevant to the new century. As the UNDP cautions, without enhanced, humane, governance,

> the dangers of global conflicts could be a reality of the 21st century – trade wars promoting national and corporate interests, uncontrolled financial volatility setting off civil conflicts, untamed global crime infecting safe neighborhoods and criminalizing politics, business and the police. (1999: 8)

Our concern is with development studies as well as IPE/IR (Dickson 1997; Dunn and Shaw 2000; Shaw 1997): the former needs to bring in civil society just as much as the latter. Strange was rightly critical about the 'failure of both IR theory and liberal economic theory' (2000: 86). The former has had a different problematic: the relations between states, not the relation of authority over markets. The latter has made unrealistic assumptions about the structures of global finance and production. In turn, we would argue that both these established and interrelated fields need to bring in civil society: a heterogeneous set of actors and agendas, interests and activities that lie outside both formal state and formal economy (Holden 2000; Schechter 1999; Van Rooy 1999). Such a perspective means that non-state actors as well as states and their regional or global organizations have their own 'foreign policies' and 'diplomatic relations'. In turn, it means that sanctions and incentives can be effected vis-à-vis not only 'rogue' states but also unacceptable corporate and NGO policies and practices: the real international relations of direct and indirect pressure around Monsanto, Nestlé, Nike, Shell and others.

In addition, however, the relatively new perspective of 'development studies' needs to heed the cautions of Strange: recognize the dynamics of global trade in goods and services, particularly in finance and technology. Otherwise it is in danger of being moribund and idealistic in the new century (Court 1999; Shaw 1997). As the World Bank's own somewhat revisionist reflections on 50 years of 'development' suggest:

> Globalization and localization offer exceptional opportunities, but can also have destabilizing effects. National governments have a leading role, but international organizations, subnational levels of government (including urban governments), the private sector, NGOs, and donor organizations all play vital supporting parts. (1999/2000: 11)

These dialectical responses to globalization and the range of actors that are implicated are captured in Robert Cox's concept of the 'new realism' (that differs from classical realism by extending analysis to actors other than the state and from neorealism by its historical analysis of structural change). In the introduction to his edited volume on the topic, Cox (1997: xv) refers to Strange's observation of a growing 'antithesis' to the dominant forces of the global political economy. Noting that her primary concern was with the forms of political and economic resistance that were created within the system itself, Cox argues that 'increasingly, however, the challenge to systemic forces comes from movements in civil society that are of a more radical antisystemic kind' (ibid.). As we noted above, before her death, Strange also had become increasingly interested in the growing counterhegemonic potential of civil society. Exploring the prospects for civil society's contributions to a 'bottom-up' democratic governance for the 21st century seems therefore to be a worthy tribute to her and her legacy to both academic disciplines and policy debates.

Notes

1   Cerny's (2000: 300) description of the 'competition state' captures this complexity and paradox. States, as 'the greatest promoters of further globalization', are becoming ever-more interventionist and regulatory in the 'name of competitiveness and marketization'; yet, by doing so, they are destroying the 'autonomy of their own national models', becoming 'more and more socially fragile' and 'undermining the capacity of political and social forces within the state to resist globalization'.
2   This term, taken from one of Strange's last academic papers, is a play on the 'Westphalian System'. The system derived from the Peace of Westphalia (1648), which contained the core principles that first established the international system of states.
3   'The battle for Seattle' refers to the street battles and heated debates surrounding the November/December 1999 World Trade Organization meeting in Seattle, Washington.
4   For further details, see the *Canadian Journal of Development Studies* special issue in honor of Gerry K. Helleiner (1999).

Bibliography

Aulakh, P. and M.G. Schechter (eds) (2000), *Rethinking Globalization(s): from corporate transnationalism to local interventions*, London: Macmillan.
Beere, M.E. and R.T. Naylor (1999), 'Major Issues Relating to Organized Crime: within the context of economic relationships', *Law Commission of Canada*.
Boas, M., M.H. Marchand and T.M. Shaw (eds) (1999), 'Special Issue: new regionalisms', *Third World Quarterly*, 20(5), October, 987–1070.

Cerny, P.G. (2000), 'Political Globalization and the Competition State', in R. Stubbs and G.R.D. Underhill (eds), *Political Economy and the Changing Global Order*, 2nd edn, Don Mills, Ontario: Oxford University Press, pp.300–309.

CODRESIA/UNDP (1999) 'Civil Society Empowerment Programme for Poverty Reduction in Sub-Saharan Africa', Steering Committee Meeting, Dakar, April.

CODRESIA/UNDP (2000), 'Civil Society Programme Empowerment for Poverty Reduction in Subsaharan Africa', The Observatory Progress Report for the 2nd Programme Steering Committee Meeting, Kampala, January.

Court, J. (1999), 'Development Research: directions for a new century', *UNU Work in Progress*, 16(1), Winter:,1–20.

Cox, R. (ed.) (1997), *The New Realism: perspectives on multilateralism and world order*, London: Macmillan.

Cox, R. (1999), 'Civil Society at the Turn of the Millennium: prospects for an alternative world order', *Review of International Studies*, 25(1), January, 3–25.

Dickson, Anna K. (1997), *Development and International Relations: a critical introduction*, Cambridge: Polity.

Dunn, K. and T.M. Shaw (eds) (2000), *Rethinking World Politics: international relations from an Africanist perspective*, London: Macmillan.

Germain, Randall D. (ed.) (2000), *Globalization and its Critics: Perspectives from Political Economy*, London: Macmillan.

Griffith, I. (ed.) (2000), *The Political Economy of Drugs in the Caribbean*, London: Macmillan.

Held, D., A. McGrew, D. Goldblatt and J. Perraton (1999a), *Global Transformations: politics, economics and culture*, Cambridge: Polity Press.

Held, D., A. McGrew, D. Goldblatt and J. Perraton (1999b), 'Globalization', *Global Governance*, 5(4), October–December, 483–96.

Hettne, B., A. Inotai and O. Sunkel (eds) (1999), *Globalism and the New Regionalism*, London: Macmillan for UNU/WIDER.

Holden, B. (ed.) (2000), *Global Democracy: key debates*, London: Routledge.

Keck, M.E. and K. Sikkink (1998), *Activists beyond Borders: advocacy networks in international politics*, Ithaca: Cornell University Press.

Kleinberg, R.B. and J.A. Clark (eds) (2000), *Economic Liberalization, Democratization & Civil Society in the Developing World*, London: Macmillan.

Lindberg, S. and A. Sverrisson (eds) (1997), *Social Movements in Development: the challenge of globalization and democratization*, London: Macmillan.

Lipschutz, R.D. with J. Mayer (1996), *Global Civil Society and Global Environmental Governance*, Albany: SUNY Press.

MacLean, S.J., F. Quadir and T.M. Shaw (eds) (2000), *Prospects for Governance in Asia and Africa*, Aldershot: Ashgate.

Murphy, C. (ed.) (2000), *Egalitarian Social Movements in Response to Globalization*, London: Macmillan.

Naylor, R.T. (1999), *Patriots and Profiteers: on economic warfare, embargo-busting & state-sponsored crime*, Toronto: McClelland & Stewart.

Nzomo, M. (2000), 'Facing the 21st Century: trends and impacts of civil society action towards poverty reduction in Africa', in S.J. Maclean, F. Quadir and T.M. Shaw (eds), *Prospects for Governance in Asia and Africa*, Aldershot: Ashgate.

'Rethinking the Third World' (1999), *Current History*, 98(631), November, 355–93.

Schechter, M.G. (ed.) (1999), *The Revival of Civil Society: global & comparative perspectives*, London: Macmillan.

Shaw, T.M. (1997), 'Prospects for a New Political Economy of Development in the Twenty-First Century', *Canadian Journal of Development Studies*, 18(3), 375–94.

Shaw, T.M. (2000a), 'Overview: global/local – states, companies and civil societies', in K. Stiles (ed.), *Global Institutions and Local Empowerment*, London: Macmillan, pp.1–8.

Shaw, T.M. (2000b), 'Preface: global to local and empirical contexts/challenges' in I.L. Griffith (ed.), *The Political Economy of Drugs in the Caribbean*, London: Macmillan.

Shaw, T.M. (2000c), 'New Regionalisms in Africa in the New Millennium: comparative perspectives on renaissance, realisms and/or regressions', *New Political Economy*, 5(3), November.

Shaw, T.M. and S.J. MacLean (1999), 'The Emergence of Regional Civil Society: contributions to a new human security agenda', in Ho-Won Jeong (ed.), *The New Agenda for Peace Research*, Aldershot: Ashgate, pp.289–308.

Shaw, T.M. and J.E. Nyang'oro (2000), 'African Renaissance in the New Millennium? From anarchy to emerging markets?', in R. Stubbs and G.R.D. Underhilll (eds), *Political Economy and the Changing Global Order*, 2nd edn, pp.274–83.

Shaw, T.M. and J. van der Westhuizen (2000), 'Towards a Political Economy of Trade in Africa: states, companies and civil societies', in B. Hocking and S. McGuire (eds), *Trade Politics: international, domestic & regional perspectives*, London: Routledge, pp.246–60.

Shaw, T.M., S.J. MacLean and K. Orr (1998), 'Peace-Building and African Organizations: towards subcontracting or a new and sustainable division of labour', in K. van Walraven (ed.), *Early Warning and Conflict Prevention: limitations and possibilities*, The Hague: Kluwer for NIIA, pp.149–61.

'Special Issue in Honor of Gerry K. Helleiner' (1999), *Canadian Journal of Development Studies*, 20(3), 439–632.

Stiles, K. (ed.) (2000), *Global Institutions and Local Empowerment: competing theoretical perspectives*, London: Macmillan.

Strange, S. (1990), 'The Name of the game', in N.X. Rizopoulos (ed.), *Sea Changes: American Foreign Policy in a World Transformed*, New York: Council on Foreign Relations Press, pp.238–73.

Strange, S. (1991), 'Big Business and the State', *Millennium*, 20(2), 245–51.

Strange, S. (1994), 'Rethinking Structural Change in the International Political Economy: states, firms and diplomacy', in R. Stubbs and G.R.D. Underhill (eds), *Political Economy and the Changing Global Order*, Toronto: McClelland & Stewart, pp.103–15.

Strange, S. (1997), 'Territory, State, Authority and Economy: a new realist ontology of global political economy', in R. Cox (ed.), *The New Realism*, London: Macmillan, pp.3–19.

Strange, S. (1999), 'The Westfailure System', *Review of International Studies*, 25(3), July, 345–54.

Strange, S. (2000), 'World Order, Non-State Actors, and the Global Casino: the retreat of the state' in R. Stubbs and G.R.D. Underhill (eds), *Political Economy and the Changing Global Order*, 2nd edn, Don Mills, Ontario: Oxford University Press, pp.82–90.

Stubbs, R. and G.R.D. Underhill (eds) (1994), *Political Economy and the Changing Global Order*, Toronto: McClelland & Stewart.

Stubbs, R. and G.R.D. Underhill (2000), *Political Economy and the Changing Global Order*, 2nd edn, Don Mills, Ontario: Oxford University Press.

Van Rooy, A. (ed.) (1999), *Civil Society and Global Change: Canadian Development Report 1999*, Ottawa: North–South Institute.

Wapner, P. (1996), *Environmental Activism and World Civic Politics*, New York: SUNY Press.

Whitworth, S. (2000), 'Theory and Exclusion: gender, masculinity and international

political economy', in R. Stubbs and G.R.D. Underhill (eds), *Political Economy and the Changing Global Order*, 2nd edn, Don Mills, Ontario: Oxford University Press, pp.91–101.
UNDP (1999), *Human Development Report 1999*, New York: Oxford University Press.
World Bank (1999/2000), *World Development Report 1999/2000*, New York: Oxford University Press.

PART VII
CONCLUSIONS

21 Reflections: Blurring the Boundaries and Shaping the Agenda

DAVID C. EARNEST, LOUIS W. PAULY,
JAMES N. ROSENAU, THOMAS C.
LAWTON AND AMY C. VERDUN

Introduction

The published work of Susan Strange defies easy classification, so it is not surprising that the diverse American and European reactions – both sympathetic and critical – also fail to fit neatly into concise categories.[1] Strange's scholarship crossed numerous academic boundaries and disturbed generally conservative disciplinary cultures. She eschewed what she considered simplistic borderlines between academic disciplines and she disparaged cliquish research. The confines she sought to transcend were not only epistemological and disciplinary, however; they were sociocultural and national as well. Trained as a journalist, she detested social science jargon. An academic without a doctorate or even a formal disciplinary affiliation, she argued with economists as well as political scientists. An empiricist, she had little use for abstract theories. A British citizen who participated actively in American policy debates of American scholars, she urged her colleagues to provide analysis and interpretation relevant to policy makers. She was, in short, an articulate and passionate student of a rapidly changing global order.

Strange reveled in the paradoxes confronting all scholars of international affairs. She urged colleagues to make normative judgments but criticized those who called for a curtailment of American international commitments; she argued that the power of markets and extragovernmental authority was eroding the capacities of states to manage their own future, but at the same time she contended that the capacity of the United States to manage the international system remained predominant and was not declining (1987; 1998a). Inherent in her thinking, however, was a rejection of the utility of traditional disciplinary boundaries in academia: between positivist and critical theory, between economics and political science, between European and American philosophical traditions, and between the academic community and the state. Strange's attempts to transcend such artificial barriers understandably left some scholars wedded to them dubious about the value of her work.

In this regard, common themes emerge in the arguments and criticisms directed toward Strange, especially by American scholars. Indeed, many of the objections to her work reflected a deepening fissure between those Strange saw as trying to build a positive social science in the arena of global affairs analogous to the natural sciences in method and aspiration, and those, like her, who understood analysts of political economy to be inextricably embedded in their subject matter itself. Strange continually pointed out, in this vein, that American scholars failed to understand their complicity in the efforts of the American government often to steer the international economic order in unwise directions. She also regularly derided a hidden assumption shared by many American economists that efficiency is and must be the primary criterion for the analysis of markets. Moreover, she disagreed with their belief that efficiency is normatively the most desirable outcome to seek. In this sense, much as she would have objected to being categorized, Strange fundamentally was a critical thinker, if not a critical theorist.[2] Her well-known criticism of hegemonic stability theory was about much more than an empirical disagreement concerning the scope of American power, despite the readiness of some American theorists to portray it as such. She regarded the theoretical debate about hegemonic decline as serving to excuse American policy makers from the responsibilities of leadership. She believed that by hiding behind the positivist prohibition against making normative judgments, American 'declinists', as she called them, were in part responsible for the instability about which they so often fretted.

As underlined in several previous chapters (notably those by Story, Cutler and Tooze), Strange largely succeeded in her effort to bridge a number of established 'academic borders' in the fields of international relations and international political economy. She transcended the disciplinary boundary between economics and political science and the cultural boundary between American and European scholarship in international studies. She also managed to knock large holes in the wall separating positive political science and normative political theory.[3] All of those impediments to interdisciplinary dialogue are in fact closely interrelated.

Strange's overarching effort to promote such dialogue was rooted in her core belief in scholarship as a fundamentally social, political and moral enterprise. As she wrote in the early 1980s:

> For only when the study of international relations once again allows, and even encourages scholars to pass fundamentally moral judgments, however subjective these may be, on the issues of international public policy will the discipline regain some of its lost appeal. (Strange and Tooze 1981: 220)

Perhaps, then, the heart of her deepest disagreement with many American scholars lay in what she saw as their failure to pass such 'fundamentally moral judgments' about the insufficiency of American leadership in the international economic order the United States itself did so much to build in the wake of a turbulent century. She wanted the United States – and its citizens, including its scholarly citizens – to be better leaders, more far-sighted, more enlightened.

The First Border: between Economics and Politics

As a leading advocate of the interdisciplinary study of International Political Economy (IPE), Strange was profoundly critical of economics as a discipline, of economists in particular but also of business schools, for not reaching beyond their disciplinary confines. Nor did she spare political scientists in this regard: 'Although both address the who-gets-what questions, most business schools and most departments of politics carry on in ignorance and indifference to the other,' she wrote (1998a: 709). While the formal models of economists especially bothered her, Strange was hardly less critical of political scientists for failing to consider extragovernmental forms of authority and the concentration of political power in markets (1994). She felt the disciplinary divide between international economics and international relations – what she once called an academic 'enclosure movement' (1984: xi) – 'results in theories that are out of touch with global changes,' as Guzzini *et al.* (1993: 9) phrased it. Despite a long and deep commitment to the US-based International Studies Association and to the British International Studies Association, she faulted both for narrowly defining their foci: 'they are not associations of people engaged in international studies but of people engaged in international relations' (Strange 1989: 435). Strange viewed IPE as a way to transcend the shortcomings of existing disciplinary approaches to the 'who-gets-what' questions. The goal of the study of IPE, she argued, is to integrate the discipline of IR with international economics and ultimately to supersede both:

> The whole point of studying international political economy rather
> than international relations is to extend more widely the conventional
> limits of the study of politics, and the conventional concepts of who
> engages in politics, and of how and by whom power is exercised to
> influence outcomes. Far from being a subdiscipline of international
> relations, IPE should claim that international relations are a
> subdiscipline of IPE. (Strange 1994: 218)

Strange's frustration with the disciplinary divide found voice in many
of her works, often in acerbic form. One reviewer of *Casino Capitalism*
(1986) noted that she 'can at times scarcely disguise her irritation
with economists and their way of proposing economic policy' (Bliss
1987: 779). Her caustic criticism did little, however, to persuade economists of the value of IPE. One economist dismissed *Casino Capitalism*
because it was symptomatic of a British tendency to blame the United
States for the world's ills (Minsky 1987). Another noted that 'one of
the reasons why political economy analysis stands in relatively low
repute among many economists is that many so-called political economists have a tendency to practice facile overgeneralizations. At the
extreme some such analysis has carried little more scholarly content
than does a typical political speech' (Willett 1979: 376–7).

Given such skepticism among economists about the IPE enterprise, Strange's attempts to transcend the boundaries satisfied few.
Reviewing Strange's co-authored book, *Rival States, Rival Firms* (1991),
Yoffie found 'the joint venture has left the analysis between disciplines. It is neither rigorous political science nor business scholarship'
(Yoffie 1993: 1463). Even complimentary reviewers found that her
work was 'not altogether convincing' (Fahey 1971: 997), that 'it tries
to cover too much ground, so that it sometimes reads like a student's
lecture notes' (Bliss 1987: 779). Due to being in the vanguard of the
interdisciplinary study of the world economy, she faced understand-
able criticism from scholars unconvinced about either her goal or her
methods. Many of her economist critics were persuaded that IPE as
an integrative enterprise was stillborn. Despite pervasive skepticism,
however, a few economists saw merit in her promotion of the idea
that politics had to be included in economic models (Willett 1979:
375).

Strange's advocacy of IPE reflected her conviction that the disciplinary boundary between economics and politics was stultifying.
Though her criticism of this divide could at times be quite caustic,
most critics seemed less bothered by her rhetoric than by the inad-
equacies of an interdisciplinary approach to political economy: the
'it's neither political science nor economics' criticism. Such a criticism misses the point, however, since Strange (and other IPE
practitioners) have never claimed that the discipline *is* political sci-

ence or economics. It is unclear, in other words, whether or not the critics of such an interdisciplinary approach ever engaged Strange on the terms and goals she laid out for the interdisciplinary study of political science and economics. Ironically, to reject Strange's approach to IPE for its failure to be neither one nor the other is (unintentionally) both to affirm and to ignore her larger criticism.

The Second Divide: American and European Scholarship

With characteristic tenacity and biting wit, Strange frequently criticized not only American foreign policy but also the practice of American IR theorists. In part, she embedded these criticisms within her larger critique of the hegemonic-decline school of thought (Strange 1987). This was unfortunate because her critics often failed to recognize the quality of her general scholarly critique within this theoretical debate. As so often occurred, barbed phrases obscured her deeper intentions. We suspect this was by no means coincidental, since Strange often cited the objections of American IR theorists as supportive of her critique.[4] She recognized that her criticism of US foreign policy ruffled many feathers.

> From outside the United States, it seems fairly clear to non-Americans why this sort of explanation [of policy instability] is not very palatable to American academics – and even less so to American policymakers. It is not easy for either to admit that the conduct of American policy toward the rest of the world has been inconsistent, fickle, and unpredictable, and that United States administrations have often acted in flat contradiction to their own rhetoric. (Strange 1987: 573)

Such stinging comments drew equally pointed retaliation from many of her reviewers. One cited her work as evidence of a 'common British addiction, which is to blame the United States for all that goes wrong, at the same time never holding it responsible for things going well' (Minsky 1987: 1884). Such analysis overlooks, however, Strange's deeper concern with the real-world implications of American scholarly practices.

It is clear that Strange saw such intellectual finger pointing as symptomatic of a broader underlying failure of American scholarship that transcended any particular theoretical debate. She cited three particular failures. First, she regularly attacked what she perceived as a common American practice of laying the blame for international disorder at the door of others abroad, as Guzzini *et al.* noted: 'if something went wrong, it was because of Vietnam, US generosity toward its allies, the liquidity need of the Bretton Woods system, the oil shocks, and so on' (1993: 10). Second, she perceived a growing 'trend to parochialism' in American IR theory (Strange 1994: 209):

> Books or articles in foreign languages are almost never read or cited. Only a few non-American writers, even in English, are regularly assigned to students in U.S. universities. American awareness of how others see the failure of international cooperation in relation to the continuing power of the United States is actually less now than it might have been a generation ago. (Strange 1987: 574)

Third, she criticized American scholars' lack of historical perspective and contended that Europeans generally were more serious in the attention they paid to historical evidence and more sensitive to the possibilities of divergent interpretations of 'facts' (1983: 339). Such parochialism and ahistoricism, it seemed to her, infused American scholarship not only with an inability to appreciate the perspectives of non-US researchers but also with value-laden theories that rested on implicit and unexamined assumptions. Throughout her writings she regularly questioned such assumptions.

Strange held that such unexamined assumptions had potentially dangerous consequences for the international system. Not only did she regard American faith in the efficiency of markets as a barrier to dialogue with other states about the management of the international economy, but she also viewed American intellectual insularity as reinforcing associated misunderstandings. When this was combined with the myth of hegemonic decline and a readiness to blame others abroad for the United States' troubles, Strange saw an insular intellectual community contributing to the mismanagement of the international economic system. As she wryly stated, for American scholars the United States was becoming 'a little old country much like any other' (1987: 552).

The persistence of the divide between many American and European IR theorists underscores, for Strange, the degree to which IR theories have tangible consequences for everyday social and political life. Theorists on both sides of the Atlantic contest the meaning of this intellectual divide precisely because the debate has implications for the maintenance of international order.

The Third Boundary: 'Normative' and 'Positive' Social Science

Strange's call for IR scholars to make 'fundamentally moral judgments' seems at odds with the positivist epistemology characterizing much IR theory. If positive knowledge requires researchers to avoid

making value-laden judgments about their subject matter, then scholars must reserve judgment on questions of public policy. Strange,
and perhaps more than a few American IR theorists, would find such
an extreme interpretation of positivism to be objectionable. After all,
many positivist scholars argue that researchers can and should make
judgments about policy issues provided they do not bias their research designs. Strange's criticism of the prohibition against normative
judgments went further than this, however, which helps to explain
why many American IR theorists were uncomfortable with her position. For Strange, the solution of social problems should be the point
of departure, not the terminus, for the theory-building enterprise:

> The mismatch between, on the one hand, the increasingly global prob-
> lems and their bitterly needed solutions, and on the other, the incapacity
> of both academics and politicians to understand and live up to this
> challenge, is the starting point for Strange's theoretical work. Theory
> is conceived as the necessary bridge between the understanding of the
> 'real world' and the possibility of changing it. (Guzzini *et al.* 1993: 9)

To study politics is, for Strange, 'to clarify where power is located,
and how it restricts the art of the possible' (ibid.: 7). Stated another
way, politics is inseparable from values, since political actors use
authority to resolve value conflicts. The mere act of theorizing, by
implicitly ignoring some value conflicts at the expense of others,
only serves to perpetuate such conflicts. For this reason, scholars
who study politics, be it domestic or international, unavoidably must
make value judgments before undertaking their analyses, not after-
wards.

Accordingly, Strange took exception to theories that removed choice
and agency from political processes long before 'constructivists' made
it fashionable to do so. She viewed choice as always possible. Deterministic 'theories', she believed, merely served to obscure power in
the international economy rather than to illuminate it, and absolve
actors from blame or responsibility (Guzzini *et al.* 1993). She was
consequently critical of two different kinds of determinism: that embedded in rational-choice theory – which she labeled 'phony science,
not social science' (Strange 1994: 217) – and that grounding various
brands of Marxism. Once again, such a stance did not make her
popular in many circles.

More broadly, Strange saw values infusing political analysis in
more ways than one. Normative judgments, she felt, could enlighten
researchers and bridge the gap between the real world and its needed
changes. Without them, power could be obscured, injustices disguised and inequalities perpetuated, and conflicts encouraged. The
prevalence of deterministic theories in American scholarship Strange

depicted as providing cover for political actors unwilling to accept what she saw as their responsibilities. Moreover, for Strange, it is the positivist objection to drawing moral conclusions that enabled some scholars to ignore their broader complicity in perpetuating this behavior. In this way, Strange argued that much 'non-normative' social science developed in the United States was fundamentally conservative, itself a normative orientation favoring the continuity of existing power relationships (Guzzini *et al.* 1993: 6).

The New Global Agenda: an Unfinished Dialogue

From the rich tapestry of human experience, Strange often emphasized in her writings as well as in her teaching the thread of political authority and its potential transformation in a world where certain structures of power – especially financial structures – appeared rapidly to be becoming global. Along this line, she explicitly built the intellectual bridges noted above. She was working on just this specific topic when she died, and an overview of the agenda she left behind is a fitting way to end this chapter and this book.

As an anti-determinist, Strange believed that all power, not just financial power, can and should be subject to a certain degree of control by those subject to it. Indeed, she commonly considered the measurement of just such degrees to be the measurement of the quality of the human condition. For progressive students of the international economy, like her, who reached maturity during the hey-day of the so-called Keynesian revolution, the metric of self-governance seemed to reach an historic high-point after World War II. At that moment, it appeared that the anarchy of competitive national financial systems, which had overwhelmed the plutocracy of the 19th-century gilded age, had itself been transcended. International monetary control, it seemed, could be maintained by interdependent political authorities willing to subordinate their traditional distrust of one another to the cause of, at least, avoiding common aversions and, at most, achieving common interests.

As both journalist and scholar, Strange was among the first to trace the conditions undercutting the realization of that idealistic view in the late 20th century. As a liberal democrat and, by nature, social critic, she was also among the first to survey the implications of that conceit becoming remote from the actual practice of monetary politics. In that survey, as always, she eschewed romanticism and dogmatism. Perhaps for these reasons, her research on those implications was widely and mistakenly viewed as lacking in rigor.

The rigor of Strange's work, in fact, was really a function of its teleological character. She was ahead of most of her readers in asking a simple question and ruthlessly seeking its answer. How could an apparently re-emerging global financial plutocracy be reconciled with a democratic understanding of the nature of political authority? It cannot be, pessimistic realists now say. It should not be, many mainstream and Marxist economists now say. It must be, replied Strange, who, as noted above, refused to make a sharp distinction in her thinking between the 'is' and the 'ought'.

Strange's imagined alternatives to an order that could be conceived either as a reconstructed quasi-imperialism or as a market-led transition to a new kind of globalism were still obscured when she left us. But she was probing for them right until the end as she mused about the transformation of political authority that seemed to be taking place before her eyes. Leaving a rich agenda for research behind for her students and peers, she was particularly focused on moments of financial crisis.

From the United States in the early 1970s, to Mexico in 1982 and 1995, to Russia, East Asia and Latin America in the late 1990s, many national financial disasters threatened to become catastrophes for the system. But who was truly responsible for the necessary bailouts and for their sometimes perverse effects? Who would actually be held responsible if the panicked reaction to financial turbulence in one country actually began to bring down large commercial and investment banks and bank-managed investment funds around the world? Who had the authority to call the citizens of the privileged and the relatively rich countries once more into the breach? Moreover, who would speak for the citizen, the weaker segments of society and the poorer countries?

In her last years, Strange gave a number of answers to such questions. As she very suggestively began thinking about structural power, she often tended in the direction of responding: 'No one would be, and that's the problem.' Then she would add the observation that the actual authority to manage global finance was dispersing or was effectively being privatized. In light of her earlier work on the crises of the mid-20th century, however, it is arguable that what she meant was that a new grasping was taking place for the ultimate levers of coercive power and that no clear victor capable of reconciling demands for both justice *and* efficiency was in sight. By conflating that power struggle with ancient debates over the nature of political authority, she likely intended to shake her readers up – especially Americans, for whom the underlying dilemma remained quite hypothetical. She also surely meant to provoke among her students further work on the theory and practice of 'global governance' in the dawning new era.

Strange had a deep understanding of the complex relationship between political legitimacy and coercive power in the constitution and reconstitution of public authority, a relationship that must form the foundation for any progressive as well as hard-headed view of the present moment of transformation (Greven and Pauly 2000). In today's capital markets, the subject of Strange's last book, the emergence of what can look like the private usurpation of public authority might well be a contingent and fleeting phenomenon. The fragility of those markets, which worried her, could itself still be viewed as reflective of the public authorities lying beneath their surface and of the quality of relationships between those authorities (Pauly 1997; 1999). Moreover, as they had before – during her own lifetime – those markets could collapse if, in the end, no true public authority remained to underpin them.

The really interesting questions in this regard are the ones to which Strange was beginning to lead us. A now-commonplace metaphor became in her hands a profound question. What if global financial markets were becoming a true casino, where at least the possibility of non-zero-sum games was replaced by the certainty that in the long run only the house can win? And what if the true owners of the house were becoming a new class of plutocrats – more numerous than their 19th-century predecessors, perhaps, but behaviorally not dissimilar – a new class essentially accountable to no one but with technocrats at various levels of formal governance accountable to them?

On just such a theme, Strange was pointing the way to a new agenda for research, one that incorporated her past concerns but also moved forward. She believed that advanced industrial states and their citizens were now engaged in very real struggle over the restructuring of the world's financial house. As ever, she saw American political and financial leaders in the vanguard, and not necessarily always guided by an enlightened awareness of the broader global good. Not coincidentally, she advised scholars to conduct a parallel inquiry into the ideological and practical factors conditioning that restructuring. In other words, she wanted them to find out how political authority was actually being restructured and she wanted them to form their own convictions as to how it should be, precisely in order to help avoid the realization of her deepest casino nightmare. Never willing to concede that even the deep structures of the world economy were impossible to change, she sought the roots of resistance not just in the transnational sphere, but also much closer to home.

At the end of her last book, *Mad Money*, Strange concluded as follows:

> We are talking about relative values and social preferences – the preference, for example, for more equity and more stability ... for the

quality of economic growth rather than its quantity. ... That is what debates in international political economy and in theoretical economics ultimately boil down to. [But] political choices are formed by people's experience. Our problem in the next century is that the traditional authority of the nation state is not up to the job of managing mad international money, yet its leaders are instinctively reluctant to entrust that job to unelected, unaccountable (and often arrogant and myopic) bureaucrats. We have to invent a new kind of polity but we cannot yet imagine how it might work. Perhaps, therefore, money has to become very much more mad and bad before experience changes preferences and policies. (Strange 1998b: 190)

If crisis and catastrophe had to be the mechanism for the reconstitution of public authority, for Strange it remained an open question as to where the act of reconstitution might happen. But note the emphasis on imagination in that penultimate sentence, and the indeterminacy intentionally left in the last. At the end of her life, Strange challenged scholars and practitioners alike to become passionately engaged in both the theory and the practice of political economy. If they did so, it remained possible that the necessity for catastrophe could be avoided. It remained possible, in short, that even eclectic academic scribblers just might help construct a better world. The challenge and the possibility are central to her intellectual legacy.

Notes

1   For favorable comments, see Fahey (1971) and Willett (1979). For critical comments, see Minsky (1987).
2   This argument is elaborated by Cutler in Chapter 9 of the present volume.
3   A fourth boundary that Strange sought to transcend is that between positivist and critical theory. This has been discussed at length in earlier chapters. Moreover, the disconnection between Strange and her US colleagues on the issue of hegemonic decline is illustrative of the schism between critical academic thinkers in Europe and elsewhere and scholars working in the positivist tradition in the United States. This issue is discussed in Chapters 2, 5, 13 and 14, and referred to in a number of other chapters. Consequently, we will not labor the point here.
4   For a discussion of this theme of her work, see Guzzini *et al.* (1993).

References

Bliss, Christopher (1987), 'Casino Capitalism' (book review), *The Economic Journal*, 97(387), September, 779–80.
Fahey, David M. (1971), 'Sterling and British Policy: A Political Study of an International Currency in Decline' (book review), *Journal of Economic History*, 31(4), December, 996–7.

Greven, Michael T. and Louis W. Pauly (eds) (2000), *Democracy beyond the State? The European Dilemma and the Emerging Global Order*, Lanham, MD: Rowman and Littlefield and Toronto, Ontario: University of Toronto Press.

Guzzini, Stefano, Anna Leander, Jochen Lorentzen and Roger Morgan (1993), 'New Ideas for a Strange World: Mélanges pour Susan', in Roger Morgan, Jochen Lorentzen, Anna Leander and Stefano Guzzini (eds), *New Diplomacy in the Post-Cold War World: Essays for Susan Strange*, New York: St Martin's Press, pp.3–23.

Minsky, Hyman P. (1987), 'Casino Capitalism' (book review), *Journal of Economic Literature*, 25(4), December, 1883–5.

Pauly, Louis W. (1997), *Who Elected the Bankers? Surveillance and Control in the World Economy*, Ithaca, New York: Cornell University Press.

Pauly, Louis W. (1999), 'Capital Mobility and the New Global Order', in Richard Stubbs and Geoffrey R.D. Underhill (eds) (2000), *Political Economy and the Changing Global Order*, 2nd edn, Oxford and New York: Oxford University Press.

Stopford, John M. and Susan Strange (with J.S. Henley) (1991), *Rival States, Rival Firms: Competition for World Market Shares*, New York: Cambridge University Press.

Strange, Susan (1983), '*Cave! Hic Dragones*: a critique of regime analysis', in Stephen D. Krasner (ed.), *International Regimes*, Ithaca, New York: Cornell University Press.

Strange, Susan (1984), *Paths to International Political Economy*, Winchester, MA: George Allen & Unwin.

Strange, Susan (1986), *Casino Capitalism*, Oxford: Basil Blackwell.

Strange, Susan (1987), 'The persistent myth of lost hegemony', *International Organization*, 41(4), Autumn, 551–74.

Strange, Susan (1989), 'I Never Meant to be an Academic', in Joseph Kruzel and James N. Rosenau (eds), *Journeys Through World Politics: Autobiographical Reflections of Thirty-four Academic Travelers*, Lexington, MA: Lexington Books, pp. 429–36.

Strange, Susan (1994), 'Wake up, Krasner! The World *Has* Changed', *Review of International Political Economy*, 1(2), Summer, 209–19.

Strange, Susan (1998a), 'Globaloney?', *Review of International Political Economy*, 5(4), Winter, 704–11.

Strange, Susan (1998b), *Mad Money*, Manchester: Manchester University Press.

Strange, Susan and Roger Tooze (1981), 'Conclusions: the Management of Surplus Capacity and International Political Economy', in Susan Strange and Roger Tooze, (eds), *The International Politics of Surplus Capacity: Competition for Markets in the World Recession*, London: George Allen & Unwin.

Willett, Thomas D. (1979), 'International Monetary Relations: International Economic Relations of the Western World', (book review), *Journal of Money, Credit and Banking*, 11(3), August, 375–80.

Yoffie, David B. (1993), 'Rival States, Rival Firms: Competition for World Market Shares' (book review), *Journal of Economic Literature*, 31(3), September, 1462–3.

Addendum: Fifty Years of International Affairs Analysis: An Annotated Bibliography of Susan Strange's Academic Publications

CHRISTOPHER MAY

Introduction

This bibliography maps the development of Susan Strange's approach to International Political Economy through work she published in the 50 years from 1949 to 1999. In a few cases, book reviews have been included where the content has some relevance to the development of her perspective. Her extensive work as a journalist has not been included; this bibliography only attempts to record her broadly 'academic' work (while recognizing this is not a distinction that she would have necessarily been happy with). From 1947 to 1955, Susan Strange also reported on both economic and sociological aspect of international relations for the *Yearbook of World Affairs*. These shorter notes have not been included and the bibliography commences with the substantial pieces she started to write in 1949.

This bibliography was compiled over a number of years and has benefitted from the comments and assistance of Mary Bone, Stephen Chan, Christopher Farrands, Margaret Law and Roger Tooze. The convention adopted is for each year to list journal articles, then chapters in books and then books (or stand-alone publications).

*The two publications marked * have proven impossible to track down.*

The Works

1   'Palestine and the UN', in *Yearbook of World Affairs: 1949* (London: Stevens, 1949) pp.151–68
Strange comments on the UN deliberations concerning the future of Palestine and highlights the central factor that gave the Zionists an inbuilt advantage at the assembly. She also discusses some of the limitations and problems with such negotiations within the forum of the UN, and alludes to structural impediments to the 'fair' settlement of differences.

2   'Truman's Point Four', in *Yearbook of World Affairs: 1950* (London: Stevens, 1950) pp.264–88
Strange notes that American 'internationalism' could be broken under the stresses of changing political and strategic circumstances. She points to the linkage between economics and politics, as a way of highlighting questions concerning the degree of freedom to use funds as recipients of US-controlled aid and loans wish.

3   'The Schuman Plan', in *Yearbook of World Affairs: 1951* (London: Stevens, 1951) pp.109–30
Again discussing the linkage between politics and economics, Strange points out it is not possible for economic integration to move forward without political will. However, the clear aim of the Schuman Plan was to redress the balance of economic power in Western Europe in favor of France and at the expense of Germany, rather than *necessarily* provide for increased integration.

4   'The Atlantic Idea', in *Yearbook of World Affairs: 1953* (London: Stevens, 1953) pp.1–19
Strange suggests that, in a bipolar world, the United States must be conciliatory to her allies because it is neither possible, nor does the United States wish, to further its ends by force. Strange also recognizes the force of 'the Atlantic idea' as part of this project, and notes its defining role for these debates.

5   'The economic work of the United Nations', in *Yearbook of World Affairs: 1954* (London: Stevens, 1954) pp.118–40
Strange argues that governments have increased power over domestic economic forces, and feel that this power is necessary and desirable. But freedom of trade in the dollar area is seen as much more important to the creation of world free trade than relations between other trading states. The UN has failed in its overoptimistic aims because the responsibility for economic stability and progress was assumed

by its members to take precedence over a wider responsibility for international economic progress *and* stability.

6 'British Foreign Policy', in *Yearbook of World Affairs: 1955* (London: Stevens, 1955) pp.35–53
Strange argues that a state whose power is waning is more liable to make fatal mistakes. A small fall in American consumption led to a large cut in American imports from the sterling area, revealing this dependence. She suggests that, as a result a major role of British foreign policy is to sustain the United States's role in the international economy to ensure continued expansion and growth.

*7 (with W. Eady and B. de Jouvenel) *Money and Trade* (London: Batchworth Press, 1955)

8 'Strains on NATO', in *Yearbook of World Affairs: 1956* (London: Stevens, 1956) pp.21–41
Strange argues that policy between NATO members is barely coordinated, that its membership is too skewed towards colonial powers and that therefore to outsiders (especially African and Asian states) it is seen as a 'rich man's club'. She concludes that inequality is disruptive and problematic, and military alliances in the long run could do little to halt the pressure for some sort of change in the international system itself.

9 'Suez and After', in *Yearbook of World Affairs: 1957* (London: Stevens, 1957) pp.76–103
Strange explores the idea that Britain or France had a 'vital interest' in the international (rather than national control) of the Suez canal, and argues that the diplomatic problems that Suez prompted were easily foreseeable. Suez revealed the weakness of Britain and France as declining powers but, while some minor illusions had been shattered, the lessons of the crisis do not seem to have been fully appreciated.

10 'The strategic trade embargoes: sense or nonsense', in *Yearbook of World Affairs: 1958* (London: Stevens, 1958) pp.55–73
Strange argues that the policy of strategic trade embargoes, a central plank of American cold war policy, should be reassessed in light of the launch of Sputnik and Britain's decision to part from the United States on an embargo on trade with China. Strange reviews the policy, set out in the Battle Act, and the political psychology underlying it, to conclude that it should be dispensed with, as it has been neither useful not effective.

11   'The Commonwealth and the Sterling Area', in *Yearbook of World Affairs: 1959* (London: Stevens, 1959) pp.24–44
Strange discusses the problem of sterling's link with the politics of the Commonwealth, the interactions between the sterling area and the rest of the world economy and policy responses to national pressures. In addition, she is critical of the separation of the national from the international in the analysis of international relations, a theme to which she would return repeatedly.

12   *The Soviet Trade Weapon* (London: Phoenix House, 1959)
Strange concludes that Soviet economic (and political) influence is reliant on economic 'trouble-spots' and the aversion by many developing states to the West's recent history of colonialism. Money spent on military aid might be better spent helping developing countries deal with agricultural surplus capacity in the global market, a theme she would return to in (32). Political activism by the West could do much to counter the 'war without weapons' represented by Soviet trade and aid policy.

13   Review of J.L. Allen, *Soviet Economic Power* (Washington: Public Affairs Press, 1960), *Economica*, Volume 28, No.109 (February 1961)
Strange challenges the implicit assertion by the author that the interpretation of Soviet interest, or its choice of the means to an end, is static. She also doubts the ascription by the author of Finnish subservience to the Soviet Union as being *solely* one of economic dependence rather than strategic vulnerability, dismissing monocausality.

14   'Changing Trends in World Trade', in *Yearbook of World Affairs: 1962* (London: Stevens, 1962) pp.139–58
Strange notes that, while manufacturing growth has accelerated, there has been less growth in the demand for raw materials and agricultural goods. This distorted or uneven growth in trade has not only had an unsettling effect on world trade, but has also required developing states to take out loans to support their development. Strange suggests that in the long term such an approach is not sustainable, and identifies not a lack of policy choice in developed state inaction but rather a lack of political will.

15   'Cuba and After', in *Yearbook of World Affairs: 1963* (London: Stevens, 1963) pp.1–28
Strange sides with the 'man in the street', arguing that the crisis was a very real moment of possible war and as such profoundly affected the US system of alliances. As in her later work, Strange was concerned about the manner in which the United States was a hegemonic power and the problem of political will when it was threatened

outside its traditional regional sphere of domination, or by the needs of multilateralism.

16 'A New Look at Trade and Aid', *International Affairs*, Volume 42, No.1 (January 1966) pp.61–73
Strange suggests that 'Prebisch's thesis', allowing subsidized exporting by developing states, and the dropping of tariff barriers, while unpopular would be a useful way forward. Strange posits the structural problems of international trade, while suggesting the way forward through a *combination* of economics and politics.

17 'Debts, Defaulters and Development', *International Affairs*, Volume 43, No.3 (July 1967) pp.516–29
Strange suggests that problems of national debt default have not been solved, merely suppressed by the expansion of credit provision. Developing states' dependence on 'supplier credit', and frequent rescheduling of other debts, will lead to eventual widespread default unless action is taken and to political problems in the international system. She argues that finance is central to international relations, a recurring theme in her subsequent work.

18 *The Sterling Problem and the Six* (London: Chatham House/PEP, 1967)
Strange analyzes the twin roles of sterling in the international economy, as reserve currency and vehicle currency (in which transactions are carried out), in a precursor to her typology of currencies; see (24). She argues that, while the City has benefitted from the expansion of the 'Euro-currency' markets, in its 'middleman' role, this has led to a number of problems for sterling. She is skeptical about the possibility of Britain enjoying any financial benefit from joining the 'six'.

*19 *Research on International Organisation* (London: Heinemann Education, 1968)

20 'The Meaning of Multilateral Surveillance', in R.W. Cox (ed.), *International Organisation: World Politics, Studies in Economic and Social Agencies* (London: Macmillan, 1969) pp.231–47
Strange argues that multilateral surveillance is not as draconian as it is presented, and states were still able to manipulate their creditors through political pressures. Interestingly, Strange notes, with great prescience, that while at that time states could still play this role, with the continuing internationalization of money markets (and the emergent technologies that made such developments possible), this would in the future present a strategic problem for governments.

21   'International economics and international relations: a case of mutual neglect', *International Affairs*, Volume 46, No.2 (April 1970) pp.304–15
Strange's first call for the development of International Political Economy as a separate discipline. She identifies a major void between the academic study of international relations and the study of international economics. The failure to fill this void will lead to the inability to analyze the two main tendencies in the international economic system: growing international cooperation and organization, and increased domestic defensiveness over national welfare issues.

22   'The Politics of International Currencies in World Politics', *International Organization*, Volume 23, No.2 (Fall 1970/71) pp.215–31
Here Strange argues that because of interdependence states are not so much defenders of national territories or peoples but of national currencies and monetary systems. Conflict can be caused by one monetary system damaging another. She starts to map out a political theory of international currencies which is further developed in (24).

23   'Sterling and British Policy: A Political View', *International Affairs*, Volume 47, No.2 (April 1971) pp.302–15
Strange sets the decline of sterling and the rise of the dollar in the context of international politics, and stresses the need to integrate economic studies with those of international relations. These views are then developed in (24), while the importance of monetary factors is a theme which underlies all of her subsequent work.

24   *Sterling and British Policy* (London: Oxford University Press, 1971)
Strange proposes a four element theoretical framework for international currencies in the international political economy – Neutral currencies, Top currencies, Master currencies and Negotiated currencies – where each category exhibits certain economic *and* political characteristics. The discussion of the implications for Britain is firmly placed in its international political context, prefiguring Strange's argument in (30) that sectoral analysis should precede general analysis of the international political economy.

25   Review of R.J. Barber, *The American Corporation: Its Power, Its Money, Its Politics* (New York: Dutton, 1970), *International Journal*, Volume 27, No.2 (Spring 1972) pp.308–9
Strange feels that the author overstates the political power and influence of multinationals in themselves. She identifies a close connection between the US government and larger corporations. This is a position she gradually moved away from in subsequent work, identifying transnational firms as actors in their own right by (67).

26 'The Dollar Crisis 1971', *International Affairs*, Volume 48, No.2 (April 1972) pp.191–215
Using the 'Dollar Crisis' as a way of examining the problems which beset academic approaches to international relations, Strange suggests that political economy is crucial to understanding international relations. She concludes that international institutions were powerless when the United States wished to follow a specific policy (revealing its power). Strange continued to refine this position during the next two decades.

27 'International Economic Relations I: The Need for an Interdisciplinary Approach' in R. Morgan (ed.), *The Study of International Affairs: Essays in Honour of Kenneth Younger* (London: RIIA/Oxford University Press, 1972)
Strange's second major attack on the discipline of international economics as it then stood, see also (21). She derides the academic 'apartheid' that separates political considerations from the economic and argues that what is required is a single international studies discipline that encompasses both the politics and economics of international relations (what would eventually become International Political Economy).

28 'IMF: Monetary Managers', in R.W. Cox and H.K. Jacobson (eds), *The Anatomy of Influence: Decision Making in International Organization* (New Haven: Yale University Press, 1974)
A detailed case study of the IMF, which Strange uses to back up her warning that there can be no justification for an analytical division between the economic and the political. Though not a full argument for structural power, this chapter recognizes that relational power is insufficient to fully explain power relations within the IMF.

29 'What is Economic Power, and Who has it?', *International Journal*, Volume 30, No.2 (Spring 1975) pp.207–24
Here Strange commits to print an early version of the structure of power theory which she would develop over the next 13 years. In this manifestation, there are three dimensions of power in the international political economy – security, 'ideology' and economic, and the importance of the history of bargains for the international structure is identified, but not developed fully.

30 'The Study of Transnational Relations' and 'Who Runs World Shipping?', *International Affairs*, Volume 52, No.2 (April 1976) pp.333–45; pp.346–67
In the first article Strange sets out an outline method for sectoral analysis in the international economy. This is prefaced by a critical

engagement with the Nye and Keohane 'transnational politics' approach. Only by building up from systematic sectoral analyses can the asymmetrical bargaining processes, the impact of technology, the influence of markets and the politicization of the international economy be understood. She then offers in the second article one such sectoral analysis.

31   'International Monetary Relations' Volume 2 of A. Shonfield (ed.), *International Economic Relations in the Western World 1959–71* (London: Oxford University Press, 1976)
While much more than an expanded and internationalized version of (24), this work covers much of the same period and material. After an extended narrative of international monetary relations for the period, Strange concludes that the increasing politicization of the international monetary system is dominated by the United States. However what later would be 'structural power' is not theorized at this stage, although the central role of 'bargains' emerges as a subject of concern.

32   'The Management of Surplus Capacity: Or how does theory stand up to protectionism 1970's style?', *International Organization*, Volume 33, No.3 (Summer 1979) pp.303–35
In this article, which is a clear precursor to (36), Strange discusses the management of surplus capacity in three sectors of the international economy – steel, textiles and shipbuilding – and the recourse to protectionism. She then goes on to discuss the problems this implies for mainstream theories of international economics. She concludes that theories that only deal with international *or* domestic policy will fail.

33   'Germany and the World Monetary System', in W.L. Kohl and G. Basevi (eds), *West Germany: A European and Global Power* (Lexington: Lexington Books, 1980)
After discussing recent developments in the political economy of Germany and Europe, Strange suggests that Germany must find the political will to match its growing economic importance in the global system.

34   'Reactions to Brandt. Popular Acclaim and Academic Attack', *International Studies Quarterly*, Volume 25, No.2 (June 1981) pp.328–42
Strange's 'review of the reviews' concludes by arguing that the report cannot be safely dispensed with, whatever its faults and shortcomings, as it identifies major problems that will continue to beset the global system without some sort of political determination to address the problem of maldistribution of welfare. The recognition

of the importance of global political processes continued to be a central theme in her work.

35 'The world's money: expanding the agenda for research', *International Journal*, Volume 36, No.4 (Autumn 1981) pp.691–712
Strange argues that work on the international monetary system must go beyond a mere mechanical explanation and move towards a more political analysis (which would also include an assessment of the impact of technology on global finance). She compares the study of the financial system unfavorably with the increasingly sophisticated account of the global ecological system, and briefly notes the creation of credit and the transfer of risk, which would be taken up subsequently in (42) and (43).

36 (with R. Tooze) *The Politics of International Surplus Capacity* (London: Allen & Unwin, 1981)
A collection of 17 essays resulting from a conference with an editorial overview of theoretical approaches to IPE and a conclusion concerning the agreements and differences among the contributors. Writing with Tooze, Strange notes that it is not intended to dispense with the 'insights' of the realists, but it is necessary to widen their approach considerably. Any analysis should start by recognizing the key historical bargains that were made within the economic structure. Strange also identifies some key structures in international society: security, finance, distribution of knowledge, provision of welfare, transport services and communications, and exchange and employment structures, without extensive analysis.

37 '*Cave! Hic Dragones*: A Critique of Regime Analysis', *International Organization*, Volume 36, No.2 (Spring 1982) pp.479–97
Strange's classic *critique* of regime theory, often used as a touchstone for those regime theorists wanting to make the point that they recognize that there have been criticisms of their approach. Strange argues for five shortcomings of regime theory: that it is a passing fad, is imprecise, has a value bias, is too static and is too state-centered. The rather brief structural power analysis conflates what Strange would come to term primary and secondary structures.

38 'The Politics of Economics: A Sectoral Analysis', in W.F. Hanrieder (ed.), *Economic Issues and the Atlantic Community* (New York: Praeger, 1982)
Strange here proposes a structural approach that is implied by her argument that an analysis of the global political economy must be concerned with its 'environment'. She again repeats her critique of the recent history of the discipline of IPE, before suggesting that the

'bargains' that IPE should be concerned with include those between firms and governments *and* those between labor and firms.

39   'Still an Extraordinary Power: America's Role in the Global Monetary System' (Paper 3) (with discussants section), in R. Lomra and B. Witte (eds), *The Political Economy of International and Domestic Monetary Relations* (Ames: Iowa State University Press, 1982)
Strange makes a provisional analysis of structural power in the international political economy. This includes elements of her later ideas – the idea of the authority/market balance and the security structure – but her arguments here are not fully developed. A central part of the dispute between her and the discussants reproduced in impressionistic form are veiled accusations of a lack of rigor, a not unfamiliar criticism.

40   'Europe and the United States: The Transatlantic Aspects of Inflation' in R. Medley (ed.), *The Politics of Inflation: A Comparative Analysis* (New York: Pergamon Press, 1982)
While containing little explication of structural power, being more of an historical overview of the international financial sector, this includes Strange's discussion of the reasons for American domination of international finance. There is a hint of the structural analysis that was implicitly being developed, not least of all because much of the evidence she cites re-emerges in later works regarding American economic hegemony.

41   Review of C.F. Bergsten, *The World Economy in the 1980s – Selected Papers* (Toronto: D.C. Heath, 1981), *International Journal*, Volume 38, No.2 (Spring 1983) pp.355–6
Strange criticizes Bergsten's exaggeration of US decline in hegemonic power and absolution of the United States from bearing prime responsibility for the deteriorating economic situation. Indeed, much of her work in the 1980s revolved round the dual need to recognize US responsibility for global economic crises, and the problem of such a responsibility being denied by the United States (both policy makers and academics).

42   'The Credit Crisis: A European View', *SAIS Review* (Summer 1983) pp.171–81
Strange suggests the world economic crisis has three interrelated aspects: unemployment, 'flagging trade' and unstable money. As in (32), she shows some skepticism towards the arguments that demonize protectionism. As she would subsequently argue more extensively, she sees the role of America as destabilizing because of the priority given to the interests of the domestic political system. She concludes

by suggesting a civilizing mission to educate the United States into responsible leadership.

43 'Structures, Values and Risk in the Study of the International Political Economy', in R.J.B. Jones (ed.), *Perspectives on Political Economy* (London: Francis Pinter Publishers, 1983)
In this chapter, Strange argues for the centrality of questions surrounding the nature of risk and how it is mitigated, managed and transferred in the international economy. She also suggests five structures of power in IPE: the production, financial, security and knowledge structures she would theorize more fully in (57), as well as an element she termed the 'welfare structure'. This fifth structure was to account for politically determined arrangements which allocate the risks to human life and contentment.

44 'The Global Political Economy, 1959–1984', *International Journal*, Volume 39, No.2 (Spring 1984) pp.267–83
After discussing some terms she would like to see the back of ('actors', 'issue-areas'), and reviewing 25 years of the global political economy, Strange again proposes four structures (security, production, knowledge and finance) as a taxonomy for looking at change. This is the first time the four structures appear in their final configuration. She also stresses that, while these structures are not hierarchical, disruptions in the financial structure have caused most upheaval over the period examined.

45 'GATT and the Politics of North–South trade', *Australian Outlook*, Volume 38, No.2 (August 1984) pp.106–10
Strange identifies three 'shaky assumptions' underlying the call to revive the GATT negotiations: protectionism was the main cause of the 1930s depression, the GATT was necessary for post-war recovery, and free trade is a widely followed 'norm'. But, if proposed alternatives are a hegemonic system run by the United States or a multilateral system managed by the GATT, she argues the reality is a cobweb of bilateral agreements which accords with people's desire to have their own state manage their affairs.

46 (Editor), *Paths to International Political Economy* (London: Allen & Unwin, 1984)
A collection of nine essays looking at various sectoral aspects to the study of IPE, together with a brief preface by Strange. Here she singles out development economists, applied economists and economic historians, and praises their openness to insights and evidence from other disciplines. There is an epistemological issue here, against theoretical closure, though as elsewhere this remains implicit.

Writing with Calleo, Strange discusses 'Money and World Politics', criticizing economists for supposing questions of values and power are questions of market 'imperfections' and not of central importance. The authors conclude with a plea for a return to more 'objective' analysis of global problems, not driven by government-set academic objectives. In her conclusion, Strange poses the question, 'What about International Relations?' She notes radical theorists have concentrated too much on the production structure, and states that the other three (finance, security and 'knowledge') are as important. She also suggests that even multinationals in the final analysis bow to the wishes of their home state. This view is in sharp contrast to the transnational structural theory of power which would emerge over the next few years.

47   'Protectionism and World Politics', *International Organization*, Volume 39, No.2 (Spring 1985) pp.233–59
Strange argues that trade is only a 'secondary structure' which is influenced and shaped by the primary structures. Disruption of the international system and trade relations is a symptom of disruptions within the primary structures, especially the financial structure. This represents a forceful precursor to (57) and is the first time that Strange lays her structural approach to power within the international political economy in its final form, including primary *and* secondary structures.

48   'The poverty of multilateral economic diplomacy', in G. Berridge and A. Jennings (eds), *Diplomacy at the United Nations* (London: Macmillan Press, 1985)
After reviewing the four values authority might pursue (wealth, security, justice and freedom), an argument further developed in (57), she interrogates the three main paradigms used to think about the international political economy: liberalism, structuralism and nationalism. She concludes that, as each approach continues to look to international organization to sustain its values, despite its failings multilateralism will continue to be regarded as worthwhile.

49   'International Political Economy: The story so far and the way ahead', in W. Ladd Hollist and F. LaMond Tullis (eds), *An International Political Economy* (*International Political Economy Yearbook No.1*) (Boulder: Westview Press, 1985)
Strange uses an appreciation of the worth of development economics to argue for the reinclusion of values into the study of IPE. Part of the job of IPE must be to make clear what choices certain priorities represent and to discuss different value hierarchies.

50 'Interpretations of a Decade', in L. Tsoukalis (ed.), *The Political Economy of International Money: In Search of a New Order* (London: RIIA/Sage Publications Ltd, 1985)
After reiterating her criticism of overspecialization in the study of international economic relations, Strange goes on to discuss the short-comings of a large spectrum of perspectives on economic development. The bulk of this article subsequently appeared as Chapter 3 of (52).

51 'Supranationals and the State', in J.A. Hall (ed.), *States in History* (Oxford: Basil Blackwell, 1986)
Partly a precursor to (67), here Strange argues there is a paradoxical symbiosis between states and TNCs and Inter-Governmental Organizations (IGOs) that remains underexamined. There has also been a shift in the basis of economic power, from land-based power to capital and knowledge. This part of her overall argument about the transnational power of capital and American TNCs is the beginning of a shift away from the suggestion of a final authority of states over transnationals in (46).

52 *Casino Capitalism* (Oxford: Blackwell Publishers, 1986)
Strange argues that uncertainty and risk in the financial sector/structure have provoked major economic disturbances. After a detailed sectoral history and analysis, she argues that the United States must once again take up the leadership role and, more radically, suggests that financial regulation of credit creating agencies should not be a territorially based jurisdiction, but be based on the currencies themselves wherever transactions take place. Alongside (57) and (67), this represents a major part of the influential core of Strange's work on international political economy.

53 'The persistent myth of lost hegemony', *International Organization*, Volume 41, No.4 (Autumn 1987) pp.551–74
Strange's classic attack on the 'declinist school' in international relations. Once she has discussed 'sociological' reasons for academics holding this view (the most powerful or cynical is that it is a convenient denial of responsibility by Americans for their effect on the international system), she suggests the domestic and international cannot be separated analytically. A structural analysis of power explains the effects of American domestic politics on the international political economy.

53(a) 'The persistent myth of lost hegemony: Reply to Milner and Snyder ('Lost Hegemony')', *International Organization*, Volume 42, No. 1 (Spring 1988) pp.749–52

There was a brief, inconclusive methodological exchange in the pages of *International Organization* in reference to (53) where, in response to the criticism that her evidence left her arguments unproved, Strange answered that the real evidence to prove her argument empirically would be too difficult to collect, though in theory possible to compile. What is clear is that Strange is not dealing with 'evidence' in its strict form and has a permissive view towards its acceptability.

54   'The Future of the American Empire', *Journal of International Affairs*, Volume 42, No.1 (Fall 1988) pp.1–17
Strange argues that, increasingly, power in the international political economy is not territorially defined, and what has emerged is an empire that is not territorially based; and secondly, that it is controlled by information-rich US corporations. This argument is carried further in (58).

55   'Defending Benign Mercantilism' (Review Essay), *Journal of Peace Research*, Volume 25, No.3 (Autumn 1988) pp.273–7
In this review of R. Gilpin, *Political Economy of International Relations*, Strange again argues against 'Hegemonic Stability Theory' – see (53) – but has started to develop a theory of transnational empire and the increasing non-territoriality of structural power, which is developed in a number of works below.

56   'A Dissident View', in R. Bieber, R. Dehouse, J. Pinder and J.H.H. Weiler (eds), *1992: One European Market? A Critical Analysis of the Commission's Internal Market Strategy* (Baden-Baden: Nomos Verlagsgesellschaft, 1988)
Strange argues that, in the national competition for market shares, there are two important strategies: state procurement used as a stimulus to R&D, or control of market access used as a bargaining lever. Without one or the other Strange envisages Europe (even with closer union) still losing out to the United States and Japan. Strange revealed her mercantilist side, as she had done in (32), (47) and (55).

57   *States and Markets* (London: Pinter Publishers 1988)
Subtitled 'An Introduction...' to IPE, this represents the only book-length discussion of Strange's theory of the four dimensions of power in IPE. It is at once an introduction to the subject and a forceful agenda-setting exercise for further research. This is Strange's defining book, around which the rest of her work revolves. She discusses her ideas on theory building and methodology as well as the four structures of power in the international political economy: security, finance, production and knowledge. This discussion is mobilized around the balance of authority and markets and the questions of

value preferences, and *'cui bono?'* (who benefits?). She then applies this analysis to a number of 'secondary structures'.
The second edition of 1994 had no substantive changes to the text.

58 'Towards a Theory of Transnational Empire', in E-O. Czempiel and J.N. Rosenau (eds), *Global Changes and Theoretical Challenges: Approaches to World Politics for the 1990s* (Lexington: Lexington Books, 1989)
In Strange's second explicit excursion into epistemology, following a similar section in (57), she argues that theories must explain some aspect of the international system not obvious to 'common-sense'. She then proposes a non-territorial theory of imperialism based on her four structures of power. She identifies a transnational empire centered on Washington DC, and argues that new studies of empire are needed to understand this new type of transnational empire.

59 'I Never Meant to Be an Academic', in J. Kruzel and J.N. Rosenau (eds), *Journeys Through World Politics: Autobiographical Reflections of Thirty-four Academic Travelers* (Lexington: Lexington Books, 1989)
This brief autobiographical essay gives some clues to the personal foundations for Strange's approach.

60 'The persistence of problems in EC-US relations: conflicts of perception?' in J. Schwarze (ed.), *The External Relations of the European Community, in particular EC–US relations* (Contributions to an international colloquium, organized by the European Policy Unit of the European University Institute, held in Florence on 26–7 May 1988), (Baden-Baden: Nomos Verlagsgesellschaft, 1989)
Strange suggests that the two primary activities of any political organization are the furtherance of security and the control of money, and it is these issues that remain at the center of the problem of US–Europe relations. While the Europeans see an America unwilling to act, the US government claims it cannot act.

61 'Finance, Information and Power', *Review of International Studies*, Volume 16, No.3 (July 1990) pp.259–74
Strange discusses the difference between US structural power and Japanese relational power and the impact of communications technology changes on the operation of international financial markets. She suggests that part of US structural power stems from the privileged position of 'American-English' in the knowledge structure.

62 'Economic Linkages 1967–87', in R. O'Neill and R.J. Vincent (eds), *The West and the Third World: Essays in Honour of J.D.B.Miller* (Basingstoke: Macmillan Academic and Professional, 1990)

Strange sets Miller's work into the context of the analysis of international relations. She argues that changes in the international political economy can only be understood by analyses of structural power; the role of the state remains central, if changing. This accounts for the continuing appeal of Realism. She attributes to her former colleague a perspective consistent with her own.

63   'The Name of the Game', in N.X. Rizopoulos (ed.), *Sea Changes: American Foreign Policy in a World Transformed* (New York: Council on Foreign Relations Press, 1990) pp.238–73
Strange argues that the competition for territory has been superseded by the competition for world market shares. Though different from the analysis in (58), this still leaves the United States as the most powerful actor in the world. This marks a significant step towards the analysis of firms as being as important as states, fully developed in (67).

64   *Europe 1992 – Some personal observations* (SAIIA occasional paper), (Johannesburg: South African Institute of International Affairs, 1990)
Strange suggests that the 1992 project served both the European collective interest (in the face of Asian and American competition) and the national interests of the major European states (France and Germany), though she notes that Britain's position is less clear-cut. She then discusses some possible problems which might appear post-1992.

65   'Big Business and the State', *Millennium: Journal of International Studies*, Volume 20, No.2 (Summer 1991) pp.245–50
Strange argues that TNCs should be placed at the center of IPE analysis, along with the state, and should not be left on the periphery. The global system is being transformed by changes in the production and financial structures, and she implicitly argues for the centrality of changes in the 'knowledge' structure.

66   'An Eclectic Approach', in C.N. Murphy and R. Tooze (eds), *The New International Political Economy* (*International Political Economy Yearbook No.6*) (Boulder: Lynne Rienner Publishers, 1991)
Strange reiterates the structural dimensions of power from (57) and adds three factors that influence them: states, markets and technology. Here she makes the contribution of the technological dynamic to the four structures more explicit. She concludes by again stressing the need for interdisciplinary understanding of IPE.

67   (with J.M. Stopford and J.S. Henley) *Rival States, Rival Firms: Competition for world market shares* (Cambridge: Cambridge University Press, 1991)

In keeping with Strange's views, this book discusses the interdependence between politics and economics without foregrounding one at the expense of the other. The authors suggest that diplomacy is now triangular: (traditional) state–state diplomacy has been joined by state–firm and firm–firm diplomacy. They also note that the linking of TNCs with specific nations is increasingly difficult, due to the decreasing centrality of territorial considerations of power.

68 'States, Firms and Diplomacy', *International Affairs*, Volume 68, No.1 (January 1992) pp.1–15
A brief summation of (67) which outlines the central argument of the book concerning the diplomacy between firms and states, and discusses some areas for further research.

69 'The Transformation of the World Economy', in L. Babic and B. Huldt (eds), *Mapping the Unknown: Towards a New World Order. Yearbook of the Swedish Institute for International Affairs 1992–1993* (London: Hurst and Co., for the SIIA, 1993)
Strange argues that the transformation of the world economy is not so much the product of state–firm interactions; rather, it is firms that are playing (and will continue to play) the more important role in structural change. This finally represents a complete reversal of the position of (46).

70 'Wake up, Krasner! The world *has* changed', *Review of International Political Economy*, Volume 1, No.2 (Summer 1994) pp.209–19
Strange offers a criticism of Krasner's realist position, drawing on her recent work and an understanding of structural power. Realism and liberalism lack the heuristic power of her own (and others') structuralist approach. All the different groups of actors and interests in the international system must be recognized and analyzed, not just states.

71 'Who Governs? Networks of Power in World Society', *Hitotsubashi Journal of Law and Politics*, Special Issue (1994) pp.5–17
Starting from a response to Waltz's famous LSE lecture (*Millennium*, 22(2), Summer 1993), Strange argues for a wider reading of politics. Financial and environmental issues have moved to center stage, but states have been losing relative power over these areas. However, she argues that the United States retains structural power, which will enable it to again *act* as hegemon for the general good. For once, she makes her underlying prescription for American leadership completely explicit.

72   'Finance and capitalism: the City's imperial role yesterday and today', *Review of International Studies*, Volume 20, No. 20 (October 1994) pp.407–10
In this short review of P.J. Cain and A.G. Hopkins, *British Imperialism* (2 vols) (London: Longman 1993), Strange again emphasizes the structural characteristics of US power in the global system and suggests that Britain's structural power was more long-lasting than is sometimes presumed, with clear implications for the continuing power of the United States in the global economy.

73   'The Power Gap: Member States and the World Economy', in F. Brouwer, V. Lintner and M. Newman (eds), *Economic Policy Making and the European Union* (London: Federal Trust, 1994)
Strange suggests that, except for the Commission, there is little to distinguish the EU from some other intergovernmental organizations. Only by recognizing the problems for sovereign political authorities in the global political economy and planning for new constitutional developments in Europe to address this problem can this 'power gap' be narrowed.

74   'From Bretton Woods to the Casino Economy', in S. Corbridge, N. Thrift and R. Martin (eds), *Money, Power and Space* (Oxford: Blackwell, 1994)
Strange argues for the importance of historical understanding if power in the international financial structure is to be analyzed. She focuses on credit creation to examine the upheavals in the financial structure and the decline of the Bretton Woods system. While larger states have (at least for the time being) managed to retain some of their power in the financial structure, smaller states have seen a decline in their ability to resist the pressures from the international money markets.

75   'Global government and global opposition', in G. Parry (ed.), *Politics in an Interdependent World. Essays presented to Ghita Ionescu* (Aldershot: Edward Elgar, 1994)
After recognizing the relevance of discussions of a 'new mediaevalism' in the global political economy, Strange suggests that the best way of addressing the nature and use of power is her structural model. The deterritorialization of power and the increasing importance of 'diplomacy' between firms, as laid out in (67), suggests a more complex view of 'interdependence'.

76   'The Structure of finance in the world system', in Y. Sakamoto (ed.), *Global Transformation: Challenges to the State System* (Tokyo: United Nations University Press, 1994)

Strange suggests much of the work on the international financial has been compromised by its emphasis on the state due to the foregrounding of the exchange rate part of the financial structure. Using a global monetarist perspective, she sees global inflation linked to the oversupply of credit by banks, but US power remains, measured by US ability to act unilaterally in the field of global finance.

77 'Rethinking Structural Change in the International Political Economy: States, Firms and Diplomacy', in R. Stubbs and G.R.D. Underhill (eds), *Political Economy and the Changing Global Order* (Basingstoke: Macmillan Press, 1994)
This is an abridged and slightly revised version of (68).

78 'The Defective State', *Daedelus*, Volume 24, Part 2 (Spring 1995) pp.55–74
Strange argues that, while states remain superficially important as major actors within the global system, the underlying power relations have hollowed out their authority. This has led to an asymmetry of structural authority in the global system. She also criticizes the state-centric nature of the discipline of International Relations and suggests a new research agenda based around her conception of structural power and the importance of non-state actors in the functioning of authority.

79 'European Business in Japan. A Policy Cross-roads?', *Journal of Common Market Studies*, Volume 33, No.1 (March 1995) pp.1–25
Strange argues that it may now be beyond any nationally elected government (even in the United States) to reimpose its hegemonic intent on other states. But some coordinated pressure from Japanese and European policy bodies may support the reintroduction into global politics of a more interdependent (and less free-market) approach to commercial and financial diplomacy.

80 'The Limits of Politics', *Government and Opposition*, Volume 30, No.3 (Summer 1995) pp.291–311
Strange explicitly engages with the notion of globalization, which she defines as the development of products for explicitly global markets, the decline distinctions between national economies, partial labor mobility in addition to capital mobility, and the speeding up of transport and communications. These trends have led to an increasingly globalized but asymmetrical array of structural power.

81 '1995 Presidential Address: ISA as a microcosm', *International Studies Quarterly*, Volume 39, No.3 (September 1995) pp.289–95

Strange argues for the constructive engagement with other disciplines interested in the international system, from political geographers to business economists. She points to the relative decline of state–state violence relative to civil and local violence, the increasing interest in the environment, and the dangers stemming from the financial markets, as reasons for widening the ISA's implicit agenda.

82 'Political Economy and International Relations', in K. Booth and S. Smith (eds), *International Relations Theory Today* (Cambridge: Polity Press, 1995)
Noting that it is over twenty years since she and others argued for the end of the false division between politics and economics, Strange argues that the development of modern IPE has been in reaction to events within the global system. She again makes many of the criticisms she has before regarding the discipline's deference to international economics. The way forward is to conceptualize politics more widely, building on the work of moral philosophers and to apply her conception of structural power, as well as the more usual considerations of relational power.

83 'A Reply to Chris May', *Global Society*, Volume 10, No.3 (1996) pp.303–5
In her reply to May's article ('Strange Fruit: Susan Strange's theory of Structural Power in the International Political Economy', *Global Society*, Volume 10, No.2 (1996) 167–89), she engages with two criticisms made of her theory of structural power. She suggests that the knowledge structure itself is not *necessarily* prior, even if her process of agenda-setting power is regarded as central. While agreeing that she lacks a general theory of change, she asserts that such a general theory is not possible, noting that she is, however, sensitive to particular forms of change.

84 *The Retreat of the State. The Diffusion of Power in the World Economy* (Cambridge: Cambridge University Press, 1996)
In what might effectively be regarded as the third part of a trilogy, together with (57) and (67), Strange examines states' transition towards the sidelines of global political economic relations. The decline of state efficacy has been obscured by their increasing intervention in the lives of their citizens, giving an impression of a retention of power. Lacking the means to change its interactions with the global political economy autonomously, the state has lost the most important and significant aspect of its potential.

85 'The Erosion of the State', *Current History*, Volume 96, No. 613 (November 1997), pp.365–9

Strange briefly revisits the globalization debate and suggests that those who argue that, as the state still exists, globalization can be ignored are very mistaken. A concentration on the state misses the 'new diplomacy' between firms and other non-state actors as well as states themselves, as outlined in (67). To deny the decline of the state is to deny the possibility that the system may in the future be ruled by big business.

86 'Territory, state, authority and economy. A new realist ontology of global political economy' in R.W. Cox (ed.), *The New Realism: Perspectives on Multilateralism and World Order* (Basingstoke: Macmillan Press/United Nations University Press, 1997)
Strange argues that the global economy is in the midst of a transition; the close incidence of political authority, economic activity and geographical territory no longer holds. Authority has shifted, or is shifting, from states to other actors in the international political economy.

87 'The Future of Global Capitalism; or Will Divergence Persist Forever?', in C. Crouch and W. Streeck (eds), *The Political Economy of Modern Capitalism. Mapping Convergence and Diversity* (London: Sage, 1997)
Strange distances herself from comparative political economists studying different forms of national capitalism, and argues for a global perception of a more systemic view of capitalism. She is dismissive of a focus on diversity, suggesting that the more important problems will be the result of the increasing convergence of capitalism.

88 'The problem or the solution? Capitalism and the state system', in S. Gill and J.H. Mittelman (eds), *Innovation and transformation in International Studies* (Cambridge: Cambridge University Press, 1997)
Again Strange criticizes International Relations for not focusing on the systemic problems. Thus IPE is open to approaches from political geography, historical sociology and elsewhere that have not been fixated on the relations between states as the key causal factor in the global system.

89 (Editor), *Globalisation and Capitalist Diversity: Experiences on the Asian Mainland* (Florence: European University Institute/Robert Schuman Centre, 1997)
This volume collects together papers presented at a conference organized by Strange at the EUI. She contributes an introduction outlining the papers in the volume and discussing the organizational background to the conference.

90   'Who are EU? Ambiguities in the Concept of Competitiveness', *Journal of Common Market Studies*, Volume 36, No.1 (March 1998) pp.101–14
Building on the argument of Robert Reich that the location of economic activity (in a state) was more important for its competitiveness than the ownership of companies (whose production was carried out abroad), Strange suggests that, unless European policy recognizes the importance of society-based competitiveness rather than firm-based competitiveness, Europe's economic problems cannot be overcome.

91   'The New World of Debt', *New Left Review*, No.230 (July/August 1998) pp.91–114
An extract from (94), in which Strange focuses on the problems of international indebtedness in the 1990s to suggest the key problem has not been the indebtedness of poor states itself, but the sorts of credit historically extended and the timidity of the solutions to the problems that have arisen.

92   'International Political Economy: Beyond Economics and International Relations', *Economies et Sociétés*, Volume 34, No.4 (1998) pp.3–24
This is a slightly revised version of (82).

93   'Globaloney?' (review essay), *Review of International Political Economy*, Volume 5, No.4 (Winter 1998) pp.704–11
In this review of the influential P. Hirst and G. Thompson, *Globalisation in Question* (Oxford: Polity Press, 1996), alongside two other books arguing a similar position, Strange makes a major intervention in the debate over the 'myth' of globalization. Arguing that the authors (like others) miss the deterritorialization of commercial power in the global system, she identifies a failure to examine what is really happening in the global political economy.

94   *Mad Money* (Manchester: Manchester University Press, 1998)
In this sequel to (52), Strange returns to a concentration on the financial structure. Her final book finds Strange once again emphasizing the need to recognize the problems of instability in the global financial sector. Arguing that the system itself needed to be reformed, she once again refused to accept that the current upheavals were inevitable or unavoidable.

95   'The Westfailure System', *Review of International Studies*, Volume 25, No.3 (July 1999) pp.345–54
Strange briefly outlines the parallel histories of the territorial system of states and the economic system of markets and suggests that, until

the last quarter of the 20th century, each benefitted the other. However, only by understanding the role of non-state authority through the study of both international and comparative political economy and a move away from International Relation's state-centricism can the 'Westfailure' system be understood and alternatives assessed.

96   'World Order, Non-State Actors and the Global Casino: The Retreat of the State?', in R. Stubbs and G.R.D. Underhill (eds), *Political Economy and the Changing Global Order*, 2nd edn (Oxford: Oxford University Press, 2000)
Strange reprises arguments from (67) and (84) to argue that the disciplines of International Relations and International Economics fail to understand contemporary globalization. In her final published work, she revisits the criticisms she has leveled at much of mainstream International Studies literature and remains as angry as ever at the myopia of many of her contemporaries, leading to a failure to recognize the real problems of the 'global casino'.

Index